Included under one cover

🖙 Six Novels

Sub-Umbra, or Sport Among the She-Noodles
Miss Coote's Confession, or the Voluptuous Experiences
of an Old Maid
Lady Pokingham, or They All Do It
La Rose d'Amour, or The Adventures of a Gentleman
in Search of Pleasure
My Grandmother's Tale, or May's Account of Her In-
troduction to the Art of Love
Flukeyania, or Belgravian Morals

🖙 Short Stories

Young Beginners
An Adventure with a Tribade
The Sultan's Reverie
How He Lost His Whiskers
And many more

🖙 Ballads, Poems

Charlie Collingwood's Flogging
The State's New Duty
The Old Dildoe
The Good Nobleman
The Joys of Coming Together
Sweet Polly
The Novice
And many, many more

Plus "Letter from Harriet Keene," "Sally's Mistake,"
"Fables and Maxims," "Fowls and Pickled Pork," &c.,
&c.
Plus Limericks, jokes, witticisms, puns, ditties, acrostics,
songs, facetiæ, gossip, rumors, scandal, and much, much
more!

THE Pearl

A Journal of Facetive and Voluptuous Reading

BALLANTINE BOOKS • NEW YORK

Copyright © 1968 by Grove Press, Inc.

Library of Congress Catalog Card Number: 68-18322

ISBN 0-345-29456-4

This edition published by arrangement with Grove Press, Inc.

Manufactured in the United States of America

First Ballantine Books Edition: September 1973
Nineteenth Printing: May 1992

CONTENTS

The Pearl No. 1
[page 1]

The Pearl No. 2
[page 37]

The Pearl No. 3
[page 73]

The Pearl No. 4
[page 107]

The Pearl No. 5
[page 143]

The Pearl No. 6
[page 179]

The Pearl No. 7
[page 213]

Contents

The Pearl No. 16
[page 537]

The Pearl No. 17
[page 573]

The Pearl No. 18
[page 609]

THE PEARL

THE PEARL,

A Journal of Facetiæ and Voluptuous Reading.

| No. 1 | PUBLISHED MONTHLY. | July 1879 |

AN APOLOGY FOR OUR TITLE.

Having decided to bring out a Journal, the Editor racks his brains for a suitable name with which to christen his periodical. Friends are generally useless in an emergency of this kind; they suggest all kinds of impossible names; the following were some of the titles proposed in this instance: "Facts and Fancies," "The Cremorne," "The All Round," "The Monthly Courses," "The Devil's Own," and "Dugdale's Ghost"; the two first had certainly great attractions to our mind, but at last our own ideas have hit upon the modest little "Pearl," as more suitable, especially in the hope that when it comes under the snouts of the moral and hypocritical swine of the world, they may not trample it underfoot, and feel disposed to rend the publisher, but that a few will become subscribers on the quiet. To such better disposed piggywiggys, I would say, for encouragement, that they have only to keep up appearances by regularly attending church, giving to charities, and always appearing deeply interested in moral philanthropy, to ensure a respectable and highly moral character, and that if they only are clever enough never to be found out, they may, sub rosa, study and enjoy the philosophy of life till the end of their days, and earn a glorious and saintly epitaph on their tombstone, when at last the Devil pegs them out.

EDITOR OF THE "PEARL."

SUB-UMBRA, OR SPORT AMONG THE SHE-NOODLES.

The merry month of May has always been famous for its propitious influence over the voluptuous senses of the fairer sex.

I will tell you two or three little incidents which occurred to me in May, 1878, when I went to visit my cousins in Sussex, or as I familiarly call them, the She-Noodles, for the sport they afforded me at various times.

My uncle's is a nice country residence, standing in large grounds of its own, and surrounded by small fields of arable and pasture land, interspersed by numerous interesting copses, through which run footpaths and shady walks, where you are not likely to meet anyone in a month. I shall not trouble my readers with the name of the locality, or they may go pleasure hunting for themselves. Well, to go on, these cousins consisted of Annie, Sophie, and Polly, beside their brother Frank, who, at nineteen, was the eldest, the girls being, respectively, eighteen, sixteen, and fifteen. After dinner, the first day of my arrival, paterfamilias and mamma both indulged in a snooze in their armchair, whilst us boys and girls (I was the same age as Frank) took a stroll in the grounds. I attached myself more particularly to cousin Annie, a finely developed blonde, with deep blue eyes, pouting red lips, and a full heaving bosom, which to me looked like a perfect volcano of smothered desires. Frank was a very indolent fellow, who loved to smoke his cigar, and expected his sisters, who adored him, to sit by his side, reading some of the novels of the day, or tell him their love secrets, &c. This was by far too tame an amusement for me, and as I had not been there for nearly three years, I requested Annie to show me the improvements in the grounds before we went in to tea, saying to Frank, banteringly, "I suppose, old fellow, you're too lazy, and would prefer your sister taking me round?"

"I'm too comfortable; lazy is an ugly word, Walter, but the fact is, Soph is just reading a most interesting book, and I can't leave it," he replied; "besides, sissie is quite as well, or better qualified than I am to show off the grounds. I never notice anything."

"Come on, Annie," said I taking her hand; "Frank is in love."

"No, I'm sure he never thinks of a girl, except his sisters," was the reply.

We were now out of earshot, in a shady walk, so I went on a little more freely. "But, surely you, coz, are in love, if he is not. I can tell it by your liquid eye and heaving bosom."

A scarlet flush shot over her features at my allusion to her finely moulded bosom, but it was evidently pleasing, and far from offensive, to judge by her playfully spoken, "Oh! Walter, for shame, sir!"

We were a good distance away by this time, and a convenient seat stood near, so throwing my arms around the blushing girl, I kissed her ruby lips, and drawing her with me, said, "Now, Annie, dear, I'm your cousin and old playfellow, I couldn't help kissing those beautiful lips, which I might always make free with when we were little boy and girl together; now you shall confess all before I let you go."

"But I've nothing to confess, sir."

"Do you never think of love, Annie? Look me in the face if you can say it's a stranger to your bosom," putting my hand familiarly round her neck till my right hand rested on one of the panting globes of her bosom.

She turned her face to mine, suffused as it was by a deeper blush than ever, as her dark blue eyes met mine, in a fearless search of my meaning, but instead of speaking in response to this mute appeal, I kissed her rapturously, sucking in the fragrance of her sweet breath till she fairly trembled with emotion.

It was just beginning to get dusk, my hands were caressing the white, firm flesh of her beautiful neck, slowly working their way towards the heaving bubbies a little lower down; at last I whispered, "What a fine, what a lovely bust you have developed since I saw you last, dear Annie, you won't mind your cousin, will you, when everything used to be so free to each other; besides, what harm can there be in it?"

She seemed on fire, a thrill of emotion seemed to shoot through both of us, and for several moments she lay almost motionless in my arms, with one hand resting on my thigh. Priapus was awake and ready for business, but she suddenly aroused herself, saying, "We must never stop here, let us walk round or they will suspect something."

"When shall we be alone again, darling? We must arrange that before we go in," I said quickly.

It was impossible to keep her on the seat, but as we walked on she said, musingly, "To-morrow morning we might go for a stroll before lunch, Frank lies in bed, and my sisters are keeping house this week; I shall have to mind the tarts and pies next week."

I gave her another hug and a kiss, as I said, "How delightful that will be; what a dear, thoughtful girl you are, Annie."

"Mind, sir, how you behave to-morrow, not so much kissing, or I shan't take you for a second walk; here we are at the house."

Next morning was gloriously warm and fine; as soon as breakfast was over we started for our stroll, being particularly minded by papa to be back in good time for luncheon.

I gradually drew out my beautiful cousin, till our conversation got exceedingly warm, the hot blood rushing in waves of crimson over her shamefaced visage.

"What a rude boy you have grown Walter, since you were here last; I can't help blushing at the way you run on, sir!" she exclaimed at last.

"Annie, my darling," I replied, "what can be more pleasing than to talk of fun with pretty girls, the beauties of their legs and bosoms, and all about them? How I should love to see your lovely calf at this moment, especially after the glimpses I have already had of a divine ankle," saying which I threw myself under a shady tree, close by a gate in a meadow, and drew the half-resisting girl down on the grass at my side, and kissed her passionately, as I murmured, "Oh! Annie, what is there worth living for like the sweets of love?"

Her lips met mine in a fiery embrace, but suddenly disengaging herself, her eyes cast down, and looking awfully abashed, she stammered out, "What is it? what do you mean, Walter?"

"Ah, coz dear, can you be so innocent? Feel here the dart of love all impatient to enter the mossy grotto between your thighs," I whispered, placing her hand upon my prick, which I had suddenly let out of the restraining trousers. "How you sigh; grasp it in your hand, dear, is it possible that you do not understand what it is for?"

Her face was crimson to the roots of her hair, as her hand grasped my tool, and her eyes seemed to start with terror at the sudden apparition of Mr. John Thomas; so that taking advantage of her speechless confusion my own hand, slipping under her clothes, soon had possession of her mount, and in spite of the nervous contraction of her thighs, the forefinger searched out the virgin clitoris.

"Ah! oh! oh!! Walter don't; what are you about?"

"It's all love, dear, open your thighs a wee bit and see what pleasure my finger will make you experience," I again whispered, smothering her with renewed and luscious kisses, thrusting the velvet tip of my tongue between her lips.

"Oh! oh! you will hurt!" she seemed to sigh rather than speak, as her legs relaxed a little of their spasmodic contraction.

My lips continued glued to hers, our otherwise disengaged arms clasped each other closely round the waist, her hand holding my affair in a kind of convulsive grasp, whilst my fingers were busy with clitoris and cunny; the only audible sound resembling a mixture of kisses and sighs, till all in a moment I felt her crack deluged with a warm, creamy spend whilst my own juice spurted over her hand and dress in loving sympathy.

In a short while we recovered our composure a little, and I then explained to her that the melting ecstasy she had just felt was only a slight foretaste of the joy I could give her, by inserting my member in her cunny. My persuasive eloquence and the warmth of her desires soon overcame all maiden fears and scruples; then for fear of damaging her dress, or getting the green stain of the grass on the knees of my light trousers, I persuaded her to stand up by the gate and allow me to enter behind. She hid her face in her hands on the top rail of the gate, as I slowly raised her dress; what glories were unfolded to view, my prick's stiffness was renewed in an instant at the sight of her delicious buttocks, so beautifully relieved by the white of her pretty drawers; as I opened them and exposed the flesh, I could see the lips of her plump pouting cunny, deliciously feathered, with soft light down, her lovely legs, drawers, stockings, pretty boots, making a tout ensemble, which as I write and describe them cause Mr. Priapus to swell in my breeches; it was a most delicious sight. I knelt and kissed her bottom, slit, and everything my tongue could reach, it was all mine, I stood up and prepared to take possession of the seat of love—when, alas! a sudden shriek from Annie, her clothes dropped, all my arrangements were upset in a moment; a bull had unexpectedly appeared on the opposite side of the gate, and frightened my love by the sudden application of his cold, damp nose to her forehead. It is too much to contemplate that scene even now.

(To be continued.)

MISS COOTE'S CONFESSION,

OR THE VOLUPTUOUS EXPERIENCES OF AN OLD MAID; In a series of Letters to a Lady Friend.

LETTER I.

My Dear Girl,

I know I have long promised you an account of the reason of my penchant for the rod, which, in my estimation, is one of the most voluptuous and delicious institutions of private life, especially to a supposed highly respectable old maid like your esteemed friend. Treaties must be carried out, and promises kept, or how can I ever hope for the pleasure of making you taste my little green tickler again. Writing, and especially a sort of confession of my voluptuous weakness, is a most unpleasant task, as I feel as shamefaced in putting these things on paper as when my grandfather's housekeeper first bared my poor blushing little bottom to his ruthless attack. My only consolation at commencing is the hope that I shall warm to the subject as it progresses in my endeavour to depict, for your gratification, some of the luscious episodes of my early days.

My grandfather, as you well know, was the celebrated Indian General, Sir Eyre Coote, almost as well known for his eight-penny fiasco with the Bluecoat boys as for his services to the Hon. E. I. Company. He was a confirmed martinet, and nothing delighted him so much as a good opportunity for the use of the cat, but I cannot tell you anything about that, as that was before my time. My first recollection of him is after the aforesaid City scandal, when he had to retire from public life in comparative disgrace. My parents both died when I was just upon twelve years of age, and the old General, who had no other relatives to care for, took entire charge of me, and, at his death, I was left his sole heiress, and mistress of nearly £3,000 per annum.

He resided in a quiet country house some twenty miles from London, where I spent the first few months of my orphaned life, with only his housekeeper, Mrs. Mansell, and the two servants, Jane and Jemima. The old General being away in Holland searching, so I afterwards heard, for original editions respecting the practices of Cornelius Hadrien, a curious work on the flagellation of religious penitents by a father confessor.

It was the middle of summer when he returned, and I soon found the liberty I had been enjoying considerably restricted. Orders not to pluck the flowers, or the fruit in the garden; and a regular lesson set me every day by the old autocrat himself. At first they were tolerably simple, but gradually increased in difficulty, and now, in after years, I can plainly understand his wolf and lamb tactics, by which I must eventually fall under his assumed just displeasure.

What gave me considerable pleasure at this time was his decided objection to mourning, or anything at all sombre in my dress. He said my parents had been shown every possible respect by wearing black for months, and I must now be dressed as became a young lady of my good expectations.

Although we scarcely ever received company, and then only some old fogy of his military acquaintance, I was provided with a profusion of new and elegant dresses, as well as beautiful shoes, slippers, drawers, and underlinen, all trimmed with finest lace &c., not even forgetting some very beautiful garters, a pair of which with gold buckles, he would insist upon putting on for me, taking no notice of my blushing confusion, as he pretended to arrange my drawers and skirts afterwards, but merely to remark: What a fine figure I should make, if they ever had to strip me for punishment.

Soon my lessons began to be harder than I could fairly manage. One day he expostulated, "Oh! Rosa; Rosa!! why don't you try to be a better girl. I don't want to punish you."

"But grandfather," I replied, "how can I learn so much of

that horrid French every day. I'm sure no one else could do it."

"Hold your tongue, Miss Pert, I must be a better judge than a little girl like you."

"But, grandfather dear, you know I do love you, and I do try my best."

"Well, prove your love and diligence in future, or your posterior must feel a nice little birch, I shall get ready for you," said he sternly.

Another week passed, during which I could not help observing an unusual fire and sparkle in his eyes, whenever I appeared in evening dress at the dinner table (we always dined in quiet state), and he also suggested that I ought to wear a choice little bouquet of fresh flowers in my bosom, to set off my complexion.

But the climax was approaching, I was not to escape long; he again found fault, and gave me what he gravely called one last chance: my eyes were filled with tears, and I trembled to look at his stern old face, and knew any remonstrance on my part would be useless.

The prospect of punishment made me so nervous, it was with the greatest difficulty I could attend to my lessons, and the second day after, I broke down entirely.

"Oh! Ho! it's come to this has it, Rosie?" said the old gentleman, "nothing will do, you must be punished."

Ringing the bell for Mrs. Mansell, he told her to have the punishment room and the servants all ready, when he should want them, as he was sorry to say "Miss Rosa was so idle, and getting worse and worse with her lessons every day, she must now be taken severely in hand or she would be spoiled for life."

"Now, you bad girl," said he, as the housekeeper retired, "go to your room and reflect upon what your idleness has brought to you."

Full of indignation, confusion, and shame, I rushed to my chamber, and bolted the door, determined they should break the door down first before I would submit to such a public exposure, before the two servants; throwing myself on the bed, I gave vent to my tears for at least a couple of hours, expecting every moment the dreadful summons to attend the old man's punishment drill, as he called it, but, no one disturbing me, I at last came to the conclusion it was only a plan of his to frighten me, and so I fell into a soothing sleep. A voice at the door awakened me, and I recognized the voice of Jane, as she said, "Miss Rosa, Miss Rosa, you'll be late for dinner."

"No dinner for me, Jane, if I'm going to be punished; go away, leave me alone," whispered I through the keyhole.

"Oh! Miss Rosie, the General's been in the garden all the afternoon, quite good-tempered, perhaps he's forgotten it all; don't make him angry by not being ready for dinner, let me in quick."

So I cautiously drew the bolt, and let her assist me to dress.

"Cheer up, Miss Rosie, don't look dull, go down as if nothing had happened, and most likely all will be forgotten; his memory is so short, especially if you put in your bosom this sweet little nosegay to please him, as you have never done it since he said it would set off your complexion."

Thus encouraged, I met my grandfather with a good appetite, and, as if the "bitterness was past," like Agag before Samuel, little suspecting I should be almost hewed in pieces afterwards.

The dinner passed most pleasantly, for such a formal affair as my grandfather made it, he took several glasses of wine, and in the middle of the dessert seemed to contemplate me with unusual interest; at last suddenly seeming to notice the little bouquet of damask and white roses, he said, "That's right, Rosa, I see you have carried out my suggestion of a nosegay at last; it quite improves your appearance, but nothing to what my birch will effect on your naughty bottom, which will soon look like one of those fine peaches, and now's the time to do it," said he, ringing the bell.

Almost distracted, and ready to faint, I rushed for the door, but only in time to fall into the arms of strong Jemima.

"Now for *punishment drill*; march on, Jemima, with the culprit, you've got her safe; Mrs. Mansell and Jane, come on," said he to them, as they appeared in the background.

Resistance was useless. I was soon carried into a spare room I had never entered; it contained very little furniture, except the carpet, and one comfortable easy chair; but on the walls hung several bunches of twigs, and in one corner stood a thing like a stepladder, but covered with red baize, and fitted with six rings, two halfway up, two at bottom, and two at the top.

"Tie her to the horse, and get ready for business," said the

General, as he seated himself in the chair, to look on at his ease.

"Come, Rosa, dear, don't be troublesome, and make your grandfather more angry," said Mrs. Mansell, unfastening my waistband. "Slip off your dress, whilst the girls put the horse in the middle of the room."

"Oh! No! No! I won't be whipped," I screamed. "Oh! Sir! Oh! Grandfather, do have mercy," said I, throwing myself on my knees before the old man.

"Come, come, it's no use showing the white feather, Rosa, it's for your own good. No more nonsense. Mrs. Mansell, do your duty, and let us get the painful business over; she isn't one of my stock if she doesn't show her pluck when it comes to the pinch."

The three women all tried to lift me, but I kicked, scratched, and bit all round, and, for a moment or two, almost beat them off in my fury, but my strength was soon exhausted, and Jemima, smarting from a severe bite, carried me in vengeful triumph to the dreaded machine. Quick as thought, my hands and feet were secured to the upper and lower rings; the horse widening towards the ground caused my legs to be well apart when drawn up closely to the rings at my ankles.

I could hear Sir Eyre chuckle with delight, as he exclaimed, "By God! she's a vixen, and it must be taken out of her, she's a Coote all over. Bravo, Rosie! Now get her ready quickly."

I submitted in sullen despair, whilst my torn dress and underskirts were turned up and pinned round my shoulders, but when they began to unloose my drawers, my rage burst out afresh, and turning my head, I saw the old man, his stern face beaming with pleased animation, whisking in his right hand a small bunch of fresh birchen twigs. My blood was in a boil, and my bottom tingled with anticipated strokes, especially when Jemima, pulling the drawers nearly down to my knees, gave me a smart little slap on the sly, to let me know what I might soon expect, and I fairly shouted, "You must be a cruel old beast to let them treat me so."

"Old beast, indeed!" said he, jumping up in a passion. "We'll see about that, Miss; perhaps you'll be glad to apologize before long."

I saw him stepping forward. "Oh! Mercy! Mercy! Sir! I

didn't mean it; they've hurt me so; I couldn't help what I said."

"This is a really serious case," said he, apparently addressing the others. "She's idle, violently vicious, and even insulting to me, her only natural guardian, instead of treating me with proper respect. There can be no alternative, the only remedy, however painful the scene may be to us who have to inflict the punishment, is to carry it out, as a matter of duty, or the girl will be ruined. She has never been under proper control all her life."

"Oh! Grandfather, punish me any way but this. I know I can't bear it; it's so dreadfully cruel," I sobbed out through my tears.

"My child, such crocodile tears have no effect on me; you must be made to feel the smart. If we let you off now, you would be laughing at it all, and go on worse than before. Stand aside, Jane, we can't waste any more time." So saying, he made a flourish with the rod, so as to make quite an audible "whisk" in the air. I suppose it was only to clear the way, as it did not touch me; in fact up to this time, he had treated me like a cat which knows the poor mousey cannot escape, but may be pounced upon at any time.

I could see the tears in Jane's eyes, but Jemima had a malicious smile on her face, and Mrs. Mansell looked very grave, but no time was allowed for reflections; the next instant I felt a smart but not heavy stroke right across my loins, then another, and another, in rather quick succession, but not too fast for me to think that perhaps after all it would not be so dreadful as I feared; so setting my teeth firmly without uttering a word, I determined to give as little indication as possible of my feelings. All this and a great deal more flashed through my brain before six strokes had been administered, my bottom tingled all over, and the blood seemed to rush like lightning through my veins at every blow, and my face felt as my poor posteriors.

"Now, you idle puss," said the General, "you begin to feel the fruits of your conduct. Will you? Will you call me an old beast again?" giving a harder stroke at each ejaculation.

My courage still sustained my resolution not to cry out, but only seemed to make him more angry.

"Sulky tempered and obstinate, by Jove!" he continued;

"we must draw it out of you. Don't think, Miss, I'm to be beaten by a little wench like you; take that, and that, and that," whisking me with still greater energy, concluding with a tremendous whack which drew up the skin to bursting tension, and I felt another like it would make the blood spurt forth, but he suddenly paused in his fury, as if for want of breath, but as I now know too well, only to prolong his own exquisite pleasure.

Thinking all was over, I entreated them to let me go, but to my sorrow soon found my mistake.

"Not yet, not yet, you bad girl, you're not half punished for all your biting, scratching, and impudence," exclaimed Sir Eyre.

Again the hateful birch hissed through the air, and cut into my bruised flesh, both buttocks and thighs, suffering and smarting in agony, but he seemed careful at first not to draw the blood; however, I was not to escape, it was only his deliberate plan of attack, so as not to exhaust the poor victim too soon.

"Bite, and scratch, and fight against my orders again, will you? Miss Rosie, you'll know next time what to expect. You deserve no mercy, the idleness was bad enough, but such murderous conduct is awful; I believe you would have killed anyone in your passion if you could. Bite, scratch, and fight, eh! Bite, will you?" Thus lectured the old man, getting warmer and warmer in his attack, till the blood fairly trickled down my poor thighs.

I was in dreadful agony at every cut, and must have fainted, but his lecturing seemed to sustain me like a cordial; besides, with the pain I experienced a most pleasurable warmth and excitability impossible to be described, but which, doubtless, you, my dear, have felt for yourself when under my discipline.

But all my fortitude could not much longer suppress my sighs and moans, and at last I felt as if I must die under the torture, in spite of the exquisite sensation which mingled with it; notwithstanding my ohs and ahs, and stifled cries, I would not ask for mercy again; my sole thoughts ran upon the desire for vengeance, and how I should like to whip and cut them all in pieces, especially the General and Jemima, and even poor tearful Jane.

Sir Eyre seemed to forget his age, and worked away in frightful excitement.

"Damme, won't you cry for mercy? Won't you apologize, you young hussy," he hissed between his teeth. "She's tougher and more obstinate than any of the family, a real chip of the old block. But to be beaten by the young spitfire, Mrs. Mansell, is more than I can bear. There! there! there!" cried he; and at last the worn-out stump of the rod fell from his hand, as he sank back quite exhausted in his chair.

"Mrs. Mansell," he gasped, "give her half-a-dozen good stripes with a new rod to finish her off, and let her know that although she may exhaust an old man, there are other strong arms that can dispense justice to her impudent rump."

The housekeeper, in obedience to the command, takes up a fine fresh birch, and cuts deliberately, counting, in clear voice, one, two, three, four, five, six (her blows were heavy, but did not seem to sting so cruelly as those given by Sir Eyre). "There," she says, "Miss Rosa, I might have laid it on more heavily, but I pitied you this first time."

Nearly dead, and frightfully cut up, although victorious, I had to be carried to my room. But what a victory? all torn and bleeding, as I was, besides the certainty that the old General would renew his attack the first favourable opportunity.

Poor Jane laughed and cried over my lacerated posteriors as she tenderly washed me with cold arnica and water, and she seemed so used to the business that when we retired to rest (for I got her to sleep with me) I asked her if she had not often attended bruised bottoms before.

"Yes, Miss Rosie," she repled; "but you must keep the secret and not pretend to know anything. I have been whipped myself, but not so bad as you were, although it's cruel. We all rather like it after the first time or two; especially if we are not cut up too much. Next time you should shout out well for mercy, &c., as it pleases the old man, and he won't be so furious. He was so bad and exhausted with whipping you, Mrs. Mansell was going to send for the doctor, but Jemima said a good birching would do him more good, and draw the blood away from his head; so they pickled him finely, till he quite came to himself, and begged hard to be let off."

Thus ended my first lesson; and, in further letters, you

shall hear how I got on with Jane, continued the contest with the General, my adventures at Mrs. Flaybum's school, and my own domestic discipline since left to myself.

> Believe me, Dear Nellie,
> Your affectionate friend
> ROSA BELINDA COOTE.

(To be continued.)

LADY POKINGHAM; OR THEY ALL DO IT:

Giving an Account of her Luxurious Adventures, both before and after her Marriage with Lord Crim-Con.

INTRODUCTION.

To the Reader,

Very little apology will be needed for putting in print the following highly erotic and racy narrative of a young patrician lady, whose adventures I feel assured every genuine lover of voluptuous reading will derive as much or more pleasure afforded your humble servant.

The subject of these memoirs was one of the brightest and most charming of her sex, endued with such exquisite nervous sensitiveness, in addition to an unusual warmth of constitution that she was quite unable to resist the seductive influences of God's finest creation; for God made man in his own image, male and female, created he them; and this was the first commandment, "Be faithful and multiply, and replenish the earth"—see Genesis, chap. 1.

The natural instinct of the ancients instilled in their minds the idea that copulation was the direct and most acceptable form of worship they could offer to their deities, and I know that those of my readers who are not bigoted Christians will agree with me, that there cannot be any great sin in giving way to natural desires, and enjoying, to the utmost, all those delicious sensations for which a beneficent Creator has so amply fitted us.

Poor girl, she did not live long, and in thoroughly enjoying her few briefs years of butterfly life, who can think her wicked!

The scraps from which my narrative is compiled were found in a packet she had entrusted to a devoted servitor, who, after her sudden and premature death at the early age of twenty-three, entered my service.

As author, I feel the crudeness of my style may be a little offensive to some, but hope my desire to afford general pleasure will excuse my defects.

THE AUTHOR.

PART I.

My dear Walter,

How I love you! but alas! you will never know it till I am gone; little do you think, as you wheel me about in my invalid chair, how your delicate attentions have won the heart of a poor consumptive on the verge of the grave. How I long to suck the sweets of love from your lips; to fondle and caress your lordly priapus, and feel its thrilling motions within me; but such joys cannot be, the least excitement would be my death, and I can but sigh as I look at your kind loving face, and admire the fine proportions of my darling, as evidenced by the large bunch of keys you always seem to have in your pocket; indeed you look to have a key of keys, whose burning thrusts would unlock any virgin cabinet.

This is a strange fancy of mine (the writing for your perusal a short account of some of my adventures); but one of the only pleasures left me is to indulge in reveries of the past, and seem to feel over again the thrilling emotions of voluptuous enjoyments, which are now denied to me; and I hope the recital of my escapades and follies may afford you some slight pleasure, and add to the lasting regard with which I hope you will remember me in years to come. One thing I ask of you, dear Walter, is to fancy you are enjoying Beatrice Pokingham when you are in the embraces of some future inamorata. It is a pleasure I have often indulged in myself when in the action of coition, and heightened my bliss by letting my fancy run riot, and imagined I was in the arms of someone I particularly wished for, but could not come at. My income dies with me, so I have no cause to make a will, but you will find notes for a few hundred pounds enclosed with this outline of my adventures, which is all I have been able to save. You will

also find a fine lock of dark brown hair, which I have cut
from the abundant chevelure of my Mons Veneris; other
friends and relatives may have the admired curls from my
head, your memento is cut from the sacred spot of love.

I never remember my father, the Marquis of Pokingham,
but have my doubts as to whether I am really entitled to the
honour of claiming him as a parent, as he was a used-up old
man, and from papers and letters, which passed privately between him and my mother, I know that he more than suspected he was indebted to his good-looking footman for the
pretty baby girl my mother presented to him; as he says in
one note, "that he could have forgiven everything if the
fruits of her intercourse with James had been a son and heir,
so as to keep his hated nephew out of the estates and title,
and wished her to let him cultivate her parsley bed for another crop, which might perhaps turn out more in accordance with his wishes." The poor old fellow died soon after
writing that note, and my mother, from whom this dreadful
consumption is transmitted to me, also left me an orphan at
an early age, leaving me her jointure of £20,000, and an
aristocratic title which that amount was quite inadequate to
properly support.

My guardians were very saving and careful, as they sent me
to school at eight years of age, and only spent about £150 a
year for schooling and necessaries, till they thought it was
time for me to be brought out in the world, so that I bene-
fitted considerably by the accumulated interest of my money.

The first four years of my school passed away uneventfully,
and during that time I was only in one serious scrape, which
I will relate, as it led to my first taste of a good birch rod.

Miss Birch was rather an indulgent schoolmistress, and only
had to resort to personal punishment for very serious offenses,
which she considered might materially affect the future character of her pupils, unless thoroughly cut out of them from
the first. I was nearly seven years old when I had a sudden
fancy for making sketches on my slate in school. One of our
governesses, Miss Pennington, was a rather crabbed and severe
old girl of five-and-thirty, and particularly evoked my abilities
as a caricaturist, and the sketches would be slyly passed from
one to the other of us, causing considerable giggling and gross
inattention to our lessons. I was infatuated and conceited with
what I considered my clever drawings and several admonitions

and extra tasks as punishment had no effect in checking my mischievous interruptions, until one afternoon Miss Birch had fallen asleep at her desk, and old Penn was busy with a class, when the sudden inspiration seized me to make a couple of very rude sketches; one of the old girl sitting on a chamber utensil; but the other was a rural idea of her stooping down, with her clothes up to ease herself, in a field. The first girl I showed them to almost burst with laughter, and two others were so anxious to see the cause of her mirth, that they were actually stooping over her shoulder to look at my slate, when, before I could possibly get to it to rub them off, old Penn pounced upon it like an eagle, and carried it in triumph to Miss Birch, who was awakened chagrined by the amused smile which our principal could not repress at first sight of the indecent caricatures.

"My young lady must smart for this, Miss Pennington," said Miss Birch, with suddenly assumed gravity; "she has been very troublesome lately with these impudent drawings, but this is positively obscene; if she draws one thing she will go to another. Send for Susan to bring my birch rod! I must punish her whilst my blood is warm, as I am too forgiving, and may let her off."

I threw myself on my knees, and implored for mercy, promising "Never, never to do anything of the kind again."

Miss Birch.—"You should have thought of the consequences before you drew such filthy pictures; the very idea of one of my young ladies being capable of such productions is horrible to me; these prurient ideas cannot be allowed to settle in your mind for an instant, if I can whip them out."

Miss Pennnington, with a grim look of satisfaction, now took me by the wrist, just as Susan, a stout, strong, fair servant girl of about twenty, appeared with what looked to me a fearful big bunch of birch twigs, neatly tied up with red velvet ribbon.

"Now, Lady Beatrice Pokingham," said Miss Birch, "kneel down, confess your fault, and kiss the rod," taking the bunch from Susan's hands, and extending it to me as a queen might her sceptre to a supplicant subject.

Anxious to get over the inevitable, and make my punishment as light as possible, I knelt down, and with real tears of penitence begged her to be as lenient as her sense of justice would admit, as I knew I well deserved what she was going to inflict, and would take care not to insult Miss Pennington again, whom I was very sorry to have so caricatured; then I kissed the rod and resigned myself to my fate.

MISS PENNINGTON, maliciously.—"Ah! Miss Birch, how quickly the sight of the rod makes hypocritical repentance."

MISS BIRCH.—"I quite understand all that, Miss Pennington, but must temper justice with mercy at the proper time; now, you impudent artist, lift your clothes behind, and expose your own bottom to the justly merited punishment."

With trembling hands I lifted my skirts, and was then ordered to open my drawers also; which done, they pinned up my dress and petticoats as high as my shoulders; then I was laid across a desk, and Susan stood in front of me, holding both hands, whilst old Penn and the French governess (who had just entered the schoolroom) each held one of my legs, so that I was what you might call helplessly spread-eagled.

MISS BIRCH, looking seriously round as she flourished the rod.—"Now, all you young ladies, let this whipping be a caution to you; my Lady Beatrice richly deserves this degrading shame, for her indecent (I ought to call them obscure) sketches. Will you! will you, you troublesome, impudent little thing, ever do so again? There, there, there, I hope it will soon do you good. Ah! you may scream; there's a few more to come yet."

The bunch of birch seemed to crash on my bare bottom with awful force; the tender skin smarted, and seemed ready to burst at every fresh cut. "Ah! ah! oh!!! Oh, heavens! have mercy, madame. Oh! I will never do anything like it again. Ah—r—re! I can't bear it!" I screamed, kicking and struggling under every blow, so that at first they could scarcely hold me, but I was soon exhausted by my own efforts.

MISS BIRCH.—"You can feel it a little, may it do you good, you bad little girl; if I don't check you now, the whole establishment would soon be demoralized. Ah! ha! your bottom is getting finely wealed, but I haven't done yet," cutting away with increasing fury.

Just then I caught a glimpse of her face, which was usually pale, but now flushed with excitement, and her eyes sparkled with unwonted animation. "Ah!" she continued, "young ladies beware of my rod, when I do have to use it. How do you like it, Lady Beatrice? Let us all know how nice it is," cutting my bottom and thighs deliberately at each ejaculation.

LADY BEATRICE.—"Ah! oh! ah—r—r—re! It's awful! Oh I shall die if you don't have mercy, Miss Birch. Oh! my God, I'm fearfully punished; I'm cut to pieces; the birch feels as if it was red hot, the blows burn so!"

Then I felt as if it was all over, and I must die soon; my cries were succeeded by low sobs, moans, and then hysterical crying, which gradually got lower and lower, till at last I must have fainted, as I remembered nothing more till I found myself in bed, and awoke with my poor posteriors tremendously bruised and sore, and it was nearly a fortnight before I got rid of all the marks of that severe whipping.

After I was twelve years of age they reckoned me amongst the big girls, and I got a jolly bedfellow, whom I will call Alice Marchmont, a beautiful, fair girl, with a plump figure, large sensuous eyes, and flesh as firm and smooth as ivory. She seemed to take a great fancy to me, and the second night I slept with her (we had a small room to ourselves) she kissed and hugged me so lovingly that I felt slightly confused at first, as she took such liberties with me, my heart was all in a flutter, and although the light was out, I felt my face covered with burning blushes as her hot kisses on my lips, and the searching gropings of her hands in the most private parts of my person, made me all a tremble.

"How you shake, dear Beatrice," she answered. "What are you afraid of? you may feel me all over too; it is so nice. Put your tongue in my mouth, it is a great inducement to love and I do want to love you so, dear. Where's your hand? here, put it there; can't you feel the hair just beginning to grow on my pussey? Yours will come soon. Rub your finger on my crack, just there," so she initiated me into the art of frigging in the most tender loving manner.

As you may guess, I was an apt pupil, although so young. Her touches fired my blood, and the way she sucked my tongue seemed most delicious. "Ah! Oh! Rub harder, harder —quicker," she gasped, as she stiffened her limbs out with a kind of spasmodic shudder, and I felt my finger all wet with something warm and creamy. She covered me with kisses for a moment, and then lay quite still.

"What is it, Alice? How funny you are, and you have wetted my finger, you nasty girl," I whispered, laughing. "Go on tickling me with your fingers, I begin rather to like it."

"So you will, dear, soon, and love me for teaching you such

a nice game," she replied, renewing her frigging operations, which gave me great pleasure so that I hardly knew what I was doing, and a most luscious longing sensation came over me. I begged her to shove her fingers right up. "Oh! Oh! How nice! Further! Harder!" and almost fainted with delight as she at last brought down my first maiden spend.

Next night we repeated our lascivious amusements, and she produced a thing like a sausage, made of soft kid leather, and stuffed out as hard as possible, which she asked me to push into her, and work up and down, whilst she frigged me as before, making me lay on the top of her, with my tongue in her mouth. It was delightful. I can't express her raptures, my movements with the instrument seemed to drive her into ecstasies of pleasure, she almost screamed as she clasped my body to hers, exclaiming, "Ah! Oh! You dear boy; you kill me with pleasure!" as she spent with extraordinary profusion all over my busy hand.

As soon as we had recovered our serenity a little, I asked her what she meant by calling me her dear boy.

"Ah! Beatrice," she replied, "I'm so sleepy now, but to-morrow night, I will tell you my story, and explain how it is that my pussey is able to take in that thing, whilst yours cannot at present; it will enlighten you a little more into the Philosophy of Life, my dear; now give me a kiss, and let us go to sleep to-night."

ALICE MARCHMONT'S STORY.

You may imagine I was anxious for the next morning to arrive. We were no sooner in our little sanctum, than I exclaimed, "Now, Alice, make haste into bed, I'm all impatient to hear your tale."

"You shall have it dear and my fingers, too, if you will but let me undress comfortably. I can't jump into bed anyhow; I must make the inspection of my little private curls first. What do you think of them, Beatrice? Off with your chemise; I want to compare our pusseys," said she, throwing off everything, and surveying her beautiful naked figure in the large cheval glass. I was soon beside her, equally denuded of covering. "What a delightfully pouting little slit you have, Beatrice," she exclaimed, patting my Mons Veneris. "We shall make a beautiful contrast, mine is a light blonde, and yours will be brunette. See my little curly parsley bed is already half-an-inch long." She indulged in no end of exciting tricks, till at last my patience was exhausted, so slipping on my chemise de nuit, I bounced into bed, saying I believed it was all fudge about her having a tale to tell and that I would not let her love me again, till she had satisfied my curiosity.

"What bad manners to doubt my word," she cried, following me into bed, taking me by surprise, uncovered my bottom, and inflicted a smart little slapping, as she laughingly continued, "There, let that be a lesson to you not to doubt a young lady's word in future. Now you shall have my tale, although it would really serve you right to make you wait till to-morrow."

After a short pause, having settled ourselves lovingly in bed, she began:

Once upon a time there was a little girl about ten years old, of the name of Alice, her parents were rich, and lived in a beautiful house, surrounded by lovely gardens and a fine park, she had a brother about two years older than herself, but her mama was so fond of her (being an only daughter), that she never would allow her little girl out of her sight, unless William, the butler, had charge of her in her rambles about the grounds and park.

William was a handsome, good-looking man about thirty, and had been in the family ever since he was a boy. Now Alice, who was very fond of William, often sat on his knee as he was seated under a tree, or on a garden seat, when he would read to her fairy tales from her books. Their intimacy was so great that when they were alone, she would call him "dear old Willie," and treat him quite as an equal. Alice was quite an inquisitive girl, and would often put Mr. William to the blush by her curious enquiries about natural history affairs, and how animals had little ones, why the cock was so savage to the poor hens, jumping on their backs, and biting their heads with his sharp beak, &c. "My dear," he would say, "I'm not a hen or a cow; how should I know? don't ask such silly questions"; but Miss Alice was not so easily put off, she would reply, "Ah! Willie, you do know, and won't tell me, I insist upon knowing, &c.," but her efforts to obtain knowledge were quite fruitless.

This went on for some time till the little girl was within three or four months of her twelfth birthday, when a circumstance she had never taken any notice of before aroused her curiosity. It was that Mr. William, under pretense of seeing to his duties, was in the habit of secluding himself in his pantry, or closet, from seven to eight o'clock in the morning for about an hour before breakfast. If Alice ventured to tap at the door it was fastened inside, and admittance refused; the keyhole was so closed it was useless to try and look through that way, but it occurred to my little girl that perhaps she might be able to get a peep into that place of mystery if she could only get into a passage which passed behind Mr. William's pantry, and into which she knew it used to open by a half-glass door, now never used, as the passage was closed by a locked door at each end. This passage was lighted from the outside by a small window about four feet from the ground, fastened on the inside simply by a hook, which Alice, who mounted on a high stool, soon found she could open if she broke one of the small diamond panes of glass, which she did, and then waiting till the next morning felt sure she would be able to find out what Willie was always so busy about, and also that she could get in and out of the window unobserved by anyone, as it was quite screened from view by a thick shrubbery seldom entered by anyone.

Up betimes next day she told her lady's-maid she was going to enjoy the fresh air in the garden before breakfast, and then hurried off to her place of observation, and scrambled through the window regardless of dirt and dust, took off her boots as soon as she alighted in the disused passage, and silently crept up to the glass door, but to her chagrin found the panes so dirty as to be impervious to sight; however, she was so far lucky as to find a fine large keyhole quite clear, and two or three cracks in the woodwork, so that she could see nearly every part of the place, which was full of light from a skylight overhead. Mr. William was not there, but soon made his appearance, bringing a great basket of plate, which had been used the previous day, and for a few minutes was really busy looking in his pantry book, and counting spoons, forks, &c., but was soon finished, and began to look at a little book, which he took from a drawer. Just then, Lucy, one of the prettiest housemaids, a dark beauty of about eighteen, entered the room without ceremony, saying, "Here's some of your plate off the sideboard. Where's your eyes, Mr. William, not to gather up all as you ought to do?" William's eyes seemed to beam with delight as he caught her round the waist, and gave her a luscious kiss on her cheek, saying: "Why, I keep them for you, dear, I knew you would bring the plate"; then showing the book, "What do you think of that position, dear? How would you like it so?" Although pleased, the girl blushed up to the roots of her hair as she looked at the picture. The book dropped to the floor, and William pulled her on to his knee, and tried to put his hand up her clothes. "Ah! No! No!" she cried, in a low voice; "you know I can't to-day, but perhaps I can to-morrow; you must be good to-day, sir. Don't stick up your impudent head like that. There—there—there's a squeeze for you; now I must be off," she said, putting her hand down into his lap, where it could not be seen what she was after. In a second or two she jumped up, and in spite of his efforts to detain her, escaped from the pantry. William, evidently in a great state of excitement, subsided on to a sofa, muttering, "The little witch, what a devil she is; I can't help myself, but she will be all right to-morrow." Alice, who was intently observing everything, was shocked and surprised to see his trousers all unbuttoned in front, and a great long fleshy-looking thing sticking out, seemingly hard and stiff, with a ruby-coloured head. Mr. William took hold of it with one hand, apparently for the purpose of placing it in his breeches, but he seemed to hesitate, and closing his right hand upon the shaft, rubbed it up and down. "Ah! What a fool I am to let her excite me so. Oh! Oh! I can't help it; I must." He seemed to sigh as his hand increased its rapid motion. His face flushed, and his eyes seemed ready to start from his head, and in a few moments something spurted from his instrument, the drops falling over his hands and legs, some even a yard or two over the floor. This seemed to finish his ecstasy. He sank back quite listless for a few minutes, and then rousing himself, wiped his hands on a towel, cleared up every drop of the mess, and left the pantry.

Alice was all over in a burning heat from what she had seen but instinctively felt that the mystery was only half unravelled, and promised herself to be there and see what William and Lucy would do next day. Mr. William took her for a walk as usual, and read to her, whilst she sat on his knee, and Alice wondered what could have become of that great stiff thing which she had seen in the morning. With the utmost apparent innocence, her hands touched him casu-

ally, where she hoped to feel the monster, but only resulted
in feeling a rather soft kind of bunch in his pocket.

Another morning arrived to find Alice at her post behind
the disused glass door, and she soon saw Mr. William bring
in his plate, but he put it aside, and seemed all impatient for
Lucy's arrival. "Ah!" he murmurs. "I'm as stiff as a rolling
pin at the very thought of the saucy darling," but his ideas
were cut short by the appearance of Lucy herself, who carefully bolted the door inside. Then rushing into his arms, she
covered him with kisses, exclaiming, in a low voice, "Ah!
How I have longed for him these three or four days. What
a shame women should be stopped in that way from enjoying themselves once a month. How is he this morning?" as
her hands nervously unbuttoned Mr. William's trousers, and
grasped his ready truncheon.

"What a hurry you are in, Lucy!" gasped her lover, as she
almost stifled him with her kisses. "Don't spoil it all by your
impatience; I must have my kiss first."

With a gentle effort he reclined her backwards on a sofa,
and raised her clothes till Alice had a full view of a splendid
pair of plump, white legs; but what rivetted her gaze most was
the luscious looking, pouting lips of Lucy's cunny, quite
vermilion in colour, and slightly gaping open, in a most inviting manner, as her legs were wide apart; her Mons Veneris
being covered with a profusion of beautiful curly black hair.

The butler was down on his knees in a moment, and glued
his lips to her crack, sucking and kissing furiously, to the
infinite delight of the girl, who sighed and wriggled with
pleasure; till at last Mr. William could no longer restrain
himself, but getting up upon his knees between Lucy's legs,
he brought his shaft to the charge, and to Alice's astonishment, fairly ran it right into the gaping crack, till it was all
lost in her belly; they laid still for a few moments, enjoying
the conjunction of their persons till Lucy heaved up her bottom, and the butler responded to it by a shove, then they
commenced a most exciting struggle. Alice could see the
manly shaft as it worked in and out of her sheath, glistening
with lubricity, whilst the lips of her cunny seemed to cling
to it each time of withdrawal, as if afraid of losing such a
delightful sugar stick; but this did not last long, their movements got more and more furious, till at last both seemed to
meet in a spasmodic embrace, as they almost fainted in each

other's arms, and Alice could see a profusion of creamy moisture oozing from the crack of Lucy, as they both lay in a kind of lethargy of enjoyment after their battle of love.

Mr. William was the first to break the silence: "Lucy, will you look in to-morrow, dear; you know that old spy, Mary, will be back from her holiday in a day or two, and then we shan't often have a chance."

LUCY.—"Ah; you rogue, I mean to have a little more now, I don't care if we're caught; I must have it," she said, squeezing him with her arms and gluing her lips to his, as she threw her beautiful legs right over his buttocks, and commenced the engagement once more by rapidly heaving her bottom; in fact, although he was a fine man, the weight of his body seemed as nothing in her amorous excitement.

The butler's excuses and pleading of fear, in case he was missed, &c., were all of no avail; she fairly drove him on, and he was soon as furiously excited as herself, and with a profusion of sighs, expressions of pleasure, endearment, &c., they soon died away again into a state of short voluptuous oblivion. However, Mr. William was too nervous and afraid to let her lay long; he withdrew his instrument from her foaming cunny, just as it was all slimy and glistening with the mingled juices of their love; but what a contrast to its former state, as Alice now beheld it much reduced in size, and already drooping its fiery head.

Lucy jumped up and let down her clothes, but kneeling on the floor before her lover, she took hold of his limp affair, and gave it a most luscious sucking, to the great delight of Mr. William, whose face flushed again with pleasure, and as soon as Lucy had done with her sucking kiss, Alice saw that his instrument was again stiff and ready for a renewal of their joys.

LUCY, laughing in a low tone.—"There, my boy, I'll leave you like that; think of me till to-morrow; I couldn't help giving the darling a good suck after the exquisite pleasure he had afforded me, it's like being in heaven for a little while."

With a last kiss on the lips as they parted, and Mr. William again locked his door, whilst Alice made good her retreat to prepare herself for breakfast.

It was a fine warm morning in May, and soon after breakfast Alice, with William for her guardian, set off for a ramble in the park, her blood was in a boil, and she longed to experience the joys she was sure Lucy had been surfeited with; they sauntered down to the lake, and she asked William to give her a row in the boat; he unlocked the boat-house, and handed her into a nice, broad, comfortable skiff, well furnished with soft seats and cushions.

"How nice to be here, in the shade," said Alice; "come into the boat, Willie, we will sit in it a little while, and you shall read to me before we have a row."

"Just as you please, Miss Alice," he replied, with unwonted deference, stepping into the boat, and sitting down in the stern sheets.

"Ah my head aches a little, let me recline it in your lap," said Alice, throwing off her hat, and stretching herself along on a cushion. "Why are you so precise this morning, Willie? You know I don't like to be called Miss, you can keep that for Lucy." Then noticing his confusion, "You may blush, sir, I could make you sink into your shoes if you only knew all I have seen between you and Miss Lucy."

Alice reclined her head in a languid manner on his lap, looking up and enjoying the confusion she had thrown him into; then designedly resting one hand on the lump which he seemed to have in his pocket, as if to support herself a little, she continued: "Do you think, Willie, I shall ever have as fine legs as Lucy? Don't you think I ought soon to have long dresses, sir! I'm getting quite bashful about showing my calves so much." The butler had hard work to recover his composure, the vivid recollection of the luscious episode with Lucy before breakfast was so fresh in his mind that Alice's allusions to her, and the soft girlish hand resting on his privates (even although he thought her as innocent as a lamb) raised an utter of desire in his feverish blood, which he tried to allay as much as possible, but little by little the unruly member began to swell, till he was sure she must feel it throb under her hand. With an effort he slightly shifted himself, so as to remove her hand lower down on to the thigh, as he answered as gravely as possible (feeling assured Alice could know nothing): "You're making game of me this morning. Don't you wish me to read, Alice?"

ALICE, excitedly, with an unusual flush on her face.—"You naughty man, you shall tell me what I want to know this time: How do babies come? What is the parsley bed, the nurses and doctors say they come out of? Is it not a curly lot of hair at the bottom of the woman's belly? I know that's what Lucy's got, and I've seen you kiss it, sir!"

(To be continued.)

A PROLOGUE.

Spoke by Miss Bella de Lancy, on her retiring from the Stage to open a Fashionable Bawdy House.
(Written by S. Johnson, LL.D.)

When cunt first triumphed (as the learned suppose)
O'er failing pricks, Immortal Dildo rose,
From fucks unnumbered, still erect he drew,
Exhausted cunts, and then demanded new;
Dame Nature saw him spurn her bounded reign,
And panting pricks toiled after him in vain;
The laxest folds, the deepest depths he filled;
The juiciest drained; the toughest hymens drilled.
The fair lay gasping with distended limbs,
And unremitting cockstands stormed their quims.
Then Frigging came, instructed from the school,
And scorned the aid of India-rubber tool.
With restless finger, fired the dormant blood,
Till Clitoris rose, sly, peeping thro' her hood.
Gently was worked this titillating art,
It broke no hymen, and scarce stretched the part;
Yet lured its votaries to a sudden doom,
And stamped Consumption's flush on Beauty's bloom.
Sweet Gamahuche found softer ways to fame,
It asked not Dildo's art, nor Frigging's flame.
Tongue, not prick, now probes the central hole,
And mouth, not cunt, becomes prick's destined goal.
It always found a sympathetic friend;
And pleased limp pricks, and those who could not spend,
No tedious wait, for laboured stand, delays
The hot and pouting cunt, which tongue allays.
The taste was luscious, tho' the smell was strong;

The fuck was easy, and would last so long;
Til wearied tongues found gamahuching cloy,
And pricks, and cunts, grew callous to the joy.
Then dulled by frigging, by mock pricks enlarged,
Her noble duties Cunt but ill discharged.
Her nymphæ drooped, her devil's bite grew weak,
And twice two pricks might flounder in her creek;
Till all the edge was taken off the bliss,
And Cunt's sole occupation was to piss.
Forced from her former joys, with scoff and brunt,
She saw great Arsehole lay the ghost Cunt.
Exulting buggers hailed the joyful day,
And piles and hœmerrids confirmed his sway.
But who lust's future fancies can explore,
And mark the whimsies that remain in store?
Perhaps it shall be deemed a lover's treat,
To suck the flowering quims of mares in heat;
Perhaps, where beauty held unequalled sway,
A Cochin fowl shall rival Mabel Grey;
Nobles be ruined by the Hyæna's smile,
And Seals get short engagements from th' Argyle.
Hard is her lot, that here by Fortune placed,
Must watch the wild vicissitudes of taste;
Catch every whim, learn every bawdy trick,
And chase the new born bubbles of the prick;
Ah, let not Censure term our fate, our choice,
The Bawd but echoes back the public voice;
The Brothel's laws, the Brothel's patrons give,
And those that live to please, must please to live;
Then purge these growing follies from your hearts,
And turn to female arms, and female arts;
'Tis yours this night, to bid the reign begin,
Of all the good old-fashioned ways to sin;
Clean, wholesome girls, with lip, tongue, cunt, and hand,
Shall raise, keep up, put in, take down a stand;
Your bottoms shall by lily hands be bled,
And birches blossom under every bed.

———————

THE ORIGIN SPECIES.

Air.—"Derry Down."

When Adam and Eve were first put into Eden,
They never once thought of that pleasant thing—breeding
Though they had not a rag to cover their front,
Adam sported his prick, and Eve sported her cunt.
                                        Derry down.

Adam's prick was so thick and so long—such a teaser;
Eve's cunt was so hairy and fat—such a breezer;
Adam's thing was just formed any maiden to please,
And his bollocks hung down very near to his knees.
                                        Derry down.

Eve played with his balls, and thought it no harm:
He fingered her quim and ne'er felt alarm;
He tickled her bubbies, she rubbed up his yard,
And yet for a fuck, why they felt no regard.
                                        Derry down.

But when Mrs. Eve did taste of the fruit,
It was then that her eyes first beheld Adam's root;
Then he ate an apple, and after he had done't,
Why then he first found out the value of cunt.
                                        Derry down.

Then they say they made fig leaves, that's fiddle-de-dee.
He wanted a quim, and quite ready was she;
They gazed on their privates with mutual delight,
And she soon found a hole to put jock out of sight!
                                        Derry down.

Then Adam soon laid Mrs. Eve on the grass,
He pop't in his prick, she heaved up her arse;
He wriggled, she wiggled, they both stuck to one tether
And she tickled his balls, till they both came together!
                                        Derry down.

Since then, all her children are filled with desire,
And the women a stiff-standing prick all require!

And no son of Adam will e'er take affront,
For where is the man that can live without cunt.

Derry down.

THE WANTON LASS.

Air.—"Derry Down."

There was a lass they called bonny Bet,
With a jolly fat arse, and a cunt black as jet;
Her quim had long itched, and she wanted, I vow,
A jolly good fucking, but couldn't tell how.

Derry down.

She thought of a plan that might serve as the same,
That herself she might shag without any shame;
So a carrot she got, with a point rather blunt,
And she ramm'd it and jamm'd it three parts up her cunt.

Derry down.

She liked it so well that she oft used to do it,
Till at length the poor girl had occasion to rue it;
For one day, when amusing herself with this whim,
The carrot it snapped, and part stuck in her quim.

Derry down.

She went almost mad with vexation at this,
Indeed it was time, the poor girl couldn't piss.
The lass was in torture, no rest had poor Bet,
So at last an old doctor she was forced to get.

Derry down.

The doctor he came, and she told him the case,
Then with spectacles on, and a very long face,
He bid her turn up, though she scarcely was able,
And pull up her petticoats over her navel.

Derry down.

Her clouts she held up, round her belly so plump,
And he gave her fat arse such a hell of a thump,
That he made her cry out, tho' he did it so neat,
And away flew the carrot bang into the street.

                                        Derry down.

Now a sweep passing by, he saw it come down,
Picked it up and he ate it, and said with a frown,
By God! it's not right, it's a damned shame, I say,
That people should throw buttered carrots away.

                                        Derry down.

THE MEETING OF THE WATERS.

A Parody on Moore's Melody.

There is not in this wide world a valley so sweet,
As that vale where the thighs of a pretty girl meet:
Oh, the last ray of feeling and life must depart,
Ere the bloom of that valley shall fade from my heart.

Yet it is not that Nature has shed o'er the scene,
The purest of red, the most delicate skin,
'Tis not the sweet smell of the genial hill;
Ah, no! it is something more exquisite still.

'Tis because the last favours of woman are there,
Which make every part of her body more dear.
We feel how the charms of Nature improve,
When we bathe in the spendings of her whom we love.

LOVE.

Nature, ev'rywhere the same,
Imparts to man a lustful flame;

In Russian snow or Indian fire,
All men alike indulge desire,
All alike, feel passion's heat,
All alike, enjoyment greet,
So that wheresoe'er you go,
Still the same voluptuous glow
Throbs through every purple vein,
Thirsts enjoyment to obtain;
'Mongst the dark, or with the fair,
Woman is empress everywhere.

THE PLEASURES OF LOVE.

Pressed in the arms of him I so adored,
The keeper of my charms, my pride, my lord!
By day experiencing each sweet delight,
And meeting endless transports every night.
When on our downy bed we fondly lay,
Heating each other by our am'rous play;
Till Nature, yielding to the luscious game,
Would fierce desire and quenchless lust inflame!
Oh! then we join'd in love's most warm embrace,
And pressed soft kisses on our every grace!
Around my form his pliant limbs entwined,
Love's seat of bliss to him I then resigned!
We pant, we throb, we both convulsive start!
Heavens! then what passions thro' our fibres dart!
We heave, we wriggle, bite, laugh, tremble, sigh!
We taste Elysian bliss—we fondle—die.

THE RIVAL TOASTS.

An English and an American vessel of war being in port
together, Captain Balls, of the former, invited the officers of

the Yankee frigate to dine in board of his ship, but stipu-
lated, in order to avoid any unpleasantness, that no offensive
or personal toasts should be proposed, to which the Ameri-
cans cheerfully assented. However, after dinner, during dessert, when the conversation happened to turn warmly upon
the respective merits of the two nations, a Yankee officer
suddenly stood up, and said he wished to propose a toast,
which he should take as a personal offense if anyone refused
to drink it.

Captain B. mildly expressed a hope that it was nothing offensive, but consented to drink to whatever it might be, with
the proviso that, if he thought fit to do so, he should propose
another afterwards.

Then shouted the American, exultingly: "Here's to the
glorious American flag: Stars to enlighten all nations, and
Stripes to flog them."

Captain B. drained a bumper to the American's toast; then
turning to the old ship's steward, standing behind his chair,
said quietly: "You can beat that, can't you, Jack?"

"Ay! Ay! Sir! If you fill me a stiff'un."

The Captain mixed him a good swig of hot and strong.
Then handing the steward the glass, he thundered out:
"Silence for Jack's toast, and any gentleman here present,
refusing to drink to it, I shall not take it as a personal
offense, but at once order the gunner's mate to give him
three dozen. Now then, Jack."

Jack, with a grim smile, and bowing to the Yankee officer,
said: "Then here's to the ramping, roaring British Lion, who
shits on the stars, and wipes his arse on the stripes."

NURSERY RHYMES.

There was a young man of Bombay,
Who fashioned a cunt out of clay;
    But the heat of his prick
    Turned it into a brick,
And chafed all his foreskin away.

There was a young man of Peru,
Who had nothing whatever to do;
    So he took out his carrot
    And buggered his parrot,
And sent the result to the Zoo.

There was a young girl of Ostend,
Who her maidenhead tried to defend,
    But a Chasseur d'Afrique
    Inserted his prick,
And taught that ex-maid how to spend.

There was a young man of Calcutta,
Who tried to write "Cunt" on a shutter.
    When he got to C-U,
    A pious Hindoo
Knocked him arse over head in the gutter.

There was a young man of Ostend,
Whose wife caught him fucking her friend;
    "It's no use, my duck,
    Interrupting our fuck,
For I'm damned if I draw till I spend."

There was a young man of Wood Green,
Who tried to fart "God Save the Queen."
    When he reached the soprano,
    He shot his guano,
And his breeches weren't fit to be seen.

There was a young man of Dundee,
Who one night went out on the spree;
    He wound up his clock
    With the tip of his cock,
And buggered himself with the key.

There was a young lady of Troy,
Who invented a new kind of joy:
    She sugared her thing
    Both outside and in,
And then had it sucked by a boy.

There was a young man of Santander,
Who tried hard to bugger a gander;
    But the virtuous bird
    Plugged his arse with a turd,
And refused to such low tastes to pander.

There was a young lady of Hitchin,
Who was skrotching her cunt in the kitchen;
    Her father said "Rose,
    It's the crabs, I suppose."
"You're right, pa, the buggers are itching."

There was an old person of Sark,
Who buggered a pig in the dark;
    The swine, in surprise,
    Murmured "God blast your eyes,
Do you take me for Boulton or Park?"

AMEN.

Oh! cunt is a kingdom, and prick is its lord;
A whore is a slave, and her mistress a bawd;
Her quim is her freehold, which brings in her rent;
Where you pay when you enter, and leave when you've spent.

THE PEARL,

A Journal of Facetiæ and Voluptuous Reading.

| No. 2. | PUBLISHED MONTHLY. | Aug. 1879 |

SUB-UMBRA, OR SPORT AMONG THE SHE-NOODLES.

(Continued.)

Annie was ready to faint as she screamed, "Walter! Walter! Save me from the horrid beast!" I comforted and reassured her as well as I was able, and seeing that we were on the safe side of the gate, a few loving kisses soon set her all right. We continued our walk, and soon spying out a favourable shady spot, I said: "Come, Annie dear, let us sit down and recover from the startling interruption; I am sure, dear, you must still feel very agitated, besides I must get you now to compensate me for the rude disappointment."

She seemed to know that her hour had come; the hot blushes swept in crimson waves across her lovely face, as she cast down her eyes, and permitted me to draw her down by my side on a mossy knoll, and we lay side by side, my lips glued to hers in a most ardent embrace.

"Annie! Oh! Annie!" I gasped. "Give me the tip of your tongue, love." She tipped me the velvet without the slightest hesitation, drawing, at the same time, what seemed a deep sigh of delightful anticipation as she yielded to my slightest wish. I had one arm under her head, and with the other I gently removed her hat, and threw aside my own golgotha, kissing and sucking at her delicious tongue all the while. Then I placed one of her hands on my ready cock, which was in a bursting state, saying, as I released her tongue for a moment: "There, Annie, take the dart of love in your hand." She grasped it nervously, as she softly murmured: "Oh, Walter, I'm so afraid; and yet—oh yet, dearest, I feel, I die, I must taste the sweets of love, this forbidden fruit," her voice sinking almost to a whisper, as she pressed and passed her hand up and down my shaft. My hand was also busy finding its way under her clothes as I again glued my mouth to hers, and sucked at her tongue till I could feel her vibrate all over with the excess of her emotion. My hand, which had taken possession of the seat of bliss, being fairly deluged with her warm glutinous spendings.

"My love; my life! I must kiss you there, and taste the nectar of love," I exclaimed, as I snatched my lips from hers, and reversing my position, buried my face between her unresisting thighs. I licked up the luscious spendings with rapturous delight from the lips of her tight little cunny, then my tongue found its way further, till it tickled her sensitive clitoris, and put her into a frenzy of mad desire for still further enjoyment; she twisted her legs over my head, squeezing my head between her firm plump thighs in an ecstasy of delight.

Wetting my finger in her luscious crack, I easily inserted it in her beautifully wrinkled brown bum-hole, and keeping my tongue busy in titillating the stiff little clitoris, I worked her up into such a furious state of desire that she clutched my cock and brought it to her mouth, as I lay over her to give her the chance of doing so; she rolled her tongue round the purple head, and I could also feel the loving playful bite of her pearly teeth. It was the acme of erotic enjoyment. She came again in another luscious flood of spendings, whilst she eagerly sucked every drop of my sperm as it burst from my excited prick.

We both nearly fainted from the excess of our emotions, and lay quite exhausted for a few moments, till I felt her dear lips again pressing and sucking my engine of love. The effect was electric; I was as stiff as ever.

"Now, darling, for the real stroke of love," I exclaimed. Shifting my position, and parting her quivering thighs, so that I could kneel between them. My knees were placed upon her skirts so as to preserve them from the grass stain. She lay before me in a delightful state of anticipation, her beautiful face all blushes of shame, and the closed eyelids, fringed with their long dark lashes, her lips slightly open, and the finely developed, firm, plump globes of her bosom heaving in a state of tumultuous excitement. It was ravishing, I felt mad with lust, and could no longer put off the actual consummation. I could not contain myself. Alas; poor maidenhead! Alas! for your virginity! I brought my cock to the charge, presented the head just slightly between the lips of her vagina. A shudder of delight seemed to pass through her frame at the touch of my weapon, as her eyes opened, and she whispered, with a soft, loving smile, "I know it will hurt, but Walter, dear Walter, be both firm and kind. I must have it, if it kills me." Throwing her arms around my neck, she drew my lips to hers, as she thrust her tongue into my mouth with all the abandon of love, and shoved up her bottom to meet my charge.

I placed one hand under her buttocks, whilst, with the other, I kept my affair straight to the mark; then pushing vigorously, the head entered about an inch, till it was chock up to the opposing hymen. She gave a start of pain, but her eyes gazed into mine with a most encouraging look.

"Throw your legs over my back, dear," I gasped, scarcely relinquishing her tongue for a moment. Her lovely thighs turned round me in a spasmodic frenzy of determination to bear the worst. I gave a ruthless push, just as her bottom heaved up to meet me, and the deed was done. King Priapus had burst through all obstacles to our enjoyment. She gave a subdued shriek of agonized pain, and I felt myself throbbing in possession of her inmost charms.

"You darling! You love me! My brave Annie, how well you stood the pain. Let us lay still for a moment or two, and then for the joys of love," I exclaimed, as I kissed her face, forehead, eyes, and mouth in a transport of delight, at feeling the victory so soon accomplished.

Presently I could feel the tight sheath of her vagina contracting on my cock in the most delicious manner. This challenge was too much for my impetuous steed. He gave a gentle thrust. I could see by the spasm of pain which passed over her beautiful face, that it was still painful to her, but, restraining my ardour, I worked very gently, although my lust was so maddening that I could not restrain a copious spend; so I sank on her bosom in love's delicious lethargy.

It was only for a few moments, I could feel her tremble beneath me with voluptuous ardour, and the sheath being now well lubricated, we commenced a delightful bout of ecstatic fucking. All her pain was forgotten, the wounded parts soothed by the flow of my semen now only revelled in the delightful friction of love; she seemed to boil over in spendings, my delighted cock revelled in it, as he thrust in and out with all my manly vigour; we spent three or four times in a delirium of voluptuousness, till I was fairly vanquished by her impetuosity, and begged her to be moderate, and not to injure herself by excessive enjoyment.

"Oh! can it be possible to hurt one's self by such a delightful pleasure?" she sighed, then seeing me withdraw my limp tool from her still longing cunt, she smiled archly, as she said with a blush, "Pardon my rudeness, dear Walter, but I fear it is you who are most injured after all; look at your bloodstained affair."

"You lovely little simpleton," I said, kissing her rapturously, "that's your own virgin blood; let me wipe you, darling," as I gently applied my handkerchief to her pouting slit, and afterwards to my own cock. "This, dearest Annie, I shall treasure up as the proofs of your virgin love, so delightfully surrendered to me this day," exhibiting the ensanguined mouchoir to her gaze.

We now arose from our soft mossy bed, and mutually assisted each other to remove all traces of our love engagement.

Then we walked on, and I enlightened the dear girl into all the arts and practices of love. "Do you think," I remarked, "that your sisters or Frank have any idea of what the joys of love are like?"

"I believe they would enter into it as ardently as I do, if they were but once initiated," she replied. "I have often heard Frank say when kissing us, that we made him burn all over"; and then blushing deeply as her eyes met mine, "Oh! dear Walter, I'm afraid you will think we are awfully rude girls, but when we go to bed at night, myself and sisters often compare our budding charms, and crack little jokes about the growing curls of mine and Sophie's slits, and the hairless little pussey of Polly; we have such games of slapping, and romps too, sometimes; it has often made me feel a kind of all-overishness of feverish excitement I could not understand, but thanks to you, love, I can make it all out now; I wish you could only get a peep at us, dear."

"Perhaps it might be managed; you know my room is next to yours, I could hear you laughing and having a game last night."

"I know we did, we had such fun," she replied, "it was

Polly trying to put my pussey in curl papers, but how can you manage it, dear?"

Seeing she fully entered into my plans for enjoyment, we consulted together, and at last I hit upon an idea which I thought might work very well; it was that I should first sound Frank and enlighten him a little into the ways of love, and then as soon as he was ripe for our purpose, we would surprise the three sisters whilst naked bathing, and slap their naked bottoms all round; that Annie should encourage her sisters to help her in tearing off all our clothes, and then we could indulge in a general romp of love.

Annie was delighted at the idea, and I promised the very next day to begin with Frank, or perhaps that very afternoon if I got a chance.

We returned to the house, Annie's cheeks blushing and carrying a beautiful flush of health, and her mama remarked that our walk had evidently done her very great good, little guessing that her daughter, like our first mother Eve, had that morning tasted of the forbidden fruit, and was greatly enlightened and enlivened thereby.

After luncheon I asked Frank to smoke a cigarette in my room, which he at once complied with.

As soon as I had closed the door, I said, "Old fellow, did you ever see *Fanny Hill*, a beautiful book of love and pleasure?"

"What, a smutty book, I suppose you mean? No, Walter, but if you have got it I should wonderfully like to look at it," he said, his eyes sparkling with animation.

"Here it is, my boy, only I hope it won't excite you too much; you can look it over by yourself, as I read the *Times*," said I, taking it out of my dressing-case, and handing it to his eager grasp.

He sat close to me in an easy lounging chair, and I watched him narrowly as he turned over the pages and gloated over the beautiful plates; his prick hardened in his breeches till it was quite stiff and rampant.

"Ha! Ha! Ha!! old fellow, I thought it would fetch you out!" I said, laying my hand upon his cock. "By Jove, Frank! what a tosser yours has grown since we used to play in bed together a long time ago. I'll lock the door, we must compare our parts, I think mine is nearly as big as yours."

He made no remark, but I could see he was greatly excited

by the book. Having locked the door, I leant over his shoulder and made my remarks upon the plates as he turned them over. At length the book dropped from his hands, and his excited gaze was rivetted on my bursting breeches. "Why, Walter, you are as bad as I am," he said, with a laugh, "let's see which is the biggest," pulling out his hard, stiff prick, and then laying his hands on me pulled my affair out to look at.

We handled each other in an ecstasy of delight, which ended in our throwing off all our clothes, and having a mutual fuck between our thighs on the bed; we spent in rapture, and after a long dalliance he entered into my plans, and we determined to have a lark with the girls as soon as we could get a chance. Of course I was mum as to what had passed between Annie and myself.

(*To be continued.*)

MISS COOTE'S CONFESSION,

Or the Voluptuous Experiences of an Old Maid; In a series of Letters to a Lady Friend.

Letter II.

My Dear Nellie,

To continue my tale where I left off. Jane and I had some further conversation next morning, which, to the best of my recollection, was as follows:—

Rosa.—"So, Jane, you have been whipped, have you. What was it for?"

Jane.—"The first time was for being seen walking with a young man coming from church. The General said I had never been, and only pretended to be religious for the chance of gadding about with young fellows, which must be checked, or I should be ruined."

Rosa.—"Well; didn't you feel revengeful at being whipped for that?"

Jane.—"So I did, but forgot all about it in the delight I had in seeing Jemima well cut up. Oh, she did just catch it, I can tell you; but she's as strong and hard as leather."

Rosa.—"So I could forget and forgive too, if I could but cut you all up well. I've got a good mind to begin with you, Jane, when I don't feel quite so sore."

Jane.—"Ah! But I know you hate Jemima, and would rather see her triced up to the horse. Perhaps we shall be able to get her into a scrape between us, if we put our heads together."

Rosa.—"Oh! you sly girl. Don't you think I'll let you off, much as I long to repay the others. Just wait till I feel well enough, and I'll settle you first. There will be plenty of opportunities, as you are to sleep with me in my room every night. I haven't forgotten how you persuaded me to dress for dinner, when you knew, all the time, what was coming."

Jane.—"Dear Miss Rosie, I couldn't help it. Mrs. Mansell sent me up to dress you. The old General put it off till after dinner, as he likes to see the culprits dressed as nicely as possible. If he punished any of us, we have to attend punishment drill in our very best clothes, and if they get damaged, Mrs. Mansell soon fits us out again, so we don't lose much by a good birching. I have known Jemima to get into trouble so as to damage her things, but Sir Eyre made her smart well for them."

I was very sore for several days, but managed to make and secrete a fine bunch of twigs, ready for Miss Jane when she would little expect it; in fact, she did not know I had been into the garden or out of the house. Of course she was a much stronger and bigger girl than myself, so I should have to secure her by some stratagem. I let her think I had quite forgotten my threat, but one evening, just as we were both undressed for bed, I said, "Jane, did Mrs. Mansell or Jemima ever birch you without grandfather knowing it?"

Jane.—"Yes, dear Miss Rosie, they've served me out shamefully, more than once."

Rosa.—"How did they manage that?"

Jane.—"Why, I was tied by my hands to the foot of the bedstead."

Rosa.—"Oh! Do show me, and let me tie you up to see how it all looked."

Jane.—"Very well; if it's any pleasure to you, Miss."

Rosa.—"What shall I tie you up with? You're as strong as Samson."

JANE.—"A couple of handkerchiefs will do, and there's a small comforter to tie my legs."

By her directions I soon had her hands tied to the two knobs at the foot of the bed, and her feet stretched out a little behind were secured to the legs of the table.

"Oh! My!" said Jane. "You have fixed me tight. What did you tie so hard for? I can't get away till you release me."

"Stay! Stay!" I cried. "I must see you quite prepared now you are properly fixed up"; and I quickly turned up her night-dress and secured it well above her waist, so as to expose her plump bottom and delicately mossed front to my astonished gaze.

"Oh! What a beauty you are, Jane," said I, kissing her, "and you know I love you, but your naughty little bum-be-dee must be punished. It is a painful duty, but I'll let you see it's no joke, Miss. Look, what a fine swishtail I've got," producing my rod.

"Mercy! Mercy!" cried Jane. "Dear Miss Rosie, you won't beat me; I've always been so kind to you!"

"It won't do, Jane, I must do my duty. You were one of the lot against me, and the first I can catch. It may be years before I can pay off the others."

The sight of her beautiful posteriors filled me with a gloating desire to exercise my skill upon them, and see a little of what I had to feel myself. Nervously grasping my birch, without further delay, I commenced the assault by some sharp strokes, each blow deepening the rosy tints to a deeper red.

"Ah! Ah! What a shame. You're as bad as the old General, you little witch, to take me so by surprise."

"You don't seem at all sorry, Miss," I cried; "but I'll try and bring down your impudence; in fact, I begin to think you are one of the worst of them, and only acted the hypocrite, with your pretended compassion, when you were, in reality, it all the time. But it's my turn now. Of course, you were too strong for me, unless I had trapped you so nicely. How do you like it, Miss Jane?" All this time I kept on, whisk, whisk, whisk, in quick succession, till her bottom began to look quite interesting.

"You little wretch! You vixen!" gasped Jane. "Your grand-father shall hear of this."

"That's your game, is it, Miss Tell-tale. At any rate, you'll be well paid first," I replied. The sight of her buttocks only seemed to add to my energy, and it was quite a thrill of pleasure when I first saw the blood come. She writhed and wriggled with suppressed sighs and ahs, but each time she gave utterance to any expression, it seemed only for the purpose of irritating me more and more. My excitement became intense, the cruel havoc seemed to be an immense satisfaction to me, and her bottom really was in deplorable state through my inconsiderate fury. At last, quite worn out and fatigued, I could hold the rod no longer, and my passion melted into love and pity, as I saw her in an apparently listless and fainting condition, with drooping head, eyes closed, and hands clenched.

The worn-out birch was dropped, and kissing her tenderly, I sobbed out, "Jane, dear, Jane, I both love and forgive you now, and you will find me as tender to you as you were to me after my flogging."

Her hands and feet were soon released, when to my astonishment, she threw her arms round my neck as with sparkling eyes and a luscious kiss she said softly, "And forgive you too, Miss Rosie, for you don't know what pleasure you have given me, the last few moments have been bliss indeed."

This was all a puzzle to me at the time, but I understood it well enough afterwards. She made quite light of her bruised bottom, saying, "What was awful to you was nothing to me, Miss Rosie, I am so much older and tougher; besides, the first time is always the worst; it was too bad of Sir Eyre to cut you up as he did, but your obstinacy made him forget himself; you'll grow to like it as I do."

This and much more in the same strain passed as we bathed and soothed the irritated parts, and we finally fell asleep with a promise from me to let her give me a pleasant lesson in a day or two.

Things went on smoothly for a few days, my punishment had been too severe for me to lightly dare a second engagement with the General; still I burned for a chance to avenge myself on anyone but Jane, who was now my bosom friend. We discussed all sorts of schemes for getting anyone but ourselves into trouble, but to no purpose. The old gentleman often cautioned me to take care, as the next time he should not fail to make me cry, "Peccavi."

One fine afternoon, however, being in the garden with the housekeeper, I remarked to her, "What a pity it was grandfather let the nectarines hang and spoil, and no one allowed to taste them."

"My dear," said Mrs. Mansell, "if you take two or three he'll never miss them, only you must not tell that I said so, it's a shame to let them rot."

"But, Mrs. Mansell, that would be stealing," I replied.

"When nothing's lost nothing can have been stolen; it's only a false sense of honesty, and you, the little mistress of the house," she urged.

"Well, you are the serpent, and I'm Eve, I suppose; they really do look delicious, and you won't tell, will you?" I asked in my simplicity; so the fruit was plucked, and Mrs. Mansell helped to eat it, which put me quite at my ease.

Just before dinner next day we were surprised by the General calling us all into his sitting-room, "How's this, Mrs. Mansell?" he said, looking fearfully angry. "I can't leave my keys in the lock of that cabinet without someone tasting my rum; I've long known there was a sly sipping thief about, so I have been sly too. Finding it was the rum that was most approved, the last time the decanter was filled I put a little scratch with my diamond ring, to mark the height of the liquor in the bottle, and have only used the brandy for myself. Look! whoever it is has got through nearly a pint in three or four days. Come here, Rosa, now Mrs. Mansell, and now Jemima," said he, sternly, smelling the breath of each in turn.

"Woman," he said, as she faltered and hesitated to undergo this ordeal, "I don't think you were a sneaking thief, if you really wanted a little spirit, Mrs. Mansell would have let you have it, I dare say, as you have been with us some years, and we don't like change, but you shall be cured of thieving to-morrow; you should have been well thrashed at once, but we have a friend to dinner this evening, it will do you good to wait and think of what's coming. Be off, now, and mind the dinner's served up properly or you'll catch it in Indian style to-morrow, and be a curried chicken if ever you were."

Our visitor was an old fox-hunting colonel, our nearest neighbour, and my spirits were so elated at the prospect of Jemima's punishment that it seemed to me the pleasantest evening I had ever spent in that house.

All next day grandfather spent looking over the garden, and a presentiment came over me that the nectarines would be missed; if he had been so cunning in one thing, he might be in another.

My fears were only too well founded, for catching sight of me with the housekeeper, cutting a nosegay for the criminal's wear, he said, "Mrs. Mansell, you had better make another bouquet whilst you are about it, someone has been at the nectarines; do you know anything about it, Rosa?"

"Oh! Grandfather, you know I was strictly forbidden to touch the fruit," said I, as innocently as possible.

"Mrs. Mansell, do you know anything of it, as she won't give a direct answer," said he, eyeing me sternly.

I was covered with confusion, and to make it worse, Mrs. Mansell with affected reluctance to tell an untruth, confessed the whole affair.

"'Pon my word, a nice honest lot you all are, as I dare say Jane is like the rest; Mrs. Mansell, I'm astonished at you, and I think your punishment will be enough, when you consider how seriously I look upon such things, but as to that girl Rosa, prevarication is worse than a lie, such cunning in one so young is frightful, but we'll settle Jemima first, and then think of what's to be done."

Left in this state of uncertainty, I fled to Jane for consolation, who assured me it was a good thing Jemima stood first, as the old man would get exhausted, and perhaps let me off lightly, if I screamed and begged for mercy.

Thus encouraged, I managed to eat a good dinner, and took an extra glass of wine on the sly (I was only supposed to take one). Thus fortified I marched to the punishment drill with great confidence, especially as I so wished to see Jemima well thrashed.

When first I set eyes upon her, as she curtseyed to the General, who was seated in the chair, rod in hand, her appearance struck me with admiration; rather above medium height, dark auburn hair, fresh colour, and sparkling blue eyes, low cut dark blue silk dress, almost revealing the splendours of her full rounded bosom, the large nosegay fixed rather on one side under her dimpled chin, pink satin high-heeled shoes, with silver buckles; she had short sleeves, but fawn-coloured gloves of kid, and a delicate net, covering her arms to the elbows, took off all coarseness of her red skin or hands.

"Prepare her at once," said the General, "she knows too

well all I would say. Here, Rosie, hand me down that big
bunch of birch, this little one is no use for her fat rump.
Ha! ha! this is better," said he, whisking it about.

Jane and the housekeeper had already stripped off the blue
silk, and were proceeding to remove the underskirts of white
linen, trimmed with broad lace; the bouquet had fallen to the
floor, and presently the submissive victim stood with only
chemise and drawers. What a glimpse I had of her splendid
white neck and bosom, what deliciously full and rounded legs,
with pink silk stockings and handsome garters (for the General was very strict as to the costume of his penitents).

I assisted to tie her up, and unfastening her drawers, Jane
drew them well down, whilst Mrs. Mansell pinned up her
chemise, fully exposing the broad expanse of her glorious buttocks, the brilliant whiteness of her skin showing to perfection by the dazzling glare of the well-lighted room. I gave
her two or three smart pats of approval just to let her know
I hadn't forgotten the slap she gave me, then drew aside to
make way for Sir Eyre.

My thoughts were so entirely absorbed by the fascinating
spectacle that I lost all remembrance of my own impending
turn. Whack! came the big birch, with a force to have made
her jump out of her skin, if possible, but only a stifled,
"Ah—r—r—re!" and a broad, red mark were the results; the
blood mounted to her face, and she seemed to hold her
breath for each blow as it came, but the rod was so heavy,
and the old General so vigorous, that in less than a dozen
strokes her fair bottom was smeared with blood and bits of
birch were lying in all directions. "Ah! Ah!! Oh!!!" she
screamed, "do have mercy, sir, I can't stand it. Oh! oh! indeed I can't."

"You sly thief, don't think I'll let you off before you're
dead; if I don't cure you now I shall lose a good servant," exclaimed Sir Eyre, cutting away.

My blood boiled with excitement of a most pleasurable
kind, young as I was, and cruel as I knew it to be, no pity for
the victim entered my breast; it is a sensation only to be
experienced by real lovers of the rod.

"You like rum, do you, Miss?" said the General. "Did you
take it raw or mixed? I'll make your bottom raw."

The poor old man was obliged now to sit down for want of
breath. Mrs. Mansell, understanding his wishes, at once took

his place with a fresh birch, without giving the victim any respite.

"She must, indeed, be well punished, sir. I'm sure they're never denied anything so long as they behave themselves," said she, with a stern relentless face; in fact, after a stroke or two, her light-brown hair was all in disorder from the exertion, and her dashing hazel eyes, and well-turned figure, made me think her a goddess of vengeance. "Will you? Will you do so again? You ungrateful thief," she kept on saying, with a blow to each question.

Poor Jemima moaned, sobbed, and sometimes cried out for mercy, whilst the blood fairly trickled down her thighs, but the housekeeper seemed to hear nothing, and Sir Eyre was in an ecstasy of gloating delight. This could not last long, however strong the victim might be. Becoming exhausted with her accumulated sensations, she at last fairly fainted, and we had to dash cold water over her face to recover her; then covered with a cloak, she was led off to her room, and left to herself.

"Now, Rosa," said the General, holding out a light green bunch of fresh birch, "kiss the rod, and get ready for your turn."

Hardly knowing what I was about, I inclined my head and gave the required kiss. Mrs. Mansell and Jane had me prepared in no time, as I was quite passive; and as soon as I was fairly exposed and spread-eagled on the horse, the old General rose to his task.

"You have seen how severe I can be, by Jemima's punishment," said he; "but, perhaps, you did not think your answer to me yesterday was any offense, and I am almost inclined to forgive you, but remember in future, if you get off lightly this time, a plain lie is better than prevarication. I think the last flogging must have done you great good, your conduct is quite different to-night. But now, remember—remember—remember!" he cried again, giving sharp, cutting strokes at each word. My poor bottom tingled with agony, and I cried loudly for mercy, promising to be strictly truthful in future; so, after about twenty strokes, he said: "You may go this time," finishing me off with a tremendous remembrance, which made me fairly shake with the concussion, and was the only blow which actually drew the blood, although I had some fine tender weals. This must finish my second letter. Believe me my true-born child of the rod,

Your loving friend,
Rosa Belinda Coote.

(To be continued.)

LADY POKINGHAM, OR THEY ALL DO IT;

Giving an Account of her Luxurious Adventures, both before and after her Marriage with Lord Crim-Con.

PART I.
(Continued.)

William felt ready to drop; the perspiration stood on his brow in great drops, but his lips refused to speak, and Alice continued in a soft whisper: "I saw it all this morning, Willie dear, and what joy that great red-head thing of yours seemed to give her. You must let me into the secret, and I will never tell. This is the monster you shoved into her so furiously. I must look at it and feel it; how hard it has got under my touch. La! What a funny thing! I can get it out as Lucy did," pulling open his trousers and letting out the rampant engine of love. She kissed its red velvety head, saying: "What a sweet, soft thing to touch. Oh! I must caress it a little." Her touches were like fire to his senses; speechless with rapture and surprise, he silently submitted to the freak of the wilful girl, but his novel position was so exciting, he could not restrain himself, but the sperm boiled up from his penis all over her hands and face.

"Ah!" she exclaimed. "That's just what I saw it do yesterday morning. Does it do that inside of Lucy?"

Here William recovered himself a little, and wiping her face and hands with his handkerchief, put away the rude plaything, saying, "Oh! My God! I'm lost! What have you done, Alice? It's awful! Never mention it again. I mustn't walk out with you any more."

Alice burst into sobs.

"Oh! Oh! Willie! How unkind! Do you think I will tell? Only I must share the pleasure with Lucy. Oh! Kiss me as you did her, and we won't say any more about it to-day."

William loved the little girl too well to refuse such a delightful task, but he contented himself with a very short suck at her virgin cunny, lest his erotic passion should urge him to outrage her at once.

"How nice to feel your lovely tongue there. How beautifully it tickled and warmed me all over; but you were so quick, and left off just as it seemed nicer than ever, dear

Willie," said Alice, embracing and kissing him with ardour.

"Gently, darling; you mustn't be so impulsive; it's a very dangerous game for one so young. You must be careful how you look at me, or notice me, before others," said Mr. William, returning her kisses, and feeling himself already quite unable to withstand the temptation of such a delicious liaison.

"Ah!" said Alice, with extraordinary perception for one so young. "You fear Lucy. Our best plan is to take her into our confidence. I will get rid of my lady's-maid, I never did like her, and will ask mama to give Lucy the place. Won't that be fine, dear? We shall be quite safe in all our little games then."

The butler, now more collected in his ideas, and with a cooler brain, could not but admire the wisdom of this arrangement, so he assented to the plan, and he took the boat out for a row to cool their heated blood, and quiet the impulsive throbbings of a pair of fluttering hearts.

The next two or three days were wet and unfavourable for outdoor excursions, and Alice took advantage of this interval to induce her mother to change her lady's-maid, and install Lucy in the situation.

Alice's attendant slept in a little chamber, which had two doors, one opening into the corridor, whilst the other allowed free and direct access to her little mistress's apartment, which it adjoined.

The very first night Lucy retired to rest in her new room, she had scarcely been half-an-hour in bed (where she lay, reflecting on the change, and wondering how she would now be able to enjoy the butler's company occasionally), before Alice called out for her. In a moment she was at the young lady's bedside, saying: "What can I do, Miss Alice, are you not warm enough? These damp nights are so chilly."

"Yes, Lucy," said Alice, "that must be what it is. I feel cold and restless. Would you mind getting in bed with me? You will soon make me warm."

Lucy jumped in, and Alice nestled close up to her bosom, as if for warmth, but in reality to feel the outlines of her beautiful figure.

"Kiss me, Lucy," she said; "I know I shall like you so much better than Mary. I couldn't bear her." This was lovingly responded to, and Alice continued, as she pressed her hand on the bosom of her bedfellow, "What large titties you have, Lucy. Let me feel them. Open your nightdress, so I can lay my face against them."

The new femme de chambre was naturally of a warm and loving disposition; she admitted all the familiarities of her young mistress, whose hands began to wander in a most searching manner about her person, feeling the soft, firm skin of her bosom, belly, and bottom; the touches of Alice seemed to fire the blood, and rouse every voluptuous emotion within her; she sighed and kissed her little mistress again and again.

ALICE.—"What a fine rump! How hard and plump your flesh is, Lucy! Oh, my! what's all this hair at the bottom of your belly? My dear, when did it come?"

LUCY.—"Oh! pray don't, Miss, it's so rude; you will be the same in two or three years' time; it frightened me when it first began to grow, it seemed so unnatural."

ALICE.—"We're only girls, there is no harm in touching each other, is there; just feel how different I am."

LUCY.—"Oh! Miss Alice," pressing the young girl's naked belly to her own, "you don't know how you make me feel when you touch me there."

ALICE (with a slight laugh).—"Does it make you feel better when Mr. William, the butler, touches you, dear?" tickling the hairy crack with her finger.

LUCY.—"For shame, Miss! I hope you don't think I would let him touch me"; evidently in some confusion.

ALICE.—"Don't be frightened, Lucy, I won't tell, but I have seen it all through the old glass door in his pantry. Ah! you see I know the secret, and must be let in to share the fun."

LUCY.—"Oh! My God! Miss Alice, what have you seen? I shall have to leave the house at once."

ALICE.—"Come, come, don't be frightened, you know I'm fond of Mr. William, and would never do him any harm, but you can't have him all to yourself; I got you for my maid to prevent your jealous suspicions and keep our secret between us."

Lucy was in a frightful state of agitation. "What! has he been such a brute as to ruin you, Miss Alice! I'll murder him if he has," she cried.

ALICE.—"Softly, Lucy, not so loud, someone will hear you; he's done nothing yet, but I saw your pleasure when he put that thing into your crack, and am determined to share your joys, so don't be jealous, and we can all three be happy together."

LUCY.—"It would kill you dear; that big thing of his would split you right up."

ALICE.—"Never mind," kissing her lovingly, "you keep the secret and I'm not afraid of being seriously hurt."

Lucy sealed the compact with a kiss, and they spent a most loving night together, indulging in every variety of kissing and tickling, and Alice had learnt from her bedfellow nearly all the mysterious particulars in connection with the battles of Venus before they fell asleep in each other's arms.

Fine weather soon returned, and Alice, escorted by the butler, went for one of her usual rambles, and they soon penetrated into a thick copse at the further end of the park, and sat down in a little grassy spot, where they were secure from observation.

William had thoughtfully brought with him an umbrella, as well as a great coat and cloak, which he spread upon the grass for fear Miss Alice might take cold.

"Ah! you dear old fellow," said Alice, seating herself, and, taking his hand, pulled him down beside her. "I understand everything now, and you are to make me happy by making a woman of me, as you did Lucy; you must do it, Willie, dear, I shall soon make you so you can't help yourself." Uubuttoning his trousers and handling his already stiff pego, "What a lovely dear it is; how I long to feel its juice spouting into my bowels; I know it's painful, but it won't kill me, and then, ah! the heavenly bliss I know you will make me feel, as you do Lucy when you have her; how will you do it? will you lay over me?"

William, unable to resist her caresses and already almost at spending point, makes her kneel over his face, as he lay on his back, so that he may first lubricate her maiden cunny with his tongue. This operation titillates and excites the little girl, so that she amorously presses herself on his mouth as she faces towards his cock, which she never leaves hold of all the while; he spends in ecstasy, whilst she also feels the pleasure of a first virgin emission.

"Now's the time, Alice, dear, my affair is so well greased, and your pussey is also ready; if I get over you I might be too violent and injure you; the best way is for you to try and do it yourself by straddling over me, and directing its head to your cunny, and then keep pressing down upon it, as well as the first painful sensations will allow; it will all depend on your own courage for the success of the experiment," said William.

ALICE.—"Ah! you shall see my determination," as she began to act upon his suggestion, and fitting the head of his pego into her slit, soon pressed down so as to take in and quite cover the first inch of it.

Here the pain of stretching and distension seemed almost too much for her, but she gave a sudden downward plunge of her body, which, although she almost fainted with the dreadful pain, got in at least three inches.

"What a plucky girl you are, my dear Alice," said William, in delight. "As soon as you can bear it, raise yourself up a little, and come down with all your force. It is so well planted, the next good thrust will complete my possession of your lovely charms."

"I don't care if I die in the effort," she whispered, softly. "Never mind how it hurts me, help all you can, Willie dear, this time," as she raised herself off him again, and he took hold of her buttocks, to lend his assistance to the grave girl.

Clenching her teeth firmly, and shutting her eyes, she gave another desperate plunge upon William's spear of love, the hymen was broken, and she was fairly impaled to the roots of his affair. But it cost her dear, she fell forward in a dead faint, whilst the trickling blood proved the sanguinary nature of Love's victory.

The butler withdrew himself, all smeared with her virgin blood, but he had come prepared for such an emergency, and at once set about using restoratives to bring her round, and presently succeeded in his efforts; her eyes opened with a smile, and whispering softly, Alice said:—

"Ah! that last thrust was awful, but it's over now. Why did you take him away? Oh! put it back at once, dear, and let me have the soothing injection Lucy said would soon heal all my bruised parts."

He glued his lips to hers, and gently applied the head of his pego to her blood-stained crack, gradually inserted it till it was three-fourths in; then, without pressing further, he commenced to move slowly and carefully. The lubricity soon increased, and he could feel the tight loving contractions of her vagina, which speedily brought him to a crisis once more, and with a sudden thrust, he plunged up to the hilt, and shot his very essence into her bowels, as he almost fainted with the excess of his emotions.

They laid motionless, enjoying each other's mutual pressures, till Mr. William withdrew, and taking a fine cambric handkerchief, wiped the virgin blood first from the lips of her cunny, then off his own weapon, declaring, as he put the redstained mouchoir in his pocket, that he would keep it for ever, in remembrance of the charms she had so lovingly surrendered to him.

The butler prudently refrained from the further indulgence in voluptuous pleasure for the day, and, after a good rest, Alice returned to the house, feeling very little the worse for her sacrifice, and very happy in having secured part of the love of dear and faithful William.

How suddenly unforeseen accidents prevent the realization of the best plans for happiness. The very same day, her father was ordered by his medical adviser to the South of Europe, and started next morning for town, to make the necessary arrangements, taking the butler with him, leaving Alice's mama to follow as soon as the two children were suitably located at school.

Lucy and her young mistress consoled each other as well as possible under the circumstances. But in a few days, an aunt took charge of the house, and Alice was sent to this school, and is now in your arms, dear Beatrice; whilst my brother is now at college, and we only meet during the holidays. Will you, dear, ask your guardians to allow you to spend the next vacation with me, and I will introduce you to Frederick, who, if I make no mistake, is quite as voluptuously inclined as his sister.

Part II.

I will pass over the exciting practices myself and bedfellow used to indulge in almost every night, and merely remark that two more finished young tribades it would have been impossible to have found anywhere.

I had to wait till the Christmas vacation before I could be introduced to Frederick, who, between ourselves, we had already devoted to the task of taking my virginity, which we did not think would prove a very difficult operation, as with so much finger frigging, and also the use of Alice's leather sausage, which, as I learnt, she had improvised for her own gratification, my mount and cunny were wonderfully developed, and already slight signs of the future growth of curly brown hair could be detected. I was nearly thirteen, as one fine crisp morning in December we drove up to the Hall on our return from school. There stood the aunt to welcome us, but my eyes were fixed upon the youthful, yet manly figure of Frederick, who stood by her side, almost a counterpart of his sister, in features and complexion, but really a very fine young fellow, between seventeen and eighteen.

Since hearing the story of Alice's intrigue with William, I always looked at every man and boy to see what sort of a bunch they had got in their pockets, and was delighted to perceive Mr. Frederick was apparently well furnished.

Alice introduced me to her relatives, but Frederick evidently looked upon me as a little girl, and not at all yet up to the serious business of love and flirtation, so our first private consultation, between Alice and myself, was how best to open his eyes, and draw him to take a little more notice of his sister's friend.

Lucy, who I now saw for the first time, slept in the little room adjoining Alice's chamber, which I shared with her young mistress. Frederick had a room on the other side of ours, so that we were nextdoor neighbours, and could rap and give signals to each other on the wall, as well as to try to look through the keyhole of a disused door, which opened direct from one room to the other, but had long since been locked and bolted to prevent any communication between the occupants.

A little observation soon convinced us that Lucy was upon most intimate terms with her young master, which Alice determined to turn to account in our favour.

She quickly convinced her *femme de chambre* that she could not enjoy and monopolize the whole of her brother, and finding that Lucy expected he would visit her room that very night, she insisted upon ringing the changes, by taking Lucy to sleep with herself, and putting me in the place of Monsieur Frederick's ladylove.

I was only too willing to be a party of this arrangement, and at ten P.M., when we all retired to rest, I took the place

of the *femme de chambre*, and pretended to be fast asleep in
her snug little bed. The lock of the door had been oiled by
Lucy, so as to open quite noiselessly, but the room was pur-
posely left in utter darkness, and secured even from the intrusion of a dim starlight by well-closed window curtains.

About eleven o'clock, as nearly as I could guess, the door
silently opened, and by the light of the corridor lamp, I saw a
figure, in nothing but a shirt, cautiously glide in, and approach the bed. The door closed, and all was dark, putting
my heart in a dreadful flutter, at the approach of the long
wished for, but dreaded ravisher of my virginity.

"Lucy! Lucy!! Lucy!!!" he whispered, in a low voice, almost in my ear. No response, only the apparent deep breathing
of a person in sound sleep.

"She hasn't thought much about me, but, I guess, something between her legs will soon wake her up," I heard him
mutter; then the bedclothes were pulled open, and he slid
into bed by my side. My hair was all loose, the same as
Lucy's generally was at night, and I felt a warm kiss on my
cheek, also an arm stealing round my waist and clutching my
nightdress as if to pull it up. Of course I was the fox asleep,
but could not help being all atremble at the approach of
my fate.

"How you shake, Lucy; what's the matter? Hullo! who's
this; it can't be you?" he said rapidly, as with a sigh and a
murmur, "Oh! oh! Alice." I turned round just as he pulled
up my chemise, clasping my arm firmly round him, but still
apparently lost in sleep. "My God!" I heard him say, "It's
that little devil of a Beatrice in Lucy's bed; I won't go, I'll
have a lark, she can't know me in the dark."

His hands seemed to explore every part of my body; I could
feel his rampant cock pressed between our naked bellies, but
although in a burning heat of excitement, I determined to let
him do just as he liked, and pretend still to be asleep; his
fingers explored my crack, and rubbed the little clitoris; first
his leg got between mine, and then presently I could feel him
gently placing the head of his instrument in the crack, and I
was so excited that a sudden emission wetted it and his fingers
all over with a creamy spend. "The little devil's spending in
her sleep; these girls must be in the habit of frigging each
other, I believe," he said to himself again. Then his lips met

mine for the first time, and he was quite free from fear on that account as his face was as beardless as a girl's.

"Ah! Alice!" I murmured, "give me your sausage thing, that's it, dear, shove it in," as I pushed myself forward on his slowly progressing cock; he met me with a sudden thrust, making me almost scream with pain, yet my arms nervously clung round his body, and kept him close to the mark.

"Gently," he whispered, "Beatrice, dear, I'm Frederick, I won't hurt you much; how in heaven's name did you come in Lucy's bed?"

Pretending now to awaken for the first time with a little scream, and trying to push his body away from me, I exclaimed, "Oh! Oh! How you hurt! Oh! for shame, don't. Oh! let me go, Mr. Frederick, how can you?" And then my efforts seemed exhausted, and I lay almost at his mercy as he ruthlessly pushed his advantage, and tried to stop my mouth with kisses. I was lost. Although very painful, thanks to our frequent fingerings, &c., the way had been so cleared that he was soon in complete possession, although as I afterwards found by the stains on my chemise it was not quite a bloodless victory.

Taking every possible advantage, he continued his motions with thrilling energy, till I could not help responding to his delicious thrusts, moving my bottom a little to meet each returning insertion of his exciting weapon (we were lying on our sides), and in a few moments we both swam in a mutual flood of bliss, and after a spasmodic storm of sighs, kisses, and tender hugging pressure of each other's body, we lay in a listless state of enjoyment, when suddenly the bedclothes were thrown, or pulled off, then slap—slap—slap, came smarting smacks on our bottoms, and Alice's light, merry laugh sounded through the darkness, "Ha! Ha! Ha! Ha! Mr. Frederick, is this what you learnt at college, sir? Here, Lucy, help; we must secure and punish the wretch; bring a light."

Lucy appeared with a candle and locked the door inside at once, before he could have a chance of escaping, and I could see she was quite delighted at the spectacle presented by our bodies in conjunction, for as I had been previously instructed, I clung to him in apparent fright, and tried to hide my blushing face in his bosom.

Frederick was in the utmost confusion, and at first was afraid his sister would expose him, but he was a little reassured as she went on, "What shall I do? I can't tell an old maid like aunt; only to think that my dear little Beatrice should be outraged under my very eyes, the second night of her visit. If papa and mama were at home, they would know what to do; now I must decide for myself. Now, Frederick will you submit to a good whipping for this, or shall I write to your father, and send Beatrice home disgraced in the morning, and you will have to promise to marry her, sir? Now you've spoilt her for anyone else; who do you think would take a *cruche cassée* if they knew it, or not repudiate her when it was found out, as it must be the first night of her marriage. No, you bad boy, I'm determined both to punish you and make you offer her all the reparation in your power."

I began to cry, and begged her not to be too hard, as he had not hurt me much, and in fact had, at the finish, quite delighted my ravished senses.

"Upon my word," said Alice, assuming the airs of a woman, "the girl is as bad as the boy; this could not have happened, Beatrice, if you had not been too complaisant, and given way to his rudeness."

Frederick, disengaging himself from my embrace, and quite unmindful of his condition, started up, and clasping his sister round her neck, kissed her most lovingly, and the impudent fellow even raised her nightdress and stroked her belly, exclaiming, as he passed his hand over her mossy mount, "What a pity, Alice, you are my sister or I would give you the same pleasure as I have Beatrice, but I will submit to your chastisement, however hard it may be, and promise also that my little love here shall be my future wife."

ALICE.—"You scandalous fellow, to insult my modesty so, and expose your blood-stained manhood to my sight, but I will punish you, and avenge both myself and Beatrice; you are my prisoner, so just march into the other room, I've got a tickler there that I brought home from school, as a curiosity, little thinking I should so soon have a use for it."

Arrived in Alice's own room, she and Lucy first tied his hands to the bedpost, then they secured his ankles to the handle of a heavy box, which stood handy, so as to have him tolerably well stretched out.

ALICE, getting her rod out of a drawer.—"Now, pin up his shirt to his shoulders, and I will see if I can't at least draw a few drops of his impudent blood out of his posteriors, which Beatrice may wipe off with her handkerchief as a memento of the outrage she has so easily forgiven."

The hall was a large house, and our apartments were the only ones occupied in that corridor, the rooms abutting on which were all in reserve for visitors expected to arrive in a few days, to spend Christmas with us, so that there was not much fear of being heard by any of the other inmates of the house, and Alice was under no necessity of thinking what might be the result of her blows. With a flourish she brought down the bunch of twigs with a thundering whack on his plump, white bottom; the effect was startling to the culprit, who was evidently only anticipating some playful fun. "Ah! My God! Alice, you'll cut the skin; mind what you're about; I didn't bargain for that."

ALICE (with a smile of satisfaction).—"Ho! Ho! did you think I was going to play with you? But, you've soon found your mistake, sir. Will you? will you, again take such outrageous liberties with a young lady friend of mine?"

She cut him quite half-a-dozen times in rapid succession, as she thus lectured him, each blow leaving long red lines, to mark its visitation, and suffusing his fair bottom all over with a peach-like bloom. The victim, finding himself quite helpless, bit his lips and ground his teeth in fruitless rage. At last he burst forth: "Ah! Ah! You she-devil! Do you mean to skin my bum? Be careful, or I will take a rare revenge some day before long."

ALICE, with great calmness and determination, but with a most excited twinkle in her eyes.—"Oh! You show temper, do you? So you mean to be revenged on me for doing a simple act of justice, sir? I will keep you there, and cut away at your impudent bottom, till you fairly beg my pardon, and promise to forgo all such wicked revengefulness."

The victim writhed in agony and rage, but her blows only increased in force, beginning to raise great fiery-looking weals all over his buttocks. "Ah! Ha!" she continued. "How do you like it, Fred? Shall I put a little more steam in my blows?"

Frederick struggles desperately to get loose, but they have secured him too well for that! The tears of shame and mortification stand in his eyes, but he is still obstinate, and I could also observe a very perceptible rising in his manly instrument, which soon stood out from his belly in a rampant state of erection.

ALICE, with assumed fury.—"Look at the fellow, how he is insulting me, by the exhibition of his lustful weapon. I wish I could cut it off with a blow of the rod," giving him a fearful cut across his belly and on the penis.

Frederick fairly howled with pain, and big tears rolled down his cheeks, as he gasped out: "Oh! Oh! Ah! Have mercy, Alice. I know I deserve it. Oh! Pity me now, dear!"

ALICE, without relaxing her blows.—"Oh! You are beginning to feel properly, are you? Are you sincerely penitent? Beg my pardon at once, sir, for the way you insulted me in the other room."

FREDERICK.—"Oh! Dear Alice! Stop! Stop! You don't let me get my breath. I will! I will beg your pardon. Oh! I can't help my affair sticking up as it does."

ALICE.—"Down sir! Down sir! Your master is ashamed of you," as she playfully whisks his pego with her rod.

Frederick is in agony; his writhing and contortions seemed excruciating in the extreme, he fairly groaned out: "Oh! Oh! Alice, let me down. On my word, I will do anything you order. Oh! Oh! Ah! You make me do it," as he shuts his eyes, and we saw quite a jet of sperm shoot from his virile member.

Alice dropped her rod, and we let down the culprit who was terribly crestfallen.

"Now, sir," she said, "down on your knees, and kiss the rod."

Without a word, he dropped down, and kissed the worn-out stump, saying: "Oh! Alice; the last few moments have been so heavenly. It has blotted out all sense of pain. My dear sister, I thank you for punishing me, and will keep my promise to Beatrice."

I wiped the drops of blood from his slightly-bleeding rump, and then we gave him a couple of glasses of wine, and allowed him to sleep with Lucy, in her room, for the rest of the night, where they had a most luscious time of it, whilst Alice and myself indulged in our favourite touches.

You may be sure Frederick was not long before he renewed his pleasures with me, whilst his sister took pleasure in our happiness; but she seemed to have contracted a penchant for the use of the rod, and, once or twice a week, would have us all in her room, for a birch seance, as she called it, when Lucy or myself had to submit to be victims; but the heating of our bottoms only seemed to add to our enjoyment when we were afterwards allowed to soothe our raging passions in the arms of our mutual lover.

(*To be continued.*)

A gentleman, who is blessed with a beautiful and lewdly disposed wife, has long been very unhappy and disappointed at the results of his endeavours to become a parent. But returning home from the City, very unexpectedly, the other morning, he caught the Vicar of the parish gamahuching his spouse. "Ho! Ho!" he exclaimed, in a fury. "So you're the bugger who swallows all my children."

PART OF A LETTER FROM HARRIET KEENE.

I'll tell you a funny dream I had the night before last. I thought I was sitting on a green bank, and a man was sitting by the side of me; he fell to kissing and talking, but did nothing else. Well, after a while, he got up and went away; then, at the side of me, as I sat there, lay the largest prick I ever saw. It was at least half a yard long, and as thick as the calf of my leg; it had four bollox, but it tapered towards the end. I thought I took it up and felt it. It was warm flesh and blood, and I said to myself, "Why the man has left his prick behind him; what a pity! and it is such a fine one too! what will he do without it?" So I thought to myself, "I wonder if it will spend if I suck it," so I kept sucking it, but it was so big and thick that it made my mouth ache, and I said to myself, "Never mind, it will do to frig myself with." So I got up, and put it under my cloak, and cuddled it so close to me that I felt as lewd as could be. As I was going along I met the man coming back, and when he came up to me, he said, "Have you seen my trumpet?" "Your trumpet," said I, "why you mean your prick!" Says he, "You nasty, lying woman, it's

my best trumpet." "Well," said I, "if this is a trumpet, why
a trumpet's a prick, and a prick is a trumpet," and I held it
up to look at. He snatched it out of my hand. "Now, then,
I'll show you if it's a prick or a trumpet," and he began to
blow away on it so loud that I awoke and lost my prick and
trumpet too.

What woke me up was the sound of a trumpet in the
street, so I suppose that was the cause of my funny dream.

THE WISE LOVER.

Woman and man whene'er inclined,
In mutual goodness pleasure find,
The lawful spouse 'tis sweet to embrace,
In hopes to see a lengthen'd race,
      But let who will the truth contest,
      Another's wife is still the best.

When I was young and slightly skill'd,
In blisses womankind can yield;
I lov'd the maid, I lov'd the piece;
But as my wit and years increase,
      I own the sweetest sport in life,
      Is to enjoy your neighbour's wife.

A virgin coy with sidelong eye,
Your mere approach, at once will fly,
Abhors your nasty hot desires,
Nought less than marriage she requires,
      Such maidenheads the wise detest,
      The adultery maidenhead's the best.

The vagrant nymph who sells her charms,
And fills in turn a thousand arms,
Besides the loss of gold and fame,
May set Priapus in a flame,
      Such fire-tailed comets God confound.
      A wife is always safe and sound.

The genial flame I've oft allayed,
With buxom Kate, my chambermaid,
And dozens such as her, but found
Such sport with ills beset around;
>> He who at liberty would feast,
>> Will find another's wife the best.

A mistress kept at first is sweet,
And joys to do the merry feat;
But bastards come, and hundreds gone,
You'll wish you'd left her charms alone;
>> Such breeding hussy's are a pest,
>> A neighbour's wife is far the best.

If you are rash, a wife at first
May into horrid fury burst,
"Sir, you shall rue throughout your life
The day you've kissed another's wife."
>> Reply, "My dear, this gives the zest,
>> I always like my neighbour's best."

Jove, I remember, when inclined
To feast himself on womankind,
Though maids enough to him were free,
Always preferr'd adultery;
>> He took the shape of bird and beast,
>> To prove Adultery the best.

But while this naughty sport we sing,
Who can forget our gracious King (Geo. IV);
Him many a lady pleasures gives,
For which her husband pay receives,
>> God bless King George! His Majesty
>> Is patron of Adultery.

I own the dangers of the suit,
The sweetest is forbidden fruit,
And laws as thick as hairs are set,
Around the center of delight;
>> This peril gives the highest zest,
>> And guarded hoard is sure the best.

The wandering nymph your purse desires,
The chambermaid to rank aspires;
Your wife content with marriage dues,
All further license will refuse;
     He who has put them to the test,
     Must own his neighbour's wife's the best.

QUEEN BATHSHEBA.

A Temperance Ballad.
(Attributed to Sir Wilfrid Lawson.)

Grass widows and princes! a warning I sing,
Of the sad wicked doing of David, the King;
With Bathsheba, wife of poor Major Uriah,
Who was bathing one day, when the King chanc'd to spy her.

He was drinking up-stairs, and the weather was hot;
And her window was open (a thing she forgot);
And the stark-naked beauty had not an idea,
That while she was washing, a creature could see her!

She and her little sister were sporting together,
Enjoying the heat of the bright summer weather;
They bath'd in the fountain, and while they were washing,
Were romping all naked, and leaping and splashing.

What man could resist such an awful temptation?
He forgot he was King of the sanctified nation;
He was fill'd with delight, and lewd admiration,
And was mad for the raptures of fierce fornication.

Beware of the Devil, who seldom lies sleeping!
So while she was washing, and while he was peeping,
The King's living sceptre grew stiff as a rod,
"Nice mutton!" cried David, "I'll fuck her, by G—!"

So calling a page, he desir'd him to go,
And enquire all about her.—He answered, "I know

The lady your Majesty's pleas'd to admire,
Is the wife of the valorous Major Uriah."

His Majesty answer'd: "Go, fetch her! Be quick!
Much conscience, indeed, has a stiff-standing prick!"
The page ran to call her; she put on her smock,
And hurried to wait on his Majesty's cock.

One touch to her hand, and one word in her ear,
And she fell on her back, like a sweet willing dear;
He was frantic with lust, but she seiz'd his erection,
And put it at once in the proper direction.

She was girlish and lively, a heavenly figure,
With the cunt of an angel, and fucking with vigour;
He got her at once with child of a son,
And he said a long grace when the swiving was done.

So the lady went home, and she very soon found
Her belly was growing unluckily round.
"This an honour," said she, "I could hardly expect,
Your Majesty now must your handmaid protect."

"Never fear," cried the King, "I'll be your adviser,
I'll send for the Major, and no one's the wiser."
So he sent for Uriah, who speedily came.
But unluckily never laid hands on the dame.

King David was puzzled, he made the man tipsy,
But still he avoided the lewd little gipsy;
David laid a new plot, and his wish was fulfill'd,
In the front of the battle Uriah was kill'd.

THE HORRIBLE FRIGHT.

Poor Sally! I hear from your loving Mamma,
That you're in a horrible fright of Papa;
Take courage, dear girl, for the sweetest delight,
Is closely akin to a horrible fright.

In your dreams, did you ne'er see a horrible man,
Who crushes and conquers you, do all you can?
He treats your poor innocent mouse like a rat
That's touzled and claw'd, and devour'd by a cat.

He produces a horrible fright of a thing,
That fits like a finger in conjugal ring;
He thrusts, and he pokes, and he enters your belly,
Till the horrible monster is melted to jelly.

When you draw a new glove on your finger so tight,
The glove is, you know, in a horrible fright;
But soon it is taught your dear finger to love,
The man and the woman are finger and glove.

Away with your horrible fright, and away
With the wretch of a father, who hinders the play;
If he dares interfere, when you kiss on the sly,
Just pull up your petticoat, piss in his eye.

Ah! Sally, my darling, I wish that this night,
I might put you, my love, in a horrible fright;
You might lie down a maiden, in five minutes more,
I would open a secret, ne'er open'd before.

You then would behold, long, ruddy, and thick,
That horrible monster, a stiff-standing prick;
You'd cry out, "Oh, softly! Oh, gently! Ah! Ah!
Oh lordy, oh lordy, oh harder, la! la!"

At last, dearest Sally, your horrible fright
Would end in a shudder of tipsy delight;
You'll open your buttocks, as wide as you can,
To admit every inch of the dear cruel man.

You'll devour every inch of his horrible yard,
Till the testicles hit on your bottom so hard;
Your terrible fright, my dear girl, will be over,
You'll breathe out your soul, on the lips of your lover.

There's an end of this horrible fright of a song,
Your mother shall read it, and say if it's wrong;

No, she will approve it—her greatest delight
Is the prick which you fancy such a horrible fright.

PAYNE'S HILL (Mons Veneris).

In Middlesex a hill we meet,
　For beauty known to fame;
Where wealthy Payne has built his seat,
　Payne's Hill they call its name.

"Pray, Mr. Burke," said Lady Payne,
　"What Latin word is this?
(I've searched the dictionary in vain),
　Pray what's *Mons Veneris?*"

He look'd into her beauteous eyes,
　So innocent of ill;
And gave the happiest of replies,
　"It signifies *Payne's Hill!*"

INSTANCE OF SELF-DENIAL.

Mohammed Sadig, a gentleman at Hyderabad, received a
female slave, belonging to his brother at Kurnool, who was
going to Bengal, and requested Sadig to keep his property for
a year. Her beauty excited his passions greatly. He told the
story to my friend, Captain Keighley, and ended thus: "To
lie with her carnally would have been wrong, as my brother
had not permitted it, so I governed my love by the holy rules
of moderation and virtue, and contented myself with merely
fucking her in the arse."

George Stokes, the cheesemonger in Snowhill, had Dr. Cullen one night as a guest. Cullen did not fancy the cheese on the table, and said, "You do not know how to select cheese; let me go into the warehouse and pick one out." He did this, and the cheese he selected was delicious. Everyone declared it most excellent. "How did you pitch upon it, and in the dark, too?" said Stokes. "I'll tell you," said the Doctor. "I tried several, till I came to one which made my prick stand. This is it; a prime cheese smells exactly like a blooming, ripe, girl's cunt."

NURSERY RHYMES.

There was a young lady of Gaza,
Who shaved her cunt clean with a razor;
    The crabs in a lump
    Made tracks to her rump,
Which proceeding did greatly amaze her.

There was a young lass of Surat,
The cheeks of whose arse were so fat
    That they had to be parted,
    Whenever she farted,
And also whenever she shat.

There was an old priest of Siberia,
Who of fucking grew wearier and wearier;
    So one night after prayers,
    He bolted upstairs,
And buggered the Lady Superior.

There was an old man of Natal,
Who was lazily fucking a gal,
    Says she, "You're a sluggard,"
    Said he, "You be buggered,
I like to fuck slowly, and shall."

There was a young farmer of Nant,
Whose conduct was gay and gallant,
    For he fucked all his dozens
    Of nieces and cousins,
In addition, of course, to his aunt.

There was an old man of Tantivy,
Who followed his son to the privy,
    He lifted the lid,
    To see what he did,
And found that it smelt of Capivi.

There was a young man of this Nation,
Who didn't much like fornication;
    When asked, "Do you fuck?"
    He said, "No, I suck
Women's quims, and I use Masturbation."

There was a young parson of Eltham,
Who seldom fucked whores, but oft felt 'em.
    In the lanes he would linger,
    And play at stick finger,
'Twas on the way home that he smelt 'em.

There was a young lady of Rheims,
Who was terribly plagued with wet dreams;
    She saved up a dozen,
    And sent to her cousin,
Who ate them and thought they were creams.

There was a gay parson of Tooting,
Whose roe he was frequently shooting;
    Till he married a lass,
    With a face like my arse,
And a cunt you could put a top-boot in.

A learned divine down at Buckingham,
Wrote a treatise on cunts and on fucking 'em;
    A learned Parsee,
    Taught him Gamahuchee,
So he added a chapter on sucking 'em.

NOT THE THING.

Said Lady Macneill, to Sir John, eating ling,
I'm afraid, Sir, that fish a'nt exactly the thing;
Why really, he answer'd, I do not dislike it,
It's not the thing, but it's mightily like it.

THE PEARL,

A Journal of Facetiæ and Voluptuous Reading.

| No. 3 | PUBLISHED MONTHLY. | Sept. 1879 |

SUB-UMBRA, OR SPORT AMONG THE SHE-NOODLES.

(Continued.)

In the course of the evening, Frank and myself were delighted by the arrival of a beautiful young lady of sixteen, on a visit to his sisters, in fact, a school fellow of Sophie and Polly, come to stop a week at the house.

Miss Rosa Redquim was indeed a sprightly beauty of the Venus height, well proportioned in leg and limb, full swelling bosom, with a graceful Grecian type of face, rosy cheeks, large grey eyes, and golden auburn hair, lips as red as cherries, and teeth like pearls, frequently exhibited by a succession of winning smiles, which never seemed to leave her face. Such was the acquisition to the feminine department of the house, and we congratulated ourselves on the increased prospect of sport, as Frank had expressed to me considerable compunctions as to taking liberties with one's own sisters.

The next morning being gloriously fine and warm, myself and friend strolled in the grounds, smoking our cigarettes, for about an hour, till near the time when we guessed the girls would be coming for a bath in the small lake in the park, which we at once proceeded to; then we secreted ourselves secure from observation, and awaited, in deep silence, the arrival of sisters and friend.

This lake, as I call it, was a pond of about four or five acres in extent, every side thickly wooded to the very margin, so that even anglers could not get access to the bank, except at the little sloping green sward, of about twenty or thirty square yards in extent, which had a large hut, or summer-house, under the trees, where the bathers could undress, and then trip across the lawn to the water. The bottom of the pond being gradually shelving, and covered with fine sand at this spot, and a circular space, enclosed with rails, to prevent them getting out of their depth.

The back door of this hut opened upon a very narrow foot-path, leading to the house through the dense thicket, so that any party would feel quite secure from observation. The interior was comfortably furnished with seats and lounges, besides a buffet, generally holding a stock of wine, biscuits, and cakes, during the bathing season.

Frank, having a key to the hut, took me through onto the lawn, and then climbing up into a thick sycamore, we re-lighted our cigarettes, awaiting the adventure with some justifiable impatience.

Some ten minutes of suspense, and then we were rewarded by hearing the ringing laughter of the approaching girls. We heard the key turned in the lock, then the sounds of their bolting themselves in, and Annie's voice, saying: "Ah! Wouldn't the boys like the fun of seeing us undress and bathing, this lovely warm day"; to which we heard Rosa laughingly reply: "I don't mind if they do see me, if I don't know it, dears. There's something delightful in the thought of the excitement it would put the dear fellows in. I know I should like Frank to take a fancy to me; I'm nearly in love with him already, and have read that the best way a girl can madly excite the man she wishes to win is to let him see all her charms, when he thinks she is unconscious of his being near."

"Well, there's no fear of our being seen here, so I am one for a good romp. Off with your clothes, quick; it will be de-licious in the water," exclaimed Sophie.

The undressing was soon accomplished, excepting chemises, boots, and stockings, as they were evidently in no hurry to enter the water.

"Now," said Sophie, with a gay laugh, "we must make Rosa a free woman, and examine all she's got. Come on, girls, lay her down, and turn up her smock."

The beautiful girl only made a slight feint of resisting, as she playfully pulled up their chemises, exclaiming: "You shan't look at my fanny for nothing. La! Polly has got no hair on her fly trap yet. What a pretty pouting slit yours is, Annie. I think you have been using the finger of a glove we

made into a little cock for Sophie, and told her to bring home
from school for you."

She was soon stretched on her back on the soft mossy
grass, her face covered with burning blushes, as her pretty
cunt was exposed to view, ornamented with its chevelure of
soft red hair; her beautiful white belly and thighs shining like
marble in the bright sunlight. The three sisters were blushing
as well as their friend, and delighted at the sight of so much
loveliness.

One after another, they kissed the vermilion lips of their
friend's delightful slit, and then turning her on her face,
proceeded to smack the lily white bottom of their laughing,
screaming victim, with their open hands.

Smacks and laughter echoed through the grove, and we
almost fancied ourselves witnesses to the games of real
nymphs. At last she was allowed to rise on her knees, and
then the three sisters in turn presented their cunts to their
friend to kiss. Polly was the last, and Rosa, clasping her arms
firmly round my youngest cousin's buttocks, exclaimed: "Ah!
Ah! You have made me feel so rude, I must suck this little
hairless jewel," as she glued her lips to it, and hid her face
almost from sight, as if she would devour Polly's charms there
and then. The young girl, flushed with excitement, placed her
hands on Rosa's head, as if to keep her there, whilst both
Annie and Sophie, kneeling down by the side of their friend,
began to caress her cunt, bosom, and every charm they could
tickle or handle.

This exciting scene lasted for five or six minutes, till at last
they all sank down in a confused heap on the grass, kissing
and fingering in mad excitement.

Now was our time. We had each provided ourselves with
little switches of twigs, and thus armed we seemed to drop
from the clouds upon the surprised girls, who screamed in
fright and hid their blushing faces in their hands.

They were too astonished and alarmed to jump up, but we
soon commenced to bring them to their senses, and convince
them of the reality of the situation.

"What rude! what lascivious ideas! slash away Frank!" I
cried, making my swish leave its marks on their bottoms at
every cut.

"Who would have thought of it, Walter? We must whip

such indecent ideas out of their tails!" he answered, seconding
my assault with his sharp, rapid strokes.

They screamed both from pain and shame, and springing to
their feet, chased round the lawn; there was no escape. We
caught them by the tails of their chemises, which we lifted up
to enable us to cut at their bums with more effect. At last we
were getting quite out of breath, and beginning fairly to pant
from exhaustion, when Annie suddenly turned upon me, saying, "Come, come, girls, let's tear their clothes off, so they
shall be quite as ashamed as we are, and agree to keep our
secret!" The others helped her, and we made such a feeble
resistance that we were soon reduced to the same state in
which we had surprised them, making them blush and look
very shamefaced at the sight of our rampant engines of love.

Frank seized Miss Redquim round the waist, and led the
way into the summer-house, myself and his sisters following
The gentlemen then producing the wine, &c., from the buffet,
sat down with a young lady on each knee, my friend having
Rosa and Polly, whilst Annie and Sophie sat with me; we plied
the girls with several glasses of champagne each, which they
seemed to swallow in order to drown their sense of shame. We
could feel their bodies quiver with emotion as they reclined
upon our necks, their hands and ours groping under shirts and
chemises in every forbidden spot; each of us had two delicate
hands caressing our cocks, two delicious arms around our
necks, two faces laid cheek to cheek on either side, two sets of
lips to kiss, two pairs of bright and humid eyes to return our
ardent glances; what wonder then that we flooded their hands
with our spurting seed and felt their delicious spendings
trickle over our busy fingers.

Excited by the wine, and madly lustful to enjoy the dear
girls to the utmost, I stretched Sophie's legs wide apart, and
sinking on my knees, gamahuched her virgin cunt, till she
spent again in ecstasy, whilst dear Annie was doing the same
to me, sucking the last drop of spend from my gushing prick;
meanwhile Frank was following my example, Rosa surrendered
to his lascivious tongue all the recesses of her virginity as she
screamed with delight and pressed his head towards her mount
when the frenzy of love brought her to the spending point;
Polly all the while kissing her brother's belly, and frigging him
to a delicious emission.

When we recovered a little from this exciting *pas de trois,* all bashfulness was vanished between us, we promised to renew our pleasures on the morrow, and for the present contented ourselves by bathing all together, and then returned to the house for fear the girls might be suspected of something wrong for staying out too long.

(*To be continued.*)

Sporting Life, 6th August, 1879.—Mr. F. Jacobs.—We are pleased to hear that this gentleman, although severely crushed and bruised by his fall while riding Mrs. Jones at Southport in the Consolation Stakes, is going on as well as his friends could wish, and it is hoped he is quite out of danger. Query.—Was he riding a St. George, or was it a genuine toss off with its neck nearly broken?—*Ed.*

MISS COOTE'S CONFESSION,

Or the Voluptuous Experiences of an Old Maid; In a series of Letters to a Lady Friend.

Letter III.

My Dear Nellie,

I told you in my last how easily for me the affair of the nectarines passed over, but I was not long to go free with a whole skin. The General had evidently booked me in his mind for a good dressing the first time I should give him a pretext for punishment.

Strange to say, my first terrible punishment and dreadful cutting up of poor Jemima, related in my last letter, had very little effect, except, if possible, to render me rather more of a daredevil. I longed to pay off both Sir Eyre and Mrs. Mansell, but could think of no possible plan of effecting my revenge at all satisfactorily; if I could but do it properly, I was quite indifferent to what they might wreak upon me.

Jane could offer no suggestion, so I resolved to act entirely alone, and pretended to let it all drop, but sundry little annoyances were continually happening to different members of the family, even to myself. The General was very angry, and particularly furious, when, one day he found some of his flagellation books seriously torn and damaged, but could fix the blame on no one; indeed, I rather fancy he strongly suspected Jemima had done it out of revenge. Next Mrs. Mansell got her feet well stung one night by nettles placed in her bed; she and Sir Eyre always were the principal sufferers, and, as a climax, two or three days afterwards, the General got his flesh considerably scratched and pricked by some pieces of bramble, cleverly hid in his bed, under the sheet, so as to be felt before they could be seen, it being his practice to throw back the upper bed clothes, and then, laying himself full length, pull them over him again. His backside first felt the pricks, which made him suddenly start from the spot, but only to get his hands, feet, legs, and all parts of his body well lacerated before he could get off the bed. I saw the sheet next day all spotted with the blood, for he was fearfully scratched, and pieces of the thorns stuck in his flesh.

Mrs. Mansell had to get out of bed in a hurry to attend the poor old fellow, and was occupied a long time in putting him to rights, retiring in about an hour's time, and making haste into bed, quite unsuspicious of any lurking danger (she had already been in it) when, prick—prick—prick! "Ah! my God! The devil's been here whilst I was away," she screamed. Jemima, Jane, and myself, ran to her room, and found her terribly scratched, especially on her knees; there were suppressed smiles on all our faces, and Jemima looked really pleased.

MRS. MANSELL.—"Ah! What a shame to serve me so. It's one of you three, and I believe it's Jemima."

JEMIMA.—"I couldn't help smiling, ma'am; you did scream so, and I thought you had no feeling."

MRS. MANSELL.—"You impudent hussey, Sir Eyre shall know of this."

Jemima, Jane, and myself, all declared our innocence, but in vain; there evidently would soon be a grand *punishment drill* for her, if not for all three.

The housekeeper and the General were both too sore for nearly a week, and, in fact, many of the thorns remained in their flesh, and one in Mrs. Mansell's knee kept her very lame, Sir Eyre had to wait ten days before he could enter into any kind of an investigation.

At last the awful day arrived; we were all mustered in the punishment room, the General seated in his chair (it was after dinner, as usual), and we were all in evening costume.

SIR EYRE.—"You all know why I have called you together. Such an outrage as Mrs. Mansell and myself suffered from cannot be passed over; in fact, if neither Miss Rosa, Jemima, nor Jane will confess the crime, I have resolved to punish all three severely, so as to be sure the real culprit gets her deserts. Now, Rosa, was it you? for if not you, it was one of the others."

ANSWER.—"No grandfather, besides, you know all sorts of tricks have been played upon me."

SIR EYRE.—"Well, Jemima, what do you say, yes or no?"

JEMIMA.—"Good Lord, sir! I never touched such thorns in my life."

SIR EYRE.—"Jane, are you guilty or not, or do you know anything of it?"

JANE.—"Oh! Dear! No, sir! Indeed, I don't!"

SIR EYRE.—"One of you must be a confounded story-teller. Rosa, as a young lady, I shall punish you first. Perhaps we may get a confession from one of you before we've done."

Then turning to Mrs. Mansell, "Prepare the young lady; she didn't get such a birching as she ought to have had the other day, but if it takes all night, the three of them shall be well trounced. Jane and Jemima lend a hand."

My thoughts were not so much upon what I should feel myself, as the anticipation of the fine sight the others would present, and hoping to again realize the pleasant sensations I had experienced when Jemima was so severely punished. They soon removed my blue silk dress, and fixed me to the horse, but the General interposed; he had a different idea.

"Stop! Stop!" he cried. "Let Jemima horse her." So I was released, and having my petticoats well fastened over my back, I was at once mounted on her strong stout back, my arms round her neck, being firmly held by the wrists in front, and my legs also tied together under her waist, leaving me beautifully exposed and bent so as to tighten the skin. Mrs. Mansell was about to open my drawers when Sir Eyre says: "No! No! I'm going to use this driving whip. Jemima, just trot around the room. I can reach her now."

Then giving a sharp flick with the whip, which quite convinced me of its efficacy:—

"Now, miss! What have you to say for yourself? I believe you know all about it." Slash! Slash! Slashing with the whip, as Jemima, evidently enjoying it, capered round the room; each cut made my poor bottom smart with agony.

"Oh! Oh! Ah! Grandfather!" I cried. "It's a shame to punish me, when you know I'm innocent. Oh! Ah—r—r—re," as he slashed me without mercy. I could feel I was getting wealed all over, but my drawers prevented the flesh from being cut.

Presently he ordered a halt, saying: "Now, Mrs. Mansell, let's have a look at her naughty bottom, to see if the whip has done any good."

Mrs. Mansell, carefully opening my drawers behind, exclaims, "Look, look, sir, you've touched her up nicely, what beautiful weals, and how rosy her bottom looks."

Sir Eyre.—"Aye, aye, it's a beautiful sight, but not half pretty enough yet. Mrs. Mansell, do you finish her off with the birch."

I felt assured of catching it in good earnest now. The General lit a cigar, and composed himself in his easy chair to enjoy the scene. Mrs. Mansell selected a fine birch of long, thin, green twigs, and leaving my drawers open behind, ordered Jemima to stand in front of her.

Mrs. Mansell, whisking her birch, said, "I feel sure this young lady is in the secret, but we shall get nothing out of her, she is so obstinate, but I will try my best, Sir Eyre. Now, Miss Rosa, tell the truth if you want to save your bottom; are you quite as sure as ever of your own innocence?" whisking and slashing me smartly and with great deliberation, making the blows fall with a whacking sound, not inconsiderably adding to the previous warmth of my posteriors, which smart and tingle terrifically at each cut.

"Oh! ah! how unjust," I screamed, to relieve myself as much as possible. "Oh, ah! If I do know I can't tell, it's a secret. Oh! have mercy!" thus trying to serve a double purpose to be let off lightly myself, by making them think someone else did it, and so transfer their fury to Jane and Jemima, whose whipping I hoped to enjoy.

Mrs. Mansell.—"Ha! ha! 'tis wonderful how the birch has improved you, my dear Miss Rosa, you're not nearly so obstinate as you were, but if you won't tell, you must be punished as an accessory. I'm sorry to do it, but it doesn't hurt you quite so awfully, does it?" thrashing away without a moment's respite; my poor bottom is beginning to be finely pickled, and I can feel the blood trickling down my legs inside my drawers.

"Hold! Hold!" cries the General, excitedly; "it's that devil Jemima; you've punished Rosa enough, try Jane next, if she knows anything we'll make her confess, and then the impudent red-headed Jemima shall catch it finely. We're getting at the truth, Mrs. Mansell."

I am let down, and the General orders Jane to take my place on the stout back; I let my clothes down with a thrill of excitement, and thanking Sir Eyre for his kindness, make myself busy in helping to arrange poor Jane's posteriors for slaughter, and pin up her skirts to her shoulders, exposing her fine, plump bottom, and beautiful thighs and legs, the latter encased in pink silk stockings, set off by red satin slippers and blue garters with silver buckles.

SIR EYRE.—"How now, Jane, you hussey, do you dare to come into my presence without drawers, how indecent, it's like telling me to 'ax my arse,' you impudent girl; how do you like that," giving her a tremendous under cut so that the birch fairly well wealed the flesh right up to her mossy crack; "it's all very well, in the heat of a birching, but to expose your nakedness like that so impudently is quite another," continuing to cut away in apparently great indignation.

JANE.—"Ah! Ah! Ah—a—r—re! My God, sir, have pity, Mrs. Mansell didn't allow us time to dress, and in the hurry I couldn't find my drawers to put on, and she was angrily calling me to come, and not keep her waiting. So I thought duty must be considered before decency. Oh! Oh! Oh! sir, you are cruel. Oh! have mercy, I'm as innocent as a babe!" as she is in terrible agony from the under cuts, which have already drawn the blood; she writhes and struggles so, Jemima can hardly stand under her plunging figure.

SIR EYRE.—"Well, well, I'm inclined to forgive you about the drawers, as I always like everybody to consider duty before everything, but how about putting the thorns in the bed; you must know about that, and it's your duty to confess."

JANE.—"Oh! Oh! Ah—r—r—re, I can't tell, I'm innocent,

how can I split upon another? Oh, you'll kill me, sir! I shall be confined to my bed for weeks if you cut me up so!"

SIR EYRE.—"Fiddlesticks, bottoms get well quicker than that, Jane, don't be alarmed, but I shall punish you a good deal more if you don't confess it was Jemima did it. Now wasn't it Jemima? Wasn't it Jemima! wasn't it Jemima!" thundering at her both with voice and rod and drawing the blood finely.

The victim is almost ready to faint, still I could see the usual indications of voluptuous excitement, notwithstanding the agony she must be in, but at last she seems quite exhausted, and ceasing to writhe and wriggle as if she no longer felt the cruel blows whilst her shrieks sink to a sobbing. "Yes, yes! oh! yes."

SIR EYRE.—"Ha! Ha! Ha!" laughing in anticipation of getting the real culprit. "Yes! yes! she's confessed at last, let her down now, poor thing," throwing away the stump of the worn-out rod; "she took a lot before she would give way, but it's bound to come out."

Poor Jane is let down in a pitiable condition, and Jemima hisses something about "lying chit" between her teeth, as I assist Mrs. Mansell to tie her to the horse, and having pinned up her skirts, I opened her drawers so as fully to expose the snow-white beauties of her fine rump.

SIR EYRE.—"Open them as wide as possible, Rosa; the mean creature, to let others suffer for her own crime, and even take delight in helping to punish them."

JEMIMA.—"It's all a lie, Sir Eyre, I never had anything to do with it, and they have turned round on me so they may enjoy the sight of my flogging. Oh! oh! this is a cruel house, pay me my wages and let me go."

SIR EYRE, chuckling.—"You'll get your wages, or at least your deserts, you sneaking wretch."

JEMIMA (is crimson with shame and fury), exclaiming— "I'm not so much a sneak as somebody else who's done it; I'll die before I own what I never did."

SIR EYRE.—"Don't let us waste any more time on the obstinate hussey. Let's try what a good birch will do," slashing her two or three times severely on her bottom, and bringing out the rosy flush all over the surface of its firm broad cheeks.

"See how her bottom blushes for her," laughed the General, "but it will soon have to weep blood," increasing the force of his blows, and drawing weals at every stroke.

JEMIMA.—"Oh! Oh! Sir Eyre! how can you believe a lying girl like Jane, won't I box her ears for her when I get over this, the spiteful thing, to say it's me!"

SIR EYRE.—"You're the spiteful one. Will you box her ears? Do you really mean that, you strong, impudent donkey! I shall soon have to try something better than a birch on you, it's not severe enough; you shall beg Jane's pardon before I've done with you; you may be strong and tough, but we'll master that somehow; how do you like it? I hope you don't feel it, Jemima; I don't think you do, or you would be more penitent," said he, in a fury. "I wish I had a good bramble here to tear your bottom with, perhaps you might feel that."

JEMIMA.—"Oh! No! Pray don't. I didn't do it, and wouldn't have done such a thing to my worst enemy. Oh! Oh! Sir! Have mercy, I'm being murdered. You'll bleed me to death," as she feels the blood trickling down her thighs.

SIR EYRE.—"You're too bad to be easily killed. Why don't you confess, you wicked creature?" Then turning to Mrs. Mansell: "Don't you think, ma'am, she's got too many things on? I am not given to cruelty, but this is a case requiring greater severity than usual."

MRS. MANSELL.—"Shall we reduce her to her chemise and drawers, so you can administer the extreme penalty?"

SIR EYRE.—"Yes! Yes! It will give a little time to recover my breath. She's taken all the strength out of me."

We now strip all her petticoats off, and undo her stays, fully displaying the large fine plump globes of her splendid bosom, with their pretty pink nipples; then she is fastened up again, and stands with her wrists fastened well above her head. She has her fawn-coloured kid gloves, and the net, as usual, up to her elbows, so as to set off her arms and hands to the best advantage. She has nothing but chemise and drawers to hide her fine figure; but before commencing again, the General orders the latter to be entirely removed and her chemise to be pinned up to the shoulders; then turning to me, he said:

"Rosa, my dear, it's all through that wicked young woman you have been punished. I don't wish to teach anyone to revenge themselves, but as Mrs. Mansell is hardly well enough, and I am in want of a little more rest, I think you could take this whip," handing me a fine ladies' switch, with a little piece of knotted cord at the end. "There, you know how to use it; don't spare any part of her bottom or thighs."

This was just what I had been longing for, but did not like to volunteer. With a glance of triumph towards poor Jane (who was gradually getting over her own punishment, and beginning to take interest in what was going forward), I took the whip, and placed myself in position to commence. What a beautiful sight my victim presented, her splendid plump back, loins, and buttocks fully exposed to view, whilst the red wealed flesh of her bottom, smeared with blood, contrasted so nicely with her snow-white belly in front, ornamented on the Mons Veneris with a profusion of soft curly hair of a light sandy colour; and her legs being fixed widely apart, I could see her pink bottom-hole, and the pouting lips of her cunny just underneath; further down stretched the splendid expanse of her well-developed thighs, as white as her belly; then she was also dressed in crimson silk stockings, pretty garters and fawn-coloured slippers to match her gloves. My blood seemed to boil at the sight of so much loveliness, which I longed to cut into ribbons of wealed flesh and blood.

SIR EYRE.—"Go on, Rosie, what makes you so slow to begin? You can't do too much to such an obstinate thing; try and make her beg Jane's pardon."

ROSA.—"She looks very nice, but I'm afraid the whip will cut her up so, grandfather. Now, Jemima, I'm going to begin, does that hurt you?" giving her a light cut on her tender thighs, where the tip of the whip left a very plain red mark.

JEMIMA.—"Oh! Oh! Miss Rosa, be merciful; I've never been unkind to you; how nicely I rode you on my back when you were punished."

ROSA.—"Yes! and enjoyed the fun all the time, you cruel thing; you knew what I was getting, but I could tell you were delighted to horse me," giving three or four smart cuts across her loins, and registering every blow with a fine angry-looking weal. "There! There! There! Ask my pardon, and Jane's pardon for your threats. Will you box her ears, will you!" cutting sharply at every question in some unexpected part; no two strokes follow each other in the same place.

VICTIM.—"A—r—r—re, have mercy. I was sorry for you,

Miss Rosie. Oh! You're as hard as Sir Eyre. You'll cut me to pieces with that whip," she sobs out, her face crimson with the conflicting emotions of fear, rage, and obstinacy.

Rosa.—"Now, Jemima, your only chance is to beg our pardon, and confess your crime; you know you did it, you know you did it, you obstinate wench," cutting the flesh in every direction, and making the blood flow freely all down the thighs on to her stockings.

The victim writhes and shrieks with pain at every blow, but refuses to admit her fault, or beg pardon. The sight of her sufferings seemed to nerve my arm, and add to my excitement, the blood seemed delicious in my eyes, and I gradually worked myself up, so that I felt such gushing thrilling sensations as to quite overcome me. The whip was dropped in exhaustion, and I sank back on a seat in a kind of lethargic stupor, yet quite conscious of all that was going on.

Sir Eyre.—"Why, Rosie, I thought you were stronger than that. Poor thing, your punishment was too much for you. I'll finish the culprit. If she won't confess, she must be executed, that's all," snatching up another whip, much heavier than the one I had used, and with three tips of cord on the end. "You won't confess, won't you, you obstinate wicked creature? My blood boils when I think how I punished the other two innocent girls," he exclaimed, cutting her fearfully on the calves of her legs, knocking the delicate silk of the stockings to pieces, and wealing and bruising her legs all over. The victim cannot plunge about, as her ankles are fastened, but she moans with agony, and shrieks and sobs hysterically in turns at this terrible attack. The General seems beside himself with rage, for he next turns to her beautiful white shoulders, and slashes them about, fearfully cutting through the skin and deluging poor Jemima with her own blood.

Sir Eyre.—"I shall murder her; I can't help it; she's made me quite mad." His cuts wind round her ribs, and even weal the beauties of her splendid bosom, and stains the snowy belly with their blood.

Jemima (in low broken sobs).—"Oh! Oh! Mercy! Let me die! Don't torture an innocent thing like me any longer." She seems going to faint, when Mrs. Mansell interposes, saying: "It is enough; more may do serious injury."

SIR EYRE (gasping for breath).—"Oh! Oh! I know you are right to take me away, or I shall really murder her."

The bleeding victim is a pitiable and terrible sight as we release her from the ladder; she is scarcely able to stand; her boots covered with blood, and little pools of the sanguineous fluid stand on the floor; and we had to administer a cordial before she was able to be supported to her room, where she was confined to her bed for several days.

I had now had all the revenge I was so anxious to inflict; but the great avenger of all, to my great grief, soon removed poor old grandfather from this world, and left me indeed an orphan. Being still very young, my guardians under Sir Eyre's will placed me at Miss Flaybum's Academy to finish my education, and the old home was broken up, and inmates scattered.

I shall send you some of my school experiences in my next, and remain, Dear Nellie,

Yours affectionately,
ROSA BELINDA COOTE.

(To be continued.)

"Pray, mama," said Sally, "what's the meaning of Hush?"

"My dear," said mama, "what makes you ask such a question?"

"Because I asked Fanny what made her belly stick out so, and she answered, 'Hush.'"

CHARLIE COLLINGWOOD'S FLOGGING,

BY ETONIENSIS.

Seventeen years of age, with round limbs, and broad shoulders, tall, rosy and fair,
And all over his forehead and temples, a forest of curly red hair;

Good in the playing fields, good on the water, or in it, this
lad:

But at sums, or at themes, or at verses, oh! ain't Charlie
Collingwood bad?

Six days out of seven, or five at the least, he's sent up to be
stripped;

But it's nuts for the lower boys always, to see Charlie
Collingwood whipped;

For the marks of the birch on his bottom are more than the
leaves on a tree,

And a bum that has worn so much birch out, as Charlie's,
is jolly to see.

When his shirt is turned up, and his breeches, unbuttoned,
hang down to his heels,

From the small of his back, to the thick of his thighs is one
mass of red weals.

Ted Beauchamp last year began keeping a list of his floggings
and he

Says, they come, in a year-and-a-half, to a hundred and sixty
and three.

And you see how this morning, in front of the flogging block
silent he stands,

And hitches his waistband up slightly, and feels his backside
with his hands.

Then he lifts his blue eyes to the face of the Master, nor
shrinks at his frown,

Nor at sight of the birch, nor at sound of the sentence of
judgment, "Go down."

Not a word, Charlie Collingwood says, not a syllable, piteous
or pert;

But goes down with his breeches unbuttoned, and Errington
takes up his shirt.

And again we can see his great naked red bottom, round,
fleshy, and plump,

And the bystanders look from the Master's red rod, to the
schoolboy's red rump:

There are weals over weals, there are stripes upon stripes,
there are cuts after cuts,

All across Charlie Collingwood's bottom, and isn't the sight
of it nuts?

There, that cut on the fleshiest part of the buttocks, high up
on the right,

He got that before supper last evening, oh! isn't his bottom
    a sight?

And that scar that's just healed, don't you see where the birch
    cut the flesh?

That's a token of Charlie's last flogging, the rod will soon
    stamp it afresh.

And this morning you saw he could hardly sit down, or be
    quiet in Church;

It's a pleasure to see Charlie's bottom, it looks just cut out
    for the birch.

Now, look out, Master Charlie, it's coming: you won't get
    off this time, by God!

For your Master's in, oh, such a wax! and he's picked you out,
    oh, such a rod!

Such a jolly good rod, with the buds on, so stout, and so
    supple and lithe,

You've been flogged till you're hardened to flogging, but
    won't the first cut make you writhe?

You've been birched till you say you don't care as you used
    for a birching! Indeed?

Wait a bit, Master Charlie, I'll bet the third cut or the fourth
    makes you bleed.

Though they say a boy's bottom grows harder with whipping,
    and times make it tough,

Yet the sturdiest boy's bottom will wince if the Schoolmaster
    whips it enough.

Aye, the stoutest posteriors will redden, and flinch from the
    cuts as they come,

If they're flogged half as hard as the Master will flog Charlie
    Collingwood's bum.

We shall see a real jolly good swishing, as good as a fellow
    could wish;

Here's a stunning good rod, and a jolly big bottom just under
    it—Swish!

Oh, by Jove, he's drawn blood at the very first cut! in two
    places by God!

Aye, and Charlie's red bottom grows redder all over with
    marks of the rod.

And the pain of the cut makes his burning posteriors quiver
    and heave.

And he's hiding his face—yes, by Jove, and he's wiping his
    eyes on his sleeve!

Now; give it him well, Sir, lay into him well, till the pain
    makes him roar!

Flog him, then, till he stops, and then flog him again, till he
    bellows once more!

Ah, Charlie, my boy, you don't mind it, eh, do you? it's
    nothing to bear.

Though a small boy may cry for a flogging, that's natural,
    but Charlie don't care.

That's right, Sir, don't spare him! that cut was a stinger, but
    Charlie don't mind;

All the rods in the kingdom would only be wasted on
    Charlie's behind,

At each cut, how the red flesh rises, the red weals tingle and
    swell!

How he blushes! I told you the Master would flog Charlie
    Collingwood well.

There are long red ridges and furrows, across his great, broad,
    nether cheeks,

And on both his plump, rosy, round buttocks, the blood
    stands in drops and in streaks.

Well hit, Sir! Well caught! how he drew in his bottom, and
    flinched from the cut!

At each touch of the birch on his bum, how the smart makes
    it open and shut!

Well struck, Sir, again, how it made the blood spin! there's a
    drop on the floor,

Each long, fleshy furrow grows ruddy, and Charlie can bear it
    no more.

Blood runs from each weal on his bottom, and all Charlie's
    bottom is wealed,

'Twill be many a day ere the scars of this flogging are
    thoroughly healed.

Now just under the hollow of Charlie's bare back, where the
    flanks are aslope,

The rod catches and stings him, and now at the point where
    the downward ways ope;

Round his flanks, now like serpents, the birchen twigs twin-
    ing bend round as they bite,

And you see on his naked, white belly, red ridges, where all
    was so white.

Where between his white thighs, something hairy, the body's
    division reveals,

Falls the next cut, and now Charlie Collingwood's bottom
  is all over weals.
Not a twig on the rod, but has raised a red ridge on his flesh,
  not a bud,
But has drawn from his naked and writhing posteriors, a
  fresh drop of blood.
And the Schoolmaster warms to his work now, as harder and
  harder he hits,
And picks out the most sensitive places, as though he'd cut
  Charlie to bits.
"So you'll fidget and whisper in school-time, and make a
  disturbance in Church?
"Can't sit still, Master Charlie, eh, can't you? Well, what
  do you think of the birch?
"Oh, it hurts you so, does it, my boy, to sit down, since I
  flogged you last night?
"It was that made you fidget all church time? Indeed, you
  can't help it, please God—
"By the help of the birch, Master Charlie, I'll teach you to
  help it, please God—
"If you don't mend your manners in future, it shan't be for
  want of a rod.
"You're a big boy, no doubt, to be flogged; the more shame
  for you, Sir, at your age—
"But as long as you're here, I shall flog you," he lays on the
  cuts in a rage.
"Aye, and if you were older and bigger, you'd come to the
  flogging block still—
"Boys are never too big to be beaten!" he lays on the birch
  with a will.
"If a boy's not too old to go wrong, Sir, he can't be too old
  to be whipped;
"So take that!" and he lays on the rod, till the twigs all with
  crimson are tipped.
There are drops of the boy's blood visible now, on each tender
  young bud—
Blood has dropped on his trousers, and Charlie's bare bottom
  is covered with blood.
But I'd rather be shut up for days, in a hole you would scarce
  put a dog in,
And brought out once a day to be birched, than have missed
  Charlie Collingwood's flogging.

How each cut brings the blood to his forehead, and makes
    him bite half through his lips!

How the birch cuts his bottom right over, and makes the
    blood spin from his hips!

How his brawny bare haunches, all bloody, and wealed, with
    red furrows like ruts,

Shrink quivering with pain at each stroke, that revives all the
    smart of past cuts!

How the Schoolmaster seems to hit harder, the birch to sting
    more at each blow!

Till at last Charlie Collingwood, writhing with agony, bellows
    out, "Oh!"

That was all; not a word of petition; a single short cry and
    no more;

And the younger boys laugh, that the birch should have made
    such a big fellow roar.

For a moment, the Master too pauses; but not for a truce or
    a parley:

Then the birch falls afresh, on the bloody wealed flesh, with
    "Take that, Master Charlie."

All the small boys are breathless and hushed; but they hear
    not a syllable come,

They hear only the swish of the birch, as it meets Charlie
    Collingwood's bum.

And the Master's face flushes with anger; he signs to Fred
    Fane with a nod;

And Freddy reluctantly hands him another stout, supple birch
    rod.

And again as he flogs Charlie Collingwood's bottom, his face
    seems aflame;

At each cut he reminds him of this thing or that, and rebukes
    him by name.

Each cut makes the boy's haunches quiver, and scores them
    all over afresh;

You can trace where each separate birch twig has marked
    Charlie Collingwood's flesh.

Till the Master, tired out with hard work, and quite satiate
    with flogging for once,

With one last cut, that stings to the quick, bids him rise for
    an Obstinate Dunce.

From the block Charlie Collingwood rises, red faced, and with
    tumbled red hair,

And with crimson hued bottom, and tearful blue eyes, and a
    look of "Don't Care."
Then he draws up his breeches, and walks out of school with
    a crowd of boys dogging
The heels of their hero, all proud to have seen Charlie Col-
    lingwood's flogging.

FINIS.

"Jack, my boy, what a devil of an appetite you have this
morning," said one friend to another as they were breakfast-
ing at their hotel. "And so would you," replied Jack, "if you
had only had a whore's tongue and a toothbrush in your
mouth since yesterday!"

Madame Rollin had three monkeys, of which one was a
she; and the lady used to amuse herself with watching their
tricks. "It is curious," said she, "to observe them, for while
one of them is caressing the other, the third comforts himself!"

Her expression was "suffices for himself"!!

Meaning Masturbation of course!!!

LADY POKINGHAM, OR THEY ALL DO IT:

Giving an Account of her Luxurious Adventures, both before and after her Marriage with Lord Crim-Con.

PART II.
(Continued.)

Christmas came, and with it arrived several visitors, all young ladies and gentlemen of about our own ages, to spend the festive season with us; our entire party consisted of five gentlemen and seven ladies, leaving out the aunt, who was too old to enter into youthful fun and contented herself with being a faithful housekeeper, and keeping good house, so that after supper every evening we could do almost as we liked; myself and Alice soon converted our five young lady friends into tribades like ourselves, ready for anything, whilst Frederick prepared his young male friends. New Year's Day was his eighteenth birthday, and we determined to hold a regular orgy that night in our corridor, with Lucy's help. Plenty of refreshments were laid in stock, ices, sandwiches, and champagne; the aunt strictly ordered us all to retire at one A.M. at latest, so we kept her commands, after spending a delicious evening in dancing and games, which only served to flush us with excitement for what all instinctively felt would be a most voluptuous entertainment upstairs.

The aunt was a heavy sleeper, and rather deaf, besides which Frederick, under the excuse of making them drink his health, plied the servants first with beer, then with wine, and afterwards with just a glass of brandy for a nightcap; so that we were assured they would also be sound enough, in fact two or three never got to bed at all.

Frederick was master of the ceremonies, with Alice as a most useful assistant. As I said before, all were flushed with excitement and ready for anything; they were all of the most aristocratic families, and our blue blood seemed fairly to course through our veins. When all had assembled in Alice's apartment they found her attired in a simple, long *chemise de nuit.* "Ladies and gentlemen," she said, "I believe we are all agreed for an out and out romp; you see my costume, how do you like it?" and a most wicked smile, "I hope it does not display the contour of my figure too much," drawing it tightly about her so as to show the outline of her beautiful buttocks, and also displaying a pair of ravishing legs in pink silk stockings.

"Bravo! Bravo! Bravo Alice! we will follow your example," burst from all sides. Each one skipped back to his or her room and reappeared in mufti; but the tails of the young gentlemen's shirts caused a deal of laughter, by being too short.

ALICE.—"Well, I'm sure, gentlemen, I did not think your undergarments were so indecently short."

Frederick, with a laugh, caught hold of his sister's chemise, and tore a great piece off all around, so that she was in quite a short smock, which only half-covered her fair bottom.

Alice was crimson with blushes, and half inclined to be angry, but recovering herself, she laughed, "Ah! Fred, what a shame to serve me so, but I don't mind if you make us all alike."

The girls screamed, and the gentlemen made a rush; it was a most exciting scene; the young ladies retaliated by tearing the shirts of their tormentors, and this first skirmish only ended when the whole company were reduced to a complete state of nudity; all were in blushes as they gazed upon the variety of male and female charms exposed to view.

FREDERICK, advancing with a bumper of champagne.— "We've all heard of *Nuda Veritas*, now let's drink to her health; the first time we are in her company, I'm sure she will be most charming and agreeable."

All joined in this toast, the wine inflamed our desires, there was not a male organ present but what was in a glorious state of erection.

ALICE.—"Look, ladies, what a lot of impudent fellows, they need not think we are going to surrender anyhow to their youthful lust; they shall be all blindfolded, and then we will arm ourselves with good birch rods, then let it be everyone for themselves and Cupid's dart for us all."

"Hear, hear," responded on all sides, and handkerchiefs were soon tied over their eyes, and seven good birch rods handed round to the ladies. "Now, gentlemen, catch who you can," laughed Alice, slashing right and left into the manly group, her example being followed by the other girls; the room was quite large enough and a fine romp ensued, the girls were as lithe and active as young fawns, and for a long time sorely tried the patience of their male friends, who tumbled about in all directions, only to get an extra dose of birch on their plump posteriors before they could regain their feet.

At last the Honble. Miss Vavasour stumbled over a prostrate gentleman, who happened to be the young Marquis of Bucktown, who grasped her firmly round the waist, and clung to his prize, as a shower of cuts greeted the writhing pair.

"Hold, hold," cried Alice, "she's fairly caught and must submit to be offered as a victim on the Altar of Love."

Lucy quickly wheeled a small soft couch into the centre of the room. The gentlemen pulled off their bandages, and all laughingly assisted to place the pair in position; the lady underneath with a pillow under her buttocks, and the young marquis, on his knees, fairly planted between her thighs. Both were novices, but a more beautiful couple it would be impossible to conceive; he was a fine young fellow of seventeen, with dark hair and eyes, whilst her brunette style of complexion was almost a counterpart of his; their eyes were similar also, and his instrument, as well as her cunny, were finely ornamented with soft curly black hair; with the skin drawn back, the firey purple head of his cock looked like a large ruby, as, by Frederick's suggestion, he presented it to her luscious-looking vermilion gap, the lips of which were just slightly open as she lay with her legs apart. The touch seemed to electrify her, the blushing face turned to a still deeper crimson as the dart of love slowly entered the outworks of her virginity. Fred continued to act as mentor, by whispering in the young gallant's ear, who also was covered with blushes, but feeling his steed fairly in contact with the throbbing matrix of the lovely girl beneath him, he at once plunged forward to the attack, pushing, shoving, and clasping her round the body with all his strength, whilst he tried to stifle her cries of pain by glueing his lips to hers. It was a case of *Veni, Vidi, Vici.* His onset was too impetuous to be withstood, and she lay in such a passive favourable position that the network of her hymen was broken at the first charge, and he was soon in full possession up to the roots of his hair. He rested a moment, she opened her eyes, and with a faint smile said, "Ah! It was indeed sharp, but I can already begin to feel the pleasures of love. Go on now, dear boy, our example will soon fire the others to imitate us," heaving up her bottom as a challenge, and pressing him fondly to her bosom.

They ran a delightful course, which filled us all with voluptuous excitement, and as they died away in a mutual spend, someone put out the lights. All was laughing confusion, gentlemen trying to catch a prize, kissing and sighing.

I felt myself seized by a strong arm, a hand groped for my cunny, whilst a whisper in my ear said: "How delightful! It's you, dear little Beatrice. I can't make a mistake, as yours is the only hairless thing in the company. Kiss me, dear, I'm bursting to be into your tight little affair." Lips met lips in a luscious kiss. We found ourselves close to Alice's bed, my companion put me back on it, and taking my legs under his arms, was soon pushing his way up my longing cunny. I nipped him as tightly as possible; he was in ecstasies and spent almost directly, but keeping his place, he put me, by his vigorous action, into a perfect frenzy of love. Spend seemed to follow spend, till we had each of us done it six times, and the last time I so forgot myself as to fairly bite his shoulder in delight. At length he withdrew, without telling his name. The room was still in darkness, and love engagements were going on all round. I had two more partners after that, but only one go with each. I shall never forget that night as long as a breath remains in my body.

Next day I found out, through Fred, that Charlie Vavasour had been my first partner, and that he himself believed he had had his sister in the melee, which she afterwards admitted to me was a fact, although she thought he did not know it, and the temptation to enjoy her brother was too much for her.

This orgie has been the means of establishing a kind of secret society amongst the circle of our friends. Anyone who gives a pressure of the hand and asks: "Do you remember Fred's birthday?" is free to indulge in love with those who understand it, and I have since been present at many repetitions of that birthday fun.

Part III.

We returned to school, and I kept up a regular correspondence with Frederick, the letters to and fro being enclosed in those of Alice. Time crept on, but as you can imagine as well or better than I can relate all the kinds of salacious amusements we girls used to indulge in, I shall skip over the next few years till I arrived at the age of seventeen; my guardians were in a hurry to present me at Court, and have me brought out in hopes that I might soon marry and relieve them of their trust.

Alice was so attached to me that since my first visit to her home, she had solicited her aunt to arrange with my guardians for my permanent residence with her during my minority, which quite fell in with their views, as it enabled me to see more society, and often meet gentlemen who might perhaps fall in love with my pretty face.

Lady St. Jerome undertook to present both Alice and myself; she was an aunt, and mentioned in her letter that unfortunately a star of the first magnitude would also be presented at the same drawing room, but still we might have a faint chance of picking up young Lothair, the great matrimonial prize of the season, if he did not immediately fall in love with the beautiful Lady Corisande, and that we should meet them both at Crecy House, at the Duchess's ball, in celebration of the presentation of her favourite daughter, for which she had obtained invitations for us. For nearly three weeks we were in a flutter of excitement, making the necessary preparations for our debut. My mother's jewels were reset to suit the fashion of the day, and every three or four days we went to town to see our Court milliner.

In company with Alice and her aunt, we arrived at Lord St. Jerome's town residence in St. James' Square, the evening before the eventful day; her ladyship was a most charming person of about thirty, without family, who introduced us before dinner to her niece, Miss Clare Arundel, Father Coleman, the family confessor, and Monsignore Berwick, the chamberlain of Pio Nono. The dinner was exquisite, and we passed a delightful evening, amused by the quiet humour of the confessor, and the sparkling wit of Monsignore, who seemed to studiously avoid religious subjects. Miss Arundel, with her beautiful, pensive, violet eyes, and dark brown golden hair, seemed particularly fascinated by the sallies of the latter, whilst there was a something remarked by both Alice and myself, which led us to suspect the existence of some curious tie between the two ecclesiastics and the ladies of the household.

Lord St. Jerome was not in town. At our special request Alice and myself shared the same room, which opened into a spacious corridor, at one end of which was a small chapel or oratory. Our minds were so unsettled by the thoughts of the morrow, and also hopes of meeting some of our old friends in town, especially the Vavasours, that sleep was quite banished from our eyes; suddenly Alice started up in bed with, "Hist! there's someone moving about the corridor." She sprang out of bed, and softly opened our door, whilst I followed and stood close behind her. "They're gone into the oratory," she said. "I saw a figure just in the act of passing in, I will know what is going on; we can easily slip into some of the empty rooms, if we hear anyone coming."

So saying, she put on her slippers and threw a shawl over her shoulders, and I followed her example; ready for any kind of adventure, we cautiously advanced along the corridor, soon we arrived at the door of the oratory, and could hear several low voices inside, but were afraid to push the door ajar for fear of being observed.

"Hush!" whispered Alice, "I was here when quite a little girl, and now remember that old Lady St. Jerome, who had been dead some time, used to use this room next to the chapel, and had a private entrance made for herself direct from the room into the oratory. If we can get in here," she said, turning the handle, "we shall be in a fine place to see everything, as the room is never used, and said to be haunted by the old lady." The door yielded to her pressure, and we slipped into a gloomy room, just able to see a little by the light of the moon.

(*To be continued.*)

A TASTE FOR FOREIGNERS.

(*Imitated from Martial.*)

To the French, to the Germans and Swedes,
    Easy Harriet, you give up your charms;
Italians and Russians besides
    Have all had their turns in your arms;

You despise not the Dutch, nor the Danes,
  Mulattoes, or Negroes, or Finns;
In you they may all quench their flames,
  Whatever the tint of their skins.

You reject the capless concerns,
  Or the circumcised Turk or the Jew;
In short, every nation by turns,
  Has had an erection in you;
Your fancy is truly uncommon,
  The reason I wish I could find;
While by birth you're a true Enlishwoman,
  That no true English prick's to your mind.

ADULTERY'S THE GO!

(A Song before the time of the New Divorce Court.)

When we were boys the world was good,
  But that is long ago;
Now all the wisest folks are lewd,
  For Adultery's the go.
      The go, the go, the go,
      Adultery's the go!

Quite tired of leading virtuous lives,
  Though spotless as the snow,
Among the chaste and pious wives,
  Adultery's the go.
      The go, the go, the go, &c.

Long life then to the House of Lords,
  They know a thing or two;
You see from all their grand awards,
  That Adultery's the go.
      The go, the go, the go, &c.

And Lady Barlow, Mrs. Hare,
  Case, Clarke, and Bolders;

Teed, Ashton, James, and all declare
    Adultery's the go.
        The go, the go, the go, &c.

Some husbands still are jealous,
    And guard the furbelow,
But spite such prudish fellows,
    Adultery's the go.
        The go, the go, the go, &c.

Horn'd cuckolds were mad raging bulls,
    A century ago;
Now, they're tame oxen, silly fools,
    For Adultery's the go.
        The go, the go, the go, &c.

Then, hey for Doctors' Commons,
    With horned beasts arow;
For man's delight, and woman's,
    Adultery's the go.

HER VERY SOUL.

On Sundays, in a church like this,
I joy to face the blushing Miss,
Eye within eye, agog for bliss,
Through touching not, I only kiss,
    Her very soul! Her very soul!

She falls at once into my plan,
I guess she prays, behind her fan,
"Oh, for a man! A real man!
To satiate, as he only can,
    Her very soul! Her very soul!

Heavens! what a glance! see her suck,
And lick her lips, on fire for cock.

I see her frisky bottom buck,
While with the prick of lust I fuck,
    Her very soul! Her very soul!

FIRST RONDEAU.

Ten years ago, on Christmas day,
Fair Helen stole my heart away,
I went to church—but not to pray,
        Ten years ago.

To pray? Yes—pray to Helen's eyes;
Ah! would that we had been more wise;
To-day, she would not recognize
Him, whom she kissed in ecstasies,
        Ten years ago.

SECOND RONDEAU.

Again we've met, and now I find,
Her still more luscious to my mind;
She was not to such pranks inclined,
        Ten years ago.

Though now a second time she's wed,
Hers is a most lascivious bed;
Though thirty years she now has sped,
She fucks still better than she did,
        Ten years ago.

LINES WRITTEN UNDER HER PORTRAIT.

Such Helen was! religious, young and fair;
A faithful spouse, and blest with babies dear;

But in the church, while week by week she prayed,
An amorous noble long her charms surveyed;
Sunday by Sunday, seated near her pew,
He kept the goddess of his heart in view;
And when the Tenth Command was duly read,
"I covet thee," his burning glances said—
Her humble rank forbade acquaintance free,
Yet high enough it was to guard her modesty;
Her husband was a gamester fierce and rude,
He fled the town, and other loves pursu'd;
She on her jointure fair remained at home,
Close guarded by his mother and her own;
Two months at church, she stood the siege of sighs,
Silence, that spoke, and eloquence of eyes;
Could virtue longer last? at length she fell;
No more, no more, can happy lovers tell.
And mark the sequel! rashly she had sworn
She ne'er would to her faithless lord return;
Her prudent lover urged a course more wise,
His vigour had more force than his advice;
She would not listen, till her swelling zone,
Proved his kind counsel wiser than her own.
Just at that juncture her good man returned,
In time to adopt the babe, that proves him horn'd;
The wedding ring upon her hand you see
Is not her wedding ring, 'twas given by me;
The one her husband gave her, here, here, behold!
Around my finger wreaths its hallow'd gold;
Her diamond brooch and clasps all brightly shine,
His gifts indeed! the locks they hold are mine;
Far, far away, I now her absence mourn,
Grant me, O Venus! grant a quick return;
Keep Helen virtuous, till again we meet,
And revel in the bliss so naughty and so sweet.

UP THE CHIMNEY.

When Captain Jones of Halifax,
    Was put in winter quarters,

His landlady, a widow, had
    The prettiest of daughters.

The Captain sued her lovingly,
    The girl was gay and ready
To join her lot with his and be
    The noble Captain's lady.

Their wedding was deferred; but soon,
    Impatient for the pleasure,
He found his way into her room,
    And swiv'd her at his leisure.

The chambermaid, who set to rights
    The different pots and pans,
Warn'd mistress there was ne'er a drop
    In that of this young man's.

The mother asked him tenderly,
    "As you're to wed my daughter,
Pray tell me why—my dear young man,
    Why—why—you make no water?"

"Ah, Madam!" cried he, "cannot you
    The real reason guess?
The fact is that I go to bed,
    So full of tenderness.

I get eager for the bliss,
    I feel so stiff and hot,
That really I'm obliged to piss
    Right up the Chimney Pot."

In the wars in India, in the year 1800, Major Torrens's party was pursuing some of the enemy. One day, while they were dining and very merry, a sergeant came and reported to the Major that two prisoners were brought in, one old and one young. The Sergeant requested orders regarding them. The Major merrily answered: "Oh, take them away and frig them." The Sergeant retired. In an hour he returned, and respectfully made this report: "Please your honour, we have frigged the young one, but we can't make the old man's cock stand."

This story was related to me, in 1818, by Torrens, who was then an old General at Madras.

NURSERY RHYMES.

There was a young lady of Harrow,
Who complained that her Cunt was too narrow,
    For times without number
    She would use a cucumber,
But could not accomplish a marrow.

There was a young lady of Glasgow,
And fondly her lover did ask, "Oh,
    Pray allow me a fuck,"
    But she said, "No, my duck,
But you may, if you please, up my arse go."

There was a young man had the art
Of making a capital tart,
    With a handful of shit,
    Some snot and a spit,
And he'd flavor the whole with a fart.

There was an old man of Connaught.
Whose prick was remarkably short,
    When he got into bed
    The old woman said,
"This isn't a prick, it's a wart."

There was a gay Countess of Bray,
And you may think it odd when I say,
    That in spite of high station,
    Rank and education,
She always spelt Cunt with a K.

There was an old parson of Lundy,
Fell asleep in his vestry on Sunday;
    He awoke with a scream,
    "What, another wet dream,
This comes of not frigging since Monday."

There was a strong man of Drumrig,
Who one day did seven times frig;
    He buggered three Sailors,
    Four Jews and two Tailors,
And ended by fucking a pig.

There was an Old Man of the Mountain,
Who frigged himself into a fountain,
    Fifteen times had he spent,
    Still he wasn't content,
He simply got tired of the counting.

There was a young man of Nantucket,
Who went down a well in a bucket;
    The last words he spoke,
    Before the rope broke,
Were, "Arsehole, you bugger, and suck it."

A native of Havre de Grace
Once tired of Cunt, said "I'll try arse."
    He unfolded his plan
    To another young man,
Who said, "Most decidedly, my arse!"

———————

At the Parish Church, South Hackney, by the Rev. C. A.
White, John Henry Bottomfeldt, of Hamburgh, to Sarah
Jane Greens, of South Hackney. (*Vide* "Daily Telegraph,"
January 3, 1875).

    How lovely everything now seems
        When joined in one by Hymen's belt,
    For now John Henry has his *Greens*,
        And Sarah Jane her *Bottom-feldt*.

THE PEARL,

A Journal of Facetiæ and Voluptuous Reading.

| No. 4 | PUBLISHED MONTHLY. | Oct. 1879 |

SUB-UMBRA, OR SPORT AMONG THE SHE-NOODLES.

(Continued.)

After luncheon Frank smoked his cigarette in my room; the events of the morning had left both of us in a most unsettled and excited state.

"I say, old fellow," he exclaimed, "by Jove! it's quite impossible for me to wait till to-morrow for the chance of enjoying that delicious Rosa; besides, when there are so many of us together there is just the chance of being disappointed; no, no, it must be this very night if I die for it; her room is only the other side of my sisters."

I tried to persuade him from doing anything rashly, as we could not yet be certain that even excited and ready as she had shown herself, that she was prepared to surrender her virginity so quickly. However, arguments and reasonings were in vain. "See," he exclaimed, "the very thoughts of her make my prick ready to burst," opening his trousers and letting out his beautiful red-headed cock, as it stood in all its manly glory, stiff and hard as marble, with the hot blood looking ready to burst from his distended veins; the sight was too exciting for me to restrain myself, the cigarette dropped from my lips, and going upon my knees in front of him, I kissed, sucked, frigged, and played with his delicious prick till he spent in my mouth with an exclamation of rapture, as I eagerly swallowed every drop of his copious emission. When we had a little recovered our serenity, we discussed the best plans for the night, as I was determined to have my share of the amusement, which Frank most willingly agreed to, provided he was to go first to Rosa's room, and prevail upon her to consent to his ardent suit; then when all seemed to be en règle, I was to surprise them in the midst of their fun, and join in the erotic frolic.

After dinner we adjourned to the drawing-room, where a most pleasant evening was enlivened by music and singing, leaving Frank turning over the leaves for Rosa and Polly, as they sang "What Are the Wild Waves Saying." Annie and Sophie whispered to me that they should like a short stroll in the garden by moonlight, so opening the window, a few steps brought us on to the soft gravel path, where we could walk with an almost noiseless tread. Papa and Mama were in the library playing cribbage, and we felt sure that Frank and Rosa would not run after us, so passing rapidly down a shady walk, with one arm round each of the dear girl's waists, and alternately kissing one and the other of them, we soon arrived at a very convenient spot, and the instinct of love allowed me to guide the willing girls into a rather dark arbour without the least demur on their part.

"How lovely the honeysuckle smells!" sighed Sophie, as I drew them both down by my side in the corner, and began a most delicious kissing and groping in the dim obscurity.

"Not so sweet as your dear little pussey," said I, playfully twisting my fingers in the soft down around the tight little grotto of love which I had taken possession of.

"Oh! Oh! Mind, Walter dear!" she sighed softly, as she clung round my neck.

"Will you let me kiss it as I did Annie's this morning, my little pet, it will give you such pleasure; there's nothing to be bashful or shamefaced about here in the dark; ask your sister if it wasn't delicious."

ANNIE.—"Oh! let him Sophie dear, you will experience the most heavenly sensations."

Thus urged she allowed me to raise her clothes, and recline her backwards in the corner, but this would not admit of Annie having her fair share of the game, but as she was now all aflame with excited expectation, there was no difficulty in persuading her to kneel over my face as I reclined on my back at full length on the seat; lovely hands at once let my eager prick out of his confined position in my trousers, and as I commenced to suck and gamahuche Sophie, I felt that the dear Annie had taken possession of my cock for her own special benefit.

"Oh! let me kiss you, Sophie dear, put your tongue in my

mouth," said Annie, straddling over me, and putting away my excited engine of love up her own longing crack, and beginning a delightful St. George; I clasped the younger girl firmly round the buttocks with one arm, whilst with my right hand I found and rubbed her stiff little clitoris to increase the excitement from the lascivious motions of my tongue in her virgin cunny.

Annie was in a frenzy of voluptuous enjoyment, she bounced up and down on my prick, and now and then rested for a moment to indulge in the exquisite pleasure of the devil's bite, which she seemed to possess to a most precocious extent, the folds of her cunt contracting and throbbing upon my swelling prick in the most delicious manner.

Sophie was all of a tremble, she wriggled herself most excitedly over my mouth, and I licked up her virgin spendings as they came down in a thick creamy emission.

"Oh! Oh! Oh!" she sighed, hugging and kissing Annie in fondest abandon. "What is it, dear? I shall choke, Walter. There's something running from me; it's so delicious. Oh! What shall I do?"

Annie and myself met at this moment in a joint spend, which left us in an ecstatic lethargy of love, and the two sisters almost fainted upon my prostrate body.

When we had recovered a little, I sat up between the loving sisters.

Sophie, throwing her arms round my neck, quite smothered one with her burning kisses, as she whispered in my ear: "It was indeed pleasure, dear Walter. Is that one of the delights of love, and what was Annie doing, for she was as excited as I was?"

"Can't you guess, darling?" I replied, taking her hand and placing it upon my still rampant cock. "That is what she played with."

"But how?" whispered the innocent girl. "She was kissing and sucking my tongue deliciously all the while, but seemed as if she could not keep still a moment."

"She had that plaything of mine up her cunny, my dear, and was riding up and down upon it till we all fainted with the pleasure at the same time. You shall have a real lesson in love next time, and Annie won't be jealous, will you, dearest?"

ANNIE.—"No, no, we must all be free to enjoy all the

games of love without jealousy. I wonder how Frank is getting on with Rosa by this time. We must now make haste back to the house."

Sophie was anxious for more explanations as to the arts of love, but was put off till another time; and all being now in a cooler state of mind, we returned to the house, where we found Frank repeating the game of the morning, by gama-huching Rosa, whilst Polly was gone out of the room.

The red-haired beauty was covered with blushes, as she suddenly dropped her clothes on our entrance, and only recovered from her crimson shamefacedness when Annie laughingly assured her that we had been enjoying ourselves in the same manner.

"Oh! How rude and indecent of us all," exclaimed Rosa, "but who can resist the burning touches of a handsome young fellow like your brother; he was so impudent, and it sends such a thrill of voluptuousness through the whole frame," commencing to sing, "It's naughty, but it's nice."

The supper bell rang, and, after a light repast, we all separated to our rooms. Frank came into my chamber to join in a cigarette and glass of grog before finally retiring.

"It's all right for to-night, old fellow," he exclaimed, as soon as we were seated for our smoke. "I begged Rosa to let me kiss all her charms, in her own room without the inconvenience of clothes. She made some objections at first, but finally consented not to lock the door, if I promised not to go beyond kissing, on my honour as a gentleman."

He was too impatient to stop long, and, after only one smoke, cut off to his room. Undressing myself as quickly as possible, I went to him, and escorted him to the door of his lady-love; it was unlocked, and he glided noiselessly into the darkened chamber. She was evidently awake and expecting his visit, for I could hear their rapturous kissing and his exclamation of delight as he ran his hands over her beautiful figure.

"My love, I must light the candles to feast my eyes upon your extraordinary beauties. Why did you put out the lights?" She made some faint remonstrances, but the room was soon a blaze of light from half-a-dozen candles.

I was looking through the keyhole, and eagerly listening to every word.

"My love, let us lay side by side and enjoy feeling our

bodies in naked contact before we begin the kissing each other's charms."

I could see that his shirt and her *chemise de nuit* were both turned up as high as possible, and his prick was throbbing against her belly. He made her grasp it in her hand, and pulling one of her legs over his thighs, was trying to place the head of his eager cock to the mark between her legs.

"Ah! No! No! Never! You promised on your honour, sir!" she almost screamed in alarm, and struggling to disengage herself from his strong embrace. "No! No! Oh! No! I won't, indeed!"

His previous soft manner seemed in a moment to have changed to a mad fury, as he suddenly rolled her over on her back, keeping his own legs well between her thighs.

"Honour! Honour!" he laughed. "How can I have honour when you tempt me so, Rosa? You have driven me mad by the liberties I have been allowed. Resistance is useless. I would rather die than not have you now, you dear girl."

She struggled in desperate silence for a few moments, but her strength was unequal to his; he gradually got into position, and then taking advantage of her exhaustion, rapidly and ruthlessly completed her ravishment.

She seemed insensible at first, and I took advantage of her short unconsciousness to steal into the room, and kneel at the foot of the bed, where I had a fine view of his blood-stained weapon, thrusting in and out of her shattered virginity. After a little she seemed to begin to enjoy his movements, especially after the first lubricating injection of his love juice. Her buttocks heaved up to meet his thrusts, and her arms clung convulsively round his body, and seemed reluctant to let him withdraw, until both seemed to come together in a luscious spend.

As they lay exhausted after this bout, I advanced and kissed the dear girl, and as she opened her eyes, I placed my hand across her mouth to stop any inconvenient scream of surprise, and congratulated her on having so nicely got rid of her troublesome virginity, and claimed my share of the fun, drawing her attention to the rampant condition of my cock in contrast to Frank's limp affair. I could see she was now eager for a repetition of the pleasure she had only just begun to taste. Her eyes were full of languishing desire as I placed her hand upon my prick.

In accordance with our previously devised arrangements she was persuaded to ride a St. George upon me, my cock was inserted in her still tender cunt, with great care, and allowed slowly to get his position, but the excitement was too great for me, with an exclamation of delight I shot a stream of sperm up into her very entrails, this set her off, she began slowly to move upon me, her cunt gripping and throbbing upon the shaft most deliciously, and we were soon running another delightful course; this was too much for Frank, his cock was again as hard as iron, and eager to get in somewhere, so kneeling up behind her he tried to insert his prick in her cunt alongside of mine, but found it too difficult to achieve, then the charming wrinkled orifice of her pink bottom-hole caught his attention, the tip of his affair was wet with our spendings, and his vigorous shoves soon gained an entrance, as I was holding her fast and she was too excited to resist anything, only giving a slight scream as she found him slip inside of the part she thought was only made for another purpose. I asked them to rest a few moments and enjoy the sensation of feeling where we were, our pricks throbbing against each other in a most delicious manner, with only the thin membrane of the anal canal between them; it made us spend immediately to the great delight of Rosa, who at once urged us to go on.

This was the most delightful bout of fucking I had ever had; she made us do it over and over again and, when we were exhausted, sucked our pricks up to renewed cockstands. This lasted till the dawn of day warned us of the necessity of precaution, and we retired to our respective rooms.

(To be continued.)

MISS COOTE'S CONFESSION,

Or the Voluptuous Experience of an Old Maid; In a series of Letters to a Lady Friend.

Letter IV.

My Dear Nellie,
    I promised in my last to relate a few of my school experiences, so now I will try and redeem the promise.

Her house was situated at Edmonton, so famous for Johnny Gilpin's ride. It was a large spacious mansion, formerly belonging to some nobleman, and stood in its own grounds. What were called the private gardens, next the house, were all enclosed in high walls, to prevent the possibility of any elopements.

Beyond these, in a ring fence, there were several paddocks for grazing purposes, in which Miss Flaybum kept her cows and turned the carriage horses, when not in use (which was all the week), for we only took coach, carriage, or whatever the conveyance might be, on Sundays, when we were twice regularly driven to the village church, nearly one-and-a-half miles distant, for Miss Flaybum's ladies could not be permitted, upon even the finest days, to walk there. We always called the vehicles coaches, although they were a kind of nondescript vehicle, and having nearly three dozen young ladies in the establishment, we filled three of them, and formed quite a grand procession as we drove up to the church door, and there was generally quite a little crowd to see us alight or take our departure, and, as the eldest girls assured us, it was only to see if we showed our legs, or displayed rather more ankle than usual. We were very particular as to silk stockings, and the finest and most fashionable boots we could get to set off our limbs to greatest advantage, and, in wet weather, when we were obliged to hold up our dresses rather more, I often observed quite a titter of admiration amongst the spectators, who curiously, as it seemed to us, were mostly the eldest gentlemen of the place, who evidently were as anxious to keep their sons away from the sight of our blandishments as Miss Flaybum could possibly wish; at any rate, it seemed to be understood to be highly improper for any young gentleman ever to present himself at what we called our Sunday levee.

We were never allowed to walk in the country roads, but on half-holidays or any special occasions, in fine weather, our governess would escort us into paddocks, and a little wood of three or four acres, which was included within the ring fence, where we indulged in a variety of games free from observation.

The school was very select, none but the daughters of the aristocracy or officers of the army or navy being admitted to the establishment; even the professions were barred by Miss

Flaybum, who was a middle-aged maiden lady, and a very strict martinet.

Before I went to this school, I always thought such places were conducted with the greatest possible propriety as to morals, etc., but soon found that it was only an outward show of decorum, whereas the private arrangements admitted of a variety of very questionable doings, not at all conducive to the future morality of the pupils, and if other fashionable schools are all conducted upon the same principles, it easily accounts for that aristocratic indifference to virtue so prevalent in my early days.

The very first night I was in the house (we slept, half-a-dozen of us, in a fine large room), I had not been settled in bed with my partner more than an hour before quite a dozen girls invaded the room, and pulled me out of bed, to be made free of the establishment, as they call it.

They laid me across one of the beds, stuffed a handkerchief in my mouth to prevent my cries, and every one of them slapped my naked bottom three times and some of them did it very spitefully, so that my poor rump tingled and smarted as if I had had a good birching.

Laura Sandon, my bedfellow, who was a very nice kind-hearted girl of sixteen, comforted and assured me all the girls had to go through the same ordeal as soon as they came to the school. I asked her if the birch was ever used in the establishment.

"Bless you, yes," she replied; "you are a dear love of a girl, and I shall be sorry to see you catch it," kissing me and rubbing my smarting bottom. "How hot it is, let's throw off the bedclothes and cool it," she added.

"Let's look at her poor bottom," said Miss Louise Van Tromp, a fine fair Dutch girl; "shall we have a game of slaps before Mdlle. Fosse (the French Governess) comes to bed?"

"Yes, come, Rosa dear, you'll like that, it will make you forget your own smarts; get up Cecile and Clara for a romp," addressing the Hon. Miss Cecile Deben and Lady Clara Wavering, who with the French Governess made up the six occupants of our room. "You know Mdlle. won't say anything if she does catch us."

We were soon out of bed, with our nightdresses thrown off, and all quite naked: Laura, a thin, fair girl with soft large blue eyes, always such a sure indication of an amorous

disposition; Cecile, about fifteen, a nice plump little dear
with chestnut hair and blue eyes. Lady Clara, who was just
upon eighteen, was dark, rather above the middle height,
well-proportioned, with languid, pensive hazel eyes, whilst
Louise Van Tromp was a fat Dutch girl of seventeen, with
grey eyes and splendidly developed figure.

It was a beautiful sight, for they were all pretty, and none
of them showed any shamefacedness over it, evidently being
quite used to the game; they all gathered round me, and
patted and kissed my bottom, Cecile saying, "Rosie, I'm so
glad you've no hair on your pussey yet, you will keep me in
countenance; these other girls think so much of their hairi-
ness, as if they were old women; what's the use of it, Laura,
now you have got it," playing with the soft fair down of Miss
Sandon's pussey.

LAURA.—"You silly thing, don't tickle so, you'll be proud
enough when you get it."

LADY CLARA.—"Cecile, dear, you've only to rub your belly
on mine a little more than you do, that's how Laura got
hers."

LOUISE.—"Rosie, you shall rub your belly on mine; Clara
is too fond of Cecile. I can make yours grow for you, my
dear," kissing me and feeling my mount in a very loving way.

LAURA.—"Listen to Grey Eyes Greedy Guts, you'd think
none of us ever played with the Van Tromp. Rosie, you belong to me."

We now commenced the game of slaps, which in reality
was similar to a common children's sport called "touch."
Ours was a very large room, the three beds, dressing tables,
washstands, &c., all arranged round the sides, leaving a good
clear space in the centre.

LADY CLARA.—"I'll be 'Slappee' to begin," taking her station in the middle of the room.

Each girl now placed herself with one hand touching a
bedstead or some article of furniture, and as Clara turned her
back to any of us we would slip slyly up behind and give a
fine spanking slap on her bottom, making it assume a rosy
flush all over; but if she could succeed in returning the slap
to anyone before they regained their touch, the one that was
caught had to take her place as "Slappee."

We all joined heartily in the game, keeping up a constant
sound of slaps, advancing and retreating, or slipping up now

and then to vary the amusement, in which case the unfortunate one got a general slapping from all the players before she could recover herself, making great fun and laughter. You would think such games would soon be checked by the governess, but the rule was never to interfere with any games amongst the pupils in their bedrooms. Just as our sport was at its height the door opened, and Mdlle. Fosse entered, exclaiming, "Ma foi, you rude girls, all out of bed slapping one another, and the lamp never put out, how indelicate, young ladies, to expose yourselves so; but Mdlle. Flaybum does not like to check you out of school, so it's no business of mine, but you want slapping, do you? How would you like to be cut with this, Mdlle. Coote?" showing me a very pretty little birch rod of long thin twigs, tied up with blue velvet and ribbons. "It would tickle very differently to hand slapping."

"Ah! Mademoiselle, I've felt much worse than that three times the size and weight. My poor old grandfather, the General, was a dreadful flogger," I replied.

MADEMOISELLE.—"I thought girls were only whipped at school. You must tell me all about it, Miss Rosa."

"With great pleasure. I don't suppose any of you have seen such punishment inflicted as I could tell you of," I replied.

The young French lady had been rapidly undressing herself as this conversation was going on. She was very dark, black hair over a rather low forehead, with a most pleasing expression of face, and fine sparkling eyes, hid under what struck me as uncommonly bushy eyebrows. She unlaces her corset, fully exposing a beautiful snowy bosom, ornamented with a pair of lovely round globes, with dark nipples, and her skin, although so white, had a remarkable contrast to our fairer flesh. There seemed to be a tinge of black somewhere, whereas our white complexion must have been from an original pink source, infinitely diluted.

MADEMOISELLE.—"Ah! You Van Tromp, où est ma robe de chambre? Have you hidden it?"

LOUISE.—"Oh! Pray strip and have a game with us. You shan't have the nightdress yet."

MADEMOISELLE.—"You shall catch it if you make me play; your bottom shall smart for it."

We all gathered round her, and although she playfully resisted, she was soon denuded of every rag of clothing. We pulled off her boots and stockings; but what a beautiful sight she was, apparently about twenty-six, with nicely rounded limbs, but such a glorious profusion of hair, that from her head, now let loose, hung down her back in a dense mass, and quite covered her bottom, so that she might have sat on the end of it, whereas her belly, it is almost impossible to describe it, except by calling it a veritable "Forêt Noire." The glossy black curling hair, extending all over her mount, up to her navel, and hanging several inches down between her thighs.

"There, Mdlle. Rosa," she exclaimed, sitting on the edge of her bed, "did you ever see anyone so hairy as I am? It's a sign of a loving nature, my dear," nipping my bottom and kissing me as she hugged my naked figure to hers. "How I love to caress the little featherless birdies like you. You shall sleep with me sometimes. The Van Tromp will be glad to change me for Laura."

"We cannot allow that," cried two or three of the others together. "Now you shall be 'Slappee' with your birch, Mdlle."

"Very well," said the lively French lady. "You'll get well touched up if I do catch any of you."

Then we commenced our game again, and she switched us finely, leaving long red marks on our bottoms when she succeeded in making a hit. Her own bottom must have smarted from our smacks, but she seemed quite excited and delighted with the amusement, till at last she said: "Oh! I must be birched myself, who will be the schoolmistress?"

LAURA.—"Oh! Let Rosa! She will lecture you as if you were a culprit, and give us an idea of good earnest punishment. Will you, Rosa? it will amuse us all. Just try if you can't make Mademoiselle ask your pardon for taking liberties with you, do, there's a dear girl."

"Yes! yes! that will be fine," cried the others, especially Lady Clara, who was already seated on her bed with Cecile as her partner.

LOUISE.—"Mdlle. wants Rosa for her bedfellow to-night, so let her tickle her up with the birch; don't spare her, Rosie, she's so hard to hurt; come Laura, let us enjoy the night together."

Thus urged I took up the rod and, flourishing it lightly in the air, said, laughing, "I know how to use it properly, especially on naughty bottoms, which have the impudence to challenge me; now, Mdlle., present your bottom on the edge of the bed, with your legs well apart, just touching the floor, but I must have two of them to hold you down; come, Laura and Louise, each of you hold one arm, and keep her body well down on the bed, there, that will do just so, hold her securely, don't let her get up till I've fairly done."

ROSA.—"Mdlle. Fosse, you are a very wicked young lady to behave so rudely to me as you have done; will you beg my pardon, and promise never to do so any more; do you feel that and that?" giving a couple of stinging little switches across her loins.

MADEMOISELLE.—"Oh! no! I won't apologize, I do love little featherless chits like you!"

ROSA.—"You call me a chit, do you? I'll teach you a little more respect for your schoolmistress; is that too hard, or perhaps you like that better," giving a couple of slashing cuts on her rounded buttocks, which leave long red marks, and make her wriggle with pain.

MADEMOISELLE.—"Ah! Ah! Ah—r—r—re, that's too hard. Oh! Oh! you do cut, you little devil," as I go on sharper and sharper at every stroke, making her writhe and wriggle under the tingling switches which mark her bottom in every direction.

ROSA.—"Little devil, indeed, you shall beg my pardon for that too, you insulting young lady, how dare you express yourself so to your governess, your bottom must be cut to pieces, if I can't subdue such a proud spirit. There—there—there!" cutting away, each stroke going in on the tender parts of her inner thighs. "Will you be rude again? will you insult me again, eh? I hope I don't hurt you too much, pray tell me if I do. Ha! Ha!! Ha!!! you don't seem quite to approve of it by the motions of your impudent bottom," cutting away all the while I was speaking, each stroke with deliberation on some unexpected place, till her bum was rosy all over, and marked with a profusion of deep red weals.

Mademoiselle makes desperate efforts to release herself, but Lady Clara and Cecile also help to keep her down, all apparently highly excited by the sight of her excoriated blushing bottom, adding their remarks, such as, "Bravo, Bravo, Rosie, you didn't think she would catch it so, how delightful to see her writhe and plunge in pain, to hear her scream, and help to keep her down," till at last the surprised victim begs and prays for pardon, crying to be let off, with tears in her eyes.

This is the end of the night's amusements, for all now resume their night chemises and retire, Mdlle. taking me to sleep with her. "Ah! Ma cherie," she exclaimed, as the lamp was put out and I found myself in her arms, "how cruelly you have warmed my poor bottom, and have you really seen worse than that, Rosie?"

"Oh! far, far worse, Mdlle., I've seen the blood flow freely from cut up bottoms," I replied, at the same time repaying her caresses and running my hand through the thick curly hair of her mount, as she was feeling and tickling my pussey. "There, there," she whispered, "nip me, squeeze that little bit of flesh," as my hand wandered to the lips of her hairy retreat, "tickle me as I do you," putting me in great confusion by her touches, for I had never experienced anything like it before, except the melting, burning sensations of the same parts at the conclusion of my previous flagellations.

This dalliance continued between us for some months, and I soon became an apt pupil in her sensual amusements, being emboldened by her freedoms, and heated by a most curious desire to explore with my fingers everything about that hairy paradise. Meanwhile she tickled and rubbed the entrance of my slit in a most exciting manner, and suddenly she clasped me close to her naked body (our chemises were turned up so we might feel each other's naked flesh), and kissed my lips in such a rapturous, luscious manner as to send a thrill of ecstasy through my whole quivering frame, her fingers worked nervously in my crack, and I felt quite a sudden gush of something from me, wetting her fingers and all my secret parts, whilst she pressed me more and more, wriggling and sighing, "Oh! oh! Rosa, go on, rub, rub"; then suddenly she stiffened herself out straight and seemed almost rigid as I felt my hand deluged with a profusion of warm, thick, sticky stuff.

After a few moments' rest she recovered herself, and said to me: "Listen! listen! The others are all doing the same. Can't you hear their sighs? Oh! Isn't it nice, Rosa dear?"

"Yes! Yes!" I whispered, in a shamefaced manner, for I seemed to know we had indulged in some very improper proceeding. "Oh! Mademoiselle, do they all do it? It's so nice of you to play with me so."

MADEMOISELLE.—"Of course they do. It's the only pleasure we can have in school. Ah! You should be with Lady Clara or the Van Tromp, how they spend and go on in their ecstasy."

"What is spending?" I whispered. "Is that the wet I felt on my fingers when you stiffened yourself out?"

MADEMOISELLE.—"Yes, and you spent too, little bashful. Didn't the birching make you feel funny?"

ROSA (in a whisper).—"Even when I have been cut so that the blood flowed down my legs, at last I suddenly got dulled to the pain, and came all over with a delicious hot burning melting feeling which drowned every other sensation."

MADEMOISELLE.—"Rosa, you're a little darling. Would you like to feel it over again? I know another way, if you only do to me exactly as I do to you, will you?"

I willingly assented to the lovely Française, who, reversing our positions, laid on her back, and made me lay my body on hers, head downwards. Our chemises were turned up close under our arms, so as fully to enjoy the contact of our naked bodies, and I found my face buried in the beautiful mossy forest on her mount, and felt Mademoiselle, with her face between my thighs, tickling my little slit with something soft and warm, which I soon found out was her tongue. She passed it lovingly along the crack and inside as far as it would reach, whilst one of her fingers invaded my bottom-hole, and worked in and out in a most exciting way.

Not to be behind hand, I imitated all her movements, and burying my face between her thighs, revelled with my tongue and fingers in every secret place. She wriggled and tossed her bottom up and down, especially after I had succeeded in forcing a finger well up the little hole and worked it about, as she was doing to me. Although it was all so new to me, there was something so exciting and luscious in it all; to handle, feel, and revel in such a luxuriously covered pussey and bottom excited me more and more every moment; then the fiery touches of her tongue on my own burning orifices so worked me up that I spent all over her mouth, pressing my slit down upon her in the most lascivious manner, just as her own affair rewarded me in the same manner. After a little time we composed ourselves to sleep, and with many loving expressions and promises of future enjoyment.

This was my experience the first night of my school life, and I need not weary you with repetitions of the same kind of scene, but simply tell you that it was enacted almost every night, and that we constantly changed our partners, so that was the cause of my acquiring such a penchant for female bedfellows, especially when they have been previously well warmed by a little preparatory flagellation.

Miss Flaybum was a stern disciplinarian in her school, and we often came under her hands, when she wielded the birch with great effect, generally having the culprit horsed on the back of a strong maid servant, who evidently delighted in her occupation.

I must be drawing this letter to a close, but will give you one illustration of how we were punished in my time.

I cannot exactly remember what my offense was, but it was probably for being impertinent to Miss Herbert, the English governess, a strict maiden lady of thirty, who never overlooked the slightest mark of disrespect to herself.

Miss Flaybum would seat herself in state upon a kind of raised dais, where she usually sat when she was in the schoolroom. Miss Herbert would introduce the culprit to her thus:

Miss Herbert.—"Madame, this is Miss Coote, she has been disrespectful to me, and said I was an old frump."

Miss Flaybum.—"That is a most improper word to be used by young ladies, you have only to take away the f, and what remains, but a word I would never pronounce with my lips, it's too vulgar. Miss Rosa Belinda Coote (she always addressed culprits by their full name), I shall chastise you with the rod; call Maria to prepare her for punishment."

The stout and strong Maria immediately appears and conducts me into a kind of small vestry sacred to the goddess of flagellation, if there is such a deity; there she strips off all my clothes, except chemise and drawers, and makes me put on a kind of penitential dress, consisting of a white mobcap and a long white garment, something like a nightdress; it fitted close up round the throat with a little plain frill round the neck and down the front, being fastened by a band round the waist.

Maria now ushers me again into the presence of Miss Flaybum, all blushing as I am at the degrading costume, and ridiculous figure I must look to my schoolfellows, who are all in a titter.

Maria lays a fine bunch of fresh birch twigs (especially tied up with ribbons) at my feet, I have to pick it up and kiss it in a most respectful manner, and ask my schoolmistress to chastise me properly with it. All this was frightfully humiliating, especially the first time, for however free we might have been with one another in our bedrooms there was such a sense of mortifying shame, sure to be felt all through the proceedings.

Miss Flaybum, rising with great dignity from her seat, motions with her hand, and Miss Herbert assisted by the German governess, Frau Bildaur, at once mounted me on Maria's broad back, and pinned up the dress above my waist, then the English governess with evident pleasure opened my drawers behind so as to expose my bare bottom, whilst the soft-hearted young German showed her sympathy by eyes brimming with tears.

Miss Flaybum.—"I shall administer a dozen sharp cuts, and then insist upon your begging Miss Herbert's pardon," commencing to count the strokes one by one, as she whisks steadily, but with great force, every blow falling with a loud "whack," and making my bottom smart and tingle with pain, and giving assurance of a plentiful crop of weals. My red blushing bottom must have been a most edifying sight to the pupils, and a regular caution to timid offenders, two or three more of whom might expect their turn in a day or two; although I screamed and cried out in apparent anguish it was nothing to what I had suffered at the hands of Sir Eyre or Mrs. Mansell; the worst part of the punishment was in the degrading ceremony and charity girl costume the victim had to assume.

The dozen duly inflicted, I had first to beg Miss Herbert's pardon, and then having again kissed the rod, and thanked Miss Flaybum for what she called her loving correction, I was allowed to retire and resume my own apparel. I could tell you about many punishment scenes, but in my next shall have the grand finale to my school life, and how we paid off Miss Flaybum and the English governess before leaving.

And remain, dear Nellie,
Your ever loving
Rosa Belinda Coote.

(To be continued.)

YOUNG BEGINNERS.

"Now, dear Nelly, as we are both snug in bed, give me the account you promised of all that passed at your uncle's during your visit."

Well, don't frig me so hard, or you'll cut short my story. My uncle, you know, is a widower. He has three children, Gussy, who is fourteen, Johnny eleven, and Janey nine years of age. I was only just fifteen. So we were all well suited together, and soon became great friends. The two boys had lately come home for their holidays, and were up to every kind of fun. Our favourite place for play was the hay loft; and our chief amusement rolling down the hay one after the other. On one occasion my frock flew up in the descent, so that when I reached the bottom, my legs were all uncovered, and the little slit between them (just newly fringed with hair) was fully exposed to view.

"Oh, look!" cried Johnny, pointing to it, and throwing himself upon me. "See what she has there."

"For shame," I said, struggling to get up.

"Hold her down," cried Gussy spreading my thighs, and opening my cunt with his fingers.

"What a funny little place, Nelly. Let us have a good look. Why need you mind? You may see mine if you like. Let's all look at one another, and see which has the nicest."

"Oh, do!" cried John and Janey, "it will be great fun."

So the two boys pulled out their little pricks, and Janey, holding up her dress and pulling aside her drawers, showed us her small unfledged cunt.

"Yours is far the nicest," said Gussy to me. "For yours has hair; we have none yet, but we shall bye-and-bye."

"How do you know?" asked Janey.

"Because I have often seen men bathing, and they all had hair about their pricks, as they call them."

"But what of women; you've never seen them bathing?"

"No, but I have seen nurse's, and she has plenty. One night, about a year ago, she was giving me a warm bath, and when she was drying me, she began tickling my little cockey; I was ashamed, but she said it was nothing to mind, that I would soon be proud enough of it, and that then I would be wanting to stick it into the chink that women have at the bottom of their belly. I coaxed her to let me feel hers. She did, and let me see it too."

"What was it like, Gussy?"

"Just like a great mouth with a beard all around it. I could nearly put my hand up into it, it was so big."

It was quite funny to see how the boys' pricks stiffened up as they felt and examined my cunt. Janey too looked on eagerly and frigged her own little slit with the handle of a battledore.

"But," said Johnny, "you have no place for getting into you here, like nurse."

"Yes, she has. See! I can push my finger up."

"Stop, Gussy, you are hurting me."

"Well, let me put my prick in. That won't hurt, I am sure."

"Do let him," cried John and Janey. "It will be such fun."

"You may try if you like," I said.

He then knelt between my open thighs, and pushed his prick about the lips of my cunt.

"Oh, he can't get it in," said Janey, "what a pity."

I began to grow excited, so I put down my hand and held his prick at the right entrance, while with my other hand on his bottom I helped to push him in.

"Oh, now it's going in, every bit of it; does it hurt you Nelly, does it hurt?"

"No dear, it feels very nice; that's the way."

Gussy, impelled by nature, shoved eagerly in and out, John and Jane laughed, but Gussy began to breathe hard, his face flushed, his eyes sparkled. "Oh!" he cried, "what's going to happen, hold me Nelly," and he fell forward on my breast, as he poured forth for the first time his maiden treasure.

After that we never lost an opportunity of playing with each other's privates. Janey and I used to frig and suck the boys' pricks, and they tickled and kissed our cunts; but Gussy and I always ended with a fuck, for he had a wonderful tool for so young a lad, and enjoyed the sweet exercise thoroughly.

He told me that he had seen his father fucking a girl in the hayfield, after the labourers had gone home. She had come back to look for something. Uncle met her, drew her behind one of the cocks, tossed up her clothes, and made her lie on her back with her legs up. He then unbuttoned his trousers, took out his prick, and kneeling between her thighs, shoved it into her cunt.

"It was at the other side of the hedge, and I heard him saying, 'Come here, Maggy, I want to give you something.'

" 'Thanks, sir, you are very good.'

" 'But I want a kiss in return.'

"He kissed her loudly. Then she said: 'Oh, but, dear sir, you need not push your knee between my thighs. Ah! stop, you'll make me fall.'

" 'Be quiet, Maggy, and I'll give you something more when I have done.'

"I had been searching for an opening in the hedge, and at length between the bushes I caught sight of them just as he had got her on her back, with her belly and legs all exposed. When I first saw his big red-headed prick standing out stiffly from the hair at its base, I did feel ashamed to look, but I was so eager to see Maggy's cunt, and to observe how a real fuck was performed, that I would not for the world have turned away my eyes.

"He soon got his prick in, and drove it up her cunt. She seemed used to the sport, and as he went on fucking she heaved up and down, crying, 'Give it me, dear sir, give it me, hard and strong, oh! oh!'

" 'That's right, Maggy, give tongue, lift your arse, and tickle my balls.'

"Maggy called out prick, cunt, arse, at every push, and their bellies smacked together, until giving one tremendous lunge, Father darted his prick into her cunt, pressed her in his arms, and kissed her in great delight.

"Then he gave her something, and when she had arrange her dress, she stole quietly away."

"You should not be talking of these things, Gussy."

"No more I do, only to you, and you know I tell y everything."

About this time a new governess arrived. She was a pret flaxen-haired girl, named Lizzy. I soon remarked that Unc was very attentive to her, and was always bringing her flowe and small presents.

She slept in a room next mine, and separated from it by wooden partition, the two having formed but one apartmen I could hear every stir she made. I knew when she got out bed, when she took her bath, and even when she sat on th chamber pot. I observed one day that in one spot the pap over the boards had cracked, and that there was a small ope slit between them. On putting my eye close I could see in Lizzy's room quite plainly. A few nights after, when I was bed, I heard whispering in her room. I got up softly and wer to the slit. By the light of her fire, I saw Uncle with his ar round Lizzy, and heard her saying:

"Mr. C., do go away. Oh, my! Where are you dragging m I won't sit on the bed with you. What do you mean by pusl ing me back. Don't attempt to raise my clothes. Oh! Whe are you putting your hand? Take it away, you are very nast Don't lift my legs. I won't let you. You'll ruin me. You a hurting my hands."

"Well, take your hands out of the way. Here; put them o my prick if you like. Open. Open more. I tell you to kee quiet, or you'll waken Nelly."

"I won't let you put it in. You must not do it."

"Do let me, love—only just a moment. There, let it in What's the use of all this struggling?"

"You'll kiss me. I'm so tired. What is it you want?"

"Only to fuck you my darling. To put my prick in here— into your sweet cunt, and fuck you. There! There! It's gettin in. Don't you feel it going up—up! How hot your cunt i Isn't it nice?"

"Yes, that's very nice. I like that. You may fuck me nov Push it in well. Oh, yes; push. Oh!"

"Push what in, my love?"

"Your prick! Your prick; dear Mr. C."

"Where do you like me to push my prick?"

"Into my cunt! Into my cunt!"

"What is my prick doing in your cunt, Lizzy?"

"Fucking me! Fucking me! Oh! so nicely. You may fuck me as hard as you like. Oh! Oh!"

Uncle had placed her on her back with her bottom projecting over the edge of the bed, her clothes were all up, her thighs stretched wide open, and her legs resting on his shoulders. He had let down his trousers, and tucked up his shirt, so I could see his great muscular rump working vigorously back and forward, driving his stiff moist prick in and out between the hairy lips of her cunt.

I felt greatly excited, and my cunt seemed burning with heat. I could not help putting my hand on it, and squeezing the lips as hard as I could.

Just then I felt someone's arm stealing round me, and a hand placed on my mouth to stifle my cry.

Gussy whispered in my ear:

"It's me. Don't say a word. Feel my prick, how stiff it is. I'll put it into your cunt this way, and fuck you from behind, but keep watching, and tell me all they are doing. What do you see?"

"I see your father fucking Lizzy. She is on her back with her bottom over the edge of the bed, her legs up on his shoulders. I can see her cunt."

"What is it like?"

"A large hairy mouth sucking his prick."

"Is he fucking still? Go on, dear Nelly; it's just coming."

"He is heaving backward and forward, faster and faster. Now he is stooping over her, clutching her in his arms. How he drives his prick into her cunt! How she bounds to meet it. There! He is done! Push, Gussy! Hold me, or I shall fall! Oh! what a nice fuck! You have a darling prick, Gussy. Now let us rest, and I'll suck it for you to make it strong again."

After a while we heard them whispering again.

"Now," said Gussy, "let us change places. Sit here with your back to the partition, and you can play with my prick, while I look through and tell you all they are doing."

I took the head of his soft little tool in my mouth, and played with his balls and bottom while he looked through the opening.

"He is kneeling down and kissing and sucking her cunt; there, he has opened wide the lips, and is looking into its deep red chink; now he is licking round it with his tongue, while he rubs his nose against the hair—listen."

"What a delicious cunt you have, Lizzy; it smells so sweet, and has such thick round full lips, and although so large, the entrance itself is as tight as possible, and holds my prick like a glove. Now lie along the edge, put your hand on this poor fellow, and pet him a little before we try another bout."

"Now he is standing up, and she has her arm round his hip so as to reach his balls from behind, with her other hand she holds his prick; she is drawing up and down the soft skin, now she places its rosy head to her lips.

"Take it in your mouth, my love."

"I declare she has taken nearly half of it in; what a mouthful she has; she is sucking it, just as you are sucking mine. How nice it feels to have one's prick sucked. Oh! Nelly, I can't go on, let it out, it's just coming," and he tried to draw it away, but I was enjoying so much the taste of his prick in my mouth, and, at the same time, had such a wonderful feel in my cunt that I would not let it go, so holding the cheeks of his bottom I moved him backward and forward, and made him fuck me in my mouth. His prick swelled, I felt it throb, and then a hot stream of sperm spurted into my mouth and flowed down my throat. We soon heard Uncle leaving Lizzy's room, then Gussy went too and all was quiet.

Uncle went to her room nearly every night, and though, during the day they were most particular in their conduct towards each other, and she, with her large blue eyes, looked the very picture of innocence, yet at night they gave themselves up to the most unbounded license. He fucked her in every conceivable attitude and way. He made her use every amorous term, even words that are generally thought vulgar and coarse. He used to lie on the rug before the fire on his back, when she, all naked, would straddle over him, and with her cunt resting on his mouth, would stoop down and suck his prick. Then, when she had it standing up stiff and strong, she would place its head between the lips of her cunt, and sitting down would force it up. Then he would place his hands under her bottom, and help her to rise up and down. At other times he would lean back in the armchair, and she would sit in his lap, her naked bottom rubbing against his belly, while his prick was soaking in her cunt, and her hand on his balls.

I heard her say she liked this plan best, as his prick seemed to get further into her cunt.

Gussy and I watched them with the greatest interest, as long as my visit lasted, and tried to follow them in their various evolutions, frigging, sucking, fucking, holding the chamber pot for each other to make water; and every possible idea we could think of to vary the fun.

AN EPISTLE TO A LADY.

Mrs. T. T., wife of a lawyer; she had first been the
wife of Dr. F., another lawyer.

Some moments in life, I could wish very long,
Because as the monkey said, pleasant but wrong;
'Tis sweet to remember some frolics I've had,
Though the angel who suffered them cries out, "Too bad."

Yes, grant me that angel, another man's wife,
She is by law, but to me she is life;
That rich feast of pleasure, that rapture, I'd call it,
That devil that tickles my intellect's palate.

I'm well read in woman, I seldom can find,
One that brings a new relish of joy to my mind;
But she's quite a treat, one that never can pall,
Think all you can think, she surpasses it all.

Oh would that I had her!—and had her just now,
I can make love much better, than verses, I vow;
Her, I ardently covet, and love, and esteem,
I saw but last night, in a sweet Golden Dream.

The dress that she wore, fitted close as her skin,
'Twas of Paradise fashion, ere fig leaves came in;
Her smooth birthday suit, all of flesh colour'd buff,
With a furbelow too, a divine little muff.

But a creature so fair's a mere victim for evil,
So she straightway received an address from the devil;
He came drest like a lawyer, so grand and severe,
And assured her she suited him, just to a hair.

O how could she bear such a lifeless old lover,
She who palpitates warm with excitement all over;
She who throbs like my heart, on the ravishing stretch,
How could she endure such a cold-blooded wretch?

She smiled at his pleadings—and then she saw me,
It was just before tasting the wit-giving tree!
And the barrister prim, a great man in his college,
Was to introduce her to the fair tree of knowledge.

But alas; with that knowledge, came misery too,
And the Eve of my vision, evanished from view;
The devil soon died, but the very next glimpse,
Betrayed she had now married one of his imps!

To escape the dull phiz of this crabbed attorney,
She to Italy flew, on a classical journey;
Next I met her, more lovely, though after twelve years,
In her dear little parlour, so private, up-stairs.

There knee pressing knee, and kind eyes within eyes,
Our converse still broken, with fluttering sighs;
We talked about books, and the way to improve,
But our tremors confessed the sweet fever of love.

Ah! would that we both had had wisdom at will,
Though it might have prevented us kissing our fill!
Those blisses are short, that most heavenly seem,
I woke, and behold, it was merely a dream!

————————

LADY POKINGHAM, OR THEY ALL DO IT;

Giving an Account of her Luxurious Adventures, both before and after her Marriage with Lord Crim-Con.

PART III.
(Continued.)

Alice led me by the hand, having closed the door behind us; a cold shiver passed over my frame, but plucking up courage, I never faltered, and we soon found a little green baize door, bolted on our side. "Hush!" she said, "this opens into quite a dark corner, behind the confessional box," as she gently withdrew the bolt, and we then noiselessly entered the chapel into a little kind of passage, between the box and the wall, and fortunately protected from observation by a large open-work screen, which completely hid us, but afforded quite a good view of the interior of the chapel. Guess our astonishment when we beheld both Lady St. Jerome and her niece in earnest conference with the two priests and overheard what passed.

FATHER COLEMAN.—"Well, Sister Clare, the Cardinal has ordered that you are to seduce Lothair, by all the arts in your power; every venial sin you may commit is already forgiven."

MONSIGNORE, addressing Lady St. Jerome.—"Yes, and Sister Agatha here will assist you all she can; you know she is a nun, but by the modern policy of Holy Church, we allow certain of the sisters to marry when their union with influential men tends to further the interests of the Church; the secret sisterhood of St. Bridget is one of the most powerful political institutions in the world, because unsuspected, and its members have all sworn to obey with both body and soul; in fact, Sister Clare, this holy sisterhood into which we have just admitted you, by this special faculty from his Eminence, will permit you to enjoy every possible sensual pleasure here upon earth, and insure your heavenly reward as well."

The bright light shows us plainly the blushing face of Clare Arundel, which is turned almost crimson, as the confessor whispers something to her. "Ah! No! No! No! not now," she cried out.

MONSIGNORE.—"The first act of sisterhood is always to do penance directly after admission, and you have taken the oaths to obey both in body and mind, sister Agatha will blindfold you, throw off your robe, and submit your body to the mortification of the flesh."

Lady St. Jerome quickly removed the dressing-gown in which her niece was enveloped, and left the fair girl with nothing but her chemise to cover her beautiful figure; the bandage was speedily adjusted over her lovely eyes, and she was made to kneel on a cushion, and rest her arms and face on the rails of the altar. Father Coleman armed himself with a light scourge of small cords, fixed in a handle, whilst her ladyship turned up the chemise of the victim so as to expose her bottom, thighs, legs and back to his castigation; then she withdrew, and seated herself on the knee of Monsignore, who had made himself comfortable in a large chair close to the victim; he clasped her round the waist, and pressed his lips to hers, whilst their hands seemed to indulge in a mutual groping about each other's private parts.

The scourge fell upon the lovely bottom; each stroke drawing a painful sigh from the victim, and leaving long red weals on the tender flesh.

The confessor continually lectured her on her future duties, and made her promise to do all his commands.

The poor girl's bottom was soon scored all over, and dripping with blood; the sight of which seemed to inflame the others, so that the confessor's affair stood out between the opening of his cassock, whilst Lady St. Jerome spitted herself on the pego of Monsignore, and rode a most gallant St. George as he sat in the chair.

The Confessor.—"Now, sister, for the last mortification of your flesh, you must surrender your virginity to the Church." Saying which, he produced several fine large cushions, took the bandage from her eyes, and laid her comfortably on her back for his attack, with an extra cushion under her buttocks, in the most approved fashion. Then kneeling down between her thighs, he opened his cassock, and we could see he was almost naked underneath. He laid himself forward on her lovely body, and whispered something in her ear, which was apparently a command to her to take hold of his lustful weapon, for she immediately put down her hand, and seemed (as far as we could see) to direct it to her crack herself. She was evidently fired with lust, and longing to allay the raging heat of the part which had been so cruelly whipped, for she heaved up her bottom to meet his attack, and so seconded his efforts that he speedily forced his way in, and the only evidence of pain on her part was a rather sharp little cry, just as he entered to break through the hymen. They lay for a moment in the enjoyment of the loving conjunction of their parts, but she was impatient, putting her hands on the cheeks of his bottom, and pressing him to herself in a most lascivious manner, and just then Monsignore and Sister Agatha, who had finished their course, got up, and one with the scourge, and the other with a thin cane (after first lifting up his cassock and exposing a brown hairy-looking bottom), began to lay on to Father Coleman in good earnest. Thus stimulated, and begging and crying for them to let him alone, he rammed furiously into Miss Clare, to her evident delight; she wriggled, writhed, and screamed in ecstasy, and gave us such a sight of sensual delirium as I have never seen before or since. At last he seemed to spend into her, and, after a while, withdrew himself from her reluctant embrace, as she seemed to try hard to get him to go on again.

We could see they were preparing to leave the chapel, so thought it time to make our retreat.

Next day we were presented, and nothing in the manner of the lively Lady St. Jerome, or the demure Miss Clare Arundel, would have led anyone to imagine the scene that we had witnessed in the small hours of the morning.

In the evening we were all at the Duchess's ball. Lord Carisbrooke, to whom I was specially introduced, was my partner in the set, in which danced Lothair and Miss Arundel as *vis-à-vis* to Lady Corisande and the Duke of Brecon.

Bye-and-bye the hero of the evening led me out for the Lancers, and afterwards we strolled into the conservatory, quite unobserved; his conversation was much livelier than I had expected, for Lady St. Jerome had represented to us that he was seriously bent on religion, and about to join the Romish Church. The conservatory was large, and we strolled on till the music and laughter seemed quite at a distance, and coming to a seat with a delightful fountain in front of us we sat down, but just as he was observing, "How delightful it was to withdraw from the whirl of gaiety for a few minutes," we heard some light footsteps approaching, and evidently a very loving couple, the lady exclaiming, with a saucy laugh, "Ah! No! How dare you presume so; I would never be unfaithful to Montairy even in a kiss"; there was a slight struggle, and, "Ah, Monster, what a liberty!" and we heard the smack of lips upon a soft cheek, and then, "Oh! No! Let me go back," but the gentleman evidently remonstrated, as I could hear him say, "Come, come, compose yourself, dear Victoria, a little, there is a seat here by the fountain, you must rest a moment."

LOTHAIR, with a start, whispered—"They must not catch us here, they'd think we had been eavesdropping; let's hide ourselves and never say a word about it," dragging me by the hand around a corner, where we were well screened by the foliage of the delicious exotics.

My heart was in a flutter, and I could perceive he was greatly moved. We stood motionless, hand in hand, as the lady and gentleman took possession of the cool seat we had just vacated; the latter proved to be the Duke of Brecon. I could see them plainly, and have no doubt Lothair did also.

LADY MONTAIRY.—"Now, sir, no more of your impudent pranks. Pray let me recover my serenity."

The Duke knelt down and took her hand, which she affectedly tried to withdraw, but he retained it, saying:

"Dearest Victoria, pity my passion. How can I help loving those killing eyes, and luscious pouting lips. That very fact of its being wrong makes my determination the greater to enjoy you the first opportunity. It is useless to resist our fate. Why has the God of Love given me such a chance as this?"

She turns away her head with affected prudery; but not a blush rises to assert her horror at his speech. One hand presses her fingers to his lips; but where is the other? Under her clothes. He first touches her ankle, and slowly steals it up her leg. She fidgets on the seat, but he is impetuous, and soon has possession of her most secret charms. Her languishing eyes are turned on him, and in an instant, he is on his legs, and pushing her clothes up, displays a lovely pair of legs in white silk stockings, beautiful blue garters with gold buckles, her thighs encased in rather tight–fitting drawers, beautifully trimmed with Valenciennes lace. His lips are glued to hers at the same instant, and his hands gently part her yielding thighs, as he placed himself well between them. It is but the work of an instant. He places her hand on the shaft of love, which he has just let out, and it is guided into the haven of love. Both are evidently too hot and impetuous, for it seems to be over in a minute.

She hastily kisses him, and puts down her clothes as she says: "How awful; but I could not resist Your Grace without disordering all my dress. It's been quite a rape, sir," with a smile. "Now, let's make haste back before we are missed." He kisses her, and makes her agree to an assignation, somewhere in South Belgravia, for the morrow, to enjoy each other more at leisure, and then they were gone.

It would be impossible to describe the agitation of my partner during this short scene; Lothair seemed to shiver and shudder with emotion, I was also all of a tremble, and nestled close to him, my arm designedly touching the bunch in his trousers, always so interesting to me; I could feel it swell and seem ready to burst from its confinement; he nervously clasped my hand, and was speechless with emotion all during the scene which I have described; as soon as they were gone he seemed to give a gasp of relief, and led me out of our hiding place. "Poor girl," he said, "what a sight for you, how I trembled for my own honour, lest the scene should make me lose my self-control. Ah! wretched woman, to betray your husband so!" Then looking at me for the first time he said, "Do you not think it is best for a man never to marry?"

Used as I had been to such things, his terrible emotion made me quite sympathize with him, and my own agitation was quite natural, as I replied, "Ah! my Lord, you little know the ways of the world; I saw a more awful scene than what we have witnessed, only last night, enacted by men sworn to perpetual celibacy, and you yourself were mentioned as a victim to their infernal plot."

"My God! Lady, pray tell me what it was," he ejaculated.

"Not now, we shall be missed, do you know any place where I can have a private conference with your lordship? If so, meet me to-morrow afternoon at two o'clock, in the Burlington Arcade. I shall come disguised," I answered.

(To be continued.)

A Jew who wanted to get hold of a Miss Bacon, said:

> If I took but a slice,
> Of pig's flesh, so nice,
> Our rabbis would bluster and take on.

But I'd brave all their damns,
      For a touch at the hams,
Of this delicate red and white Bacon.

When Molly the housemaid, who lived at the "Blue
Boar," at York, was married to John the Ostler, her mistress
gave the poor couple a bedchamber, in a garret, to celebrate
their nuptials. But Robert and Harry, who had long well
known all Poor Molly's in and outs, were seriously anxious to
know the result. They crept to the door, and at last heard
Molly exclaim: "Ah! Johnny dearest, you are where man
never was before!" "Zounds, Harry!" whispered Robert; "he
must have got into her arse."

SONG.

How lovely did Venus at first seem to be,
When her birth she received from the spring of the sea;
As red as a rose looked her cunt's lovely rim,
And the foam slowly dripped from the hairs of her quim!

Her belly was whiter than marble, I ween,
And above it her bubbies like snow balls were seen;
But Venus was still discontented, alas,
She wanted a prick and two balls at her arse!

Her thighs were so pure, so graceful and round,
None fairer and lovelier e'er could be found;
But her cunt, I dare say, great pleasure it sips,
With a stiff-standing penis to part its red lips!

Oh, poking is a pleasure, we all must enjoy,
Tho' I had it for ever, it never would cloy;
To any young man on the grass I would fall,
And if cunt would allow it, take bollox and all!

THE REVERIE.

What dull and senseless lumps we'd be,
If never of felicity
We tasted; and what bliss is there
To equal that of fucking rare?
An age of grief, an age of pain,
I would endure and ne'er complain;
To purchase but an hour's charms,
While wriggling in a maiden's arms!
And hugging her to heavenly rest,
My hand reposing on her breast!
Her arse my own, her thighs my screen,
My penis standing in between!
My bollox hanging down below,
And banging 'gainst her arse of snow;
Or else grasped firmly in her hand,
To make my yard more stiffly stand.
How soon the blood glows in the veins,
And nature all its power now strains;
The belly heaves, the penis burns,
The maiden all its heat returns,
Till passion holds triumphant sway,
And both the lovers die away.

A MAIDEN'S WISH.

When wishes first enter a maiden's breast,
She longs by her lover to be carest;
She longs with her lover to do the trick,
And in secret she longs for a taste of his prick!
Her cunt it is itching from morning till night,
The prick of her lover can yield her delight;
She longs to be fucked, and for that does deplore,
For what can a young maiden wish for more?

If fever or sickness her spirits doth shock,
Why, we know what she wants, 'tis a stiff-standing cock!

Give her a prick, it will soon make her well,
Though perhaps in the long run, her belly may swell!
She'd like very well to be laid on the grass.
To have two ample bollox sent bang 'gainst her arse;
She longs to be fucked, and for that does deplore,
For what can a young maiden wish for more?

It's a pity any quim hungry should go,
All maids wish them filled, as you very well know,
And if the young men would be ready and free,
They'd up with their clouts in a trice, d'ye see!
She wants to be ask'd, but to ask is afraid,
And fearful she is that she'll die an old maid;
She wishes for prick, and for that does deplore,
For what can a young maiden wish for more?

THE JOYS OF COMING TOGETHER.

Tell me where are there such blisses
   As the sexes can impart?
When lips join in heavenly kisses,
   When they both convulsive start!
     Throbbing, heaving,
     Never grieving;
     Thrusting, bursting,
     Sighing, dying!
All nature now is in a glow,
Now they're coming, oh! oh!! oh!!!
Mutual keeping to one tether,
Sweet it is to come together!
Decrepid age is only teasing,
   Shrivelled-up pricks, who can abide?
Vigorous youth, oh, that is pleasing,
   It is worth the world beside!
     Craving, wanting,
     Sobbing, panting,
     Throbbing, heaving,
     Never grieving,

Thrusting, bursting,
Sighing, dying!
All nature now is in a glow,
Now they're coming, oh! oh!! oh!!!
Mutual keeping to one tether,
Sweet it is to come together.

NURSERY RHYMES.

A parson who lived near Cremorne
Looked down on all women with scorn;
    E'en a boy's white fat bum,
    Could not make him come;
But an old man's piles gave him the horn.

A cheerful old party of Lucknow,
Remarked, "I should like a fuck now!"
    So he had one and spent,
    And said, "I'm content!
By no means am I so cunt-struck now."

There was a young man of Peru,
Who lived upon clap juice and spew;
    When these palled to his taste,
    He tried some turd paste,
And said that was very good too.

There is a new Baron of Wokingham;
The girls say he don't care for poking 'em,
    Preferring "Minette,"
    Which is pleasant, but yet,
There is one disadvantage, his choking 'em.

There was an Archbishop of Rheims,
Who played with himself in his dreams;
    On his nightshirt in front,
    He painted a cunt,
Which made his spend gush forth in streams.

There was a young man of Newminster Court,
Bugger'd a pig, but his prick was too short;
 Said the hog, "It's not nice;
 But pray take my advice;
Make tracks, or by the police you'll be caught."

There was a young man of Cashmere,
Who purchased a fine Bayadere!
 He fucked all her toes,
 Her mouth, eyes, and her nose,
And eventually poxed her left ear.

There was a young party of Bicester,
Who wanted to bugger his sister;
 But not liking dirt,
 He bought him a squirt,
And cleaned out her arse with a clyster.

There was a young man of King's Cross,
Who amused himself frigging a horse,
 Then licking the spend
 Which still dripped from the end,
Said, "It tastes just like anchovy sauce."

A president called Gambetta,
Once used an imperfect French Letter;
 This was not the worst,
 With disease he got cursed,
And he took a long time to get better.

There was a young girl from Vistula,
To whom a friend said, "Jef has kissed you, la!"
 Said she, "Yes, by God!
 But my arse he can't sod,
Because I am troubled with Fistula."

A new patent shoe-horn, for the insertions of big pricks
into tight bum-holes, is reported to have been invented by
a lady member of the *Comédie Française*, who is said to
place the half skin of a peach, turned inside out, upon the

tip of a lover's penis, before he is allowed to enculer his chère amie, who prefers bum-fucking to the old orthodox plan of coition.

———

"I see you have your everlasting stocking on," said her fond papa, at Southend, to a Whitechapel young lady of twelve, who was wading bare-legged on the beach. "I don't know about that, father, for my arse is covered with the same stuff, and that's got a hole in it."

———

THE PEARL,

A Journal of Facetiæ and Voluptuous Reading.

No. 5   PUBLISHED MONTHLY.   Nov. 1879

SUB-UMBRA, OR SPORT AMONG THE SHE-NOODLES.

(Continued.)

Next morning Annie and her sisters rallied us upon our late appearance at the breakfast table, remarking with a pouting look, "that we could not care much for their company if we laid a-bed and left them to themselves for the best half of the day, and that Rosa was just as bad, for she was actually still in dishabille, taking her breakfast in her own room."

Here mama interposed, by adding, "Besides, Walter, I am astonished you should copy Frank's lazy ways, you who on your first arrival here were so eager for early morning walks; look at Annie, she is not half so rosy and animated as she looked after your first walk."

A deep flush passed across Annie's face at this allusion to our first eventful walk, when we had the adventure with the bull, but I prevented her parents' observing it by replying: "That residents in town were always in such a hurry to enjoy the fresh air, and that it seemed to have an extraordinary somnolescent effect upon me, as I could hardly keep my eyes open at supper time, or rouse myself from sleep in the morning."

FRANK.—"I'm glad you have found out it is not all laziness now. Walter will take my part when I assert it is the natural drowsiness of youth, which is readily induced by the keen bracing air we breathe all day."

Papa made a few incredulous, ironical remarks about the youth of the present day, and then breakfast being over, as he rose from the table, said: "Walter, would you mind riding a dozen miles to oblige me. Frank would not be ready to start for an hour at least; besides, I would rather trust you than him with the lady my note is for; Mrs. Colonel Leslie is both young and gay, and I would rather not run the risk of Frank being one day a corespondent in the Divorce Court, and caution you to take care of yourself."

I readily assented, more especially when I noticed a shade of jealous anxiety flit across Annie's tell-tale face. The horse was already at the door, so springing into the saddle I rode off with a fluttering anticipation of something racy being likely to turn up. I shall not trouble about my reflections during this delightful hour's ride; the atmosphere was most deliciously bracing, and my thoughts were so amorously bent that when I reined up at the lodge-gate, at the entrance to the Colonel's grounds, I felt that I could fuck anything in petticoats, from a witch to a gatepost; the gatekeeper soon passed me in, and springing from my saddle before the door of a fine old Elizabethan hall, my knock was promptly responded to by a most handsome young coloured fellow with a Hindoo cast of features.

Mrs. Leslie was at home, and he begged I would excuse her coming down to the drawing-room, as she was still at her toilette, and would immediately see me in her private boudoir.

This courteous message revived all my romantically amorous ideas, with which I had indulged myself during my ride.

Ushered into the boudoir, I found the lady of the house to be a beautiful brunette of about three-and-twenty, with a most bewitching expression of countenance, whilst her large, full, dark eyes seemed to read my very soul as she extended her hand and drew me to a seat by her side, saying: "So, you are cousin Walter, I suppose; how is it that Frank did not ride over with his papa's note? But tell him," she added with a very arch look, "that I was quite as well pleased to see you, and that I consider his cousin quite as fascinating as himself."

Then ringing the bell, she continued, "Will you take a cup of chocolate with me after your ride? it will invigorate me for the serious business of your uncle's note," opening a drawer and laying several bundles of papers like legal documents on the table, just as the servant entered (he was the good-looking Hindoo who had first introduced me).

Mrs. Leslie.—"Vishnu, bring up the chocolate, with two

cups and some biscuits, and mind not to forget the flask of noyau," remarking to me as he disappeared, "Is he not a good looking heathen? The Colonel had him long before he married me, and I call him his principal Hindoo deity; whenever I look at him it puts me in mind of Joseph and Potiphar's wife, especially now the Colonel is away; do you not think it a burning shame to leave a young wife all alone by herself?"

She continued to run on in this curious way, without giving me a chance to make a reply or observation in return, as she busied herself laying out the papers, making pretence of an awful lot of business to be gone through.

The servant now brought in the chocolate, &c., and was dismissed with the order to tell Annette that her mistress would be too busy for some time, and was not to be disturbed until she rung for the completion of her toilette.

My fair hostess was a most charming object as she moved about in her dressing-gown, which was rather open at the neck, so as to display the upper part of the snowy prominences of her luscious bosom, besides which I caught glimpses of her naked feet, with nothing on but the most petite blue satin slippers.

Presently she poured out two cups of chocolate, put in a little of the noyau, and presenting me with one of them took her seat by my side, on the soft yielding lounge. "Drink it off as I do," she said; "it will do you far more good than sipping and allowing it to get cold."

We both drank our small cups at a draught, and I almost instantly felt a thrill of voluptuous warmth rush through my frame, and looking at my fair companion, her eyes seemed to sparkle with a strange amorous fire.

The devil was in me; in less time than it takes to write it, my empty cup was put on the table, and my disengaged arm placed round her neck; I drew her face to mine, and imprinted several kisses on her lips and cheeks as my other hand took possession of that inviting bosom; she was covered with blushes as she exclaimed, "Fie! Fie, sir!! how can you take such liberties when I can't help myself without dropping my cup?"

"Dear lady, excuse my liberties, and d n't distress yourself, I am really greatly obliged to the cup for its assistance; how can I look upon such loveliness without being tempted, yes,

tempted! driven mad by the sight of such charms; you wi
excuse, you will pardon my presumption, I am sure,"
ejaculated, throwing myself upon my knees before her an
hiding my face in her lap, as I clasped my arms nervousl
round her waist, and could feel her whole frame tremble wit
emotion.

Suddenly she seemed to start with pain as she exclaimed
"Ah! Goodness! Oh! Oh!! Oh!! the cramp in my legs. Ol
Oh!" as the cup was thrown down by her side. "Oh, releas
me, sir! Oh, Walter, excuse me, I must rub it!"

Here was a splendid opportunity to improve a luck
chance. "Permit me, poor dear lady, you are in such dreadf
pain, and I am a medical student," I said, making bold t
raise her dressing-gown and chafe her lovely calves with m
eager hands; what lovely legs I now beheld, with not a vestig
of anything on them; my blood was on fire, my fingers grad
ually wandered higher and higher, and I could not refrai
from imprinting kisses on the delicious soft, pinky flesh, a
she seemed rather to sigh than speak, "Oh! thank you, pra
don't, it's so indelicate, and the cramp is gone now."

"No, no, dear Madame, the nervous contraction of you
beautiful thighs convince me that it is higher up, and wi
return again in a few moments, unless I can relieve yor
indeed you must not mind me, as I am a medical man,"
quickly replied, making bolder advances every moment, an
taking advantages of the warm temperament I knew she po
sessed.

"You rogue, you young villain, your touches and kiss
have undone me, how can I resist a handsome student? Ol
Walter, Walter, I must have you! I had only been trying t
draw you out a little, never thinking you were such a youn
gallant; and now I am caught in my own net!"

"Ah! What a hurry. You'll spoil it all by your impetuosit
you shall never have me without first kissing the shrine
love."

"Sir!" pushing me away, as I was endeavouring to g
between her lovely thighs. "Strip, strip, sir, I must see m
Adonis, as your Venus now unveils herself to you," throwir
off her dressing-gown (which I now saw was her only artic
of clothing); and drawing my face down to hers, she thru
her tongue into my mouth, "tipping the velvet" in the mo
delicious style of voluptuous abandon, and delightfully ha

dling my prick and balls at the same time. It was too much for my impatient steed, my spendings flew all over her hands and body almost instantly.

"Ah! What a naughty impatient boy, to come so quickly! Pull off your clothes, sir, and let us take our fill of love on yonder bed. My husband deserves this, for leaving me open to such temptation. You dear boy, how I shall love you; what a fine prick you have, and so—so—what do they call it?— (blushing at her own words) so randy! That's what the Colonel says of the young fellows. Isn't it a dreadfully rude word, Walter? But so full of meaning. Whenever he said so, I couldn't help wishing for a handsome, randy young gentleman, such as your uncle has sent me to-day."

This is how she ran on, as I threw off everything, and I was as naked as herself in a trice; then, hugging, kissing, belly to belly, and handling each other's charms in every possible way, we slowly progressed towards the inviting bed in the other room; once or twice I stopped and tried to get my prick into her standing up, but she would none of that, and at last, when her bottom rested against the edge of the bed, she ordered me to kneel down and kiss the seat of love; how my tongue searched out her fine stiff clitoris, which projected quite an inch-and-a-half from the lips of her vagina. I sucked it in ecstasy, and titillated her sensitive organs so that she spent profusely in a minute or two, holding my head with her hands to make me go on; it was a most deliciously enjoyable gamahuche; my tongue revelled in her creamy emission, till she begged me to slip off my shirt and come on the bed and let her enjoy my fine prick. So I ended this prelude with a playful, loving bite on her excited clitoris, and then, springing to my feet, we rolled on to the bed, her ready hand grasping my cock, as I mounted on her lovely body.

"What a shame!" she sighed. "How you have been spending, you naughty boy, you won't have much left for me now; but he's fine and stiff!" as she squeezed it in her hand, and brought the head of my affair to the mark.

I found her deliciously tight, and assured her she was quite a virgin.

"So I should be, my dear Walter, but for you. The Colonel has got so little to please me with, that, tight as I am, I can hardly feel him! now your jewel of pleasure makes me feel gorged with delight!"

Her motions were as lascivious as her words. She writhed
and threw up her buttocks with extraordinary rapidity and
energy, whilst I was equally eager and rapid in ramming into
her delicious cunt.

I was ready as if I had never spent, and we swam in a mutual emission almost immediately, both of us being so overcome by our feelings that we almost swooned in delight; this
only lasted for a minute; the throbbing and contracting of
the folds of her vagina on my enraptured prick awoke me
to renewed efforts, and we were rapidly progressing towards
another spend, when she checked me, and begged I would
withdraw for a little, when she would amuse me till she felt
she must have him again, and she added, "I shall enjoy it
so much more if I can make you last longer. Sit on my body,
Walter dear, and lay your beautiful prick between the globes
of my bosom; you shall spend there next time. I can't help
telling you what a fine one it is, over and over again!"

She went on caressing it with her hand, and making her
two bubbies close upon it, so that I could work between
them. It was another delicious idea, but she had not exhausted all her ways of exciting me. Her other hand passed
under my thigh, and I thought she was frigging herself, but
it was only to wet her finger, preparatory to frigging my
bottom-hole with it. This made me come again almost directly.

"Now," said she, "I mean to ride on you, and make it last
as long as possible, so let us reverse positions."

This was done, and she rode me and stopped alternately
for about twenty minutes, when we met in a glorious flow of
sperm.

"What do you think of that?" she exclaimed, as soon as
she recovered her breath. "We will get up and answer your
uncle's letter now, and you shall promise to come again
soon."

(To be continued.)

MISS COOTE'S CONFESSION,

Or the Voluptuous Experiences of an Old Maid;
In a series of Letters to a Lady Friend.

LETTER V.

My Dear Nellie,

I was nearly four years with Miss Flaybum before my education was considered to be complete. The last half-year had arrived, and you may be sure how I looked forward to my emancipation from the thralldom of Miss Herbert and her mistress; Lady Clara, Laura, and the Van Tromp had all left. Cecile now was my bosom friend, we had both grown our feathers as they were called, and I loved Mademoiselle Fosse so dearly that my guardians had arranged with her to live with me as a companion in future, as they intended making me a sufficient allowance to set up a genteel household of my own. Besides myself and Cecile there were at school no less than nine or ten big young ladies, who as well as Mademoiselle would leave for good when we broke up for the approaching Christmas holidays. Miss Flaybum seemed to be much annoyed at the prospect of losing quite a third of her pupils all at once; she became decidedly spiteful in her little tyranny, and in the punishments inflicted, seeming to take an especial delight in horsing the biggest girls; we were birched for the most trifling offences, often in threes and fours at a time; such doings could not fail to breed resentment in our breasts, and we all longed for some chance of revenge. I had become quite a leader in the school, and with the other girls often made what we called sacrifices to the rod, especially of the younger pupils, in our respective bedrooms, who dared not complain to Miss Flaybum for fear of worse happening to them.

The last few days were approaching, and in less than a week I hoped to take leave of old Edmonton for good, and not wishing to abandon the field without paying off old scores I had a consultation with Mdlle. and Cecile, as to the practicality of wreaking our revenge. The result was we engaged all the big girls who were leaving to help us, besides taking about a dozen more of the others into our confidence, who promised at least to remain neutral frightened spectators. Miss Flaybum in her careful wisdom had all the servants, except Maria, sleep in a distant part of the house, and a heavily barred door prevented all access for them to us at night.

Miss Flaybum also invariably gave the young ladies a breaking-up party the evening before they were to go home, so we determined to bribe Maria to forfeit her allegiance and aid in our treason; the plan being at the end of the evening's entertainment to seize upon Miss Flaybum, Miss Herbert, and Frau Bildaur, and well birch them all, especially the two former tyrants. We had no difficulty with Maria, who had recently drawn most of her wages. I promised her a handsome douceur and a place in my own establishment, which she gladly accepted, being as she said quite tired out with the Misses' tantrums.

She also agreed to provide everything necessary for our purpose, cords, and especially three of the penitential dresses to put on our victims.

The eventful evening arrived, the conspirators had agreed between themselves to irritate Miss Flaybum by making very free with her champagne, which upon such occasions was made a great display of, but very sparingly served out to the company. Maria, assisted by two other servants, was principal waitress, and at supper, by her connivance, nearly all of us took about three glasses of the sparkling gooseberry, instead of one, as usual on such occasions. Miss Flaybum opened her eyes in astonishment as she saw us indulging in a second glass, but when she saw us still further encroaching on her profuse hospitality she fairly exploded, "Miss Coote, Miss Deben, I'm astonished at you; how dare you, Mademoiselle, to encourage those young ladies in such intemperance," rising from her seat in rage, "why half of my pupils will get intoxicated; Maria, remove those bottles this instant, you must have lost your head."

Maria, who had watched the storm brewing, had, just the previous instant, succeeded in dismissing the other two servants and well bolting the door leading to the domestics' quarters, having, with good tact, provided them with a considerable amount of refreshment, to regale themselves withal.

Perceiving the field was all clear, I rose up, glass in hand, saying, with a bow of mock deference, "Wait a moment, Maria, we are not quite ready to dispense with the champagne. Miss Flaybum, Miss Herbert, and you young ladies (looking round the table), we shall, many of us, part to-morrow morning, never to return to this happy establishment, and I, for one, feel sure you will all join with me in drinking a real bumper to the health of our much respected and beloved schoolmistress."

Miss Flaybum gasped with agitation, but subsided into her chair, as if resigned to her fate, and apparently unable to help herself.

The young ladies all received the proposal with rapturous applause; glasses were filled without stint.

"Now, then," I exclaimed, stepping on to my chair and placing one foot on the table, "we must drink to the health of such an illustrious and amiable lady, with all honours, in the Scotch fashion, one foot on the table, and throw your glasses over your shoulders as you drain them to the bottom, in her honour. To the health of Miss Audrey Clementine Flaybum,—

> For she's a jolly good fellow,
> For she's a jolly good fellow,
> For she's a jolly good fellow,
> And so say all of us,
> And so say all of us,
> And so say all of us,
> With a hip, hip, hurrah,
> With a hip, hip, hurrah,
> Hurrah, hurrah, hurrah."
>   (Crash of glasses)

My confederates joined and gave the health in regular chorus and, I must say, in rather a masculine manner.

"My God! my God!" screamed Miss Flaybum, as the glasses crashed on the floor, or wherever they fell, "the young ladies are all drunk; what shall I do, Miss Herbert, how awful, where did they learn all this pot-house slang?"

"What an insult!" I exclaimed. "Are we drunk, young ladies? Cecile, Mdlle. Fosse, will you stand still to be stigmatized as drunkards?" We all crowded round Miss Flaybum and the English and German governesses, the two former red with passion, whilst Frau Bildaur was trembling with fear.

"This is no laughing matter," I continued, "we have all

been insulted. Miss Audrey Clementine Flaybum, our turn is
come now, you shall be made to smart for this, and make a
most abject apology for insulting a number of young ladies
of the highest aristocracy, and you Miss Dido Herbert, shall
be punished too because you evidently approved it all. I
think we will begin upon Frau Bildaur, but I won't be hard
upon her, as she is rather tenderhearted. Maria, do your duty,
no retiring, strip them, and put the penitential garments
on before us all here."

Miss Flaybum, now pale and trembling with rage and fear.
—"How dare you address me so; Maria, clear the room of
these impudent young ladies, they are all flushed with wine."

Her appeals to Maria are all in vain; she first strips and
robes Frau Bildaur; the poor creature, ready to faint with fear
and shame, offers no resistance, but Miss Herbert is indignant, and resists strenuously, whilst Miss Flaybum is held
down in her chair by half-a-dozen strong young ladies.

"Never mind about dressing that old frump," I exclaimed;
"stretch her on the table, and turn up her clothes."

Almost by magic the supper table is half cleared, all the
debris of the entertainment being swept to the other end of
the table. The struggling victim is powerless as soon as Maria
with the assistance of Cecile and Mdlle. Fosse resolutely
drag her to the table; she is stretched over the mahogany,
and Mdlle., having turned up her clothes and pinned them
well up, sits on her shoulders, to keep her down, whilst one
or two others hold her arms. Cecile opens her drawers and
exposes a rather thin bottom, saying, "She's not very plump,
dear Rosa, but no doubt you can make her squeak."

Rosa.—"Tear off her drawers and fully expose her, I must
pay off all scores at once."

This is speedily done, the victim appeals for mercy and
exclaims against such indecency, but in vain; whilst Miss
Flaybum looks on in speechless horror, gasping and sighing
with indignation, and the thoughts of what shameful indignities may be in store for herself.

Rosa, giving a light swish on the exposed rump.—"Have
you got any feeling, Miss Dido Herbert? I hope this won't
hurt you much, but you've been a spiteful old thing to us
for a long time." Swish, swish, swish, harder and harder, till
the devoted bum begins to get quite rosy. "Will you beg our
pardon, and promise to be kinder to your pupils in future?"

giving a whack with all her force, which weals and almost draws the blood.

Miss Herbert.—"Oh! Oh! we never punished like that! Oh! shameful, Miss Coote!"

Rosa.—"How dare you, Miss Dido, tell me it's shameful, do you really mean what you say?" slashing away in earnest, and soon making little drops of blood begin to ooze from the bruised weals.

Miss Herbert, sobbing hysterically.—"Oh! Oh! I didn't mean to say that. Oh! Oh! Ah—r—r—re! Have mercy! My God! how cruelly you cut!"

Rosa.—"I thought you would come round, Miss Dido; pray, don't you admire my style of birching, don't you wish me to do it a little harder," keeping up a vigorous stroke all the time, and beginning to make quite a beautiful display of raw buttocks.

The victim shrieks with agony and cries for help.

Rosa.—"You may scream, it's delightful to hear it, and know you have some feeling. Will you beg our pardons now?"

Miss Herbert.—"Oh! Yes! Yes! I will, I will. Oh! Oh! pray stop, pray have mercy, I'll never be unkind any more!" sobbing hysterically, "Oh, dear!" Oh, dear! I shall faint, I know I'm bleeding! Oh! dear Miss Coote, how can you be so cruel?"

Rosa.—"Do you think we're any of us intoxicated? Don't you think it was very improper and unladylike of Miss Flaybum to say what she did, and insult us so, just as we had done her a great honour; what do you think of it, Miss Dido?"

Miss Herbert.—"Oh! Ah! Ah! Ah! Ah! Ah—r—r—re! Oh! it was so wrong of her! Oh! I do apologize. Oh! let me go. Oh, Mercy!" as she writhes and twists in the most agonizing manner.

Rosa.—"You must thank me, and promise to retire quietly to your room when you are allowed to go, and profit by the lesson you have received; it is not half so bad as it might have been, there, there," giving her a couple of slashing undercuts between her thighs. "Kneel down and kiss the rod, and thank me."

Miss Herbert.—"Ah! Ah! dreadful. Oh! I shall die! Oh! have pity," sobbing and moaning.

She is now released, and has to kneel and kiss the rod, and make most humble thanks, apologies, and promises, to the infinite delight of the audience, who thoroughly enjoy her humiliation as she kneels bathed in tears of pain and shame, and greet her with a storm of hisses as she slinks from the room crestfallen and smarting with her degradation.

Rosa.—"Now, Miss Aubrey Clementine Flaybum, it's your turn; resist us, and you shall be punished ten times worse than that woman Herbert."

The schoolmistress is quite cowed by the previous scene. She implores for mercy, and begs them not to degrade her before the whole school, but Rosa and her accomplices are determined and relentless.

Maria gradually strips her mistress, who is a fine looking woman of the fat, fair and forty class, with quite prominent blue eyes and flaxen hair. The disrobing process displays in turn her fine neck and bosom, crimson with shame and heaving with agitation, whilst tears of bitter vexation course down her cheeks. Then she presently stands with only chemise and drawers, the latter so well filled out as to give promise of a splendid bottom within, and the ends beautifully trimmed with expensive lace, below which are seen a fine pair of plump legs, in flesh-coloured silk stockings, and high-heeled shoes, with jewelled buckles, but when the penitential-dress and mobcap are assumed, she looks quite a benevolent Mrs. Fry, grieving over some kind of human depravity.

"There," said Rosa, "she's wise not to resist. Let her stand and see Frau Bildaur receive her punishment, and I will rest too; you dear Cecile, take a new rod and punish her lightly."

It was a beautiful sight to see the chestnut-haired, plump, merry-looking Cecile as she whisked her birch against the trembling Frau, who was presently horsed on Maria's back, and, with drawers let down and skirts up, was soon ready for her punishment, displaying a very fine, full bottom on which to operate.

Cecile.—"Frau Augusta Bildaur, I will only give you a dozen smart cuts, and let you go when you kiss the rod, and thank me for chastising you."

Thus saying, she slowly counts the number of each blow, as she strikes her well-aimed, deliberate cuts, which quickly raise all the exposed surface to a warm, rosy tint, and leave a lot of very red marks.

The victim receives her punishment very firmly, with closed lips all the while, but when released is very profuse in her thanks, as she kisses the instrument of her flagellation. The timid look is gone, and instead of the tears, her eyes are lighted up with a warm sensual light, and she begs, in a whisper, to be allowed to witness Miss Flaybum's castigation.

Rosa.—"What a pity there is no proper whipping post to tie her up to: we must make shift with the table. Put Miss Flaybum up in the same way as you did Miss Herbert."

The victim does not resist, as she sees it is quite hopeless, and would only entail greater pain on herself. Her drawers are removed altogether, displaying to the curious girls a beautiful plump bottom and white belly, ornamented by a fine Mons Veneris, covered with a profusion of light curly hair, with the tip of a luscious looking clitoris just peeping out between the lips of her pussey. They spread-eagle her on the table, four girls holding her legs wide apart, whilst others secure her arms, and Mademoiselle again sits on the victim's back to make sure of her.

Rosa.—"What a fine sight; how delightful to have to subdue the spirit belonging to such a splendid figure. Miss Audrey Clementine Flaybum, you have been guilty of grossly insulting myself and other young ladies, and you must retract all your accusations of drunkenness, and I trust to thoroughly convince you of our sober earnestness. Do I whip you like a drunkard, or were you not rather intoxicated with passion when you said so?" whipping her slowly at first. "Did we use pot-house slang? I hope I don't hurt your poor delicate bottom, it begins to look rather flushed, but perhaps it's only blushing at our rudeness," warming to her work, and slashing away in good earnest.

Miss Flaybum's face shows the depth of her indignation, whilst her fat, plump bottom writhes at every stroke, so that it is as much as the young ladies can do to hold her legs; she seems determined not to cry out, but Rosa increases her pain with such skillful and maliciously planted strokes, she is compelled at last to sigh for relief.

Rosa, laughing.—"Ha! Ha! Ha! she's obstinate and won't answer; she wishes me to cut harder; Maria, get another good heavy birch ready, this one won't last long. I begin to think Miss Audrey Clementine Flaybum is really drunk herself (roars of laughter), or she would have the sense to apologize, but I'll bring her to her sober senses. How do you like that, and that, and that," cutting each stroke as to go in well between the cheeks of her bottom, and touch the pouting lips of her pussey, which could be quite plainly seen behind; they were indeed painful cuts, and elicited a sudden sharp cry of pain.

MISS FLAYBUM.—"Ah! Ah! Oh! Oh! How cruel. What fiendish creatures to cut me up so!"

ROSA, laughing again.—"Ha! Ha! she's just beginning to get sober, a little more will thrash all the champagne out of her; drunken people always accuse others of being drunk," cutting up her bottom, and making the blood run in little streams, so that it soon began to run down her thighs, and drip from the hairs of her pussey; the flagellatrix and her friends are getting quite excited at the spectacle, but not the least in sympathy with the victim, whose sufferings seem to afford them exquisite voluptuous sensations, many of the elder girls being stretched on the floor together, or in other positions of sensual enjoyment.

The victim now screams indeed for "Mercy, Mercy! Oh! Oh! Have pity, Miss Coote. Oh! Oh! I shall faint, I shall die."

ROSA, in a state of furious excitement.—"No, no, no fear of your dying, your fat bottom will stand a good deal more yet; you are too obstinate to be let off, the birch will keep you from fainting. Why—why—why—don't you apologize?" giving a terrific undercut between the tender surface of her thighs at every question, making the poor schoolmistress gasp and moan in agony; still her proud spirit refused to do what was required of her.

She is almost fainting, when Rosa, who is getting rather tired with her exertions, calls for a bottle of champagne. "Now, then girls," she exclaims, "she's so plucky we must drink her health again." In response to this call, half-a-dozen young ladies take a bottle each, and at a signal from Rosa, all the corks are fairly discharged at the bleeding bottom, which presents a famous mark, and elicits peals of laughter at the joke, as they drink to "the plucky old girl," who is humiliated more than ever at this unexpected indignity.

Rosa, refreshed, throws away the stump of the birch she has been using, and takes up another heavy swishtail.

"This is something like a rod. Will you, now, Miss Audrey Clementine Flaybum, beg our pardon, and own you were drunk yourself, or must I cut your fat rump in pieces? Aha! That's the vulgar word you would never allow your lips to mention. Perhaps you did not think you had such a thing as a rump yourself, when you used to birch and humiliate us." Whacking away with great earnestness all the while she is lecturing the victim, who screams and shouts in agony as the thundering strokes of the fresh heavy rod crash on her bottom, scratching and tearing the already bruised and bleeding skin in a frightful manner.

Miss Flaybum is almost done for, and really thinks she is going to die, and in an agony of fear and pain forgets the indignity of her position, as well as her firm resolves never to debase herself before her pupils. She screams for mercy.

"Mercy! Oh! Oh! Oh!" she sobs. "Let me go now, dear Miss Coote. Oh! I will beg your pardon. I must have been intoxicated myself. Oh! Forgive me, and I'll never say a word about this. Oh! Oh! Indeed I won't if you spare my life," sobbing in a low hysterical voice.

Rosa.—"And you will forgive us all, and thank us for making you sober again? Fie! Fie! Miss Flaybum. You were indeed overcome. Was it not so?" giving a sharp cut right up under her pussey, to keep her from fainting, and steady to her promises.

Victim.—"Yes! Yes! Oh! Ah—r—r—re! I'm sorry to have forgotten myself, and—and—I do thank you for correcting me with firmness. Oh! Oh! Have mercy now, let me kneel and kiss the rod."

What a pitiable object she looked, kneeling in front of me, as she kissed the broken stump of the birch, which was now well dyed in her own blood. Such a sight of abject terror and degraded, humiliated pride, as well as the burning shame of all she had to endure; her cheeks were stained with tears, and her face and neck blushing nearly as red as her still exposed bottom; for, to humiliate her as much as possible, she had to kneel with her clothes still pinned up behind.

I don't know what possessed me, but I felt such extraordinary excitement that I hardly knew what I was doing; my only idea being that she was getting off too easily. So,

suddenly stooping, I said, "Ha! Ha! Miss Audrey Clementin
Flaybum, you know what a good birching is like now. I mus
look and see how I have pickled your delicate rump for you
I haven't cut it up too much," passing my hand all over th
raw lacerated posteriors. "It will be well in a week, althoug
there is a good deal of blood. See, see," wiping my hand a
over her face, to her intense shame and disgust, just as sh
was beginning to slightly recover herself.

This was the last indignity before we allowed her to re
treat to her room.

As to ourselves, we were indeed intoxicated with success, s
that I shall never forget the goings on of that last night a
school, how the girls rushed about to each other's rooms, an
revelled in every kind of lasciviousness one with anothe
Sleep was banished from our eyes, and nothing but the ad
vent of breaking-up day put an end to our orgie of sensuality

Miss Flaybum was not visible next day, and the only refer
ence she ever made to our memorable scene of retributiv
justice was an enormous charge for damaged glass in m
school bill.

This will end my letter for the present, but, dear Nellie
when I return from my tour, perhaps I can tell you a littl
more of my experiences.

> Your affectionate friend,
> ROSA BELINDA COOTE.

(To be continued.)

THE SPELL OF THE ROD.

When Lucy's fine rump was first bared to the twigs,
    She was finely cut up and her flesh torn in shreds;
She cried out for mercy in her dire distress,
    Promising amendment as we lowered her dress.

She had been most naughty, and a bad rude girl,
    Who presumed the hair on her fanny to curl;
But the birch reached her quim as well as her bum,
    The height of her agony was glorious fun.

Her frightened looks, and deep blushes of shame,
  Set our hearts pit-a-pit, and our senses in flame;
The old cockolorums our cunnies would grope,
  Then tossed us on sofas and had a fine stroke.

So all those slow coaches, who a rise scarce can get,
  Come, pay your respect to Our Lady St. Bridget;
She'll warm up your blood till it boils in your veins,
  And your penis all his pristine vigour regains.

Let the birch be your love, St. Bridget your saint,
  Never flinch from the rod, nor think of a faint;
Swish—swish—let it fall, till the glow of desire,
  Will run thro' your senses, and set them on fire.

Ah! then you can fuck! and fuck, ah! so well!
  That my Muse quite fails your joys to foretell;
But with oceans of spending, the fuck never ending,
  Your ecstasy goes on, for a long time extending.

THE STATE'S NEW DUTY.

*An old Ballad upon the proposed Extension of the Contagious
Diseases Acts to the Civil Population.*

[The memorial to the Government for the extension of
these Acts was signed by several Peers, six Bishops, ten Deans
and Canons, forty-two Clergymen and Ministers, twenty-four
Heads of Colleges and Masters of Public Schools, fourteen
Professors of different Universities, nineteen Mayors, ten
Chairmen of Quarter Sessions and Boards of Guardians,
twenty-nine Sheriffs and Magistrates, &c.]

Vide letter of Messrs. J. B. Cuyenven and Berkely Hill to the
  Daily News, March 8th, 1871.

It was certain Holy Bishops, Noble Lords and bold M.P.'s,
Deans, Rectors, Heads of Colleges, and numberless M.D.'s,
They met in solemn Council, to discuss in grave debate,

And solve a weighty question, they thought worthy of the
   State.
It was not Education, it was not Irish Church,
The Ballot and Permissive Bill, were both left in the lurch.
There may be other evils, but said they, the greatest evil is,
That a man can't have a woman, without the risk of Syphilis;
Said they, the state takes measures that tradesmen shall not
   cheat,
In selling meat, or fish, or fruit, that isn't fit to eat;
It supervises Mutton, and is down on faulty weight,
So to guarantee safe Harlots is the duty of the State.
(Now the women had no voice, or else they might have said,
"If you regulate the sale of Human flesh, like meat and bread,
You should grant to us the tradesman's right, by action to
   recover
The wages of our labour against a bilking lover.")
So a noble Act was passed, the Preamble whereof ran,
"Whereas to fornicate is the right of every man,
"And whereas in exercise of that right are oft contracted
"Disagreeable reminiscences! Be it hereby enacted:
"That a special force of Peelers, henceforth each city pay,
"To apprehend all women, they suspect of being gay;
"Who if they don't disprove the charge before some worthy
   Beak,
"Shall by this Act, be Speculumed in batches, once a week;
"That in every Town a Surgeon, be appointed to the Post,
"With Speculums provided at the British Nation's Cost;
"And five hundred pounds per annum, to be quarterly paid
   down,
"To guarantee the soundness of the women of the Town."
Then happy were the Peelers of that sanctified Division,
That was specially deputed to this female supervision;
Thieves, Drunkards, and Garrotters, no longer were their care,
But they played the spy on women who were volatile and fair;
If they saw a flaunting Petticoat that showed too much of
   calf,
Or a naughty Girl, responding to an Ogle with a Laugh,
If she wouldn't let the Peeler have a cut in with the Swell,
Or tip from her earnings, the Justice not to tell,
Straightway the injured Peeler's virtuous conscience was re-
   lieved,
By yielding to the Justice information he'd received;

And such unhappy damsels as a Peeler might select,
For reasons of his own, to be pronounced "suspect,"
Were all served with a Summons to disprove it to the Beak,
Or submit them to be *Speculumed* in batches once a week;
Then cried every youthful student, "That examining M.D.,
With £500 per annum, would be just the Post for me,
No wealthy wife with Coach and Pair, or Patients, would I
    seek,
But I'd *Speculum* the ladies at £9 10s per week!"
And thus began the era of Sexual legislation:
To man alone the State allows Free-trade in Fornication;
Diseased or sound—no matter—let him riot fancy free,
And gaily pox the ladies that the Peelers guarantee;
Is not Man the Nobler sex, for whom was Woman made?
And shall harrassing Inspections his liberties invade?
For Man alone, the Bill of Rights, and Magna Charta passed;
And shall Free-born Fornicators be with dirty Harlots classed?
The sauce that suits the Goose, o'er the nobler Gander pour?
Or the State restrict the God-like Sex's privilege to whore?
Since clandestine harlots will in spite of Statutes lure,
In spite of all espionage to keep the men secure;
Methinks the Act is faulty, in not finding means to know
The Article that's warranted, from her that is not so.
A list should be placarded conspicuous to see,
Or some special Chignon ordered, for the Girls we guarantee.
And since on Prostitution 'tis resolved to legislate
(Like Cab fares and Pawnbroking, and the sale of bread by
    weight);
Methinks 'twere only logical to extend the Act's protection,
And not limit our paternal care to personal infection.
Why not advance another step, extortion to put down,
And regulate the charges of women of the town?
A Commission might be ordered, a scale of fees to draw,
Composed of the supporters of this Sanitary Law
(These Bishops, Deans and Doctors, who have found a new
    vocation
In preaching up the doctrine of the right of Fornication.)
How early that Commission could assemble every morn,
Taking evidence from Regent Street, the Argyle and Cre-
    morne,
Making curious calculations, how to regulate aright

The charge for short engagements, and engagements for all
  night,
Meditating from the Cab rules, of suggestions the adoption,
A charge for work done, or by time, at the Engager's option.
For reference the Reverends their Bibles might turn over,
To see the charge of Tamar to her Israelitisch lover;
And ponder if the object of the Heaven-inspired Narrator
Was suggestions for the guidance of each future fornicator?
While all Schoolmasters—Bishops, who had on the subject
  brooded,
Could advise them whether birching should be extra or in-
  cluded.

LADY POKINGHAM, OR THEY ALL DO IT;

Giving an Account of her Luxurious Adventures, both before and after her Marriage with Lord Crim-Con.

PART III.
(Continued.)

He hastily wrote the assignation on his tablets, and we made haste to return to the saloons from which we had been absent quite twenty minutes. A little while after, as I was sitting by the side of Alice, whispering my adventure in her ear, Lady Montairy, to whom I had previously been introduced, came and seated herself by my side. "Ah!" she said, with a sly look, "you're in a fair way to carry off the great prize; my sister Corisande will stand no chance."

"I've only danced one set with him," I replied, demurely.

"Ah!" she laughed, "it was not the Lancers I referred to, but your quiet stroll into the recesses of the conservatory. You had quite a lover's *tête-à-tête*."

"But we did not indulge in a *Pas Seul*, as you did with His Grace," I laughed, enjoying her confusion. She was speechless with surprise, her eyes fairly started with affright, and I hastened to reassure her, "I'm your friend, dear Lady Montairy, your secret is safe with me, and I hope you will not make any remarks in connection with myself and Lothair."

She squeezed my hand nervously, and asked, "Do you remember Fred's birthday? I was not there, but my brother Bertram was with his cousins the Vavasours, and passed as their brother Charlie, who happened to be too ill to go with them. I'm initiated into your society. We shall meet again," she added with a smile; "I must go now to keep my engagements."

The supper was a fairy feast, except for its substantial reality, and we returned home to Lady St. Jerome's charmed with everything, and especially with the fine prospect we seemed to have of future enjoyment.

Next day I made an excuse to go out alone to pay a visit to an old schoolfellow, and two o'clock found me sauntering through Burlington Arcade. Lothair was there to the minute, and gently whispered in my ear, as I was looking in a doll-shop, "Now, this is really kind of Your Ladyship, and proves you can be depended on; I have made a most excellent arrangement, we have only to step across the road to the Bristol Hotel in Burlington Gardens, where I have ordered luncheon for myself and cousin, in a private apartment, and they know me too well to pry into my affairs."

The chamber-maid attended me in the bedroom, and as soon as I had laid aside my cloak, hat, &c., I rejoined Lothar in the adjoining apartment, where a sumptuous luncheon was set out.

Lothair, whose shyness of the previous evening seemed considerably dispelled, most gallantly insisted upon my partaking of refreshment, before a word of my communication should be uttered. "Besides," he said, "a little champagne will give you courage, if it is at all disagreeable; the scene last night was such a shock to both of us that if you now prefer to be silent I won't press you about what you mentioned in the excitement of such a moment."

His conversation was very lively all through the repast, and when we had nearly finished I asked him to ring for a little milk, which was brought to me; he was at the moment abstractedly examining the debris of a pâté de foie gras. I poured part of the milk into two champagne glasses, and slyly added about ten drops of tincture of cantharides, with which Alice had provided me, to his portion. "Now, my Lord," I said, "I challenge you to pledge me in a glass of my favourite beverage, champagne and milk, I think it is delicious," pouring out the fizzing wine, and handing him the glass, which I first touched with my lips.

His eyes sparkled with delight as he drained it to the bottom, and flung the empty glass over his shoulder, exclaiming, "No one shall ever put their lips to that again, it was indeed a challenge, Lady Beatrice, after which nothing but the reality will satisfy me," then rising, he persisted in claiming the kiss I had, as he alleged, challenged him to take.

"Now," he continued, drawing me to a sofa, "let us sit down and hear the awful communication you hinted at; who were those wretched men?"

"Monsignore Berwick and Father Coleman," I replied; "did you ever hear of a secret sisterhood of St. Bridget, the nuns belonging to which devote both soul and person to the service of the Church?"

"No, never, go on," said Lothair, so I continued: "These nuns are all aristocratic ladies, who devote themselves, as I said, implicitly to the interests of Holy Mother Church, to satisfy and appease the lusts of her priests, as well as marry any influential man they think they can lead by the silken tie of matrimony; such, my Lord, are Lady St. Jerome and Miss Arundel."

"Incredible," exclaimed Lothair, "but I cannot doubt your word, dear Beatrice—permit me to call you," his eyes looking amorously at me, and evidently already slightly moved by the exciting dose I had given him. I took his hand in mine, it was feverishly warm, then looking him full in the face: "My dear Lord, I would not have been here if for one moment I had thought you could doubt my word."

"Call me Lothair, darling, throw away all awkward reserve," he said, putting his arm around my waist, and giving another kiss on my cheek, "go on; tell me all about those fiendish priests who have been plotting to ensnare me."

"Take my advice, Lothair," I went on, "you will find Miss Clare quite changed, her demure and reserved aspect turned to alluring and captivating glances; the Cardinal's orders are positive that she is not to spare even her honour if necessary, but that is an article I saw her surrender to the confessor." Then I described to him the scene we had witnessed in the chapel, which, added to the effects of the tincture, seemed quite to work him up to a state of amorous excitement.

"Honour! Honour!" he exclaimed, excitedly. "Alas! dear Beatrice, last night I felt able to lose life rather than that, and now it's gone, fled like a shadow, but what is it after all, but a mean, mistrustful shame; you must be mine, I can't restrain the fire of love which is consuming me; the very sin makes the idea more delicious." My faint efforts were useless, he was a fine strong young fellow; in an instant I was thrown backwards on the sofa, and his hands took possession of my longing cunny; the furor of lust was upon him, but I made a fair show of resistance, and seemed only to yield to force, shutting my eyes as if afraid to see how he was exposing himself.

He roughly forced my thighs apart, and throwing himself upon me, I could feel the hot soft head of his cock forcing its way between the lips of my vagina. I struggled and contracted myself as much as possible, and having previously well bathed the parts in a strong solution of alum and water, he experienced as great tightness and difficulty in penetration as if I had really been a virgin. My subdued cries of pain were real, for his big affair hurt me very much, but he gradually won his way, which was at the last moment facilitated by a copious spend.

"Ah! Darling; how delightful," he cried, as he lay with his weapon up to the hilt, throbbing and enjoying the lascivious contractions to which I now treated him.

His lips were fixed to mine, the soft velvety tip of his tongue was a titbit I could not refuse, and I sucked it till I almost choked for want of breath. He spent again under the stimulating emotions with which I inspired him. He lay still for a few moments as we recovered our breath, then, with an upward motion of my buttocks, I challenged him to go on.

It was a most erotically voluptuous love engagement. I could not exhaust him; he was continually shooting his love juice into my very insatiable womb, and it was more than an hour before either of us would consent to a cessation of the game.

All that time we had been as closely joined together as the Siamese twins, only one heart and one soul seemed to animate us, whilst we were constantly returning the flow of sperm one after the other in the most thrilling manner.

After we had washed and refreshed ourselves, he begged my forgiveness for his impulsiveness, and promised to make me his wife, but I recalled to him his words of the previous evening: "That it was better for a man never to marry," and that for my part I thought that such sweet liaisons could never be enjoyed by "married people."

"Ha! Ha!" I laughed. "You have the two nuns of St. Bridget to enjoy. Be advised by me, and seem to fall into their traps. I will introduce you to another secret society which you have little idea of. It is devoted to the pleasure of love, without being under the control of a lustful priesthood. You shall meet me again this day week and tell me how you get on."

He parted from me very lovingly; and on my return to St. James' Square, I found that Lady Montairy had brought an invitation from the Duchess for us to spend a few days at Crecy House before our return to the country.

"How delightful," said Alice. "The Duke has gone to Paris on business, and the Duchess is often indisposed; we shall find ourselves in Paphian bowers."

Lothair dined with us that evening, but neither of us betrayed, by word or look, the new link between us.

Miss Arundel was attractive, and even alluring, in her manner towards him. Her face was all smiles as she addressed him in tones of sympathy, even of tenderness. Bewitching enough to turn the head of any less susceptible (even than Lothair) to the influence of the softer sex. She looked divine, dressed in a wondrous white robe, garlanded with violets just arrived from Paris; on her head a violet wreath, deep and radiant as her eyes, and which admirably contrasted with her dark golden brown hair.

I could see he was fascinated. He asked us all to drive down to Richmond and dine with him the next day, but Alice declined for me and herself, alleging as a reason the short time we had to stay in town, and that we should at once have to avail ourselves of the Duchess's invitation, and with Lady Jerome's permission would remove to Crecy House early in the morning.

I could see this plan afforded them infinite satisfaction. So next day saw us welcomed at Crecy House by Lady Bertha St. Aldegonde on behalf of the Duchess, who was confined to her room. Lady Montairy conducted us to our apartments, and dismissing the attendants as soon as possible, she embraced me first, and then Alice, saying: "How nice of you two dears to come so soon. You're just in time for a most important ceremony. To-morrow Mama thinks we are all going to the Academy, but in reality it is quite a different place. The fact is, Corisande is going to be received as a member of the Paphian Circle, as we call the society which you helped to originate. St. Aldegonde, indifferent and 'ne'er do well' as he seems, is the life and soul of it; Bertha indulges him in everything. Jealousy is unknown in our family. You will meet Bertram, Carisbrooke, and Brecon all there. We only want Lothair to make it perfection, as Corisande means to taste and try which she likes best."

ALICE.—"But surely we're not obliged to wait till to-morrow. Can't you, Victoria, give us a little party in your room to-night?"

"Yes," she answered. "But only a hen party; ourselves and Corisande. My room is the next to yours. The gentlemen will be at the clubs. St. Aldegonde never will have a woman at night, and says the morning is the proper time, because his cock always stands best on an empty stomach before breakfast."

(To be continued.)

A BLACK JOSEPH.

[The Trial of Mrs. Inglefield, wife of J. R. Nicholson Inglefield, Esq., Captain of Her Majesty's Ship Scipio, for Adultery with John Webb, a black servant, in the Consistory Court, 1786.]

John Webb—a second Joseph—a black footman to Captain Inglefield, was the only material evidence against the lady. Previous to his deposition he had lived with the parties two years, mostly at Singlewell, a small village near Gravesend. When he first went there, the family consisted of three small children, all girls; in two or three months afterwards his mistress was delivered of a boy.

From the first moment of his being engaged he thought she took more notice of him than became her. She frequently smiled on him and took hold of his hand, and gently pressed it. About a month after her accouchement, happening to be alone with his lady, she put her hand about his neck, and kissed him. Upon the black drawing off, she laughed at him.

The next day after this occurrence, as he was dressing her hair, she put her hand under his apron, and unbuttoned one of the flaps of his breeches, and began handling and playing with his privities, but the witness, not liking this, declared he would not finish her hair if she did not let him alone. The lady, therefore, was again obliged to laugh it off.

The next day after this, in the forenoon, being summoned by the sound of the chamber bell, he went into the room, where he found his mistress alone, sitting on the foot of the bed. Mungo—according to his own account—avoided going near her as much as possible, but at length she caught him by the skirt of his coat, placed him on her lap, and handled his privities on the outside of his breeches, at the same time

asking him—"Can you do anything? Do not be afraid; your
master will know nothing about it." All this, however, made
no impression on the generative powers of our African hero.
He was a eunuch in spirit, though not in parts, and he tore
himself away, but whether at this period he left his mistress
laughing or crying does not appear.

The succeeding day, however, Mrs. I. renewed the glorious
strife; while under the operation of hair-dressing, she once
more applied her delicate hand to the rude parts of Master
Comb, and was proceeding to unbutton when he drew himself off, leaving his mistress laughing out an intimation that
she should leave her bedroom door open that night, and that
he must come.

Master Webb, failing to improve the hint, was the next
day met in an angry mood by his enraged mistress, who now
spoke very harshly to him.

During these attempts it seems the Captain was from
home, which was the time, he says, when his mistress tor-
mented him the most. But what affected him more than all
was that one day she absolutely kissed him before her daughter, a child of about four years old.

Towards the end of the summer the Captain and his lady
resided on board the Scipio, then laying at Scheerness, for
about a month, and one morning about 10 o'clock, when they
had been there a fortnight, the Captain being gone on shore,
his mistress called him into the after-cabin of the ship, and
told him to empty a basin of water, which, when he had
done, she shut the cabin door, took him round the waist with
both her arms, kissed him and then, as a matter of course,
handled him about his privities on the outside, he preventing
her from unbuttoning.

All these warm attacks our youthful Negro of nineteen
manfully withstood, and after some struggling he liberated
his sweet desirable person from the fangs of his mistress, but
passing from the room he was observed by Charles McCarthy,
the steward of the ship, who questioned him as to what he
had been doing, to which he replied—"nothing."

Two or three days after this aquatic adventure, he was questioned by his master as to all the previous particulars, when,
like a faithful servant, he told him all that he knew. In consequence of which Captain Inglefield from that time ceased
to cohabit with his wife. The concluding declaration of Webb

is: "That he and his mistress, notwithstanding the critical situations in which he was placed, never had once the carnal use and knowledge of each other's bodies."

McCarthy, the Steward, corroborated the cabin incident, but in the end the Judge declared there was no proof of the lady's guilt, and ordered Captain Inglefield to take his wife home and treat her with matrimonial affection, and to certify his having so done by the first session of the next term.

INTO THE BARGAIN.

Two lads were out on Hertford Heath
   And being flush of money,
Offered two shillings to a wench,
   To let them view her cunny.

They viewed it with extreme delight,
   Stark naked and provoking;
They paid their shillings for the sight,
   The touching and the stroking.

"Now," said the cunning little slut,
   "Just add a sixpence each;
And you shall see my very scut!
   I'll let you see my breech."

"What fun!" exclaim the simple boys,
   So they the shilling paid;
Then pulling up her smock behind,
   Her bottom she displayed.

And so they peeped, and felt their fill;
   Then cried the giggling lass,
"Your bargain shall be better still;
   Say 'Please,' and kiss my arse!"

ORIGIN OF COPULATION.

Success to dame Nature, for 'twas by her plan,
That woman first thought of enjoyment from man;
She knew that of pleasure they'd never be sick,
And so out of kindness, invented a prick!
    A stiff-standing, glorious prick!
    Voluptuous, rubicund prick!
Oh, surely, of fortune it came in the nick,
Good-natured dame Nature to give us a prick!

Without it how lost would a poor maiden be,
It tickles her quim, makes her water run free;
Most women a handle would have to their front,
So they've only to thrust a long prick in their cunt!
    Their hairy, voluptuous cunt!
    Their sweet little, queer little cunt!
What damsel no handle would have to their front?
And prick e'er has been a great friend unto cunt!

When nature to woman gave two mouths, she will'd,
Of course, that they both should be equally filled,
And if women will look after one mouth, you know
That prick will look after the mouth that's below!
    Stiff-standing, glorious prick!
    Voluptuous, rubicund prick!
Oh, surely, of fortune it came in the nick,
Good-natured dame Nature to give us a prick!

When sorrow torments lovely woman, oh dear,
A mighty good fucking will banish despair;
If her belly but aches, why we all know the trick,
There's nothing can ease it so well as a prick!
    A nice luscious prick!
    A stiff-standing prick!
For any young maiden it can do the trick.
Oh, joys there are plenty, but nothing like prick!

TAKING A MAIDENHEAD.

Air—"Gee, ho Dobbin."

Oh, Maidenhead-taking's a very great bore,
It makes cunt and prick so confoundedly sore;
But fucking the third time's like heaven above,
For your prick then glides in as you draw on a glove!
    Gee up, Roger,
     Wag up, Roger,
Roger's a thing that all women admire!

Oh, give me a damsel of blooming fifteen,
With two luscious thighs and a mouse-trap between,
With the fringe on the edge, and two red lips I say,
In her cunt I'd be diving by night and by day!
                      Gee up, &c.

That woman would be a disgrace to our land,
Who would not take a prick, when it stiffy does stand;
And when it droops low as if it were in dread,
She must tickle the balls, till it lifts up its head!
                      Gee up, &c.

Cunt is a treasure which monarchs admire,
Cunt is a thing that my theme doth inspire;
Cunt is a mighty temptation to sin,
But cunt is a hole that I'd ever be in!
                      Gee up, &c.

Prick is its friend, its first cousin, I ween,
Tho' prick I confess is a rare go-between;
Prick to a woman much joy can impart,
And prick is a thing that she loves in her heart!
                      Gee up, &c.

Then here's to the female who yields to a man,
And here's to the man who'll fuck when he can,
For fucking creates all our joy on earth,
And from fucking you know, we all date our birth.
    Gee up, Roger,
     Wag up, Roger,
Roger's a thing that all women admire.

EPITAPH.

Here lies the amorous Fanny Hicks,
The scabbard of ten thousand pricks,
And if you wish to do her honour,
Pull out your cock, and piss upon her.

THE TRIUMPH OF SCIENCE OVER PHYSIC.

Home they brought the warrior, fed
    To repletion more than just;
And the servants, chuckling, said,
    "He must shit or he will bust."

Then they gave him castor oil,
    Pills and drugs of many a sort;
Yet despite their loving toil,
    He would not be taken short.

Stole a maiden to the spot,
    And emetics, laughing, dared;
Yet in vain she held the pot,
    For he only belched and glared.

Came a nurse of ninety years,
    An enema huge she bore;
Shoved it up amidst their jeers,
    And he shat for evermore.

SONG.

If anxious Venus, beauty's queen!
    Your empire should endure,
Borrow Cecilia's face and mien,
    Our homage to ensure.

Though perfect all the charms may seem,
   That famed Apelles drew.
Not half so sweet are they, I deem,
   As fair Cecilia's Cu.

The feelings of my faithful heart,
   My mouth shall still express,
Upon that Cu—, delicious part,
   In rapture's wild caress.

Oh! ye, who ne'er disquiet felt,
   Nor aught but virtue knew.
Whence is it? But your eye ne'er dwelt
   Upon Cecilia's Cu.

Cecilia, think not, from my brain,
   The souvenir can remove,
Of thy sweet Cu, 'twill there remain,
   Imprinted fast by Love!

But if my thread of life should break,
   Expire thy lover true.
May I flight 'mid kisses take,
   Imprinted on thy Cu!

GONE TO CA-CA.

Tom brought home some friends,
   And not finding his dear,
But only young Harry,
   Who look'd rather queer.

(Papa) Hush, Harry! What nonsense!
      Run, call your Mama!
(Boy) Mama and de Captain
      Are gone to Ca-Ca.

(*Papa*) Hush, Harry! What nonsense!
            Just hear the child talk!
(*Boy*)   Captain pull down his breeches,
            Ma pull up her frock!

THE PATIENCE OF JOB.

A farmer and his wife, who had been to church one Sunday morning, were walking home through a country lane, when John said, "Excuse me, my dear, for a minute or two, I want to get over the hedge to do something for myself." After rather a long interval his loving wife, who had walked on a little, returned to look for him, and could hear her good man on the other side of the hedge, blasting, swearing, and damning at an awful rate. She managed to get over to him, and then seeing him stooping down as if troubled by a very hard motion, exclaimed, "John! John! how can you swear so, don't you remember what the parson said about the patience of Job?"

"Blast that damned Job," exclaimed the furious John, "he never had his balls caught in a rabbit trap! Why don't you make haste to help me?"

The poor fellow stooping down to ease himself, had really been caught, and his wife had to release him and help him home.

LATEST SPORTING NEWS.

RESULT OF THE WHORING HANDICAP.

Syphilis 1
Chancre 2
Bubo 3

Immediately the flag dropped Gonorrhea began making the running for Injection (a brown colt out of Syringe). Coming round the Chordee Bend, Poultice showed well to the front, but when once in the Straight was soon left behind.

They passed the Grand Stand in the following order: Syphilis first, Chancre second, Bubo third, and Suppuration a bad fourth, closely followed by Unction, Black Wash, Lint, and Copaiba. Testicle pulled up much distressed, Capsules bolted. Doctor's Bill (extra weight) came in last.

The Sporting Prophets say that if French Letter had not been scratched she would have altered the result of the race.

NURSERY RHYMES.

There was a young man of Berlin,
Whom disease had despoiled of his skin;
    But he said with much pride,
    "Though deprived of my hide,
I can still enjoy a put in."

There was a young woman of Cheadle,
Who once gave the clap to a beadle.
    Said she, "Does it itch?"
    "It does, you damned bitch,
And burns like hell-fire when I peedle."

There was an old Chinaman drunk,
Who went for a sail in his junk,
    He was dreaming of Venus,
    And tickling his penis,
Till he floated away in the spunk.

There was a young man of Rangoon,
Who farted and filled a balloon.
    The balloon went so high,
    That it stuck in the sky,
And stank out the Man in the Moon.

There was a young man at the Cape,
On a maiden committed a rape.

Said she, "You damned shit,
  You can't fuck a bit,
And you're knocking my quim out of shape."

There was a young parson of Harwich,
Tried to grind his betrothed in a carriage.
  She said "No, you young goose,
  Just try self-abuse,
And the other we'll try after marriage."

There was a young man of St. Paul's,
Possessed the most useless of balls.
  Till at last, at the Strand,
  He managed a stand,
And tossed himself off in the stalls.

There was a young lady of Treadle,
Who sat down in Church on a needle,
  The needle, not blunt,
  Penetrated her cunt,
But was promptly removed by the beadle.

There was a young girl of Newcastle,
Whose charms were declared universal.
  While one man in front
  Wired into her cunt,
Another was engaged at her arsehole.

There was a young parson of Goring,
Who made a small hole in the flooring;
  He lined it all round,
  Then laid on the ground,
And declared it was cheaper than whoring.

When Mrs. Conwell was in this country, she showed me a
copy she had made of a large picture of a Turkish soldier on
horseback. She had made the horse's testicles very conspicuous, and then shamming ignorance, pointed at them, saying,
"That is the rider's foot on the other side." "Yes," said I,
with a low bow, "very like a foot!" This made her giggle.

THE PEARL,

A Journal of Facetiæ and Voluptuous Reading.

| No. 6 | PUBLISHED MONTHLY. | Dec. 1879 |

SUB-UMBRA, OR SPORT AMONG THE SHE-NOODLES.

(Continued.)

Nothing of moment occurred during the evening, after my visit to Mrs. Leslie, but I could see that Annie was rather piqued because I had nothing to tell her, except that I thought the Colonel's lady a most charming person, and had been pressed to stay with her to luncheon before she would write a reply to my uncle's note.

Next day being the last representation of a celebrated piece at the theatre of the County Town, by a first-rate London company, papa expressed a wish that we should all go in the evening, but Annie and Sophie, giving me a knowing look on the sly, declared they had already seen it once and did not care to go again. For my part, of course, I had seen it half-a-dozen times in town, so it was finally arranged that Frank, Rosa and Polly only would go with papa and mama; they had a drive of more than an hour before them, so started at 6 P.M., and as soon as they were out of sight we three started for the bathing place at the lake. It was such a deliciously warm evening, and it would be just the place for our anticipated pleasures, as I had suggested to Annie and Sophie during the day.

Bolting the summer-house door on the inside as soon as we got in, I suggested first of all to stimulate our mutually ardent desires by a bottle of champagne; this so exhilarated the two lovely girls that we indulged in a second bottle before stripping for a romp. Seven o'clock found us bathed in a flood of golden light from the declining sun, which now shone directly in upon us; this warned us to make haste and improve the opportunity, so each one assisting the others and at the same time indulging in many loving tricks and liberties, we were soon in Adam and Eve costume.

"Now," I exclaimed, "Annie dear, you won't be jealous if I make a woman of your sister, as we promised the other day," taking the youngest one up in my arms with my rampant cock throbbing against her belly, as I carried her to the lounge.

"What a naughty boy you are, Walter, anything or anybody for a change is what fickle men like, but I won't be jealous of Sophie, although I am of Mrs. Leslie. I know you had her yesterday; that sheepish tell-tale look, sir, when you met me on your return, was enough to confirm my suspicions of what would happen when you were tête-à-tête with that killing lady," she replied.

"For shame, Annie, darling, you told me yourself the other day love ought to be free everywhere; I don't deny my guilt, but will do my best to earn forgiveness now," I said, pushing Sophie back upon the soft yielding lounge, "help me to ease this darling of her troublesome virginity, and I will then repay your own longing cunny for all your love and forbearance; I am sure Mrs. Leslie would like to make you one of our party without any feelings of jealousy; there are so many ways of voluptuous enjoyment that if only one man to three beautiful girls it can be so varied as to give everyone the most intense delight."

At this both the girls gave me rapturous kisses, with every possible assurance that they never would be selfish, and would be only too happy to extend the circle of those they could be free and loving with, adding with special emphasis, "We are such noodles, dear Walter, we knew nothing till you introduced us to the arts of love, and as long as you can stay with us shall look to you to guide us in everything; we know it's wrong, but what heavenly pleasure there is in the loving mixture of the sexes."

ANNIE, taking my prick in her hand.—"Now, sir, I will show this gentleman the way into Sophie's cabinet of love; be firm, dear, he won't hurt you more than can be helped, and the after joy will soon drown all recollection of the first short suffering."

SOPHIE, opening her legs as wide as possible.—"I'm all on fire to taste the real tree of love, don't spare me, Walter, dear, I'd rather die than not have it now!"

The red head of "Cupid's Battering Ram" was now brought to the charge; Annie opened the rosy lips of her sister's cunt and placed my cock in the exact position, but her touches, together with the thoughts of the delicious titbit I was about to enjoy, caused me to spend in a moment all over her fingers and into the virgin passage in front. "Push on, push on; now's the time to gain your victory," she whispered; "that will make it easier to get him in," at the same time lifting up Sophie's buttocks with her disengaged hand, so as to make her meet my attack in a more favourable manner. My first lunge lodged the head of Mr. Priapus fairly within the tight folds of the victim's vagina, and I had already won the first outworks of the virgin's defences.

Poor Sophie moaned under the sharp pain of my assault, but biting her lips to repress any cries of pain she courageously placed one hand on the shaft of my prick, as if jealous of her sister's loving help, and anxious to have the honour of herself showing me the way to achieve love's dearest triumph, or perhaps it was for fear of my withdrawing before completely accomplishing my task.

"You love!" I exclaimed, enraptured by this exhibition of pluck, "I will soon make a real woman of you," then pushing fiercely on, on, I gradually forced the tight sheath to dilate. Every obstruction gave way to my determined energy, and with a final plunge, I was buried to the roots of my affair, and shooting at the same moment my warm spendings into her inmost vitals. This exhausted me for a few moments, and I lay supine upon the heaving bosom of the lovely Sophie, till I could feel Annie's fingers busy tickling my balls and feeling the shaft of my cock. Just at the same moment Sophie, who had almost fainted under the painful ordeal, opened her eyes, and with a loving smile pouted her lips as an invitation for a kiss, which I instantly responded to, almost sucking her breath away in my ardour. My excitement was now raised to the highest possible pitch by her sister's titillations, and the loving challenge of Sophie herself to renew my motions with her, by heaving up her bottom and nipping my prick in her cunny in the most delightful way imaginable.

This time I prolonged the pleasure as much as possible, beginning slowly, and often stopping to feel the delicious throbbings of cock and cunny in their delightful conjunction. "Ach! this is indeed love; it repays for all the pain I felt at first. Oh! oh! dear Walter, it feels as if my very soul was flowing from me in ecstasy!" she almost screamed out, kissing, biting, squeezing me with all her might at the moment of emission, which I again responded to with a flow of my own sperm.

I now declared we must refresh ourselves a little before going further, so she reluctantly allowed me to withdraw. A short plunge in the lake had a most invigorating effect. I felt as strong as a giant again, then another bottle of fizz renewed our loving ardour; the girls were handling my prick, which stood again as hard as ivory. So slipping on my shirt, as I intended to be the uppermost of the trio, I laid Sophie on her back, and then telling the obedient Annie to kneel over her sister and gamahuche her in return for Sophie's doing the same by her, I mounted up behind her, saying, "I've made a woman of your dear sister, and will now treat you, my darling, to a new sensation." But just at the moment Sophie, who had no idea of my intentions, seized hold of my cock, saying, "She must kiss the dear sweet thing, which had afforded her such exquisite bliss." Holding it tight in her hand, she took the head between her pearly teeth and kissed and treated him to such love bites that I soon spent in her mouth, which she greedily swallowed, with all the abandon of voluptuous enjoyment. Meanwhile, I had been frigging Annie's bottom with my two fingers, which I had managed to insert together, and that dear girl was sucking her sister's quim, and wriggling herself in the most excitable way possible.

Sophie was now going to insert my prick in her sister's cunt, but Annie, almost beside herself with excitement, exclaimed, "No, no, my dear, put him where Walter has got his fingers; I should like to try that, it is so exciting; the very thought of it makes me mad with desire to know what it is like. His fingers have given me such pleasures that I am sure the dear thing in your hand will greatly improve the sensation!"

No sooner said than done; the obedient girl directed my cock to the beautifully wrinkled tight little brown hole of her sister's bottom at the very moment I withdrew my fingers. When I found they so thoroughly appreciated the idea I had resolved to initiate them into, being well lubricated and as

tiff as possible, it soon passed the portals of Annie's second
irginity. But, Heavens, what a delicious bout we had, she
ounded about so with delight, that I had to hold tight round
er neck to prevent being thrown out, whilst Sophie, below,
amahuched her delighted sister, and with her right hand
ontinued to press my balls and prick, keeping time to every
isertion in her sister's bottom. We all spent together, almost
creaming with delight, and then lay in a confused heap, en-
)ying all the sensations of our delicious exhaustion.

As soon as they could kiss and persuade my rather ener-
ated tool into renewed stiffness, Sophie declared I must
blige her with a taste of the new-found joy, and ravish her
ottom as well as her sister's.

This was another delicious love engagement; the sisters
amahuching each other with the utmost erotic ardour, whilst
iy delighted prick revelled in the tight-fitting fundamental
f the sweet girl, who wriggled and plunged about so ex-
itedly that I had to hold fast to keep my place.

After this, we returned to the house, and passed the time
ery pleasantly till the return of the party from the theatre. I
ras anxious to hear Frank's account of how he had got on
ith Rosa during the evening, and especially as they drove
ome.

"Walter," he said, as we were once more alone in his room
fter all had gone to rest, "I've had a most enjoyable time of
: since we started. Of course, as we went, it was daylight, so
osa and I maintained a proper decorum, but at the theatre,
apa and mama were separated from us by Polly, and we all
ve sat in the front row of the dress circle. How the sight of
osa's swelling bosom (which her low-necked dress allowed
ie fully to see) made my prick stand at once; so I took her
loved hand and made her feel how hard and excited it was.
s no one could see, she indulged me with quite a gentle
igging outside my trousers, till I spent profusely, to the
reat delight of the roguish beauty, as I could tell by the
mile on her face and the excited looks with which she met
iy ardent gaze.

" 'What a shame,' she whispered in my ear. 'I know what
ou have done, you naughty boy. You should have reserved it
or a more favourable opportunity.'

" 'Look out, darling, as we drive home; see if I don't repay
our kind attentions,' I whispered in return.

" 'Both papa and mama were rather sleepy before the con
clusion of the last piece, and to make them go off, as soon as
we were seated in the carriage, I offered them my flask of
brandy to keep out the effects of the night air. It had a pretty
good strong dose of narcotic in it, and they were soon sound
asleep in their corners. Polly also pretended to be dozing.

"Rosa was on my lap directly, and my hands were at once
groping their way to the seat of pleasure whilst she was
equally busy unbuttoning my trousers and handling the staff
of life.

"Our lips met in long-drawn rapturous kisses, which fired
every drop of blood in our veins, and both were too impatient
for the real business to prolong our toyings with each other's
privates; besides, I felt she was already spending over my
busy fingers. She had my cock in a glorious state of erection
so opening her delicious thighs as she raised her clothes, she
was at once impaled on the spike she so burned to have
thrust into her. It was quite equal to the first time I fucked
her. The long evening passed in expectation of what I might
be able to do on our return journey; it so added to the
piquancy of my arduous longings that I seemed in Heaven
itself, and swimming in a very ocean of love, we spent over
and over again; our melting kisses and tongue-sucking con
tinually stimulating us to renewed exertions, till the near ap
proach to home warned us of the necessity of bringing our
pleasures to an end for a time. Even now, I tell you, Walter
my cock keeps throbbing and standing at the very thought
of the delightful pressures she treated me to; her cunt bites
so deliciously."

(To be continued.)

MISS COOTE'S CONFESSION,

Or the Voluptuous Experiences of an Old Maid;
In a series of Letters to a Lady Friend.

Letter VI.

My Dear Nellie,
     During my late tour in Italy and Germany I often amused
myself with making notes for further letters to you on my re

turn to England, collecting all the incidents I could think of
or remember as likely to interest you, and now I am at home
once more I will amuse myself on dull evenings by writing you
another series of letters. Well, then, to begin.

When I left school my guardians entrusted me to the care
of Mdlle. Fosse, and we were soon settled in a house of my
own in the western suburbs of London. My establishment
consisted of ourselves, Jane, my grandfather's late servant
(who acted as our lady's-maid), a cook called Margaret, and
two housemaids, Mary and Polly, besides a nice young page, a
brother of Jane's who was called Charlie.

My guardians thought that until I was of age we could dispense with a footman or coachman, and hire from time to
time such carriages as we might require to visit our friends, or
go shopping, or to the theatres, and my allowance was limited
to £1000 a year, out of which Mademoiselle had a liberal salary
of £200, which I never begrudged in the least; she was such a
dear, loving soul, and always did all she could to further my
amusements and keep me out of serious mischief.

Myself and Mademoiselle occupied separate bedrooms com-
municating with each other, so that we could, if we wished,
enjoy each other's society by night as well as day. The cook
and Mary occupied a room at the top of the house, whilst the
page had a little cell of a room to himself on the same corridor as our bedrooms, and Jane and Polly (we were obliged
to call her so, to distinguish her from the other Mary), were
also in a room on the same flight, which also contained a
couple of spare rooms for visitors. On the top floor there were
several spare rooms, one of which was very large, and after
consultation with Mademoiselle I determined to fit it up as
a punishment chamber, and maintain strict discipline in my
family. I had hooks fixed in the ceiling, and also provided a
complete paraphernalia of ropes, blocks, and pulleys, a whipping post and ladder, also a kind of stocks in which to fix a
body so as only to expose the legs and bottom behind, and
prevent the victim from seeing who was punishing her.

Mademoiselle and myself frequently indulged in our
"Soirées Lubriques," as she called them, and for an occasional extra excitement, we got Jane, and either birched her
in our bedrooms, or got her to assist us in birching one another, for I was now thoroughly given to the pleasures of the
rod and the excitement to be raised by its application. These

little bits of fun, as we called them, were wanting in that piquancy so appreciable when the victim is a thorough stranger to the birch, and feels its tickling effects for the first time. This made us particularly on the look-out for some culprit whom we might immolate to our prurient desires.

Our gardener was a steady man, rather over forty, and his wife, a very pretty woman of about thirty. They had two nice little girls of nine and ten years old, and lived in a small cottage at the back entrance of our garden, which was pretty large.

Mrs. White, the gardener's wife, was very fond of finery, and her husband's wages not being sufficient to satisfy her cravings in that respect, she hit upon the ingenious plan of supplying some of our neighbours (who were not so well off for garden produce as we were) with some of the fruit and vegetables which otherwise would have been wasted, and as she thought might as well be sold for her own profit. The father did not see much harm in it, as he afterwards said, Miss Coote was so good and generous, and did not seem to mind what they took for themselves.

The two little girls, Minnie and Lucy, were employed by their parents to carry things out at the back gate, but they happened to be seen by Jane early one morning, and duly reported to me.

I had long an unaccountable wish to birch these little dears, but could think of no excuse how to bring it about, so that Jane's report was most welcome.

In company with Mademoiselle, early in the morning, we repaired by a roundabout way to the back entrance of my garden, and placed ourselves so as to see exactly what was going on, and were soon rewarded for our trouble by seeing the little girls carry several baskets of fruits into their mother's cottage.

Having satisfied ourselves as to the facts of the case, I returned to the house, and ordered the gardener and all his family to be summoned to my presence.

In company with Mademoiselle, I received them in the drawing-room. White and his wife, leading in the little girls by the hand, and with a respectful obeisance, enquired the reason of my sending for them.

Miss Coote.—"Your pretended innocence is well assumed.

How is it, White, that your children carry away fruit from the garden as they do every morning?"

WHITE, stammering in great confusion.—"They only have a little for ourselves, Miss."

MISS COOTE.—"You're only adding falsehood to theft. White, your wife does not get all her finery out of your wages."

WHITE.—"Oh! Sally! (To his wife:) Pray speak. I don't know anything about it."

MRS. WHITE (scarlet with shame, and bursting into tears).—"Oh! Oh! It's all my fault. William don't know I ever sold anything, and the dear children are innocent. Oh! Pray forgive me, Miss Coote."

MISS COOTE (sternly).—"He must know. He's as bad as you, and you're bringing up those little girls to be thieves."

White and his wife and children all went on their knees, imploring me for mercy, and protesting that very little had been sold.

MISS COOTE.—"Nonsense! You make me think you even worse, because I know it has been going on for some time. Now make your choice. Shall I punish you severely myself, or have you taken before a magistrate? You know they will hang both of you."

White and his wife both implore for mercy, and beg me to punish them any way I may think best. "Only, only, pray Miss Coote, spare the dear little things, they only did what we told them."

MISS COOTE.—"You are wise to leave it to me. I may have some mercy; the law has none for poor wretched thieves. I don't know how to punish you, White, as you are a man, so I will forgive you, and hope you will be honest in the future; but Mrs. White and the children must be properly whipped and corrected. They must attend me here, dressed in their Sunday clothes, at seven o'clock this evening. Now you understand. Go home till then. I will cure them of thieving, or my name's not Rosa Coote."

Poor White and his wife are covered with confusion and retire for the present, whilst I congratulate Mdlle. Fosse on our good fortune in securing such victims.

Seven o'clock, and I am ready in the punishment chamber to receive the culprits. They enter with a very dejected appearance, although dressed smartly in the highest style of rustic fashion with their bouquets.

Miss Coote.—"I am glad, for your sake, Mrs. White, you have left me to punish you, as I hope after this you will be thoroughly trustworthy. Mademoiselle Fosse, will you assist Jane in preparing Minnie for the birch? Stop! Tie Mrs. White to the ladder, or her motherly feelings may cause her to interfere, then get Lucy ready also. If they haven't got drawers on, we must find a pair for each of them."

Mrs. White (with tears in her eyes).—"Oh! Oh! Miss Coote, my dear young lady, don't be too hard on the children. Cut me to pieces rather."

She is soon tied by her wrists to the ladder, but left as she is, in all her clothes, for the present. Then they strip little Minnie and Lucy, and expose their pretty plump figures to our gaze. Mademoiselle takes Lucy on her knee, and I have the youngest, Minnie, only nine years old. The little creatures are all blushes, and quite crimson with shame as we turn them on our laps bottom upwards. They are evidently quite unused to inspection by strange ladies.

Miss Coote (to Minnie).—"How you do blush, my dear; are you afraid I shall hurt you so much? What a lovely little bottom, does your mother often slap it?" giving two or three fair spanks, which very much improve the lovely colour of the firm flesh, and makes the little thing twist about beautifully, as she feels the smart.

Minnie.—"Oh! Oh! Pray don't! How you hurt! I can't bear it, Miss Coote," beginning to cry, and the pearly tears dropping on my lap.

Mademoiselle.—"So you little girls sold the fruit for your mother; did you, Lucy?"

Lucy.—"Father gave it to us to carry home."

Mademoiselle.—"The old story of Adam and Eve. One tempted the other. So it was all father; mother quite innocent, eh?"

Miss Coote.—"I think I can make Minnie tell us a different tale to that, Mdlle. Fosse. They are little story-tellers as well as thieves," giving Minnie a good slap with her open hand. "Just try my plan, Mademoiselle."

Minnie shrieks and kicks about in pain as Miss Coote slaps away, and Mademoiselle does the same by Lucy, till both their bottoms are as rosy as peaches. Both little girls screaming loudly for mercy; laying the blame first on father, and then mother, as they find it is no use to deny it.

"Now, Jane," says Miss Coote, "hand us a couple of light birches. We must thoroughly cure them before they are let off." Then taking hold of the birch, she directs Jane to tie both little victims to the whipping post, and puts a tight pair of drawers on each to hide their blushing rumps.

Jane ties them up, side by side, by their wrists, the arms well stretched above their heads, and their toes only just reaching the floor. Then she produces two little pairs of very thin lawn drawers almost as delicate as muslin, so that the rosy flesh was slightly perceptible through the material. They were, if anything, rather too small, and fitted quite tightly (the youthful bottoms are so finely developed, considering the age of their owners) and leave a space of nearly six inches wide behind, where they gave a delightfully seductive view of the pink roseate flesh and the cracks of the anus; altogether their shamefaced confusion and distress, as they gracefully lift their little legs, one by one, into the drawers, and go through all three positions Jane manages to put them in, as she fastidiously arranges them for sacrifice, was a most delightful sight to me, gloating as I was in the anticipation of the pleasure the whipping would be sure to afford.

Miss Coote.—"Now, Mademoiselle, will you assist me in the whipping? I will do all the talking."

The mother here is so distressed at the sight of her children tied up for whipping that she tries to fall on her knees, but soon remembers herself, when her hands being tied up prevent her intention. "Oh! Oh! Miss Coote, do have mercy on my little girls," she sobs. "To think I should bring this on them. Oh! Oh!" trying to wring her hands.

Miss Coote.—"Hold your foolish noise, woman. I'm just going to begin. How do you like it, Minnie? How is it, Lucy?" beginning to switch them finely, soon making a lot of thin red marks all over their backs and bottoms. "Will you ever take my fruit again, you little hussies? Warm their bottoms well for them, Mademoiselle. Take the thieving impudence out of their posteriors."

The victims shriek in a series of shrill screams, their faces are scarlet, and the tears roll in a little stream down their pretty pitiful faces, and they beg and pray to be let off. "Oh! Oh! we will be good, &c."

Miss Coote and her friend are delighted; the sight is so stimulating, their blood rushes through their veins and raises their voluptuous feelings of sensuality to the highest pitch, the cries of pain are so much music to their ears, and they cut the little bottoms dreadfully till the blood starts from the weals; the poor agonized mother is another spirit, which only adds to their enjoyment, as although only a spectator she seems to feel every blow, and cries and sobs as if her heart would break.

MADEMOISELLE.—"Look at the silly woman, you'll have something to cry for presently, Mrs. White."

The thin drawers are cut up, and torn into rags, the birches almost worn out, and the two flagellatrices would never have stopped, but Jane interposes, for little Minnie has fainted, and Lucy seems likely to go off too.

They untie them, and with a little water and pungent smelling salts soon revive the little one, then both mother and children are refreshed by some champagne, slightly dashed with a most stimulating liqueur.

Mrs. White, who had also been released, nurses her children on her lap, caressing and kissing them, crying and hysterically sobbing over their sore bottoms. "Poor little dears; oh! Miss Coote, you have been cruel to the innocent things."

MISS COOTE.—"How dare you say innocent things when you taught them to steal. I'll make you confess your guilt, you bad woman."

MRS. WHITE, all of a tremble.—"Oh! My heart bleeds for their poor rumps, I can't help what I say."

MISS COOTE.—"Take them away, and let Mary see to their bruises, then come back and help us to cheer up the mother a little; she's dreadfully depressed, poor thing," laughing ironically at Mrs. White.

Jane soon returns, and begins to prepare the mother for her punishment.

MISS COOTE.—"Stretch her properly on the ladder; she's the worst of the lot, first tempting her husband, and then making the children help to steal."

MRS. WHITE.—"Oh! I didn't think you cared about the garden stuff, it would have been spoilt."

MISS COOTE.—"Then why didn't your husband ask me what to do with it? Did you not use the money to buy ribbons and dresses?"

The poor woman groans for very shame, and has nothing to say for herself. Jane and Mademoiselle pull off her bright blue dress, and expose a fine pair of white shoulders, showing that her blushes have extended all down her neck, which was slightly flushed as they uncover it. She is a fine woman with reddish brown hair and hazel eyes, fine plump arms, and hands which do not look as if they worked too hard at home, her underclothing, skirts, and petticoats, although not of the finest material, are beautifully white and tastefully trimmed with cheap lace; they soon remove everything, and find her quite *sans culottes* like the little girls; the poor woman blushes scarlet at the exposure of all her luscious-looking charms, her splendid prominent mount being covered with a profusion of long, curly hair, similar to what she has on her head.

MISS COOTE.—"My gracious, Mrs. White, how could you come here for a whipping and have nothing on to cover your modesty; it's shockingly indelicate; what can we do?"

MADEMOISELLE.—"I guessed what would happen; look here, Miss Coote, I amused myself before dinner, and have made her an apron of real fresh vine leaves; how pretty they will look on her, and set off the pink flesh."

The poor woman fairly sobs with shame at our remarks, and laughing jokes about what a fine set of rumpsteaks she has got, and how nicely they will be grilled for her. They adjust the apron of vine leaves very tastefully about her loins, and then present her to me, to kiss the rod, a fine heavy bunch of long, green fresh birchen twigs, tastefully ornamented with gaily coloured ribbons. She is made to kneel, and giving the required kiss, stammer out as whispered in her ear by Jane. "Oh! Oh! My dear young lady—Miss Coote—do—do—whip me—soundly—for I have been a wicked—dishonest woman. Oh! Oh! forgive me, don't be too hard," she exclaims, forgetting the orders and in a tremble of anticipation, the tears coursing down her scarlet cheeks, as she gets upon her feet; and they lay her at full length along the ladder, which is at a great angle, both arms and feet stretched out as far as possible, and tied tightly so she can scarcely move her bottom, or wiggle in the least.

All being in readiness:—

MISS COOTE.—"You have only half confessed your guilt, but your bottom well warmed will bring you to a full sense of it," as she waves the tremendous rod about and makes it fairly hiss through the air, keeping the victim in agitated expectation for several seconds, when—whack—whack—whack.

Three resounding blows sound through the room, the victim's bottom immediately shows the result of a confused appearance of long red marks and weals, whilst the green leaves are flying in all directions.

MRS. WHITE, screaming in dreadful pain.—"Ah! Oh! Ah—r—r—re! I can't bear it! Oh! Oh! Spare me, have mercy!" The muscles of her back and loins showing by their contortions the agonizing sensations caused by the cuts in her distended and distressing position.

MISS COOTE.—"How she screams! where's your courage? why the little girls bore it better than you do; scream away, it will keep you from thinking too much of the pain, I'm only just beginning and have not got warm to my work yet," going on whack—whack—swish—swish, all the while.

VICTIM.—"Oh! Oh! Frightful! Oh! you'll kill me! do have mercy now."

MISS COOTE.—"You bad woman, will you be a thief again? will you bring your little ones up to be honest in future? what do you think of a good birching, does it make your posteriors feel warm?" cutting blow after blow, with great force and deliberation; the poor woman is in most excruciating pain, and sobs and moans in her distress.

VICTIM, hysterically.—"Oh! Oh! I know I deserve it. Oh! I will never do it again. Oh! Ah—r—re, how terrible, I feel like being burnt with hot irons!" The blood flows freely from the often bruised weals, and the operator varies her blows so as to inflict the greatest possible torture on the poor woman by cutting her round the loins, making long weals over the lower part of her belly, and stinging the front dreadfully, then across the tender thighs, making the tips of the birch go well in between her legs, causing intense agony.

The fig leaves are all cut off and scattered, making the stems which have been interlaced look like an exploded firework as they still hang about her lacerated loins and buttocks; Miss Coote works herself up into a perfect fury of excitement, and cuts away regardless of the victim's apparent exhaustion, upbraiding her continually and making her promise to take her children to church regularly every Sunday in future, and pay particular attention to the seventh commandment, "Thou shalt not steal."

Mrs. White is almost too far gone to hear half of this objurgation, but slightly moans, "Oh! my God, I shall faint. Let me die in mercy. Thou shalt not steal. My God how I am punished," and fairly swoons under the rod, to the great pleasure of Jane and Mademoiselle, who have exquisitely enjoyed the scene.

The victim is released, when the marks on her wrists and ankles almost cut into the flesh by the tightly tied cords fully attest what she must have suffered from her fearfully stretched position, whilst her bottom and thighs and loins are a perfect pickle of weals and bleeding cuts; the drops of blood quite clotted the beautiful hair on her mount and round the red lips of her "Venus' wrinkle."

Jane and Mary and Polly sponge and relieve the poor woman's soreness, as well as they can, and revive her by plenty of cold water and fresh air, &c., and send her home refreshed by a little more champagne.

Next day, as I was walking the garden with my dear Mademoiselle, we asked White how his wife felt after her whipping, and being a blunt illiterate man he gave us young ladies rather an indelicate answer as follows:—

"I'm darned, Miss, I never had such a night before; I was abed and asleep before she got home with the children, but she was so hot she left them to shift for themselves, and mounted me as you often see the cow do to the bull when she wants him to do his duty; she didn't care how tired I was with my day's work, she was off and on all night. I can't understand her being so on heat, for we always leave that to quiet days like Sundays, but she said it was delightful. Darn me, though, if I liked it quite so much. We shall be having twins, or three or four at once after such a tarnation game as that."

I will send another letter soon, but one thing you must excuse in my rough composition; that is my so often speaking of myself in the third person, which makes it easier to tell my tale.

Yours affectionately,
ROSA BELINDA COOTE.

(*To be continued.*)

THE BUDDING ROSE.

(These lines were written to amuse a girl of fifteen. They delighted her mother.)

Wonderful are Cupid's arts!
　　He, the god of soft persuasion,
At his pleasure stirs our hearts,
　　To flames of eager passion.

Long I've loved thee, darling Sarah,
　　Gradually more ripe and blooming;
Daily, hourly, plumper, fairer,
　　In the swelling charms of woman.

Sarah, when I saw you first,
　　In the church, at sister's side;
Oh my heart, with ardour burst!
　　Could I call thee once my bride!

But your father is my foe,
　　Hating me, so long his friend;
Could he once my passion know,
　　In thy misery it might end.

But a bonnet and a fan
　　Are slight tokens of my passion;
Such a girl for such a man
　　Is a fatal strong temptation.

Happy bonnet! that can cover,
　　Such a darling, maiden-head;
Happy fan!—a vigorous lover
　　Should be in your hand instead!

Yesterday you were a child,
　　Now a blooming blushing virgin;
Female passions warm and wild
　　Are to actual pleasure urging.

Mr. B—— was very cruel,
　　"Virtue was at last rewarded,"

He obtained the mossy jewel,
　　Pamela so long had guarded.

Fancy them in bed (and lying,
　　She beneath, and he above;
Kissing, cuddling, fainting, dying,
　　In the ecstasies of love!)

Though he is a horrid sinner,
　　Pamela forgives the crime,
In again! again he's in her!
　　Drinking pleasures quite divine!

See! his amorous lips and hands
　　Fondle all her naked part;
And his upright vigour stands,
　　In her open ravished heart.

Shirt and shift are off together,
　　Naked is the sweet embrace;
Not one part's concealed by either,
　　All's as naked as your face.

Even her modest brother Joseph,
　　Joseph Andrews with his Fanny;
When they once had got their clothes off,
　　Had as little shame as any.

Such, dear Sarah, was the pleasure,
　　Pamela at last enjoyed;
Take them in their fullest measure,
　　Kissing never, never cloyed.

Oh, if I could once behold you,
　　Lying (naked on my bed);
In my arms I would enfold you,
　　I would (take your maidenhead!)

Sarah, live to love and pleasure,
　　Careless what the grave may say;
When each moment is a treasure,
　　Why should lovers waste a day?

Setting suns may rise in glory,
    But, when little life is o'er,
There's an end of all the story,
    We shall live and love no more!

Give me then, ten thousand kisses,
    Give me all thy blooming charms;
Give me heavenly, melting blisses,
    Lying naked in my arms!

A philosophical dandy thus vented his musings upon
Copulation: "The idea is old; the attitude queer; and the
motion fully ridiculous; but all tends to the acme of felicity."

MISSY'S THOUGHTS.

(At a Boys' School.)

I'll tell my mammy when I go home,
The boys won't let my twat alone;
They pull my frock, and beg to see.
What can they want to do with me?

My sister Mary's twice as wild,
For she's fourteen, and I'm a child;
And if they tried to plague her so,
I think what bouncing Moll would do.

But why do the boys all tease me so,
And ask if I have a mouse to show?
They say there's a mouse in Bruce's clothes,
And when he was cuddling me, it rose!

When yesterday, I climbed for pears,
The boys all came to get their shares;
They giggled, and pointed into my slit,
I didn't know they were laughing at it.

The usher pretends to be my friend,
But I don't know where his love will end;
For while he keeps his sober talk,
I catch his fingers under my frock.

They often make me lie down to show
The very inside of my belly below,
I do as they please, because they pay
A shilling among them for the play.

They're not content, though I open wide,
They grope for something or other inside;
You'd think them fools, to see how they kiss,
The smarting hole, by which I piss!

And then they show me all their shames,
And teach me all the nasty names;
I'll tell my mammy when I go home;
The boys won't leave my Cunt alone!

A Brahmin at Madras introduced a relation of his to the
Collector, who asked him whether this man was his brother.
"No," said he, "he is not my brother, but he is one of my
bloody relations."

A sailor on board the Duke of Edinburgh's yacht had a
reputation as an impromptu poet. The following was one of
his efforts before the Duchess:

> He was a bloody sparrow,
> Lived up a bloody spout;
> There came a bloody thunderstorm,
> And washed the bugger out.
>
> But in a bloody minute,
> They stopped the bloody rain;
> So the bloody little sparrow,
> Went up the spout again.

After which, he said: "I don't think much of it myself,
marm, but my mates say it's bloody fine."

LADY POKINGHAM, OR THEY ALL DO IT;

*Giving an Account of her Luxurious Adventures, both before
and after her Marriage with Lord Crim-Con.*

PART III.

(Continued.)

The indisposition of the Duchess was a good excuse for all
the ladies of the family to retire early, and after having dis-
pensed with the lady's-maids, we met in Lady Montairy's
chamber, all attired "*en robes de nuit.*"

Bertha St. Aldegonde was a really splendid woman, a dark
brunette of a fully developed figure, prominent dark flashing
eyes, and a most sensual chin. Victoria Montairy was also a
fine woman, with a very beautiful classic cast of countenance,
whilst the darling Corisande seemed more beautiful than ever,
for want of ornament, in her spotless *chemise de nuit.*

Alice and I both kissed her with rapture, which she lovingly responded to.

"Now, what is the programme?" said Alice to Lady Bertha.

"St. Aldegonde and Montairy are both keeping themselves
in reserve for the grand ceremony of to-morrow," she replied;
"what weak things these men are; as if we wanted to be kept
in reserve. Why Victoria and myself never get enough; the
more we have the more we seem to require, and the less able
they become to satisfy us. Talk about women's rights, they
ought to compel husbands to find substitutes, when they
can't do it for us."

"Well, if you have a pair of good godemiches, Beatrice and
myself will try and satisfy you a little, whilst dear Corisande
shall keep us up to the work with a good rod," said Alice.

The godemiches were brought forth, and proved to be of
monstrous size, to our ideas; they were made of the finest
vulcanized india rubber, beautifully moulded and finished,
with all appendages complete; we strapped them on as soon
as they were charged with a creamy compound of gelatine
and milk. All were stripped to the buff.

Lady Bertha took me on her knee, kissing me lusciously,
and handling the dildoe as if it had been alive. "What a fine
fellow," she laughed, "but not a bit too large to please me."
Meanwhile my fingers were busy, nipping and pinching her

clitoris; she glued her lips to mine and fairly sucked my breath away, excited by my touches which had caused quite an erection of her finely developed clitoris. She drew me on to a couch, and I thrust the affair into her already spending cunny; her bottom responded to every shove, whilst I felt the smarting cuts of the birch, which Corisande was applying alternately to myself and Alice; it was most delicious. I responded with all my ardour to the loving caresses of Lady Bertha, who clasped me firmly by the buttocks, whilst with two fingers of the right hand she frigged both my bottom and cunny at once; Alice and her partner were quite forgotten; I thought I had never experienced anything so delicious in my life. The combination of emotions quite carried me away, the lovely woman bounding under me in rapture, our luscious kisses, the warmth and exquisite titillations of my fundament arrangements seemed such an acme of bliss that when I made the godemiche spend into her my own nature seemed to melt into a sea of lubricity.

After a few moments I entreated her to be the gentleman, and let me have her stiff clitoris, which I was sure could give me great pleasure. "Certainly, dear," she said, "I often do it to Victoria; throw off the dildoe." As quickly as possible we change places, and I begged her first to bring herself forward over my mouth that I might kiss her pussey, and caress that exciting clitoris of hers. It was done at once, and I had a glorious view of the paraphernalia of love. A splendid mount covered with glossy black hair; the serrated vermilion lips of her cunny slightly parted, from which projected quite four inches a stiff fleshy clitoris as big as a man's thumb. I opened the lips with my fingers, passed my tongue lasciviously about the most sensitive parts, took that glorious clitoris in my mouth, rolling my tongue around it, and playfully biting with my teeth; it was too much for her; with a cry of "Oh! Oh! you make me come, darling!" she spent profusely all over my mouth and chin.

She sank down upon me, and I opened my legs to admit her. "Now it's my turn to repay the delicious pleasure I owe you," she sighed, kissing me rapturously, and sucking my tongue into her mouth, so that I could scarcely catch my breath; with her fingers she opened my slit as wide as possible, then directing her clitoris to the passage she seemed to stuff lips and all in, then closed my affair upon it, holding them together tightly with her hand. I can't express to you how novel and delightful this conjunction was to me; we were both so heated and excited, our spendings seemed to mingle together and add to our erotic fury; without separating for a moment she rubbed and pushed about inside of me, the lips and hair of her cunny titillating the sensitive parts in a most thrilling way. We swam in a sea of lubricity, whilst Corisande added to her sister's enjoyment by the stimulating effect of her rod.

At last all was over, and we retired to rest, and did not rise till late next morning. Refreshed by a cold bath we had only just time to breakfast and prepare for our visit to the Academy. We drove to Burlington House, but only stayed half-an-hour, entered the carriage again and were driven to a large house facing the Thames, in Cheyne Walk; it was detached, and stood back in its own grounds.

We were received at the door by a quiet-looking old lady, who was the housekeeper and manager to the Paphian Circle; she ushered us into a large drawing-room, which occupied nearly all the space of the first floor, being supported in the centre by elegant fluted columns of black and gold, and the whole apartment looked like a hall of the veritable Alhambra, the windows closed by gorgeous black and gold curtains, and although it was daylight outside, lighted up by a constellation of wax lights, artistically arranged all round the walls.

The Duke of Brecon was there as a novice, with Bertram and Lord Carisbrooke as sponsors; Lords Montairy and St. Aldegonde, with several other gentlemen and ladies, were also present. Alice and myself were overwhelmed with compliments as being two of the original founders of the society.

Lord St. Aldegonde, as president, now asked Corisande and the Duke if they pledged their words to keep all the secrets of the Paphian Circle, remarking that oaths were quite useless, as he felt sure those who introduced them had every faith in their honourable intentions. Being answered in the affirmative, and having shaken hands with them, he requested all to prepare for dancing, as no one else was expected.

The company retired to the dressing rooms, and in a few minutes we were all back in the drawing-room, everyone in a state of nudity with the exception of silk stockings, garters, and elegant dancing shoes. To prevent jealousy or any undue

preference there was a deep box on a sideboard, where the
refreshments stood; in this box were deposited slips of parch-
ment, each bearing the name of one of the gentlemen
present, and the ladies had each to draw for her partner in
the first waltz, and the pas de deux after it. Corisande drew
Lord Carisbrooke, and my prize was St. Aldegonde.

I must not omit to mention that one of the ladies would
get a slip with "Piano" on it, and the last gentleman had to
turn over the music for her. This fell to Lady Bertha, who
was a brilliant pianist, and at once struck up a well-known
favourite from the Argyll Rooms, and we were instantly in
motion. It was far more exciting than the blindfold romp on
Fred's birthday; she kept us going till one by one, the couples
subsided on the inviting couches, which stood around the
room; my partner was in a brilliant state of erection, but he
whispered to me, "Not yet, Beatrice dear, we must see to
Corisande." Everyone seemed to act without the necessity
of orders; all the couples ranged up in a semi-circle, round
the couch where Carisbrooke was caressing and kissing her,
whilst the beautiful girl, her eyes languishing with love, was
sighing and looking at his fine cock, which she held in her
hand. "Now, love," said the gallant, "as a novice you must
kiss every gentleman's affair, and then we will initiate you
into the mysteries of Venus." Corisande, all blushes, took
each throbbing pego tenderly in her hand, and softly kissed
the velvet heads. "Now, Brecon," said my partner, "you do
the same to the ladies, and that part of the ceremony will be
over."

"With pleasure, on my knees," said the Duke, and we
each presented our cunnies to his lips. Carisbrooke now
gently inclined Corisande backwards, and put a soft pillow
under her bottom, then proceeded to place himself in position, but unable to restrain his excitability, he spent all over
her lovely mossy mount and belly, some of the sperm going
quite up to the alabaster globes which adorned her heaving
bosom.

He blushed with shame and vexation, whilst Corisande was
crimson, and gasping with excited expectation.

Lady Bertha, who was the coolest of the company, at once
wiped all the sperm off her sister's belly with her fingers, with
which she lubricated her crack; then taking hold of His Lord-

ship's affair, directed it properly to the longing gap of love.

"Shove away. Shove, my boy. Heave up your bottom to meet him, dear," she laughed, giving Corisande a good sounding slap on the side of her buttocks with her other hand.

With a furious plunge, the dart of love made its effort just at the right moment. The collision with her hymen was most destructive, the virgin defences gave way as with an awful shriek of pain, she lost all consciousness. He completed the conquest of his victim's virginity, and then lay soaking, and trying to revive her sensibility by his lascivious throbbing inside of her, whilst we applied salts and restoratives to bring her round.

She very speedily came to herself, evidently forgetting the fearful pain of her ravishment; there was a delightful languor in her eyes, as she patted his bottom and hugged him to her bosom. He responded to the gentle challenge, making her revel in all the delights of coition, and never withdrew his blood-stained priapus till they had mutually spent several times.

My partner now led me to a couch, as the others dispersed on the same kind of business. He was still as stiff as ever, and I longed to feel him within me, but, to my surprise, he mounted the reverse way upon me, presenting his bottom to my face and asked me to press my firm bubbies together, so that his cock might spend between them whilst he gama-huched me. It was a luscious position, and I lent all my ardour to second his fancy, and his lascivious tongue made me spend in delight just as his sperm deluged my bosom and belly.

Alice had had Lord Montairy.

After this, the gentlemen's names were replaced in the box, and the ladies made another selection, but in case of anyone drawing the same partner a second time, she had to return the slip and draw another.

Thus we passed a most delicious afternoon, refreshing ourselves from time to time with champagne and ices, or something more substantial, for the worship of Venus and Priapus requires continual stimulating with the most invigorating viands.

In this short sketch of my adventures it would be impossible to describe everything at great length, but I can assure you the ladies fairly exhausted the gentlemen before they allowed themselves to be driven home to dinner.

(To be continued.)

THE OTHER WAY.

Henry lived six gay years in Rome,
    His mistress was a kind Machese.
Her daughter bright in childish bloom,
    Charmed him with pretty loving ways.

Mama encouraged him to take
    The budding virgin's maidenhead,
But this displeased the virtuous rake,
    The girl was soon about to wed.

Mama replied, "Why should you hesitate?
    True it is disapproved by some,
But if you are so very delicate,
    Can't you just fuck her in the bum?"

TWO EXTRAORDINARY LETTERS;
Produced in the Case of the Duchess of Cleaveland, in a Tryal against her husband, Robert Fielding, Esq., in the Arches Court of Canterbury, in the year, 1707.

Dear Wife,—

Puggy's indisposition has made me against my will indebted to my dear wife, for a kind billet she brought me before this she sent me this morning, which I hope will safely kiss her hands, for the contrivance of conveying it is very ingenious. You'd have reason to pity Puggy if you knew all, that is to say, I believe she is in your condition, which news from my dearest wife, if it be confirmed, I fancy I should hardly ever survive the joy and transport, therefore for God's sake, confirm it, as soon as you are sure matters are fixed. I hope you remember the dear, dear day of my having you in my naked arms and seized, possessed myself of all those charming treasures my dear had till then denied me. But then! blest be the memory of so much bliss, then, I say, opened those flood gates of happiness, and sure you must remember that.

> "Like night and heat incorporate we lay,
> We blest the night and cursed the coming day."

Nay, even still, whenever I think of that night's way of passing our time, and how my dear assisted me to get into the inmost closet of her dearest womb; methinks I fucked again with height of pleasure, and fucked and fucked till I dissolved with pleasure; make haste, then, my dearest Nannette, to your husband's arms to-morrow night, as you promised me by Puggy, that we may again repeat those pleasures. And though I believe I made my love a little sore, as I was myself the first time we tryed, yet now matters will be more easy. I am sure the head of your poor playfellow was so swelled by the eagerness of thrusting it into your seat of Paradise, that you took all the skin off the face of it; so pray bring some of the same balsam you carry about you to heal it, as the dear liquor my dear carries about between her legs, which she must promise to open as wide as she can, that my great prick may yet again arrive at the summit of felicity. Adieu.

Your own husband,
FIELDING.

Dear Mary,—

I am glad my dearest wife got safe home, and without being whipped, for I should be very jealous if anyone should peep into Nannette's backside but myself. I assure you when I have got you once more in my arms, I'll so belabour it I'll make it black and blue, and cram it full of my elixir to nourish young Lord Tunbridge. Adieu my soul's life; think of your own,

FIELDING.

To my better-half,
    The Countess of Fielding,
        At Waddon.

FABLES AND MAXIMS.

Translated from the Indian of Shitpot, the great Brahmin Confucius.

THE TWO WOLVES.

"What a nasty smell there is in this den," said one wolf to another; "have you shit yourself?" "No," said the other. "Then," said the first wolf, "I must have done so myself." So he had. The moral of this fable is that though ever ready to spy into the defects of others, we are apt to overlook our own imperfections.

THE DOG AND THE COCK.

"What a large fellow you are!" said the Cock to the Dog. "I can fuck half-a-dozen hens, while you are getting half way in." "Very likely," said the Dog, "but when I am in I stay there fancy; look at my prick compared to yours. I don't call yours fucking at all, it's over before it's well begun." This fable teaches that I like a long prick best.

THE MONKEY AND THE DILDOE.

A pet monkey who had watched his mistress fill her dildoe with cream, waited a chance when she had ceased using it, being called away for a few minutes. "Now," said he, "I will have my fill of cream," so he sucked away, but unfortunately the lady had contracted syphilis, and the monkey

died in convulsions. The moral of this fable is, that you
should never suck dildoes.

The Fox and the Gander.

"You want a good stiff prick up your arse," said the Fox,
when he found he could not catch the Gander. "I've got one;
I always wear it there," said the Gander, chuckling. "Sold
again! Yah! Bloody Fool!" The Fox slunk off abashed.
This shows that the same repartee does not suit everyone.

CUNT ON CO-OPERATIVE PRINCIPLES.

It has been suggested to the Editor of THE PEARL that
there is a great necessity for a club where gentlemen might
get their greens much cheaper and better than at present.

Women are so dear, and at the same time so deceptive in
appearance, that one often pays heavily and yet only gets
a stinking article for his generous outlay.

To obviate this, it is proposed to start a club, where at
least twenty pretty governesses would be engaged at salaries
of £100 per annum; there would be French, English, German, Russian, Italian, and even Zulu and Hottentots, so as
to assimilate to every variety of taste. These ladies would
accommodate the members whenever they might visit the
club, and everything in the shape of dress and generous living
and indulgence would be extended to these houris, to make
them as agreeable as possible, and happy and contented with
their fucktious situations.

Gentlemen members would have to pay a subscription of
£1 per week, wines and refreshments of course being extra,
but supplied at the lowest possible prices compatible with
economy and efficiency.

Gentlemen desirous of submitting their names for admission as members, should do so at once to the Editor, Pearl
Office, Cock Lane, London, E. C., as the number will be
strictly limited to one hundred.

CHARACTERS OF HUSBANDS.

If a husband came home and found his wife being had by another man, what would he do?

That depends on his disposition.

The Polite husband would beg him not to draw until he'd spent.

The Considerate husband would offer soap, towel, and warm water, as soon as he drew.

The Funny husband would cry "Boh!" and tickle his arse with a feather.

The Good-Natured husband would remark that he liked buttered buns.

The Ceremonious husband would wait for an introduction.

The Just husband would sneer at the size of his balls.

The Modest husband would think his balls looked larger than his own.

The Refined husband would pull his shirt over his bottom.

The Cautious husband, with a large family, would ask if he had on a French Letter, and if not, request him to spend outside.

The Jealous husband would be annoyed, although he had on a French Letter.

The Suspicious husband would make his wife wash afterwards.

The Excitable husband would begin to frig himself.

The Shy husband would blush and walk away.

The Avaricious husband would want to charge for it.

The Mean husband would look to see if he'd used his cold cream.

The Epicurean husband would gamahuche his wife immediately afterwards.

The Conscientious husband would fear that he had neglected his wife.

The Cynical husband would be surprised that anyone should care to fuck his wife.

The Prompt husband would be up his arse before he could say, "Jack Robinson."

A poet, whose water taps had been stolen, as well as those of his landlady and another neighbour, affixed the following to a board in his front garden:

My landlady's cock has been stolen away;
As well as my own, and also my neighbour's.
Let us hope in contentment they lay,
Released for a while from their watery labours.

Bad luck to the rascal that cut off our cocks;
Surely one was sufficient his water to pass.
The bugger deserves to be stuck in the stocks,
With a cock in each eye, and the third up his arse.

BEFORE.

Thou heavenly sun whose golden light
Displays the hills with verdure bright;
Sink thee, oh sink thee, in the west,
And bring the hour I love best.
      This evening shall my bosom prove,
      The richest ecstasies of love.

Soon as thy glorious light retires,
I look for her my heart admires;
A matron she of sober grace,
With wisdom printed on her face.
      This evening shall my bosom prove,
      The richest ecstasies of love.

And is my heart then grown so cold,
As to be pleased with matrons old;
When I might feast on younger things,
Ah, no! a lovely girl she brings!
      This evening shall my bosom prove,
      The richest ecstasies of love.

To war her soldier son has hied,
She offers me his blooming bride;
And if the girl my taste should please,
Her husband I advance with ease.
                    This evening shall my bosom prove,
                        The richest ecstasies of love.

She tells me of her daughter's form,
Her swelling bubbies ripe and warm,
Her rosy cheeks, her sapphire eyes,
The jutting fullness of her thighs.
                    This evening shall my bosom prove,
                        The richest ecstasies of love.

Her little mouth, her snowy skin,
The other mouth her smock within;
The more I questioned, more she told,
In thought the darling I behold.
                    This evening shall my bosom prove,
                        The richest ecstasies of love.

The stirring raptures of her tale,
Made beauty over age prevail;
At length, with many a "Fie! for shame!"
She quenched for once my raging flame.
                    This evening shall my bosom prove,
                        The richest ecstasies of love.

And said I that the dame was old,
And thought I that my heart was cold!
Her vigorous limbs are firm and fresh,
And rich she blooms in prime of flesh.
                    This evening shall my bosom prove,
                        The richest ecstasies of love.

And if the daughter brings the gust,
Of youth to aid the mother's lust;
And plays the game as well as she,
She must a perfect angel be.
                    This evening shall my bosom prove,
                        The richest ecstasies of love.

AFTER.

No more; no more; I can no more!
Adieu, ye pair whom I adore,
Adieu my love! one dear, dear kiss,
Thy lord shall reap the good of this!
    And once again, oh let me prove,
    These heavenly ecstasies of love.

CONUNDRUM.

My first expresses, or joy, or woe,
Each passion that touches the soul;
My second's as far as you can throw;
And my whole—you may suck my whole.

My first tells every passion of man's,
Each feeling that moves his soul;
My second supports the pots and pans;
And my whole—you may suck my whole.
       O—range.

NURSERY RHYMES.

There was a young man of Calcutta
 Who thought he would do a smart trick;
So anointed his arsehole with butter,
 And in it inserted his prick.
  It was not for greed after gold;
  It was not for thirst after pelf;
  'Twas simply because he'd been told,
  To bloody well bugger himself.

There was a young lass of Dalkeith,
 Who frigged a young man with her teeth;

She complained that he stunk;
Not so much from the spunk;
But his arsehole was just underneath.

There was a young Jew of Torbay,
Who buggered his father one day;
    Said he, "I'd much rather,
    Thus bugger my father,
Because there is nothing to pay."

There was a gay parson of Norton,
Whose prick, although thick, was a short 'un;
    To make up for this loss,
    He had balls like a horse,
And never spent less than a quartern.

There was a young man of the Tweed,
Who sucked his wife's arse thro' a reed;
    When she had diarrhoea,
    He'd let none come near,
For fear they should poach on his feed.

There was an old man of Balbriggan,
Who cunt juice was frequently swigging;
    But even to this,
    He preferred tom-cat's piss,
Which he kept a pox'd nigger to frig in.

A cabman who drove in Biarritz,
Once frightened a fare into fits;
    When reprov'd for a fart,
    He said, "God bless my heart,
When I break wind I usually shits."

A young woman got married at Chester,
Her mother she kissed and she blessed her.
    Says she, "You're in luck,
    He's a stunning good fuck,
For I've had himself myself down in Leicester."

THE PEARL,

A Journal of Facetiæ and Voluptuous Reading.

| No. 7 | PUBLISHED MONTHLY. | Jan., 1880 |

SUB-UMBRA, OR SPORT AMONG THE SHE-NOODLES.

(Continued.)

In the morning, papa and mama had scarcely slept off the effects of the sleeping dose they had imbibed from the brandy flask of their dutiful son, and lay abed very late, in fact, almost to luncheon time; meanwhile, we, the younger members of the family, had privately agreed upon a plan of amusement for the afternoon and evening.

Finding that two pretty young girls of fourteen and fifteen were living close by, with an invalid mother, whilst their brother was away, being a Midshipman in the Royal Navy, I proposed that Annie should send the Misses Bruce an invitation to spend the afternoon with us, en famille, without the least ceremony, and join us in an alfresco tea party at a little hut in the woods, which formed part of my uncle's estate.

At luncheon we informed the governor of what we had done and hoped that both he and mama would join in our outdoor party in the woods.

"No thank you, my dears, we are too much afraid of the damp grass and rheumatics. Besides, we have not yet gotten over the fatigue of yesterday. We will stay quietly at home and hope you may enjoy yourselves thoroughly, as we should do if we were younger," replied the jolly, kind-hearted old gentleman.

This was exactly what we had wished for and expected; so Frank and Annie at once sent off the servants with every requisite for our open-air tea party.

About three o'clock, the two young ladies arrived, and as all were ready, we at once set off for the scene of our anticipated fun, which was a rough bower covered with flowering honeysuckle and clematis, at the end of a long, shady, private walk, more than half-a-mile from the house.

Frank and myself particularly attached ourselves to the two fresh young ladies as being the greatest strangers, and therefore justly expectant of the most attention.

Emily Bruce, the eldest, was a charming dark-eyed brunette, her rather large mouth having a fascinating effect as you regarded her. In fact, such a display of pearly white teeth, I never saw before, and the very thought that they might perhaps be soon employed in love bites on my tenderheaded prick filled me with maddening lust to possess myself of their owner.

Nor was her sister, Louisa, a bit less prepossessing, she being almost the counterpart of Emily, except that one could easily see there was a slight difference in age.

Arrived at the bower, the servants were at once sent home, being told that they could clear away the things next morning, as it would be too late for them to return in the evening, and at the same time, without asking the consent of her young friends, dear Annie scribbled a pencil note to their mama, to say that if they at all were late, she would insist upon them staying with her all night, and not to make herself at all anxious on their behalf—this was quietly sent off by one of the servants.

As soon as we were alone, Frank and I, uncorking the champagne, lighted our cigars, and saying that the sun was still too warm for outdoor romping, pressed the girls to try some very mild cigarettes of Turkish tobacco.

At last Annie and Rosa set the example by lighting up, and were at once laughingly followed by the others. Our two young friends protested they never took wine. Still, they evidently sipped it with great delight, and we bantered them upon being so tied to their mother's apron strings, etc., till they began to be quite free as my cousins and Rosa.

We had a good stock of fizz, besides sandwiches and cake, so that no one seemed at all anxious to take the trouble of tea-making.

Still we were careful that only enough should be taken to warm our friends up to a slightly excitable state, in fact, just to induce that state of all-overishness, which tingles through a young girl's sensitive frame when she feels the first vibrations of amorous desires, which she can as yet hardly understand.

Their sparkling eyes, slightly flushed faces and above all, the dazzling beauties of their teeth, as they indulged in gay laughter at our badinage, set all of us aflame. I could see that Rosa and my cousins were longing to help in enjoying these innocent and ravishing young girls.

Now a game of hunt the slipper was proposed, and we at once joined to the soft, mossy green sward, outside the bower. This was a most delicious and excitable romp.

Whenever it came our turns, Frank and myself indulged in all kinds of quick and startling touches, which made the two little dears blush up to their eyes at first, and when we managed to catch one of them with the slipper we claimed a hearty kiss as penalty, which they submitted to with tolerable grace, yet evidently in a state of great excitement, it was all so new to them. We finished the game, had a little more champagne, then proposed a game of hide and seek in the wood, with the reservation that no one was to go too far off.

We were to be in pairs, I chose Emily, and Frank took Louisa. Polly and Sophie went together, whilst Annie and Rosa had to search for us when we called out.

It so happened that there was an old sand pit close by, in which several years before Master Frank had amused himself by making a Robinson Crusoe's cave, and planted bushes in front of it, so that the entrance was perfectly out of sight, and no one would fancy anyone could be screened by the small amount of cover which seemed to grow on the side of the pit; this was just the place for our purpose, and it had been beforehand arranged that we were not to be found for a long time. Gliding into the cave Frank let fall the old curtain that hung at the entrance, and we were at once in the dark, the place was large enough for us all to sit together on a heap of fine soft sand at the further end.

"What a dear girl you are!" I whispered in Emily's ear, as I took a kiss in the dark, and drew her trembling body quite close by an arm around her waist. "Pray don't," she whispered in return, "if you do not keep quiet I won't stop in this dark place."

"Don't say so, it would be cruel, especially if you knew all I feel towards you, Emily dear. I must call you Emily, yes, and kiss you again and again; I love you so, your breath is so fragrant, what are you afraid of, there's nothing to fear among friends, darling," I whispered, kissing my partner rapturously.

"Oh, ah, you take my breath away Walter, I'm so unused to such goings on. Oh, fie, sir, for shame, you make me feel all of a tremble, you take such liberties!" as I was working one hand inside the bosom of her dress, and getting possession of two hard round bubbies which throbbed with emotion under my loving caresses.

"It's all love, darling, and no one can see, can't you hear how Frank and Louisa are kissing; is it not delicious to think they are doing the same, and will be sure to keep our secret?"

A deep sigh was my only answer, and again our lips met in a long luscious kiss. My tongue was thrust into her mouth, and tickled the tip of her own velvety organ of speech. I could feel the nipples of her virgin bosom stick out as stiff as little cocks and whispered to her to allow me to kiss them.

"I can refuse you nothing," she whispered; "you are such a bold lover. I'm all in flame from head to foot at the numberless liberties you are taking with me. Ah, if mama only knew," she sighed, as I was now sucking her titties, and running my disengaged hand up her thighs; they were nipped tightly together, but gradually relaxed under the gentle pressure of my hand, till I actually got possession of her cunny, which I could feel was slightly covered with soft downy hair, and soon began to frig her gently with my forefinger. How the dear girl wriggled under this double excitement, and I could feel one of her hands groping outside my trousers over my bursting prick to return the pleasure I was giving her. One by one she unfastened the buttons, then her soft delicate hand soon had possession of my stiff affair, naked and palpitating with unsatisfied desire.

"Ah," she whispered, "I am satisfied at last! we had a servant at home, a few months ago, who slept in our room, and used to tickle and play with us so. She told us that men had a long thing as hard as iron, which they pleased the ladies by shoving up their bellies, and that was how the babies were made. Do you believe it? She was always shoving her fingers into us as you are doing to me now, and—and—and," here she hesitated and seemed to shudder with delight, just as I spent all over her hand, and I could also feel her spendings come in a warm gush over my fingers. It was deli-

cious. Her hand first held tight the top of my throbbing
prick, then gently worked up and down the shaft, lubricated
by my spendings. It was indeed a voluptuous treat; I begged
her to thrust her tongue into my mouth, and we continued
the mutual frigging till she almost fainted away in her
ecstasy.

Slightly recovering, I asked her what it was she was going
to tell me about the maid servant, when she hesitated.

"Do, dearest, tell me everything," I implored, in a loving
whisper. "We are now without reserve to each other; you can
have no secrets from your loving Walter."

"It was so funny, I don't know how she could do it, but
Mary was so fond of sucking and kissing us where you have
your hand, dearest," she replied, "but it was so nice you can't
imagine how we enjoyed having her do it to us."

"My love, my Emily, let me kiss you now, and it would
be sublime if you would kiss me. I long to feel the love bites
of your beautiful teeth in my Cupid's Dart. Frank and Louisa
are too busy to notice what we do," I whispered in her ear,
as I inclined the willing girl backwards on the soft pillow of
sand, and reversing my position, we laid at full length, side
by side, both of us eager as possible for the game; my head
was buried between her loving thighs, with which she pressed
me most amorously, as my tongue was inserted in her loving
slit; this was a fine gamahuche. I stirred up all the lasciviousness of her ardent temperament till she screamed with delight, and caused Frank and Louisa to enquire what we were
doing, but we made no reply. She sucked my delighted prick,
handled and kissed my balls, till I spent in her mouth, as her
teeth were lovingly biting the head of my penis. She sucked
it all down, whilst I repaid her loving attentions to the best
of my ability with my own active tongue.

As soon as it was over, I took Emily by the hand, and we
groped towards our companions, who, I found, were equally
busy as we had been. Frank thoroughly understood my intention; we all got together, and joined in a grope of cocks
and cunnies without the least restraint, till suddenly the curtain was pulled down, and we heard the laughing voices of
Rosa and Annie, as they exclaimed, "See, here they are.
What are these rude boys doing to you young ladies?"

Emily and Louisa were covered with confusion, but the
girls lovingly assured them they would keep the secret, and

introduce them to more fun after they had retired to bed, as
it was now getting late, and we must all return to the house.

As I have before observed, the wing of the mansion in
which we all slept was quite apart from the other wing in
which papa, mama, and the servants were located, so as soon
as we had retired, Frank and myself joined the girls in their
room, or rather rooms, for they occupied two. The Miss
Bruces blushed crimson at seeing us only in our shirts,
especially as one was seated on the pot de chambre, whilst
the other was exhibiting her charms to my inquisitive cousins
before a cheval glass.

"All right," exclaimed Annie, "my dears, everything is free
between us and the boys, but we mean to punish you for
allowing the impudent fellows to presume upon such liberties
with you in the cave. Your bottoms shall smart, young ladies,
I can assure you," as she produced a couple of light birch
rods from a drawer; in fact, I had provided them for her, the
idea having been suggested to me by reading a book called
The Romance of Lust.

A fine large bed stood by the wall, facing another at the
end of the room, but our programme only required one
couch. Annie and Rosa were determined to have their enjoyment now; everyone was ordered to strip off shirt or chemise,
then I horsed Emily on my back whilst Frank did the same
by her sister.

Sophie and Polly were entrusted with the rods, and gaily
switched us and our riders' bottoms as we trotted round the
room, the sisters hardly knowing whether to laugh or cry,
when a more stinging cut than usual made them cry for
mercy; our pricks were as rampant as possible, and we were
not in need of any extra stimulation; still the girls were very
hard on our rumps, although not quite so severe with the
sisters. The darling Emily had so twined her legs round me
as I held them close under my armpits that her pretty feet
in their bewitching little slippers were frigging my cock between them most deliciously.

The sight of our red smarting bottoms and bursting pricks
was too much for Annie and Rosa, and they were inflamed
by lust, so throwing themselves backward on the bed, with
their legs wide open and feet resting on the floor, the two
dear girls presented their quims to our charge, as with both
hands they held open the lips of their delicious cunts, invit-

ing our eager cocks to come on. We charged them at once,
under the impulsive urging of the rods, gave a few delightful
fucking motions, then withdrew and trotted round the room
again, this we constantly repeated to prolong our enjoyment,
till at last the dear girls could stand it no longer, their arms
clasped us firmly, whilst the rods cut away with extra force to
make us complete their pleasure; it was a most luxurious
finish, we all spent with screams of delight, and lay for a few
moments in a delicious state of lethargic exhaustion till we
awoke to find Sophie, Polly, Emily, and Louisa all rolling on
the floor in the delights of gamahuching.

After this the two dear girls begged, with tears in their
eyes, that Frank and Walter would make women of them, so
that they might really taste the wildest delights of love.

"Then, dears," said Rosa, with a sly laugh, "you must kiss
them, and make their exhausted cocks stiff again, and then
we will lend the two boys to you."

We sat on the bed by the side of our late fucking partners,
who we kissed, fondled and frigged, whilst Emily and Louisa,
kneeling between our knees, sucked our pricks up to standing
point, as their hands drew back our foreskins or played with
our balls.

Stiff and rampant as we were we entreated them to go on
for a little longer, till feeling ourselves almost at spending
point, Polly and Sophie arranged two bolsters and some pillows on the floor in the most advantageous manner, the sisters
were each placed with two pillows under their bottoms, whilst
their heads rested on the bolsters. Annie and Rosa then
conducted us to the victims, who impatiently awaited their
immolation to the god of love with open legs and longing
cunts. The two mistresses of the ceremonies took our pricks
in hand, and directed them to the path of bliss. Emily was
my partner again; she threw her legs over my back and
heaved up to meet the fatal thrust which was to be the
death of her troublesome virginity. I had no time to see how
the others progressed, but heard a smothered shriek of agony
from Louisa, as no doubt Frank achieved her fate for her;
my partner was more courageous, she glued her lips to mine,
sucking in my tongue in the most ardent manner imaginable,
even whilst my prick was tearing through her hymen; my
spending deluged her wounded quim, and we soon lost all
thoughts of pain when we recommenced a lovely fuck, mov-

ing slowly at first, till her rapid motions spurred me on to faster plunges, her deliciously tight cunt holding me like a hand, in fact so tight that I could feel my foreskin drawn backwards and forwards at every shove.

"Ah! you dear fellow, push on, kill me with delight!" she screamed in ecstasy, as we came again together, and I was equally profuse in my words of endearment.

As we lay still after it was over her tight-fitting cunt seemed to hold and continually squeeze my delighted prick so by its contractions and throbbings that I was ready again directly, and we ran another thrilling course before she would let me try to withdraw.

Frank and Louisa had been equally delighted with each other, and thus the two sisters each lost her maidenhead almost at the same moment.

(To be continued.)

A COPY OF A LETTER.

Was given mee by my cozen SC of Kempston, and written in a Tarpaulin style.

Madame,—

Premising you are safe returned to Towne, I made bold to acquaint you that Mr. F— is lately arriv'd att ye haven of Matrimony; He had been long in ye middle state of Purgatory between ye Church & ye Ladyes Chamber; ere she with ye advice of her mother, & some other experienced Ladyes, was lanced forth into ye marriage bed. The Vessell had been 14 years & three months on Building, that it is thought she will care well under Sail. It is a fine smooth ship, I will promise you, & one of ye first-rate; and likely to doe ye King good Service if ably & well man'd. The only fault there is (if any) she is too narrow in ye Poope. She hath a fine shroud, & all difficulty soone vanish'd saving only ye maine yard may prove too burly for the midle Deck. The Capt. it is thought this night will goe on board or her; hee is bound for ye Straites Mouth, and cannot come off without bloodshed: Nay worse; 'tis fear'd if opposition be made, hee may be forced to spend his provision in ye channell, & soe returne without doeing ye Kingdome a penny worth of service.

ODE.

By the Rev. Mr. Bray, on the Death of his favourite Donkey.

> How well do I remember yet
> How very proud I used to get
> When, like a little king, I'd sit,
>   Upon my Ass!

> When seated in his nice warm back
> My tiny, little whip I'd crack,
> And with my youthful hand I'd smack
>   My Ass!

> And when we galloped o'er the lea
> I shouted with delight and glee,
> For all the girls came out to see
>   My Ass!

> With him my frugal meals I'd share
> And nurture him with greatest care,
> And dally with the long, soft hair
>   Upon my Ass!

> In meadows green he'd love to play
> And, when tired out, at close of day,
> You then, of sweet delicious hay,
>   Could smell my Ass!

> And when through dirty lanes we'd scud
> And get bespattered o'er with mud,
> I'd get some water when I could,
>   And wash my Ass!

But someone served him such a trick—
At first they hit him with a stick,
And then with heavy boots did kick
                    My Ass!

One day he got beyond my reach,
Into a pond. I gave a screech,
For a blood-thirsty, hungry leech
                    Did suck my Ass!

And oh! his fate I do bewail,
He backed one day against a rail,
And a long, pointed, rusty nail
                    Stuck in my Ass!

Alas his end I soon did see;
A woodman cutting down a tree,
Did slip, and, barely missing me,
                    Did axe my Ass!

I saw him die, I watched the gore
Run from the wound as home they bore
My dearest friend—my wounded, sore,
                    And bloody Ass!

My grief for him was most sincere,
The pain was more than I could bear,
So now, kind friend, come shed a tear
                    Upon my Ass!

Perhaps this epitaph is odd—
"A better donkey never trod,
Here lies beneath this friendly sod,
                    My Ass!"

THE SWING.

How oft I've sworn to Caroline,
    The world no sight can show,

To match her locks, her lips divine,
  Her bosom's hills of snow.

But oh! I find myself forsworn,
  Two lips I have beheld;
Still lovelier, on this happy morn,
  A mount that those excell'd!

For chance has shewn me all that lies
  Beneath her virgin zone;
Sure never seen by any eyes
  Of man, save mine alone!

As o'er my face the swing I drove,
  As wider flew her thighs;
The opening heaven itself o' love
  Met my delighted eyes!

Her bosom boasts no swell so fair
  No tints that these eclipse;
Her head has no such auburn hair,
  Nor such enchanting lips!

Yes I've beheld the mossy mount,
  Where all the graces centre;
I've seen the rosy, nectar'd fount,
  Where he she loves shall enter!

While from within her petticoat,
  A warm and savoury breeze,
Full in my face, would sweetly float,
  Loaded with ecstasies!

Then be not wrath my matchless maid,
  Nor blush so deep with shame;
Nor I attack'd nor you betray'd,
  Let chance then bear the blame!

Oh pardon me, and I'll confess,
  That henceforth when I gaze
Upon the beauties of thy face,
  My fancy elsewhere strays!

Then if a reddy conscious blush,
  Thy angel forehead warms;
Upon our souls the hour shall rush,
  That shew'd thy inmost charms.

When John Scott was minister of Dundee, he reproved
Alick Anderson for ill-treating his wife; Alick tried to justify
his conduct, but the minister observed, "Ou Alick mon, there
must be something wrong on both sides!" "True very true,"
cried Alick, "she has neither bubbies nor buttocks!"

There was a young lady of Harwich,
  Who said on the morn of her marriage:
    "I shall sew my chemise,
    Right down to my knees,
  For I'm damned if I fuck in the carriage!"

MISS COOTE'S CONFESSION,

Or the Voluptuous Experiences of an Old Maid;
In a series of Letters to a Lady Friend.

Letter VII.

My dear Nellie,—

In my last letter you had an account of some pretty everyday larceny, but in this you will read about a pretty young
lady who was also a thief by nature, not from any necessity;
in fact, it was a case of what they call in these degenerate days
Kleptomania; no wonder when downright thieving is called by
such an outlandish name that milk-and-water people have
almost succeeded in abolishing the good old institution of the
rod.

Miss Selina Richards was a cousin of Laura Sandon, my old
schoolfellow and first bedfellow at Miss Flaybum's; bye-the-
bye, can you explain or did you ever understand how girls can
be *fellows*, but I know of no other term which will apply to

the relationship in question. Is there no feminine to that word? It certainly is a defect of the English language.

Well, being on a visit to Laura when I was about eighteen, she mentioned the case to me, saying that her cousin Selina was such an inveterate thief her family were positively afraid to let her go anywhere from home for fear she should get into trouble, and that her parents were obliged to confine her to her room when they had visitors in the house, as the young thief would secrete any trifles, more especially jewelry, she could lay her hands upon, "and you know, Rosa, what an awful disgrace it would be to all the family if she should ever be accused of such a thing."

ROSA.—"But have they never punished her properly, to try and eradicate the vice?"

LAURA.—"They confine her to her room, and often keep the child on bread and water for a week, but all the starving and lecturing in the world won't do any good."

ROSA.—"Have they never tried a good whipping?"

LAURA.—"It never seems to have entered the stupid heads of her father and mother; they are too tender-hearted for anything of that kind."

ROSA.—"Laura, dear, I don't mind confessing to you I should dearly love to birch the little voleuse; ever since I left school our last grand séance at the breaking-up party has quite fascinated me—when I think over the beautiful sight of the red bleeding posteriors, the blushes of shame and indignation of the victims, and above all the enjoyment of their distress at being so humiliated and disgraced before others. We often enjoy our old schoolbirchings in private, and a little while ago I administered an awful whipping to our gardener's wife and her two little girls for stealing my fruit, etc., and effected quite a cure, they are strictly honest now. You are coming to see us soon, can't you persuade your uncle and aunt to entrust Selina to your care, with the promise that I am to be thoroughly informed of her evil propensity; on second thoughts I think you should say you have told me, and that I offer to try and cure the girl, if they will only give me a carte blanche to punish her in my own way. You will have a great treat, we shall shock the girl's modesty by stripping and exposing her, you will see how delightful the sight of her pretty form is added to the distressing sense of humiliation we will make her feel; the real lovers of the birch watch and enjoy all the expressions of the victim's face, and do all they can to increase the sense of degradation, as well as to inflict terrible and prolonged torture by skilful appliance of the rod, and placing the victim in most painful, distended positions to receive her chastisement."

LAURA.—"What an ogress of cruelty you have become Rosa!"

ROSA, kissing her.—"So will you my dear, with a little more experience, you are much older than me, but really younger in that respect; by judicious use of the rod a club of ladies could enjoy every sensual feeling of pleasure without the society of men. I mean to marry the birch (in fact I am already wedded to it), and retain my fortune as my independence."

LAURA.—"What a paragon of virtue, do I really understand you pander to your sensuality without intercourse with men?"

ROSA.—"Come and see, that is my only answer to such a dear sceptic, only manage to bring the pretty voleuse with you, and you will have every reason to be satisfied with your visit."

Laura was quite successful in her application to the parents of Selina; they thought the visit might perhaps result in some good to their daughter, and readily gave all the required assurances as to liberty of inflicting punishment for any little dishonesty we might detect.

On their arrival at our house Selina was alloted a small room to herself, whilst Laura asked and was allowed to be my bedfellow again. Nothing was put out of the way, as I was so thoroughly assured of the honesty of all about me, and felt certain that if Miss Selina did steal anything, she could only secrete it and would have no opportunity to dispose of the plunder, so we might be sure to recover all our lost property.

Miss Richards had received a very careful education, and, in general, was a most interesting young lady, and apparently very modest and retiring.

Several days passed very pleasantly, and it almost seemed as if Missie's fingers had forgot their cunning. I was just beginning to fear we might lose our victim for want of a fair opportunity, but it turned out to be only a kind of natural shyness, which would disappear when she found herself quite at home.

Things began to vanish, my jewelry seemed much preferred, first a small diamond ring, then an opal brooch set with pearls, gloves, scarfs, and any small articles walked off mysteriously, but no one could ever detect her even setting her foot in my room in the day time, and so Laura and I determined to watch at night. We usually went into Selina's room the last thing before retiring ourselves, when her eyes were invariably closed.

Our resolve was put in practice the first night, and about two hours after we were supposed to be safely asleep, the creaking hinge of the door gave us a slight admonition of the stealthy approach of someone.

We could hear no footstep, but caught a glimpse of Miss Prig putting her head just inside the door to see all was right.

We were motionless, our heads being well within the shade of the bed curtains, whilst a dim moonlight partially lighted up the rest of the chamber. The little voleuse, as stealthily as a Red Indian, actually crawled on her hands and knees to the dressing table, and then without raising her body, groped with her hand on the top of the table for anything that might be lying about; in fact, we could see nothing of her as we were in bed, but could plainly hear the slight movement of the articles as they were touched or moved.

Off went the bedclothes, with a cry, "Now we have her safe, the sly thief." I sprang to the door and cut off her retreat, whilst Laura acted the policeman, by sternly arresting the confused prisoner.

Turning the key in the lock, we at once laid her over the foot of our bed, with her feet resting on the floor, and turning up her nightdress, administered with our hands a good slapping till she fairly screamed for mercy.

"Oh! Oh! Pray, Miss Coote, forgive me. Let me go, I won't come here again. Oh! Ah—r—r—re! Indeed I won't," struggling and writhing under our smarting slaps. We could see even by the faint light how red her bottom was, and at last we released her with the assurance of a full enquiry next day, and advised her to give up all she had stolen or it would be worse for her.

By my orders, she was confined to her room in the morning, and Jane acted as gaoler. After dinner, about six o'clock, she brought the prisoner before me in the punishment room.

To make my proceedings more impressive, all the establishment were present, except Charlie the page, who being masculine, I did not think it would be decent to have him admitted.

Miss Coote.—"Selina Richards, you stand before me a convicted thief caught in the act. Have you restored all your booty, you sly young cat?"

Selina (with a crimson face and downcast eyes).—"Oh! Oh! I have indeed, ask Jane, she has searched the room and can't find any more but what I gave up to her. Ah! Miss Coote, I don't know how I could have done it; I'm so ashamed of myself and sorry to have been so wicked. Oh! Oh! What shall I do?" quite overcome and bursting into tears.

Jane.—"If you please Miss, I've got everything but your ring, that I can't find anywhere."

Miss Coote.—"You bad girl, I know your character; don't think you can deceive me by your feigned tears and repentance. What have you done with my ring, eh?"

Selina (appealing in great and apparently genuine distress and consternation).—"Oh! I have never seen it. Indeed, I didn't take that, Miss Coote. Ah, you must believe me, I am so degraded to feel how guilty I am. I had the brooch, but have given that and everything else up to Jane."

Miss Coote.—"I don't believe what you say about the ring, and will birch you well till you really confess the truth. Now strip the little thief, and examine every article of clothing as it is taken off. Shake out all the braids of her hair, she may have it there."

Notwithstanding her confusion, I noticed a slight gleam of satisfaction pass across her countenance, for which, at the time, I was puzzled to account.

They proceeded with the undressing, and I could not help noticing her continued satisfaction as each garment was overhauled, as much as to say, "You haven't found it yet," which convinced me she had the ring very cunningly secreted somewhere, but for the life of me, I was quite at a loss to think how she could have disposed of it, as Jane assured me there was not a chink in her room where it could possibly be put, she had even ripped up the bed in her search.

At last they let down all the braids of her hair, and she stood in her chemise, blushing crimson at the exposure, her usually damask cheeks as rosy as ripe cherries. She evidently now considered the search at an end, as she kicked off the drawers and protested against my order to "remove the last rag."

"Oh! Oh! Pray don't expose me, there can't be anything in that."

Miss Coote.—"But there may be somewhere else."

The suddenly abashed look that came over her face convinced me I was now getting near a discovery. Her legs were closely nipped together, and she covered her hairless mount with her hands.

Miss Coote.—"Give me a birch Jane, I'll make her jump," then taking the switch in hand cuts smartly over Miss Selina's knuckles, "remove your hands, Miss Prig, now jump will you," repeating the blow on the naked bottom with such effect that the poor girl screamed with pain, but still kept her legs close; again the rod descended with a terrific undercut, "won't you open your legs and jump Miss." This time it was effective; with a fearful scream the victim threw herself down on the carpet, but she was unable to prevent the escape of the ring which rolled out on the floor.

It would be impossible to describe the poor girl's distress and confusion now her guilt was so thoroughly established; she was crimson all over, and tried to hide her face in her hands as she cried for shame; her bottom had some fine looking red marks, and also in between her thighs, which the last cut had inflicted.—

Miss Coote.—"Look at the little thief, she thinks to hide herself by covering her face, she doesn't care about exposing all her private parts, or using them to hide my ring, what a disgustingly clever trick; Jane, put on her chemise and drawers; if she does not care I do, and like to do birching decently with all propriety."

Jane and Polly lift her up, and put on the required articles, then as she stands before me still sobbing with shame and pain, I had never seen a more delicious looking victim; she had such a beautiful brunette complexion, her almost black hair hanging all down her back to her loins, pretty white rounded globes with dark brown nipples looked impudently above her chemisette, which only reached a little way down her thighs; it was tastefully trimmed with lace all round, and seemed to draw attention to her beautiful thighs and legs, the latter set off by blue silk stockings with handsome garters and lovely boots.

Jane whispers in the culprit's ears, and Selina humbly kneels before me, saying in broken accents:—

"Oh! how can I speak to you, dear Miss Coote. I—I—have so disgraced—myself. Will—will—you ever forgive me. Oh! What shall I do—will you punish me properly and cut—the —the—awful propensity out of me—indeed, dear Miss Coote —I can't help myself—my fingers—my fingers will take the things—even—when I don't—wan't them," as she kisses the rod and bursts into a torrent of hysterical tears.

By my orders the victim is well stretched out on the ladder, as I generally preferred it to the whipping post, and having armed myself with a very light rod made of fine pieces of whale-bone, which would sting awfully without doing serious damage, I went up to the ladder for a commencement, but first made them loosen her a bit, and place a thick sofa bolster under her loins, then fasten her tightly again with her bottom well presented, the drawers pinned back on each side, and her chemise rolled up and secured under her arms; poor Selina seemed to know well enough what was coming, it checked her tears, but she begged and screamed piteously for me to forgive and wait and see if she ever stole anything again.

MISS COOTE, laughing.—"Why what a little coward you are. I should have thought such a bold thief would have more spirit, and I have hardly touched you yet; you won't be hurt more than you can fairly bear; you would do it again directly if I don't beat it out of you now."

SELINA.—"My arms and limbs are so dreadfully stretched, and my poor behind still smarts from the three whacks you gave. Oh! Have pity! Have mercy! Dear Miss Coote."

MISS COOTE.—"I must not listen to such childish non-sense, you're both a thief and a dreadful liar, Miss Selina, will you—will you—do it again," giving three smart stinging cuts, the whalebone fairly hissing through the air as she flourishes it before each stroke to make it sound more effective.

SELINA.—"Ah! Ah! Ah—r—r—re! I can't bear it, you're thrashing me with wires, the blows are red hot. Oh! Oh! I'll never, never do it again!" her bottom finely streaked already with thin red lines, the painful agony being greatly increased by the strain on her wrists and ankles as she cannot restrain her writhing at each cut.

MISS COOTE.—"You don't seem to like it, Selina, but indeed it's for your good, how would you like to be branded B. C. with a really red hot iron, you'd sing a still different tune then; but I'm wasting my time—there—there—there —you've only had six yet, how you do howl you silly girl!"

SELINA.—"Ah—r—r—r—re!" with a prolonged shriek. "You're killing me. Oh! I shall soon die!" her bottom redder than ever.

MISS COOTE.—"You'll have a dozen whalebone cuts," counting and cutting deliberately till she calls twelve, then giving a little pause as if finished; she lets the victim compose the features with a sigh of relief, and just then gives another thundering whack, exclaiming, "Ah! Ha! Ha! Ha! you thought I had done, did you, Miss Prig; it was a baker's dozen you were to get, I always give thirteen as twelve for fear of having missed one, and like to give the last just as they think it is all over."

SELINA.—"I know it's well deserved, but oh! so cruel, you will let me go now; pray forgive me, indeed, you may depend upon me in the future," still sighing and quivering from the effects of the last blow.

MISS COOTE.—"You're not to get off so easily, Miss Prig, your bottom would be all right in a few minutes, and then you would only laugh when you think of it. The real rod is to come, look at this bum-tickler, it's the real birch grown in my own grounds, and well pickled in brine these last two days, to be ready for you when caught. It will bring your crime to mind in a more awful light, and leave marks to make you remember it for days to come."

SELINA.—"Pray let me have a drink, if I must suffer so much more, my tongue is as dry as a board, Miss Coote, you are cruel, I am not old enough to bear such torture."

MISS COOTE.—"Be quiet, you shall have a drink of champagne, but don't talk about your tender age, that makes your crime still worse, for you have shown such precocious disgusting cunning, far beyond your years."

She has the refreshing draught and the rod resumes its sway.

MISS COOTE.—"You bad girl, your bottom shall be marked for many a day; I'll wager you don't steal as long as the marks remain. Two dozen's the punishment, and then we'll see to your bruises, and put you to bed. One—two—three—four," increasing the force of the blows scientifically with each cut, and soon beginning to draw the skin up into big bursting blood-red weals.

VICTIM.—"Mother! Mother! Ah! Ah—r—r—re! I shall die. Oh! kill me quickly, if you won't have mercy." She writhes in such agony that her muscles stand out like whip-cord, and by their continued quivering, straining action, testify to the intensity of her pain.

MISS COOTE, laughing and getting excited.—"That's right, call your mother, she'll soon help you. Ha! Ha! She didn't think how I should cure you, when your papa gave his consent for me to punish you as I like. Five, six, seven," she goes on counting and thrashing the poor girl over the back, ribs, loins, and thighs, wealing her everywhere, as well as on the posteriors. All the spectators are greatly moved, and seem to enjoy the sight of Selina's blood dripping down, down till her stockings are saturated and it forms little pools beneath her on the floor.

The victim has not sufficient strength to stand this very long, her head droops, and she is too weak to scream, moaning and sighing fainter and fainter, till at last she fairly swoons, and the rod is stopped at the twenty-second stroke.

Miss Coote is quite exhausted with her exertions, and sinking on a sofa, fondly embraces her friend Laura, describing to her all the thrilling sensations she has enjoyed during the operation, which the flushed cheeks and sparkling soft large blue eyes of Laura show she is beginning to duly appreciate.

Mademoiselle Fosse and the servants lay Selina on the floor, and sprinkle her face with water, whilst one of them uses a very large fan most effectively; her lacerated bottom is sponged with strong salt and water, and she soon shows signs of regaining animation. Sighing and sobbing, "Where, where am I? Oh! I remember, Miss Coote's cut my bottom off. Oh! Oh! Ah! How it smarts and burns!" They pour a little liqueur down her throat, and she is soon quite conscious again, and cries quite hysterically over her pickled state.

MADEMOISELLE.—"Now for the finishing touch. Mary, fetch that pot from the kitchen, and bring the bag of feathers."

SELINA (piteously).—"Oh, haven't you done yet? What have I to suffer?" wringing her hands in apprehension.

MADEMOISELLE.—"Here it is. We won't keep you in suspense," taking the brush from a pot of warm tar, held by Mary. "This will heal your bruises, and prevent the flies getting at your sore bottom, this warm weather."

They make her stand up, and Mademoiselle paints all over her posteriors, and the lower part of her belly inside her thighs, and even the crack of her bottom, with the hot stuff, regardless of the great pain she is inflicting.

SELINA (shrieking in fearful distress and shame at this degradation).—"Ah! This is worse than all, you're actually scalding me; my skin will peel off," dancing about in excruciating agony.

MADEMOISELLE (laughing).—"My dear, it is to heal and keep your skin on. We're going to cover you with nice warm feathers. You never felt so comfortable in your life as you will presently."

The ceremony was both amusing and exciting, but it would be impossible to describe the poor girl's misery and dreadful shame. Her shrieks and appeals of "Oh! Ah! It will never come off," especially as they lift her up and roll her bottom and front in a great heap of feathers, taking care to shove them in everywhere, so as to thoroughly cover all the tar.

This is the finale, and she is led from the scene of her punishment and degradation; but that was not all; every day for nearly three weeks she had to strip and exhibit her feathery bum for inspection and laughing remarks. I need scarcely say the ordeal she went through effected a radical cure of the Kleptomania.

Do you not think, dear Nellie, my plan would cure the Kleptomaniacs of the present day? It would be well worth a trial.

> Yours affectionately,
> ROSA BELINDA COOTE.

(To be continued.)

PLEASURES OF MEMORY.

Sweet is the memory of the scenes
    In boyhood I enjoyed,
Hot vigour thrilling in my veins,
    By no fruition cloy'd.

So innocent a child I seem'd
    That Catherine, Jane, Eliza,
Would treat me as a girl, nor dream'd
    That I was e'er the wiser.

I many a naked frolic spied,
    Nor seem'd a whit to care,
With changeless glance serene I eyed
    Their sexual members bare.

All fear'd the strict severities
    Of Mistress and of Master,
Who thought to crush propensities
    That only throve the faster.

But when I was thirteen I grew
    Too big a boy for this,
The girls grew timid—well they knew
    I might do more than kiss.

No longer Jane would offer me
    The clean shirt nice and warm,
And turn me up and cuddle me,
    Without supposing harm.

And Catherine never called me now
    The bathroom door to keep,
The while she bathed, lest any came
    And say, "You must not peep."

Nor Harriet, when she climb'd the trees,
    Would let me now stand under,
All seem'd to guard their modesties
    With care that made me wonder.

But fostering Venus kindly led
   Her young disciple still,
Although I kept my maidenhead
   Sorely against my will.

For though from British blood I sprung
   Yet born in India's land,
I felt while callow, raw and young
   Cythera's guiding hand.

And night by night, when fast asleep,
   Wits, nerves upon the stretch,
My melting heart I could not keep,
   I was an amorous wretch.

One day I chanced to climb outside
   My cousin's bathing room,
And found a hole through which I spied
   The place I'd used to roam.

I sigh'd to think how oft the girls
   Had idly let me in,
"It's nobody but little Charles,
   No matter though he's seen."

Yes, I was their sole favourite,
   No other boy was suffer'd
To share in many a luscious sight
   To me so freely offer'd.

"Those joys (thought I) are now no more!"
   I started—at that minute,
Dear Kate came to the bathroom door,
   She lock'd herself within it.

"Oh, do I dream, or is it true?
   And is she going to bathe,
And treat me to the fullest view
   Of all above, beneath?"

She dropt her gown, and one by one
   She stript her of her clothes,

Her smock is all she now has on,
    "Oh, will she nought expose?"

There, now it's off—and Catherine stands
    In utter nudity,
And neither of her rosy hands
    Conceals her modesty.

I saw her right before my eyes
    Naked, stark naked stand,
The blooming centre of her thighs
    As naked as my hand.

What see I now! what see I not!
    Is Kate a woman grown?
She was a little girl I thought,
    But lo, she's fully blown:

Oh look at her sweet fie for shame,
    With pouting lips so red.
Oh look at her dear frisky game,
    Her open maidenhead!

THE TRIAL OF CAPTAIN POWELL.

For *Ravishing Margaret Edson, a child under the Age of 12
Years, at York Assizes, March 31st, 1775.*

Mary Edson stated: I am the child's mother. On the Fri-
day before New Year's Day, I perceived my daughter was ill,
I asked her what she had done to herself (as she had trouble
in making water), if she had fallen and hurt herself; she said
no. On Sunday, the 1st January, when I stripped her I saw
her shift very much daubed with what had come from her,
which gave me a great shock.

Q.—What colour was it?

A.—A yellow colour mixed with red. When I saw her in
that condition, I said if you do not tell me what you have
done with yourself I will take the skin off your backside. As
she would not tell me I got a birch rod, and twining her over

my lap gave her bum a sharp tickling, when she said that Captain Powell sent for her brother and her, and he gave her brother a halfpenny to buy some sweets. After the boy went out the Captain barred the door, and then he put his finger up her body and hurt her very much. I was much surprised, and sent for Mrs. Nurser, a neighbour, who advised me to send for Dr. Lee, who lives at Knaresborough. In the afternoon too we asked her what Captain Powell did to her, and she then said Captain Powell unbuttoned his breeches and took out his cock and put it into her. I asked her if she felt anything come from him. She said she thought he made water in her. She said he sat in his chair and took her before him, and she shewed the motion he made in the chair, then he took her upstairs and did the same again.

Q.—From the appearance of the colour on the shift did you think it had the same appearance as that which comes from a man on those occasions?

A.—To the best of my judgment I thought it was.

Mr. John Lee, a surgeon, said that Mr. Edson, the father of the child, making application to him to examine his daughter, he attended at his house, when he inspected the child, and found her private parts much inflamed and swelled, which convinced him she had received some injury; there was likewise a discharge from the parts, which made him afraid it was venereal. He attended and administered to her about six weeks.

Q.—Did it appear to you there had been any violence used by a man's penis?

A.—I cannot say I formed any judgment as to the cause.

Q.—Suppose a man had introduced his private parts, would it have occasioned this?

A.—Yes it would.

Q.—Would a finger being put there occasion the excoriation?

A.—Yes it might. If a man had entered the vagina of the child and entered into her body, I should have thought it would have had a different appearance. It would have brought away blood, but I observed none.

Margaret Edson (the child).

COURT.—What age are you?

A.—Ten-and-a-half.

Q.—Do you tell lies?

A.—No.

Q.—Will you tell me the truth?

A.—Yes.

Q.—Do you know Captain Powell? Look round and see if he is here.

A.—There is Captain Powell, pointing to the prisoner.

Q.—Now tell us what Captain Powell did to you.

A.—I and my brother was at Mrs. Raper's playing with her little boy; we did not stay long. My brother and I were going home, and Captain Powell said, "Come hither, Peg, come hither." My brother went with me to Captain Powell, and he gave my brother a halfpenny to go and buy sweets. My brother went, and then Captain Powell bolted the door.

Q.—What did he do after that?

A.—He put one hand round my waist and turned up my clothes.

Q.—Where was he?

A.—He was sitting in a chair.

Q.—How was you standing?

A.—On the floor before him, between his legs.

Q.—What did he do?

A.—He unbuttoned his breeches and took his cock out.

Q.—How did you know it was his cock?

A.—I saw it; I saw him take it out.

Q.—What did he do after that?

A.—He put his cock in my arsehole.

Q.—Tell us that again?

A.—He unbuttoned his breeches, took out his cock, and put it in my arsehole.

The jury did not wish to hear any more, and he was indicted at the next assizes for a common assault, and found guilty.

FOWLS AND PICKLED PORK.

The wife of a City gentleman one day found in his pocket a billet from a ladylove of his, asking him to come that evening to supper, and that she had fowls and pickled pork.

The husband came home at his usual time, and told his

wife that he had some particular business to transact that evening, which would keep him out rather late.

"Very well, dear, but you can't go out in that soiled shirt, come upstairs and change it," responded his tender better half.

She went with him to their bedroom, and with her jokes and larking soon gave him such a cockstand that he tossed her on the bed and had a good fuck.

Proceeding to finish dressing she again interrupted him with the remark that "he could not go out with such dirty stockings, now John let me pull them off and put on a clean pair for you."

This led to further dallying, especially when she remarked, "how silly his cock looked with its head hanging down, now she had taken the life out of it; la, I wonder if it can stand again dear," as she played with and kissed his limp concern. This led to another loving fuck, which ended by her giving him a rapturous kiss, as she exclaimed, "I believe, John, you have made me a baby at last. Now, my dear, I don't mind if you go and have the 'fowls and pickled pork.'"

But the husband declared "he would be damned if he did now."

N.B.—The Editor of The Pearl would advise married ladies not to trust too implicitly in the belief "that if they fuck their husband well before he goes out, they may safely trust him." Our experience is that it only tends to make the men more excitable; we once knew a person (not ourself of course), who would have three different women on the way home from business, and then fuck his wife well when he went to bed, which he would not have thought of otherwise.

LADY POKINGHAM, OR THEY ALL DO IT;

Giving an Account of her Luxurious Adventures, both before and after her Marriage with Lord Crim-Con.

PART IV.

I must now return to my liaison with Lothair; he had promised to meet me again in a week, when I hoped to hear the particulars of his drive to Richmond.

We lunched again at the Bristol Hotel, and without having recourse to the tincture, I found him almost as hot and impulsive as before. "Ah! Beatrice," he said, as we lay exhausted on the sofa, after a series of delicious encounters, "I cannot express half the gratitude and devotion I ought to have; for you, not satisfied with making me happy yourself, quite unselfishly advised me how to enjoy the two nuns. But first tell me of that Society of Love, which you promised to introduce me to, and then you shall have my adventure."

So briefly I described to him the Paphian Circle, and took his promise to allow me to introduce him at the next séance.

"I know," he said, "you thought me quite captivated by Miss Arundel, but I never forgot your advice, and resolved to seem to lend myself as a proselyte, accept all the advantages they might offer as baits, and get a thorough insight into all the plans of the Jesuits before I open their eyes, but it is a game that will last a long time. Now, as to the Richmond drive. Lady St. Jerome and Miss Arundel were most vivacious and alluring, as we drove down by road; then we had a beautiful row on the river whilst waiting for dinner, which we sat down to with excellent appetites. I plied the two ladies with wine, and requested them as a special favour not to leave me to myself at dessert, as I did not smoke, and there were no other gentlemen present. Everything was sparkling and agreeable, religion seemed to be avoided by mutual consent, the ladies had withdrawn from the table to a sofa in a recess, where their faces were screened from the light of the brilliant chandelier; they had each had two or three glasses of champagne and seemed very careful not to exceed the limits of decorum, when, taking a fresh bottle, I challenged them to drink to the prosperity of the Christian Church.

" 'Ah!' said Miss Arundel, with flashing eyes, 'but what Church do you refer to?'

" 'Dear ladies,' I replied, 'you shall word the toast as you please, and I will drain a real bumper to it in your company.'

" 'Then,' said Clare, 'we drink to the prosperity of the Holy Roman Catholic Church, and long life to His Holiness Pius IX.'

"Their eyes sparkled, and both seemed unusually excited.

" 'What would we not do to assure your conversion, dear

Lothair,' said Lady St. Jerome. 'Come and sit between us whilst we talk seriously to you.'

"I sat down on the sofa, and being well flushed with wine, impudently put an arm round each of their waists, and said, without thinking, 'Ah! that's mere nonsense; but in truth, I would sell both body and soul for the happiness you and your niece could confer on me.'

"Miss Arundel drew a deep sigh, but Lady St. Jerome softly whispered, as she laid one hand on my thigh, most awkwardly near to an important member, 'Ah! what do you mean? Join our Church, and there is nothing we will deny to you.'

" 'Nothing! nothing! you will get indulgences and dispensations for everything then,' whispered Clare, as she laid her head on my shoulder.

" 'No! no traffic with priests; I want my indulgence from you, dear ladies, if you care for my soul, now's the time to save me; drive me away in unsatisfied desperation, and such a chance will never occur again. Ah! how awfully I am tempted by the proximity of such charms!' I exclaimed, falling on my knees, and clasping their legs, as I hid my face in Clare's lap.

"They were both trembling with emotion, and I was equally agitated, but I seemed to guess from their looks and manner towards me, the present moment was too favourable for them to let slip.

"Lady St. Jerome was the first to speak. 'Dear Lothair, we do indeed pity your distress. Oh! Oh! for shame, sir, what liberties! Will you? Will you, promise us?' as she fidgeted about in confusion, feeling my hand slowly advancing up her legs beneath the clothes; both my hands were busy, but Clare had closed her thighs, and firmly stopped my advance in silence, whilst her aunt's ejaculations seemed to encourage me more and more.

" 'By all that's sacred, I promise everything you may demand of me, they shall receive me into the Church, as soon as they please, if you two will but be ministering angels to my impulsive passions,' I cried, taking advantage of her confusion to gain complete possession of the grotto of love.

" 'Clare, dear,' sighed Her Ladyship, 'can we possibly sacrifice ourselves for a nobler purpose; by now subduing his carnal lusts, we shall also draw a lost sheep to the foot of the cross.'

"I felt Miss Arundel's tightly compressed thighs relax in their resistance, and she gave a spasmodic sigh as I victoriously advanced my rude hand also to her mossy retreat. 'Ah! how delicious to have possession of a double set of the loveliest charms, I will kiss you, and enjoy you by turns,' I said in rapture, at the prospect before me.

LADY ST. JEROME.—'Excuse me a moment, dear Lothair, Clare is all blushing confusion, let me spare her modesty as much as possible,' as she rose and locked the door, then almost turned out the gas.

"Pulling up her skirts, I threw Miss Arundel backwards on the sofa, and releasing my bursting weapon, threw myself between her yielding thighs, as I exclaimed, 'You have indeed relieved me of making an invidious selection, as I cannot restrain the heat of my passion, Clare must be the first victim to it.'

"It was almost, if not quite, dark in the recess where we were, but my lips sought those of the lovely girl, her entire frame seemed to quiver under me, and she gave a faint shriek as the head of my cock first touched the lips of her cunny. 'Courage, darling,' I whispered in her ear, 'I won't hurt you more than I can help; open your legs, and give way to me as much as you can, you suffer for a noble object.' As if I did not know she had already lost her virginity.

"Lady St. Jerome had now returned to the sofa, where she encouraged Clare to bear the dreadful pain with all her fortitude. Then Her Ladyship took my affair in her hand, saying, 'Let me, dear Lothair, direct you right. I'm a married woman, and know exactly how it ought to be done.' Her touch only added to my excitement. She kept drawing the foreskin back, and took care to present the head rather above the proper entrance to the vagina, to make me think the resistance I felt was genuine, but it gave me infinite pleasure, and made Mr. Pego spend all over the entrance of Clare's longing cunny. At last, after great difficulty, they let me fairly in, and I begged Her Ladyship to still keep her hand there and stimulate my exertions. I spent three times, each time more excitedly than the last, whilst the dear girl was a constant flood of lubricity, and seemed to melt with love, clinging to me with all the tenacity of her voluptuous furor.

"At last, notwithstanding her entreaties for me to go on, on, on, I managed to withdraw, as I told her she would leave nothing for me to repay all her dear aunt's kindness. 'But, Clare darling,' I said, 'I will still give you pleasure with my tongue.' So I made her give way to Lady St. Jerome, who eagerly slipped off some of her skirts, as she said, to give me greater freedom, but in reality so that she might enjoy herself more. Her pussey was quite wet with spendings, which had flowed in sympathy with our enjoyment.

"Miss Clare was an apt pupil, and quickly arranged herself over her aunt's face, so as to present her excited cunny to my lips.

"Lady St. Jerome had an extraordinary gift of contraction in her vagina, it took hold of my cock, like a delicately soft hand and with a frigging motion, as she wriggled and met my thrusts, of the most delicious kind. I grasped and moulded her lovely breasts with both hands, for she held me convulsively to her body, and I had no necessity to clasp her myself. Our conjunction was so exciting that I spent again immediately, under the touches of what I called her invisible hand, then steadying myself I revelled in love and lubricity for more than half-an-hour, both the dear ladies gasping, sighing, and sometimes when they spent giving vent to subdued shrieks of pleasure and dearment. Clare seemed quite as excited as her aunt, who I found was frigging her bottom-hole, and rousing all her lustful propensities to the utmost, with a disengaged hand, as soon as she found I was so safely rooted in herself that one arm could hold me.

"I can't tell you how we finished, for there seemed to be no end to it; however, about eleven o'clock we apparently woke from a kind of delicious lethargy, into which we had all fallen, and we soon sufficiently composed ourselves to ring for the carriage and start for town; on the plea of keeping out the chilly night air, the windows were put up, and I had one or the other of them astride of my lap and spitted on the shaft of love till the noise of granite pavement under the wheels of the carriage warned us of the near approach to St. James' Square.

"I have promised not to marry, but expressed my wish to be received into the Church by the Holy Father himself soon after Christmas, when I will visit Rome on purpose; this will give me plenty of time to carry on my game, and prove to

the Jesuits that I am now quite equal to the tricks they
played on me, when they had me down at Vauxe before, and
imposed on the weak senses of a poor boy, quite green to the
ways of the world. I can love Clare, when I don't think of
it, but if I do I should hate her even in the midst of our love
transports."

Our time in town was getting short, so at my suggestion
Bertram and St. Aldegonde arranged an early day with
Lothair, for his initiation to the Paphian Circle.

We were still at Crecy House, and this time the affair was
managed under cover of a small private party at the Duke of
Brecon's, where we dismissed our carriages, and then drove
out in those of his Grace for a country excursion, which of
course only extended to Cheyne Walk. Everything was in
readiness, and Lothair being admitted as usual, we quickly
appeared in the garb of Madre Natura as before. Partners
were drawn for the first dance, my lot fell to the Duke of
Brecon, whilst Lothair was drawn by Alice, and Lady Corisande presided at the piano, where her brilliant execution
helped to add to the excitement engendered by the lascivious
motions of the dance, in which, when the gentlemen and
ladies changed partners as they went through the figure, they
gave our bottoms a fine smarting spank, which we repaid by
sharp little slaps on their extended cocks, soon getting
tremendously warm and excited over our quadrille, and at the
conclusion could scarcely restrain ourselves sufficiently to allow Lothair to give the usual kiss all round to our palpitating
cunnies.

I noticed Lady Bertha very busy whispering to everyone,
and soon found out that she was proposing a little bit of
extra fun for us, of which the novice was of course to be the
victim, whilst both pleasure and profit would accrue to the
Paphian Circle.

(To be continued.)

PROGRESS.

Let those who never tried, believe,
    In woman's chastity!

Let her who ne'er was asked, receive,
   The praise of modesty!

Again I've been at Church to-day,
   And eyed that angel stranger;
Whose yielding glances seem to say,
   "I love, but dread the danger."

Too truly sung the Indian sage,
   That "Father, Brother, Son,
To her who feels the sexual rage
   Are lawful—all are one."

Tho' woman's virtue's true as steel
   Before you touch her soul;
Still let it once the *Magnet* feel
   'Twill flutter tow'rds the *Pole!*

EXPOSTULATION WITH A FIERCE PREACHER.

Oh, jealous Cotterill, why so warm?
   Because your congregation,
In spite of all you preach and storm,
   Persist in fornication.

And so you think a ball-room dress
   Unfitted for a pew,
And fain would check the wantonness
   That gives the breasts to view.

"Indecent" is a cruel word
   To use to strict church-goers,
It's very awful by the Lord
   To call us rogues and whores.

In pews, like sheep in pens we sit,
   While you indulge in barking,
If sheep will cast sheep's eyes a bit
   It is not worth remarking.

The ball-room and the play-house gay
    In India are so rare,
That church for those who play or pray
    Is crowded by the fair.

Poor Cotterill—why then should he grieve
    Because our glances roam?
He merely wants us all to leave
    Our "Hearts and Souls" at home.

I joy the lecherous girl to squeeze,
    I joy thy rage to see,
So first I sin myself to please
    And next to anger thee.

The silliest goose that swims the lake
    Is known to be the Dotterel,
That spelling must be a mistake,
    The name I'm sure is Cotterill!

HYMN TO THE GENIUS OF WOMAN.

(A statue in the Florentine Gallery.)

Genius of woman, glorious form
    Of perfect loveliness,
I worship thee, with beauty warm,
    Released from every dress.

Oh smile on him to Thee who bows,
    Who worships Thee alone;
And pays his deep impassioned vows,
    At none but Beauty's throne.

And bless thou Her whose pencil gave,
    Thy dazzling limbs to light,
Naked, as rising from the wave,
    They shone all rosy bright.

It was a homage due to Thee,
  By grateful Chloris paid;
For Thou with every conquering charm,
  Has't blest the golden maid.

And every touch her pencil gave,
  To each alluring part;
Has bound in firmer spells the slave,
  Of pleasure, love, and art.

Oh sacred, fervent, silent be,
  Our worship at Thy shrine;
No eye profane shall ever see,
  Thy lineaments divine.

THE PEARL,

A Journal of Facetiæ and Voluptuous Reading.

No. 8   PUBLISHED MONTHLY.   Feb., 1880

LA ROSE D'AMOUR;

Or the Adventures of a Gentleman in search of Pleasure.
Translated from the French.

"Thus every creature, and of every kind,
The sweet joys of sweet coition find."—DRYDEN.

CHAPTER I.

At the age of seventeen, through the mistaken but paternal fondness of my father, the Count de L—, I was still immured in an old chateau, on the coast of Brittany, with no society but that of my tutors, an eternal round of daily lessons, to be gotten only by poring over some dozens of musty volumes. Naturally of an indolent disposition, I became ennuyed to such a degree by the monotonous routine of my life that I verily believe I could not have survived three months longer had it not been for an accession of company which the old chateau received.

I was most agreeably surprised, while at my studies one morning, by the noise of carriage wheels driving rapidly over the stone pavement of the courtyard. I threw my book into one corner, bounded down the stairs, and met my father at the hall door; he was accompanied by my uncle, Count C—, and his two sons, who were about my own age.

In the course of the day my father told me that he was about to start for Russia as ambassador, and that after remaining at the chateau for a week or two, my uncle and cousins would return to Paris, taking me with them, as during his absence I was to reside with my uncle.

The next day my father, after giving me a great deal of good advice and his blessing, started en route for St. Petersburg.

My cousins, Raoul and Julien, I found to be two as wild young colts as ever were let loose upon the inhabitants of a country village, setting at defiance everything, and leading me, who proved an adept scholar, into all kinds of mischief, whilst their father, who had some business in the neighbourhood, could not look after our conduct.

Going one day into my cousin Raoul's chamber in search of him, on opening the door, I was perfectly astounded at what I saw. There lay Raoul on the bed, in the arms of one of the *femmes de chambre*, Manette, a most lusty, finely formed, rosy-cheeked wench.

When I entered the room my cousin was lying on the top of Manette, clasped in a tight embrace, a pair of large white legs crossed over his back, and from the heavings and motions of their bodies, I perceived that they were enjoying themselves in a manner altogether satisfactory; and so intent and enraptured were they, with the exercise they were taking, that they did not notice my having entered the room.

Although, during the three days my cousins had been with me, they had, by licentious conversation, uprooted all my preconceived notions of virtue in woman, so strictly had I been reared, never having been allowed to enter the company of females, not even in the village adjoining the chateau, that seeing the two on the bed in that manner I was so amazed that I stood at the door watching them till Raoul raised himself off the girl.

He got up, standing with his back to me, while Manette still lay with her eyes closed, her petticoat and shift thrown up, her thighs wide apart, revealing to my ardent gaze a round white belly, the bottom part of which was covered with a large growth of jet black curly hair, and lower down, between her thighs, I discovered what I had so often heard of, but never before seen—a cunt; from between the locks of curly hair that grew over the mount above, and around the dear delicious slit, I could perceive two fat and rosy lips slightly gaping open, from which oozed out a little whitish-looking foam.

My senses were so confused with what I saw, and the strange emotions which had been called up in me, that I stepped forward towards the bed. The moment my step was heard Manette buried herself under the bedcovers, while

Raoul came to meet me, and taking me by the hand led me up to the bed, saying,—

"Cousin Louis, what have you seen? how long have you been in the room?"

I answered and told him I had witnessed their whole performance.

Raoul threw the cover off the girl, and raising her to a sitting posture, with one arm round her waist, said,—

"Cousin Louis, you who have never tasted the pleasures to be received in the arms of a pretty girl, do not know what it is to resist the temptation of making use of every opportunity and means in one's power, to gratify the appetite, and see what a beautiful, charming mistress Manette is; who could deny her? Having done me the honour to invite me to her chamber last night I could not but return the courtesy this evening, and know the sequence."

I replied, "Yes, she is very charming," and feeling a desire to get an insight into the pleasures derived from the conjunction of the sexes, I laid my hand on the bare knee of Manette, who still sat on the edge of the bed, her clothes scarcely covering her cunt and thighs, and slipped it under her chemise, till it rested on the hairy mount that overtopped the delicious slit beneath.

But Raoul stopped me, saying, "Excuse me, cousin, but Manette is mine, at least for the present, but as I see you are anxious to initiate yourself in the mysteries of the Cyprian goddess, I think that with the help of Manette I shall be able to find you a companion for the night; can we not Manette?" said he, turning to her.

"Oh, yes," said the girl, jumping to her feet, and assuming a smiling look, "we will get Monsieur Louis my little sister Rose, who I am sure is a much prettier girl than myself, and she has larger and whiter breasts than I have," said she, covering a pair of fine round white globes, which I was greedily devouring with my eyes. "I am sure," she went on, "that you will be pleased with Rose, when we bring her to you tonight."

Telling Manette that on condition she brought her sister at night to my chamber, I would be secret and mention to no one what I had seen, I retired and left them.

Going to my chamber early in the night I spent an hour in a fever of excited expectation till Manette entered the room,

leading her sister by the hand. Rose was a most beautiful girl,
and the moment she entered the room and the door was
closed, I sprang forward, caught her in my arms, and led her
to a sofa, where I sat down and drew her to my side. I un-
pinned the handkerchief that covered her breasts, and clasping her again in my arms covered them with burning kisses.
This caused Rose to blush exquisitely and struggle somewhat
to release herself from my embrace, when Manette stepped
before us, saying,—

"Monsieur Louis, Rose was never in company with a man
before now, and of course is a little backward, but is very
willing to remain with you, and by yourselves you will, I am
sure, find her all you wish; is it not so, sister?"

To which Rose replied, "Oh yes," and hid her face in the
cushion of the sofa.

Manette told me that as wine was a great reviver of the
spirits and provocative of love, she would go and bring me
some, telling Rose to ply me plentifully with it. She went,
and soon returned with a tray of wine, cakes, &c., and retired,
wishing us "a happy night of it."

When Manette retired I locked the door, then drawing up
a sofa to the table I led Rose to it, and seating myself by her,
endeavoured to put her at her ease by not proceeding to any
liberties at first, till I had plied her with some half-dozen
glasses of wine. After she had drunk pretty freely, the natural
vivacity of her character began to show itself, in her open and
free conversation. I now put my arms around her waist and
neck, and pressing her close to my breast, imprinted burning
kisses upon her rosy pouting lips. I then slipped one hand
into her bosom, feeling and moulding her firm round bubbies. After dallying thus awhile I stooped and slipped a hand
under her chemise, raised her clothes up on her knees.
Squeezing and playing with her legs, I slid my hand along her
thigh till my fingers rested on a bunch of silken mossy hair,
which overhung the entrance of her virgin cunt.

Playing with the silken curls, twining and twisting my
fingers through them, I dropped one finger lower down, and
putting just the tip of it between the lips, I titillated her so
well that she began to wriggle about in her seat. I could
stand it no longer. I was on fire; the blood was boiling
through my veins. I raised her on her feet, and began stripping her, fairly tearing her clothes off in my haste, till she

stood perfectly naked before me. Ye Gods! what beauties, what charms, were exposed to my ardent fiery gaze, what delicious breasts, how firmly moulded, small, yet so round and firm. I press them, kiss them, take the nipples in my mouth, I draw her to me, till feeling her naked body against me, I drop on my knees and transfer my love kisses to the lips of her luscious little hairy slit. I was in a perfect frenzy, I burned, I raged. In a trice I threw off everything, and clasping her body to mine, I raised the trembling girl in my arms, and carried her to the bed.

Placing a pillow on which to rest the plump, luxurious cheeks of her backside, I lay her down, springing on the bed by her side. I open wide her thighs, and my prick being up in arms and eager for the fray, I lay my length on her. With the tips of my fingers I unclose the pouting lips, and with the utmost trouble insert the head of my virgin rod into the entrance of her no less virgin cunt.

No sooner did I feel the head lodged aright than I drove and shoved in with the utmost fury; feeling the head pretty well in I thrust and drove on, but gained so little that I drew it out, and wetting it with spittle I again effect the lodgement just within the lips. At length by my fierce rending and tearing thrusts the first defences gave way, and I got about half-way in, but had become wrought up to such a pitch that the floodgates of love's reservoir gave way, and I sank upon her breast in a delirium of transport as I oiled her torn and bleeding cunt with a perfect flood of virgin sperm.

Poor Rose had borne it most heroically, keeping the bed-clothes between her teeth, in order to express any cry of pain, whilst her hands clasped my body to hers, or even handled the shaft of love to assist its murderous intentions on her virginity.

As I lay panting and gasping on Rose, glowing with the fierce excitement, my eyes darting forth their humid fires, the stiffness which had perceptibly remitted, returned with re-doubled vigour, and I again began to make headway into her. The sperm that I had spurted into her cunt had penetrated and oiled the dark and narrow passage, making my further entrance somewhat easier. I now recommenced my eager shoves, my fierce lunges, and I felt myself gaining at every move, till with one tremendous and cunt-rending thrust I buried myself into her up to the hilt. So great was the pain

of this last shock that Rose could not suppress a sharp shrill
scream, but I heeded it not; it was the note of final victory,
and only added to the delicious piquancy of my enjoyment as
I buried myself, if possible, yet further within the soft, luscious folds of her love sheath. We lay for a short time in the
closest conjunction with each other, so that the hair on both
of us was interwoven in one mass.

Putting my arm around her neck, I drew her to a yet closer
embrace, and planting numberless kisses on her rosy lips and
damask blushing face, which was wet with tears of suffering
which the brave little darling could not prevent from starting
from her lovely eyes, I drew out the head and slowly thrusting it in again; my fierce desires goaded me to challenge her
to a renewal of the combat. A smile of infinite love crossed
her lovely countenance, all signs of past pain seemed to
vanish, and I could feel the soft and juicy folds of her cunt,
throbbing and clasping tightly on my enamoured prick; my
movements quickened in an instant, and so exciting was the
to-and-fro friction, aided by the delicious jingling of my magnificent stones against her backside, despite all her pain, Rose
was thrown into such an ecstasy that she clasped me in her
arms, and throwing her legs over my back paid down her
first and virgin tribute to man, forced from her by the soul-
stirring motions of my rod of love, while I met her and
spurted another stream of burning sperm into the utmost
recesses of her fount of love, commingling together, partially
cooling the fires which were raging within us.

So novel, so new, exquisitely delicious, so transporting, so
heavenly were the sensations, ecstatic were the joys we both
felt that we twined and writhed in each other's arms like
serpents, while Rose exclaimed,—

"Oh God! I die! Oh heaven! What joy, what pleasure. Oh!
oh! ah! ah!—h!—h—"

Ending in one long deep-drawn sigh. With a few convulsive jerks and struggles of her delicious backside she loosened
her holds, and stretching herself out with a shudder, fainted
away, and I, who was at my last gasp, also sank into oblivion.

When we had recovered from our delirium I got up and
poured out some wine, gave it to Rose, and tossed off a
bumper myself, I then planted a soft kiss on the lips of her
torn and bleeding cunt, exclaiming,—

"True fount of love, sole seat of never failing joys and

pleasures to man, dear, delicious, hairy little slit, from this moment my whole life and soul are forever devoted to you."

I spent the night with Rose, in one continued round of pleasure, revelling in the full enjoyment of her virgin charms. Again and again did we renew our embraces, swimming in a sea of pleasure. So furiously did we enter into our combats of love that nature soon became exhausted, and we fell asleep in each other's arms.

In the morning when I awoke Rose was sitting up in the bed, looking with anxious eyes on the now diminutive, shrunken instrument which the night before had ripped open the entrances to her virginity, robbing her of her maidenhead. When she perceived that I was watching her she threw herself into my arms and hid her face in my bosom.

Gently raising and reassuring her, I made her take hold of it, and began dallying with her breasts, tickling her, pressing them, sucking their rosy nipples, while the touch of her hand renewed in me the fires which were already springing into flame. Rose had the pleasure to see the small shrunken thing she first took into her hand spring up into a magnificent rod, smooth and polished as ivory, its large uncapped head red and glowing with the heat that was raging in it. I determined that she should reap the reward of her labour, and gather into her storehouse the rich harvest of love that was awaiting her.

Gently laying her down, and placing a pillow under the firm half-moons of her backside, she stretched open her legs to the utmost, exhibiting to my gaze the gaping lips of her cunt, ready open to receive the delicious morsel which, panting and throbbing like a high mettled courser, raised his foaming head erect against my belly.

Laying myself down on Rose I made her take hold of my prick to put it in, but so firm and erect was it that she could barely bend its head down to the entrance. So magnificent was the erection that with all the stretching her cunt had received the night before it would not enter. Drawing myself back to wet the head within the lips, and slowly shoving it into her, she could not move, but lay quietly till I stirred her up so powerfully that we soon melted away, making her feel the pleasures more sensibly, and giving her the full enjoyment of that which she had but tasted the night before.

We had barely recovered ourselves when we were aroused

by a knocking at the door. Slipping on a loose *robe de chambre* I immediately opened it, and Raoul and Manette came in. I led them up to the bed, and pulling off the coverlet showed them the blushing Rose, more beautiful in the morning from the fatigues she had undergone the night past.

I called their attention to her, saying, "Behold her chemise; see how it is dyed by the juice and crimson tide, which flowed from the parent stem after I had plucked *la rose d'amour* from my lovely Rose."

My cousin Raoul now congratulated me. He said that he was "overjoyed that he had been in a manner instrumental in procuring for me such a delicious rose as Rose turned out to be." That he was sincerely glad he had been partially the cause of my being thus happily initiated into the mysteries of the divine art of love, and at the same time of my having had a virgin partner in my delicious combats.

Manette, too, congratulated her sister.

"How pleased she was to learn that she had secured such a lover as M. Louis, how happy you will be together now you have once tasted the supreme joys to be obtained in each other's embraces, sipping of the pleasures of which I am sure you will never tire."

I now spent all my nights with Rose, sometimes in her own chamber, again in my own, and not content to wait for the night I would sometimes get her into my room in the day, and enjoy myself with her.

One day, while in my room with Rose, she stretched across the foot of the bed, her clothes raised up, and exposing to my view all her beauties, I standing between her legs with my prick (which was a very large one, few men being able to boast of one as large), in my hand, Manette suddenly entered the room, I having neglected to lock the door.

She got a fair view of my prick, and stood looking at it, apparently amazed at its being so big, but seeing the manner in which I was engaged, she retired.

(To be continued.)

Strictly Private, except to Brothers,

BY ORDER,

THE LADY FREEMASON.

As a brother of old, from his lodge was returning,
He called on his sweetheart, with love he was burning,
He wanted some favours, says she, "Not so free,"
Unless you reveal your famed secrets to me."

"Agreed—'tis a bargain—you must be prepared,
Your legs well exposed, your bosom all bared."
Then hoodwinked and silent, says she, "I'll be mum,
In despite of the poker you'll clap on my bum."

To a chamber convenient his fair charge he bore,
Placed her in due form, having closed tight the door,
Then presented the point of his sharp *Instrumentis*,
And the Lady was soon made an "entered apprentice."

His working tools next to her gaze he presented,
To improve by them seriously she then consented,
And handled his jewels his gavel and shaft,
That she in a jiffey was passed "fellow craft."

She next wanted raising, says he, "There's no urgency,"
She pleaded that this was a case of emergency,
His column looked to her in no particular way,
But she very soon made it assume perpendicular.

He used all his efforts to raise the young elf,
But found he required much raising himself;
The task was beyond him. Oh! shame and disaster,
He broke down in his charge, and she became master.

Exhausted and faint, still no rest could betide him,
For she like a glutton soon mounted astride him,
"From refreshment to labour," says she, "let us march.
Says he, "You're exalted—you are now royal arch."

In her zeal for true knowledge, no labour, no shirking,
His *jewels* and *furniture* constantly working,
By night and by day, in the light or the dark,
With *pleasure* her lover she guides to the *mark*.

FABLES AND MAXIMS.

Translated from the Indian of Shitpot, the great Brahmin.

THE LADY AND THE EEL.

A young lady was frigging herself with a small live eel,
when it slipped from her fingers and disappeared in her cunt;
making its way into the womb, it entered, and stretching out
its head said, "I am much obliged to you Madam, for finding me so warm and comfortable a residence; I shall make
myself quite at home." This fable teaches how much better
it is to use large eels which could not enter.

THE DISCONTENTED CRAB.

A crab who had for some time lived very happily on the
person of a very dirty whore, one day became discontented.
"How much nicer would it be to live with some cleaner and
more reputable person," he thought, so watching his opportunity he effected his escape on to the person of a well-dressed
and delicately clean young gentleman. "This," said the crab,
"is something like," but to his disgust the gentleman took a
warm bath after leaving his late mistress, and spying him out
cracked him.

This fable conveys two morals. First, one should always
leave well alone; secondly, a dirty person is very much nicer
than a clean one (*to crabs*).

MISS COOTE'S CONFESSION,

Or the Voluptuous Experiences of an Old Maid; In a series of Letters to a Lady Friend.

Letter VIII.

My Dear Nellie,

I do not intend to trouble you with all the little incidents of domestic discipline which my strict regulations so often brought under notice, and required the exercise of the beloved rod, but only write out for your amusement a few of my most remarkable recollections.

The cure of Selina Richards brought me very considerable fame amongst a large circle of acquaintances and friends, but I steadily refused to take charge of my more *mauvais sujets*, but devoted myself to promoting a Ladies Club enclusively for the admirers of Birch Discipline. The meetings were to be held at my house, where my servants would be sworn to secrecy, and to act as sub-members, not on an equality with the ladies of our Club.

The rules specially enjoined secrecy on every member, so that novices might not obtain the slightest inkling of the ordeal they would have to undergo when initiated into the mysteries of Lady Rodney's Club, as it was called, our object being to make our séances for the receiving of new members the means of affording us the most exquisite enjoyment, by bringing out all their modest bashfulness, and studying their distress and horror at finding themselves stripped and exposed for flagellation before all the sisters of the rod.

My old schoolfellows, Laura Sandon, Louise Van Tromp, Hon. Miss Cecile Deben, Lady Clara Wavering, and three other ladies besides Mdlle. Fosse and myself, as president and manager, were the first members; two of them were married, but we agreed that everyone should be known to the other sisters by her maiden name only.

Lady Clara was the first to propose a novice for admission to the Club; it was a younger sister of hers, who she informed us had a great penchant for young gentlemen, having several times seriously misconducted herself with youthful friends of the opposite sex, so that her lecture and castigation would be of a most piquant description.

We fixed an evening for her introduction, and were all present to inaugurate the Club's first séance of admission.

Our large punishment room was tastefully draped all around with elegant curtains, and brilliantly illuminated by clusters of wax candles projecting from the walls, above handsome mirrors set in bouquets of lovely flowers.

The ladies of the Club were all dressed in the same costume, viz., blue silk corsets with scarlet silk laces, and short skirts of white tulle, only coming a little below the knee, so as to show all the beautiful legs in pink silk stockings and high-heeled Parisian boots. All were in these short skirts, the outer dresses being discarded to allow a greater freedom of action, and also display for the glorious necks and bosoms of the members, who were every one young and beautiful, flushed with excitement and anticipation, their snow-white globes heaving at each breath, and set off to the greatest advantage by bouquets of red roses adjusted between the lovely hillocks of love.

As president, I was seated in a chair of state, supported on either side by four ladies, whilst Jane and Mary stand behind me.

A knock at the door; Lady Clara advances to open it, and introduces her sister, Lady Lucretia Wavering, about sixteen, but otherwise a very counterpart of herself, dark, well proportioned, rather above the medium height, languid expression, and large pensive hazel eyes. She holds a beautiful bouquet in one hand, and is dressed in simple white.

Advancing right up to where I was seated, she makes a profound bow, and Lady Clara says, "Permit me, Miss President and ladies of the Lady Rodney Club, to introduce to you my sister, Lady Lucretia, who is desirous of being admitted a member."

PRESIDENT.—"Lady Lucretia, we welcome you to our sisterhood. Are you willing to take the oaths of secrecy, and be initiated into the mysteries of the rod?"

LADY LUCRETIA.—"Yes, and to be submissive to all your rules and regulations."

PRESIDENT.—"You must now strip and assume the costume of a member, and must truthfully answer any questions I may put to you."

Jane and Mary as servants assist to disrobe the novice, who

blushes slightly as they proceed to remove her skirts after taking away her dress.

LUCRETIA, turning to me.—"You surely don't strip us quite naked, I thought I had only to change the dress."

PRESIDENT.—"Yes, everything, because you have to taste the birch before assuming our costume."

LUCRETIA, blushing deeply.—"Ah! Oh! I never expected that, it's so indecent."

PRESIDENT.—"Make haste, such improper remarks must be checked; Sister Lucretia, you have already broken the rules by objecting to lawful orders, your bottom shall smart soundly for it."

LUCRETIA, in great confusion and faltering voice.—"Pray permit me to apologize, I had no idea the members were liable to chastisement, but thought they amused themselves whipping charity children sent up by schools for punishment."

PRESIDENT.—"You will have to do that under the rod; we are quite above tickling the bottoms of school children here, although it is the duty of every member to exercise proper discipline in any house or place where she may have authority."

Lucretia is silent, but the scarlet face and nervous twichings of the corners of her mouth attest how she feels about the approaching taste of the rod; her eyes are cast down in shame, and presently with nothing but her drawers, chemise, boots, and stockings on, they lead her to the ladder, the president and ladies all rising and clustering round the victim.

PRESIDENT.—"Have the ladder nearly upright, with her wrists secured high up, and let her toes only just touch the floor; woe to her bum if she dares to step on the bottom rung of the ladder without orders."

The victim with tears of shame and apprehension protests against this disposition of her body as being too painful, and cries out for mercy as she feels her chemise rolled up and fastened under her armpits, and her unbuttoned drawers pulled down to her knees. "Ah! Ah! Oh! You'll never be so bad as that to a novice! Oh! have mercy, dear Miss Coote."

PRESIDENT.—"Don't show the white feather, young lady; we're going to initiate you into a most delightful society. You will soon be one of the most active of the sisterhood," taking from Jane a very elegantly tied-up rod, ornamented with blue and gold ribbons, then just lightly switching the victim's bare bottom, "Now ask me to birch you properly, and beg pardon for your frivolous objections."

LUCRETIA, in a tremor of fear, and with faltering voice.—"Oh! is there no getting off; why must I be cruelly whipped?"

PRESIDENT, with a smart cut across her beautiful buttocks, which at once brings the roses to the surface.—"There, that's a slight taste, you stupid, obstinate girl, I can't waste more time, there, there, there," giving three more sharp cuts in succession, each leaving their respective long red marks. "Perhaps in a minute or two you will think it worth while to obey orders, and beg pardon, &c."

VICTIM.—"Ah! Ah—r—r—re! it is cruel, oh! oh! I am sorry for saying so! the cuts smart so it's impossible to think what one's saying. Oh! pray forgive me, and punish me properly. But—but—oh! be merciful!" as she writhes and wriggles under the painful strokes which already begin to weal her delicate, tender skin.

PRESIDENT.—"Very well, you've done it after a fashion; but now as you're becoming one of our members, pray have you got a sweetheart?"

VICTIM, just then receiving an extra sharp cut.—"Ah—r —r—r—re! Oh! oh! I can't bear it, it's like a hot knife cutting the skin! Indeed, I have not got a lover, if that's not allowed!" putting her feet on the rungs of the ladder to ease the painful strain on her wrists.

PRESIDENT, with a tremendous whack across the calves of the legs, which makes Miss Lucretia fairly spring with agony. —"How dare you alter my disposition of your body by putting your feet on the ladder?" switching her legs again and again with great heavy cuts, till the poor girl capers like a cat on hot bricks. "Perhaps you won't do that again, but wait till I give you the order presently. Now about lovers, of course you have had one, if not just at present?"

LUCRETIA, in smarting pain.—"Oh! Oh! My poor legs! Oh! Yes! Ah—r—r—re! But I gave him up six months ago. Have mercy, or how can I speak to answer your questions?"

PRESIDENT, without relaxing her smarting strokes.—"Out of order again, Sister Lucretia. Your rosy-looking bottom must be enjoying the fun, or you would never keep questioning my discretion as you do. How do you like it? Does it smart very much? Tell us a little more about your lover, if you please."

LUCRETIA, writhing in agony.—"My wrists are breaking, and my bottom—oh! my bottom burns and smarts so! Ah! You want to know about my lover. I gave him up because —because he behaved improperly to me."

PRESIDENT.—"Are you speaking the truth, Sister Lucretia? as that is a most essential thing with us. We call the birch the Rod of Truth, for it is sure to bring everything out. What did he do to you? Cry out if you are in great pain, we like to hear it, and it will do you good."

LUCRETIA.—"Ah, indeed! I must shriek! You cut me so dreadfully. Oh! He took liberties with me, and put his hands up my clothes, that's all. Ah! Have mercy! You don't give time for me to get my breath."

PRESIDENT.—"Are you sure that's not a bit of a fib?" slackening a little with the rod.

LUCRETIA, thinking she is now going to be let off.—"It's quite true, my dear Miss Coote, that's what he did," and beginning to feel a deliciously voluptuous warmth and lubricity in her sensitive parts, she shut her eyes, whilst a sensuous smile betrays her pleasurable emotions.

PRESIDENT.—"What are you thinking of, Sister Lucretia, with that satisfied smile? How your buttocks seem to quiver with some curious emotion. Has my question about your lover revived anything in your mind of past enjoyments. Out with the truth. I believe you have been telling a lot of fibs," cutting the astonished victim in a terrible rage with a perfect shower of blows, which weal and bring blood for the first time.

VICTIM.—"Oh! Oh! Ah! Ah! How cruel! Just as I thought it was all over, and began to feel a delicious warmth in my posteriors. Indeed, I was not thinking of my lover," casting down her eyes, and blushing more than ever in a very confused manner.

PRESIDENT, sternly.—"How dare you persist in telling so many fibs. We happen to know a little of your goings on with young Aubrey. Speak the truth at once, or I will cut your impudent bottom into ribbons of scarified flesh. You can't deceive us, we know the effects of the rod, and the voluptuous feelings it induces." All the while, whack—whack—whack sound the blows of the birch, as they ruthlessly cut and weal the victim's bottom. The operator gets quite excited, and feels all the thrilling sensation; each stroke has an electrical effect on her nerves; the cries and screams of Lucretia seem most delightful to her, and all the spectators are in ecstasies of voluptuous emotions. The victim fairly shrieks in agony, she writhes her body about, displaying her lovely figure in a variety of contortions, shifting continually at every scathing touch of the birch.

The ladies at first watched the scene with rapt attention, but gradually the blood courses in warm excitement through their veins, mantling their cheeks with a flesh-like bloom; their eyes sparkle with unusual animation, and at last, by a common impulse the eight ladies, with Jane and Mary, each take a fine long light rod of green twigs; they form a circle round the President as she continues to flagellate the victim on the ladder; each raises her skirts under her arms so as to leave all exposed from the waist downwards. For a moment there is a lovely scene of plump white buttocks and thighs, fascinating legs encased in silk stockings, pretty garters and attractive elegant shoes, set off with jewelled buckles, and, above all, such an inviting collection of impudent looking cunnies, ornamented with every shade of chevelure, black, auburn, or light brown; then all is motion, the birch rods soon put a rosy polish on the pretty bums, each one doing her best to repay on the bottom in front of her the smarting cuts she feels behind. Laughter, shrieks, and ejaculations fill the apartment, and their motions are so rapid as to make quite a rainbow of excited peris round the central figures; but this luscious scene only lasts three or four minutes; the victim, under the President's rod, gets exhausted, her shrieks sink into sobs, and at last she sighs lower and lower, then fairly faints, with her head hanging helplessly back, and her limp form a picture of weals and blood, which oozes from the cuts, and slowly trickles down the white flesh of her thighs.

PRESIDENT, throwing aside her broken and used-up rod.— "There ladies, stop your game and all help to bring her round, she'll soon recover; how pretty your rosy bottoms look, I shall join in the next ring that is formed."

The victim is loosed from the ladder, and by use of a large fan, Lucretia soon shows signs of returning animation, her eyes open, and she looks around in bewilderment. "Where am I? What a beautiful dream!" she murmurs in a low voice, then a little more refreshed by a strong cordial poured down her throat, "Ah! I remember, my bottom smarts so!" Putting her hand down to feel her posteriors she looks at the blood which stains her fingers, and sobs hysterically, "What a cruel girl that Miss Coote must be, and how she seemed to gloat over my sufferings. Ah! let me only handle the tickler over her bum someday."

At this we all burst out into a loud laugh, and thoroughly enjoyed poor Lucretia's shame and confusion.

Miss Coote.—"Cheer up, Sister Lucretia, you have only to do what we call stepping the ladder, someday you will have a chance of revenge, but you will find Louise Van Tromp quite as cruel as I am, when she uses the birch in her skilful style on your half-cooked bum. Come Jane, I think she is ready for the second edition of her punishment."

Louise Van Tromp.—"Ah! trust me, Sister Rosa, to do my duty, she has not half confessed to us yet," taking up and switching a fine birch rod, making it fairly hiss through the air, to the evident terror of the victim.

Lucretia, with sobs and tears running in streams down her cheeks.—"Oh! Oh! how horrible, will you never have mercy; my bottom is so sore I really can't bear it to be touched," shrinking back as Jane tries to draw her to the ladder. "Oh! No! Not again on that awful thing!"

Louise brings down her rod with a tremendous whack across the poor girl's bare shoulders, exclaiming, "What are you hanging back for, look sharp, quick, or I'll cut your shoulders again," looking with delight on the red marks her cut has left on the white flesh of the victim.

Lucretia.—"Oh! Oh! I will! I will!" holding up her wrists for Jane to secure them, which is quickly done.

Louise.—"Now, step on the rungs of the ladder one at a time, as I call out the number beginning at the bottom, if you take two at once you must do it over again. Now, one" —giving a terrible whack on the victim's bruised rump.

"Ah—r—r—r—re!" shrieks Lucretia, in terrible agony as the birch cuts into the already lacerated skin, but careful only to take one step.

Louise, making her birch flourish through the air with a hissing noise.—"Pretty well, now—now—now," keeping her in trembling suspense. "Two—three," giving a couple of crashing strokes with a good interval between them, to make the victim feel the effect as much as possible.

Lucretia gives a fearful shriek at each cut, and sobs out hysterically, "Ah! How dreadful, the skin of my bottom will burst, it's getting so tight."

LOUISE.—"Glad you enjoy it so, dear, I'm sorry to hurt you much," looking delightedly round at the other members. "Now—now—now—"—with another flourish—"four—five," each blow draws the blood afresh from the already crimsoned surface, and puts the spectators into a flutter of excitement.

Lucretia fairly groans, but only once makes a false step, which she corrects before Louise can find fault. "Only two more," she sighs, as if calculating the steps yet to be done.

LOUISE.—"Steady, keep your bottom well out," switching her lightly underneath so as to tickle the exposed pussey, then another grand flourish. "Six—seven," these are awful crackers, but the victim keeps herself steady, and her pluck is greeted by clapping of hands all round. Jane takes advantage of the opportunity to secure the victim's ankles so that she is fixed in a most inviting attitude for further flagellation.

LOUISE.—"Thanks, Jane, very thoughtful of you. Now, Sister Lucretia, before you are let off you must tell us all about yourself and young Aubrey. Miss Coote did not half get it out of you," whisking the tightly bent bottom in a playful way with her rod, but the victim is evidently so sore that even light strokes make twinges of pain pass across her scarlet face.

LUCRETIA.—"Oh! Oh! Pray don't begin again. I told you he took liberties with me, what more can I say? Oh! Oh! Don't touch me; the least whisk of that thing gives awful pain."

LOUISE.—"Then, you silly girl, why do you persist in keeping back the truth? Did you not encourage him?" making the victim writhe under her painful touches, which, although not very heavy, seem to have great effect on the raw bottom in such a tightly bent position.

LUCRETIA, in great shame and confusion, and seeming to crimson all over at the thoughts of her degradation before them all.—"Oh! Oh! Spare me! If you know all, have mercy consider my feelings, how painful such a confession must be Ah—r—r—rre! You are shameful girls to enjoy my pain and shame so," sobbing as if her heart would break.

LOUISE.—"Come! Come! It is not so bad as that. Make a clean breast and be one of us in future. You will enjoy such scenes yourself when the next novice is admitted; but I can't play with you. There—there—there!" cutting three brisk strokes on the bent bottom.

LUCRETIA.—"Ah! Oh! Oh! I shall faint again. It's like burning with red hot irons. Ah! You know he seduced me, and—I must confess I did not resist as I ought. Something tempted me to taste the sweets of love, and your President's birching brought all the thrilling sensations back to me, and when I fainted my dream was all about the bliss enjoyed in my lover's arms."

LOUISE, still lightly using her rod.—"A little better, and getting nearer the truth, but you still prevaricate so in trying to excuse your own fault. Now, did you not seduce the youth instead of his taking advantage of you?"

LUCRETIA.—"Oh! Pity me. I saw him lying asleep on the grass in a secluded part of the garden; he was so sleepy that I failed to wake him, but I since believe he was shamming. Noticing a lump of something in his breeches, I gently pressed it with my fingers to see what it was, when it gradually swelled under my pressure and became like a hard stick throbbing under the cloth; my blood was fired; I can't tell how I did it, but presently, when he opened his eyes and laughed at me, I found myself with his exposed shaft in my hand. He jumped up, sprang upon me, and taking advantage of my confusion, I own he had an easy conquest. But something of the sort will happen to every loving girl at some time or other. Now I have told you all, have pity and let me go," sobbing and looking dreadfully confused and distressed.

She was let down, and we all crowded round her, giving affectionate kisses and welcoming her to be a real sister of Lady Rodney's Club.

The poor girl was very sore, and sobbed over her poor bruised bottom. "Oh! Oh! I can't sit down, it will be weeks before I can do anything with comfort. Ah! You pretend to be kind now after all that dreadful cruelty. I only wish we could get Aubrey and give him a good thrashing, it would do the impetuous boy good." We had another laugh at this, but assured her our rules didn't provide for admitting any of the opposite sex to the séances of the Club; but in my next you shall see what happened, and how Lucretia tricked us by

introducing young Aubrey as a young lady novice desirous of
admission to our Society. I remain, dear Nellie,

> Yours affectionately
> —Rosa Belinda Coote.

(To be continued.)

LADY POKINGHAM; OR THEY ALL DO IT:

Giving an account of her Luxurious Adventures, both before
and after her Marriage with Lord Crim-Con.

Part IV.

The kissing ceremony was over, and then Alice told him he
had yet another little penance to perform before he could be
admitted to full rights of membership, pointing to a fine
"Berkeley Horse," which was being wheeled into the centre of
the drawing-room, a thing something like a common pair of
steps, only covered with red baize, and provided with a cush-
ioned footboard for the victim to stand on, whilst his hands
were well stretched above his head, so as to only allow of his
standing on tiptoe. Lothair in his simple ignorance stepped up
gallantly and was instantly secured by his wrists to the top-
most rings of the horse.

St. Aldegonde, grinning with delight, tightened the cords
unmercifully, making Lothair expostulate with him at the
painful tension.

"That's nothing, my boy," said St. Aldegonde, "don't cry
out before you're hurt. Wait until you feel the rods tickle and
warm your posteriors, it will do you good, as it did me; it's the
most invigorating thing in the world; ask Bertha if I did not
give her all she required that night."

All the company were now furnished with beautiful
bunches of long thin elegantly tied-up birch.

Alice, stepping to the front.—"Now, sir, mind you answer
all my questions under pain of severe punishment. In the
first place none but orthodox members of the English
Church can be admitted to the Paphian Circle, and a member has just hinted to me that you are going to Rome, and

may be a Jesuit in disguise. Now, my Lord, what do you say to that?" giving his bottom a smart cut, which made him wince with pain, and left a long red mark across the white skin of his manly buttocks.

LOTHAIR.—"My God! you punish without waiting."

Before he could finish speaking all the ladies attacked him with their rods, raining a perfect shower of painful cuts on his helpless bottom, exclaiming, "Answer! Answer!! Answer!!! No prevarication! Don't spare him! &c.," whilst the gentlemen, who stood behind, cut into the fair bottoms of their partners, calling out, "Pass it on to him; cut away, ladies; he's a Jesuit, &c."

Lothair at first lost his breath, but soon shouted out lustily, "Hold! Hold!! It's not true! Don't kill me!"

His bottom and back were scored all over, and little drops of blood trickled down from places where the skin was broken.

ALICE.—"Well, my Lord, pray excuse our virtuous indignation, if you are not really a Jesuit. But how about a Cathedral you intend to build for them, eh?" cutting him several deliberate strokes as she was speaking, each one making him quiver under its smarting force.

LOTHAIR.—"Oh! My God! How do you know that? I've only had the plans drawn."

ALICE.—"But, my Lord, allow me to drive the thoughts of such a foolish thing from your mind. Can you not think of some better applications for your money? Will you promise me not to make yourself a fool?" cutting harder and harder every moment, till he fairly howled with pain, ejaculating,—

"Ah! Oh! Damme! How cruel of you Miss Marchmont! Ah—for God's sake let me off now. I—I—won't do it; I give my word for that."

ALICE.—"Beg my pardon instantly, my Lord, or you shall feel what cruelty really is like. Cruel indeed! to a young lady who is only doing a painful duty!" catching hold of a fresh rod, and slashing his bleeding bottom with all her might.

Lothair writhes his body about in dreadful pain, and his fine cock stands out rampantly in front, in a most outrageous state of stiffness, the head quite purple from the extraordinary pressure of blood which distended it. "Ah! ah! oh! oh! I do beg your pardon, I'm sure you will forgive me, and let me off now," he groaned in agony.

ALICE.—"I've only a trifling thing to ask you, now you have apologized. My duty is far more painful and disagreeable to me than it can possibly be to you; bodily suffering cannot for a moment be compared to anguish of mind," as she still cuts into his raw-looking posteriors, and looks round delightedly on the spectators for encouragement, then goes on again. "If you're not going to build that Cathedral, will you devote a fourth part of what it would have cost to the building of a proper temple for the meetings of our Paphian Circle?"

LOTHAIR, gasping in pain.—"Oh! Oh! Yes! That I will, £50,000, if you will let me down at once!"

There was a general clapping of hands all round, and cries of, "Enough! Enough! He's a good boy now," and then there was a scuffle all round to secure victims, which were mostly of the weaker sex, but Ladies Bertha and Victoria, by the aid of diplomacy, had got both their husbands prisoners on a sofa, and lashing into them most unmercifully, laughing and shrieking out, "Keep the game alive! Keep the game alive!"

Alice had meanwhile let down poor Lothair, who was into her in a moment, to the dear girl's great delight, both of them frequently spending and screaming with ecstasy.

My partner threw me across his knee, and made my bottom smart under his loud slaps. I screamed and struggled desperately, and at last equalized matters by grasping his stiff cock, and making him feel that two could play at the game of inflicting pain. He cried a truce, and I speedily righted myself, sitting up with my bottom in his lap, and his pego right up into my vitals. He clasped his arms round me, taking one globe of my bosom in each hand, which he moulded delightfully with his fingers as I rose and fell on his tight-fitting shaft, leaning back my head so as to meet his kisses and give him my tongue. This was a delicious position, his spendings seemed to shoot with extraordinary force into my womb, and my own helped to make quite a stream of sperm, which spurted all over his thighs at each insertion, and fairly drowned the hair round the roots of his pego.

St. Aldegonde and Montairy were having each other's wives for a change after their whipping, but cunt seemed decidedly at a discount with them, as each of them was indulging in a bottom-fuck, which those ladies seemed to relish immensely, and to add to the voluptuous excitement of

the scene, the darling Corisande struck up "They a' Do't" to
the tune of "A man's a man for a' that."

> The grit folk an' the puir do't,
> The blyte folk and the sour do't,
> The black, the white,
> Rude an' polite,
> Baith autocrat an' boor do't.
>
> For they a' do't—they a' do't,
> The beggars an' the braw do't,
> Folk that ance were, and folk that are—
> The folk that come will a' do't.
>
> The auld folk try't,
> The young ane's do't,
> The blind, the lame,
> The wild, the tame,
> In warm climes an' cauld do't,
> For they a' do't, &c.
>
> The licensed by the law do't,
> Forbidden folk and a' do't,
> And priest and nun
> Enjoy the fun,
> And never once say nay to't.
> For they a' do't, &c.
>
> The goulocks an' the snails do't
> The cushie doos and quails do't,
> The dogs, the cats,
> The mice, the rats,
> E'en elephants an' whales do't.
> For they a' do't, & c.
>
> The wee bit cocks an' hens do't,
> The robbins an' the wrens do't,
> The grizzly bears,
> The toads an' hares,
> The puddocks in the fens do't.
> For they a' do't, &c.

> The boars an' kangaroos do't,
> The titlins an' cuckoos do't,
>   While sparrows sma',
>   An' rabbits a'
> In countless swarms an' crews do't,
>   For they a' do't, &c.
>
> The midges, fleas, and bees do't,
> The mawkes an' mites in cheese do't,
>   An' cauld earthworms
>   Crawl up in swarms,
> An' underneath the trees do't,
>   For they a' do't, &c.
>
> The kings an' queens an' a' do't,
>   The Sultan an' Pacha do't,
> An' Spanish dons—loup off their thrones,
>   Pu' doon their breeks, an' fa' to't.
>
> For they a' do't, they a' do't
> The grit as weel's the sma' do't,
>   Frae crowned king
>   To creeping thing,
> 'Tis just the same—they a' do't!

Her clear melodious voice sounding distinctly through the apartment had such a thrilling effect that we all joined in the chorus at the end of each verse, and never before felt so excited or saw such a scene of delicious wantonness as was displayed on every side, till at last exhaustion compelled us reluctantly to give up the engagement, and after a short rest we returned in the carriages to the Duke's mansion, as if we had only had an afternoon's drive.

This was altogether a memorable day, for as soon as we got back to Crecy House, Corisande whispered to me that as the gentlemen had all been fairly used up, her sisters had resolved to have an evening to ourselves whilst the gentlemen were in Parliament or at their clubs recruiting their enervated abilities by wine, smoke and cards. We might be sure of them till six A.M. at least, and the afternoon had left us all in such a burning unsatisfied state that they had impressed into our service four handsome young fellows, two footmen and two pages, who had never yet been admitted to any freedom with their mistresses, but Lady St. Aldegonde had already sworn them to secrecy as to what they might see in the evening, and given her instructions to have everything prepared in her own private drawing-room, so as to be ready as soon as the rest of the establishment had retired for the night.

It was past ten o'clock when we arrived home, but Bertha was so clever, it was all devised and ordered in a few minutes, the footmen, and pages little suspecting the scene they were to be introduced to when taking their oaths of secrecy. Everything promised a deliciously enjoyable affair, especially as we had to undertake to seduce them to our purposes.

In less than an hour-and-a-half, it was all ready; the Duchess was still keeping her room, so Bertha dismissed all except John, James, Charles and Lucien (the latter a fine handsome French page) as well as two pretty lady's-maids, Fanny and Bridget. There were five of us ladies who sat down to a game of cards, for which the party was ostensibly designed, all of us very lightly attired in the most négligé style as if quite indifferent to any little exposures we might make of our charms.

"My luck is dead this evening," exclaimed Lady Montairy, throwing her cards down; "I shall be ruined if I sit here; what do you say to a dance; let's get the servants to join us for fun; come Lucien, have a waltz with me round the room, I feel so low spirited I don't care what I do to drive it away."

"Fie, sister! how you make the boy blush, but I wouldn't mind a dance myself if it were not for the thing getting known," replied Corisande.

"Let's have a downright spree for once, John, James, and all of you will keep it secret, I should so like to know how you enjoy yourselves downstairs," laughed Bertha.

"Your Ladyship's slightest wish is binding upon us," replied John, most respectfully, speaking for the others, "and I am sure none of us would betray such a secret, when ladies condescend to a little familiar fun with their domestics."

Bertha seated herself at the piano, and everything was cleared out of the way for a waltz. Lady Montairy led off with Lucien, I proposed to Charles, a very handsome youth of seventeen, whilst Alice and Corisande had the two good-looking footmen, John and James for partners, Bridget and Fanny making a female couple.

What fun we had, how flushed and excited our partners looked as we clung to them in the voluptuous evolutions of this inspiriting waltz, as the strains of Lady Bertha's talented execution seemed to thrill through our souls; the young fellows quite delighted us by their easy graceful motions and manners, having evidently profited by their everyday experience in seeing their superiors conduct themselves in society.

At last we stopped from sheer exhaustion, Lady Montairy giving Lucien quite an amorous kiss, as she led him to a sofa, pretending she did it to put him at his ease, and we all followed her example, my partner excitedly returning my embrace with ample interest and ardour, his hot burning lips sending a thrill of desire through my frame.

Pretending to wish to cool myself a little I walked him into the next room, which was only lighted by the brilliant moon, and we opened the window, which looked out over a lovely garden, and then sat in a rather dark recess to enjoy the slight breeze which was loaded with perfume of flowers and had a soft sensuous effect on my excited nerves. I longed to enjoy my young partner, but did not exactly like the idea of being the first of the party to break through the slight barriers that still existed in favour of decency, although I knew perfectly well it was intended to be done by Lady Bertha and her sisters; still they seemed so slow in arriving at a thorough explanation with their company that I could wait no longer. "Charles," I whispered, "do you know what love is, have you ever had a sweetheart?"

"No, my Lady, I never had a chance yet, as I look at all the beautiful creatures, and think how hard it is that I dare not kiss one of them. Dear Lady, did you but know the intense pleasure your lips afforded me just now you not would think that kiss was thrown away, as I expect you did it in fun," he responded with emotion.

"Silly boy," I laughed in a whisper, "to think that should make you so happy, why I don't mind giving you another here in the dark, if it is such a pleasure, and costs me nothing," kissing him again in a very amorous manner. He clasped my heaving form to his bosom, and I could feel quite a shiver of delight rush through his trembling frame.

"What makes you tremble so, Charles?" I asked in the most innocent manner, laying my hand carelessly on his thigh just where I hoped to make an important discovery.

Nor was I displeased to touch the engine of love which my hand gently prodded, as if quite unconscious of anything wrong. What a start he gave as he exclaimed, "I am so ashamed, oh lady, you have driven me mad," then suddenly letting his rampant love dart loose, it stood throbbing and spending over my hand, whilst I seemed to be unable to realize what I was doing.

"Oh; darling! Oh, Beatrice! Forgive me! What pleasure!" he seemed to gasp out, kissing me rapturously, and taking all sorts of liberties with my bosom, which he was moulding and pressing with his hands.

"What am I doing? Pray Charles, don't be so rude," I said hastily, dropping the hold of his affair, and pretending to want to free myself from his embrace, but the amorous lad had gone too far to realize his prize, and almost quicker than I can relate it, his hands were under my skirts, forcing their way to the very shrine of love itself.

(*To be continued.*)

SUB-UMBRA, OR SPORT AMONG THE SHE-NOODLES.

(*Conclusion.*)

Not a day passed but we had some voluptuous games, whilst as to Rosa and Frank, they were openly engaged to be married, which was an especial gratification to the old people.

Time flew so rapidly that my visit drew to its close, and we were all thinking of devising some signal display of love, to be enacted as a parting scene ere I took my departure from my uncle's hospitable and happy domicile, when one fine morning in June, who should favour us with a call, but my lovely brunette Mrs. Leslie. She had driven over to invite myself and cousins to spend an early day before the Colonel's return. "You know," she said, turning to my uncle, "how stiff and starch all his ideas are, and I must have one day of real fun before he comes home from Paris. Will you let them come tomorrow and stop till the next day?"

My uncle being too kind to refuse, the arrangement was

made at once. Mrs. Leslie stayed to luncheon, and we took
an afternoon stroll in the park afterwards. From time to time
her intelligent glances assured me she was anxious for a tête-à-
tête with me, so asking her to take my arm, we soon managed
to give the others the slip, and lost ourselves in a dense copse.
Sitting down on the soft mossy turf, under a shady little yew
tree, we were quite hidden from observation.

"How I longed to kiss your sweet lips once more," I exclaimed, clasping her in my eager embrace, and sucking her
breath almost away in a luscious osculation.

"If that is all you thought of, sir, you have been vastly
unfaithful to your protestations of love, and I should really
feel awfully jealous of your pretty cousins and Miss Redquim
did I not see the unruly state of the jewel in your trousers,"
she laughingly replied, as she took speedy steps to release
and secure the impatient prisoner in her grasp, continuing,
"I wonder how he has amused himself since that ever
memorable day when I first had the pleasure of both seeing
and feeling the noble fellow. Now tell me true Sir Walter,
have you seduced your cousins and their friend?"

I at once made a full confession of all our amours, and
begged she would indulge us in every possible way on the
morrow, as it would be the last grand chance I should have
before returning to town.

"Most delightful state of things I am sure, but what a
shame not to have run over and invited me to join in your
amorous festivities. Surely you knew it was just what I should
have delighted in. I have a great mind to disappoint you now,
only I should also be punishing myself, so come on, you
naughty young fellow, and I will consider between this and
to-morrow what your penance will be," she said, reclining herself backwards, her fine dark eyes full of a humid languishing
fire, which too truly indicated her voluptuous requirements.

Lifting her skirts quickly, I paid my devotions at the shrine
of love by a kiss and playful bite of her clitoris, then, unable
to dally any longer, placed myself between her readily yielding thighs, and was soon revelling within the soft juicy folds
of her divine organ of bliss, delighted beyond expression by
the throbbing compressions to which it treated me as I lay
quietly enjoying the sense of complete possession, which is
so delicious to contemplate, before commencing more vigorous action; our lips met again and our billing and cooing

would have lasted some time had we not heard Frank declaring to Rosa and his sisters, "what a damned shame it was of Walter and Mrs. Leslie to give them the slip, but he would find us and spoil our fun."

This caused my charming inamorata to heave up her buttocks as a challenge to me, not to waste more time, so I put spurs to my steed, but none too soon, for just as we died away in a mutual spend, Frank, Sisters, and Co. burst upon the scene with a triumphant exclamation of "here's Walter and his grass widow," and before we could recover ourselves the laughing party inflicted an awful slapping on our bottoms, till a truce was made and we all agreed to wait patiently for the morrow's party at Mrs. Leslie's.

Next day, favoured by splendid weather, we were early at the Colonel's residence, and the handsome swarthy Vishnu ushered us into the luxurious boudoir of his voluptuous mistress. "You have arrived early, it is scarcely one o'clock, my toilette's not yet made, but how very welcome you all are to my house, I need not trouble to say, after the frank understanding we came to yesterday, as to our amusements now you are here. The chocolate is just ready, and I have infused in it an imperceptible something (a secret, my dear, which the Colonel brought from India), which will soon set all your young amorous blood in such a glow of desire that you will not know how to satisfy your intense cravings for the delight of love, and then naughty Walter shall be served out for his unfaithfulness to me."

This speech made up all smile as we took up the small cups of delicious chocolate which Vishnu handed round, and as he disappeared our hostess, who had nothing on but her dressing-gown, having drawn Frank to her side on the lounge, asked us, as the day was so warm, to throw aside as much as possible of our superfluous clothing, which was speedily done.

"We must have a romp before luncheon, then repose or stroll about during the afternoon, and in the evening we shall, I hope, enjoy some novel idea I have quite set my mind upon," she continued during the short time we took to disrobe. "That's right, only keep on the chemiserie now, at night we will discard the last rag; I have no chemise to take off, so will keep on this convenient robe de chambre, but you may look Frank, if you don't think Rosa will be jealous," as she opened the front, and displayed to his ardent gaze all the beauties of her person.

"If it makes her jealous, I can't help admiring such charms!" said Frank, "but Rosa is far too sensible for that, and thoroughly enters into all our fun, in fact I am sure she loves Walter as well as she does me, only she can't marry both of us."

"Ha! ha!! that accounts for Walter forgetting me, so to be revenged on them both you must have me now," she replied, lifting up his shirt to see if he was ready, "why your love-dart is almost exactly the size of his," and without more ado she was on his lap, and spitted herself on Frank's cock, throwing off entirely the robe de chambre that she might enjoy him without impediment.

This instantly excited the girls, who lay down in pairs for a mutual gamahuche and bottom-frig, Rosa playfully telling me to let Mrs. Leslie have the double pleasure by fucking her bottom as she was riding Frank.

"Hold her tight, my boy," I said, "and I will let her beautiful little fundament know what it is to keep a stiff prick waiting for his turn," as I took a little cold cream from the dressing-table, and putting some on the head of my prick as well as on the delightful brown wrinkled hole exposed to my attack, the head began to slip in at once, despite her struggles and screams, "that we should injure her between us." Further and further I gradually worked in, till I could feel my cock rubbing against Frank's with only the thin divisional membrane between them, our joint spendings deluging both cunt and bum, spurting the warm, frothy sperm over our balls at every thrust. This was not enough to satisfy her, but she kept us at our work until we repeated our emissions with screams of delight, and rolled on the floor in a confused heap amongst the dear girls, who were so excited by the sight of our ecstasies that they were revelling in every species of tribadism to allay their lustful yearnings.

After this Mrs. Leslie opened a side door, conducted us into her bathroom, where we refreshed ourselves and indulged in a variety of kissing, frigging, &c., but by her advice the girls refrained from exhausting us too much, and accepted cigarettes of Turkish tobacco to join us in a smoke, as we lighted some of the Colonel's fine cigars. It was a picture worthy of any Apelles, as we could see the reflection of all our naked charms on the bathroom walls, which constituted one vast mirror of the very finest silvered glass, two rather good-looking young fellows with big pricks, as rampant as could be wished, and five lovely ladies all smoking and puffing pretty curls or rings of vapoury nicotine, alternating that sober enjoyment for more active fun, by trying to burn the tips of their cunts with the fiery ends of cigarette or cigar.

About half-past two, we dressed, and then took luncheon, then strolled in the grounds or on the bank of a small stream, where some of us passed the time trying our piscatorial luck, till the bell rang for dinner, which passed pleasantly enough, and about 9 P.M., we assembled in the drawing-room, for a grand erotic séance.

Mrs. Leslie dismissed all her servants for the night, except Vishnu, who she said would be quite sufficient to attend to our little requirements.

The room was large and lofty, the windows closed and artistically draped with gorgeous black and gold curtains, the spaces between filled up with mirrors and branching candelabra, the opposite side of the apartment being also quite a tableau of flowers, mirrors, and lighted wax candles, which shed a brilliant and yet soft luxurious effulgence over the whole scene; two doors at one end gave access to retiring rooms, where we undressed, and in a very few minutes the whole party, in a state of ravishing nudity, were grouped round Mrs. Leslie as she sat on an ottoman, awaiting her decision as to the programme.

She first persuaded us to sip a little of her chocolate, then went on to say, "As we are five to two you will find I have a stock of fine, soft, firmly made dildoes to make up the deficiency in males, which alternated with the real article will enable us to thoroughly enjoy ourselves. First, I believe Miss is a virgin, notwithstanding all she knows and has seen; her delicate little pussey must be itching to be emancipated from the thraldom of virginity. Walter must do the service for her at once, on Rosa's lap, so now to business, as I see our gentlemen are in a beautiful state of readiness.

Polly blushed deeply, but readily seated herself on her friend's lap with her legs wide open, presented to my staff of life, whilst Rosa, passing her hands round the dear girl's waist, held open the lips of her cunny, and guided the head of my affair in the proper direction. Much as she had been

frigged and gamahuched, it was a hard task; her cunt was so
deliciously small and tight that in spite of her favourable position, I could only just get the head of Mr. Priapus within
the nymphæ before she started with the intense pain, and
gave a suppressed scream of anguish, the tears starting to her
eyes and trickling over her blushing face.

"Courage, darling, it will soon be over," I whispered, kissing her excitedly, whilst Mrs. Leslie encouraged me by saying, "Sharp and quick, Walter, a good thrust will force better
than those gentle pushes; gentleness is not real kindness when
taking a maidenhead"; at the same moment I felt she was at-
tacking my virgin bottom-hole behind with a well-lubricated
dildoe, its head being well in before I knew exactly what she
was doing; this and the desire to possess Polly so stimulated
me that I thrust furiously at the opposing obstacle, her
heartrending cries adding to my pleasure, and making me
mad with desire. At last I was halfway in, then a fierce lunge
seemed to break quite through as I, at the same time, deluged
the tight passage with a copious emission.

The poor little victim had swooned, but Mrs. Leslie, working her dildoe behind, ordered me to let my cock throb
inside Polly's tight sheath, as it would tend to bring her
round, and excite her amorous sensibility to the utmost.

What delightful sensations I experienced, my prick feeling
all the spasmodic contractions of her vagina, and having my
bottom well dildoe-fucked at the same time, I spent again
under the influence of this accumulated excitement just as
my partner was coming round under the influence of some
cordial which had been poured down her gasping throat, whilst
strong smelling salts had been applied to her nostrils. She
opened her eyes, giving a violent sneeze at the same time,
which vibrated on my delightful prick, who instantly began
gently to bestir himself in her tight scabbard; this roused her
little by little, till throwing her arms round my neck, and
returning my hot kisses with all the ardour of her nature, she
cried and laughed by turns, as she begged me to make haste
and complete her happiness.

By a side glance I could see Frank was in Mrs. Leslie's
bottom, Annie in him with a dildoe, and Sophie doing the
same to her sister, in fact, a perfect string of pederastic
branchings from my own violated bum. It was such a scene
as I had never seen before, and added additional fury to my

already maddened lust. I came again and again before we finished, each spend more ecstatic than the last. The chocolate had so invigorated us, that we went through an almost interminable series of spendings, till at last nature could stand it no longer, we rolled on the floor in a confused heap, and wound up in a mutual gamahuche; Mrs. Leslie secured the blood-stained quim of little Polly, which she sucked till she had enjoyed the last drop of ensanguined spunk she could extract from the wounded slit of her young friend, who writhed in delight under the soothing touches of such a lascivious tongue.

It was between eleven and twelve o'clock, when just as we were recovering from a state of lethargic oblivion, and thinking of some re-invigorating refreshment, the sound of carriage wheels on the gravel drive up to the house, and then, rat-a-tat-tat on the loud knocker made us all start to our feet and rush for our clothes.

"The Colonel, by all that's unfortunate," exclaimed Mrs. Leslie, "make haste or he will catch us; who would have thought of his arriving this time of night."

The prudent Vishnu, pretending to be awaking out of his first sleep, so bungled and delayed opening the front door, that we were tolerably presentable by the time the Colonel made his appearance, and whatever his suspicions may have been, he went through the formality of introduction in the most friendly way possible, the presence of so many young ladies evidently quite disconcerting him for the moment.

I afterwards learnt from his wife that under promise of secrecy she had confessed all to him, and vastly amused her husband by an account of our doings; but, at any rate, it stopped our fun at the time, and next day I was obliged to return to town, and thus brought to conclusion "My Sport amongst the She-Noodles," anything but "Noodles" after I had so enlightened them, in fact quite as knowing as Adam and Eve after they found out they were "Naked," having tasted the "Tree of Knowledge," which, in my humble opinion, meant found out "L'Arte de faire l'amour."

FINIS.

THEN—AND—NOW.

Nine years ago I Betsy knew,
　　When she was but thrice five;
With eyes that flash'd in amorous glow,
　　The prettiest girl alive!

Behold her now! a married dame,
　　Huge, burly, fat and coarse;
With a plump, lusty, dumpy frame,
　　Hind quarters of a horse!

She then was light, and slim, and fresh,
　　Rosy, and light'ning ey'd;
She then was Spirit—now—O Flesh!
　　How are thou finished!

SECOND PART.

Her sister Athenais sits
　　Beside her in the pew;
I wonder if that lass forgets,
　　What I once used to do?

She then was nine; I put my hand,
　　Into her frock behind;
And strok'd her, you will understand,
　　Just as I felt inclin'd.

She giggled and she winc'd about,
　　But liked the picked rudeness;
She eyes me kindly—she no doubt
　　Remembers all my lewdness.

Yes—eyes me most luxuriously,
　　With glances bright beseeching!
How pleasantly the moments fly,
　　While Mr. Cotterill's preaching!

I see she feels the amorous smart,
　　She muses on the men,
Comprising in her virtuous heart,
　　The thoughts of now and then.

TEMPTATION.

Papa and Mamma, Arabella and I,
  Were sitting at supper with nobody by;
Now because they believe me a cozy old fellow,
  They want to induce me to wed Arabella.

I like the girl well, but I don't choose to wed,
  Fair Bella perceives I'm not easily led;
But while Papa told me some prosy old fable,
  She was scratching her marrowbones under the table.

She look'd in my face, and on our eyes catching,
  I just turn'd my head to see what she was scratching;
She had got her right ankle upon her left knee,
  Up to her left garter I fairly could see.

She look'd in my face without shame or aversion,
  While scratching her nakedness for my diversion;
While I sat electrify'd stuck like a fool,
  She put down her petticoats easy and cool.

And ten minutes after she did it again,
  Though knowing I look'd and saw it quite plain;
Come—there was a prank for a delicate virgin,
  Who thought an old bachelor wanting some urging!

A SENSIBLE WOMAN.

Mrs. Johnson, going into the cellar one day, caught her husband fucking the servant girl. A short time after, finding that Kate was packing her boxes to leave, she enquired the reason.

Kate.—"I couldn't think of stopping mum, after what you saw in the cellar."

Mrs. J.—"Go along girl, do you think I mind? Perhaps with what you do in the cellar, and I do upstairs, we may keep the old whoremonger at home between us."

A SENSIBLE WOMAN.

Mrs. Johnson, going into the cellar one day, caught her husband fucking the servant girl. A short time after, finding that Kate was packing her boxes to leave, she enquired the reason.

Kate.—"I couldn't think of stopping mum, after what you saw in the cellar."

Mrs. J.—"Go along girl, do you think I mind? Perhaps with what you do in the cellar, and I do upstairs, we may keep the old whoremonger at home between us."

THE PEARL,

A Journal of Facetiæ and Voluptuous Reading.

| No. 9 | PUBLISHED MONTHLY. | March, 1880 |

LA ROSE D'AMOUR;

Or the Adventures of a Gentleman in search of Pleasure.
Translated from the French.

(Continued.)

The following day in the afternoon, Manette came into my room and asked me to follow her to her chamber, whither she led, saying, "I have something to show you that will please and satisfy you much more than your mistress could do."

I followed to her chamber, which after entering, she locked. I stood looking out of a window while Manette went behind the bed, the curtains of which were drawn. Hearing a light step advancing towards me I turned round, and Manette stood before me entirely naked; she sprung into my arms, clasping me round the neck, and led me to the bed, on which she seated herself.

I now saw what it was she had to show me, and being no ways loath to enter into the combat with her, to which she had invited me, I threw off my coat and vest, while she let down my pantaloons, and drew out my blunt but ever ready weapon, then falling back on the bed, drew me on top of her. My cock soon ran its full length into the soft and luscious sheath which nature intended for it. Twice before I got off her did I open the floodgates of love's reservoir, and pour into her a stream of fiery sperm, as each time she met me, letting down the very cream and essence of her body so copiously that our thighs were bedewed with it.

From this time till my cousin left the castle did I enjoy Manette in the same manner each day.

At the end of the second week after his coming my uncle announced his departure for Paris on the following day, and told me to make all preparations to go with him. When this was announced to my cousins and myself we determined to make the best possible use of the day by spending it in the woods on the banks of a small creek, with our respective mistresses.

It was Sunday morning, Raoul, myself, and Julien (for although I have not mentioned him in connection with our love affairs, it must not be supposed that he was idle in such things all the time, far from it; while Raoul and myself amused ourselves with Manette and Rose he consoled himself in the arms of Marie, one of the dairy maids, a large lusty brunette, and very good-looking, to whose bedchamber he stole every night) set out, meeting the three girls at the place appointed, they having gone on some time before us, carrying provisions and wine.

Having saluted our beauties we proceeded to arrange matters for a lunch, and sat down or rather reclined on the green sward, and discussed the merits of some of the good things they had provided for us, and after satisfying our appetites felt inclined to taste of the other good things they had left, but which were not visible.

Accordingly, as a preparatory note, we would slip our hands in their bosoms, and dallying awhile would roll them over on their backs, but in spite of our endeavours we could not raise a petticoat, more than to just get a glimpse of a thigh, resisting all our endeavours to get further into matters, saying, they would not consent to such naughty things in sight of each other, and if we did not behave better they would run off and leave us.

I then purposed we should undress and take a bath. "We will strip ourselves to our shirts, and then strip you, and at the word of command each shall throw off their nether garments."

To this there was some demurring on the part of our young ladies, as they felt some shame at being seen by each other thus, especially Marie, whom neither Raoul nor myself had seen till the present time, but we overruled their objections and stripped to our shirts, then each going up to his mistress, commenced unhooking and unlacing, and taking off frock and petticoats, till nothing but their shorts were left on them. I gave the word of command, "off shirts." We threw our shirts off, but on looking at our girls found them still standing in their shifts.

Finding they would not take their shifts off I proposed that one after the other throw off and stand naked, and each as they did so to be examined in all parts by the men, and their relative beauties compared, and offered to the one that would first do so a handsome diamond ring.

Manette stood for the saying, "that having come there to meet and enjoy ourselves with our lovers, and they having thrown off all covering, she would not spoil the sport, as she was not ashamed to let them see all what she had, for she was sure she had as pretty a leg and as sweet a little cunt as any girl in Brittany."

I was so much taken with the lusty Marie, Julien's mistress, her immense large titties, her extraordinary large hips and thighs, above all her beautiful cunt, which was covered up and hidden in a most luxuriant growth of jet black hair, which hung down fully eight inches long, and from out of which peeped two large red pouting lips, which looked most temptingly luscious, that I proposed we should each, after our first bathe, change mistresses, so that each one should have enjoyed the mistresses of the other two.

To this my cousins consented—with it the girls were much pleased as Manette was very anxious to have me once more bury myself within the juicy folds and recesses of her cunt; and Marie was also very willing, as she had whispered to me while examining her, telling me that although she was large she had a little cunt, but that Julien's prick was too small to give her much pleasure when he was in her; that mine was nearly twice as large as his, and she was sure that if I would consent to try her, I would like her much better than Rose.

I now led the way into the brook, leading Rose by the hand, the others following us. Once in, we played and sportively wantoned in the water, playing all manner of tricks, plunging them in over head and ears, and provoking them in every possible way, and under pretence of washing our fair partners, we gave our hands every liberty, going over every part, the breast, squeezing and moulding their titties, their soft bellies, rubbing their thighs, their cunts, and all other parts; the girls at the same time going over us in pretty much the same manner.

As we thus stood in the water, which was only about waist deep, our engines erect, and in good working condition, with my arm around Rose's waist, I tried to insert the nozzle of my engine into the mouth of her water-tight furnace, for the purpose of putting out the fire which was raging within it, but could not succeed, as we were unable to support one another.

My attention was drawn to a considerable splashing I heard, and on looking round I perceived that Raoul and Julien had laid their nymphs down on the edge of the water, their heads resting on the bank, and had got into them in that manner, the motions of their backsides and bellies coming together making the water fly all over them.

This was an example set before us, which Rose and I could not resist, so leading her out of the water we sat down on the grass, under the shade of a tree, there setting her across my thighs, her legs lapping around my backside, her soft, beautiful white belly rubbing against mine. I dallied with her ruby-nippled titties, firm and springing to the touch, with one hand, while with the other I was trying to make out the entrance to the harbour of love, in order to make room for my masterpiece of nature, that stood reared up between her thighs, and pressed hard against her belly, as if demanding admittance and shelter within the soft and luscious sheath, which nature had so bountifully supplied to a woman, and of which Rose possessed a most lovely specimen. She in a fit of humour affected to elude my efforts to gain entrance into her, trying to protract the desire she was wishing for, but managing her manœuvers so that they made the fire which was burning in us rage fiercer, and redoubled my excitement.

I covered her with burning kisses, and her eyes shot forth humid fires, and, languishing, seemed to melt beneath the long dark silken lashes which half concealed them. We rolled and twined about on the green sward, locked in each other's arms, till I at last got her under, with my knees between her thighs, and I was soon fairly into her, while she, feeling the dart of love entering into the very depths of the retreat, gave up, and lay at my mercy. But the fight growing fiercer and fiercer, she soon brought me to a crisis, at the same time paying down her own tribute to man.

Closing her eyes and breathing a sigh she stretched out her limbs with a faint shudder; the muscles instantly relaxing gave me to know that she had experienced the greatest pleasure that woman is capable of receiving or man of giving.

We had not recovered out of our trance when the others came up, and slapping us on our bare backsides soon brought us to.

Immediately on coming out of the water we changed partners, Raoul taking Rose, Julien, Manette, and I, Marie, and on receiving her I lay down between her beautiful legs, my cheek pillowed on the mossy hair that surmounted the gaping lips of the delicious entrance below.

Reclining thus for some time, sipping wine, eating bonbons and sweatmeats, we dallied away an hour or two, till our passions began to rise in such a manner as to be not long kept in subjection. My cousins, I suppose, thinking that being in the water added to the pleasure they received from the girls while fucking them, or from the novelty of the thing, proposed our going into the water again, and there enjoy our mistresses. They did so, but I remained under the tree with Marie. When the others got under the bank, I rose up, and spreading down all the dresses and petticoats, and making a pillow of a coat, I made a comfortable bed for Marie to lie on. I invited her to the combat. She got up and lay on the bed I had prepared for her, placing herself in an excellent position to favour my entrance. I laid myself down on her gently, she taking hold and guiding the head of the instrument into the opening, which was to pierce her to the very vitals. After she had lodged the head between the lips of her cunt, I titillated her with it for a moment and then slowly drove it into her, so slowly that it was a full minute before it was all in, so tight was her cunt and so large was my prick that they were stretched and gorged to the fullest extent.

Marie's cunt was small, very small indeed, most lusciously tight, and slowly drawing my rod out to the head—the tightness of it causing so great a suction that it sent a thrill of most exquisite pleasure through the whole body—then darting it into her, and again drawing it out, and darting it in till I could no longer master myself, my motions became so rapid and vigorous that we soon let down and mixed the essence of our souls together.

Although I loved my little Rose, with her dear little cunt and all her charms, although I found great pleasure when in the arms and enjoying the riper beauties of her sister

Manette, yet the sensations of delight and pleasure I had ju
received from Marie were, in my mind, superior to the
both.

I was the second time tasting and sipping of the sweets t
be had in the arms of Marie when the rest of the party brok
in upon us, but we did not mind them, and kept on till w
had finished our work. After resting from our labours fo
some time, and our appetites being sharpened, we got ou
nude syrens to rearrange the luncheon, then after satisfyin
our appetites, and taking another bathe, we dressed and se
out for home. On the way I called for a consultation as t
whether our exchange of mistresses should stand good for th
night or not.

Raoul answered that as we had spent the day together s
we ought to do the night, for all of us to lie together in on
room, and if either of the girls wished to be fucked by eithe
of us, that she should say so, and be accommodated, and vic
versa, to which we all consented.

That night we met in my chamber at eleven o'clock, th
girls fetching in beds from another room, and making the
up on the floor. I stretched myself naked on a pallet, an
Manette ran up and lay down by me. Raoul took Marie fo
trial, and Julie Rose.

After I had given the plump Manette a double proof of th
powers within me, another change was made, and I got th
lusty Marie. Towards daylight we were each lying with ou
own particular mistress, and after making all arrangement
for the future we fell asleep, I in my favourite position, layin
between the legs of Rose, having them thrown over me, m
head pillowed on her soft white belly, my cheek resting o
the silken mossy hair that surrounded her cunt.

We breakfasted at ten o'clock, after which I slipped up t
Manette's room, where I found her, Rose and Marie. T
each I made handsome presents, and told them if they woul
be true to me, that on my return from Paris, I would tak
and keep the whole three of them. Each one of them wa
anxious to have me tumble her once more on the bed, but a
I could only do one they drew lots for my last fuck, whic
fell to Marie. She lay down across the bed, and while I le
down my pants the other two girls threw up her clothes, an
each raised a leg, and after I had made good my entranc
they rested her thighs on my hips, so that I soon put her i

ecstasy by the delicious manœuvers of love's piston-rod. Half-an-hour after, I was on the road to Paris, where I will introduce myself to you in new scenes in a new chapter.

Chapter II.

We spent five days on the road, and if our amorous pleasures had in any way debilitated us, we were thoroughly restored to full vigour by the journey.

We arrived at the Count's hotel in Paris late in the evening, too late, so said my cousins, to give me an introduction to any of their *filles d'amour*, and after partaking of a slight supper we retired to our (at least for that night) virtuous couches.

The next day we spent at the Palais Royal, and on the Boulevards. At ten o'clock we went up to Raoul's chamber and had not been seated more than a minute or two before three beautiful girls entered, bearing trays, on which were wines, comfits, bon-bons, sweetmeats, &c. Having arranged them on a round table, Raoul introduced the pretty dears to me.

After the introduction we sat down to the table and passed an hour or so in drinking, eating, and chatting with our lovely guests till the champagne began to get into our heads, when we were not content with kissing and feeling the bubbies of our charmers, with other little liberties, but we tried to get deeper into matters, and found ourselves repulsed by our ladies, who, on our attempting to use a little gentle force, got up and ran out of the room. No sooner were they gone than Raoul said,—

"Don't be afraid, cousin, they will return shortly, and we will give them a great surprise by stripping ourselves perfectly naked."

We did so, and when done Raoul told me to choose which of the girls I would have for my partner for the night when they entered into the room again.

Presently the door opened, and the girls entered one after the other, and were in as naked a state as ourselves, with the exception of a large green gauze, which each of them was wrapped in, and which only served to heighten their charms, instead of hiding any part of their bodies from our view. Their hair falling down over their shoulders in long ringlets increased their beauty in combintaion with the gauze, so much that I stood perfectly bewildered, and not until my cousin spoke to me did I think of choosing a partner. But Louise, a lovely little sprite of eighteen, fair, finely formed, with a large bust, wide expanding hips, large firm buttocks, and pretty plump withal, shot forth at me such fiery glances from a pair of most bewitching dark-blue eyes that I immediately chose her.

The moment I named her she ran up to me, and opening her gauze enveloped me in it with herself. No sooner had she done so than the other two were in the arms of my cousins.

We again sat down to the table, our mistresses sitting on our laps. Louise hugged up as close to my naked body as she could; her delicious fat backside resting on my thighs, her large, firm bubbies pressed against my breast, a plump little arm thrown round my neck, her soft cheek nestling against mine, her rosy pouting lips glued to mine, in burning, fiery kisses, were enough to set on fire the soul of an anchorite, and as if this was not enough the bewitching little devil parted her thighs, and slipping her hand between them, caught hold of my prick, which had been rooting up against her backside, trying to find some hole or other in which to put his head and hide himself, and drawing it up between her thighs put the head of it between the fat juicy lips of her already spending cunt, rubbing the head between the nymphæ till I became so much excited that I told her if she did not want me to spill my liquor on her thighs she must let me in, as I could not possibly contain myself much longer.

Finding that she had worked me up to the pitch that suited her purpose, Louise raised one leg, and giving it a swing, threw it over my head, making herself revolve on her own "axass," bringing her round, soft and smooth belly against mine. Being now seated cross-legged, she raised herself on her toes, and taking fresh hold of my prick, lodged the head of it in her cunt, then letting her weight fall upon me, impaled herself on it, piercing her up to the very quick. She would thus move herself up and down; so rampant was I that I gave way before Louise was quite ready, but feeling the hot juice flooding the recesses of her cunt, it brought down her second tribute in time to mix with mine. We kept glued together, till my pego drawing itself up into littleness, fell out from the juicy folds of its nest.

Louise got up, and ran out of the room, soon followed by the two other girls, who I now saw had been engaged in the same game that Louise and myself had been playing. In a short time they returned, and we sat drinking till a late hour.

My amorous little devil of a partner had at last got me so excited that I proposed we should not go to bed for the night. My mistress, taking a light, led me to her chamber, which it was easy to see was fitted up as a sanctuary for love alone, a place in which nothing else was done or thought of. We first refreshed ourselves by bathing the most excited parts in icy cold water, then full of undiminished vigour, I carried her to the bed. We spent the night in one continued round of voluptuous pleasure.

The time thus passed for two weeks, without any other variety than occasionally slipping into the rooms of the mistresses of my two cousins and enjoying them for an hour or so during the day.

At last, Raoul advised me not to engage myself with either of the girls for a few days, as I should require all my vigour renewed, for he was going to introduce me to an establishment rivalling anything heard of in the "Arabian Night's Entertainment," an establishment of girls, supported by the nobility alone, the admission fee of which was one thousand francs. In it, he said, there were the most beautiful females in all France. He repeated his caution to me about holding any sexual intercourse with either of our girls, as I must do honour to his recommendation, that being a stranger about to be initiated I would be obliged to perform in public the first round with the girl I should choose for the night.

On the evening of the third day after my cousin's announcement I went with him to the house in which the orgies were celebrated. It was a large and gloomy-looking mansion, situated in the Rue St. Honore. We arrived at the gate, and were admitted by the porter. Crossing a paved courtyard we ascended a broad flight of stone steps, and my cousin, giving his name to the doorkeeper, led the way through a dimly-lighted hall, into a small, neatly furnished apartment at the left hand side, in which he left me for a few minutes, as he said, to bring in the examining committee. He returned very soon, accompanied by three gentlemen,

to whom he introduced me, saying my desire was to become
a member of the club.

The initiation was very simple; it merely consisted in my
handing over to them the entrance fee of one thousand
francs, and one thousand francs more for the benefit of the
house.

I was then led up another large flight of stairs, and invited
into a dressing room. They there informed me that I must
adopt the costume of the house, which was simply a large
dressing-gown open in front, put on over the shirt. I stripped
as they did, and we were soon en règle. Leading me to a pair
of large folding doors, which noiselessly opened at our approach, I was almost blinded by the flood of light which
streamed through them. Entering the room, a scene of the
utmost magnificence and gorgeousness presented itself to my
view, rivalling any fairy tales I had ever read. It was a large
saloon of lofty height and great length, supported on both
sides by rows of columns of marble of variegated hues; between each of the pillars supported on alabaster pedestals
stood a number of masterpieces of sculpture, in the finest
Carrara marble, representing nude females in every position
possible in which could be combined grace and lasciviousness.

So natural did they appear with a piece of gauze thrown
across their shoulders, one would have sworn they were living witnesses, flesh and blood, so admirably was their hair
chiseled out, representing the mode of wearing it by women
of different countries, so well was the rounded swell of the
breasts imitated, and then, further down, the short curly hair
that ornamented the beautiful life-like pouting lips below,
that one were almost tempted to advance and feel if they
were not living. Some, too, were most ludicrous; one I saw
representing a woman, her knees slightly bent and wide apart,
with a prick about halfway into her cunt. Another was made
to hold one in her hand, the head just without the lips of
her love notch, which appeared to have just fallen out of her
cunt, and shrunken up in her hand; and others in different
attitudes.

At the end of the hall there played a fountain of perfumed
waters, which diffused through the room a most delicious
and fragrant coolness. There were painted on the walls, pictures, the most lascivious that nature could conceive, women

in every variety of posture and position, nearly all of whom were represented as fucking with a man.

But the ceiling was the chef d'œuvre of this gorgeous apartment. The centre piece represented an immense cunt painted in the finest colours, from between the lips of which depended a large carved prick, with stones attached, from which hung a magnificent chandelier. On the outer side, and around the large cunt in the centre, were pricks with wings flying at it, from some of which you could see a stream of sperm spurting into the centre piece. Again, on the outside of the ring of pricks was a circle of naked nymphs, who appeared to be in pursuit of the pricks; they seemed to be leaning forward with outstretched hands ready to grasp them; the whole thing, intermixed with gold and silver stars, and surrounded with clouds of cerulean hue, formed a most splendid scene.

In the centre of the apartment was a long table, on which was laid out a most luxurious repast, served up on gold and silver plate, which partook of a character similar to the other adornments of the room. There were chased on the seats nude figures of men and women in all shapes and positions. Here were goblets supported on a stem, shaped like a prick; others there were, the bowls in shape of a cunt, supported on legs beautifully formed, and vases of every description, one of which in particular caught my eyes; it represented a nude female standing on her head, her legs bent at the knees, the feet resting on the hips, and forming the handles, the cunt representing the mouth, in which was set a bouquet of rare flowers.

After being introduced to the gentlemen present, and having time given me to notice the different beauties of the apartment, I was told that the goddesses of the establishment would soon enter to their supper, and that as they came into the room I should choose the one I most fancied, as they were all perfectly free, there being no jealousy among the men in that respect.

(To be continued.)

A FACT.

When tipsy Harry fumbled Kate,
   And felt her hairless belly;
"What's this," he cried, "thou's but a babe,
   This is no cunt, I tell ye!"

To whom the indignant lass replied,
   "Pray, why should you upbraid me?
It is not my fault, I am just
   As God Almighty made me."

"What's that to me?" replied the brute,
   "To stroke a child's unlucky;
If God Almighty made you so,
   Let Mr. Spurgeon fuck ye!"

AN ADVENTURE WITH A TRIBADE;

Related in a Letter From a Young Lady to Her Sister.

The next day at dinner time the impatient Caroline came herself to fetch me. As soon as we were in the carriage, she gave loose to her joy; she looked at me, embraced, and pressed me in her arms, never had I inspired more lively transports.

When we arrived she introduced me into the saloon, but this place not being convenient she was obliged to constrain herself rather more. After half an hour's animated conversation, in which she convinced me that she was not less well-informed than singular, dinner was announced. Placing ourselves at table she appeared almost instantaneously to abandon the reserve she had imposed on herself in the saloon. I never partook of a more delicious repast, the meats were exquisite, and the wines like nectar. Caroline helped me abundantly, pressing me to empty my glass by invitation as well as example, whilst a prefect harmony of celestial music poured in a flood through the perfumed air, which was fragrant with all the perfumes of Arabia; every moment she committed fresh thefts; the most passionate lover could not have attached more value to such insignificant trifles.

We were only waited on by two young girls, extremely pretty, and who were doubtless initiated in the sweet pleasures of their mistress, for their presence did not prevent her lavishing on me the most tender caresses. The diversity of wines and liqueurs which I had been forced to drink, that delicious harmony whose varied modulations alternately inspired the most lively transports and the most voluptuous languor, the advances of Caroline, her free discourse, all, in short, contributed to make me share her delirium, so that when she passed from the table to the boudoir, not only her sex was no longer an obstacle to my impetuous desires, but the novelty of that piquante and singular scene seemed to add to their intensity.

The most exquisite perfumes were burning at the feet of the principal statue.

"Do you see," said Caroline, regarding it, her cheeks on fire, "do you see with what greedy curiosity Venus examines the charms of Algae, the most beautiful of the graces? The marble seems to become animated at the sight of such attractions. Ah, my Julia, let me imitate it; let my hands, my eyes, do so also. But let us divest ourselves of these inconvenient robes, let there be no obstacles to our burning transports, every veil which covers you robs me of a pleasure!"

In a moment Caroline reduced me to a state of pure nature; far from resisting, I imitated her eagerness; the new beauties which discovered themselves to our view extorted a cry of admiration, and suspended our burning caresses.

Our hands, which for an instant seemed to have respected so many charms, wander with fresh delirium. Caroline takes me in her arms, drags me on to the ottoman, and obliges me to assume the attitude of Algae! I recline with my head resting on one of my arms, the right foot on the ottoman, the knee raised, whilst the left leg, unsupported, gently balances itself.

My chere amie, not less curious than Venus, takes the same posture, and places herself exactly in front of the throne of felicity, one of the beautiful knees rests on a cushion, the other serves for a footstool. Caroline, at her ease, contem-

plates the object of her dearest desires. Her delicate hand
opens the rose, and the new Sappho exclaims with transports
of joy, impossible to describe, "She is still a virgin! Good
God, what a source of pleasure!"

I confess I could never have imagined this discovery of
such great value to her; virgin or not, what need she care?
But we cannot account for the eccentricity of the passions,
and doubtless the most singular of all is to find one female
amorous of another.

Love! thou who inflamed Caroline with the most ardent
fires for one of her own sex, lend me thy burning pencil that
I may worthily describe this voluptuous scene, as even in
forcing us to give way to thy caprices, thy only object is to
render us happy!

Caroline rises transported, presses me in her arms, giving
a thousand kisses, then resuming her first attitude, contemplates anew the prettiest of bijous. "Yes," she exclaims, "that
flower is untouched. What colour! What freshness! Similar
to the bee, I will extract the ambrosia! I will intoxicate myself with its delicious juice. I will drain it with pleasure!"

Then by a thousand means, which I dare not describe, but
which occasioned me the most delicious sensations, Caroline
made me attain the last period of delight. Her design was not
merely to procure me delight; the skilful bee, wanting in the
natural engine necessary to extract the honey from the rose,
made use of her lascivious tongue to draw down my ambrosial
tribute to love, titillating and sucking in such a rapturous
manner that her face was almost drowned by my impetuous
emission, as I went off into a most delicious state of almost
unconscious lethargy.

Expressions would vainly endeavour to give an idea of Caroline's excitement; she seemed to have lost her reason as the
source of life, her words were as incoherent as her conduct was
extravagant. But what do I say? Was she not more sensible
than ever, since all she said, everything she did, only tended
to increase our intoxication, and add to its fury. Caroline,
whose desires no longer knew any restraints, in order to
satisfy them, made me pass through all the gradations of
pleasure. I tasted in the same evening all those indescribable
enjoyments which I should not have been acquainted with
until after a long novitiate, had not the extraordinary passion

I inspired her with induced her to initiate me at once in the most secret mysteries.

What charming pictures could I describe were I permitted to give the reins to my pen.

My imagination, exalted by these enchanting souvenirs, longs to retrace the image! But, alas! I must confine in my bosom the secret ready to escape, and deprive the most beautiful half of the human race of a fruitful source of pleasures and voluptuousness, of which the experience alone can conceive the extent!

TEN LITTLE NIGGERS.

Ten little niggers did a farting match design,
One got excited and died, so there were nine;
Nine little niggers laid his body straight,
One chanced to touch his prick, then there were eight;
Eight little nigger boys took a trip to Devon,
One fucked a peasant girl, and soon they were seven;
Seven little niggers got fooling with their pricks,
One got his foreskin back, and then they were six;
Six little niggers a frig loop did contrive,
One overspent himself, then they were five;
Five little nigger boys each picked a whore,
One had his in the arse, then there were four;
Four little nigger boys for a prize did pee,
One pissed himself away, then there were three;
Three little niggers had connection with a Jew,
The Chief Rabbi caught one, and then there were two;
Two little niggers were gamahuched for fun,
One got his prick bit off, then there was one;
The last little nigger met a Countess at a ball,
Married her, got the pox and died, and now that is all.

MISS COOTE'S CONFESSION,

Or the Voluptuous Experiences of an Old Maid;
In a series of Letters to a Lady Friend.

Letter IX

My dear Nellie,—

I have been looking over some of my grandfather's papers, and found the following curious little bit written by his brother Dean Coote, "Remarks on the influence of Female Beauty":—

I shall reverse the general practice, and instead of beginning with the head, commence with the leg, and hope to get credit for so doing. A pretty face, sparkling eyes, rosy cheeks, delicate complexion, smiles, dimples, hair dark, auburn or blonde, have all, it is acknowledged, great weight in the business of love; but still let me appeal to every impartial and unprejudiced observer, which he is most curious to behold, the legs or the face of his favourite lady.

Whether does the face or the legs of a pretty girl that is clambering over a style, or mounting a ladder, most attract our notice and regard?

What is it that causes my lord to smack his chops in that wanton lecherous manner, as he is sauntering up and down the lounge in Bond Street, with his glass in hand, to watch the ladies getting in and out of their carriages? And what is it that draws together such vast crowds of the holiday gentry at Easter and Whitsuntide, to see the merry rose-faced lasses running down the hill in Greenwich Park?

What is it causes such a roar of laughter and applause when a merry girl happens to overset in her career, and kick her heels in the air?

Lastly, as the parsons all say, what is it that makes the theatrical ballets so popular?

It has frequently been remarked by travellers that in no nation of the world are the ladies more nice and curious about their legs than in England; and to do them justice there is perhaps no nation in the world where the ladies have greater reason to show them like pretty girls in dirty weather, when the fear of passing for dragtails causes the pretty creatures to hold their petticoats up behind, and display their lovely calves and ankles above par. But I am infinitely more delighted with my muddy walk than were I making an excursion in the finest sunshiny day imaginable. There is a kind of magic in the sight of a handsome female leg, which is not in the power of language to describe, to be conceived it must be felt.

We read in the memoirs of Brantôme of a certain illustrious lady, who was so fully sensible of the vast importance of a handsome leg that once having the misfortune to break one of hers by a fall from a horse, and the surgeon by some inadvertency or other, failing to set the bone straight, she was so grieved at this accident that she actually had the fortitude to snap it across a second time on purpose and with design, then sending for a more skilful doctor, took care to have her leg carefully reset, by which means it was restored to its former grace and loveliness.

Some of my readers may, perhaps, condemn this conduct in the lady; for my part, I cannot but greatly admire both the soundness of her judgment and the amazing strength of her mind. But too well am I acquainted, from experience, with the magic which centres in a pretty leg, a delicate ankle, and well-proportioned calf.

The first time that I was in love (I perfectly well remember the circumstances as if it occurred but yesterday), the first time I could ever be said to feel what love is, I had to thank a pretty leg for it. I was then in my teens, as harmless and innocent a young fellow as needs be. My friends were of the strictest sect of religion. I was nolens volens brought up in their principles. Plays, novels, and all kinds of books which treat upon the subject of love were denied me; my parents were ambitious that I should be a second Joseph, and had partly succeeded in this pious design, when, lo! one single unlucky circumstance completely baffled all their endeavours.

It was a beautiful summer's day. I had strolled into the wood, laying myself down in a copse of young hazel trees, and alternately musing and dozing away, when my curiosity was excited by a rustling noise close to the spot where I lay concealed. I was all attention; and directing my inquisitive eyes to the quarter from whence the noise proceeded, discovered a lovely rosy-cheeked girl, who lay basking, as it were, in the sun, and deeming herself sufficiently remote from observation, was under no restraint in her motions. Presently up she whips her coats and ungarters her stockings, contemplates her legs, turns them this way, and that way, and in short practised a thousand manœuvers, which I have not at present leisure to expatiate upon; suffice it to say not a single movement was lost upon me, and from that hour to the present moment, I never see a pretty leg but I feel certain unutterable emotions within me, which seem to realize the observations of the poet:—

Should some fair youth, the charming sight explore,
In rapture lost he'll gaze, and wish for something more!

The Dean was quite right in his pretty delicate remarks about the influence of the leg; although only a woman, the same magic influence affects me; when I see a pretty pair of calves in silk stockings it makes me long to look higher, and have the bottom which belongs to them under a nice birch rod.

To return to my experiences, novices were rather shy of offering themselves as candidates for admission to Lady Rodney's Club, but one day, two or three weeks after the séance described in my last, Lucretia called upon me, apparently very much excited, and her errand was to tell me that Maria Aubrey, the sister of her quondam lover, wished to join us, and asked me to fix a day for her admission.

Knowing the young lady to be a very desirable subject, and to belong to a most aristocratic family, I could make no objections, and expressed my pleasure at the acquisition I hoped she would prove to the sisterhood, and appointed that day week for the reception of the novice.

When I mentioned the proposal to Lady Clara and asked what she knew of the young lady, she assured me that she had not yet the pleasure of her acquaintance as the young lady had been at school in Germany for some years, and was only just returned home.

Lucretia kept away from me till the eventful evening, but arrived punctually at seven o'clock with her protégée, who appeared slightly taller than herself, rather slim, with blue eyes, and dressed in white for the occasion; in fact, she seemed a very quiet, good-looking girl, the only thing specially attractive about her being a remarkable merry twinkle of her eyes, which seemed to look everywhere, and enjoy the sight of everything.

We were all present, and myself as usual seated as President, surrounded by the others. Lady Lucretia presented the novice without delay, taking her by the hand and leading her close up to the chair, then bowing, says, "Allow me, dear Miss Coote and sisters of Lady Rodney's Club, to present to you Miss Maria Aubrey, a dear friend of mine, who wishes to be admitted to your society."

PRESIDENT.—"Miss Maria Aubrey, are you willing to submit to our initiative ordeal and swear to obey the rules enacted by a majority of the members?"

MARIA.—"Yes, I am anxious to be admitted, we had so much of the birch in Germany, that I am an enthusiast in the use of the rod."

PRESIDENT.—"Let her be sworn as usual," after which she resumes, "Now Sister Maria, you will have to strip and assume the regular costume which we have provided for you."

The novice blushed deeply, and seemed quite at a loss what to say, and I noticed that Lucretia was hugely enjoying the scene. From some secret cause she whispered something to Lady Clara, and the latter to Mdlle. Fosse, who imparted the information to me "that our novice was not in reality Maria Aubrey, but her brother Frank, Lucretia's lover, whom she had persuaded to personate his sister, without in the least letting him know what he would have to go through, and no doubt was quite nonplussed at the idea of being stripped and exposed."

I must confess that I felt quite a flush of anger at learning the trick Lucretia had put upon all of us, but by the whispered advice of Mdlle. Fosse I proceeded as if nothing was known. "Come Sister Maria, begin to disrobe yourself; here, Jane and Mary assist the young lady."

MARIA.—"Oh! No! No! I can't be stripped, I didn't know you did that," blushing more than ever, and pushing the servants away from her. "Give me the things and I will retire to make the change but not before you all."

PRESIDENT.—"Already disobeying the regulations; you must strip this instant or the birch will be used without mercy, and we shall see if you are so fond of it."

MARIA.—"Ah! I beg your pardon, but—you really must excuse me from undressing before so many."

Here the President takes up a most formidable rod, made of a thick bunch of long birch twigs, elegantly tied together

with red and blue ribbons, and giving a sign, Jane and Mary,
assisted by four or five others, pounced upon the victim,
dragged her to the ladder, and in spite of desperate struggles,
secured both ankles and wrists with cord which were passed
through the rings of the ladder, and Miss Maria found herself quite helpless before she was well aware of what was
going to be done.

PRESIDENT, advancing to the victim rod in hand.—"Ah! I
see, this is a case of serious obstinacy; rip off that dress, and
pull up her skirts, the sooner we begin to initiate her a little
the better."

They all help to tear off the dress, etc., the victim is scarlet
with shame, and shrieks out, "Ah! Oh! Pray don't, I've been
deceived, I'm not a girl at all, don't expose me," tears of
mortification running down his cheeks.

PRESIDENT, authoritatively.—"Stop, then, who may you
be, are you a male or a hermaphrodite?"

The spectators all laugh at this question, and seeing his
tongue-tied confusion, cry out, "Go on, go on, Miss Coote,
give the impudent fellow a taste of your tickler, he must
confess everything, and take an oath of secrecy or we'll whip
him to death."

VICTIM.—"My God, what a scrape I'm in, these devils of
girls will murder me. Oh! let me go, and I will swear never
to tell anything."

PRESIDENT.—"Plenty of time for that bye-and-bye, you're
not going to get off quite as easily after your impudent con-
spiracy with Lady Lucretia; you shall both see each other
well whipped; you won't be shocked at seeing the bottom
we know you are so well acquainted with. You're secure
enough. Jane, prepare Sister Lucretia for punishment, so that
he may know what to expect for himself."

LUCRETIA.—"Ah! No! I never meant anything but a little
fun, you know I wished to birch him, and this is the only way
I could manage it."

PRESIDENT.—"Very well, Miss, we'll take that all into consideration, and perhaps let you put the finishing touches to
his bottom bye-and-bye. Put her posteriors in the stocks,
Jane."

Leaving the young gentleman securely fixed to the ladder,
they seize upon his ladylove, who knows better than to resist,
and in a few moments Frank has the pleasure of seeing her

blooming bottom and beautiful legs projecting from the wooden stocks in which she is so fixed that only the nether half of her person can be seen.

PRESIDENT.—"Now Mdlle. Fosse will administer a proper correction for the insult she has put upon the Club by introducing a person of another gender amongst us."

MDLLE. FOSSE, who has armed herself with an excellent bum-tickler of well-pickled birch.—"I don't think the impudent hussey was half punished when we admitted her, or the soreness of her bottom would surely have kept her out of this." Then whack—whack—whack—she gives four very smart strokes with great deliberation. "How do you like that, is my arm heavier than Miss Coote's?"

LUCRETIA, screams and kicks her legs about in great pain. —"Ah! Oh! Oh! I beg—I beg pardon, indeed I thought a young gentleman would be a most agreeable accession to the Club. Oh! Ah! how you cut, it's dreadful!" as the blows continue to fall with great effect and precision, each one leaving its long crimson and blood-red marks and weals.

MDLLE. FOSSE.—"I must be quick, as it will take some time to punish Master Frank. I hope he is enjoying the sight of your castigation; is it as nice as it was before? let us know when your prurient ideas are satisfied by that feeling of sensuous pleasure you told us you experienced then," touching the tips of her birch in under her exposed pussey, and between the tender inner surfaces of her upper thighs.

The male victim's face was flushed with excitement at the sight of his lady's punishment, every blow seemed to thrill through his system, and put him into such a state of feeling as he had never experienced before, bringing out all the sensuality of his disposition as he watched the scene with rapt attention.

Mademoiselle plies her rod so vigorously that the blood soon begins fairly to trickle over Lucretia's bottom and thighs. "Ah! Oh! I shall faint. I shall die!" she sobs, writhing and twisting beautifully under the continued flagellation.

The President here comes forward with her rod saying, "I think Master Frank is longing to taste what it is like; pin up his skirts as decently as possible. I only want to see his bottom, we don't want the other thing introduced to our notice."

Frank was so absorbed in watching the beautiful sight of

Lucretia's whipping that he never knew his own skirts were
pinned up till a tremendous whack on his own bum awaked
him in a most lively manner to a sense of his forlorn condition. He winces and bites his lips, the tears starting to his
eyes, and an extra crimson flushing over his face, all convince
the spectator of his renewed humiliation. Again and again
the President makes her blows sound through the apartment,
but not till seven or eight weals have been raised on his
posteriors will Master Frank gratify them by the least approach to a cry.

PRESIDENT, with a tremendous crack which fairly draws the
blood.—"I'll make you beg our pardon, sir. Will you ever
insult us by coming here as a girl again?"

Frank, trying to bear it pluckily, and ashamed to cry out
before a lot of girls, writhes his buttocks in agony, and still
bites his lips in silence till they fairly bleed.

PRESIDENT.—"Obstinate, eh, so much the more fun for
us, my boy; will you beg pardon, and swear never to tell anyone of this spree of yours?" cutting his white bottom with
all her might, each blow scoring the flesh and making it raw.

FRANK.—"Ah! I must call out, it's awful. Oh! don't quite
murder me ladies. Ah—r—r—re!"

PRESIDENT.—"Will you come here again, you impudent
fellow, will you take the oath now to keep our secret?" keeping him in constant agony by her well-applied strokes.

Frank's cries and Lucretia's sobs, in addition to the sight
of two well-pickled bottoms, made the ladies all quite excited;
each one takes up her birch, and as the President and Mademoiselle retire, they relieve each other in short spells of birching on the posteriors of the two victims, till at last Lucretia
is nearly spent; she gets oblivious to pain, and seems lost in
a kind of lethargic stupor. They let her down, and apply
restoratives, which soon bring her to herself again, whilst
Frank, who has been imploring for mercy, and praying to
be sworn to secrecy for some minutes past, is at last allowed
to take the required oath, but is greeted with renewed
laughter when he begs pitifully to be released and allowed
to go home.

"Ha! Ha! he thinks we shall let him go now, he can't
object to Lucretia finishing him off, when she's a little
recovered."

FRANK.—"It was all her fault, I should never have come, only she assured me of a warm welcome."

PRESIDENT, laughing.—"That's good, ladies, is it not? And you can't say we haven't given you one, but it must be warmer still before we let you go."

Lucretia swallows some stimulating cordial, and with sparkling eyes announces herself as ready to assume the rod; they hand her an elegant new one, and she takes her position, evidently minded to give him a little after the fashion of Louise Van Tromp's style of birching. "Do you," said she, "dare to insinuate that I tempted you to come here, sir?" flourishing the rod over her head so that he could hear it hissing through the air.

FRANK, all of a tremble.—"Ah! Ah! Lucretia, will you too prolong my torture, now I have promised everything."

Lucretia, bringing down her rod in earnest, makes his bottom wince and writhe under the stroke as she says, "Then you don't withdraw that insinuation, sir." Whisk—whisk—whisk, each blow harder than the last, and getting excited more and more, as the cuts seem to make the blood boil more tumultuously in her own veins, "Is it not true that you ravished me, sir? these ladies know all about your shameful conduct to me."

FRANK, in agony and desperate at this renewed torture.—"Ah! Oh! Ah! I'm hanged if I own all that, why you know you had my—my—you know what I mean in your hand first."

LUCRETIA, angrily.—"Don't mention the disgusting monster," cutting him desperately across the shoulders, "hold your wicked tongue, sir, if you are only going to asperse my character," again paying her attention to his raw-looking bum.

Frank, who has now lost his false hair by twisting his head about too much, looks a little more manly, but is a very fair youth withal, although his rump is not so finely developed as it would have been in a girl.

Lucretia, who feels all the stimulating warmth of her own flagellation, cuts away in fury. "See, see," she cries, "that unmentionable thing of his is quite rampant, and sticks out under his shirt in front, it's impossible to hide the disgusting creature." Striking more and more round his buttocks, which so disarranges his shirt that we continually get glimpses of a very formidable-looking weapon projecting six or seven inches from a bed of curly light hair at the bottom of his belly, the

youth's eyes roll in a kind of erotic frenzy, and every thought
of pain and shame has evidently given away to his sensuous
feelings as he writhes and twists his bottom in a most lascivious manner at every stroke. The flagellatrix is also beside herself, the sight of his bleeding bottom and erotic emotion
increases her fury more and more. "Ah!" she cries, "he not
only tries to make me out worse than himself, but see how
insultingly he is exposing himself to us all!" cutting the next
stroke so as to reach the offending member. This she does
again and again, causing such intense pain and excitement
that at last the poor fellow shouts out, "Oh! Oh! My God!
I shall burst, it's awful, and yet gives most delicious sensations! Ah—r—re! Ah—r—r—re! Oh! Oh!" and then he
seems to die away in an excess of voluptuous emotion.

Lucretia suspends her rod for a few instants and then suddenly wakes him up again with two or three tremendous
whacks upon his sore posteriors, exclaiming, "Wake up, sir,
we've had enough of that, perhaps you will now withdraw
your insinuations against me; did you not take advantage of
my confusion, when I found you so exposed in the garden?"
following up her question by a lively application of her rod,
till the blood fairly trickles down Master Frank's thighs.

FRANK, again in awful pain, and ashamed to think how he
has been exposed, now his erotic excitement has passed off
for the moment.—"Ah! Ah! you she-devil, who could believe
you could cut me up so after your loving caresses and assertions of your affection for me. Ah! Miss Coote, save me
from her, have mercy ladies!" the tears of shame and agonized
mortification running down his crimson face.

LUCRETIA.—"Not yet, you impudent boy; will you withdraw your assertions about me, or I will literally skin your
bottom before you get let off."

FRANK.—"Oh! Oh! how cruel of you Lucretia, to force me
to tell a lie, how can I?" writhing under the shower of smarting strokes, and evidently beginning to experience the return
of his voluptuous feelings.

LUCRETIA.—"Your cries are delightful. I enjoy it so much
more, knowing how we love each other. Will—will you withdraw your wicked assertions? You have made these ladies
think me a monster of lasciviousness. Do you hear, sir?" cutting well up under the crack of his bottom, so that the tips

of the birch might sting him in the tenderest and most private parts.

VICTIM.—"Ah! Oh! Oh! My God! you'll kill me," seeming almost ready to faint with the suddenly excruciating pain.

LUCRETIA.—"Then why do you obstinately persist in refusing the satisfaction I ask of you, and say I want to make you tell lies, you wicked fellow, I'll murder you with the birch if you don't retract your vile insinuations," cutting him terribly everywhere she fancies he can feel most.

FRANK, in terrible agony.—"Oh! Oh! What—what must I say—all those stories about us are quite untrue, we never did anything wrong," writhing about and hardly knowing what he says in his anxiety to get away from his torture.

LUCRETIA, with a furious blow which almost takes his breath away.—"Hold, hold, now, sir, you go to the other extreme; I only want you to confess you took advantage of me; your brain is confused, what a strange thing that after all this whipping and wealing the blood should still fly to your head."

FRANK, sobbing with mortification.—"Indeed—indeed, I remember now, how I put my hand under your clothes, when you were so overcome you could not resist me. Ah! Oh! Oh! Let me off, you never need fear I shall tell the secret of my own humiliation!"

He is fairly broken down, Lucretia drops her worn-out birch as tears of sympathy rise in her large loving eyes, and she sobs, "Poor fellow, poor fellow, what made you so obstinate?"

PRESIDENT.—"Let him down, and make him kneel before me and beg our pardon for the indelicate scandal he has caused amongst us, as I can feel and see what painful emotions the sight has caused in every lady's breast."

He is released, and Frank, humbly kneeling, declares his sorrow for having so shamefully intruded upon our private proceedings and again promises faithfully to keep our secret, and begs with fresh tears in his eyes to be allowed to remain a member after his painful initiation.

This was most favourably received, and I soon found out that Lady Clara was at the bottom of a plot for introducing the male element into our society.

I hastily closed the séance, and never knew how or what means they used to ease his sore bottom, but next day, by

advice of Mdlle. Fosse, I intimated to them all a dissolution
of the Club, as I could not possibly join in or allow my house
to be used for birching orgies in connection with the opposite
sex. My next and last letter on this subject will relate more
nearly to myself.

Yours affectionately,
ROSA BELINDA COOTE.

(To be continued.)

THE FRUITS OF PHILOSOPHY.

Said good Mrs. Besant,
To make things pleasant,
If of children you wish to be rid,
  Just after coition,
  Prevent all fruition,
And corpse the incipient kid.

To do this completely,
Securely and neatly,
That your conscience may suffer no twinge,
  Before having connection,
  Procure an injection,
Likewise an elastic syringe.

Then after the "coup,"
All the ladies need do
Is to jump out of bed on the spot,
  Fill the squirt to the brim,
  Pump it well up her quim,
And the kid trickles into the pot.

A little lady who was, and we believe is, a great speaker at
the Quakers' meetings, was once asked by Mr. Bright in his
young days, "if she did not find the spirit inspired her with
thoughts of marriage?" "No," she answered, "but I frequently
find my struggling with the flesh does."

THE COLUMBINE.

Written in London 12th January, 1837, on Fraulein Theresa
Schmidt, an opera dancer, as Columbine.

———

Night after night I've fed my eyes,
  On sweet "Theresa Schmidt, Fraulein,"
And marvell'd how cold Northern skies
  Could mould so fair a Columbine.

No verse, no rhyme could tell my mind,
  To vent the praise my heart would breathe,
But she's an English girl I find,
  And bears the vulgar name of Smith.

But whatso'er her name may be,
  No Roman dancer could surpass,
The way she shows her open C,
  And flourishes her jutting arse.

Yes—whatso'er the name she bear,
  No graces, no celestial nymphs,
Can grant to men a sight more fair,
  Of paradise a clearer glimpse.

Let others rave of Taglioni,
  Dancers from Florence or from France,
But give Theresa for my money,
  She shines the goddess of the dance.

The sculptor modelling naked truth,
  Array'd in Eve's celestial dress,
May find her here in blaze of youth,
  In all her native loveliness.

Pure English are the parts she shews,
  Although she's call'd Theresa Schmidt;
What's in a name? A bright moss rose
  By any other name's as sweet!

———

LADY POKINGHAM, OR THEY ALL DO IT;

Giving an account of her Luxurious Adventures, both before and after her Marriage with Lord Crim-Con.

Part IV.

(Continued.)

My partner was far too impetuous to heed my faint remonstrances, and in spite of all I could do to keep my thighs closed his venturesome hand soon took possession of my heated cunny. "If I die I must have you, darling lady," he whispered in my ear, as he suddenly forced me quite back on the sofa, and tried to raise my clothes.

"Ah! No! No! I shall faint. How your violence frightens me!" I sighed, trying to smother my desires by simulating helplessness, and then feigning unconsciousness I promised myself a rare treat by allowing him to think I really had fainted, which, no doubt, would urge him to take advantage of the moment to riot unrestrained in the enjoyment of my most secret charms.

It was almost dark in the shadowy recess where the sofa on which we were was situated. "She's quite gone, the darling!" I heard him say to himself, as he gently parted my relaxing thighs, "I'll kiss it first." Then I knew he was kneeling between my legs, and I felt his fingers gently parting the lips of my cunt. "How I must have excited her, she's been spending!" he went on, then I felt his lips right between the nymphæ as he kissed me rapturously just on the excitable little clitoris. What a thrill of desire it sent through my frame, as it made me literally quiver all over with emotion, so that I could scarcely refrain from clasping his head with my hand, or nipping his dear face between my thighs.

This only lasted a few moments, which seemed awfully long in my excitable state, my cunt was spending and throbbing under the voluptuous titillations of his velvety tongue. Heavens how I wanted to feel his prick inside of me! and could not have feigned my fainting state another instant, but the moment my lips were in the act of parting to implore him to fuck me at once he started to his feet, pushing my thighs as wide apart as possible, and directly I felt the hot head of his cock placed to the mark; slowly and gradually he pushed his way in, as contracting my usually tight affair I made it as difficult as I could for him to achieve possession. How he kissed my lips, calling me, "Darling lady, dear Beatrice, oh, you love, what pleasure you give me!"

I felt him spend a torrent of his warm essence right up to my vitals, and then lay still upon me exhausted for the moment by the profuseness of his emission.

Still apparently in the state of inanimation, and without opening my eyes, I made my cunt nip and contract on his throbbing prick as it was soaking within me, in such a manner that he was almost immediately aroused from his delicious lethargy, and recommenced his movements, exclaiming to himself, "What a love of a girl, even in her fainting state, the love pressure of her cunt responds to the action of my prick. What pleasure it would be if I could but arouse her to sensibility!" as he kissed me over and over again rapturously, quickening his stroke till my blood was so fired I could no longer impose upon him, so I suddenly threw my arms around the dear boy's neck, whilst my amorous kisses responding to his silently assured him of the delight he was affording me.

"Here they are, the sly things, why Beatrice is the hottest of the lot, see she has got Charles well in her," laughed Lady Bertha, bringing a light into the room, and followed by all the others, looking very excited, and as if some of them at least had been doing the same; in fact I could see the front of John's trousers were undone, whilst the flushed face of Lady Montairy, and the delighted manner in which she clung to the handsome young French page, assured me that she at least was on the best of terms with her partner, added to which, in the background, Bridget and Fanny seemed as loving as any of them from their damask cheeks and sparkling eyes.

Charles was dreadfully confused, and I felt that the surprise was taking all the vigour out of him, so with the greatest presence of mind, I threw my legs over his buttocks and embraced him more firmly than ever, as I exclaimed, "It's this naughty fellow, my dear, has taken liberties with me, that I fainted from fear, and he is in complete possession of my virginity, and having aroused all my passions to the highest pitch he wants to withdraw, slap his bottom well for me, and make him now complete my pleasure, after satisfying his own greedy lustfulness!"

He struggled hard to get away but I held him tightly, whilst all of them slapped him without mercy, making him fairly bound in the saddle to my great delight, more especially when I soon found him swelling up quite an unnatural stiffness, till his prick was almost breaking my quim, and he was furiously fucking with all his might, as he cried out for them to leave off and let him do it properly.

The noise of the slaps on his bum seemed to give me intense delight and I never remember to have had a more delicious fucking, which as he had spent twice previously lasted a long good bout, till we both came together almost frantic with delight, as our mutual essences were commingled at the same moment.

"There, don't let me catch any two of you slipping away by themselves again," said Lady Montairy, as she gave a last tremendous slap, which fairly made the poor fellow bound under her hand, in spite of his exhaustive spend. "It spoils half the fun, when some are so sly, and pretend to be mockmodest when at the same time they are quite or more inclined for the sport than anyone."

All returned to the drawing-room and refreshed ourselves with champagne, jellies and other reinvigorating delicacies, as we laughed and bantered the four young fellows and the two lady's-maids about their sweethearts and love experiences, till Bertha wrote all the names of the female members of our party on slips of paper, which she said she would hold for the boys to draw their prizes, declaring that Bridget and Fanny, if drawn, should submit to be fucked, although they protested their virginity and determination to keep it for the present, much as they enjoyed the other fun.

First of all she asked us to assist her in stripping our cavaliers quite naked, in order that we might enjoy the sight of their adolescent beauties (John, the eldest, being only nineteen). They were finely formed young fellows, but the splendid proportions of Master Charlie's penis carried off the honours of the evening, being more than eight inches long and very thick. My lady friends were in ecstasies at the sight, and almost made the other three young fellows jealous by each wishing he might draw them for a partner.

"Now there shall be no deception or cheating; I've a novel

idea how the lots shall be drawn," said Bertha, drawing up her clothes till she showed the beautiful lips of her luscious cunt, just peeping out between the slit in her drawers as her legs were wide apart; then drawing me close to her side she gave me the slips of paper and whispered in my ear to arrange them in her cunt with the seven ends just sticking out. It was soon done, then our gentlemen had to kneel down in front and each one drew his paper with his mouth.

This was a jolly bit of fun, Bertha looked as if she would have liked to be fucked by all four instead of merely having them draw lots from her gap, which was so tickled as they drew out the papers that she actually spent under the novel excitement.

John drew Bridget; James, Lady Montairy; Charles, Bertha, whilst I was lucky enough to get the handsome Lucien, who had been eyeing me with a most amorous leer, which you may be sure did not in the least offend me.

Corisande and Fanny were told to fit themselves with a couple of most artistically moulded india-rubber dildoes of a very natural size and not too large, which Lady St. Aldegonde said her husband had procured for the purpose of having his lady bottom-fuck himself occasionally, when he wanted extra stimulation. "And now my dear, they will be very useful in enabling you to give these nice youths the double pleasure as they enjoy their partners."

The ladies were now also divested of everything, till the complete party were in a state of buff, excepting the pretty boots and stockings, which I always think look far sweeter than naked legs and feet.

The interest centred in the engagement between Bertha and Charles, as the others were all anxious to see the working of his fine prick in her splendid cunt. He was in a very rampant state of anticipation, so she laid him at full length on his back on a soft springy couch, then stretching across his legs she first bent down her head to kiss and lubricate the fine prick with her mouth, then placing herself right over him gradually sheathed his grand instrument within her longing cunt, pressing down upon him, with her lips glued to his, as she seemed to enjoy the sense of possessing it all. I motioned to her bottom with my finger, and Fanny, understanding my ideas, at once mounted up behind her mistress and brought the head of her well-cold-creamed dildoe to the

charge against her brown-wrinkled bottom-hole, at the same
time clasping her hands round Bertha, one hand feeling
Charlie's fine prick, whilst the fingers of her other were tickling the fine clitoris of our mistress of the ceremonies. It was
a delightful tableau, and it awfully excited us all when they
at once plunged into a course of most delicious fucking.
Fanny was as excited as either of them as she vigorously
dildoed her mistress, and kept her hands stimulating them in
front. Corisande now attacked Fanny behind with her dildoe,
delighting her with frigging combined.

How they screamed with delight, and spent over and over
again; it is impossible to describe, but I had got Lucien's
fine prick in my hand as we were kissing and indulging in
every possible caress. It throbbed in my grasp as I repeatedly
drew back the foreskin, till at length fearing he would spend
over my hand, I sank back on a sofa, and drew him upon
me, guiding his affair to my longing cunt, whilst he clasped
me round the body and kissed more ardently than ever. I
could see all that was going on round the room, Lady Bertha
still riding furiously on Charles, stimulated by the double
exertions of Fanny and Corisande, and watched with delight
the frenzied enjoyment of the lady's-maid, as she handled and
felt how Charles was going on in front, whilst her young
mistress's dildoe almost drove her to distraction by its exciting movements in her bottom. Lady Montairy was riding
James as he sat on a chair, but John was being quite baffled
by his partner Bridget, who wriggled and avoided every attempt of his cock to get into her, as she kissed and allowed
him any liberty except the last favour of love.

At last we all finished. "Now," said Lady Bertha, "we will
rest and refresh ourselves a little, and then we will see to
Bridget and Fanny having their maidenheads properly taken;
meanwhile I will tell you a little adventure I once had down
at Brentham a few months after my marriage. Well, you must
know St. Aldegonde wanted to represent the county in parliament, and a general election was expected very soon, indeed
it was rumoured the dissolution would occur almost immediately, so no time was to be lost, and there was one great
landowner, who if we could but secure him to our side we
were sure of carrying the day. He had been an old admirer
of mine, and had been much chagrined at my lordship's success in obtaining my hand, and we both knew he was almost

certain to throw all his influence into the opposite scale. We were just going to bed one night, and about to fall asleep after a beautiful fuck (it is nice when first married) when a sudden idea made me quite laugh, it seemed so good.

"St. Aldegonde was quite anxious to know what I had been thinking of, 'My love,' I said, kissing him (I don't often do that now, except when I want to wheedle him out of something) 'would you mind giving a bit of my cunt to secure your return for the county?' 'Why, Bertha darling, just at this moment nothing would make me jealous, as you've sucked the last drop of spend from my cock,' he said, with a yawn, and then realising my idea, he continued, 'Do you mean Mr. Stiffington, my love; it's a bright idea, if you do, and damned cheap way of buying him, besides cunt could never be reckoned bribery.'

"The prospect of adventure, added to the good I might do for my husband, made me volunteer to do it, and as secrecy was everything, we determined that I should go down to Brentham disguised as a servant.

"Next day we started apparently to go to Paris, but I left St. Aldegonde at the railway station, and started off to Brentham by myself after changing my dress at a hotel. The housekeeper at Brentham was the only person whom I took into my confidence, but of course she did not know all.

"She passed me off as a niece from town, who had a holiday for a few days, and I mixed with the servants as one of themselves; the idea that I could be Lady Bertha never entered their heads, as I was supposed to be gone abroad for a tour.

"Without delay she got the coachmen to drive me over to Mr. Stiffington's place, Manly Hall, with a note to that gentleman on some special business, which I must deliver with my own hands.

"The gentleman was at home, and I was soon ushered into the library, where he was attending to his letters or other business, after breakfast, about 11 o'clock in the morning.

"'Well, young woman, let me have the particular letter you brought from Brentham; why couldn't a groom have done as messenger? By Jove! you're a nice looking girl though!' he said suddenly, seeming to notice my appearance.

"'If you please, sir,' I said, blushing, 'I'm Lady Bertha's

maid, and bring a very important note from Lord St. Aldegonde.'

"He was a fine handsome fellow of about thirty-five, full of
life and vigour in every limb; his eyes looked me through and
through, then suddenly he penetrated my disguise, as he exclaimed, 'Ah, no, you're Lady Bertha herself, what is the
cause of this mystery?'

"I was all confusion, but he told me to sit down and tell
him without reserve what I wanted, as he drew to a sofa and
seated himself by my side.

" 'Your vote and interest to secure my husband's return
for the county,' I said in a low voice, 'we know you can turn
the scale, so I ventured to solicit your influence in person.'

" 'But how can you expect me to be otherwise than hostile
to a man who deprived me of your beautiful self,' he replied,
'why did you jilt me for a lordling?'

"I looked down in pretended distress, as I answered with
an almost inaudible voice, 'If you only knew our family
necessities, it would soothe your wounded self-respect, nothing but his dukedom in perspective sealed my fate against
my own feeble will, and now it is my duty to further his
interests in every way.'

" 'Dear Bertha,' he exclaimed excitedly, 'do I really hear
right, would you have preferred me, can you not pity my
unrequited love, won't you even favour me with a smile as
I look in your face?' taking my hand and covering it with
impassioned kisses. 'I would support your husband, but—but
I must be bribed—let me think what you shall give me, dearest; of course he's had your first virginity, but I must have
the second, it will cost him nothing, and no one need know.'

"He was growing quite impetuous; with one arm around
my waist, whilst he covered my blushing face with the most
ardent kisses, I could feel his other hand wandering over my
bosom or my thighs, as he felt them through my dress, then
taking one of my hands he forced me to feel his standing
cock which he had let out of his breeches; the mere touch
sent a thrill of desire through my whole frame as I sank backwards in an assumed faint.

"He jumped up, fastened the door, then went to a drawer,
from which he took a small book and a little box, then kneeling down by my side he gently raised my clothes, kissing my
legs all the way up, inside or outside of my drawers as he

could get at them, and parting my thighs opened the slit in my drawers, till he had a fair view of my pussey. 'What a sweet little slit, what soft silky down it is ornamented with,' I could hear him say as he pressed his lips to my Mons Veneris, then I could feel his fingers parting the lips of my cunt with the greatest tenderness to enable him to kiss the little button of love. This was too much, I pressed his head down with my hands, as I spent over his tongue with a deep drawn sign of pleasure. 'She's mine, how she likes it, the touches of my tongue have made her come!'

"'Look, darling,' he continued, as he rose to his feet, 'I thought a few delicate kisses would revive you if properly bestowed in the most sensitive place, but I don't mean to have you there; this book will show you the most delightful avenue of bliss, and open up to your ravished senses heavenly bliss you have hither had no conception of.'

"Keeping my clothes up, and making me retain hold of his priapus in one hand, he showed me a series of splendid little drawings in the book, all illustrating the way to enjoy bottom-fucking. He could see I was tremendously excited, so lost no time in placing me on my hands and knees on the sofa, then anointing my tight little bum-hole with some ointment from the box, and putting some also on the shaft of his prick, he made me push my bottom well out behind, with my legs wide apart so as to give him every facility, but 'Ah! Ah! No, no, I can't bear it!' I exclaimed, the tears fairly starting to my eyes as I felt the first advance of his lovely engine, forcing its way through the tightened orifice; the pain was like a number of needles pricking the part all at once. I can describe the sensation as the sphincter muscle gradually relaxed in no other way. He frigged me deliciously in front all the while, pushing so firmly and getting in in such a gentle manner behind that I seemed to love him more and more every moment, and long for him to accomplish his task, and complete my enjoyment, as the very pain seemed a percursor to some extraordinary bliss, nor was I disappointed; the pain was soon succeeded by the most delicious sensations as his movements stirred me up to the highest pitch of excitement, and he never withdrew till we had spent thrice in rapturous ecstasies, screaming with delight and almost losing our lives from excess of enjoyment.

"Thus my mission was successful, and his lordship became a Member of Parliament."

This tale had worked us all up, so that we were mutually groping each other's privates, and as soon as Bertha had finished we seized Fanny and Bridget, but too much of the same thing being rather tedious to read I will only say that John and Charles took their virginities in splendid style, when the girls really found no more nonsense would be tolerated.

This was my last adventure in town, and in the next part I shall go on to relate what happened after my marriage with Lord Crim-Con, which took place shortly afterwards.

(*To be continued.*)

AN ANSWER TO A QUEER QUESTION.

A few young sages one bright day
   (Such conduct is not becoming)
Disputed, doth an old tale say,
   Which is the prettiest part of women:
And this, the cause of the affray is.
   Some said the cheeks, and some the eyes,
And so they sought the beauteous Lais,
   And asked her to award the prize.
The lady said, perhaps displeased,
   These thoughts I cannot understand.
If you could have them where you pleased,
   I wonder where you'd put your hand?
'Twould be, you would see,
   On their K. U. N. T.

SONG.

Translated from the Hindustani.

Oh when shall I behold, love,
   Thy noble manly face?

O when thy neck enfold, love,
   Within my close embrace?
All young, and warm, and willing,
   O when shall I receive
Those raptures, fierce and thrilling,
   Which man alone can give?

As the thirsty pearl shell opes, love,
   To imbibe prolific showers,
All, all my bosom's hope, love,
   Expect thy vigorous powers;
My dreams are full of pleasure,
   Naught else my heart employs,
Come kiss me without measure,
   Thou source of all my joys!

CAUTION TO LADIES.

A contributor wishes to remonstrate against the practice of a very nice young lady friend of his, who treats her quim as if it was a baby's arse. He says, "A nice cunt is a delicious thing to suck, but damn the violet powder, which dries up all the natural juiciness!"

ROUGE ET NOIR.

A nigger in fair St. Domingo,
Being blasé and worn, said, "By Jingo,
   Blast all women and boys,
   I'll try some new joys,"
So he went out and fucked a Flamingo.

THE PEARL,

A Journal of Facetiæ and Voluptuous Reading.

No. 10   PUBLISHED MONTHLY.   April, 1880

LA ROSE D'AMOUR;

Or the Adventures of a Gentleman in search of Pleasure.
Translated from the French.

(Continued.)

Shortly a bell sounded, and through a side door entered a troupe of the most beautiful young girls the world could produce.

The effect on me was electric, so much beauty congregated together I could not imagine. So bewitchingly graceful did they appear as they gleefully tripped into the room, exhibiting the most lascivious attitudes. So true to a fault were their figures, so charming was the clear transparent whiteness of their necks and faces, slightly tinted with the rose's hue, shaded by masses of rich black, auburn, or chestnut hair, which waved in the light like rays of molten gold, falling in ringlets over their beautifully rounded shoulders, whilst their eyes, half hid in the long silken lashes, beaming and sparkling with licentiousness, made them look like houris descended from the Moslem's paradise, rather than anything of mortal mould. And what served to heighten the enchantment their appearance cast over me was their dress.

Some entered dressed in pants and cymar, à la Turque, displaying to the utmost advantage their large busts and beautifully rounded hips.

Others (the majority) dressed in Turkish pants of fine blue or pink gauze, with a short petticoat hanging halfway to the knee, made of the same material, and which, instead of hiding any part of their bodies, only added to their beauty, and heightened every charm.

Their beautiful breasts could be plainly seen, even the rosy-tipped nipples could be distinguished as they rose and fell in undulating palpitations against their slight covering.

The shape of the legs and thighs could be seen; nay, even the masses of curling hair that overhung their delicious, luscious little cunts, even the lips of which I could see—all, all was visible.

I stood thus entranced, gazing on the fairy-like beings that were grouped around me, without a thought but of their extreme loveliness, till I was aroused from my state of dreamy delight by one of the gentlemen present asking me to give my arm to one of the ladies, and take her for my partner at the supper table. And that if after supper I should see any other lady who I might prefer to my first choice, I should be at full liberty to take her.

All that I could do in answer was to gaze around on them with a half-bewildered look, till a beautiful creature came up to me, and with a smile, putting her arm in mine, her lustrous dark eyes beaming with the very spirit of luxuriousness, asked if I would not accept her as my companion for the night.

I answered her by putting my arm around her taper waist, and drawing her into a close embrace, imprinted on her lips a dozen burning kisses, which she returned with equal ardour.

Leading the way to the table we seated ourselves on a sofa (there being no chairs, but a sofa for each couple); the repast commenced.

No sooner had we taken our seats than an unseen band of music struck up, playing the most beautiful and seductive airs; and as the dessert came on, a large curtain, which was stretched across at one end of the room, suddenly drew up, exhibiting a beautiful little stage, on which appeared four girls dancing some of the most licentious dances, throwing themselves into the most tempting postures, pirouetting till their gauze skirts stood entirely level with their navels, showing their cunts, even drawing apart the vermilion lips of those mossy temples of love by the extension of their legs, allowing us to catch a glimpse of the luscious interior which the open legs half disclosed.

After sitting at the dessert an hour or more, drinking the most exciting and heating wines with one another, on a given signal the girls withdrew to prepare for the ball, leaving us to do the same, which consisted merely in our stripping stark naked, retaining only our pumps.

I must here beg the reader's indulgence to state what I should have said before—that is, that the members of the society which held their revels in this house all belonged to the first families in the kingdom. That when any gentleman was initiated he must bring with him and present to the society some female relative, either a sister or cousin, mistress, or some beautiful female friend, so that in enjoying the relatives of other members he could have no advantage over them or their honour.

The young lady who had made herself my partner, I learned, was Mademoiselle de C——, daughter of Count C——, and sister to one of the gentlemen present. Here, on the pretence of being on a visit to each other's houses, they met once a week, and gave loose to the most unbounded licentiousness. All modesty formally banished the house, and the most lascivious abandon being substituted in its place.

After stripping we entered the ballroom, which, like the salle à manger, was painted with nude figures, and instead of seats, it was furnished at the sides and ends with richly made couches stuffed with the softest down, and having spring bottoms, sheets of the finest lace, and coverlets of silk and satin, but no curtains to them, as nothing was allowed to be done in secret.

If a gentleman and his partner were tired of dancing, they could retire to a couch and play at the game of love.

On brackets against the wall, a little raised above the couches, were shelves supporting decanters of wine, trays of comfits, and other stimulating refreshments.

We had not long to wait for our partners ere they came dancing into the room, as naked as we were, except a wide scarf of light blue or pink gauze, which each had thrown over her shoulders.

If I was pleased with my partner at supper I was much more so now that I could have a fair view of her when perfectly naked. Her skin rivalled alabaster in whiteness, her beautiful full breasts sustained themselves firm and round as two globes; her well rounded shoulders tapered down into a small waist, a small foot, with an ankle expanding upwards into a fine calf, her thighs full, large and proportionately made, swelling up into a pair of large hips, while the two half-globes of her backside were equally massive and firm. Her hair, which she had combed out, hung down to her

knees, while her cunt was surrounded and overshadowed by
a mass of jet black hair which grew upon and around her
belly as high as her navel, hanging down between her thighs
some way, forming a perfect veil or covering over the dear
little slit, contrasting most beautifully with the snowy whiteness of her belly and thighs.

On entering the room she ran up to me with extended
arms, but I caught her, and held her out at arm's length,
surveying and devouring with my eyes her every charm and
beauty, and then clasping her in a long embrace, we writhed
about in each other's arms, rubbing our bellies together, till
Mr. Pego began to snort and prance about between her
thighs, seeking for an entrance into some hospitable retreat
in which to hide his impudence.

So great was the excitement raised in me by feeling her
soft white belly rubbing against mine, as well as the springy
mossy covering of her fount of love pressing against my rampant machine, that I would have sent him in to explore the
dark little cavern concealed between her thighs, as we stood
in the centre of the room, had she not prevented me.

Hardly knowing how to contain my still increasing passion,
I slid between her arms, and dropped on my knees on the
floor, parting with my fingers the glossy ringlets that hid a
pair of rosy pouting lips, most lusciously tempting, and im-
planted my burning kisses on that amorous spot.

There was no time for further dalliance as the music began,
and she led me away to join in the dance.

After the first cotillion I led her to a couch, and reclining
on it drew her down by my side, and would soon have
brought matters to a crisis had she not prevented me again,
by saying that we should be obliged to enter the lists, and go
through our first manual exercise on a state couch in the
centre of the room, surrounded by the whole company.

Shortly after I heard the tinkle of a small bell, and immediately entered four men, wheeling in a couch of carved
rosewood, covered with sheets of the finest linen, overspread
with one of Brussels lace.

The committee, one of whom was my partner's brother,
advanced to me and led me to the couch, while three of the
ladies present took Mademoiselle de C——, and placing her
on her back turned a small screw at one side of it, which, acting on springs, raised that part on which rested her beautiful

buttocks, elevating them at least one foot higher than her head or feet, forming a sort of bow, and throwing up that portion of her belly and thighs which was most contiguous to the dear little cleft in the bottom of her belly.

So soon as they had arranged everything the three girls stepped back a little, and the men placed me on the top of her who was to share my sweet labour. She extended her thighs to the utmost to receive me.

After I was placed comfortably on her the gentlemen fastened us down on the couch by means of belts of india rubber, which extended across the bed, and held us firmly on it.

I soon perceived the necessity of this, as at the least motion I made (there were such powerful springs fixed in the body of the couch) the springing caused by it would have thrown me off my partner if not off the couch.

The sweet little creature, who was lying under me, now threw her legs across my back, and clasping me in her arms, showed that she was ready for the delicious combat.

Upon these signs the girls who had placed her on the couch advanced, and one with the tips of her fingers held open the lips of her cunt, while another took hold of my stiff-stander, and pointing his head at the entrance, directed him to the opening before him. But so highly were my passions wrought up, and such a magnificent erection had I acquired, so swelled up was its large red head, and so lusciously tight and small was the entrance to the grotto of love, that it would not enter.

After two or three trials, each of which failed, the one who had hold of my driving machine, forced my backside up from off Mademoiselle de C——, and slipping her head between my thighs, took my prick into her mouth, and palating it with her tongue, wet it well with saliva, and letting it out of her mouth, again presented it at the entrance of the fiery furnace which was gaping to receive it. Effecting a safe lodgement for the head, with one vigorous thrust I buried myself in her to the very haft.

So fierce was the concussion produced by the meeting of our bodies that my magnificent stones fairly cracked against her delicious backside. With such force did I come down on her that the springs in the bed were forced low down, and rebounding sent us some three feet into the air. The bed was so constructed that the springs could force the bed up from the body on which it rested.

I now felt that I was master of the field, and taking advantage of my position, gave my partner such a series of thrusts and drives—the springing of the bed driving her to meet me—our bodies would come together with such a force as to make all tremble.

The spectators around us were continually calling out to us and commenting upon our performance with such exclamations as the following: "O God, what a magnificent thrust." "How splendidly he drives it home to her." "See how deliciously their bodies meet together." "What a splendid prick, what beautifully large stones, how exquisitely do they flop against her buttocks," &c.

"Ah, Mademoiselle de C——, how I envy you those glorious cods and that luxurious prick, with which you are now gorging that greedy little maw of yours," exclaimed a lively young creature as she left her gallant's arm to approach the bed and get a fairer view of the fierce driving machine which so excited her imagination. "Oh, how beautiful!" she said, as stooping down she caught a full view of the whole machinery in motion. "See how the proud courser steams and smokes as he reins back his head to the starting place, and then how he makes everything foam again as he dashes onward in his mad career, towards the goal of victory!" and in her excitement she took my stones in her hand, and gently squeezed them, and brought me at once to the crisis.

Making one last lunge forward, I lay quivering and gasping on my fair partner's bosom, drenching her inmost parts with a perfect shower of the elixir of love.

My partner, who had been no ways backward in sustaining my fierce lunges and had returned them with thrusts and upheavings fully as amorous as my own, feeling the heat of the burning liquid I was ejecting in her, gave way at the same time, and dissolving her very soul into a flood of sperm, opened the gates of love's reservoir, and let flow such a stream of pearly essence as never came from woman before.

After we had recovered ourselves from the delirium in which our senses were lost for a few moments, the belts which held us together were loosened.

I arose, and raised Mademoiselle de C——; as I stood her on the floor large drops of spendings fell pattering between her feet, attesting to the vigour and warmth with which we had entered into the pleasure of love.

I now received the congratulations of the male part, as to the manner in which I had gone through the performance, and done such credit to their sex.

My mistress also received the encomiums of the females, all of whom envied her of her good luck in having me for a companion.

Then taking the dear girl to one of the side couches, we reclined for a short time, taking wine and refreshments to invigorate ourselves for further enjoyments.

Casting my eyes around the room I observed that every couch was occupied by a couple, all of them playing the same game we had just gone through with.

My fair partner and myself arose and promenaded round the room, observing the different modes and manners of frigging which some of them adopted.

At the sight of so many beautiful women in action all at once, I thought it only right my mistress should complete the set, and leading her back to the couch, I again gave her such a delicious fuck that she could not get up for half-an-hour afterwards.

Shortly after the company had recovered from the transports into which they were plunged, two servants entered the room, bearing in on trays small cups of spiced chocolate, prepared in such a way as to give the drinker strength to enter the lists of love ten or a dozen times.

Fucking was now proclaimed the order of the night.

Never in the world was there so much delicious frigging done at one time by an equal number of persons.* Never were there so many beautiful cunts to be seen so gorged and stuffed, and so well fucked by so many noble pricks. Never did woman receive such a shower of sperm as drenched them from all quarters.

The debauch was growing to its height, the chocolate began to operate fiercely on the men. The women writhed and twined themselves about the floor, fucking, screaming and shouting in ecstasy.

---

* The Editor of The Pearl thinks the author of this tale must have forgotten Belshazzer's Feast, photographs of which can be had, price £1 1s. each.

The most licentious words now issued from the mouths of those females, who, on the morrow, would meet you in their salons with a demure look and virtuous countenance.

The excitement was steadily increasing. The women became prefect Bacchantes, they drank freely of the most exciting and exhilarating wines.

Suddenly they stripped the beds from off the couches, and spread them on the floor, forming one large bed, upon which they could all lay down.

The uproar increased.

Here might be seen two women contending (amicably) for one man.

Again, two men contending for one woman, till each found a place for their inflamed pricks, one in her cunt, and the other in her bottom or mouth at the same time.

The females shouted, ran after the men, throwing themselves on the bed, dragging the men on the top of them.

My loving mistress partook of the universal excitement with the rest. She was, if possible, more furious than any of her sex, mad with the extraordinary lubricity aroused within her amorous frame, twining herself in my arms, rubbing all parts of her body against mine, smothering me with kisses, nay, even pinching and biting me with force, so highly were her erotic propensities aroused, and continually calling on me by every endearing name, to frig, fuck, or give her satisfaction with my tongue.

Placing herself in the most lascivious positions, throwing up her legs and outstretching her arms, she would invite me, in the most licentious terms, to enter the amorous lists, expatiating on each and every separate beauty of her person, declaring the superior firmness of her plump bubbies, which she would press and squeeze, then on the white and velvet softness of her belly, describing all the luscious charms of her cunt, the luxurious heat contained within its juicy folds. Then turning on her belly, would display the two full and plump moons of her backside, inviting me to enter from that quarter. Then throwing her legs back, lay with the feet resting on her buttocks.

While in this position a thought struck me, and I determined to put it in execution.

Throwing myself on my back, my feet towards her head, my bare arse against hers, my prick stiff and erect as a rod of ivory tipped with red, I told my inamorata to lower her legs on my body. As she did so I had my battering ram right to the point, and she impaled herself on its head. This was a rather novel mode of fucking, but none more so than the manner in which some of the others were frigging.

The orgies of these Bacchantes having reached its height, partially subsided for a few minutes, when the president of the club, calling for order, put to the vote whether the lights in the room should be put out or not.

Having witnessed all that had passed, this seemed a strange proceeding, and on asking my fair partner to solve the riddle, she replied that at a certain hour at each meeting the party, both male and female, stripped themselves of every ornament. The women are not even allowed to retain combs in their hair. The men then retiring to another apartment for a moment or two, the women would put out all the lights in the room, taking care, however, to leave one burning in a small side closet, when on the ringing of a bell the men would again enter the room, in which were their mistresses, and mixing indiscriminately with them, would recommence the soft pleasures of love at once.

Neither the ladies nor their lovers were allowed to open their mouths even for a whisper, for fear of being known to each other, and that for the same reasons everyone was obliged to lay aside every ornament, no matter what it might be, so that a brother and sister, in case they were together, could not recognize one another by any particular bracelet, ring or other ornament.

After the vote had been taken we did as I have just stated.

On our re-entering the room, which was totally dark, the door was locked from the outside by an attendant, and stumbling forward through the darkness, we met the women, who threw themselves into our arms, and we were soon tumbling pell mell on the floor.

I got hold of a plump little fairy, and groping my way to one corner of the large bed, I placed her in a favourable position, and finding my way in the dark as well as in daylight, I revelled in charms the most voluptuous.

Oh, ye Gods! how tight did her cunt clasp my prick. What a luscious suction was created by the juicy folds of her cylinder as my piston-rod shoved in and out. How gloriously she met all my thrusts by the most energetic heaves. Oh, how her fiery kisses were lavished on my cheeks and lips, as I pressed her to my bosom. And now the cirsis came on, and we swam in a sea of pleasure.

I lay by her side, and broke the rules by telling her in a whisper who I was. I questioned her about her adventures in the dark.

She went on to tell me that at one of the meetings, on the lights being suddenly restored, she found herself lying in the arms of her half-brother, and that she had frequently met with her cousin also.

She said that she had known brothers and sisters, and many a pair of cousins, who had been caught in each other's arms, and that on the lights being restored, so far from quitting one another they pursued the chase till the game was run down, and enjoyed themselves as they would, had they been strangers.

She said that in order to obtain the full enjoyment of the pleasures of love, it was necessary to do away with all modesty and restraint, that man was made for woman, and woman for man. That, for her part, she considered it made no difference who the actors were, so the fucking was well done and enjoyed.

All her actions and movements pronounced my partner one of the most licentious of women. She played with all parts of my body; laying her head on my thighs, she would handle my stones, put the head of my prick between other lips than those nature formed to receive it, and tickling the head of it with her tongue she tried to awaken it to renewed vigour; trying every means to arouse its dormant energies, she succeeded, and casting herself into my arms, lay on her back upon me.

My pego was in a beautiful state of erection, his head rooting up between the snowy thighs of my fair burden, and furiously butting the door, demanding an entrance into the secret chamber of love. With the tips of her fingers she opened the valves that closed the rosy-tinted aperture of her cavernous recess, and inserting the head I gave rein to my courser, and for the seventh time that night did I drown myself in bliss.

So well pleased was I with my companion that despite the attraction of the many beauties who were groping about over the room, enjoying themselves first with one man, then with another, and any of whom I might have had, that I laid myself in her arms, my cheek resting on a very large round globe of flesh, her arms clasping me close to it, while her legs were crossed with mine.

In this position I fell into a sound sleep.

When I awoke the lights were blazing with great splendor, and I found the girl in whose arms I had fallen asleep engaged in a vigorous combat with a man who lay close by me.

Continuing the debauch till the approach of day, we all dressed, each one going separately, and by different routes to their residences.

I reached home, and hastening to my apartment, completely worn out from the violent exercise I had undergone, I fell into a sleep from which it was three o'clock in the afternoon before I awoke.

Chapter III.

I attended all the orgies of the club—of which I had been made a member—where new debauches were committed every week.

At each meeting my partiality for the delicious creature I had lain with last, on my initiative night, increased to such a degree that I determined to have and retain her to myself if possible.

Celestine was the daughter of the Marquis de R——. In the club she was known by the soubriquet of La Rose D'Amour, by which name I shall continue to call her.

She combined all the graces and charms peculiar to the softer sex.

She had a temptingly small foot, giving tokens of the excellent smallness of the delicious slit, which nature had placed between a pair of ripe fleshy thighs, backed by a pair of fair buttocks, beautifully rising up, swelling out into bold relief from the adjacent parts. A belly white and soft as a bed of snow, a waist slender as a nymph, a neck like a swan, small mouth, inlaid with two rows of ivory, lips rosy and pouting, cheeks soft as the velvet down of an overripe peach, languishing dark eyes, sparkling and beaming with a lascivious fire, shaded by long silken lashes, while her auburn hair fell in a profusion of ringlets over her neck and shoulders, half concealing a pair of large globes rivalling alabaster in whiteness, tipped with nipples hard and red as rose buds, in fact she was "perfection personified."

The day following my last visit to the club, I received a letter from St. Petersburg, announcing my father's death, desiring me immediately to set out for that place for the purpose of removing his remains to France.

Now, I had never seen enough of my father to have any great fondness for him; what little filial affection I had was soon drowned by the ideas I had of enjoyment now I was to succeed at once to his vast fortune, so that I did not like to give up my pleasures, especially that of forgoing my meetings with La Rose D'Amour.

On receiving the letter I at once proceeded to the Hotel de R——, and on enquiring for Celestine was shown into the drawing-room.

The servant returned to usher me into her mistress's boudoir, where, opening the door, I passed in, and found her reclining on a sofa, in a bewitching dishabille. Her neck was uncovered, the bosom of her wrapper open, half displaying her pretty bubbies. One foot resting on the sofa, the other on an embroidered footstool, the dress lying on the knee, displaying a finely rounded calf. After locking the door I read her the letter I had received, and telling her I could not part from her, implored her to leave home and accompany me on my journey, telling her that on our return to France, I would fit up my chateau in Brittany with all the luxury of an Eastern Harem, where we might reside amid all the pleasures that love could induce, and all the luxury that wealth could purchase.

After a few short murmurs she consented, and I left her to make the necessary preparations for our departure on the morrow.

As she was to accompany me in male attire, acting as a page, I was obliged to have recourse to my faithful valet, to procure proper dresses, &c.

By eight o'clock in the evening we had everything prepared, and as we were to start at daylight, Celestine, under pretence of going to a ball, came and passed the night with me in my chamber at my uncle's.

At daylight we set off with all the speed that four good horses could give us.

My companion made a very handsome-looking boy, and

was the cause of our having some very amusing adventures on our journey.

At a small town on the frontier, at which we stopped, on showing my passport to Monsieur le Maire, he insisted on our staying at his house for the night, which I at last complied with.

He was an old man about sixty, grey-haired and bald. After arriving at his house, he sent a servant to inform his wife that there were strangers in the hall below, and desiring her presence.

In a few minutes, to our agreeable surprise, there entered the room a very charming, rosy-cheeked, vivacious-looking young woman, about twenty-two years of age.

In the course of the evening I observed by the almost scornful manner in which she regarded her husband that the union with him had been a "marriage of convenience," and furthermore, from the glances I perceived passing between her and Celestine, I knew she wanted but the opportunity to give her husband the slip, so I determined, if the chance offered, to repay M. le Maire's hospitality by making an addition to his bald pate in the shape of a pair of horns.

On retiring for the night, my mistress informed me that she had an engagement with our host's wife. That she intended to drug a glass of wine for her husband on going to bed, which would ensure her freedom for at least ten hours, and that as soon as her husband was fast asleep she would go to her room.

Telling Celestine to undress and get into my bed, I went into the room prepared for her, and stripping myself perfectly naked, awaited in darkness the coming of the charming hostess.

After waiting for an hour I heard a light step advancing towards the room, the door opened, and she entered, and whispering Rudolph, the name Celestine had taken, advanced to the bed. Slipping the bolts in the door, I caught her in my arms, and found she was as naked as myself. In kissing her she knew immediately by my whiskers that I was not the person she expected to meet, and fearing she had made a mistake in the room, she gave a slight scream, and struggled violently to free herself.

But I retained a firm hold of her naked waist, and drawing her to the bed, explained everything to her. How that my page Rudolph was my "chere amie," accompanying me in this disguise.

After calming her fears I lighted a taper that stood on the table and after a careful survey of her beauties, while I pinched and kissed everything, especially a dear hairy little cleft at the bottom of her belly, I found her to exceed the expectations I had formed at the supper table.

She could not resist my handling her person, but freely gave herself up to my touches.

The game was getting too exciting to stand dallying very long, so turning her on her back, I plunged my weapon into a bath of hot juicy flesh, and gave her a luxurious feast of the fruit of which she had had before but a very slight taste.

Five times that night did I put her through the manual exercise of love, and five times did she die away in the most ecstatic enjoyments, the pleasures of which she declared she had only known in imagination.

It was with sincere regret that Madame le Maire parted from me at dawn of day, to join her sleeping husband, to whose brows had just been added a pair of horns. They were short to be sure, but there appeared every prospect of their branching out into large antlers.

Before leaving me she made me promise to stop on my return.

After breakfast in the morning I returned my host my sincere thanks for his hospitality, assuring him that the entertainment I had received in his house was far beyond my expectations.

I ordered my carriage, and followed by my page, took the road to Vienna.

(To be continued.)

SALLY'S MISTAKE.

Sally, the servant-maid of Mr. A——, was accustomed to walk in her sleep. She one night came into her master's room, went into his bed, laid down and slept between him and his wife.

In the morning Mr. A—— got up according to his usual custom, a little after five o'clock, after having performed (as he thought) the part of an affectionate husband, not suspecting that there was anybody in bed with him but his wife.

He had not got downstairs before Mrs. A—— awoke, and accosted Sally, whom she mistook for her husband, in the following terms: "My dear Mr. A——, indeed I am not surprised that we have no children, since you are so lazy. Come closer, my dear, pray my dear, come. I am sure I am young and vigorous and perform my part as well as any woman in the kingdom."

Here Mrs. A—— paused a few minutes, waiting for an answer, but receiving none from the imagined husband (who lay all the time in a cold sweat, fearing a discovery, for she thought Mrs. A—— was her gallant the shopman, who laid with her every night, as she was afraid to sleep by herself; but they never spoke to each other during their amorous interviews for fear of being overheard).

"Fellow, do you think me worthy of an answer; I'll be revenged—I'll never get into bed with you again!"

Here her breast swelled so with anger that she could not utter another word.

Fortunately it was not yet light, so Sally jumped out of the bed and ran up to her gallant, to whom she imparted the whole affair.

This was the first time they had ever broken silence during their amours, and they were overheard by another maid who slept in the next room. She watched for the shopman's coming out of Sally's chamber, and made him go into hers to gratify those desires which I leave the reader to guess.

They all arose at their usual time, and Mrs. A—— being informed that breakfast was ready, went downstairs into the parlour, and had just seated herself when Mr. A—— entered the room, and accosted her in the following words:

Mr. A.—"Well, my dear, what do you think of me now?"

Mrs. A.—"That you are as incapable as a eunuch."

Mr. A.—"Nay, my dear, I thought you seemed so much pleased with our gambols this morning that we should have been very great friends all the day, but, alas, I find there is no satisfying a woman!"

Mrs. A.—"I'll tell you, fellow, I'll have a divorce. Not even answer me, scoundrel. Did I not make a man of you?

Had it not been for me, you would have had to carry your
cod-piece to a beggar woman ere this—whilst I know by your
unnatural abstinence you have a gay woman in keeping—
some painted little bitch or flaghopper. Not a civil answer,
when I offer you my love? You shall repent it, sir, you old
whoremonger, thus to neglect your virtuous wife" (clapping
her hands in fury).

Mr. A.—"My dear, I did. As I love my money, will you
have it cut off and preserved like a snake in a bottle—or do
you want it twice before breakfast?"

Mrs. A.—"Your money is my money, and so ought your
—— to be, but you take it elsewhere, you old adulterer!"

Mr. A.—"Nay, nay, my dear, but I believe you're too
loving, my jewel, as soon as breakfast is over I'll lock the door
and we will ——."

Mrs. A.—"Now, indeed, my dear, you speak like a man
of mettle, and I forgive all that is past."

When breakfast was over he performed his promise. Madam
was pleased, and harmony once more reigned in their loving
abode. Sally also was equally happy in having escaped from
her dangerous predicament, her fellow servant in having
gotten a gallant, and the shopman two fine girls to play and
toy with at his pleasure.

Morale.—"It's an ill wind that blows nobody any good."

PLEASURES AFAR.

Discovery of the Longitude.

A merchant of Genoa, leaving wife at home,
Kiss'd a little whore, in the town of Rome;
"You, my dear," said he, "tried full many a nation,
Then say who had the longest tool of generation?"

Said the merry girl, "Oh, that's soon decided,
You, who cross the sea, are the best provided;
What a length of tail, though the seas you roam,
Your spouses never fail, to bear you babes at home!"

MISS COOTE'S CONFESSION,

Or the Voluptuous Experiences of an Old Maid; In a series of Letters to a Lady Friend.

Letter X.

My dear Nellie,—

I have found a curious letter from a lady amongst grandfather's papers, so begin this leter with a copy of it.

Dear Sir Eyre,—

We live in an age so dissolute that if young girls are not kept under some sort of restraint and punished when they deserve it, we shall see bye-and-bye nothing but women of the town, parading the streets and public places, and, God knows, there are already but too many of them!

When fair means have been used, proper corrections free from cruelty should be administered.

What punishment, and at the same time more efficacious, than birch discipline?

Physicians strongly recommend to punish children with birch for faults which appear to proceed from a heavy or indolent disposition, as nothing tends more to promote the circulation of the blood than a good rod made of new birch, and well applied to the posteriors.

I may add my own opinion that the rod is equally good in its effects on quick, excitable temperaments. With such children the sense of shame and exposure (if corrected before other children) adds greatly to the humiliation caused by the smarting strokes on their bare flesh and makes a lasting impression on their imaginative sensibilities.

The parent who uses the rod with discretion is infinitely more respected and reverenced by his children than a more indulgent one.

Birch breaks no bones, and therefore can do no great harm; the harm it does is very trifling when put in comparison with the evils which it can prevent.

I know it is pretty well used among what are called genteel people, but in that class, where it is chiefly wanted, the children are entirely left to their depraved habits, and from want of proper corrections become too often the shame of their parents.

Is it not better to chastise when she is yet young (for bad habits are generally contracted from the age of twelve to fifteen), than to see her, when grown up, taken to a house of correction for offences which a good whipping given with a birch rod might have prevented?

She is ruined body and soul by being thrown amongst the vilest possible human beings.

There are children so obstinate and of a nature so perverse that nothing but severe corrections will amend them.

I know a young widow of fashion who has three nieces and two nephews, who live with her. They are all above twelve years old, except her own daughter, who is nearly seven.

One of the girls is tolerable, but the other two as well as the two boys are exceedingly mischievous. She is indeed a strict disciplinarian, and always punishes their faults with the birch, and though she is yet quite young (not above four and twenty), she manages the children as well as any experienced schoolmistress could.

The other day the second eldest girl, who is about fourteen, told her brother she could tell him how children were made. And indeed instructed him so well that the boy, who is thirteen, a few days after took very improper liberties with a pretty young girl of fifteen, who acts in the house as a waiting-maid to the widow.

The girl complained to her mistress, who having found out that her niece was as guilty, if not more so than the boy, sent the girl immediately for a fresh broom, wishing to give them what is called a thorough whipping.

She made two large slashing rods, with the greenest and strongest twigs she could pick out of the broom, and beginning with her niece, she pinned her shift to her shoulders and tied her hands in front to prevent her from making a rear guard of her hands. She then whipped her posteriors and thighs as hard as she could, and continued whipping her without intermission, as long as she could hold the rod.

Having rested a few minutes she seized the boy, pulled his breeches down to his heels, and with the other rod she flogged him for ten minutes, and with such vigour of arm as made the young libertine kick and plunge like a colt, screaming in agony all the while.

For my part I think she acted in that instance very properly and such a correction may be hereafter of great service to these children, for it is better not to whip a child at all than not to make him feel well the stings of the birch.

I called last week on a friend of mine, an eminent mantua-maker in the city, whom I found in a violent passion.

On enquiring the cause, she told me that one of her apprentices had stolen a large silver spoon, and just as she was going to send her maid to gaol on suspicion she received a letter from an honest Jew, to whom the culprit had sold it, intimating he had suspected his customer, and followed the girl to her house, and offering to return the article.

"Now," said she to me, "I generally correct my apprentices with the birch, but I have just bought this horsewhip (showing me a large heavy carter's whip) to flog the hussey with. I will strip her and horsewhip her, till every bit of her skin is marked with it."

"Pray don't use that murderous thing," I expostulated in reply, "you might be punished for it; people have not yet forgotten Mother Brownrigg's case, who whipped her apprentices to death for the fun and cruelty of the thing."

It was with the utmost difficulty I could prevail upon her to substitute a good birch rod for that cruel whip. However, on my persistently representing to her the cruelty of chastising a girl with a horsewhip (although I am sorry to say I have actually seen it done in many families, where those in authority were inconsiderate and hasty in their tempers, and would use the first thing that came to hand), she consented to do the whipping with a good birch.

Domestic discipline, to be most effective, ought always to be carried out calmly, and all show of temper in inflicting punishment ought especially to be avoided, as likely to conduce to a want of respect in the delinquents.

A cart full of birch brooms, just cut from the trees, happening to pass by at that moment, she sent the servant to purchase a couple of them.

We both went upstairs to the back garret where the girl was confined. She appeared to me about fifteen, exceedingly pretty, with a beautiful white and delicate skin.

At the desire of my friend I stripped her of her clothes except her shift, and then the girl was ordered to seat herself on the floor, where the two brooms were thrown down in front of her, and select the finest pieces of birch herself, and tie them up into a rod, her mistress all the while pointing out particularly fine bits as most suitable for her thievish bottom, &c., and putting the girl into the greatest possible shame and confusion, the presence of a stranger like myself evidently adding immensely to her mortification.

When the rod was finished she tied her to one of the posts of the bed, and began to whip the young pilferer's posteriors and thighs with all her strength.

"Oh! you hussey!" she would exclaim, "will you ever steal anything again? Will you? Will you? Will you? I will teach you to be honest! I'll whip it into your system."

"Oh, God! Oh, gracious heaven! Oh, mistress! Oh, mistress!" screamed the girl, wriggling and twisting like a little devil on feeling the smarting cuts of the new birch. "Do forgive me, I will never steal any more for the rest of my life! Oh! Oh! Indeed I won't!"

But the mistress, foaming with rage, kept on flogging her with unremitting fury, till the rod was worn out, and she had to drop it from sheer exhaustion.

Then she called the servant, and ordered her to wash the girl's weals and bruises with some strong brine.

She means to give her every Saturday during a month just such another whipping. I think she is quite right to do so, as such corrections will deter the girl in all probability from ever stealing again.

When we left she was ordered by her mistress to amuse herself during the week by making four more good useful rods from the brooms which were left with her.

I have myself three daughters grown up, the eldest is about fourteen; she was addicted to telling lies, but I have whipped that quite out of her; my second daughter I have also entirely cured of some very dirty habits; but the youngest, who is about twelve, is not only idle and obstinate but exceedingly mischievous. I have made no impression upon her as yet, but am determined she shall feel the stings of the birch every day, if necessary, till she amends.

> Believe me, dear Sir Eyre,
> Yours faithfully,
> MARY WILSON.

Now for my own adventure promised in the last. You will remember that in giving some account of my establishment, I mentioned Charlie the page, brother to my favourite servant Jane.

Well, he was such a nice boy as to be a universal favourite in the house, just sixteen, beardless as a girl, with a soft voice and very willing and agreeable, in fact he was such a good-looking youth as to make quite an impression upon me, but I resolutely kept the secret buried in my own bosom.

In my second letter I told all about my regard for Jane, and it was often my practice, especially when I awoke too early of a bright summer's morning, to get up in my nightdress and slip unseen into Jane's chamber, to satisfy my restlessness by a luscious embrace in the arms of my favourite.

But one morning as I approached the door, which was slightly ajar, I heard a suppressed sigh, and cautiously peeping in, to my infinite astonishment saw Master Charlie with nothing but his shirt on, and that drawn up almost under his arms, on the top of his sister Jane, who was equally nude. His lips were pressed to hers in the ardour of coition, and her legs were thrown over his loins.

My first impulse was to withdraw as silently as I had come, but the luscious sight rooted me to the spot, and like Moses at the burning bush, I felt constrained to witness the wonderful sight. There was his youthful shaft, almost as big as that of Mr. Aubrey mentioned in my last; it looked as hard and smooth as ivory, and I was forced to fix my attention on its rapid pushing and withdrawing motion, which she seemed to encourage and meet by the heaving of her bottom to every rapid shove.

The door was close to the foot of the bed, and as they were quite unconscious of my presence, I knelt down to avoid being seen, and enjoy the voluptuous sight to the end.

I felt awfully agitated and all of a tremble, it was so new to me and unexpected, brother and sister. Ah! how they seemed to love and enjoy each other; they cling to each other in ecstasy, and the lips of her vagina seemed literally to cling to his shaft, holding on and protruding in a most luscious manner at each withdrawing motion, but it soon came to an end, as both died away in a mutual flood of bliss, whilst a warm gush from my own cunny bedewed my thighs with an overflow of what was as yet a truly maiden emission.

Hot, flushed and confused I silently withdrew from the scene unobserved, fully determined to punish Mr. Charlie for his incestuous intercourse with his sister, and if possible secure him for my own enjoyment.

The temptation was irresistible; the more I thought and strove to banish it from my thoughts, the more would my blood boil and throb through my veins at the thoughts of what I had seen, and must experience for myself. It was no use; I could not struggle against the fascination of the thing.

It was a Sunday morning. Mdlle. Fosse would go to Moor-fields to her father confessor, and attend an afternoon lecture; so as soon as I had done luncheon I told Jane and the other two servants they might go out for the afternoon and return by half-past six or seven, as I would dispense with dinner if Margaret the cook would have something nice for supper, and Charlie could answer my bell if anything was wanted.

As soon as the house was clear, and I knew the cook liked the society of her pots and pans too much to think of leaving the precincts of the kitchen, I rang for my page, and ordered him to bring a lemon, some iced water, sugar, &c., and seeing that he had dressed himself with scrupulous care in case I summoned him, I said, "Charlie, I'm glad to see you are particular about your appearance, although there is no one at home."

CHARLIE, with great modesty.—"But you, Miss, are my mistress, and I always wish to show you the greatest possible respect even when you are quite alone."

ROSA.—"Indeed, sir, you profess great respect for me, and seem afraid hardly to lift your eyes, as if I was too awful to look at, but I have my doubts about your goodness; will you please fetch me a rather long packet you will find wrapped in paper on the library table."

He soon returned with the parcel, and I proceeded to open it as he stood before me, awaiting his dismissal or further orders. The paper was removed, and I flourished before his face (which rather flushed at the sight) a good long rod of fresh green birch, tied up with scarlet ribbons. "Do you know what this is for, sir?" I asked the astonished boy.

CHARLIE, in some little confusion.—"Ah! Oh! I don't know—unless it's what's used for whipping young ladies at school."

ROSA.—"And why not boys, you stupid?"

CHARLIE.—"Ah! Miss Rosa, you're making fun of me, they use canes and straps to boys—but—but—.."

ROSA.—"Out with what you are going to say, I'm the only one that can hear it."

CHARLIE.—"Why—why—(turning quite scarlet), the thought came into my head that you might be going to whip me."

ROSA, with a smile.—"Well, that shows that at least you must know you have been doing something very bad; what is it?"

CHARLIE, in confusion.—"Oh! it was only a silly thought, and I didn't mean, I knew I deserved it."

ROSA.—"That's a clever answer, Master Charlie. Now, answer me, am I your only mistress?"

He cast down his eyes at his poser, but managed to stammer out, "Why, of course you are, Miss, as I am in your service alone."

ROSA.—"Now you bad boy, I prepared this rod on purpose for you; can't you guess what I saw early this morning in Jane's room?"

Charlie seemed as if shot; he fell on his knees before me, in the deepest shame and distress, covering his face with his hands, as he exclaimed, "Oh, God! how wicked of me, I ought to have known I should be sure to be caught. Oh! be merciful, Miss Rosa, don't expose us, it shall never happen again. Punish us anyhow rather than let anyone know of it."

ROSA.—"It's awful, but I'm inclined to keep your secret, and be merciful. Do you know that you are guilty of incest, and liable to be hung for it, both of you?"

CHARLIE, sobbing and crying.—"What, for that? I only went to kiss her last night, and then laid down by her side; somehow our kisses and the heat of our bodies led from one liberty to another, till—till—I stopped all night, and you found me there this morning."

ROSA.—"You shall both smart for this. I will whip you well myself to cure such obscenity, but if ever it happens again, remember you shall swing for it. Now, sir, off with your coat and vest, and let down your breeches with your behind toward me."

He was terribly shame-faced over doing as I ordered him, but too frightened of the consequences to remonstrate, and turning his back to me, he soon stood in his shirt, with his breeches well pulled down.

"Now, sir," I said, "draw up that chair and kneel upon it,

with your face over the back, then just pull up your shirt so as to properly offer your uncovered rump to the rod. Mind you bear it like a man, and keep as I order you, or I will yet send for a constable to take you to goal."

CHARLIE, in a broken voice.—"Oh! Miss, I won't even call out if I can help it; punish me as much as you like, only don't betray us."

ROSA.—"Well sir, you'll find my hand rather heavy, but you must smart well for your awful crime," giving a couple of good stinging strokes which made their red marks, and suffused the white flesh of his pretty bum with a rosy tint all over.

"Will you? Will you? you bad boy, commit such incestuous wickedness with your sister again? There—there, I can't cut half hard enough to express my horror of the thing!" exclaimed I, striking every blow with great deliberation and force, till his skin was covered with bleeding weals, and I managed, as I walked round his posteriors in the exercise of the rod, to see that his face was a deep scarlet, but his lips were firmly closed; the sight of his bottom just beginning to trickle with blood so excited me that my arms seemed to be strengthened at every cut, to give a heavier stroke next time.

"Ah! Oh! Oh! I will never do it again. Ah—r—r—re! I can't keep my mouth shut any longer. It's awful! Oh! Oh! How it burns into my flesh!" as he was compelled to writhe and wriggle under my fearful cuts.

This went on for about twenty minutes; now and then I had to slacken a little for want of breath, but his sighs and suppressed cries urged me on; it was a most delicious sensation to me; the idea of flogging a pretty youth fired my blood so much more than if the victim had been a girl; the rod seemed to bind me in voluptuous sympathy with the boy, although I was in perfect ecstasy at the sight of his sufferings. At last I sank back on a sofa quite exhausted with my exertions, and presently found him kneeling in front of me, kissing my hand, which still held the birch, exclaiming, "Ah! Miss Rosa, how you have pickled me; but, oh! I'm sure to do something bad again to make you whip me another time, it's so beautiful I can't describe what I feel, but all the pain was at last drowned in the most lovely emotions."

ROSA, in a faint voice.—"Oh! Charlie, how wicked of you,

there, you shan't kiss my hand, my foot is good enough for you to beg pardon of."

CHARLIE, in rapture.—"My God! Miss Rosa, may I kiss that dainty little trotter of yours?" seizing one of my feet, and pressing his lips to my slightly exposed calf.

His touch was like a spark to a train of powder, I sank quite back on the sofa in a listless state, leaving my leg at his mercy, and seemed unable to repel his liberties; I felt his roving hand on the flesh of my thighs under the drawers, but the nearer he approached to the sacred spot the less able was I to resist; his hands went higher and higher, the heat of unsatisfied desire consumed me. At last with an effort I whispered, "Oh! oh! for shame, Charlie, what are you doing? come let my leg go, I want to tell you something. Ah! the punishing of you has been the undoing of me, ah! I am indeed afraid of you," hiding my face in my hands just as he raised his beautiful scarlet visage close to mine, and one of my feet also just touched something projecting in front under his shirt. "Oh! Oh! what's that in front of you Charlie," I gasped.

"Oh, dear Miss, it's what Jane calls 'the boy,' and gives such pleasure that Aaron's rod could not equal its magic power," he said softly.

ROSA, hysterically.—"Oh! Oh! Charlie, will you be good and true to me, my life, my honour are in your power, you will never use my confusion, the secret that my impulsive nature cannot restrain. Ah! you naughty boy, it was the sight of your performance with your sister fired my imagination so that I determined to score your bottom well for you, but, alas, the sight has been too much for the sensuality of my disposition—."

I could not continue what I had to say, but the dear boy covered my face and bosom with kisses, his searching hands finding out and taking possession of all my secret charms, while I could not restrain my own hands from being equally free, and repaid his hot burning kisses with interest.

Our lips were too busy to give utterance to words; in short I surrendered everything to the dear boy, and we swam in the delights of love; of course I experienced the painful tension and laceration of my hymen, but all was soon forgotten in the flood of bliss which ensued.

His efforts exhausted him, and I had further recourse to the rod to procure myself a repetition of our joys, and lastly when

I feared the dear youth might perhaps be seriously injured if I exacted from him more than nature could sustain, I prevailed upon him to use the birch on my own bottom, so as to keep my voluptuous sensations from abating.

Ah! the rod is delicious if skillfully applied after the delights of coition. The dear boy wanted to renew his attack, but I would not permit it, promising he should come to my room at night for another feast of love, but insisting upon his being rested for the present.

I enjoyed a most voluptuous liaison with my page for three or four years, till I was constrained to part with him on account of his manly appearance. By my advice and assistance he married well, entered into business, and became a thriving man. From time to time, as long as he lived, we secretly enjoyed the sweets of each other's society.

You have often wanted to know why I never married; the truth is, two things combined to prevent it. The first being my love of independence, and aversion to being subject to anyone, however I might love him; this I might perhaps have brought myself to give up, but the second reason was insurmountable. I could not get a new maidenhead, and positively gave up all idea of marriage without that article, so essential to all spinsters who enter the hymeneal state.

Poor Charlie died in the prime of his life, at thirty-five, but before his decease gave me a packet of papers relating to his amorous adventures, by which I find he was not very faithful to me, even when in my service, but "de mortuous nil nisi bonum" is my motto, I only know I loved him when I had him.

Perhaps someday I may put his memoirs into some shape for your perusal, but this letter is the finis of these selections from my own experience.

> Believe me,
> Your affectionate friend,
> ROSA BELINDA COOTE.

LADY POKINGHAM, OR THEY ALL DO IT;

*Giving an Account of her Luxurious Adventures, both before
and after her Marriage with Lord Crim-Con.*

PART V.

I now come to a most important epoch of my life, which at
once sealed my matrimonial fate.

We were to leave town the next day, and were taking a
morning walk in Kensington Gardens with Lady St. Jerome,
when who should suddenly meet Her Ladyship, and demand an
introduction to her charming young friends (meaning myself
and Alice), but a tall handsome-looking old fellow of thirty,
with the most wicked pair of dark eyes I had ever seen.

Lady St. Jerome appeared to have a most sinister smile
upon her face, as turning to us she said, "My dears, allow
me to present you to the Earl of Crim-Con, the most gallant
gentleman of the day, but be careful how you accept his
attentions." Then seeing a rather savage look cross his countenance—"Pardon me, my Lord, if in introducing you to Lady
Beatrice Pokingham and Miss Alice Marchmont, I caution
them to beware of such a dangerous lover; they are under my
protection at the moment, and I should fail in my duty if
I did not."

The angry flush was but momentary, being instantly replaced by a most agreeable smile, as he replied, "Thanks,
thanks, my dear cousin, but your piety always makes you so
hard on my little foibles. Will nothing ever make you believe
I have honourable intentions; you know how often I have
asked you to try and find me a nice little darling wifey-pifey,
who would lead me with her little finger, and keep me out
of mischief."

"You might have found a good wife long ago, you miserable hypocrite," retorted Her Ladyship, "you know that a certain place is said to be paved with good intentions, and that
is where all yours will go to, my Lord, I fear, but I only just
cautioned my young innocent friends here."

"Ah, hem, I think I know that warm place you allude to,
just between the thighs, is it not my Lady?"

Lady St. Jerome blushed up to her eyes as she exclaimed,
in an apparently angry tone, "Now, this is really unbearable,

that Your Lordship should at once commence with your obscene inuendoes; my dears, I am so ashamed of having introduced you to such a horrible specimen of modern society."

"A truce, I will really be on my best behaviour, and try not to offend the most delicate ideas again," he said with great seeming earnestness, "but really cousin, I do want to be married and kept out of harm. Now I suppose these two young ladies are eligible parties, do you think either of them would have a worn-out roué like me?"

"Really, my Lord, you are incorrigible to go on so and talk like that before two young ladies at once," expostulated our cicerone.

"Ha, you don't believe me, cousin, but, by God, I am not jesting, you shall see presently, just wait a moment," he said, then taking out his pocket-book, pencilled something on two slips of paper which he held in his hand, with the ends slightly projecting. "Now, cousin, just draw one and see which it is to be."

"Only for the fun of the thing, to see what you mean"; then she pulled one of the slips from his hand, exclaiming with a laugh as she looked at it, "Beatrice, you are to be Lady Crim-Con if you will take such a scapegrace for better or worse."

His Lordship.—"I really mean it, if you will have me dear lady; may I call you Beatrice? What a happy name, especially if you would make me happy."

It is impossible to write how I felt at that moment; I knew that he was rich, with a great title, and despite his bad reputation, that was a most tempting bait to a comparatively portionless girl.

Somehow he took my arm, and Lady St. Jerome, with Alice, walking in front, seemed to go any way but direct home, in order to give His Lordship every facility to urge upon me his sudden courtship. I can't tell you how it happened, but before we reached the house, I had promised to have him, and in less than a month we were married.

I need not trouble about the wedding ceremony, but at once give some account of the first night I had with my spouse. When I first mentioned him, I spoke of an old man of thirty; that is exactly what he was, and although still a handsome fellow, one would have guessed him to be fifty at least.

His youthful vigour had been expended long ago, by constant and enervating debauchery, and now instead of being able to enter the lists of love in a genuine manner, he had a perfect plethora of disgusting leches, which he required to be enacted before he could experience sensual excitement.

Our first night was passed at the Lord Warden Hotel, Dover, as we were on our way for a continental tour.

During our short courtship I had never allowed him the slightest liberty, as my common sense told me that such a man would discard the most beautiful girl if he could but take advantage of her before marriage.

Well, then, the ceremony at St. George's, Hanover Square, where the nuptial knot was tied, was scarcely over, and we had just taken our seats in the carriage to return to Lady St. Jerome's house, from which I was married, when he gave me a rude kiss, and thrusting his hands up my clothes, seized upon my cunt in a very rough manner, as he laughingly told me not to pretend to be prudish, as "he knew I was a little whore, and had had Lothair and lots of other fellows, in fact that was the reason he had married me, and meant I should be a damned little bitch to him, and do everything he required, which a virtuous girl might object to; besides," he added, "I always looked out for an orphan who had no blasted parents to complain to. There, don't cry like a fool," as he saw the tears of mortification run down my crimson face, "you have only to pander to my curious tastes a bit, and we shall be happy enough."

I felt his advice the best I could take at the moment; his evident knowledge of my intrigues gave him such an advantage that I dried up my tears and resolved to make the best of a bad bargain, as I returned his kiss as lovingly as possible, and begged him "not to be a bad boy before other people, and he would find me everything he could wish."

I must have been very nearly screwed that night before I retired to bed to await His Lordship's coming. I got in between the sheets perfectly naked in accordance with his orders, and commenced frigging myself at once, the many bumpers of champagne he had made me drink in his company, to various obscene toasts, which he constantly proposed, such as—

"A stiff prick for a randy cunt." "Here's to a girl who would rather be buggered, than not fucked at all," and one in particular, which awfully excited my ideas, viz.: "Here's to the girl who likes to frig herself before you till she spends, then suck your prick to a stand, and prefers to have you in her tight wrinkled bum-hole rather than anywhere else."

Presently he entered the room, with a hiccup; as he pulled the bed-clothes off me, he exclaimed, "You're a damned pretty little bitch, Beatrice, and being nearly drunk, my dear, you see my cock happens to stand for once, we will make the best of it. I had the whites of a dozen raw eggs in some milk this morning, and just now a cup of chocolate with half-a-dozen drops of the tincture of cantharides to make me randy for once."

His coat, trousers, and everything were thrown off in a trice, till he was as naked as myself, whilst his eyes had an almost demoniac kind of glare, so unnaturally brilliant did they look just then.

Springing on the bed, "Ha," he exclaimed in a husky voice, "my little beauty has been frigging herself and spending. Suck my prick or I'll kill you, you little bitch!" he said savagely, as he reversed himself over me, and plunged his head between my thighs, where he at once commenced to suck my quim most deliciously, whilst I nestled his rather long prick (it was not very thick), between my bubbies, pressing them together with my hands so as to make him fuck me there, whilst I was so excited that I readily kissed and took his balls in my mouth.

He was so furious in his gamahuching that he continually made me feel his teeth quite sharply, as he bit the clitoris and nymphæ, growling out, "Spend, spend, why don't you come, you little bitch?" getting more outrageous and cruel every moment, till his bites made me shriek with agony as I writhed about, and deluged his mouth with quite a profusion of my creamy emission.

"A devilish good spend that," he murmured between my thighs, "but I have made your poor cunny bleed a little!" as he seemed to enjoy licking up the sanguineous mixture.

"Now suck my prick," he said with renewed fierceness, turning round and presenting it full in my face. "You're a cheating little bitch, and I mean to have you dog fashion."

I took that long prick in my hands, frigging the shaft as hard as I could, whilst I just titillated the ruby head with my tongue, till I felt it was tremendously distended and as hard as iron.

"Jump up quick, on your hands and knees, you little whore," as he gave me a couple of tremendously smarting smacks on my buttocks, loud enough to have been heard a long way off, only our bedroom was at the end of a corridor, the whole of the rooms in that part of the hotel having been taken en suite for us.

Turning up my rump as desired, I thought it was only a fancy of his for entering my cunt that way, but he suddenly spit on the head of his long stiff affair, and presented it to my astonished bum-hole, as he exclaimed with a chuckle of delight, "I'm going to fancy you're a boy, and take the only maidenhead you have left, your cunt will do another time, but it must be a virginity on a wedding night!"

"Ah, no, no, no, you shan't do that to me!" I cried out in fright.

"Nonsense, you little randy bitch, shove your arse out, and let me get in, or I'll serve you out dreadfully, and pitch you out of the window into the sea, and say you committed suicide through overexcitement!"

My fright increased, I was really afraid he would murder me, so I resigned myself to my fate, and clenched my teeth as I felt the head of his prick like a hundred little pins forcing its way within my tightly contracted vent hole. At last he got in, then withdrawing his hands from my mount where he had been tearing and pulling the hair to increase my pain, he placed both arms round my neck, and beginning slowly, fucked my bottom most voluptuously, till with a scream of delight I spent again in perfect ecstasy as I felt the delicious warmth of his spendings shooting up my fundament.

Being so overexcited by the means he had taken to prepare himself for our noces, he retained his stiffness, and never gave up possession of my bottom till we had come together a third time.

As soon as he withdrew his long limp cock, now reeking with a mixture of spendings and soil, he at once secured me to the bedposts with some silken cords before I could get away, or was well aware of his purpose.

"Now, my pretty boy, I have got you nicely, and will whip another cockstand out of you as soon as I have sponged off all the effects of our late enculade," he said, bringing some cold water and a sponge in a basin; he laved and cooled my heated parts, till I began to feel quite grateful to him. At last he sponged himself, and wiping himself and me with a fine soft towel, proceeded to select his instruments of flagellation from a small long leather case, which I had supposed only held a gun.

He showed them to me delightedly, then selecting a fine switch of horse hair mounted on a cane handle, he began to whip me with it between my thighs, and on the lips of my cunt in a most exciting manner, till I was so carried away with emotion that I begged he would fuck me properly to allay the longing irritation of my burning cunt.

"My prick isn't stiff enough yet, but I'll suck your spendings for you, my beautiful randy little tit," he cried out, falling on his knees and twisting my body round so that he could get at my cunt. How delightful the thrusts of his tongue were to me in my excited state. I wriggled about in ecstasy, and getting one foot on his prick gently rolled it on his thigh under my sole, till I felt it was getting enormously stiff again, and at the same moment almost fainted away from excess of emotion, as I delighted my lecherous husband by another copious spend.

I thought he was going to fuck me properly now, his engine was so rampant, but instead of that he turned my back to him once more, and selecting a fine light birch rod, made of three or four twigs only, elegantly tied up with blue and crimson velvet ribbons, he commenced to flagellate my tender bottom; how his light switch seemed to cut and weal the flesh at every stroke; it was in vain that I cried for mercy as the tears of real agony rolled down my cheeks; he only seemed the more delighted, and jeered me upon the effects of every cut, telling me first how rosy my bottom looked, then, "now you bitch, it's getting fine, and red, and raw, it's bleeding deliciously!" till at last the rod was used up, the splinters lying all about the floor and bed, then throwing it aside he again assaulted my poor bottom-hole, apparently more and more delighted as he gave me pain, in again forcing his entrance as roughly as possible; however, when he was fairly in I soon forgot everything under the influence of his ecstatic moves, till I could remember no more, and suppose I fainted; he must have released my bonds and allowed me to sink on the bed, for when I awoke the sun was streaming in at the window, and His Lordship was snoring by my side.

His treatment on my wedding night was comparatively mild

to what he afterwards made me go through, but his penchant for getting pleasure out of me soon seemed to wear off, although now and then he would fit me with a dildoe and make me bugger him behind, whilst I frigged him with my hands in front till he spent.

Another of his amusements, and which seemed to afford him particular delight, was to show me all his collection of bawdy books, drawings, and photographs, till he could see I was awfully excited, and then he would jeer me about being married to a used-up old fellow, like himself, didn't I wish I could have Lothair now, &c.

One day having amused himself this way with me for some time he made me lie down on a sofa, and tied a bandage over my eyes, fastened my hands and feet so that I could not move, then throwing my clothes all up he tickled and frigged me with his fingers till I was quite beside myself with unsatisfied desire and begged him to fuck me, or at least to fetch his dildoe and give me some kind of satisfaction.

"It really is a damned shame to tease you so, my little whore," he laughed, "so I will get the dildoe out of my cabinet in the next room."

He was scarcely gone many seconds before he returned, and I felt his fingers opening the lips of my cunt, as I thought to insert the dildoe, but instead of that it was his prick, and throwing his arms around me he seemed to be more vigorous than ever, his cock swelling and filling my longing gap in a manner I had never felt it before. I spent in an ecstasy of bliss, as I murmured my thanks in endearing terms for the pleasure he had afforded me by such a delicious proof of his manliness.

Presently a strange hand seemed to be feeling his prick, and thrusting a pair of fingers into my cunt alongside of his still vigorous engine.

"Ah! Oh!! Oh!!! Who is that?" I screamed from under my skirts, which were thrown over my face.

"Ha! Ha!! Ha!!! She pretends to think I've been fucking her when she must have known it was James all the time!" I heard him laugh, as at the same moment all the obstructions were removed from my face so that I could really see it was the young butler on the top of me, with his prick still in full possession, and just beginning to run a second course.

"Kiss her, put your tongue in her mouth, my boy! Fuck!

Fuck away! or it will be the worse for your arse!" exclaimed
His Lordship, who was handling his balls with one hand, and
slapping his rump furiously with the other. "See how she
pretends to be ashamed; it's quite delightful Lady Beatrice,
to see you can still blush."

I screamed and protested against the outrage, but James's
delicious motions soon made me forget everything, and recalled to my mind the orgie we had with the servants at
Crecy House, and in imagination I was again in the arms of
the wondrously developed Charlie.

We spent a second time, but he kept his place and continued the love combat with unabated vigour, and His Lordship seeing that I was quite carried away by my feelings, and
responding to his man's attack with all my naturally voluptuous ardour, released both my hands and feet so that I might
thoroughly enjoy myself.

"Hold tight James," he cried out, "she's so high spirited,
you'll get unseated, but the little devil needn't think she's to
have this treat all to herself!"

Saying which he mounted on the sofa behind the young
butler, and I could see his long prick was now as stiff as possible, and he seemed to have a rather easy task in getting
into his man's bottom, no doubt having often been there
before, but wanted some extra excitement on this occasion,
so he sacrificed me to his catamite, in order to bring himself
to the necessary pitch by seeing all our lascivious movements.

You may be sure that after this James and I were upon the
best of terms, His Lordship introducing him to our bedroom
at night, and joining us in every kind of wantonness; he even
once contrived to get his long thin prick into my cunt alongside of James's as I was riding a St. George; it gave me the
most intense pleasure, and immensely delighted them both
by the novel sensation, besides the idea of having achieved
an apparent impossibility.

After this Crim-Con seemed to get quite blasé and indifferent to everything we did, and even insisted on sleeping by
himself in another room, leaving us to ourselves. However,
both myself and paramour were not so blind as to believe he
was quite used up, but consulting together we came to the
conclusion that His Lordship had fallen in love with my young
page, a youth of fifteen, who had only recently entered my

service, and slept in a small room at the end of a long corridor in which both our bedrooms were situate.

He always locked himself in when going to bed, as he said, for fear I would not let him alone, so to determine the mystery one night we floured the whole length of the corridor, and in the morning were rewarded by seeing the marks of His Lordship's footsteps, both going and returning from the page's room.

We did not want to spoil his fun, only to enjoy the sight of it, and reap a little extra excitement if possible from the scene, so next day we examined the ground, and found that a small room next to that occupied by the page exactly suited our purpose, and being furnished as an extra bedroom for visitors we had only to make some good peepholes to enable us to sit or kneel on the bed and see everything.

(*To be continued.*)

THE ARITHMETICIAN.—A FACT.

Come tell me, dear Charlotte, my goddess, I cried;
    What numbers have tasted thy charms?
Too fickle enslaver! thou ownest a pride,
    In admitting a host to thine arms!
Yet blooming in all the luxuriance of youth
    The hills of thy bosom belie thee,
Then come my enchantress, confess me the truth,
    Let not prudery idly deny me!

O never, she cried, let us reckon the "number,"
    But rather the "length" of our loves!
Ah, give me full measure! and if it be under,
    I reckon by couples my "doves,"
With my finger I spann'd every member of pleasure,
    Together I spann'd the amount,
Till the pricks put together, were twelve miles in measure,
    And then I gave o'er the account!

THE PEARL,

A Journal of Facetiæ and Voluptuous Reading.

No. 11   PUBLISHED MONTHLY.   May, 1880

LA ROSE D'AMOUR;

Or the Adventures of a Gentleman in search of Pleasure.
Translated from the French.

(Continued.)

In a fortnight more we reached St. Petersburg, where, after preparing everything for my return, I determined to devote a day or two to pleasure.

At a ball given at the Imperial Palace, to which I was invited, I became acquainted with the Countess Z——, one of the most accomplished beauties at Court, and the reigning belle of St. Petersburg.

The Countess Caroline was a widow of twenty-three! She had been married at twenty, and about a month after her marriage her husband had been killed in a duel with an Englishman.

The Countess had a gait and look proud and haughty as a Juno, her oval face and majestic figure excited my highest admiration, and I determined if possible to make her mine.

Entering into a conversation with her, I found that she was pleased with my company, and much more with my person.

Accomplished as she was, Caroline Z—— had the vice peculiar to all Russians, of drinking large quantities of brandy. In fact, she drank so much that knowing she lived in a large palace, with no one but her serfs, I formed the resolution of making her mine that same night.

Plying her with brandy till late in the morning, she became so much excited as not to be able to control herself. I kept close by her side throughout the night, till the ball broke up. I humbly asked permission to be her escort home.

Engaging her in a laughing conversation, I put the ques-

tion to her as we descended the palace stairs, which the
giddy young creature, nearly intoxicated with brandy, at once
accepted.

I handed her into the carriage, and bidding the driver go
fast, in a moment we were at her palace.

On alighting she invited me in—an invitation which I
promptly accepted, and led me up a flight of large stairs into
her own dressing-room. So much was she affected by the
brandy she had drunk that she hardly knew what she was
doing.

Laying off her bonnet and shawl she rang the bell, and two
waiting-maids entered. Asking to be excused for a few minutes,
she retired to her boudoir, followed by her attendants, and in
a short time reappeared in a different dress, a loose flowing
gown of rich cashmere.

Calling for lunch and brandy, she dismissed the attendants
who brought it in. They retired in apparent amazement at
the sight of a man being admitted into her dressing-room,
and especially at that hour.

I now watched my opportunity, and pouring a few drops
of liquid from a small vial I always carried about me, into a
glass of brandy, I presented it to her, and she drank it off.

It ran like liquid fire through her veins, her eyes sparkled
with licentiousness, her heart heaved and palpitated with the
fierce desires which were consuming her.

Advancing my seat beside her own, I poured into her ears a
tale of burning love. I put my arm around her waist, and finding she made no resistance, pressed her to my bosom, and
planting numberless kisses on her lips, sucked the breath
from her.

In a minute more she delivered herself up to me body and
soul, she threw her arms around my neck, and repaid the
kisses I had just given, with interest.

I raised up with her in my arms, and carried her into the
boudoir, in which stood a bed in a recess. I undressed her till
she stood in her shift, and then taking off my own clothes
stood in my perfect nudity. Giving Caroline a soft kiss I
drew the shift from off her, and had a fair view of all her
secret charms.

Leading her to the bedside I gave her the fillip on her
back, and soon was buried to the very utmost notch in the
most lusciously tight cunt I had ever entered.

With what fire, what enthusiasm, with what fierce upheavings did she meet and receive the piercing thrusts of my love dart.

The excitement thickens, the combat grows hotter and hotter. Heavens! what pleasure! what joy! what ecstasy! Oh, how my lively partner kept time to all my fierce desires! In what a sea of delight was I plunged! What an indescribable luxurious heat reigned in the luscious folds of her cunt! Ye gods! how often did I dart my stiffened arrow through the rich, juicy flesh of her deliciously sensitive quiver! I felt the crisis approach, our mouths met; we devoured each other's tongues; her rosy lips, how sweet and warm! What intense voluptuousness in those amorous bites, that burning struggle of our tongues, that sought, moistened, entangled, drew back, and darted together again!

I gave her the coup de grace, and so great was the flood that issued from the reservoirs of love that the precious pearly fluid flowed down her thighs, as I spurted into the deepest recess of her cunt the burning sperm.

Caroline had not all the briskness and vivacity of La Rose d'Amour, her movements were languishing but more voluptuous. I turned her over and over, I touched and handled every part. I kissed her again; everything did I devour with my fiery kisses, especially the gaping lips of her cunt, which were wet and moist with the liquid stream from the fountain of pleasure which I had poured into her.

The spark kindled, the flame blazed. We writhed and twined, over and over, in each other's arms, and the sixth time had my indefatigable courser bounded to the goal of victory without tiring. The storm grew higher, the sperm fell in torrents, but could not put out the blazing fire that raged within us.

We awoke in the morning refreshed from the fatigues of the night. Again did I survey all the charms of my lovely bedfellow. She stroked my limber instrument till it grew into a stately rod. I toyed with her enticing firm globes of alabaster, each tipped with a rosebud most lusciously tempting, which I moulded and pressed in my hand, and sucking the nipples received fresh fire.

I turned her on her back, she spread her thighs, and guiding the dart which pierced her to the very vitals, we again drank of the sweets obtained in the fountain of Venus.

Swearing eternal constancy and love I left my charming Caroline, and hastened home.

I told Celestine all that had occurred, not omitting to expatiate pretty freely on the pleasure I had enjoyed while revelling in the virgin charms of Caroline Z——.

This somewhat piqued my French charmer, but on opening to her my views she consented to the arrangement proposed. I told her my intention was to fit up the chateau in all the magnificence of Barbaric pearl and gold, and to take, nay, in fact, steal off all the handsomest women that excited my desires very strongly, and carry them to the chateau, which I would have guarded by trusty followers, in fact, to make it a fortified seraglio.

I told her that she should reign as undisputed mistress of the place, and that, greedy as she was, she should never want for the peculiar flesh which she was always willing and ready to devour. I also told her to have everything in complete readiness to start at a moment's notice, while I went to see the beautiful Russian in whose arms I had passed the night.

Calling in the evening, a servant led me immediately to Caroline. I found her in a splendid bathing-room, reclining in a bath of milk and perfumed waters.

Placing a cushion on the marble edge of the bath, I made my proposition to her of leaving Russia and going to France with me. I pictured to her imagination what should be the magnificent splendour of our abode, in which love alone should be admitted.

I described to her all the endless variety of enjoyments in which we could indulge, passing our days and nights in one uninterrupted round of pleasure.

So highly did I excite her imagination by the glowing description of the amorous life we should pass that she at once agreed to accompany us. I say us, for I had told her all of my having Celestine with me, and of my intentions of possessing every woman who might take my fancy.

She entered at once into the spirit of my proposition, and made me promise to bring Celestine to her house on the following evening, and all three spend the night together.

After spending the day in driving about the environs of St. Petersburg, Celestine (in her male attire) and I alighted at the house of the Countess, and we were at once shown into the dressing-room of which I have before told.

Caroline was reclining on a sofa in all the charming co-
quetry of a *négligé dishabille* when we entered. Instead of
rising to receive us she merely tapped a silver bell which lay
beside her, and two girls entered, who, taking Celestine into
the boudoir, remained for a full half-hour.

What was my astonishment when she re-entered to behold
her in a dress, the exact counterpart of the one Caroline had
on, who as soon as she came in got up and embraced her,
praising her beauty, admiring her figure, calling her sister,
and paying her every attention she could think of.

On asking my beauteous Russian how she had got the
dress for Celestine, she replied that from the description I
had given her she had the dress made in that short time,
as she could not think of showing off her own charms to the
best advantage, Celestine being concealed by her male attire,
saying which she opened a casket, and placed on the brow
of Celestine a coronet of diamonds of the first water, on her
neck a necklace of pearls, and in the bosom of her dress a
large rose formed of brilliants, asking her to receive them as
a present from a sister.

Celestine drew from her finger a very large brilliant, and
presented it to Caroline as a token of friendship, excusing her
present poverty for not being able to make a more handsome
return for her elegant present.

Supper being laid in the room in which we then were, we
sat down to a feast for the gods, expressly prepared for the
occasion by the voluptuous Caroline. The dishes were all
highly seasoned, while the wines were of the most heating
and exciting kind.

After the dessert had been brought in I laid my plans again
before my two mistresses.

Caroline said she would need but a week to make her
preparations, as the most of her immense fortune consisted
in money and jewels, which she would place in my hands
to be disposed of as I thought proper, telling me to make
arrangements for her leaving very secretly, for if either of her
brothers should know of her intentions they would most
assuredly detain her by force if in no other manner.

Having drunk enough wine to excite their desires pretty
strongly, my two beauties commenced tussling me about,
rolling me on the floor, and tumbling on top of me, their
dresses in most admirable disorder; a pin becoming loose

would expose the half of a breast whiter than snow; the flying up of a petticoat would display a well-turned calf, a knee,
or a firm, fleshy thigh.

But this dalliance, acting as a provocative on their already
excited lusts, could not be put up with very long. They burned
for some more substantial good than that afforded by kissing
and pinching, which were fine auxiliaries for increasing an
appetite they could not satisfy.

Jumping up I ran into the boudoir, followed by the dear
creatures, whose eyes flashed with the fires of libertinism,
while their breasts rose and fell with quick heavings.

I hid under the bed, from whence they pulled me, and
stripping me naked, glued their moist lips over every part of
me, my erect Jacob staff coming in for more than its share.

They stripped to their skin, and calling on me as umpire
to decide on the relative beauties of their charms, as they
stood before a large pier glass, handling their snowy strawberry-
tipped bubbies, sleeking down the glossy curling whiskers that
surrounded two pairs of the most temptingly pouting lips
that ever adorned women. Where both were perfect models
of voluptuous beauty and grace, although different in their
kinds, I could not decide, but admired more and more the
charms of which I was the happy possessor.

I seized on the rosy nipples of the heaving snowy hillocks,
which disdaining the use of corsets, rested on their bosoms
like globes of alabaster. I sucked them, I squeezed their soft
round bellies against mine, I kissed everything and everywhere. I laid my kisses on the hairy mounts that overhang
the delicious grottos underneath; the lips which close the
mouth of the flesh slits next receive their share; I am on fire!
I burn! The bed receives us! I wish to push matters home at
once; but no, they would bring me to the very point before I
could enter.

Celestine has seized on my prick; she cannot get it into her
cunt, so, determined not to lose it altogether, she takes it in
her mouth, she sucks its glowing head, she rolls her tongue
over the top of it. I am mad—delirious. No longer to be restrained I throw myself on to Caroline, who receives me with
open legs and arms. I dart my fiery rod into her furnace,
which consumes it. A few maddening thrusts, drove home
with such force that I touch her to the very quick—a cry of
thrilling pleasure escapes us at the same time, and all is over.

But so intense were our passions that we hardly perceived it till I felt her again moving up to me. How delicious! What voluptuous warmth pervaded her whole body. How exquisitely did the springing cheeks of her backside respond to all my motions. The little devil Celestine is playing with two large balls that keep knocking against the buttocks of my antagonist.

It is too much; I drive it home, and lie gasping and quivering on Caroline's breast, who cries out, "Oh heavens! further in! I come—I spend! Oh—oh, God, I die! Oh, dear, what plea—pleas—pleas—ure!"

She had fainted. The delicious wrigglings of her backside, the contraction of her cunt, sucked the last drop from me.

When she recovered from the delirium in which her senses were plunged, she lay with her eyes languishingly beaming, her lips apart, with the tip of her rosy tongue slightly protruded between two rows of pearl—the very picture of voluptuous pleasure.

So plentifully had I bestowed in her the liquid treasure of love's reservoir, and so delightfully had she intermingled with mine the essence of her own dear self, that when I withdrew from her the pearly stream flowed out and ran over her thighs.

I had a short respite, receiving renewed vigour from the caresses of Celestine, whose greedy little maw was gaping wide to receive the half-erect machine which she was working at, trying to make it stand, so as to win her purpose.

Her whole body glowed with an intense heat, what voluptuous warmth reigned in every part! She burns, she imparts to me the fire which is consuming her very vitals. My ever willing and ready courser comes up to the stand, with head erect, impatient for the word.

I give him the reins, and he plunges forward in his impetuous career; on, on he speeds, nothing retards him. On, on, he rushes, nor stops till the race is run. He falters, he stops, his head droops, he pours out his very life blood, sprinkling the whole course which he has run with the precious liquid. It is finished; another faint struggle; a few convulsive jerks and it is all over. I lay panting on the heaving bosom of Celestine.

After having for the eighth time renewed my embraces with my two loves, we fell asleep, only to wake to new pleasures.

At the end of the week Caroline, having completed her business, placed in my hands upwards of three millions of francs and jewels to the value of one million more, and the following day we left St. Petersburg.

Having at my request provided themselves with a full wardrobe of male attire we started for France, where I longed to be, to put into operation all my schemes of pleasure, which I was determined should rival, if not excel, anything of the kind ever seen or heard of in the East.

On passing the frontier of France, I directed my route to the chateau, where, after depositing my lovely mistresses, I kept on to Paris.

On entering the capital I drove to the most fashionable upholsterer, telling him what I wanted done, gave him carte blanche in respect to the expense to be incurred.

Telling the man to make everything of the very richest material money could purchase, I advanced him a cheque for one hundred thousand francs, with the privilege of drawing on my banker for more in case of need.

Giving orders to have everything fixed in one month, I started to seek out some of the members of the Club from which I had stolen Celestine.

My first visit was to the hotel of the Count de C——, for the purpose of seeing Mademoiselle de C——, or Rosalie, as I shall call her, who having been my partner in the initiative act on the night of my admittance to the club, I felt a considerable partiality towards her, and determined to transplant her to the chateau as soon as everything was fitted up in it.

On entering the hotel I was told that the Count and his lady were out, enquiring for Rosalie, I was shown into the music room, where I found her seated at a harp.

On the servant disappearing she ran up to me, and threw herself into my arms.

I led her to a sofa, and seating her on my knee, unfolded to her my intentions, stating what I had done and what I intended to do. Telling her how Celestine had accompanied me to Russia; how I had made a conquest of the charming Caroline; how I had brought them both to France, and left them at the chateau. I urged her by all the powers of persuasion I could employ to go with me to the chateau, where her life would be one continued round of luxurious pleasure.

She gave her consent to accompany me as soon as I had everything prepared for her reception.

During our conversation I was pressing and moulding her breasts, and as the dialogue gained interest my hand became more bold, and roamed everywhere.

When I had finished talking I found that in my absent-mindedness I had lain her down on the sofa, and was pre-paring to put her attentions of love to the proof, when an infernal servant opened the door to announce a visitor.

Ach, cursed luck! thought I, as we settled ourselves, to be thus interrupted at such a time. But on seeing the lady enter my grief was changed to joy, for she was certainly the most voluptuous and beautiful creature my eyes ever looked on. With what dignity, what grace she crossed the room. What graceful ease reigned in every motion. A well-turned ankle, a pretty little foot, that noiselessly tripped across the floor, gave me a very good opinion of what was to be found above the garter.

Rosalie introduced the lady to me as Laura, daughter of the Count de B——. Seeing there was no further oppor-tunity of paying my compliments privately to Rosalie, I took my leave to make other calls.

I spent some six or eight days in Paris, leaving orders with jewelers and silversmiths for every variety of fancy articles, not forgetting to have my banker write to his agent in Lon-don, to procure me a swift sailing yacht of the largest size, fitted up in the richest manner, without regard to cost, and to be manned with a crew ready and willing to do any service I might name. She was ordered to be sent to the chateau on the coast of Brittany, where a small creek, putting in from the open sea, made an excellent harbour for a vessel.

Having finished my business, I hastened down to the chateau, taking with me a first-rate architect and a number of workmen.

In a short time I had converted a large saloon on the sec-ond floor into a magnificent hall. Its sides and ends were covered with flowers and evergreens, making a perpetual summer. On each side stood a row of statues of nude figures, which I had purchased in Paris. At either end played a beauti-ful fountain, while in the centre was a large marble basin, in which played a third fountain. The figure that cast up the water was a statue of a female lying down, so arranged that she seemed to be floating on her back in the water, the jet d'eau burst from her cunt, and ascended nearly to the ceiling, making a shower bath to anyone who would be seated on the figure.

The side windows opened on to a balcony, which overlooked the sea.

On the opposite side of the corridor I had converted the whole suite of apartments into one large room, which as soon as the upholsterer arrived was to be furnished with fifty beds.

The suite of apartments on the same floor of the adjoining wing I had converted into one large bathing room. In this room was a marble bath, in which fifty people could bathe at the same time. A small fish pond stood in the garden. It turned into a small lake of about one hundred yards in diameter.

(To be continued.)

FRANK FANE—A BALLAD.

The master said to the Schoolboy,
    As it fell on a day,
"All the rest are to go,
    Frank Fane is to stay.
I set you all free
    From the birch and the cane,
Not a boy shall be swished,
    Not a boy, but Frank Fane."

Said the Merry Master,
    "Frank Fane is to stay,
To be flogged with a flogging,
    As good as your play.
Frank Fane is to stay,
    To be whipped in the hall,
To be whipped, till his whipping
    Atones for you all.

Any boy that enjoys
    A fine flogging to see,
I give leave to stay here,
    With Frank Fane and me:
They will see his white bottom,
    When they see it again,
I don't think they'd fancy
    It belongs to Frank Fane."

While the rest went a playing,
    In the hall there were four,
Frank Fane and his Master,
    And two fellows more.
There were three there for pleasure,
    And one there for pain;
How they giggled and grinned,
    At the funk of Frank Fane!

"Now loosen your braces,
    And lower your breeks,
And show your companions
    Your bare nether cheeks.
Make haste to the closet,
    And bring a good rod,
Or I'll cut you to ribands,
    You shuffler, by God!"

"O master! dear Master!
    Have pity for once!"
"What, pity for a truant,
    A thief and a dunce!
For once, and at once,
    You shall smart for all three,
A three-fold example
    Your bottom shall be."

Now his comrades they took him,
    Each grasping a hand,
And gaily accomplished
    The Master's command.
They swayed down his body,
    Rolled up his shirt-tail,

And poised up his buttocks,
   That a stroke mightn't fail.

Then they tied down his legs,
   That the skin might draw tight,
That each lash might draw blood
   To the Master's delight;
Then they twitched at his hair,
   And chucked up his chin,
And cried out, "Good Master!
   It's time to begin."

Now Arthur's and Redgy's
   Own bottoms were sore,
But they knew that Frank Fane's
   Would be terrible more.
And each was too glad
   To forget his own grief,
In seeing Frank's flesh
   In the state of raw beef.

Said Arthur to Redgy,
   "We've often been stripped,
All three of us together,
   And jollily whipped;
But now we're both masters,
   And, crickey! it's fun,
To see Frank Fane catching
   Three floggings in one."

The first was three dozen,
   Laid in with a will,
"Just enough," quoth the Master,
   "For a boy in the bill."
Then he sat down and rested
   His arm for awhile
And looked at his work,
   With a grim kind of smile.

Then he gave a fresh sentence—
   "So much for the Dunce!

Now five dozen for the Truant,
    But not all at once.
This rod is all splintered,
    Go fetch me two more;
No, two's poor allowance,
    So, Redgy, bring four!"

"There'll be two for the Truant,
    And two for the Thief,
And if that does not bring
    That fat bottom to grief—
Then Keate was a fumbler,
    And Busby a fool,
And I'm not a Master
    Of Whippingham School!"

Then the right trusty Master
    Went at him like mad,
And loud were the prayers
    And shrieks of the lad.
Said Arthur, "You coward!"
    Said Redgy, "Keep cool!
Your bottom's a credit
    To Whippingham School!"

But the Master is pausing!
    Is it mercy or fear?
Ah! no, it's to toss off
    A mug of strong beer.
And refreshed with his tipple,
    He's at him again,
He never seems tired
    Of swishing Frank Fane!

He pauses once more.—"Boys!"
    He cries, "Hold him tight,
I remember I've got
    A short letter to write.
If the creature's rebellious,
    Let him taste this sweet cane,
I'll be back in ten minutes
    To finish Frank Fane."

So the cane on his shoulders
    Went rat-a-tap-tap,
And in turns they examined
    His bum like a map;
Such outlines! Such islands!
    Such mountains of weals
And such pretty red rivers
    Running down t'wards the heels!

Here's the Master returning,
    A cigar 'tween his lips,
Hurrah! for the Master
    Who smokes while he whips!
He knows how to tackle
    Two pleasures at once—
The taste of the baccy
    The smart of the Dunce.

So he puffed like a demon!
    And fiercely cut in,
Till you hardly could pick out
    An inch of whole skin.
Then he took a new country,
    And he striped the white thighs,
Till the old hall re-echoed
    A tempest of cries.

O! firm was his muscle!
    And supple his wrist,
And he handled the Rod,
    With a terrible twist,
But muscles grow weary,
    And arms lose their powers,
There's an end for all nice things,
    For floggings—like flowers.

Shrieks Frank Fane, "I'm dying!"
    Says Redgy, "You a'nt,
And if you go off
    In a bit of a faint,
We'll soon thrash you back
    Into living again,

You've not done with swishing
    Just yet—Master Fane!"

Now the whipping is over,
    And the culprit is free,
I don't think he'll sit down,
    This evening for tea!
And when in a fortnight
    He's turned down once more,
I fancy he'll find
    His bottom still sore.

MY GRANDMOTHER'S TALE OR MAY'S ACCOUNT OF HER INTRODUCTION TO THE ART OF LOVE.

From an unsophisticated Manuscript found amongst the old lady's papers, after her death, supposed to have been written about A.D. 1797.

CHAPTER I.

When I was sixteen years old I was a pupil teacher at the N. School. I had a bedroom to myself, but I always chose one of the elder girls to sleep with me. My favourite, Susey P——, was about my own age, and of a warm friendly disposition. We soon became very intimate, and promised to tell each other all our secrets.

We were both exceedingly curious to know all about the secret pleasures of love, and often talked over the subject at night, all the time fondling and playing with each other's cunts.

"Did you ever hear any name for this little chink, May?"

"Yes, dear, cunt. One of the girls wrote it the other day on her slate. She said that was what the boys called it."

"And what do they call their own things?"

"Pricks."

"Why do they call them pricks?"

"I suppose it is because they prick our cunts."

"Would you like to have your cunt pricked?"

"Yes, I think, I would like it now, for my cunt feels so very hot."

"So it is, and mine is just the same. O May! if my cunt could be turned into a prick what fun we would have."

She then got over me, and rubbed her cunt against mine, while I held the cheeks of her bottom and pressed her in between my thighs.

"May, did you ever notice the lump between the legs of Mr. T——, the resident tutor?"

"Yes, dear, that's his prick, every man has that, though some have it larger than others."

"O yes, I know that, but have you seen it swell out when he talks to us girls, and leans over us to make us hold our pens right?"

"Perhaps he is then thinking of our cunts."

"I am sure of it, and especially of yours, for you are his favourite. If he were here now I know what he would like to do."

"What?"

"Just to get on top of you, and shove his prick into your cunt, and fuck you."

I only laughed, and we soon fell asleep.

On Sunday, a short time after, having a headache, I remained at home. I was not aware that anyone was in the house, until happening to pass Mr. T——'s room, he suddenly sprang out, caught me in his arms, drew me in, and closed the door.

"Oh Mr. T——. Please let me go."

"Dearest May, let me tell you how dearly I love you." And while he half smothered me with kisses, he gently drew me towards the bed.

"No, I won't sit down—let me up—don't attempt to put your hands under my clothes."

But he forced his hand up, and I felt his eager fingers exploring all my secrets there.

"Mr. T——, take your hand—I cannot allow such liberties —let me up, or I'll scream."

"Don't, my pet, for there is no one to hear."

"Do let me up, and take your hand—oh my! how dare you lift my clothes."

He held me down, and soon, in spite of my struggles, he

uncovered all my belly and thighs, and my cunt lay bare and exposed to view.

It was the first time it had been seen by man, and I felt horribly ashamed. But a peculiar sensation of pleasure quickly turned the idea of exposure into a source of delight.

His face flushed, and his eyes sparkled as he looked down, and exclaimed, "What a lovely cunt you have, May; this rising mound is covered with such a profusion of rich brown hair, and the swelling lips, how deliciously they pout, while the glowing red chink between is most luxurious and inviting. I must kiss it. Oh! how sweetly it smells."

He stooped and warmly kissed my cunt.

Then opening the lips he sucked the clitoris and pushed his tongue into the hot recess.

The touch of his mouth made my cunt thrill, and when I felt his tongue moving around the clitoris, and penetrating the sensitive folds inside, I could not help opening my thighs and raising myself a little, so as to afford him a freer access to that pleasurable spot.

When he stood up I saw that his trousers were down, and that his prick was sticking out pointed towards me, and nodding its great red head as if in proud defiance.

Holding it in his hand, he said, "Look at this poor fellow, May, he craves your kind indulgence, and only asks to hide his blushing head for a moment in this sweet nest; won't you take him in your hand?"

"O, for shame! Mr. T——. Put that horrid thing away. I won't look at it, or touch it. I won't let you put it in." And I covered my cunt with my hand. He pulled my hand away, and placing it on his prick, forced my fingers round it. It felt deliciously smooth and soft, but at the same time firm and stiff.

"Mr. T——, let me up. What do you mean?"

"I mean that I am going to fuck you May; to put my prick into your cunt and fuck you."

"I will never let you. It would harm me, and hurt me."

"No, my love, it will neither hurt you nor harm you. Let me put it in, do, my sweet pet."

He pushed the head of his prick in between the lips of my cunt, and moving it up and down the furrow, said, "There, that does not hurt you, I am sure." He then placed it at the inner opening, and with a sudden push forced it in.

"Oh! Mr. T——. Take it out. Oh! it is hurting me. You said you would not hurt me."

But he only pushed harder, then something gave away inside, and I felt the whole prick rush up into my belly. It had a startling effect at first, and almost took away my breath, but when he went on to work his tool in and out, and I felt it rubbing with a most delicious friction against the throbbing folds of my cunt, the feeling became one of overpowering delight. I twisted about and heaved to meet his thrusts.

"There, darling, now don't you like that?"

"Yes, I like it now, that's very nice."

"Now say it's name."

I whispered, "Prick."

"Say it out."

"Prick."

"And yours?"

"Cunt."

"And doing this?"

"Fucking."

"Go on, say what it is you like."

"I like to feel your prick fucking my cunt."

"Oh, go on, it's just coming."

"Prick—cunt—fucking—belly—bottom."

Then, drawing his prick suddenly out of my cunt, he poured a torrent of hot seed over my belly, and up to my very breasts.

After this Mr. T—— and I lost no opportunity of performing the sweet rites of Venus, and he soon initiated me into all the various ways and modes of enjoyment. I found that I could fully trust him, as he was very discreet, and particularly careful to avoid doing me harm.

Susey and I too became more and more confidential. I acknowledged to her that I had been fucked, but did not name Mr. T——.

One night I prevailed on her to give me full particulars of some love scenes between her elder sister Jane and her intended, Mr. John C——.

"They used to take me out to walk with them. They generally went to a wood, where they had a favourite resting place, well sheltered among the trees. But when there they always sent me away to gather blackberries or flowers.

"I often saw him kiss her, and sometimes when no one was

looking, push his hand up under her petticoats. This aroused my curiosity, and I resolved to watch them.

"So the next time when I went off with my basket, I made a circuit, and entered the wood behind them. I crept through the trees until I could both hear and see them plainly.

"He was lying on his back, his trousers all open, and a long fleshy thing with a purple head was standing up. She was stooping over it moving it up and down with her hand. Then she kissed it, and took it in her mouth and sucked it.

"'How nicely you suck my prick, Jane. Kneel up now, I want to see your beautiful bottom and cunt at the same time.'

"As she did so he threw up her clothes over her back, uncovering the two round cheeks of her bottom, and the thick lips of her cunt jutting out like a huge hairy mouth between.

"'My darling, you have a splendid backside, the sight of it would bring to life the prick of a dying man. Keep as you are, I'll fuck you this time from behind, in what is called dog fashion.'

"He then got up, and knelt between her legs, and drawing apart the white cheeks of her bottom, pushed his prick into her cunt.

"Then holding her hips, he worked his article rapidly in and out, telling her to push back her bottom to meet each thrust of his prick.

"She panted and pushed, while he grunted out, 'Do you feel it Jane? Do you feel my prick?'

"'Yes, dear John, I do feel your prick, ever so far up my cunt—that's right—drive it in hard. Fuck—fuck—fuck.'

"Then they fell together on the grass, and I ran away."

"How did your cunt feel, Susey, when you saw his prick, and watched them fucking?"

"Oh, it used to get very hot, and then I would rub it and squeeze it as hard as I could."

"Did you often see them doing it, Susey?"

"Yes, many a time, and in every kind of way. Would you believe it, I saw him once fuck her in her bottom, and she did not mind it a bit."

"Did they ever find you out, Susey?"

"They did. I'll tell you how. One day I crept up very close to them, she was standing with her back against a tree, holding up her clothes. He was kneeling between her legs kissing her cunt. He looked up and she said:

" 'Well, to please you—there—watch.'

"And a stream of amber fluid spurted out with a hissing noise from between the hairy lips of her cunt. She had scarcely done before he kissed it again, and sipped up the drops that hung about the hairs.

" 'Now, John, it's my turn to see you spouting.'

" 'Well, if you hold my prick I'll try.'

"She held it while he pissed, rubbing it all the time, as if she was milking a cow's teat, and when he had done, she kissed and sucked it.

" 'Your prick is in grand order to-day. Look how stiff it is.'

"She bent it down, and let it go, when it sprang up erect as before.

" 'Lie on your back, John, and I'll get over you, I know it is a way you like.'

"So he lay down, his fine prick standing up in full erection.

" 'Now tuck up, and turn your bottom to my face.'

"She did so, and straddling over him with her great white bum jutting out, she stuffed his prick, neck and shoulders, into her gaping cunt.

"Then she bounded up and down like a jockey riding. When she rose up I could see the prick standing up, all red and inflamed. Then heaving down, the prick rushed up into her cunt, and her bottom came flap against his belly.

"This scene excited me greatly. I envied Jane. She seemed to enjoy it so thoroughly. And not thinking what I was doing, I forced my middle finger right up my cunt, the sudden pain made me cry. 'Oh!' They started, and quickly drawing aside the branches, saw me, my clothes up, and my finger in my cunt.

" 'Holloa, Susey! is that you?' cried John.

" 'You wicked little minx,' said Jane, 'how dare you steal upon us in that manner?'

"I said nothing, but covering my face with my hands, began to cry.

" 'Don't scold her, perhaps she could not help it. Come here, Susey, sit down and dry your tears. Now promise you will never speak of anything you may have seen.'

"I sat down, and earnestly promised all that they desired.

"John, passing his hand up under my clothes, and pinching

the lips of my cunt, said: 'You have already given me a
glimpse of this little nook, Susey. I want a closer and fuller
view. Lean back. Open your legs. There. There. Hasn't she
a nice innocent looking little cunt, Jane? I think the cunt of a
young girl before the hair grows over it is particularly pleasant
to look upon, and to kiss too,' he said, as he held up my bottom
with his hands, and buried his face between my legs.

"I felt his whiskers brushing my thighs, and his soft tongue
pushing into my cunt.

"'Yes,' replied Jane, 'you may pet and kiss Susey's little
plaything as much as you like, but remember that is all.'

"'Tell me, Susey, what did you see?'

"'I saw you pushing something into Jane.'

"He drew out his prick, and putting my hand on it, asked,
'Was this what you saw?'

"'Yes.'

"'Do you know what it is called?'

"'Yes, I heard Jane call it prick.'

"'And what's this little slit?'

"'My cunt.'

"'Would you like to see the prick going into Jane's cunt
again, and fucking it?'

"'Oh, yes, I would very much.'

"'Well, Jane, my love, let us have another turn before we
go, my prick is awfully excited.'

"He laid her back, and opening her legs, made me look
at her cunt. I had often seen it before when she was bathing,
but had never looked into it until now. I was surprised at its
depth and extent. He put my hand on it, and said: 'See these
fine thick lips, how they swell out. That's the sort of cunt a
man loves to fuck. And this deep chink, how red and hot it
is. Put your fingers in.'

"Three fingers entered easily. The soft warm folds inside
closed on my fingers, and seemed to suck them in.

"Just like your own cunt, May. Oh! how hot it is! and how
it throbs! And mine is throbbing too. Let us have a mutual
suck before I proceed with my story."

I readily agreed, for my cunt felt all in a flame. We threw
off our shifts, and lay naked on the bed. She got over me, and
lifting up my thighs, sucked eagerly at my cunt, and twining
her arms round my hips, tickled my bottom.

My tongue was equally busy about her sweet orifice, and

as she felt it penetrating the heated parts inside, she wriggled about, and pressed her bottom on my face.

We were soon partially relieved by a copious discharge from our founts of pleasure.

Susey then resumed her exciting narrative:

"John knelt between Jane's thighs, and made me direct his prick into her open cunt. I held it by the root as it passed quickly up. He told me to stir his balls and pinch his bottom.

"Meanwhile, I watched the operation with the greatest interest and delight.

"As the prick went in, the lips enclosed it with a kind of eager suction, and when it came out they seemed to follow it, as if loath to part with such a pleasant morsel.

"John put his hands under her, and raised her up. As he warmed to the work, his great muscular bottom heaved backward and forward with increasing rapidity, making his prick plunge in and out of her hot receptacle.

" 'Are you pinching him, Susey? Pinch hard.'

"I pinched his bottom, and tickled the hole there with my finger.

" 'Push it in, Susey, oh, that is so nice. Tell us what you see, dear.'

" 'I see your bottom heaving backward and forward and your prick rushing in and out between the thick hairy lips of Jane's cunt.'

" 'What else do you see, Susey?'

" 'I see the bag below your prick, and feel two round things in it.'

" 'Stir them, Susey. What else do you see?'

" 'I see the round hole of your bottom.'

" 'Move your finger inside, Susey. Oh! Oh!!' he cried, as he drove his prick with great force into her cunt, and banged his balls against her bottom, while she clasped him in her arms."

All this time Susey had been frigging my cunt with her fingers, and now she sprang on top of me, and pounded her cunt against mine, until our cunts again overflowed with love's sweet juice, and we lay back to rest.

The next time I went to Mr. T——, after the usual preliminaries of petting, sucking, &c., he said he wished to try a new mode of enjoyment which he had seen in a picture. So he first set up a large mirror before us, and then sitting on the edge of a sofa, he lifted me up backwards, and placed my bottom on his belly. Then putting his hand under my thigh, he raised my knee up to his breast. So that, in the glass, we had a most exciting view of my open cunt, and his upstanding prick nestling its rubicund head between the hairy lips.

I rested my foot on his knee, and then pressing down, watched it slowly disappearing in the pouting gap. As I rose up, the sweet instrument of pleasure again appeared, all red and shining with the moisture of my cunt, and when I pressed down it hastily returned, leaving nothing outside but the balls in close contact with the hairy lips.

Mr. T—— smiled, as he saw his tool absorbed in the crimson recess of my greedy cunt, and said:

"How beautifully plump and pouting your cunt is, my sweet May. With what delicious pressure it sucks in my bounding prick, while the soft cheeks of your bottom rub sweetly against my belly. But let us not hurry, it is so pleasant to talk together while my prick is soaking in your cunt. I want you to tell me something about your friend Susey. Does she know much of these matters?"

"Indeed, she does, everything in fact."

"Do you speak out the names? Prick, &c.?"

"Yes, she talks freely of pricks and cunts, and of fucking too."

"Was she ever fucked, do you think?"

"I think not, but she has often seen it done."

"How was she able to manage that?"

I told him how she had seen her sister fucked by her intended before their marriage.

"Do you often pet each other's cunts?"

"Yes, nearly every night."

"How?"

"When we are stripping for bed, she often asks me to lean back; and then she kisses and pets my cunt, and I do the same for her."

"Has she a nice cunt?"

"It is a nice little cunt, much tighter than mine; the lips are very plump, and well covered with light red hair. The skin round it is white, and smooth as satin, and the inside a bright pink."

"Why, May, you have quite excited me. Would you be awfully jealous if you saw me fucking her?"

"No, I would not be such a fool."

"May, you are the dearest girl, and have the sweetest cunt in the world. But I must take out my prick now. Hold it in your hand. There—see—how it spouts."

Before leaving I consented to let him hide in my wardrobe the following evening, that he might hear and see how we got on together.

When the time came I detained Susey in the schoolroom, until I was sure that Mr. T—— was safely ensconced in his hiding place. Then we went to our room, and having carefully fastened the door, commenced undressing as usual right opposite my wardrobe. I stopped her as she was putting on her nightdress, and said:

"Susey, the night is warm, let us have some sport before we go to bed. And first give me a good peep at your nice little cunt."

I stretched open her thighs, as she leaned back on the bed, that Mr. T—— might have a better view.

I opened the soft pouting lips, and said:

"Your cunt is very red to-night, have you much feeling in it?"

"Yes, it is all aglow. Oh! pinch the clitoris—rub your finger—there—you may push it in if you like."

The door of the press opened a little further.

"Susey, my pet, I want to see you make water. I'll hold the pot between your legs, and you can do your pee into it."

I did so, and soon the hot piss came gurgling out.

I heard a stir in the press behind me.

"Now, May, it is my turn to see you perform, and I will hold the pot for you."

I spread my thighs and fired away.

"Lean back May, and let us tip cunts, for want of something better."

She got in between my thighs, and pushed hard against my cunt. Mr. T—— must have had a grand view of her peach-like bottom, as she heaved it up and down.

The door of the press opened further, and I could see the head of a prick sticking out.

"Tell me, May, once again, how you felt the first time you were fucked?"

"Well, you know, he pushed me back on the bed, pulled up my clothes, and in spite of all my efforts, laid bare my cunt. Then he forced himself in between my thighs, and with his naked prick standing up. He made me take it in my hand and rub it up and down. He praised my cunt, and sucked it, which I thought very nice, though I wondered at his doing it."

"I don't," said Susey. "I love to suck your cunt, darling May, but go on, tell me more."

"He said he wanted to fuck me. I said he shouldn't, but he forced the head of his prick into the mouth of my cunt. Then giving a great heave he drove it up. It smarted me a good deal at first, but when it got in altogether, and he commenced to work it in and out, the pleasure was so great that I could not help telling him, when he asked me, that I liked his fucking very much, and that his prick felt very nice in my cunt."

Here Susey commenced bounding between my thighs. "Oh! May! how I long for a prick. How I do wish that Mr. T—— was here. I could almost ask him to fuck me, my cunt is so burning hot."

The press door opened, and Mr. T—— stepped out perfectly naked. In a moment he was behind Susey, poking his prick against her cunt.

"Here I am then, ready and delighted to gratify each of my sweet pets."

Susey started, but when she looked back and saw Mr. T——, and felt the head of his prick in her cunt, she hid her blushing face in my neck, and resigned herself to his amorous attack.

I laughed and held her buttocks open while he drove his prick into her maiden cunt.

It did not hurt her much, as she had enlarged the opening when frigging it with her finger.

After a few strokes I asked her how she liked the feel of a prick in her cunt.

"Oh May," she replied, "why do you ask me. You know well yourself how a prick feels."

I slipped my hand between them, and felt her hot clitoris clinging to his prick, as it plunged in and out. While at every push she got behind, her belly and breasts heaved against mine.

Mr. T—— was too much excited by all that he had seen and heard to be able to prolong his fuck, so he had to draw out his prick to avoid harm.

I held it in my hand, as he rubbed it in the furrow between the cheeks of her bottom, and I soon felt the emitting spasm, as it poured a stream of hot sperm over her back.

Susey seemed disappointed, however, and asked why he took it out.

"Just because I would not injure you."

Then he explained how that unless the seed was injected on the mouth of the womb, which lay at the end of the passage, there was no danger of any woman being put in the family way. And though the pleasure of both parties is lessened by the withdrawal of the prick at the moment of highest enjoyment, yet a man must be a selfish brute if on that account he would run the risk of doing such a grievous wrong to any girl whom he respected and loved.

He now placed his pendant tool in Susey's hand, and said if she would pet it a little that it would soon be in working order again.

She raised it up, and regarding it with interest, drew back the soft movable skin, and uncovered its rosy head.

"Kiss it Susey," I said bending her down.

She kissed the end of his prick, as she gently worked it up and down. Then as it gradually stiffened she let its head pass into her mouth, while her roving hands wandered over his bottom and balls.

Then he laid her back that he might inspect and kiss her pretty love chink.

"Is not this soft red hair very nice?" I said, passing my hand over her swelling mound.

"Yes it is exceedingly nice and exciting," and he buried his mouth in the pouting slit, while I caressed his prick and balls.

Rising up, he presented his prick, which had now regained its former size and strength, and asked, "Which of you will take it in?"

Susey said, "Fuck May, Mr. T——. I would so like to put your prick into her cunt, and see you fuck her."

He leaned over me as I lay back on the bed, and Susey, looking up between his legs, popped his tool into my cunt, and held his balls as he pushed it up.

Then, at his request, she laid down beside me, with her thighs up, and her pretty little cunt open before him. He leaned over and kissed it, at the same time softly working his prick in and out of my cunt, and not being so hot as before, he was able to prolong the pleasant exercise. After a minute or two he stopped and said, "I must take it out now, as I feel it coming. Hold it in your hand Susey, and you will soon see what a man's seed is like."

She held it over my belly, while he pressed his balls against my cunt. And the white seed, like fluid starch, spouted in spurts from his excited tool.

"Oh! isn't it funny," she said, stooping down, and touching with her lips the tip of his prick, when a fresh spurt darted into her mouth.

"Oh! there is very little taste. Will it do me any harm in my mouth?"

"None whatever, not even if you swallowed it all, indeed, it is considered most invigorating."

He told us afterwards how greatly he enjoyed seeing us playing together, and especially doing our pee, for, he added, nothing excites a man so much as seeing a woman doing her pee, the water streaming out of her hairy chink is most suggestive of love's delights.

We spent many nights after this when we sported and fucked in every possible way. His great delight was to have one of us sucking his prick and tickling his bottom, while he sucked and frigged the cunt of the other. He loved to make us spend in his mouth, at the same time that we swallowed his seed.

We let him fuck us in our bottoms too.

He said this gave him great pleasure, for our bottom-holes were smaller and tighter than our cunts. We did not like it so well, but we were so fond of him we could not refuse.

Mr. T—— often lent us pictures that were a great source of amusement. Among others, a set of scenes between a handsome white girl and a negro. In the first he is sitting on a chair, playing the banjo, his trousers open, and his great black tool sticking out. She has her eyes fixed on it, while she holds up her dress, and points to a most voluptuous cunt between a pair of widely extended fat thighs, as much as to say, "Look here, Sambo, here is a place that will soon take the stiffness out of your prick."

In the next behold him on his knees, between her thighs, holding open the thick furry lips of her cunt, while with his tongue he licks round the clitoris, and the red chink below it, muttering, "Oh, sweet cunt! how I lub to taste you, to suck you, and to fuck you."

In the next she is seen stooping forward, with the full orbs of her snowy bottom naked before him. With one hand he pats those delicious prominencies. With the other he directs his prick, now larger than ever, into her cunt.

It seems to quiver with delight, as the organ of bliss penetrated its soft folds.

Now Sambo, work your active bottom; drive home your noble tool, and make this willing fair one feel the vast pleasure that can be given by the sturdy prick of the despised negro.

(To be continued.)

————————————————

LADY POKINGHAM, OR THEY ALL DO IT;

*Giving an account of her Luxurious Adventures, both before
and after her marriage with Lord Crim-Con.*

PART V.
(Continued.)

After retiring to bed at night (James and myself had been
in the drawing-room all evening going through the most exciting and lascivious ideas, to amuse His Lordship, who contented himself by leisurely watching our love gambols,
smoking his cigar, and evidently keeping himself in reserve
for something bye-and-bye), instead of settling ourselves between the sheets we adjoined to the spare room, next to that
in which Reuben, the page, slept.

We were too soon for His Lordship, as on applying our eyes
to the peepholes, the boy's room was yet in the most profound darkness, so as the night was warm, and there was no
necessity for covering, we reclined upon the bed to await the
coming of Crim-Con; meanwhile we amused ourselves by
kissing and toying with each other's parts, till my handsome
butler, notwithstanding the previous hard work of the evening, was in a most rampant, impatient state, and would fain
have cooled his ardour within my longing cunt but that
would have spoilt all, as our transport would have been
certain to be overheard by the page, and thus prevent all our
anticipated sight-seeing.

Just as I was whispering to him to keep quiet, we heard a
match struck in the next room, and applying ourselves to the
holes, were much astonished to find Reuben was not alone,
there was the butler's assistant, a rather tall fair youth of sixteen, for whom we had never reckoned in our calculations;
he had always such a cold, reserved respectful manner, even
to James, that we never for a moment gave him a thought as
likely to be mixed up with His Lordship's amusements.

Reuben lighted a couple of the candles, then turning to
his companion, who was lying on the bed frigging slowly his
standing prick, as if keeping it in a state ready for use, said,
"Will, it's time His Lordship was here now, what a good job
I broke away from you just now, or you would have spent
and spoilt all; he likes to see us looking ready and randy, but

if he thinks we have been fucking or frigging by ourselves he would damn us, and bolt off in a rage."

Reuben and Will were both quite naked, and there was a great contrast between the youths, for while the latter was rather slim, tall and fair, the former was a regular Adonis in figure, beautifully plump rosy face, dark hair, and dark fiery impetuous eyes; his prick was also in a fine state of erection, and neither of them had more than a suspicion of downy hair around the roots of their pricks.

"What a fine fellow you look Rube, no wonder His Lordship seduced you; besides, you are a dear unselfish chap for introducing me into the fun, won't I fuck you gloriously when he is here to see us. I love you warmer, hotter than ever I could the prettiest girl in the world! And then, too, think of how well it pays!"

Here the two boys lay down on the bed fondling each other's pricks, and kissing mouth to mouth, sucking tongues, and twining about in the most amorous manner, till I fully expected every moment to see them spend, but they stopped suddenly, a step was heard outside, the door creaked on its hinges, and His Lordship appeared with a large table lamp in his hand.

"Hold, hold hard, you randy rascals!" he exclaimed, "I believe you've been and had your fun already. If you have, you buggers—," he hissed between his teeth, in a frightfully suggestive manner, which seemed almost to terrify the boys, who paled slightly for a moment, and then both of their faces flushed crimson.

Rube was the first to answer. "Oh no, my Lord, we have been too careful, only Will was just telling me his love, and how gloriously you should see him fuck me."

"Bravo! So he shall my dear, and I will suck your darling pego, and find out if you have been deceiving me."

He placed his lamp on a small table at the foot of the bed, so that the room was now excellently well lighted, then seating himself on the bed he opened his dressing-gown, showing his long limp prick, and taking the pair of them on his lap, they sat on his naked thighs, whilst he kissed them, thrusting his tongue into their mouths, or handled and compared their two charming pricks.

This was only a little preliminary toying, then presently asking Rube if the cold cream was under the pillow, he threw aside his only vestige of a garment, and stretched himself on his back on the bed.

"Now my plump little beauty," he said, addressing the page, "kneel over my breast, and give me your prick to suck, and now Will, mount behind him, and I will put your tool to his arsehole."

James's assistant was too ready to need a repetition of the welcome order, he was there in a moment, his hard cock quite eight inches long, battering against the tight dark wrinkled nether hole of his love.

His Lordship was so eager for work that he scarcely had taken Rube's seven inches between his lips before his fingers were busy with the lubricant on Will's prick and the page's bottom, directing the former's delighted tool so cleverly to the mark that almost immediately he completed his insertion up to the roots of the hair, and was revelling in the delicious sensations and pressures to which his love treated him.

His Lordship sucked excitely at the morsel in his mouth, and we could just hear him mumbling out, in a half-choked voice, "Beautiful! Fuck! Go on quick. Spend, spend! Ah—r—r—," as we could see Rube's dark eyes full of fire, and his prick stiffen and shoot its juice into Crim-Con's mouth, till the drops of thick creamy spend fairly oozed from his lips, as he still sucked and smacked his lips with great gusto; besides, we could see his own prick rising into quite a manly state.

Will fucked into his love's bottom with fury, and seemed to spend almost at the same time, and so exhaustively that he must have fallen backwards had he not clung round Rube's neck.

We were not idle whilst this exciting scene was enacted under our eyes. James instinctively wetted the head of his prick and my bum-hole with spittle, and soon drove his great machine through the narrowest gate of Paradise. Its movements were indeed heavenly, blissful. I never before felt such an acme of pleasure, the sight before me, the soul stirring movements behind, and our mutual emissions almost made me groan in an agony of delight.

A perfect frenzy of lust seemed to take possession of my body, I could see His Lordship's prick was now finely erect, and the two boys were alternately kissing and sucking him.

Whispering my paramour to follow me, I quickly rushed from our concealment into the room where they were. As the door was not locked and before they could recover from their surprise, I threw myself on my back, on His Lordship's belly, almost taking the breath out of him by my sudden weight on his stomach, regardless of his "Damned Hellish Bitch" and other exclamations of displeasure. I fixed his stiff prick in my bottom-hole in triumph, nipping and squeezing, and wriggling my bum about on him as James with his tool in an awfully excited and distended state took possession of my hot raging cunt.

The boys seemed to quite understand my ideas, as they each of them knelt and presented their pricks for me to fondle, whilst Crim-Con, still cursing and swearing at me for a "Damned Hellish Bitch, &c." groaned under our weight, but I could feel he was thoroughly enjoying it, as his prick stiffened more and more every moment, under the delightful movements and pressures to which I treated him; besides, the membrane between his prick and James's was so slight that it was almost like two cocks rubbing together in my cunt.

I frigged the boys till their eyes almost started from their heads from excess of emotion, they spent over the firm round globes of my bosom, but I still kept them stiff, alternately kissing the head of one or the other prick whilst Crim-Con's hands tickled their balls, and frigged their arseholes till we made them nearly mad.

I had never felt my husband's long thin prick so well before, and James's affair was so distended by the excess of lustful excitement that I was gorged to repletion, and yet felt that I wanted more, more, more! Had I been cunt all over I should have wanted every hole well filled by a good stiff one. What a delicious moment. Ah! ah! if I could but die like that! I seemed transported to another world, my senses were leaving me, I was indeed in Paradise!

I remember no more of this extraordinary scene, but James told me next day they were frightened, I went off into such a death-like faint, they had to carry me to my room, and use restoratives till I gradually breathed a little, and sank into a restless kind of sleep, that I had bitten both the boys' pricks till they were sore and bleeding. "As for His Lordship," he added, "I am afraid he is as good as dead, he was so exhausted Dr. Spendlove had to be fetched, and he fears the worst."

This was too true, His Lordship only lived forty-eight

hours, whilst I have never been well since. The extraordinary excess of lubricity that night seemed to have quite undermined my constitution, and I have gradually declined from that time. I was advised to be very careful how I indulged in venereal pleasures in future, but in spite of my weak, nervous, excitable nature, I have found it impossible to quite abandon those pleasures which seem to me to give the only real foretaste of the future Paradise; regardless of declining strength, whenever the opportunity offered I have indulged in the delights of love myself, or in seeing others do it.

The executors settled everything, whilst the incoming earl, to show his appreciation of their services in furthering his interest, made most lavish provision for James and the two youths, as he afterwards told me that he considered they helped him to the title and estates a good five or ten years before he could reasonably expect to have come into them.

"And do you not think, my Lord," I asked him when he told me this, "that I also deserve your thanks, where is your gratitude to little Beatrice?"

He looked at me in a curious kind of way. He was a handsome young fellow of eight and twenty, but married to death by a fair fat wife, who besides having a fortune of her own, had already blessed him with nine children, and a prospect of blessing him with many more.

"I can't make you out Robert," I went on to say, "you're so different to your poor brother, and so content with the same thing every day; every look, every smile you have is for that splendid wife of yours. He was for flirting with and having every pretty woman he came across; what sort of a heart can you have, you have never seemed to pity me for my loss?"

He was so handsome, and I so disliked the new Lady Crim-Con, that I resolved to seduce him, and gratify both pique and passion at the same time.

"What are you driving at, Beatrice dear, I'm sure you puzzle me?"

"Ah! you know how delicate and how lonely I am, and never even to give a brotherly kiss of sympathy. I know Her Ladyship hates me, but I shall be gone to Hastings in a few days," I said, bursting out into sobs as if my heart would break, the tears from my downcast eyes dropping upon one of his hands which he had placed in a deprecating kind of way on my lap as he sat by my side.

He kissed me tenderly on the forehead, more like a father, as he said, "I'm sure I only wish I knew how to cheer you up, my dear."

"My dear," that sounded quite a little affectionate and as if the ice was breaking, so throwing my arms round his neck, I kissed him passionately in return for his fatherly salute, sobbing out in a low broken voice, "Oh, Robert, you do not know what it is to be left dull, miserable, and all alone in the cold, cold world, can you not spare me a little, only a little of those loving smiles your wife must be quite surfeited with?"

He gave a soft sigh, and I felt an arm steal round my waist, as he very tenderly drew me close to him, and did not seem at all loath to receive my kisses, which were getting yet more impassioned.

"If you do give me a kiss, what will Her Ladyship lose?" I whispered.

A perceptible tremulousness seemed to vibrate through his form as our lips at last met in a long, loving kiss. It was quite plain I had at last excited his amorous sensuality, which had previously been so dormant in his respectable married bosom.

"Now, I love you Robert, dear, and you needn't mention such an indifferent thing to Lady Cecilia," I whispered, when at last our lips parted.

"A slice from a cut loaf is never missed, you know Beatrice," he said, as he smilingly held me at arm's length, and gazed into my blushing face, and continued, "besides, I can easily make it up to her, so she will lose nothing."

"Your loaf is pretty well sliced dear," I replied, "considering how many children you have to eat bread and butter, Robert."

Again he drew me to him, and we exchanged the most lascivious kisses as I sat on his lap. This billing and cooing being so effective that I very soon felt his prick stiffening quite perceptibly under my bottom. His face flushed, and an extraordinary fire beamed in his usually quiet eyes; we understood each other at once. Without a word he inclined my unresisting form backwards on the couch, and as I closed my eyes, I felt him raising my clothes, his hands stole up my thighs till he gained the seat of joy. My legs mechanically opened to give him every facility, in a moment he took advantage of my tacit invitation, and I felt the nose of a fine battering ram at the entrance of my widowed cunt.

The desire for a really good fuck had been consuming me for some days, and I could not resist the impulse, however immodest it might seem to him, of putting my hand upon his glorious engine of love, and directing it into love's harbour myself. It was in, I was gorged to repletion, spending, sighing with delight, almost before he could make a move.

Opening my eyes, I could see he was delighted at my ecstasy. "Ah, you darling man, my darling Robert, you don't know what it is for a young widow to be deprived of the natural solace of her sex. Now, push on my boy, and let us be thoroughly happy, let us mix our very souls in love's emission, and then tell me if you can spare one a few crumbs of your cut loaf now and then."

A very few thrusts brought down my love juice again, and I also felt him shoot a tremendously warm flood of his essence into my longing cunt. Our lips were joined in fierce loving, tongue-sucking kisses, whilst I threw my legs over his buttocks, and heaved up my bottom to meet his manly action with the most libidinous abandon.

Her Ladyship was out with the carriage, and we were quite safe for a couple of hours at least; still, considering his family duties, I made him keep a shot or two in reserve for the night, as he contented himself by kneeling down and worshiping at the shrine of love, where he had just been paying his tribute to Venus, exclaiming in ecstasy, as he examined or kissed the various charms, "What a love of a cunt! How small and tight! What a charming chevelure, &c.!"

A day or two after this, to our mutual delight, Lady Cecilia was summoned into the country, to attend on her mother's sick bed.

My room was next to theirs, so at night it was a very simple thing for him to slip into bed with me. I found he knew very little about ornamental fucking, himself and wife had strictly adhered to the plain family style, which had produced such fruitful results. My ridicule of his ignorance made him quite ashamed of his want of knowledge, especially when I introduced him to the delights of bum-fucking, and he faithfully promised me that when Her Ladyship returned, he would insist upon his marital rights over every part of her person, and so steer clear of babies in future, and that if I only made a good peephole I might see all his fun with Lady Cecilia.

Delighted with my conquest, I determined to persuade him to degrade his wife in every possible way, that I might enjoy the sight of it. So I initiated him into every possible style of enjoyment, till I had the satisfaction of knowing that the hitherto respectable husband was completely changed into a lustful libertine.

(To be continued.)

Two things which generally come together—"Short sight and short cock."

THE PEARL,

𝔄 Journal of Facetiæ and Voluptuous Reading.

| No. 12 | PUBLISHED MONTHLY. | June, 1880 |

LA ROSE D'AMOUR;

Or the Adventures of a Gentleman in search of Pleasure.
Translated from the French.

(Continued.)

In the course of a few weeks a vessel arrived in the creek, laden with furniture for the chateau, and the upholsterer presented himself to me. I took him through the building, showing him in what style I wished such and such rooms furnished.

The room of fountains was simply furnished with cushions of rich satin and silk, and musical instruments, as I intended it merely for smoking, singing, and dancing.

The other long room opposite was furnished with bedsteads of finest rosewood, inlaid with gold, silver, pearl, and even precious stones. Each bed had springs placed in it, and was stuffed with the finest down. The sheets were cambric of the finest texture, coverlets of silks and satins, beautifully worked, while over all was a spread of Brussels or point lace.

The curtains were of crimson velvet, set off with white silk. In the alcove of each bed was placed a mirror, set in frames of silver.

The floor was covered with the richest carpets; the walls were hung with silk, on which were worked the loves of Cupid and Psyche, Rape of Europa, Leda ravished by Jupiter in the shape of a swan, Diana issuing from the bath, a Procession of naked female Bacchanalians carrying the Jolly Gods in Triumph on their shoulders, and other devices.

Instead of chairs and sofas there were cushions placed in the room, worked with pearls and precious stones, bordered with fringe of pure bullion.

Each bed stood on a raised dais of mahogany. The carpets

were of the richest texture, so soft and thick that the foot sank ankle deep in them. At one end of the chamber was the state bed; it was partitioned off from the other parts of the room by a curtain of blue velvet.

This apartment was furnished as a Turkish tent, the drapery (of green velvet) depended from a centre-piece of gold stars, and was drawn down to the sides so as to form a perfect tent.

The bed stood in the centre of the place, it was made of beautifully carved cedar from Lebanon; the posts, head and foot boards were ornamented with designs of birds, fishes, men and women, &c., of pure gold and silver, set with precious stones. Curtains of richly wrought velvet, looped up with chains of gold, completed the coup d'œil.

I had placed no ornament in this apartment, so it was designed as an initiatory bed for all the beauties I could bring to the place. And although licentious pictures, statutes, &c., may have an exhilarating effect upon men at times, they also, by their beauty, attract the attention from the dear creatures we might be enjoying.

Adjoining this large bedchamber I furnished one as a dressing-room. The walls and ceiling were inlaid with large plate mirrors, making the room one complete looking-glass. At the sides, overhead, no matter where they might look, whosoever entered it could see nothing but their reflections.

Here were placed stands and toilette table, of chased gold and silver, ivory, and pearl; all the perfumes of the East, all the cosmetics that could enhance the beauty, and give youth and fullness to those who inhabited the place, were here in profusion.

Adjoining the room of glasses was a drawing-room which looked out on the garden. The doors and windows opened on to a balcony running the full length of that side of the castle. To this room I paid more attention than to any other. The floor was covered with a carpet of purple velvet, stuffed with down. The rarest productions of the old masters adorned the walls, mirrors, framed in gold, depending from the beaks of birds wrought in silver, hung between the paintings. In each corner of the room stood a statue of one of the graces, in the bodies of which were set music boxes, made to discourse the sweetest music. On stands of alabaster were large vases, chefs d'œuvre of Dresden manufacture, containing sweet smelling flowers; while the richest spices and perfumes of Araby, burning in censors entirely concealed in niches in the wall, diffused through the room odours that enchanted the senses.

Here it was that I received my mistresses after all the rooms were furnished.

During the time the workmen were busy arranging the rooms and furniture, I had kept them in a distant wing of the chateau, refusing to see them till everything was finished. I had secured the services of a dozen or more lusty fellows and wenches, to serve as servants and guards to those I might wish to detain.

One of the men I made the servant of the bedchamber—so called, as he was the only male I allowed in this part of the castle. Him I sent to bring to me La Rose d'Amour and the voluptuous Russian, with Rose, Manette and Marie.

When they entered I was reclining on a pile of cushions, dressed in a loose robe of rich cashmere, with a Turkish cap on my head, ready prepared for a bath, to which I intended to take them.

So soon as the door was closed on them they ran up, and falling on me, devoured me with embraces and kisses. Oh, how they caught fire at the touch of me, and burned for that which I had kept them from more than a month, whilst I could scarcely restrain myself from throwing them on the floor and darting the liquid flame of love into them at once. But I restrained myself.

I took them into the garden of flowers, and showed them all my improvements there, the beautiful little lake surrounded with shrubs and trees, over the whole surface of which was a net of fine wire, which confined a quantity of rare birds.

Again we entered the chateau, and passed through to the bedchamber, where I showed them the fifty beds, telling them I intended to travel till I had procured fifty of the handsomest women in the world to lay in them.

From this we passed on to the bathing-room, and throwing off all covering, plunged into the perfumed waters.

After laying and wantoning in the bath for some time, I pulled the tassel of a bell, and four of the wenches I before mentioned entered to serve as waiting-maids.

We emerged from the water, and they dried our bodies

and hair, and giving us loose gowns, we wrapped ourselves in them, and I led my beauties to the dressing-room.

I cannot depict their astonishment on entering this apartment of mirrors. Taking their gowns, I threw them out of the door and closed it. I told them to dress in the rich clothes which lay before them.

How great was their astonishment to see themselves reflected a thousand times in the walls and ceiling! The toilet stands seemed to be in every part of the room, and it was some time ere they could get over the confusion they were in, but with the help of one another they got dressed. The dresses I had provided for them were those used by the Turks—wide, loose pants and vests of satin, and short skirts, instead of the unhandy long shift.

After having dressed ourselves, I took them to the room of fountains, where we had a rich lunch. Here I opened to them my views, telling them that after one more trip to Paris, as soon as the yacht arrived which I had ordered, I intended to sail for Constantinople, where I would buy some of the most beautiful girls I could find, and also that I intended to purchase some mutes and eunuchs for my own harem, as I could not trust the females I might buy and bring with me the same as I could the ones that were now around me.

I told them I intended to take one or two of them with me in the vessel when I went, and that to be perfectly fair and impartial they should draw to see who should be the lucky ones; and also that I intended to have two of them sleep with me that night, and they must draw for that at the same time.

I had determined beforehand that I would sleep with Celestine and Caroline, and also that I would take them with me on my voyage, so I arranged the drawing that it came out as I wished.

At an early hour I led the way to the bedroom, followed by the five girls. It took us but a moment to put ourselves in a state of nakedness.

Oh, with what joy, what transports, I hugged their warm naked bodies to mine! How delightfully the soft, smooth, white skin of their bellies felt as they twined about in my arms! With what fervour did they fasten their moist, pouting lips to mine, devouring me with kisses, while their lustrous eyes sparkled and flashed with lustful fires.

I draw the voluptuous Celestine to the bed. My passions are raised to the highest pitch. My prick is swelled almost to bursting, its vermilion head stands erect against my belly, not to be bent without danger of breaking.

Celestine is on her back, her thighs apart, showing the lips of her luscious cunt slightly open, anxiously awaiting the attack.

I precipitate myself upon her; I pierce her to the very quick. She screams with mingled pain and pleasure.

The enormous head of my prick distends the folds and lips of her cunt to their utmost stretch. The storm increases, everything trembles, the lightnings flash, the rain pours, it comes in torrents! I spend! I die! My God, what pleasure! Oh, heavens, have mercy!

We rolled, we screamed, we bit, we yelled like demons from the excess of our pleasure. Her cunt is a small lake of sperm, my prick swims in it, lolling its length. I draw it out, and the pearly liquid gushes forth, flooding her thighs and the sheets with the rich mingled essence of our bodies.

Ah, my charming Celestine, what an excess of exquisite pleasure did I experience whilst in your arms that night. Thrice did I, goaded by my fierce lusts, bedew the cunts of my two noble mistresses with a deluge of the precious liquid, bountifully supplied by the stream of pleasure from love's reservoir.

I recovered myself a little, and paid a visit to Rose, Manette, and Marie, to each of whom I did justice, always advancing to the attack with head erect and flying colours. Nor did I leave one of them without having well oiled their precious little maws with the dear liquid that women are ever looking for.

On the following morning I started for Paris, accompanied by Caroline, dressed as a page, to finish my preparation for starting to Constantinople.

After stopping at my hotel, I sallied out with my female page to call on Rosalie de C., whom I was lucky enough to find alone.

Having embraced her, I introduced Caroline to her, asking when she would be ready to go with me to the chateau; she replied that she would be ready in two days.

I then enquired after her friend, the lovely Laura B——. I told Rosalie that I was determined to possess her friend

Laura by some means or other, and that she must render me
her assistance in securing her, and as I could think of no
other plan, I proposed to Rosalie that she should go and get
her friend to take an airing with her in the Bois de Boulogne,
and that in a sequestrated place I would come up with them,
alight from my carriage, and invite her and Laura to get out
and take a walk, and that I would then throw a shawl over
Laura's head, force her into my own carriage, take herself and
Caroline, and set out with all possible speed for the castle.

Everything happened as I had arranged.

On coming up with Rosalie in the wood she accepted my
invitation to walk.

I opened the door of the carriage, and as Laura passed out
first, just as she reached the ground, Rosalie from behind
threw a large shawl over her head, and drew the corners close
around her neck, so that her voice could not be heard. I
caught her up in my arms and carried her into my own carriage. Rosalie and Caroline entered immediately, and I
dashed off with my fair prize at the top speed of four fine
horses.

On the road to the chateau I stopped at no houses but those
of persons whom I had brought over to my own interest.

Arrived at the place we stopped at for the night, I hurried
with my companions into a large room prepared for us by a
courier that I had sent in advance.

Immediately after my arrival supper was served. Dismissing
all the attendants, I turned the key in the door, and for the
first time since I had forced her into my carriage, I spoke to
Laura.

I told her of my unconquerable love for her, of the feelings
that were aroused in my heart towards her the first time that I
saw her at Rosalie's house, and that I then formed the determination of carrying her off to the chateau. That I was determined no one else should be possessed of so much beauty, nor
revel in such charms as she possessed.

I laid open to Laura all my plans. I informed her how I had
fitted up the old castle, and for what purpose, telling her that
she would there find Celestine C——, one of her old companions, and that Rosalie was another who willingly accompanied me.

I introduced her to Caroline Z——, telling her rank, how I

made a conquest of her, and her having linked her fortune with mine, and followed me to France.

I dwelt at some length on the life of luxurious ease and pleasure we should lead at the chateau, expatiating on the endless joys and ecstasies of her living with me in all the unrestrained liberty of sexual intercourse.

Rosalie and Caroline also spoke to her of the life of pleasure they led with me, describing to her, as well as they could, the extreme luxury of lying in a man's arms and being well fucked; and used all their powers of persuasion to induce her to go with them and me peaceably to the chateau.

Laura, from being at first very sulky, neither eating nor speaking to any of us, became somewhat mollified, so that she partook of the supper, and answered questions put to her by my two mistresses.

After the supper was removed I called for wine, and while we sat talking and drinking I took care to make the discourse run principally upon one subject alone—that of love and its natural consequences, the intercourse of the two sexes.

Caroline and Rosalie were very useful auxiliaries, talking with the utmost abandon, stripping and dancing about over the floor as the wine began to fly to their heads, uncovering their breasts, showing their bubbies, occasionally flirting up their petticoats, exhibiting a fine calf or knee, with other tricks, all of which tended to confuse the senses of the charming little Laura, who watched their movements all the while. I constantly plied her with wine till she became somewhat excited and a little free, making remarks on the two girls who were tussling on the floor.

I rang the bell, and ordered a bottle of white brandy, which, as soon as it was brought in, I uncorked, and pouring out glasses of it, invited my Russian to drink. She took up the glass, as did Rosalie, both declaring that Laura must drink with them. After some hesitation she took up the glass, and placing it to her lips, sipped a little of the liquor, and put it down.

Caroline and Rosalie, for the purpose of inducing the charming Laura to drink freely of the brandy, drank glass after glass of it, till Laura, from sipping, began to toss off her glass as well as either of us.

When I gave them the sign to retire for the night, Laura had become so intoxicated that she required the assistance of the other two to enable her to retire without staggering in her gait.

After they had got into their bedchamber, I stripped myself perfectly naked, and Caroline having left the door slightly ajar, I stepped into the room; hiding myself behind a bed curtain I observed the manœuvres of my two lovely pimps.

They first undressed themselves stark naked, then did the same for the inebriated Laura. And then she stood in all her naked beauty before me, exhibiting charms to my ardent gaze, more lovely, if possible, than any I had heretofore ever enjoyed.

After my mistress had stripped Laura of her clothes, they viewed and admired her naked beauties, praising them above that of the Venus de Medicis, throwing her down on the floor, turning her over and over, squeezing her breasts, pinching her backside, opening her thighs, even the lips of the dear little niche between them. They praise its beauty, admire the lascivious plumpness of its lips, and even go so far as to lay their kisses upon it. The conversation running in praise, the while, on the pleasures she would mutually enjoy with the men who should be so lucky as to tear up the virgin defences which guarded the entrance to so delicious a little cunt.

I could now see Caroline insert the tip of her finger into the dear slit with which she was playing, and commence tickling her, while Rosalie threw her arms around her neck, and drawing her to a close embrace, kissed her, putting her tongue into Laura's mouth, which, with the frigging she was receiving from Caroline, caused her to experience the most delightful sensations, if I might judge from the exclamations and the wrigglings of her backside, as she squirmed about on the floor.

Perceiving, by the motions of Laura, that she would soon, for the first time, slightly experience the ecstatic joys which women can only procure the full enjoyment of when in the arms of a man. Seeing this I slipped out from my hiding place, and went and took the place of Caroline between her thighs (unperceived by Laura, whose face was hid in the bosom of Rosalie), and inserting my finger into her cream jug, I soon brought down a copious libation of the precious liquid with which my hand was plentifully bedewed, so freely did the liquid jet out once the sluice was opened.

Crossing her thighs over my body she almost squeezed the breath from me, exclaiming in broken accents:

"Oh, now it comes! Again—oh, God! I faint. I die!"

Loosening her holds, she stretched herself out with, as usual, a gentle shudder, as the ecstasy caused her to faint away.

While Laura lay in her trance of pleasure I laid myself down in her arms, placing my cheek on her bosom, my lips touching hers, my hand still covering that dear slit, and my finger still retaining possession of its inner folds.

As I perceived Laura beginning to recover from her ecstasy, I drew her to my bosom and recommenced my titillations. I asked her if she was still angry with me for carrying her away, telling her that as soon as we arrived at the chateau she should enjoy all the reality of the unreal mockery she had just tasted through the agency of my fingers.

If her modesty and virtue were not entirely conquered, the motion of my finger reproduced in her the delicious sensations of pleasure from which she had just recovered, and which for the second time she was about to enjoy. She could make me no answer, but to throw her arms round my neck and glue her lips to mine.

My desires were excited to the highest pitch. I depicted to her the pleasure she would experience when, after arriving at the chateau, I should deflower her of her virginity, and triumphantly carry off her maidenhead on the head of this, "dear Laura," I said, as I took one of her hands and clasped it round my prick. "Then," said I, "you will know all the joys and pleasures of a real fuck."

"You will then," I continued, "experience all the sweet confusion, far different from what you now feel, of stretching wide apart your thighs to receive man between them, to feel his warm naked body joined to yours, the delicious preparatory toying with your breasts, the hot kisses lavished on them and on your lips, his roving tongue to force its way between your rosy lips in search of yours, the delicious meeting of them, their rolling about and tickling each other as mine now does yours," at the same time thrusting my tongue to meet hers.

"And then to feel him take his prick, and with the tips of his fingers part the lips of the flesh sheath into which he intends to shove it, putting the head of it between the lips, and gently shoving it in at first, stretching the poor little thing to its utmost extent, till, not without some pain to you, the head is effectually lodged in it. Then, after laying a kiss on your lips, he commences the attack by gently but firmly and steadily shoving into you, increasing his shoves harder and harder, till he thrusts with all his force, causing you to sigh and cry out, he thrusts hard, he gains a little at every move, he forces the barriers, he tears and roots up all your virginal defences, you cry out for mercy but receive none. His passions are aroused into madness, fire flashes from his eyes, concentrating all his energies for one tremendous thrust, he lunges forward, carries everything before him, and enters the fort by storm, reeking with the blood of his fair enemy, who with a scream of agony yields up her maidenhead to the conqueror, who, having put his victim *hors de combat*, proceeds to reap the reward of his hard fought and bloody battle.

"Now he draws himself out to the head, and slowly enters again. Again he draws out, and again enters, till the friction caused by the luscious tightness of the rich flesh which clasps tightly his foaming pego causes such delicious sensations that he is no longer master of himself.

"He lunges with fierceness into her, the crisis of pleasure approaches; he feels it coming, he drives it home to her—deeper, deeper. At last it comes—he spends.

"My God, the pleasure! His exclamations of Oh! ah! the deep drawn sighs, the short jerks of his backside, the quick motions of his rump, proclaim that the acme of pleasure has seized him, and that he is spurting into her the precious fluid which oils and cools the burning itchings of the dear little cunt, which has undergone the one painful trial to which all your sex is liable."

During my description Caroline had taken my pego in her hands, and had been playing with and rubbing it all the time. I still kept my finger in Laura, and perceiving by the twitching of her rump that she was about to spend—

"I—oh, dear—I—now—feel it. There, I come now, I spend. Ah, oh, oh, h—ha!" and I died away on her bosom, to awake and find that Laura had wet my hand with a most plentiful effusion of nectar ravished from her by my fingers, while I had squirted over her belly and thighs a flood of sperm.

Laura, without any murmurings, gave herself up to me and the seductive friggings of my fingers without any reserve, and not till nature was perfectly exhausted did we fall asleep in each other's arms.

In the morning, when Laura awoke and found herself lying in my arms, she sprang from my side, and snatching a coverlet from the bed, wrapped herself in it, and sat down in one corner, sobbing and weeping as though her heart would break.

I attempted to console her, but she would not listen to me, and having dressed myself I went into another room, while Caroline and Rosalie tried to bring her to herself again, and they succeeded so far as to bring her out to breakfast, which was shortly afterwards served.

At the table they rallied Laura for her coyness in the morning, after having spent so delightful a night with me, jesting her about my having procured for her with my finger the exquisite pleasure which had thrown her into such delicious swoons. Telling her how, when the fit was coming on her she would throw her arms round me, squeeze my hand between her thighs, wriggle her plump little buttocks, &c.

After having drank a few glasses of wine she had completely recovered her spirits.

I went out of the room to order the carriage, and on my return I found her tussling with the other girls, they trying to throw her down for the purpose of giving her a taste of the pleasure she had enjoyed so frequently through my agency during the night.

When I entered the two called me to come and help them, while Laura begged me to rescue her from the hands of her tormentors.

Whilst they were thus calling on me the landlord entered to announce the carriage, when taking Laura by the arm, I led her out, followed by the others. We entered the carriage and drove off.

It was late in the night when we arrived at the chateau, on the third day of our being on the road. I retired to bed and fell asleep, with all the girls sleeping around me, determined to touch none of them, reserving all the powers within me for the purpose of doing full justice to the maidenhead of the lovely Laura.

(To be continued.)

MY GRANDMOTHER'S TALE; or MAY'S ACCOUNT OF HER INTRODUCTION TO THE ART OF LOVE.

From an unsophisticated Manuscript found amongst the old lady's papers, after her death, supposed to have been written about A.D. 1797.

Chapter II.

When vacation came, and the school broke up, I returned home to my father, who was a widower. And Susey went to keep house for her bachelor uncle in Scotland.

We promised to keep up a regular correspondence, and to write a full account to each other of everything interesting.

I felt very lonely after Susey had gone, and missed Mr. T—— more than I could tell.

My cunt demanded a large share of my attention. I did not know what to do with it. In vain I looked at it in the glass, I combed it, I petted it, I frigged it with my finger, I poked it with a candle until I spent, but it was a poor substitute, I panted for that reality.

About this time I noticed Tom, the gardener's son, a lad of eighteen. He was always eager to work in my garden, and never seemed so happy as when I commended him.

One morning I was sitting in the summer-house when he returned from his breakfast.

Not seeing me he came to a corner near the summer-house, and, taking out his prick, began to make water. I could see it through the leaves as he held it in his hand. It was a large, strong-looking prick, and I feasted my eyes on its fair proportions. He seemed in no hurry to put it up, but looked at it as he drew back the skin, making its red head swell and bound in his hand. Then, with difficulty, he forced it into its usual hiding place, and went to his work.

The sight of this prick set my cunt on fire, and I resolved to get possession of it if I could.

I returned to my room, and taking off my drawers, carefully washed and dressed my cunt.

Then going back to the garden I called Tom, and told him to set up the ladder against the pear tree by the wall, as I wanted to see if the fruit was ripe. He held the ladder as

I climbed up. He was just below me, and as I moved my legs about, reaching to the pears, he must have had a full view of all I had between them.

I glanced down to observe the effect. His face was flushed, and he was gazing up with all his eyes.

"Take care, Miss, or your will fall."

"No fear, Tom," I replied, stretching out to one side, when my foot slipped, and I came sliding down, just over him, so that his head passed up between my thighs.

He caught me in his arms, and as he held me for a moment I felt him kiss my cunt.

"Oh, Miss, are you hurt?"

"Not much, only a little stunned. Carry me into the summer-house."

He took me in his arms, his hand still resting on my naked bottom, and laid me on a seat.

"Shall I call anyone, Miss? You seem very faint."

"No Tom. I shall be all right in a few mintues; it is only my knee."

I lay on my back with one leg up. He was kneeling on the ground at my side. I saw him peeping up under my dress.

"Is it here, Miss?" Putting his hand on my knee, "May I rub it?"

"Yes Tom, thank you, that makes it better."

He rubbed my knee, he touched my thigh above the stocking, he moved his hand gradually higher and higher, until at last he slightly touched the hair on my cunt. He looked up at my face. I lay with my eyes closed.

He grew bolder, he pressed the lips, he felt the chink between, he rubbed the clitoris.

"Tom, where are you putting your hand?" I said, in a languid tone.

"Oh Miss, I can't help it. You are so beautiful."

He convulsively grasped my cunt, and pushed his fingers into its glowing slit.

"Tom, I cannot allow this, let me up."

"Darling Miss May, don't be angry."

He forced his head under my clothes, and rapturously kissed my cunt.

I trembled with delight as I felt the touch of his lips, and the soft probing of his tongue, yet for appearance' sake, I cried, "For shame, Tom, let me up, you are making me very angry."

I raised myself on my elbow, and saw that his prick was out and standing in fine condition.

"Tom, how dare you expose yourself in that manner. Go away."

"Miss May, I can't help it, indeed I can't."

He still kept his hand on my cunt, opening and closing the lips, and pinching the clitoris.

He drew me across the wide seat, and getting in between my thighs, pushed the head of his prick against the lips of my cunt.

"Sweet Miss May, do let me put it in, oh do."

"No Tom, I won't allow it. Let me up now, perhaps I may some other time."

He pushed again, the head entered, it passed up, the whole prick was in, it filled my cunt.

My hungry cunt, with what eagerness it sucked in a morsel so delicious! Oh! there is nothing to be compared to a standing prick for gratifying a girl who knows and understands the supreme delights of fucking.

So I lay back and let him work away.

"Tom, what are you doing?"

"I am only—fucking—fucking your cunt—Miss May. Oh! how good you are—ain't that nice!" he said, as he drove up his prick with most thrilling effect.

"It is, dear Tom, press up to my heart."

"Do you like my fucking you, Miss?"

"Yes, Tom, you have a very nice prick, but take care or you may do me harm."

The dear fellow understood me, and just before he spent drew out his prick. I took it in my hand, and held it while it poured forth a torrent of love's juice.

I need not say that after this many happy love scenes were enacted in the summer-house.

Tom proved very docile and prudent. He had a wonderful prick, always ready for its work, and eager for a fuck. He knew well how it use it with effect, and I soon found that he was no tyro in the art of love.

He told me many curious things; among others, that papa was in the habit of fucking our milk-maid Sarah in the hay-loft. It was she herself told him, for he had been the first to open her maiden channel.

He offered to place me in a position where I could safely witness all that passed between them.

"Meet me early to-morrow morning. For it is after Sarah brings in the milk, and while Robert the groom is at his breakfast, that the master comes out."

So the next morning Tom conducted me to the hay-loft. He covered himself and me lightly with the hay.

We had not long to wait, for we soon heard papa talking in a low voice to Sarah as they came up the ladder.

They came down near us.

Papa then said: "Take him out, Sarah, I have been longing for a fuck all night."

She unbuttoned his trousers and drew out his prick. It was in good order, with a fine large ruby head.

The sight of my father's prick had a curious effect on me. At first I did not like to look at it, but at length the amorous feeling overpowered every other; and I almost envied Sarah as she held it admiringly in her hand, slowly moving it up and down. Then she took out his balls, and putting her hand underneath pushed it on to his bottom.

He had meanwhile pulled up her coats, and uncovered a fine thick-lipped cunt, which pouted in fleshy luxuriance.

"What a splendid affair you have, Sarah! It is the most lascivious cunt I ever looked at. Now tell me, who fucked you last?"

"La, sir, why do you ask me that?"

"Just because it excites me more to hear you tell. You know I don't care who fucks you, provided you hide nothing from me, and keep yourself from harm. Did not Robert fuck you last evening? Your face was so red when I met you after leaving him."

"Well, to tell the truth, sir, he did."

"Tell me how it happened."

"I went into the stable to borrow a lantern, he caught me in his arms and kissed me. Then he forced me back on a heap of straw, pushed his hand under my petticoats, and got hold of my cunt. I scolded him, and boxed his ears. He did not mind, but squeezing in between my thighs, he thrust his big tool into my cunt, and fucked me like mad."

"Has he a big tool, Sarah?"

"Yes, it is very big and strong, but he does not use it so nicely as you do, he is always in too great a hurry."

Papa now got over her, she held his prick, and with her hand directed it into her cunt. He pushed it slowly up until his balls pressed her bottom. She grasped his buttocks, and vigorously heaved up to meet every thrust he gave, saying at every heave, "Dear sir, oh, how nice—push it in—drive it home—that's the way—how your prick fills my cunt—fuck me fast—fuck me hard."

I was leaning forward on the hay, and Tom over me, his prick and balls resting on my naked bottom; but as soon as papa commenced fucking Sarah, he lodged his prick in my cunt.

He then timed his strokes, so that each time papa pushed I felt Tom's prick driving up my cunt, and his hair tickling my bum.

I spread my thighs and raised my bottom, Tom suddenly drew out his prick, and holding open the cheeks of my bottom, popped it in there. As it was well moistened with the juice of my cunt, it slipped in easily. I dared not speak, so had to let him have his own way.

He pushed it home, and bending his arms round my hips he frigged my cunt. After a few strokes, which were far from disagreeable, he administered a warm and soothing enema, just as papa with a grunt of satisfaction poured his libation at the shrine of Sarah's cunt.

He then got up and went away, after telling her to remain until he was out of the yard.

He had not gone many minutes when Robert popped up his head.

"Holloa, Sarah, so master has been just oiling your notch. I heard him fucking you, and all you said too. And now I'll have my revenge."

He seized her in his arms, threw her on the hay, and pitched her clothes over her head.

She struggled and kicked her legs about in the air, but Robert held her down while he gloated over her wriggling bum and inflamed cunt. It looked very red and open, while the rich juices of her previous fuck trickled down her bottom.

"So you say master fucks better than I do, and that I am always in too great a hurry. Well, I will be slow enough now."

He took out his prick, and held it in his hand, while he opened the lips of her cunt.

It was the largest prick I ever saw, and had a tremendous head. I was curious to see how she could take it in. He pushed it against her cunt. She plunged about.

"Be quiet," he shouted, giving her a slap on the bottom. "Keep your arse quiet, I say, and mind your fucking."

He forced the head in, and, to my surprise, it passed easily in. The huge prick must have filled her belly. He grasped the cheeks of her bottom on each side, and held her up, as he plunged his great prick with wonderful force in and out of her smoking gap.

I had seen many a fuck, but never a fuck like this. I admired the wonderful size and strength of Robert's prick, and could not repress a longing for a taste of its prowess.

Tom too was greatly excited by the scene, and fucked me in his best style. But it was the idea of Robert's prick that filled my mind.

The next afternoon, drawn by an irresistible attraction, I went into the stable.

"Robert, I have come to look after my mare, I think she wants to be clipped," and I stepped up.

"Take care, Miss," he said, putting his hand on my shoulder, "she is very restive just now."

"Oh, I am not afraid," and I began to pat her.

He made some kind of noise that caused her, I think, to plunge and kick.

"I told you so, Miss," he said, passing his hand down over my bosom, and drawing me towards him. "It is a mercy you were not killed." And he pressed me in his arms.

"Robert, let me go—where are you drawing me—you will make me fall. Oh! what do you mean—don't push your knees there—don't attempt to raise my dress. Robert, what are you about—I won't let you—take it away—you must not do it— Oh! oh!!—you are hurting me—Oh, my! what are you pushing in—yes, I do feel it—hold me in your arms—yes, I like that—you may fuck me, Robert, as hard as you like."

The monstrous prick was in my cunt. I felt it everywhere. He grasped my buttocks. He lifted me up. As he arose I clasped my arms round his neck, and crossed my legs over his back. He carried me around the stable, with his prick still embedded in my cunt. It seemed to penetrate to my very heart. Every nerve within me thrilled with rapture, as he shot into my vitals a stream of gushing sperm.

It was the first time I had ever received into my cunt the seed of man, and the feeling was intensely delicious.

"What have you done Robert? Perhaps you have ruined me for life."

"Not at all, Miss, look here," and he showed me a large syringe, "and there happens to be warm water in this bucket. Let me syringe your cunt at once, it will remove all danger."

I lay back with my thighs widely extended, while he poured such a flood of water into my cunt as must have washed out every trace.

Robert then wiped and kissed it, after which he knelt by my side, and presented before me his prick once more in splendid condition.

"What a great fellow you have, Robert," I said as I chafed it in my hand, and uncovered its rosy head. I kissed it, and with difficulty took part of it in my mouth.

"Oh, Miss May, you are very good, and you have the sweetest cunt I ever fucked, may I put it in again?"

"Not this time, Robert, I would rather pet this fine fellow, while you are tickling my cunt."

So keeping its glowing head in my mouth, with one hand I frigged the shaft, and with the other stirred his balls and touched his bottom, while he was equally busy about my seat of pleasure, deliciously frigging with his fingers each sensitive orifice.

And just as I felt my cunt flooded with love's effusion, he shot into my mouth such a torrent of seed that I could not swallow it fast enough, and it squirted out on each side of my mouth. It was pungent and pleasant to the taste.

Before I left him he swore on his oath never to speak of what had just happened, and he proved loyal and true.

I had now two esquires both able and willing to gratify me at any time, or in any way. And although I soon found out more of papa's secret amours, yet I myself exercised the greatest care and circumspection.

A few days after this adventure papa told me that as he considered I must be very lonely so much by myself, he had asked a young lady named Kate L—— to come and stay with us for some time.

In due course she arrived. She was a nice, pleasing girl, with dark hair and eyes, and three years older than I was. I found her amiable and obliging, and ready to enter into my plans and share in my amusements.

Papa paid her particular attention, and I observed she did not seem at all averse.

They were often alone together, and I guessed something was going on, but she never told me anything.

Her bedroom was separated from mine by a bathroom, into which both our rooms opened.

One night, when we went upstairs, I sat for some time with her, and after bidding her good night, I passed through the bathroom, leaving the doors slightly opened. When I had undressed I put out my candle, and sat by the fire to warm my feet before going to bed.

I had not sat long when my curiosity was excited by hearing whispering in Kate's room.

I crept softly to the open door and listened.

"Oh, sir, why have you come into my bed?"

"Because I am so fond of you, my darling."

"If you were really fond of me you would not come to me in this way—don't—I pray you leave me—oh, my!—how can you be so nasty—take your hand off me—I don't like it —no, it is not nice—let my hands go—I won't hold it—I won't move it up and down—don't separate my thighs with your knee—what are you getting over me for? What are you pushing into me?"

"My prick, darling Kate. There, don't struggle, my pet, let it in, don't be frightened, I won't harm you in any way. Open your thighs, that's the sweet girl. Now I'll push it in as gently as possible. There, it is in, it is all the way up."

Then the bed began to creak, and the clothes to rustle.

"Put your arms around me, my love. Heave up your dainty little bottom. That's right. Do you know what doing this is called?"

"No sir."

"It is called fucking. Isn't fucking very pleasant?"

"Yes, it is now. Do I heave up right?"

"My darling, you heave as if you had been fucking all your life. Pinch my bottom. May I pinch yours?"

"Yes, as hard as you like."

"Now place your hand here. Hold my prick. Hold it tight. Oh! there it comes."

And rolling off her he lay panting at her side.

I felt greatly excited, and crept into the room, close up to the bed. I heard them kissing.

"Did I hurt you, my love?"

"You did a little at first, but when your prick was well in, and you commenced fucking, there was no feeling but pleasure. Would you like me to pet your prick now?"

"I would, darling, rub it up and down, this way, put your other hand on the balls, move your fingers further back, still further, there."

"Have you much feeling there?"

"Yes, there is great feeling behind the balls; don't you feel the root of the prick extending back to the little hole? That's a dear girl, the touch of your finger there is delicious. Push it in a little, my sweet pet. Kate, did you ever look at May's cunt?"

"Yes, I have seen it when she was in the bath; it looks well covered with hair."

"I am sure if you made free with her you would have great fun together, for, unless I am greatly mistaken, she has a very randy disposition. Promise to try to-morrow night, and tell me next day all that you have succeeded in finding out."

She promised to carry out his wishes.

"But now that you have worked up my prick we must have another fuck. Lie over me this time."

I heard her getting over him.

"Now it's in, heave away my love. You must do all the fucking yourself."

She panted as she worked her nimble bottom up and down over him.

"Do you like it this way, my love?"

"Yes, as a variety, but I like better to have you lying over me, and pushing in your prick."

He now prepared to leave, and I started for my own room, and was soon fast asleep.

I had several amorous dreams that night. I thought that Robert was fucking me in the loft, when papa came behind, pulled him off, and thrust his own prick into my cunt, and fucked me most delightfully. In my dream I felt no surprise at papa's fucking me; on the contrary, the idea seemed to add greatly to my enjoyment.

The next evening Kate offered to sleep with me. I could not repress a smile as I consented.

When we were undressing Kate said: "I would like to see you quite naked, May. You know we girls need not be ashamed of one another, and I will set the example."

She threw off her shift and stood before me, then pointing to my cunt she remarked that I had a great deal of hair there.

I replied that her dark hair was prettier, for it set off the whiteness of her skin.

She put her hand on my cunt, and asked me to let her feel it, "and you may feel mine if you like."

She touched the clitoris, and passing her finger down the slit pushed it up the passage, and said:

"Dear May, you are very open, were you always as open as you are now?"

"No, I was not; but are not you very open too?"

She smiled as she said: "May, if you will give me your full confidence I will promise you mine."

"Agreed," said I.

"Did you ever see what a man has here?"

"I did, did you?"

"Yes, do you know what it is called?"

"I have heard it called a prick, is that it?"

"It is. Had you ever a prick in here?"

"I have Kate, haven't you?"

"Yes, dear. Now tell me how it happened, and I'll tell you about myself afterwards."

I related my adventure with Mr. T——, and how he was so fond of kissing and sucking my cunt.

"Would you like me to kiss it?"

"I would, dear Kate, and I'll kiss yours too."

"Well, lean back, lift your legs, open your thighs as widely as you can. There, do you like that?" Holding my buttocks with her hands she sucked my cunt with great ardour, rolling her tongue round and round, and thrusting it up the passage.

After enjoying it for a while I said, "It is my turn now, dear Kate, let me pet and kiss your sweet cunt, while you are giving me the account you promised."

I sat on a stool between her thighs, and with my mouth
buried in her open cunt, listened to her narrative.

(*To be continued.*)

A SECRET REVEALED;

or

The True Reason Why Queen Esther Pleased the King More Than All the Other Virgins.

From an Original Essay by I. van Meyen.
Amsterdam, A.D. 1629.
Text.—Esther, Chap. II, v. 2 to 17 inclusive.

The Jewish Rabbis have a tradition that it was entirely
owing to the training Mordecai gave to his cousin Hadassah
(or Esther), in order to prepare the young girl to be his own
wife, that she was enabled to bear off the palm from all the
competing virgins, when the whim of the Court suddenly
causes her to be impressed for the royal pleasures, as well as
hundreds of other beautiful girls throughout the kingdom,
which of course at once quashes all her cousin's plans for his
own future enjoyment.

Robbed of his prospective bride, Mordecai had the brilliant
idea of making Esther's advancement the stepping stone of
his own fortunes. He knew that kings regarded their numerous concubines as so many toys only to be cast aside, and
perhaps never even looked upon again, when they had once
submitted to the Royal ravisher, and his natural shrewdness
and great knowledge of human nature made him reflect how
cloyed and disgusted even a king must get with the sameness
of the pleasure,* which the taking of hundreds of maidenheads from unresisting virgins could only afford him.

Accordingly, as the tradition has it, he secretly sent her instructions to rehearse with the seven virgins, her companions
(see v. 9), all the salacious ideas which he had himself instilled into her mind in view of his own future gratification,

---

* *This king Ahasuerus is generally supposed to be identical with
Xerxes, who was so "blasé" that he offered an immense reward to the
man who should invent a new pleasure.*

and also especially enjoined upon her the wisdom of putting
aside all modesty when her turn came to enter the Royal
presence, to submit to his embraces most joyfully, also to put
on the greatest possible semblance of erotic desire and abandon, and finally when she found her sovereign completely used
up, she was to entreat His Majesty to allow her maidens to
enter his presence, and enact with her such scenes as would
restore his prostrated energies in a very short time.

The old tradition is silent as to what took place when
Ahasuerus was so delighted that he placed the crown upon
Esther's head, and made her queen in the room of Vashti,
divorced. But from many allusions contained in the writings
of ancient Talmudists, who enlarged upon such an interesting subject, I have made out something as follows:

Mordecai had managed to convey to his cousin a small box
of magic ointment, which he had procured from one of the
magi (a forbidden sect in Persia in those days), the effect of
which he assured her was most marvellous when applied to the
parts of generation in either sex.

Thus provided, she was conducted by the chamberlain to
the king's house, and ushered into his august presence, whilst
the seven virgins, her companions, were left in an ante-
chamber. Esther being simply naked, with an azure girdle
ornamented with stars of gold round her loins, sandals of gold
on her feet, a wide coral necklace around her splendid throat,
whilst the raven tresses of her silken hair were ornamented
by a profusion of splendid pearls. Thus she stood as she
bowed her head before Ahasuerus, a thin veil of gauzy texture covering her from head to foot in such a way as to set
off the splendour of her charms rather than hide them from
the eye. Her virgins had no such pearls or necklets, but
simple azure girdles, with silver stars and silver sandals.

The king was reclining upon a magnificent couch, as she
knelt down to pay her homage to her sovereign lord and
master. He was a handsome man of about forty, with a
used-up "blasé" expression of countenance.

"Come, pretty girl, and kiss my Royal prick; perchance thy
luscious lips may raise some slight desire, which I may gratify,
but alas, all virgin beauties cease to inflame my once amorous
disposition. Dost know aught, fair child, thou thinkest would
please me?"

"Most Royal Prince, whom all the earth obeys, let not

thine heart be sad, because the fires of love have paled within
thy bosom. I have a box of magic unguent will restore thy
youthful vigour, and if my maiden companions may be permitted to attend me in your Royal presence, we will play
such games, the sight of which shall rouse a perfect storm of
passionate desire!"

"Good God! do I hear aright? haste fair maiden to begin,
call thy virgins, and if thou pleaseth me thou art queen!"

Esther, kneeling down, ventured to open the front of the
Royal robe, and taking his limp priapus reverently in her hand,
drew back the foreskin, and imprinted a kiss upon its ruby
head, at the same time using her tongue so skilfully that he
experienced quite a pleasurable sensation from its touches
round the entrance to the urethra.

"Rise, maiden, and call thy fellows."

"Most Royal Prince, ere I rise from my knees, give thy
word of honour that whatever we do shall be pardoned in
advance, or we may not feel free to touch thy Royal person."

"Thou shalt be queen, and I thy subject till break of day,
do what thou wilt sweet maid!"

The other seven virgins being summoned, Esther first ordered them to strip the king perfectly naked, then she
anointed the Royal priapus and fundus with the magic ointment, working her fingers so deftly, especially in the tight
hole of the latter, that she soon perceived some signs of
virility, as the lordly member began to throb and swell.

"Enough," cried Esther, "now the king shall see me ravish
my seven virgins before he takes my own virginity," producing as she said this an imitation mandrake of tremendous size
quite ten inches long, and thick in proportion, provided with
straps, so that she could adjust it upon herself; thus furnished,
she ordered four of her companions to seize one of their
number, and hold the victim down upon a couch, with legs
and arms well stretched out, then throwing herself upon the
trembling girl, ruthlessly plunged her great machine through
all the virgin obstacles.

The screams of pain, struggles, and sighs of the different
victims as they were deflowered in turn so affected the king
that he was almost mad with lust, and ready to throw himself upon the lascivious Esther, had not the girls, two at a
time, taken in turn the trouble to play with and excite him
more and more, at the same time restraining him as long as

possible, till as Esther was in the act of sacrificing the seventh victim, he felt the crisis approaching, and springing away from their restraint, threw himself upon her bottom, clasping her tightly round her waist, as his bursting pego plunged at the door of her maidenhead from behind.

This had been expected, and his two attendants, acting upon previous instructions, at once went to his assistance, the fingers of one opening the moist lips of the haven of love, whilst her companion's hand guided the head of the restive courser, till it was fairly lodged just within that tight but luscious mouth.

Esther was now screaming in pain as well as her victim, but she was so excited, and longing to be made a woman herself, that her bottom pushed out to meet his thrust, and achieved her fate almost in a moment.

The king, finding himself buried to the hilt of his weapon, paused to enjoy the voluptuous pressures and delicious warmth of the tight-fitting sheath he had penetrated, wishing to prolong the exquisite sensations which thrilled through his frame.

The two girls who had guided him into the seat of bliss now kissed and played with the Royal appendages, handling his affair, drawing back the skin as far as possible, and working their fingers in his bottom-hole, till he could retain himself no longer, and again pushing furiously into Esther, deluged her longing gap with a profusion of the seed Royal, almost screaming, "Oh, heavens! what pleasure! I melt! I die!" and then fell prone upon her back from excess of emotion.

"Esther, thou art my queen," were the first words he uttered as soon as he could speak.

The seven (no longer virgins) now washed the king and queen, and then themselves, after which all were refreshed and reinvigorated by stimulating wines and viands. Esther again excited her Royal spouse, till his pego was as a bar of iron; she made him enter the bottoms of all her maids, but without spending his Royal seed, till at last presenting her own lovely buttocks, she received the weapon of love in her anus, and kept him there till he rewarded her devotion by another copious emission.

Thus she became queen, and, as the king said when he presented her to the nobles of the Court, she surpassed in virtue and loveliness all the women of his realm.

THE MARRIAGE MORN.

Tune—The Merry Dance.

The marriage morn I can't forget,
        My senses teem'd with new delight;
        Time, cry'd I, haste the coming night,
And Hymen, give me sweet Lisette:
        I whisper'd softly in her ear,
        And said, "The God of Night draws near."
Oh, how she look'd! Oh, how she smil'd! Oh, how she sigh'd!
        She sigh'd—then spent a joyful tear.

Now nuptial Night her curtain drew,
        And Cupid's mandate was, "Commence
        With ardour, break the virgin fence."
Then to bed sweet Lisette flew,
        'Twas heav'n to view her when she lay,
        And hear her cry, "Come to me, pray."
Oh, how I feel! Oh, how I pant! Oh, I shall die—
        Shall die before the break of day!

Soon Manhood rose with furious gust,
        And Mars, when he lewd Venus view'd,
        Ne'er felt his pow'r so closely screw'd
Up to the standing post of Lust;
        But when the stranger to her sight,
        Sweet Lisette saw in rampant plight,
Oh, how she scream'd! Oh, how she scream'd! Oh, how she
        scream'd!
        She scream'd—then grasp'd the dear delight!

Now lustful Nature eager grew,
        And longer could not wanton toy;
        So rushing up the path of joy,
Quick from the fount Love's liquor flew;
        At morn, she cry'd, "Full three times three,
        The vivid stream I've felt from thee;
Oh, how I'm eas'd! Oh, how I'm pleas'd! Oh, how I'm
        charm'd!
        I'm charm'd with rapt'rous three times three!"

LADY POKINGHAM, OR THEY ALL DO IT;

Giving an Account of her Luxurious Adventures, both before and after her Marriage with Lord Crim-Con.

PART V.
(Continued.)

The Earl was as good as his promise. "My Robert," as I called him in our loving intercourse, was so well schooled that he was quite equal to the assertion of all his rights as a husband by the time Lady Cecilia returned home.

After dinner, on the evening of her arrival from the country, he found me sitting alone in the conservatory, and sitting down by my side, whispered in my ear how delighted he was at being able to have a last word of advice with me before retiring to rest with his, no doubt, rather expectant spouse.

"You have so drained me, last night and early this morning, dear Beatrice," he said, putting his arm round my waist, and meeting my ready lips in a long breathless kiss, and then continued, "Nothing but some extraordinary excitement will enable me to do justice to her expectations. I must fuck her at least three or four times after such a long absence; how shall I be equal to the occasion?"

"Have me first," I replied, "whilst she is seeing the children put to bed, there is plenty of time; it will give you zest for the fun to come, the idea of taking the virginity of her maiden bottom-hole will excite you enough, and the more she resists and gets indignant, the more you will enjoy it."

I had been gently stroking his prick outside his trousers; my touch was magical, it stiffened immediately, and when I let the impatient prisoner out of his confinement, I thought I had never before seen his priapus so distended and inflamed with lust as at that moment.

Rising up, I first stooped to give the engine of love a warm kiss, and keeping it in my hand, raised my clothes, and turning my bottom to his belly, spitted myself on the loving object, opening my legs and straddling over his lap, so as to get the very last fraction of its length into my heated cunt. We sat still for a moment or two, enjoying the mutual sensations of repletion and possession so delightful to each of the participators in a loving fuck, before commencing those soul-stirring movements which gradually work our heated desires to that state of frenzied madness which can only be allayed by the divinely beneficent ecstasy of spending, and mingling the very essences of our nature.

The idea that I was robbing his hated wife of her just expectations added such piquancy to our loving conjunction that I literally moaned or whined with delight, as I twisted my head round in the act of emission, so as not to lose the luscious kiss which is such an extra pleasure in those supreme moments of our happiness.

He did not come at the same time, but stopped and rested a moment or two, then rising, and keeping me still impaled on his dear prick, without losing place even for a single second, he laid my body face downwards on a little table which stood handy, and then recommenced his delicious moves, with his hands under me in front, frigging and tickling my cunt, till I almost wrenched myself away from him by the violence of my convulsive contortions. Suddenly drawing quite out, with another plunge he drove the head of his tool into the smaller orifice, which is so delightfully near and convenient when in the position in which he had me.

"Ah! Oh—oh—oh—oh—o—o—o—oe!!" I screamed, swimming in lubricity as I felt him so gorging my bottom, whilst his busy fingers were adding to my erotic madness by the artistic way in which they groped within my spending cunt. "Oh, heavens, Robert, Robert! Do, do come darling! There, ah—re, I feel it, how deliciously warm!" I murmured excitedly, as his flood of boiling seed inundated the gratified and sensitive sheath which enclosed him so tightly.

After recovering from our transports, we conversed about how he should proceed with his wife, his prick all the while as stiff as a policeman's truncheon, till at last fearing Lady Cecilia might surprise us, I went into the drawing-room and played the piano whilst he smoked his cigarette amongst the flowers in the conservatory outside the window.

Her Ladyship pretending fatigue (we knew what she was in a hurry for), the family retired rather earlier than usual to rest, but I took care to be at my peephole before Cecilia and Robert entered their bedroom.

As it was a habit of his to go over the lower part of the house, and see everything safe for himself before going to bed, his lady came first and at once commenced to undress.

She was about the same age as her husband, a vastly fine, fair woman, rather above the medium height, light auburn hair, slightly golden in tint, deep blue eyes, set off by dark eyebrows and long dark lashes, a full mouth, richly pouting cherry lips, and a brilliant set of pearly teeth; then as she gradually unrobed herself, her various and luscious charms quite fired my lascivious blood, as one by one they stood revealed to my earnest gaze. What magnificent swelling breasts still round and firm, and then as she lifted her chemise over her head, and exposed the lovely whiteness of her belly (still without a wrinkle, as she had easy confinements and never suckled her children, for fear of spoiling her figure), set off below by a bushy Mons Veneris, covered with light curly silken red hair, through which I could just perceive the outline of her slit.

Now she stood before a cheval glass, surveying herself at full length, I could see a blush cross her beautiful face, as she seemed almost ashamed to look at her own nakedness. Then a self-satisfied smile parted those cherry lips, and displayed the sparkling pearls of teeth, as she patted the shiny marble skin of her belly and bottom (evidently thinking of the effect of the sight upon Robert when he should enter the room), then she playfully parted the lips of her cunt and examined it closely in the glass. The titillation of her fingers brought another blush, and she seemed as if she could not resist the temptation to frig herself a little, moving a couple of digits in a restless kind of way backwards and forwards between the vermilion lips of love.

My blood was on fire, and much as I hated her, I would have liked to gamahuche her there and then. But suddenly the door opened, and Robert stood transfixed, as he exclaimed in surprise, "Surely, Cecilia, you have lost all modesty; why have you never exposed yourself to me like that before?"

"Oh, Robert dear, how you startle me, you came up so soon and I was only just looking at the love I know you are longing to caress as soon as the light is out."

"I really did not know you were such a charming figure, Cecilia, but now you are naked I will feast on the sight, but we won't put out the lights, my dear. I must now examine in detail every charm. By the way, I may tell you that during your absence I found some bad books of my late brother's and they so fired my imagination by the extraordinary descriptions of various modes of sexual enjoyments that I quite blushed to think of our innocent ignorance, and long to try some of them with you."

He had almost torn his clothes off whilst speaking, and I could see his prick as rampant as possible, in fact I believe it had never lost its stiffness since our excitable bout a short time before.

Throwing himself into her arms, they hugged and kissed, whilst she, taking hold of his pego, slowly backed towards the bed as she tried to bring its head to the mark.

"Not there, Cecilia, love, you have another maidenhead I mean to take to-night; our plain silly way of doing it only leads to getting a lot of children, and surely my quiver is full enough of them. I'll have no more, it's positive ruination, however rich a father may be. No, no, the French style in future, do you understand, I mean to get into your bottom," he said, as seriously as possible, yet with evident excitement.

"What a nasty idea! You shall never do that, Robert, to me!" she exclaimed, crimsoning with shame to the roots of her hair.

"But I must and will, Cecilia. Look at this book, here are all the different ways of 'doing it.' Why they suck each other, fuck—ah—you start at the vulgar word—but it's fuck—fuck—fuck—that's the name for it. They fuck in bottoms, under armpits, between the bubbies—another nasty name for titties—anywhere—everywhere—it's all the same to a man, all what they call C U N T, a word I am sure you have seen some-where in your lifetime written on shutters, doors, or even on the pavement—a deliciously vulgar word, Cecilia, but the universal toast of men when they meet in company (I could see he was trying to make her look at a little French book, called La Science Pratique, with its forty pretty little plates), how my blood has been fired by fancying all these delightful ideas remained to be enjoyed when you came home."

"Why Robert you are mad, I'll burn that horrible book, I won't learn their filthy ways!" snatching at the book.

"You're my wife, every bit of your body is mine to do as I please with it; don't drive me to extremities, Cecilia, or I may be rough, for I'm determined to put my prick in your arse, now at once!" trying to turn her over.

"Robert, Robert, for shame, Beatrice will hear your disgusting language. You shall never abuse me that way!" hiding her face in her hands and beginning to sob.

"But I will, and you may blubber like a child. Your tears only urge me on, if you resist I'll smack and beat you, till you are obedient!"

She struggled, but a woman's strength is soon exhausted, and at last he got her face down on the bed, with her bottom on the edge and her feet on the floor, then giving her a tremendously painful smack on her bum, he spread her legs wide apart, opened the cheeks of that glorious bottom, anointed the head of his bursting prick with spittle, also the tight-looking brown hole he was about to attack, and then pushed on to the assault of the virgin fortress.

I could hear her moan with pain as the head gradually forced its way within the sphincter muscle. "Ah—it's pricking—oh, oh—you'll rend me, Robert—oh, pray—Ah—r—r —re.—Oh! Oh!"

At last he was in, and rested a moment or two, then slowly began his fucking motions.

Presently I could tell by the wriggling of her bottom that she enjoyed it. His hands were busy frigging her cunt in front. How excited they got, each seeming to spend at the same moment, but he kept his place, and the second finish was so excitable that they screamed quite loudly in the frenzy of emission, whilst Cecilia actually fainted away with Robert fallen exhausted on her senseless body.

Presently he recovered sufficiently to be able to apply restoratives to his fainting wife, and as soon as he had brought her round, so that she could understand what he said, proceeded to tell her "that in future they would enjoy all the novel ideas he had found in that nice French book, no more big bellies for you Cecilia, or the anxiety of children for either of us. You must now suck my prick, till it is stiff enough again," he said, presenting it to her mouth.

"No, no, I never can do such a dirty trick, besides, it's doubly disgusting, you have not even washed since you outraged my bottom," she sobbed, as her eyes filled with tears, seeing no signs of compassion in his face.

"What's that to me, you've got to suck it, so go on, my dear, without all those wry faces, which only add to my fun, it's rare sport to make you submit to my fancies. I find I've been a fool ever since I was married, not to have asserted my right to do as I please with every bit of your person, cunt, arse, mouth, or bubbies; they can all afford me intense pleasure, without getting in the family way. Now go on, and I will fuck you with a fine large dildoe. Mind you must swallow every drop of my spendings when it comes."

He forced his prick between her reluctant lips, all slimy and soiled as it was from the previous enculade, then producing an enormous dildoe, nearly twelve inches long, and big in proportion, he put a little cold cream on it, and presented the head to her notch, trying to force it in.

"Ah! No! no!! that's so awfully large!" she almost screamed, but the head was partly in, and despite her sobs, and moans of pains, he soon succeeded in passing at least ten inches of it into her distended vagina.

Her cunt was exposed towards me, so that I could see how gorged it was with that big india-rubber tool, and the sight of her slit so stretched to its utmost capacity caused quite a thrill of desire to shoot through my veins; it was almost impossible for me to prevent myself making some kind of demonstration. How I longed to be with them and join in the orgie of lust. Each shove of that tremendous affair now seemed to afford her the most intense delight. She sucked his prick in a kind of delirium, her highly wrought feelings banishing every sense of delicacy, shame, or disgust that might have previously deterred her from doing so. I frigged myself furiously, they screamed and spent, till at last both spectatrix and actors were thoroughly exhausted.

When I awoke next morning, and applied my eye to the peephole, it was just in time to see Her Ladyship awake. First she felt her cunt to see if it was all right, and not ruined by the giant dildoe she had taken in the previous night. Her eyes sparkled with desire, and she repeatedly blushed as I suppose the recollection flashed through her mind. Presently throwing the sheet entirely off her husband's body, she handled his limp affair for a few moments, then putting her face down, took the head of his prick in between her lovely lips, and sucked away with evident relish, till she had him in a glorious state of fitness, and was about to treat herself to a proper St. George, when Robert, who had only been feigning sleep to see what his randy wife would do, suddenly woke up, and insisted upon her applying it to her arse-hole instead of her cunt, wetting it with spittle.

Slowly but surely she achieved its insertion, although to judge by her face it was evidently a painful operation. But when once in how they enjoyed that glorious bottom-fuck. Even after he had spent she rode on till he met her again, and both seemed to come at the same time, kissing each other in a frenzy of erotic madness.

(To be continued.)

THE NEW PATENT FUCKING MACHINE.

Dear Mary, I promised to write directly to school I returned.
But I think when this letter is finished 'twere better by far it
    were burned;
For a girl has just now returned to us, and bought while in
    town she has been
The last improvement in dildoes—the new patent Fucking
    Machine.
At night when we go to our bedrooms, we go in for a jolly
    good spree,
And first I perform upon Fanny and then she performs upon
    me.
It beats the old "flatcocks" a long way, you know the old
    game that I mean,
Oh! mustn't a man be galoptious if he beats the new Fucking
    Machine?
It beats fingers by far too—a long way, its shape is just like
    a tool,
The girl who owns it is good-natured, she has fucked, I be-
    lieve, the whole school;
She has it herself much too often, and is getting most awfully
    lean,
And her pussey's quite tender with using the patent new Fuck-
    ing Machine.
It gives a delightful sensation, your breath comes too quickly
    to speak,
Whilst Fanny was doing it for me I bit a piece out of her
    cheek;

And when you feel yourself spending and clasp it your legs
    in between,
Oh! I should die if it ever got broken, God preserve the new
    Fucking Machine!
A new girl arrived, dearest Mary, and slept during last night
    with me;
When I put the machine to her "cunny," she said, "None of
    that sort for me!"
She turned up her nose at our patent, and said we were "aw-
    fully green,"
To injure ourselves with such habits, and not have the real
    Fucking Machine.
That the men are all dying to have us, if only we'll give them
    the chance;
She was herself had in the carriage, coming home from the
    Lord Mayor's dance.
Now directly I get home next Xmas, I'll spoon my young
    cousin Jack Green,
And I swear he'll be only too ready, to lend me his Fucking
    Machine.

ANECDOTE OF KATE SANTLEY.

One night, at the Alhambra, amongst a shower of bouquets
from the boxes, a carrot was thrown from the gallery. She
coolly gathered an armful of trophies, and after bowing again
and again to the boxes, looked up with a smile at the gods,
as she said, "Excuse me taking your carrot, now I have the
flowers," and tripped off the stage amidst a storm of applause.

THE PEARL,

A Journal of Facetiæ and Voluptuous Reading.

No. 13   PUBLISHED MONTHLY.   July, 1880

LA ROSE D'AMOUR;

*Or the Adventures of a Gentleman in Search of Pleasure
Translated from the French.*

CHAPTER IV.

The morning after our arrival, on awakening, I roused up the sleeping beauties who lay around me, and led them to the bathing-apartment.

We all entered the water, and after sporting for an hour or more, we issued from it, and entering the dressing room, made our morning toilets, the girls dressed in cymar, pants and vest, such as those worn by the Odalisques in the East.

This day was made all preparations on a splendid scale for the great sacrifice of the night, the taking of Laura's maidenhead.

We spent the time in roving about the park until noon; running, jumping and tussling, so as to keep up an excited circulation of the blood.

The dinner, which I had ordered three hours later than usual, consisted of all the most highly seasoned dishes and of the richest and most exhilarating wines, of which we partook to a slight excess and at last rose from the table with our amorous propensities aroused to the highest pitch.

We retired to the bedchamber, and stripping ourselves we again sought the bath, which was highly scented with the most costly perfumes.

Remaining but a short time in the bath, we went to the bedchamber, and Rose and Marie having drawn aside the heavy hangings, we entered the state-apartment. Here Celestine and Manette, with towels of the finest linen, absorbed the water from the body and hair of Laura, while Rosalie and Caroline did the same for me.

While they were combing out the rich auburn tresses which floated in wavy masses over her neck and shoulders, I was on my knees before her, combing out the black silken hair which grew, with a luxuriance seldom seen in girls of seventeen, out of the fattest little hillock I ever saw and almost hid the entrance to the beautiful grotto beneath.

Having combed out her precious locks, comme il faut, and parted them from around the mouth of the greedly little maw, which was shortly and for the first time to partake and eat of the flesh, with the tips of my fingers I open the pouting lips and feast my eyes with gazing on the deep carnation of the luscious love-niche, in which I was soon to put the idol. I peep, gaze, look and try to get a further insight into the hidden mysteries of the deep, dark, cavernous recess; but my sight could penetrate no further than a most tempting bit of flesh, somewhat in the shape of a heart, which appeared to be pendant, like a dazzling light from the ceiling of a room, in the centre of the passage to the unexplored cavern, through the folding doors of which I was peeping.

My enraptured eyes still gaze on the tempting titbit before me, till, recalled to my senses by feeling something moving between my thighs, and looking down, I perceive the hand of Celestine clasped around my noble shaft, and slowly drawing her hand up and down it, covering and uncovering its beauti- ʃul red head with the fine white skin which lay around the neck in folds.

This at once gave an impetus to my desires, which could not be restrained. I raised up, and catching Laura in my arms, I carried her to the bed and placed her on it, the firm semi-globes of her backside resting on the edge of the bed, supported by a cushion of white satin, covered with an embroidered cloth of fine linen.

Celestine and Caroline support each a leg, while Rose and Marie jump onto the bed, and Manette and Rosalie stand on either side to support me, in case my feelings should overpower me at the close of the performance, and also to serve as pilots for me—the one to open the gate of love, the other to guide the fiery dart aright into the entrance.

Fearing somewhat for the little maid, who was to undergo the process of defloration, and knowing that the rose was not without its thorn and that the sting would at first be pretty severe, I anointed my impatient virgin-destroyer with perfumed oil, and marched to the battlefield, determined to conquer or to die.

Her legs were held apart. I enter between and plant a soft kiss on the lips which I was about cruelly to tear open, which seemed to send a thrill of joy through her.

I slightly incline forward; the tips of Manette's fingers part the rosy lips. Rosalie grasps hold of my pego and lodges the head in the entrance.

The two girls, who support her legs, rest them on my hips, and standing behind me, cross their arms with joined hands so that the ankles rest on them as on a cushion. Gathering myself up, I make one fierce lunge forward and gain full an inch.

The sudden distention of the parts cause her to scream with pain and to wriggle her rump in such manner that instead of in any way ridding herself of me, it was a help to me in my endeavours to penetrate still further.

I thrust harder, I penetrate, I pierce her. The blood begins to flow. I feel it on my thighs. Her buttocks are convulsively twitching and wriggling in endeavours to throw me off. In her agony she utters scream after scream.

Poor little maid, it is a rough and thorny way to travel. But once gone over, the road is ever after smooth. Again I thrust forward.

"Ah, my God!" she exclaims, "I shall die! Have mercy on me!"

I have no pity on her and shove harder than ever to put her out of her pain and agony. I tear her open, carrying everything before me, and one last shove sends me crowned with victory into the very sanctum of love amidst the clapping of hands and the shouts of triumph by those who surround us.

No sooner was I buried in her to the extremest point than I lay quivering and gasping on her belly, spending into her womb a flood of boiling sperm.

I soon regained new life and vigour, and drawing myself out to the head, commenced a to-and-fro friction that caused no more than a few "ahs" and deep-drawn sighs, as the sperm I had injected into her had oiled the parts and made the way comparatively easy for the dear creature who lay under me.

She now received my thrusts and shoves with a slight quivering of her rump. She clasps me in her arms, she closes

her eyes. A few energetic heaves and the dear girl feels the
pleasure, despite that pain that a woman experiences in having drawn from her for the first time by a man the milk of
human kindness.

I too meet her and again melt away in her, fairly drenching
her with the copious draughts of the liquid I spurted into
her.

At last I rise up from off my lovely victim, leaving her a
bleeding sacrifice on the altar of love.

The girls gathered around Laura congratulating her on
being transformed from a maid into a woman. The entrance
being forced, she could henceforth drive into the boundless
pleasures and joys of love without feeling pain.

They raised her up whilst cleaning her of the blood that
dyed her thighs and buttocks, I took up the consecrated
cushion and its bloody covering and directed one of them to
prepare the bed for us. I—but no. I determined to give her
a little rest, and ordering the girls to prepare a cold supper,
told them to awake me in two hours, and we fell asleep in
each other's arms.

After sleeping for some time, Laura awoke much refreshed,
but still feeling sore from the severe battering she had received.

The table being laid alongside the bed, we reclined on it,
the others sitting around the table on cushions.

Not feeling much inclined to eat, I commenced dallying
with my bedfellow, railing her on the feelings she experienced
while I was taking her maidenhead, till the spirit began to
wax powerful within me, whereupon I laid her down flat on
her back and fell with my face downward upon her, and
thence followed what the spirit moveth. Yes, verily, we did
mighty deeds of fucking that night, and it was not until after
the sixth operation, or moving of the spirit, that we lay exhausted in each other's arms and fell asleep.

In a few days after there arrived at the mouth of the creek
a fine large steam-brig, which dropped anchor and sent a
boat ashore with the captain, who delivered me a letter from
my banker, stating who and what the officers and crew were
and upon what terms they had been engaged.

I immediately walked down to the creek and going into the
boat with the captain, we pulled on board. I examined her
decks, masts, etc., and then descended to the cabin, which

extended my most sanguine expectations, so magnificently was
it fitted up. The cabin contained six staterooms, very large
and splendidly fitted up, equalling in style and ornament the
most elegant boudoir I had ever seen in Paris.

I questioned the captain, who was English, as well as the
whole crew, in regard to the men on board.

He said that he and his men had been employed to serve
me in any way I might think proper, so long as I did not
command him to commit piracy. That he and the crew were
paid enormous wages, and that they were bound and felt
ready and willing to follow me to "heaven or hell," if I but
showed them the way.

On questioning the stewards, I found the brig to be well
stored with all the luxuries that could be procured.

I ascended to the deck with the captain, and passing the
word forward for all hands to come aft, I had a crew of most
hardy and devil-may-care looking fellows around me in a
trice, standing respectfully hats in hand.

I made them a short address, laying open to them my intentions, and stating the service I required of them.

I gave the captain his orders to be in readiness to sail in
two days and I returned to the chateau.

Summoning the steward I directed him to prepare everything for our voyage, as I determined to start in two days
for Constantinople.

I then directed a page to send the women to me.

On their entering, I made them all strip to the skin and
examined the cunts and several charms of each of them with
a critical eye, endeavouring when all were most lusciously
beautiful to select one as my compagnon de voyage; but not
being able to choose among so many loves I left it to chance.

Taking up a dice-box, I made each throw in her turn. La
Rose D'Amour and my fair Russian, Caroline, made the
highest throws and I determined to take both.

After they had cast their dies, I informed them what my
object was. Whereupon, Laura, my last love, who bye-the-
bye, was a great libertine, fell on her knees before me weeping, and begged me to take her with me.

It was impossible for me to take more than two, I told her;
it was no use to grieve about the matter as she could not go,
but that I would pass all my remaining time with her.

Leaving the chateau in the care of my trusty stewards and

followers, I embarked, taking with me over one million in francs in gold, for the purpose of purchasing slaves in Constantinople.

Chapter V.

After a pleasant voyage of about two weeks, I arrived at the capital of the Turkish Empire.

At the earliest opportunity I presented my letters to some of the most wealthy and influential foreigners under a fictitious name.

I soon became acquainted with many wealthy Turks and among them three or four slave-merchants.

I then hired an interpreter, and paying a visit to one of the merchants, engaged him as an agent to find out and procure me a lot of the handsomest females to be found in the market. And knowing that the poor class of the inhabitants were in the daily habit of selling their daughters, such as were handsome enough to grace the harems of the rich and lustful Turks, I directed him to send out some of his emissaries to search out all the families among the poor quarters who had beautiful girls and who would be apt to exchange them for gold.

In the course of a few days my agent called on me, stating that he was about to go on a three days' trip from the city to the house of an old broker-merchant of his who was continually in receipt of girls from the interior of the kingdom, and occasionally of a few from Circassia. That for certain reasons he never came to the city, but on receipt of any new beauties he always wrote, and he, my agent, went to his place of residence and either bargained for or took the females to Constantinople and sold them on commission.

He said that when I first called on him he wrote to his correspondent in the country, who replied that he had several very fine girls, one in particular whom he named Ibzaidu, who, he said, was fit to adorn the harem of the Grand Sultan.

I told my agent, Ali Hassan, to start immediately and to bring the lot, if they were beautiful, to the city.

In the interim of his absence, attended by my interpreter, I sauntered day and night through the streets and bazaars, endeavouring to spy out some of the beauties of the place;

but all in vain. I could not catch even a glimpse of a female face.

On the evening of the ninth day from his leaving me, Ali called on me, saying that he had brought with him seven slaves, who were safe in his harem, and invited me to call at his house in the morning and examine them.

He ran perfectly wild in his praises of Ibzaidu, whom he pronounced to be more beautiful than a houri, the *nee plus ultra* of Circassian beauty.

About eleven o'clock the following day, I went to Ali's house, and immediately entered on business.

He retired for a few minutes to give orders for the slaves to prepare for my visit.

In the course of half-an-hour a eunuch entered, made a salaam to his master, and retired.

Ali arose, and inviting me to follow, led the way into a large and elegantly furnished apartment in his harem.

On entering, I beheld six girls seated on the cushions at one side of the room, dressed in loose Turkish pants of white satin and vested of rich embroidered stuff.

In the centre of the room was a couch and at one end of it stood two eunuchs. After surveying them as they sat, and noting their different styles of beauty—knowing it to be customary—I told Ali that I wished to examine them in a perfectly naked state to ascertain if they were still virgins, as he represented them to be. And also that I wished to see if the several parts of their bodies corresponded in beauty with their faces.

He immediately led one of them out on the floor beside me, and spoke a few words to her and the others in Turkish. I then made a sign for him and the eunuchs to go out and leave me alone with the females.

They retired, and taking hold of the girl's hand, I signed her to strip, which she refused to do. I entreated and urged her as well as I could by signs to do so; but she crossed her hands over her breast, refusing to do it. I clapped my hands and Ali and his eunuchs entered. I merely nodded my head to him when he pointed his finger at the girl and the eunuchs caught hold of her and in a trice stripped her naked. I then went up to her, laid my hand on her firm round bubbies, pressed and moulded them, felt her waist, rubbed my hand lower down, onto the mossy covering of her cunt, she sprang from me and catching up some of her clothes, wrapped them round her body, and sat down in one corner.

Ali stamped his foot on the floor, and the eunuchs took her and carrying her threw her on her back on the couch.

One held her down by the shoulders, while the other caught hold of one leg and Ali of the other, stretching them wide apart, I fell on my knees between them, and with my fingers opened the lips of her cunt. On attempting to insert one of them into it, and finding that I could barely force the tips in, which caused her to wince and cry out, and to twist her backside about, I desisted, firmly persuaded that she had her maidenhead inviolate.

Whilst they held her on the couch, I examined, felt, and kissed every part of her; and having provided myself with such things on purpose, I placed on her wrist, neck, and finger, a bracelet, necklace, and ring. Making a sign they let her rise, and giving her her clothes, she dressed and sat down much pleased with and examining her jewels.

I now led out another girl, and made a sign for her to undress which she took no notice of, standing with her arms crossed, and her head hanging down. I took her hands and removing them from her breasts proceeded to take her vest, and as she did not resist, I told Ali and his slaves to go and wait outside the room.

I then stripped her of her pants and cymar and was much pleased with her beauty. I led her up to the couch and sitting down drew her to my side, handling her breasts, feeling her arms, belly, thighs, twining my fingers about in the luxurious growth of hair that overgrew the grotto underneath, to all of which she made no resistance.

At last I laid her down on her back and spreading her thighs apart, inspected her cunt, and found she was still possessed of all the signs of virginity. I also gave her jewels, such as I gave the first one, and inspected the balance in the same manner, picking out one after one.

Two I found not to be virgins, and one was bandy-legged although handsome in every other respect.

I called in Ali and enquired where the beautiful Ibzaidu was, desiring him to bring her to me.

Ali clapped his hands and two female slaves entered leading her in. Then they retired leaving her standing before me.

She was enveloped in a piece of fine Indian muslin and had a veil over her face.

I raised the veil and started back in amazement at the dazzling beauty of her face.

I then caught hold of the drapery in which she was enveloped, and gently drawing it from her clasp, I threw it on one side and gazed with admiration on the most ravishingly beautiful form and figure I ever beheld.

Hers was one of those oval majestic figures, such as poets and mythologists attribute to Juno.

I much admired her rich jet-black hair which clustered in ringlets over her neck and shoulders, contrasting singularly with the dazzling whiteness of her skin. Her shoulders were finely formed, her arms, plump, beautifully rounded, would cause a sigh of desire to arise in any breast, to be clasped in their embrace. Her breasts, luxuriously large, hard and firm, white as snow-flakes, tipped with deliciously small nipples, of that fine pink color which so strongly denotes virginity in the possessor.

Her waist was gracefully elegant and tapering; her belly fine, round, and with the whiteness of alabaster, soft as the finest velvet down. Her hips were very large and wide, whilst her buttocks swelling out behind into two hillocks of snowy-white flesh, firm and springy to the touch, gave token of the vivacity and liveliness with which their owner would enter into the delicious combats of love.

Her thighs were of a largeness and fleshy plumpness seldom seen in a female, with the knees small, while the calf was large in proportion to the thigh. The ankle tapering, and a foot delicately small, spoke plainly to the looker-on that the seat and centre of love, that dear part of woman which takes away the senses of all men, was an equally small and elegant pattern.

Her chin was most charmingly dimpled, her lips, full and pouting, slightly open, gave just a glimpse of two rows of ivory, which appeared set in the deep rosy flesh of her small and elegant mouth. Her nose was of the Grecian cast, her eyes of a sparkling lustrous black, and the forehead was middling high. She was, in fact, the very beau ideal of female beauty.

What ease and grace reigned in every part. With what a sylph-like springy motion she moved, as I led her towards the couch on which I stretched her out. There I examined minutely all her secret charms. I felt and handled every part.

Her cunt was ravishing, beyond all description. The mossy Mount of Venus swelled up into a hillock of firm flesh, surmounted and covered with rich, mossy, coal-black hair, straight and fine as silk. The lips were most luscious, fat, rosy, pouting beauties. On opening them, I felt for her clitoris and found it to be extremely large, while the orifice was narrow and small indeed, apparently not larger than a girl's of eleven or twelve years of age.

"God of love!" I exclaimed on viewing it, "here is a maidenhead that might have tempted Jupiter from Olympus, a prophet from the arms of the houris in Paradise, or an anchorite from his cell."

Handling and examining so many lovely things had set me on fire and I could hardly restrain myself from immolating her on the altar as a sacrificial offering to the god of voluptuous love.

I drew myself away from her and signed her to rise up and resume her drapery.

I then concluded the bargain for the purchase of Ibzaidu, and for the first three I had chosen.

After settling with Ali, I told him that he must let me have the use of a part of his house, including the harem, during my stay, so that I should be able to guard safely my slaves and to have for them proper attendance. Also, that he must instantly purchase for me six or eight mutes and eunuchs, which he immediately set about, whilst I returned to my house to get my money, jewels, etc., and also to bring away Caroline and her companion.

(To be continued.)

DR. TANNER'S FAST OF FORTY DAYS.

A correspondent in New York writes to the Editor of THE PEARL, to say that, for the last three weeks of the terrible experiment, the Doctor's penis, which in its normal condition would be eight and a half inches when in a state of erection, was shriveled up to less than an inch in length, and no handling or frigging could induce either stiffness or emission.

JULIEN'S CONCERT.

Now music being the food of love I thought that I would go
To Julien's concert; for I heard the price was very low.
It being nearly eight o'clock, so in I toddled quick,
To hear the quadrille and see great Julien shake his pr——
The little staff about, and I've been told by jokers
That the ladies they do all agree that he's the prince of pokers.
The ladies they were highly dressed—naked, almost stark,
Their muslin being thin enough to see the watermark;
I gazed on one, a beauteous maid, her smile was bright and
    sunny,
She'd a nice small mouth and golden hair and a fine full open
    cunny.
Being so, I introduced myself to her so gentle,
She said, she'd come there for an hour with something
    instrumental.
I gently sat down by her side while glowing like a fire;
The smile she gave I must admit I really did admire.
Said she: "The band is going to play." Said I: " 'Twill shake
    the walls."
"Oh, no," said she, "that's only when great Julien shakes his
    ball——
My bunch of rosy locks, his staff so well displayed is,
He knows full well a good long piece is sure to please the
    ladies."
The names of all the instruments she then enquired about
Especially of that long brass-thing that kept sliding in and
    out.
The fingering of the double-bass she thought was rather slack,
And wondered Julien should engage a man who'd got the
    clap——
Pers they were an awful bore, and still she would insist on
Me telling her who'd get the horn, and who the cornet à
    piston.

She said she liked the clarinet, likewise the German flute—
You know all well such instruments the ladies always suit;
The forty parts they were so off they almost made us start,
And the ophicleide would come in just like a thundering fart
Or peal of thunder, but not so far as India;
And the French horn would pop in, to join those things so
　　windy
The place got overpowering; our ears were tired of drumming;
Said she: "I feel I'm going, you'd better be a-coming."
She took my arm, we left the place, I acted as conductor;
I called a cab, and on the road I freely furnished her with my
　　ideas of Julien's improvements,
And so wound up with a grand duet with many pleasing
　　movements.

MY GRANDMOTHER'S TALE or MAY'S ACCOUNT OF HER INTRODUCTION TO THE ART OF LOVE.

From an unsophisticated Manuscript, found amongst the old lady's papers, after her death, supposed to have been written about A.D. 1797.

CHAPTER III.
KATE'S NARRATIVE.

You know I am a native of the West Indies. I was born in Santa Cruz, where my father had a plantation, and lots of slaves.

The little boys and girls were naked until they were eight or nine years old: I remember being greatly struck with the fine little cocks of the boys, and wondered why they differed so from girls.

The son of our overseer was just my age, about ten. He was a smart intelligent boy, and we used to play together. His name was Joe.

One day I caught him piddling and looking at his cock. I laughed and told him he ought to cut it off, it was so ugly.

He said he would be sorry for he would much rather be a

man than a woman, "and when I grow to be a man," he said, "this will grow big."

"How do you know?" I said, putting my hand on it.

"Because I have often seen men naked. Do you know what a man calls it?"

"No. What?"

"He calls it a prick."

"Oh?"

"And do you know what he does with it?"

"He piddles with it, I suppose, like yourself."

"Ah!" he said, looking very sly, "he does more than that with it."

"What?"

"He can put it into a woman between her legs, in that queer little slit you girls have."

"There's no room for it there," I said.

"Yes there is; I'll show you if you'll let me, may I?" he said, lifting my frock.

"You may, just for a minute."

He put his fingers into my cunt and felt about for the opening. At last he found it, and, to my surprise, pushed his forefinger up.

"Stop," I cried, "that hurts."

"I won't hurt you bye-and-bye," he said, with his sly look.

"How, what do you mean?"

"I'll tell you, but mind, it's a great secret. You know Jim who has the cat and flogs the slaves when they misbehave. Well, when the women are sent, he flogs their backs; but when girls are sent he flogs their bottoms. I was near the place when a fine plump girl came from your papa with a note, which I saw afterwards. It had only these words: 'Give this girl twelve lashes.—E. L.'

"Jim brought her in and shut the door but I stole round to a window on the other side and peeped in. He had her kneel on a bench and tied her hands to the block. Then he threw up her petticoat, uncovering her shining black bum, and took out his cat.

"He said: 'Be quiet, Norry. If you let me have my will of you I won't hurt you, but if you won't I'll give it you.'

"He opened his pantaloons and out started, oh! such a big one, it would have frightened you as he pushed it against her bottom. She cried more than ever.

"He brought down the cat with a smart stinging blow on her bottom.

"She jumped and yelled.

" 'Be quiet now or you'll get more.'

"She stopped, while he separated her legs as widely as he could. Then stooping, he looked up into her slit, which he kept open with his fingers. I could see that it was very red inside, had plenty of black woolly hair on it.

"Then he put in the head of his prick, and giving a great push, it went in every bit of it. Then he withdrew it out all wet and red looking, and putting his arms round her hips he went on pushing in and out with all his might.

"She did not mind but only poked out her bottom as if to get more of it.

"Then he stopped suddenly, and pressed in hard against her.

"After which he untied her, and giving her a kiss, sent her away."

"That's very odd Joe. It must have hurt her very much."

"Indeed it didn't. She liked it beyond anything. I know it by the way she stuck out her bottom. Will you just try and you'll feel how pleasant it is."

My amorous feelings were aroused, so I did not object to his having a trial.

I kneeled on the seat, as he told me, and jutted out my bottom.

He tried to get his cock into my slit, but failed. I put down my hand and kept the lips open, but whether from my immaturity or his inexperience, he could not succeed.

A few days afterwards he came running up to me in great glee, crying out: "I can do it now, Katie, I can do it now!"

"Stop your noise. What do you mean?"

"Stay, Katie, and I will tell you. You know father and I live in the cottage. He has, however, generally one or two of the slave girls with him in the evening. They like to come to him for they get plenty of rum, and are sure of a half holiday next day.

"He sends me to bed and then produces the rum, sugar and water. Last night he had three with him. He sent me off to bed as usual, but I hid behind the door.

"They soon became very merry over the drink and capered about in style. He threw up their petticoats, slapping their bottoms and tickled their cunts, while they pulled out his prick and handled his balls. Then he made them undress and chased them naked around the room. Whenever he caught one, he felt her cunt, and making her kneel would stick his prick into it from behind while the others tickled his balls and bottom. In the midst of the fun, one of them suddenly opened the door, and spying on me, seized me, and dragging me into the room, cried out: 'Oh, here's massa Joe playing bo-peep. What shall we do with him?'

" 'Let's strip him,' cried another, 'and we will make him fuck Fanny. She is the youngest and her cunt will fit his little prick best.'

"My father only laughed and said: 'All right, he'll be man enough for any of you some of these days.'

"So I was stripped, nothing loath, and placed over Fanny, who was lying on the floor. She had her legs wide apart and with her fingers kept the lips of her cunt open while one of the others, after kissing and sucking my little cock, pushed it in. Then they clapped my bottom, and sat around to watch the performance.

"Oh, Katie, you can't think how easy my prick slipped into her cunt. And I felt it growing bigger when it got in; she was so hot inside. She then hugged me in her arms and jerked up her bottom, while I worked and pushed as I had seen father do until the nice warm feeling came and I nearly fainted with pleasure.

"I was then glad to get away and creep off to bed, for I was tired and sleepy.

"Look at it, Katie, isn't it larger and stronger than before?"

He held it in his hand and drew back the skin until its head stood up round and red as a cherry.

"Put your hand on it, Katie. Feel how firm it is!"

I took it in my hand and rubbed it up and down.

"Yes, Joe, it is larger and stronger. You may put it in if you like."

He laid me back, lifted my dress and looked at and felt my cunt.

"Yours is much prettier and nicer than the black girl's, Katie. These soft round white lips are beautiful. Hold them open like a dear girl while I push it in."

I put my hands down and opening the lips with one while with the other I directed the head of his prick to the right spot and told him to push. He did so. It entered. He pushed harder. It got in more and more until it was all enclosed and I felt its head far back.

Oh, sweet sensation! Nothing can exceed the pleasure of feeling one's cunt for the first time filled up with a throbbing, heaving prick!

His eyes sparkled and his breath came hard and fast as I hugged him in my arms, and told him to push in his prick and fuck me very well.

Having now ascertained for ourselves the wondrous power we each possessed of conferring pleasure on the other, our play always turned on the practice and enjoyment of love.

We were never tired of examining and petting each other's privates.

And our senses being now fully aroused, we were always on the watch to enlarge our experience of the ways and means of enjoyment.

My father had several slaves almost white, and most of them good-looking. These were all retained in the house and never sent into the fields.

One pretty little girl named Nina was assigned to me as my waiting-maid. She always attended me in my bath, and used to dry me when I came out. She was particularly attentive to my little slit, on which the hair was just beginning to grow. She used to perfume it, and comb it, and kiss it.

"You have a beautiful cunt, Missy, the sight of it would set any young fellow wild!"

"I suppose it is much the same as other girls', your own for instance. Show it to me, Nina."

She lifted her dress, and opening her thighs, gave me a full view of her cunt. It was a pretty little mouth, with a full rosebud clitoris, and the lips covered with brown silky hair. I put my hand on it, and pushing up my finger, said: "Did this ever set any young fellow wild?"

"Oh, Missy, you must not ask me such questions, or I will have to tell you lies."

"Nina, if you want me to be your friend you will tell me everything. But this will do for the present."

My father was in the habit of walking in the garden after sunset when it was nearly dark, to smoke his cigar, and I found out that he always had with him one or the other of the white slaves.

One night I missed Nina, and guessing where she was, I threw on my shawl and went out softly into the garden. I heard voices in a sheltered walk, and as it was almost dark, I was able to get within range of hearing without being seen.

"Now, Nina, be kind and you'll be my pet, and I will give you all sorts of pretty things—there, let me feel it, that's a sweet girl, open your legs more, lean against this tree, hold up your dress, give me your hand, place it here, close your fingers round it. That's the way. You have a dear little cunt, very fat and plump. But I wonder you have much hair on it. How old are you, Nina?"

"Just fifteen, sir."

"Now then, press out in front. Hold my prick, while I push it—there it's in—put your arms round me—press my bottom. How do you like the feel of my prick in your cunt?"

"It feels very nice, push it in more."

I heard them kissing and panting as they shoved together, and then they rested in each other's arms.

She soon left him, after promising to go out at that same hour that day every week.

I often followed him out now, and found he always had one of the slave girls with him.

I then learned all the terms and ways of enjoyment, for he was fond of variety, and loved to make them talk, and say all manner of words while he fucked them. And I was astonished to hear how freely they spoke of pricks, cunts, arses, frigging, fucking, pissing, etc.

Joe had been sent to school and my cunt, not having been entered for a long time, was in an aggravated state of longing and desire.

So, when Nina's turn came next, the thought flashed upon me, why not personate her for one occasion.

I was about her height and size, and my cunt was now pretty well furnished with hair. So when the hour came, I set her to a task which would occupy her for some time, and said I was in a hurry to have it done.

Then, going out in the dark I quietly strolled up the walk. Someone met me, put his arm round me, and pushed his knee in between my thighs.

"How is your sweet cunt tonight?"

I said nothing but only pressed against him as he lifted my dress and felt my cunt.

Moving his finger about, he said: "It's very hot and juicy tonight. I am sure it is longing for a fuck. Put your hand here, my love."

I felt his firm upstanding prick. I moved the loose skin up and down as Joe had taught me. I put my other hand below and felt the two soft balls in their hairy bag.

"Take it in your mouth, dear, for a moment."

I had gone too far to recede now, so I stooped and sucked its glowing head while I tickled him behind the balls.

"Oh, Nina, that's delicious! Now lie back on this moss bank, raise your legs, open your dress, that I may press your soft bubbies, while my prick is in your cunt."

He knelt between my uplifted thighs. He leaned over me. He opened the lips of my cunt. He introduced his prick. He moulded my breasts. He kissed me and darted his tongue into my mouth.

"Say you like it, Nina, my love!"

"Oh, yes dear sir!" I whispered heaving up my bottom. "I feel your prick in my cunt—fucking—fucking—oh! so—deliciously!"

The rapturous feeling increased. He pushed and panted. I heaved and gasped: "Oh, yes, push, fuck, oh! oh! oh!"

He lay over me, his face on my shoulder and his prick buried in my cunt.

After a while he said: "I don't know how it is, Nina, but I never enjoyed fucking you so much before, your cunt closes on my prick with such a hot compression, and you nipped the head of my prick when I drove it home as you never did before, and which only a few women can do. Oh! there! I feel it now!"

(Here I interrupted Kate by asking: "What do you mean by nipping the head of his prick?"

"Well, my dear, I'll teach you. When you feel the entire prick driven in as far as it can go, draw up your bottom inside, as hard as you can. If you do it right you will squeeze the head of the prick as it rests on the mouth of your womb. Try it now while I have my finger in. Yes, that's the way."

"Well, go on, what did he say next?")

He asked me: "Is Miss Kate kind to you?"

"She is," I whispered in reply.

"Don't you attend her in the bath?"

"Yes."

"Does she let you see her cunt?"

"Yes, I dry it and sometimes kiss it."

"Is it a nice little cunt?"

"Very nice."

"Do you think she has any longing to have it fucked?"

"I am sure she has, it is always red and hot."

"I guessed as much. Indeed, I often think of it when I observe her swelling hips. How I would enjoy fucking her, if I could only do it without letting her know who it was."

"Perhaps I could manage it for you. Come to my bed to-morrow night and I'll prevail on her to take my place. I'll tell her I expect a young fellow who will take her for me, and give her the greatest pleasure but without doing her any harm. If you find the door of my room unlocked you will know I succeeded."

Next evening, papa did not go out at all and I saw he was regarding me with a peculiar look in his eyes. He was also more affectionate and made me sit on his knee when I was bidding him good-night and he pressed my bottom and thighs in the warmest way.

Nina readily agreed to my taking her place for the night when I told her I had been restless of late and thought a change of my bed would do me good.

About midnight someone entered the room and felt his way to where he heard me breathing. He quietly put off his clothes, and slipped into bed. He put his arm over me and felt my cunt. He opened the lips and rubbed about the clitoris and then tried to push his finger up.

I held his hand. "Oh, you hurt me!"

"Why, you are not my Nina at all."

"No, I am only Nina's friend."

"Well, whoever you are, you have a sweet cunt. Put your hand on this, it won't hurt you."

"But it will do me harm."

"No, trust me, my pet, I won't harm you."

He then got over me and began to push his prick against my cunt.

"Oh, no, I can't, I am afraid. Oh, pray don't, it is too big!"

I held him by the hips and pushed him back.

"I can't bear it—it will kill me!"

Every time he pushed the head of his prick at the entrance, I shrank from him.

He begged me. He prayed me just to let it in and he would be so very gentle.

He got it in a little way inside the entrance.

"Oh, push easily, or you'll kill me. Oh! Oh!"

"There, now—it is quite in. My precious I shall not hurt you any more."

He moved his prick very slowly in and out, in and out.

I began to heave and twist.

"Darling, this is exquisite! Your cunt is delightfully tight, and its soft pressure most delicious. Put your arms round me, my love! I only once before had such a fuck as this."

I pressed him in my arms, thrust up my bottom to meet every thrust of his prick. I raised my thighs and crossed my legs on his back.

He ran his prick with delightful friction in and out of my throbbing, heaving, panting cunt. I felt a soft hand on my bottom and soft fingers playing about my cunt. I knew they were Nina's, I did not mind. I was intoxicated with pleasure. I squeezed in my bottom to nip his prick.

"Oh! That's grand, who taught you that sweet trick—do it again. Oh! That's splendid!"

Nina got into the bed and pressed against his bottom.

"Oh, Nina you are just in time. Let me get on you that I may spend in your cunt."

He drew out his prick, saying to me: "You know I promised not to harm you; but Nina does not mind the risk for she knows she will be well taken care of. Let us get outside the clothes and take off everything, the night is so warm."

He then got between her uplifted thighs, and resting on her breast, told me to put it in.

I felt her cunt, it was very hot and flowing. I took his prick and rubbed its throbbing head between the soft lips, placed it at the entrance. He pushed, it passed in. I went behind him and holding him around the hips rubbed my cunt against his bottom while he fucked.

He discharged immediately and soon afterwards he bid us good-night and went away.

Nina begged me to excuse her. She said she heard all that

passed and got so excited that she could not help coming in to us.

I asked: "Did papa know who your friend was?"

She said she was not certain but thought he did.

There was something peculiar about papa's manner the next morning. He put his arms around me several times, called me his sweet girl, his darling pet. He told me he was making arrangements to send me to England, to have my education completed there. He told me that he had taken my passage in a sugar-brig which was to start in a few days, and which was commanded by a friend of his, a Captain Lemberg, who would take good care of me.

I said I would like it very much but would be sorry to leave him and put my arms round his neck kissing him.

He enfolded me in his; he lifted me off the ground, carrying me to a sofa and laid me down. He sat by me and slipping his hand under my dress put it on my naked bottom. "My darling," he said, "let me pet you, I feel so fond of you and I won't have you long."

"Dearest papa, you may do anything you please with me, I love to give you pleasure."

He kissed me warmly, turned me on my back, lifted my dress, opened my thighs, and looked at my cunt.

"You are beautifully made here. Tell me, my darling, was it you in Nina's bed last night?"

"It was I, dearest papa; was I very wicked?"

"No, my darling, you gave me the sweetest pleasure I ever had in my life. Did you enjoy what I did to you then?"

"I did indeed, it was most delightful."

"Might I do it to you again?"

"You may, dear papa, if you like."

He drew me to the end of the sofa, made me raise my legs and open them as widely as possible. Then kneeling on the floor, he kissed my cunt. He praised its shape and colour. He opened the lips, put in his tongue and licked the inside round and round. He introduced his prick, pushing it slowly up, and fucked me most delightfully.

I tried all I could to increase and intensify his pleasure. I asked if he was enjoying it much.

"Do you like it, papa?"

"Yes, my sweet pet, your cunt is perfection itself. I envy the man who gets you for a wife."

I now ventured on a request I had long in mind.

"Dear papa, I have one thing to ask you for."

"What is it my pet? I would do anything in the world to gratify you."

"Will you give Nina her freedom and send her to England with me?"

"Surely, my pet, I will do more; if she marries with your consent and approbation I will allow you to present her with £50 dowry, and besides, you may order whatever dress she may require for the voyage."

Need I describe the response I made to these kind words how I clung to him, how I tightened the pleasure girth within, what a glowing reception I gave to his prick as it darted into my quivering cunt, or how he grunted his satisfaction: "Oh, Katie! Oh! Katie, my pet!"

Nina was overjoyed when she heard that she was to have her freedom. She thanked me on her knees and promised to be the most faithful of servants.

Now, dearest May, I have told you more than ever I told anyone else, because I find in you a kindred soul and I want someone to sympathize with me. Don't judge me too harshly I was little more than a child and alone, my father has been a widower ever since I could remember. Do you love me less?

"No, dearest Kate, I love you a hundred times more for your confidence and affection; but go on and tell me about the voyage and how you first met papa."

"I will dearest; but not to-night. I am tired and sleepy Kiss me, my love, good night."

(To be continued.)

———————————

That interesting old roadside public-house, "The Cock," at Kennington, has lately been redecorated. The sign-post was surmounted by an effigy of Chanticleer, who shone re splendent in new gold-leaf. Enters Mr. Robinson, a neigh bouring pawn-broker, who thus addresses the bar-maid "Your house now looks charming, my dear! Will you te the painter who gilt your gov'nor's cock to come and gil my balls?" The bar-maid broke a wine-glass in her blushin confusion.

FLUNKEYANIA; or BELGRAVIAN MORALS.

By Charles.

Chapter I.

It is understood a useful, and it certainly is a commendable, practice, that in bringing a book before the public, the author should say a few words by way of introduction, and of excuse, I presume, for his writing the book at all. But as I have very little to say about my antecedents and even that not of a very exalted or interesting character, I shall plunge at once in medium res, and beg the reader to follow me into the study of the Earl of Pomeroy, who was in the act of investigating my character previously to engaging me in the somewhat anomalous, not to say duplicate, role as his own confidential secretary-valet and body-footman to the Countess.

This, I am aware, is unusual in high families, but it is not without its special utility as I very soon had occasion to find out.

That I had plenty of opportunity offered me of playing the spy, my reader can easily imagine, when I tell him that almost always during the forenoon and generally late in the evening I was in attendance in plain clothes on His Lordship. And in the middle of the day and afternoon dressed in handsome livery, upon the Countess; sometimes at home, sometimes with Her Ladyship's carriage.

That I should give a preference to the service with the lady perhaps was natural, for not only was Her Ladyship's personal attendant, Justine, very pretty, but she showed her admiration for your humble servant in the most distinguished manner.

But moreover, my vanity led me to suppose that my handsome mistress, the Countess, was not altogether insensible to the gratification of being attentively and devotedly waited upon by a good-looking youth, though he might be twenty years old and she thirty at least.

I think we have heard of such things before in the pages of history, dear reader! And I rather fancy we have heard of such charming characters as Catherine of Russia and one or two Queens of Spain!

At any rate, I was not insensible to the advantage of my

position, which I was determined to enjoy as long as I could, unless, indeed, anything occurred of so glaring a nature (such as an elopement for instance) that everybody must as a matter of course become aware of it, in which case it would become my duty to His Lordship (and myself) to be beforehand of everybody else and disclose the plot.

But in the meantime, I was pretty certain that my noble mistress was not quite so virtuous as she was beautiful. But when a woman is so charming as she was, a young man is apt to find excuses for her, and I reflect that if a Spanish or an Italian lady has her Cavalier Servente or a French Marchioness has her very particular friend and nobody finds any fault with it, society need not be so very hard on the Countess, if she deviates slightly from the strict line of duty. But, then, you see, my friends, we are such a very moral people! And Society is hard.

One day I particularly remember, I was on duty to attend Her Ladyship who was going to take a short walk (not a very usual habit of hers).

She was, for her, rather plainly dressed and I noticed that the neighbourhood she selected did not seem to me the most appropriate for a lady of title to take the air on foot. But as long as she was not insulted or otherwise inconvenienced that was no business of mine; but presently I considered it my duty to call the Countess's attention to the fact that it was beginning to rain.

"So it is! How provoking!" was my lady's exclamation. But to my natural suggestion that I should call a cab she replied in the negative, telling me that she was only a few doors from the house of a former servant in the family who lived at number so and so. That she would step in and rest. That I should remain at the public-house at the corner for half an hour or so and then, if the rain had not ceased, I should bring a cab for her, asking for her nurse, Mrs. Wilson.

Now, the reader will do my intellectual powers injustice if he considers that I did not understand all this thoroughly well. But I only touched my hat respectfully and repaired to the public-house, where, as the rain had not ceased and I thought it a pity to disturb my lady in her interview with her nurse, I remained about an hour and I am bound to say the Countess did not find fault with my delay. I suppose that she must have enjoyed her nurse's society so much indeed. Nor

is it to be wondered at that my suspicions were correct and
that the said nurse took the shape of a handsome young man
and that, reversing the order of things, instead of he nursing
her, she nursed her nurse!

It is to be hoped the nursing did her good; but she certainly did not seem much the better for it as she was very
quiet and pale, and on arrival home, passed two or three
hours on the sofa.

And on another occasion, I was ordered to accompany her
on a short drive, when of course, as the brougham was put
in requisition, I sat beside the coachman.

We had not gone far, and were still in the neighbourhood
of the park, when I noticed a young lady standing on the
footpath, as if in expectation of our arrival.

No sooner did my Lady Pomeroy behold her than she
pulled the check-rein and ordered me to let in her young
friend, Miss Courtney, whom she wished to take for a drive.

Of course I did so with all speed, and a most outrageously
affectionate reception inside the carriage Miss Courtney met
with, such a desperate kissing and hugging compressed into
the space of a half-minute while I was putting in her skirts
and shutting the door, I had never seen equalled!

During the transient glimpse I had of their embrace I am
almost sure I saw Miss Courtney thrust her tongue most
amorously between the Countess's lips, and also take several
indescribable liberties with the sacred person of my mistress.

And yet Justine knew something of the science of kissing
and hugging too, and had initiated me into, I supposed, every
branch of the mystery.

But on this occasion there was something more—a something almost indelicate, by which, taken in combination with
other little matters almost as trifling, my attention was excited most curiously.

It will be easily understood by my judicious readers that I
was naturally an adept where ladies were concerned, and had
in my capacity as a young footman considerably brightened
and improved any previous ideas I may have possessed. And,
in this case, I was sharp enough to see that though Miss
Courtney was well dressed, she was not very well dressed.
That is to say, though her clothes were of rich fashionable
materials, they looked as if they had not been fitted by a

first-class modiste, or put on by a lady's-maid who was up to
her business.

Then she did not step into the carriage like a young lady.
She grasped the side-handle and sprang in without touching
my arm in the first place. In the second place I have noticed
that young ladies in getting in and out of a carriage, however
modest, and even prudish they may be, are by no means
averse to display their pretty ankles and even—well, Excel-
sior, up higher—a little peep of legs besides.

In fact, I have seen the mossy grotto itself when the drawers
happened to favour me.

Well, there is nothing improper in that, and decidedly
nothing unpleasant.

But Miss Courtney exhibited her lower limbs up to the
knee, making not the slightest attempt to conceal them, and
very fine legs they were too—only, somehow—somehow they
did not appear to me like young ladies' legs.

There is a marked difference in this respect, I perfectly
well know. For example, I may say without vanity that I have
a very handsome pair of legs, well—and so has Mademoiselle
Justine; but then there is a great difference.

"Of course there is!" I fancy I hear my reader suggesting.

"Come, none of that, sir!" I reply. "I meant as to legs,
simply as to legs."

And to return to my subject. The decidedly manly look of
the young lady's legs, taken in conjunction with her dress, her
style altogether and the peculiar nature of the caresses exchanged between her and the Countess, all these little
incidents put together, I repeat, produced strong suspicions
in my mind as to the sex of our young passenger.

But I need not have troubled myself to have entertained
any suspicions at all. At any rate, they soon became certain-
ties. For presently, I took upon myself to ask Robert the
coachman where he was driving? And why was he driving so
horribly slow?

To my first enquiry he replied that he was going to drive
along St. John's Wood-Road, and in the second place he
affirmed that he was too compassionate a disposition to vex
two handsome creatures that had never done him harm.

I stared at him, for I presumed he referred to the handsome pair of chestnut horses. But when he followed up his
remark by gravely saying that it did not matter at what pace

he drove for there was "nobody in the carriage," I thought at first he must be mad or drunk, but on turning my head round, the whole truth flashed upon me at once!

Sure enough, the carriage was supposed to be empty, for all the blinds were closed!

"Don't you know the peephole," said my friend John. "Our coachbuilder made it on purpose to please me, or I ought to say, Lord Pomeroy. He put me up to it and sometimes rides on the box with me and says it's far more pleasure to see his wife fucked by a fine young fellow than to have the trouble to do it himself."

"You don't mean that," I replied.

"Yes, no humbug between ourselves! Old Pom only cares for page-boys, lady's-maids, or some other man's wife or daughters. 'Nothing like breaking the Ten Commandments' is his favourite saying. You'll find that hole in the roof. A little bit slides back just behind you."

Eager to see something of real life, the slide was noiselessly pushed back, till I could see every part of the interior of the brougham. There sat my lady billing and cooing with Miss Courtney. How flushed they looked as their impassioned kisses too plainly told the depth of their feelings.

They were sitting side by side, and the first act of their little love-drama was evidently just over, but the curtain had not yet fallen for the Countess's dress was raised to her navel and I could see the jewelled hand of Miss Courtney groping between her lovely thighs. But that was nothing to the sight of the manly root with which that young lady was furnished at the bottom of her belly, which although rather drooping, was still glistening with the cream of love, as the Countess continued to caress it in her milk-white hand, gently uncovering the fiery-looking red head of her delight, as the motion of her fingers seemed to make a mute appeal to its further gallantry. My curiosity was quite satisfied and we let them enjoy themselves in peace for the rest of the drive.

(To be continued.)

LADY POKINGHAM, OR THEY ALL DO IT;

Giving an Account of her Luxurious Adventure, both before
and after her Marriage with Lord Crim.

PART V.
(Continued.)

My peephole afforded me the sight of many more luscious
scenes between Lady Cecilia and her husband before I left
town to take up my residence at Hastings for the benefit of
my health.

My agent had secured and furnished for me a pretty little
detached residence of thirteen or fourteen rooms, surrounded
by gardens and orchards, so as to be delightfully free from
the prying curiosity of my neighbours.

The household consisted of a cook and housekeeper, both
young persons, not exceeding twenty-four or -five years of age,
the latter being the daughter of a decayed merchant, a most
pleasant and intelligent companion, but up to the time I
engaged her, strictly prudish, virtuous.

Being naturally fond of young boys and girls, we had also
two very pretty page-boys of about the age of fifteen or sixteen and two beautiful young girls about the same age,
instead of housemaid and lady's-maid.

At first I felt considerably enervated by the little excesses
I had been a party to, or witnessed, whilst staying with the
new Earl, but the soft bracing air of the southern coast soon
made me feel more like myself again, and long to indulge in
the delicious dalliances of love, to which my warm temperament made me always so inclined.

The result was that I determined to seduce every member
of my virgin household, each one of whom I believed to be
thoroughly virtuous up to their entering my service.

The two youngest girls, as my special attendants, slept in
the next room to mine, and had a door of communication by
which the two rooms entered into the other without the
necessity of going into the corridor.

I had quite a passion come over me to gamahuche these
two pretty young things, and make them thoroughly subservient to my purposes.

You may be sure I was not long in putting my plans in

operation as soon as I had sketched them all out in my brain. That very same evening, after my two pretty demoiselles had put the finishing touches to my toilet and left me sitting in my chemise de nuit, in front of a cosy fire with my feet resting on the fender, as I pretended to be reading a thrilling romance:

"Leave that door open, my dears," I said, as they respectfully bid me good night. "I feel so dull perhaps I shall call for you to keep me company, if I feel that I cannot go to sleep."

In a few minutes I heard them tittering and laughing.

"Now, girls," I cried, "come here this moment. I want to know what you are having such fun about. Come just as you are, no putting anything more on or waiting to hide your blushes. Annie! Patty! Do you hear?"

Afraid of making me angry, the two girls came blushing into my room just as they were, in their nightgowns.

"Well now, what is it that is amusing you so?"

"Please, my Lady, it was Patty," said Annie with a wicked look at her companion.

"Ah, no, you fibber! My Lady, it was Annie began it," retorted the other, looking quite abashed.

Nothing could be got out of them, each saying it was the other.

At last I said: "I can guess pretty well what you two girls were amusing yourselves about; now tell me truly, were you looking at each other's privates in the glass?"

This question hit the mark, and seeing how shame-faced and blushing they both were, I went on: "No doubt, examining to see which one showed most signs of hair on her little pussey. Let me see Annie," as I suddenly caught the bottom of her nightdress and in an instant had it reversed over her head, so as to cover up her face and expose all the rest of her beautiful little figure. "Why, the impudent little thing hasn't a hair to boast of! Give her bottom a good slapping, Patty!"

Patty was only too pleased to do it, and the slaps fairly echoed through the room, mingling with Annie's piteous cries to let her go.

My blood was up. The sight of her beautiful bum, all flushed and rosy under the sharply administered slaps, made me fairly lust to take further liberties. So I let the little victim go, whispering in her ear, and her tearful eyes were brightened in a moment. She darted at Patty and sooner than it takes to write was dragging her about the room fully exposed, with her head and arms secured in her reversed nightdress.

I amused myself by slapping poor Patty's pretty posteriors till they were almost black and blue, regardless of her sobbing and crying for mercy.

At last we let her go, and I took her on my lap to kiss away her tears. She soon smiled again and nestled herself to my body quite lovingly. This seemed to make her companion almost jealous as she appealed to me with a flushed face to kiss her also, which I readily did in the most loving manner, and I asked her to fetch a decanter of wine and some glasses from a cabinet, saying I felt so dull and sleepless I must have something to cheer me.

"Ah, my dear lady," exclaimed Patty, kissing me again and again, "you don't know how we all love you and feel for you, being left alone and unhappy. There is nothing we wouldn't do to bring a smile to your pale face."

"Then we'll sleep together and have a romp on the bed. Only mind, you are good girls, and never tell your mistress's doings," I replied, taking a glass of wine, and ordering them to do the same.

A second and a third glass seemed to open their eyes immensely; the least touch or joke sent them into fits of laughter. They blushed and seemed quite excited. In fact Patty, who had remained on my knee, was almost ready to faint with emotion as she caressed my face and bosom, the cause being a hand I had managed to slip under her nightdress, so that one finger had been tickling and playing with her almost hairless slit and gradually working her up to a state of excitement she was at a loss to comprehend.

"Let us all be naked. Throw off every rag, my dear ones, I want to feel your soft warm flesh next to mine, to cuddle you and feel you all over. Shall I read a pretty little piece of poetry about a potter who married your namesake, Patty?" I said, and seeing they were ready for anything, told Annie to bring me a manuscript called "The Haunted House" from a drawer in the cabinet.

"Now listen to 'The Tale of a Potter' and don't laugh till it is finished. You will find it rather free but nothing more than big girls like you ought to know." Then I commenced:

Young Hodge, he was a worthy wise,
 A potter he by trade;
He fell in love with Martha Price,
 She was a parson's maid.

This Hodge worked amongst his pans,
 His pots, his mugs, his delf;
He said: "A sad fate is a man's
 When he is by himself.

Now soon I'll marry Martha Price,
 A nice snug home I've got;
The parson soon the knot shall splice,
 And we'll both piss in one pot."

Then Hodge he made a pretty pot,
 And took it to his love;
Said he: "I've brought this pot to show,
 I mean your love to prove.

Now name the day, the happy day,
 Whose night shall bring me bliss;
When your sweet cunt and my stiff prick
 Shall mingle in this their piss."

They married were within a week,
 And Hodge he was in luck;
He took sweet Patty's maidenhead
 With his first vigorous fuck.

Then in her arms he fell asleep,
 But started with affright;
And in the middle of the bed
 He sat up bold and white.

"Oh, love! oh, love! I've had a dream,
 A dream to cause me fright;
I dreamed we both were in my shop
 And there I hugged you tight.

I dreamed I went your cheek to kiss,
 We romped with hugs and squeezes;

When down I knocked the pots and pans
  And broke them all in pieces."

Then Martha answered with a laugh:
  "No pots you've broke, good man;
But much I fear this very night,
  You've cracked a Patty Pan."

And from that night unto this day
  Hodge in that crack would pop,
A prick as thick as any brick,
  But the crack he cannot stop.

So maids beware, heed well your pans.
  With this my tale is ended;
If your pan's cracked by prick of man,
  It never can be mended.

Throwing down the manuscript, I had a finger in each of
their cracks sooner than it takes to write. "What darling
little pans each of you has! I long to throw you on the bed
and kiss them. What do you think of mine with its soft
curly hair? Only it's a broken pan, you know, my dears, as
I've of course had my husband."

"La, and was that really so nice, dear lady? Oh, I love you
so, do let me look," exclaimed Patty, slipping off my knee
and kneeling between my legs to get a better sight of the
object of her curiosity, which she first kissed most lovingly,
and then, parting the hair, put a couple of fingers right up
my cunt. This so tickled and delighted me that I leant back
in the chair and pulled Annie close to my bosom as I hugged
and kissed her, whilst I still had a finger in her little slit, as
far as it would go. My legs also mechanically opened to
facilitate inspection, as Patty exclaimed, "How deep my two
fingers can go right up and it is so warm and moist. It makes
me feel I could eat it!"

In a few minutes we were all tossing on my bed in a state
of nature. They laughed, screamed and blushed as I excitedly
examined and kissed their respective cunnies. How my tongue
revelled around their budding clitorises till they rewarded me
with those first virgin emissions which are always so deliciously thick and creamy. How lovingly they both repaid all

my caresses, Patty paying the most ardent attentions to my cunt, which delighted her more and more every moment, whilst Annie seemed to prefer sucking my bubbies as I gamahuched her.

"What a treat it would be to see you both lose your maidenheads at once," I exclaimed.

"Ah! couldn't the pages do it for us, dear lady? I do love that Charlie so!" appealed Patty without consideration in her excitement.

"I'll try and manage it; but we must be careful not to let them into our secrets before I can find out how they are disposed," I replied.

"Oh, I know Charlie is a rude, bold little fellow, wicked enough for anything if he had the chance. What do you think, I once actually caught him handling his affair in the pantry when he thought no one was looking and when I happened to enter suddenly; it was sticking out straight and red-looking at the top. His face was quite red and he seemed rather short of breath; but the impudent fellow, like the daredevil he is, shook it fairly in my face as he asked me to give him a kiss, saying: 'What do you think of this, Patty? That's how it gets, when'—oh, mistress I can't tell you all he said."

But I pressed her and at last she told me: "It was when we had been waiting on his mistress. 'Oh, Patty,' he said, 'isn't she lovely, such mouth and teeth and loving eyes, I feel as if I could jump at her, I do!'"

"Very well, Master Charlie," I laughed, "perhaps I shouldn't so much mind if you did, when we are alone someday I will give him the chance and let you two dears know all about it. But I will first read you another song from 'The Haunted House' and to-morrow I will give you a copy, and I expect both to be able to sing it soon."

"LIVE AND LEARN."
Tune:—Drops of Brandy

When I was little and good,
    A long time ago 'm afraid, Miss;
A stiff prick was not understood,
    I was a quiet little, shy little maid, Miss.

I knew but one use for my cunt,
  I knew not what joy 'twould afford me,
The sight of a cock would affront,
  And talk about fucking have bored me.
But now, oh, much wiser I've grown!
  I'll stretch my legs open for any,
My modest shy feelings have flown,
  And fucks, why, I can't get too many!
I like a stiff prick up my arse,
  Though too much of that makes you bandy.
When I look at my quim in the glass,
  It always pouts red and looks randy.
I like a fuck—morn, noon, and night,
  On every weekday and Sunday:
If I'm fucked on the Sabbath, all right!
  But I want to be buggered on Monday.
Oh! Let it be hot or be cold,
  I'm always alive for a cock, Miss;
Men, fair, dark, young or old,
  Here's a hole that'll take in their jock, Miss!
I can spend for an hour at a time,
  My cunt is as hot as fire, Sir;
The man that says: "Fucking is crime,"
  I say to his face, he's a liar, Sir.
Then give me a prick in each hand,
  Turn my arse north, my cunt to the south;
And get all your jocks well to stand,
  One in each hole and one in my mouth;
I'll fuck and I'll suck and I'll frig,
  Until you're all quite bloody well spent, Sir!
Then I'll take in the lodgers again,
  And never once ask them for rent, Sir!
Hurrah! for my cunt, my best friend,
  Hurrah! for a cock to kiss, Sir;
I'll fuck till this life comes to end,
  I hope too, there's fucking in bliss, Sir!"

When we awoke in the morning it was too late for a repetition of our tribadism, so I made them get up quickly and bring in breakfast, promising to look after Master Charlie during the day.

(To be continued.)

OVERHEARD AT THE AQUARIUM.

Swell.—"Damn it! all the same flaghopping faces, not a fresh bit of cunt here. I'd give anything if I could fuck the Princess Amuzulu, and bugger the "Old Man of the Woods!"

Just as we were going to press an anonymous correspondent on board Admiral Seymour's ship at Ragusa has favoured the Editor with the following:

A PROPOS OF THE NAVAL DEMONSTRATION.

Who'll bugger the Turk?
"I," said Gladstone, "as Chief of the Nation,
And Premier of England, to gain reputation.
I'll bugger the Turk,
And ne'er let him shirk
My prick's Grand Demonstration!"

THE PEARL,

A Journal of Facetiæ and Voluptuous Reading.

| No. 14 | PUBLISHED MONTHLY. | Aug. 1880 |

LA ROSE D'AMOUR,

Or the Adventures of a Gentleman in Search of Pleasure.
Translated from the French.

CHAPTER V.

In the evening I had arranged everything and was seated on a pile of rich cushions in one of the apartments of Ali's harem, my head reclining on the breast of the voluptuous Circassian, Ibzaidu, or Cluster of Pearls, as her name signified, surrounded by my other slaves whom I gave to Ibzaidu for servants and who, I was determined, should reign supreme until such time as I should find someone more beautiful than herself.

I had opened my caskets of jewels, and adorned her wrists, arms, neck, head and ankles with jewels of massy gold of Western and Oriental workmanship, and it seemed that she would never tire looking at and playing with them as a child would with a painted bauble.

Before night my host came in, bringing with him mutes and eunuchs, and he showed me through the suite of apartments devoted to my service, one of which I found to be a bedchamber, fitted up with the utmost elegance, containing twenty single beds.

Here it was that I slept among my concubines, or rather I should say that I lay with them, for I deserted all the others with whom I ought to have had sexual connection to repose in the arms of Ibzaidu, who, when she saw me advancing to her bedside, stretched out her arms to me and kicking off the cover, moved to the further side of the bed to make room for me.

I entered her bed, and lay with my cheek resting on her bosom the night long. And although my prick was in splendid condition, firm and erect as a rod of ivory, yet I never once thought of letting it force an entrance through the delicate and narrow passage into the inner court of the temple of love.

I spent about three weeks before I met with any more prizes, partly in the city, part of the time at the villa of Ali's on the banks of the Bosphorus in the company of Ibzaidu alone, leaving the other females in the city, under the care of the eunuchs.

During one of my visits at the villa, I was surprised one evening, while walking along the terrace of the garden, to see Ali dashing up the road at full speed, mounted on a full-blood Arabian. I descended to the gate and met him, to enquire the news, thinking that something might be wrong at the house I occupied in the city.

On enquiring, he informed me that there was a large lot of females ordered to be sold in a few days, by order of the Grand Sultan.

Ali said they were the females composing the harem of some officer of the State who had been dead about one year, whose only heirs, two nephews, had been quarreling about the possession of them ever since and that the Sultan had just ordered them to be sold and the proceeds to be divided among the two heirs; and he said that from reports circulating in the city, there must be some beautiful slaves amongst them, and he advised me to start directly for my own house, and that he would by bribery manage to get me a private interview with them, so that I could examine them at my leisure and choose such as I would like to have, and on the day of sale he would purchase them for me.

On the succeeding day I accompanied Ali to the house of the trader in whose keeping were the slaves.

The trader met us at the door, and took me at once into a room in which were the females. They were all enveloped in large white drapery which covered them from head to foot.

Mustapha, the trader, spoke to them, and they arranged themselves in a row round the room, then he retired, telling me that as soon as he left the room, they would all drop their mantles, and I could examine them at leisure.

Leaving me, he went out, locking the door behind him.

Stepping up to the female nearest me she cast her covering behind her. So did the others and I feasted my eyes with a picture of voluptuousness greater than I had ever dreamt of.

There stood before me about sixty females, perfectly naked, that I think could not be excelled in any harem in the East. There were the women of Circassia with their dark flowing tresses, eyes of piercing black and skin of dazzling whiteness, mostly contrasted by the deep carnation of their lips, the nipples of their breasts and the jet-black, bushy hair that surmounted their cunts.

Again, there were the languishing mild blue-eyed beauties ravished from the isles of Greece, and the voluptuous Georgians; even Africa had yielded up her sable beauties to the lusts of the sometime owner of all the lovely slaves who stood about me.

I minutely criticized each one separately, going over their respective claims to beauty with the eye of a connoisseur. Oh, how I feasted my sight on the row of lovely, luscious cunts that ran around the room. I look at, feel, touch them all, and stroke down the bushy hair that surrounds their notchs.

I became so much excited from the handling of so many cunts that I put my arm around the waist of one charming little creature, who by her looks must have been a great libertine, and led her into a small side-apartment where, presenting her with a fine gold chain which I wore, I laid her down on a pile of cushions, and twice gave her to experience the most ecstatic pleasures before I got off her.

I gave her some time to recover from the confusion I had thrown her into, ere we returned to the apartment in which the women were standing, who took no further notice of our absence than to raise their heads and to look at the chain which I had hung around her neck.

I marched the one I had just been fucking with to one side and picked out ten others, among which number was one black, a young African about fifteen years of age, who still retained her virginal rose, and who was, on the whole, the most voluptuously formed female I had ever seen and apparently better fitted for enjoying the pleasure of love than any female in my possession. Her hair was quite straight and black as a raven's wing; her breasts were full and large, as though of ivory. Her waist was slender, while her hips were spread out to a width I had never before seen. Her thighs were of a largeness to put to shame anything I had ever lain with.

Having stood on one side those whom I wished to pur-

chase, I called in the merchant and Ali and showed them
to him, and as the sale was to take place the following day,
I ordered him to be punctual in attendance to purchase them
for me, and left.

On the following day by noon Ali had conveyed to my
apartments all the slaves that I had chosen that night. I put
four of them to the test, giving them, for the first time, to
know the difference between lying in an old goat of a Turk's
arms to that of being well fucked by a young and lively
Frenchman, overflowing with the precious aqua-vitae, which
all women are so greedy after.

I now spent about two weeks in enjoying these new
beauties that I had bought, with the exception of those who
had not been deflowered of their virginal rose by the horny-
headed old lecher, their late master, and those were but three
out of the number.

Whilst I was thus idling away my time in the arms of my
handsome slaves, my interpreter called on me one morning,
and on being admitted into my presence told me that he had
found one of the loveliest girls in Constantinople in the
house of a poor mechanic and that on enquiry he had refused
to part with her on any account, or for any amount of money;
but he said it might be barely possible to steal her off, if I
was so inclined.

I promised him a large sum if he would procure her for me,
and calling on Ali, my agent consulted with him as to the
best means of bringing her off.

They agreed to go and stay about the house at night, until
they saw the old man go out, and then, with the assistance of
a couple of eunuchs, rush into the house, gag her, carry her
out, and put her into a litter and bring her to me, all of
which I approved, promising them a rich reward if they succeeded.

It was not until the third night that they were able to
carry her off and I was agreeably surprised one night while
reclining in the arms of one of my lovely slaves to see a
couple of my mutes come into my room bearing in their arms
the beautiful stolen prize.

I took her out of their arms, and seating her on a cushion,
I uncovered her face and took the gag from her mouth. I
found her to be a lovely creature as far back as I could see

and I began stripping her so that I might have a full view of her naked and view all her hidden charms.

Oh! what charms, what beauty met my fiery glance.

I had to call on several of the women to help me hold her while I was feeling and admiring her charms. I burned with desire to enjoy her, I lavished my eager kisses on every part of her body. I fastened my lips to hers. I sucked the rosy nipples of her breasts; the lips of her cunt received more than their share.

I was about to throw myself on her, but reflecting that I had determined to reserve all that had their maidenheads till after my return to France, I sprang from her, threw myself in the arms of Celestine and buried myself up to the hilt in her, just in time to prevent the liquor from spurting all over the floor.

Shortly after, Ali got me two more females, both of whom had been taken from one of the isles of the Hellespont.

I had now nearly run out of money and was preparing to start home, when, by accident, I found out that Ali was reputed to have a daughter more beautiful than any female in Constantinople, and I determined to wait a while and get possession of her by some means or other.

I had not money enough left to think of offering a sum large enough to tempt his cupidity, so I made all arrangements to steal her off, for which purpose I despatched him into the country.

The same day I found out the part of the house in which Ali had shut up his daughter in the hopes of keeping her from my sight; and I made everything ready for stealing her off the same night as soon as it was dark.

I sent all my baggage and the females with the eunuchs and the mutes on board the brig.

I got a litter, and with the assistance of the interpreter whom I largely paid to aid me in the enterprise, I succeeded in gaining the apartment of Selina, whom I saw to be asleep. Without any noise we gagged her and putting her into the litter soon had her on board the brig with my other treasures, when we instantly steered out of the harbour and made all haste; nor did I think myself in perfect safety until we floated once more in the Mediterranean.

Selina, on being released, at first made a great outcry at

being carried off, and I kept out of her sight until we had been under weigh a couple of days, when the sea-sickness had tamed her wondrously, and I could approach her without having torrents of abuse and Turkish execrations heaped on my head. In fact, the whole of my passengers were sick, with the exception of Caroline, Celestine, and the Nubian slave.

These three attended the rest, till they got over their sea-sickness, which was not until the third or fourth day with some. Then all was mirth, jollity, luscious love.

After all were perfectly recovered, we ran up to a small, verdant but uninhabited island in the Mediterranean and lay to for one day and night.

In the evening I had let down into the water a very large sheet of canvas, made on purpose, supported by the corners of the yard-arms of the vessel, for the purpose of letting the women have a bath. Ordering them to change their rich dresses for pants and shirts of plain white cotton, I took them on deck and having stationed the sailors in the boats a few yards distant from the canvas, I plunged them one after the other into the water in the belly of the sheet.

Here they amused and enjoyed themselves amazingly for an hour or more. They were then twisted up in an armchair, rigged for the purpose, and after dressing themselves, I again brought them on deck, where they romped and played about like so many young kittens or monkeys.

Calling on a eunuch, I ordered him to bring up some musical instruments that I had procured in Constantinople.

Ibzaidu and two others played on the guzla and sang some plaintive songs of home in a rich mellow voice that cast a sadness and gloom on the spirits of all, till Celestine seized the guitar and sang me some of the songs of our own dear France.

Thus we amused ourselves until late at night, having the supper brought up on the deck which we partook of by moonlight.

Stopping and enjoying myself by the way as I listed, it was nearly five weeks after sailing before I anchored in the harbour of the little creek close to the chateau in Brittany, where, after safely stowing away in the old castle my goods, women, etc., I made preparation for that which you may know in the next chapter.

CHAPTER VI.

The first thing I did after one day's rest was to assign the
eunuchs and mutes I had brought with me to their separate
duties, which consisted solely in guarding and attending the
females, either when in their apartment or when roving about
in the garden or shrubberies attached to the chateau, so that
they were never from under the sight of some of the slaves.

After having made these arrangements I made preparations
for giving a grand entertainment to the captain and the crew
of the steamer, who had conducted themselves very much to
my satisfaction during the voyage, never having once intruded
or infringed their privileges, always acting with great delicacy.

On the evening in the Mediterranean that I had the women
on the deck to bathe, the sailors would have all retired below
had I not called them back and sent them in the boats, and
now I determined to repay them their good conduct by giving
them an entertainment fit for princes.

In the evening I sent word to the captain and the crew
to come up to the castle. In half an hour they were admitted
and having shut up the women in an apartment out of the
way, I showed them through the shrubberies and garden, all
of which they viewed with amazement, wondering at the rich-
ness and taste displayed in the fitting up of the castle of
beauties, as they termed it.

About six o'clock a servant made his appearance saying that
supper was ready. I had ordered the supper to be served in
the hall of the fountains and led my guests there.

We entered and sat down at the tables and directly came
trooping in all the females of my harem and seated themselves opposite to the men.

After the supper was over, Ibzaidu and some of the other
women I had brought from Turkey took their instruments
and gave us a concert of Oriental music. After which Caroline
went to the piano, and Celestine sat down to a harp and
played some brilliant and lively pieces of French and Italian
music. Upon which, those of my lovely slaves who belonged
to the Grecian isles got up and danced the romaika and other
dances peculiar to the country.

They were followed by Ibzaidu and two other Circassians,
who were attired in the costumes of their native land, and
danced some of the native dances.

These were in their turn followed by the Georgians, after which came my sable mistress, the Nubian, dressed in petticoats reaching the knees with an overdress of fine blue gauze.

Her dance was wild and pleasing and in throwing herself about over the floor, as her legs were bare, would show her thighs, her bare buttocks and sometimes her black bushy notch.

Celestine and Caroline rose up and stepped out on the floor to dance, and Laura sat down at the piano.

They were dressed in short petticoats and dress, the same as the Nubian, and performed some lascivious dances, showing every charm which nature had graced them with.

The officers and crew of the brig applauded the dancing very much.

About twelve o'clock I sent off the common seamen, retaining only the officers, five in number.

After the seamen left us the company became mixed, the officers sitting in the midst of the women, some of whom I had not frigged for a long time, and who looked with a wistful and longing eye on the men about them, and it was very clear to me that were I not present they would soon be engaged in the soft pleasures of love.

Clapping my hands, a couple of eunuchs entered and pointing out Rose, Marie and Manette, and two others they led them away to an apartment I had fitted up with beds. When they came back I took leave of the officers, and the eunuchs left the room with them to where they had put the five girls.

What a pleasant surprise to both parties! The men to find the beds occupied by the five girls and the girls to find the same number of men enter to them. Oh, how they panted with the pleasure of the sight.

Instantly did they know why I had sent them to that apartment. After the men were gone I sent all the women to the chamber except a lovely Georgian, and repaired to an adjoining apartment to where the five couples were.

Here I had a place so constructed that I could see all that was going on in the other room without being seen.

After the men had got into the room they ran up to the beds and would have clasped the women to their breasts, but they all jumped out of bed naked, and began to undress the men, who were speedily divested of all clothing. Then what a scene of love followed!

The men threw the girls on the beds, who opened wide

their thighs as they fell on their necks, and then jumped on them with pricks stiff as iron rods, piercing through the tender folds of the cunts under them, sending joy and pleasure to their very vitals, and I could judge from the exclamations and the writhing about, and the wriggling of backsides, the hot kisses and the amorous bites on the neck that not one had but received a double or triple dose of the sacred liquor injected into them. I think I never saw men and women fuck with greater zest, or derive more pleasure and enjoyment from frigging than they did.

Looking at them had such an effect on myself and companion that we were obliged to retire to the bedchamber for the purpose of enjoying ourselves in like manner.

In ascending a flight of stairs, my slave tripped, and falling hurt herself, so that on entering the room I had to seek another in whom to pour the extra liquor from the magic spring, and which was about to run over for the want of pumping.

The first bed I cast my eye on contained the luxurious Nubian slave, and I determined to offer up her maidenhead as the sacrificial offering to the god of love.

Approaching, I motioned her to rise and follow me to the state-bed whither I went.

We entered the bed together both stark naked, and placing her at once in a favourable position with a cushion under her large fat bottom, I lay my length on her and guiding the head of my prick tried to insert it between the lips of her slit, but could not succeed.

I got up, and oiling it well with ointment I again freed the entrance and succeeded in ripping and tearing up the works and barriers that defended her virgin rose, and found her a dish fit for the gods! Heavens! with what transports of delight did I squeeze her in my arms as I drove the arrow of love into the deepest recess of the luscious quivering flesh through which I had forced a passage for it.

Despite the pain which my forcible entrance into her must have caused, the moment I began working in her, Celeste, the name I had given her, began moving up to me with vigour, elasticity, and a sense of pleasure utterly impossible to be looked for in one in her situation.

So young, not quite fifteen, and then with a notch of such a lusciously tight smallness that even after entering her to the full length, it was with the utmost difficulty that I could work in and out of her, but with the suction caused by the tightness with which the flesh worked around the piston rod, I soon drew open the sluice of love's reservoir and thence gushed forth a stream of fiery fluid which completely drenched her inmost parts, causing a shudder of pleasure to run through her whole body that at once proclaimed to me that she was about to give proof of the joy and ecstasy with which she had received from me the terrible lance thrust which had given her such a wound and was causing her to pour down the essence of her very soul through the gaping orifice.

The oiling which her parts had received from the mutual flow of our sperm made the entrance somewhat easy, but still very tight.

Towards morning she began to realize the full enjoyment of the luscious pleasure of being well frigged as the folds of her cunt from the constant friction had stretched somewhat more, causing no more than a delicious tightness, perfectly agreeable to me and which greatly enhanced the pleasure, as the first three or four times that I entered her I found it too tight for the full enjoyment of perfect bliss, as it almost tore the foreskin off my pego when entering, thus causing pain which detracted from the pleasure.

In the morning when I descended to the breakfast table I found those whom I had sent to spend the night with the officers of the brig so sore that they could hardly walk from the tremendous battering they had received from their companions during the night.

I rode out through the surrounding country during the day and on my return in the evening in passing one of the rooms I heard considerable whispering, and listening I overheard one of the women in conversation with some men.

I slyly opened the door and imagine my astonishment at beholding Caroline, Celestine, Rosalie and Laura in company with the four lubbery country-boors I had engaged at the chateau.

They were all lying on the floor, the girls with their clothes tossed up to their waists and the men with their pricks out of their breeches and the girls playing with them, trying to instill new life and vigour into the drooping instruments which had apparently just done good service.

Not being seen by them I retired, softly closing the door, to meditate on what I should do with the guilty ones.

After thinking over the subject for some time I came to the conclusion that I had no right to do or say anything on the subject, knowing that it was the instinct of nature which prompted them to act as they had done, and recollecting that I had promised to each of them that they should never want for that, to which they were then treating themselves, I decided to say nothing about the matter, unless merely to give them all a severe fright.

After supper, as I was sitting in the midst of my girls in the hall of fountains, watching some of the Grecian women as they winded through the mazes of the voluptuous romaika, to the music of the guzla, I clapped my hands and four mutes entered.

I pointed out the four I had caught frigging with the servants and ordered the mutes to seize them.

They bound their wrists with silken sashes and led them up to me.

I put on a savage frown and accused them of having debased themselves to the embraces of menials.

This they denied and persisted in denying.

I ordered the mutes to strip them and taking a slender riding switch I began tapping Celestine with it on her bare buttocks very lightly just so as to cause them to blush till they became a beautiful carmine hue, mixed in with the clear alabaster, and they all four cast themselves on their knees before me and acknowledged their fault. I then told them that it demanded a more serious punishment and that they should receive it.

Now, I had ordered up from the village four of the finest-looking stout peasants to be found, and making a sign to the mutes they went out and returned leading them in blindfolded.

After they were in the room I conversed with them, and ordered some chocolate to be served which I had prepared with certain drugs that would cause their amorous propensities to rise every few minutes for four hours.

They were stark naked, and shortly after drinking, their lances stood erect against their bellies.

I then untied the wrists of the four girls and told them to lie down on cushions prepared for the purpose. I then led a man to each and put them in one another's arms, telling

the men to go in. The men instantly mounted the women
and for three hours kept them working in a dead heat.

Fourteen times did those men frig the women under them,
changing women every now and then.

At first the women enjoyed it very much but at last got
tired to death, perfectly worn out, battered and bruised to
pieces, the lips of their slits gaping wide open, flabby and
swollen, with a perfect little lake of sperm between their
thighs.

As soon as I saw the chocolate began to lose the effect on
them I had them taken out and there lay the girls so befucked
that they could hardly move hand or foot.

I myself was not idle during their performance, for I had
three times dissolved myself in the Nubian slave. I spent the
night in her arms, arising in the morning with the intention
of husbanding myself for a couple of days, so as to be able
to do justice to the maidenhead of Ibzaidu, which I intended
sacrificing to my amorous and fierce desires.

Chapter VII.

On the evening of the second day after, I made grand
preparations for the event about to be celebrated. I had an
elegant supper served such as would have tempted old Epi-
curus himself. All the inmates of the seraglio were at the
table and I plied them so well with wine that not one except Ibzaidu arose from it sober.

When I gave the signal for retiring to the bedchamber
they reeled and staggered about like so many drunken sailors.
Arrived at the bedchamber we all stripped to the skin and
catching Ibzaidu in my arms I carried her to the state-bed and
threw her down on it, and being somewhat fearful of my
powers, as I had been sucked nearly dry by the Nubian, I
called for and drank a cup of my magic chocolate which I
knew would enable me to go through the acts like a conqueror.

I gave the word and all the girls came round the bed with
their instruments playing, and sang a beautiful song which I
had composed for the occasion.

I gave the word and getting on the bed fixed my victim
in the best position, got between her thighs and giving a

bunch of switches to one of the girls I directed her to lash my backside with them so as to smart much.

I took hold of my battering-ram and strove to force an entrance. The head is in, the soft flesh yields to my fierce thrusts. I drive in, she screams with pain but I heed it not. It is music to my ears. It tells me that I am about to arrive at the seat of bliss. I shove and thrust harder, everything gives way to me, the lashing on my buttocks gives me double force, and one fierce lunge sends it into the furthest extremity of her grotto and at the same moment I oiled the mangled tender flesh of her dear little bleeding slit with such a stream of burning sperm as never woman sucked from man before. I thought my very prick and stones were dissolving in pearly liquid.

After resting myself on her bosom for a few moments, I found that my battering-ram was prepared for another assault and I fiercely drove him into the breach.

Three times before I got off did I spend the juice of my body into her without calling from her any return.

She lay and moaned in her agony and pain, and on looking I saw that I had terribly battered and bruised the entrance of the seat of pleasure.

I raised her up and had her put into a warm bath and after drying her I again put her to bed. After giving her some wine and taking some myself, I found that again I was in trim for another bout.

With a spring I placed myself between her thighs. I entered her, not without a good deal of hard work.

God of voluptuous love, what a heat reigned through her body!

How lusciously did the sweet flesh clasp around my rod!

A few thrusts and a few moves in and out awaken her to a sense of pleasure.

She moves up to me, she catches the fever that runs through me. Quicker, quicker she heaves up to me to meet my fierce lunges as I drive my foaming steed through her gap into the rich pasturage. She clasps me in her arms, and throws her snowy thighs around my back, the bounces of her bottom fairly spring me off her. I feel she is coming. Ah, my god, she comes—she spends! The sperm comes from her in a shower. I, too—I again—I spend! It runs from me. Great God! It's

too much! I die! Oh-h! And then I breathed my spirit away in
a sigh soft and gentle as a zephyr.

My God, how voluptuous, how luscious was the beautiful
Circassian! What warmth! With what fire, what energy did
she meet all my efforts at procuring and dispensing pleasure!
How lusciously did she squeeze me when in her! How plentifully did she let down the milk when the agony of pleasure
seized her!

We swam in a perfect sea of voluptuousness totally indescribable. Man cannot imagine, pen cannot describe it, it
was an intoxication of delight—pleasure wrought up to agony,
bliss inexpressible, more exquisitely delicious than that enjoyed by the houris of Paradise when in the arms of true
Mohammedans, or that enjoyed by the spirits of the Elysian
fields.

(To be continued.)

MY GRANDMOTHER'S TALE or MAY'S ACCOUNT OF HER INTRODUCTION TO THE ART OF LOVE.

*From an Unsophisticated Manuscript found amongst the Old
Lady's papers after her Death, supposed to
have been Written about A.D. 1797.*

Chapter IV.
Kate's Narrative Continued; The Voyage;
Captain Lemberg and His Niece Hilda.

On the next occasion that May and her friend Kate were
snugly stretched in bed, their arms fondly circling one another and their hands tenderly plucking the hair of each
other's cunt, they soon grew so excited that she, throwing off
everything and May reversing her position, lay over her friend
and gamahuched her most lovingly, Kate's tongue returning
those fiery kisses of love with such interest that in a few
minutes both were dissolved in a balmy emission.

As soon as they were recovered a little and more composed,

May said softly: "Now, dear Katie, proceed with your most interesting and exciting narrative."

Well, when the time came, papa brought me word to board the brig, and after taking a most affectionate leave he left me in charge of Captain Lemberg and his niece, Hilda. I was delighted to have her as a companion for she was a merry, spritely girl, and had made the voyage before.

I had a little cabin adjoining hers and opening on the salon.

Nina was accommodated in the forepart of the ship and was with a soldier's wife, a Mrs. S and her sister Jenny. The vessel sailed early the next morning and soon began to pitch and roll. The motion made us all sick. Nina was not able to leave her berth and Hilda was nearly as bad. As for me I never felt so bad in my life.

About noon the Captain came into my cabin. I was lying down, only half dressed and so sick that I did not care what was done to me.

He said he was so sorry to find me so bad; but that if I would allow him to prescribe for me he knew what would be sure to give relief.

I said I would take anything he gave for I could not be worse than I was.

He went out and soon returned with a tumbler of hot brandy and water. When I tasted it I said: "I cannot take this, it is too strong."

"All the better, my dear, it will do you more good. Come, trust an old sailor."

He put his arm round me and supported me while I gulped it down. Then he laid me back. It relieved the sickness but threw me into a stupor.

Before he left he arranged my dress and was very particular in setting it over my breast. Seeing I did not move he passed his hand down over my stomach and pressed the mound at the bottom of my belly. Then he lightly kissed my forehead and went away.

After a short time he returned and finding me tossing about, but still in a state of stupor he softly rubbed my stomach over my chemise, bringing his hand lower and lower, until he reached my cunt. Finding I did not mind him, he passed his hands up under my chemise and boldly grasped my cunt.

"Oh, Captain," I muttered, but could say no more.

He pushed his hand between my thighs so as to feel the lips. He separated my thighs more and felt them round about. Indeed I don't know what he did, I was so stupefied, but I think he kissed it.

In the evening the sea calmed down and I felt much better.

He brought me a cup of coffee, which roused me up. He supported me with his arm while I was drinking and then stooped to kiss me. I could not refuse him my lips, he was so kind.

In a few days I recovered from the effects of my sea-sickness, and I began to feel at home in the vessel.

Hilda brought me about and showed me everything.

At the opposite side of the salon the Captain and the mate, Mr. Carle, occupied cabins corresponding to ours.

Mr. Carle was a young man, good-looking and very agreeable. He was most attentive to Hilda and did not mind me much. But the Captain was unremitting in his attentions to me. He got into the way of kissing me every night and used to squeeze my bottom when I passed near him.

With Hilda he was still more free, but then she was his niece.

In arranging my cabin I found there was a sliding panel between Hilda's cabin and mine which, when open, gave a full view either way.

The Captain generally kept the first night-watch and remained on deck until after twelve; then he would come down, take grog, and turn in.

One night I was awakened by talking in Hilda's cabin and I heard her say: "Now behave yourself, I won't have you coming this way into my cabin at night. Ah, stop, I will call out, if you don't let me alone."

"Hildy, my pet, let me, just a moment."

"No, you mustn't put your hand there—you mustn't raise my shift—you mustn't open my thighs. Oh, Uncle, do—take it away. You are a terrible man, why don't you go and fuck Kate? What would Carle say if he knew you did this to me?"

I got up, opened the panel and peeped in. Her lamp was burning. I could see that he had drawn her to the edge of her berth, over which her naked bottom projected. Her legs were raised up and resting on his arms while his large prick was darting in and out of her open cunt. I could see that she was beginning to enjoy it for she wriggled her bum and threw her arms around his neck.

"Press it, dear Uncle! You make me like it in spite of myself."

At every thrust he banged against her rump, crying: "There, there, you have it all."

Before he left I heard him talking of me and telling her to show me some books and pictures.

The next day, coming suddenly out of my cabin I caught her sitting in Mr. Carle's lap. He had his arm round her and was kissing her. They started and blushed when they saw me and he got up and went on deck.

She then told me that they were engaged to be married at the end of the voyage. "And do you know, Kate, though I am fond of Carle I dread it."

"Why?" I asked.

"Oh, don't you know what a man does to a woman when they are in bed together?"

"No," I said, looking very innocent. "What?"

"Oh, you must know that he has something that he puts into her stomach."

"What is it like, Hilda? Tell me about it."

"It's a thing called a prick, eight or nine inches long, with a purple head. It hangs between his legs and when it stiffens he can push it into our slits, which are called cunts, you know. Then after working it in and out, something comes out, and it makes the child."

"How queer! Did you ever see it, Hilda?"

"I have often seen pictures of it. Uncle has curious books with pictures, that tell all about it. Would you like to see it? I was looking over his books and I came upon a secret drawer which was open, and there I found them; come, I'll show them to you."

We went into his cabin and on opening the drawer saw a number of books full of coloured pictures of the most lascivious evolutions of love.

There were naked men and naked women with their cunts and pricks and bottoms displayed in every kind of attitude and position. They were frigging, sucking and fucking in all varied positions.

There were some large French prints also. One depicted a

beautiful girl with her bare shoulders and legs, seated on the
lap of her lover. Between her voluptuous thighs her cunt is
seen delightfully gorged with his standing prick. Her arms
are round his neck and her face is turned up, beaming with
the satisfaction she experiences in her well-filled cunt.

Another showed a fat nun with her frock up and her breasts
bare, stretched on a couch before a large mirror; she had been
working a dildoe, that is, an artificial prick into her voluptuous
cunt. She has obtained an emission and is now lying back in
delicious languor, while two randy monks, peeping round the
curtain, and beholding the luscious scene reflected in the
glass, have pulled out their pricks and contend who shall be
the first into her lustful orifice.

Then there was a scene in a café in Paris: a number of
naked men and women dancing together. As they circle
round, their pricks and cunts are presented in most exciting
points of view; one is pressing the soft buttocks of his partner,
while she holds with loving grasp his standing prick. Another squeezes the breasts of his beloved, while she supports
his pendant balls. Another couple falls, but they so manage
that he falls between her extended thighs and his eager prick
soon finds lodgement in her expectant cunt. Some are lying
their partners, nothing loath, upon the surrounding couches
and relieving their excitement by plunging into their melting
cunts. While others again regale their senses of taste and
smell between the voluptuous thighs of their delighted fair
ones.

These pictures excited me greatly. I had never seen anything like them before. "Oh, Hilda," I muttered as I pressed
together my thighs, while she pointed out each lascivious
detail.

"But we must not remain here," she said. "Let us take
some of these books into your cabin and there we can observe
them at our leisure."

So, taking three, we shut the drawer and made off.

When we had comfortably settled ourselves on a little sofa
at the side of my cabin, we opened the first. It contained a
thrilling description of a doctor's exploits with a buxom young
widow. How he gained her confidence and then excited her
amorous feelings, until he succeeded in raising her snowy
smock and in feasting his eyes on the ripe beauties of her
voluptuous form. The next depicts her standing thus at his

side with her splendid cunt protruding its full rounded lips from the midst of a thick covering of crisp curling hair, while the crimson line between gives promise of a warm reception to his prick.

He has put her hand on his standing prick, which she looks at with shy pleasure as she draws the skin down from its glowing red head.

In the next plate she is seen lying across his lap, her beautifully rounded bottom with its milk-white globes is turned up to meet his amorous gaze. He pats the cheeks and titillates the furrow between, while his prick is luxuriating in the soft folds of her melting cunt.

In another plate she is represented as astride of him, her bottom rubbing against his belly as he leans back. By the sweet suction of her mouth she has restored his prick to vigorous life, and, as it now stands up between her widely separated thighs, she presses it warmly against the lips of her longing cunt.

"How would you like to be in her place, Kate? And to feel a fine lusty prick pressing against your cunt and then pushing up into it filling you with rapture and delight?"

"I am sure it would be very pleasant if it were the prick of one I loved."

"No doubt that would vastly increase the pleasure; but don't you feel when your cunt gets excited that any prick, if it were in the right condition, would give you pleasure? How does your cunt feel now? Would you mind my putting my hand on it, Kate?"

"Not in the least, Hilda, if you want to."

"Lean back, dear, open your thighs. Might I see it?"

"I have no objection."

I now became aware that the sliding panel was slightly open and though I saw something like an eye peering through the slit, I pretended to take no notice. I replied: "You may, Hilda, provided you let me see yours afterwards."

She quickly raised my petticoats, uncovering all my belly and thighs right up before the panel, which was now opened a little further. She played with my hairy turf and praised its colour. Then, separating my legs as far as possible she drew the lips apart. "You have a sweet little cunt, Kate, with a wonderful clitoris, and a deep red recess. Oh, how hot it is inside! And how it sucks and presses my finger. If I only had a prick I would like to fuck you myself." She stooped and kissed the lips and sucked the clitoris. I then got up and made her display her secret charms before the panel, which made her blush for she well knew what was there.

She had a very pretty cunt, daintily fringed with light red hair and the inside hot and juicy.

That night the Captain changed watches with Mr. Carle and before he went to our cabins made us take some of his grog. Hilda took it very freely and made me take more than I wished; in fact, when I stood up I felt quite giddy.

The Captain took me in his arms and made me sit on his knee. While I was warding off his kisses he slipped his hand under my dress and pushed it up between my thighs.

"Oh, Captain! Stop. Take your hand away—no, I won't allow it!"

"What is he doing?" Hilda asked, laughing.

"No matter, I won't allow it—stop! Oh, stop, how can you be so impudent?"

"Don't be angry, Kate, my pet. I won't harm you. Sure every pretty girl likes to have her cunt tickled. Doesn't she, Hilda?"

"Well, I don't, and I won't let you. Oh, Hilda, don't let him raise my dress—don't let him—you make me ashamed —how can you be so wicked?"

I was now stretched on my back and he over me holding my arms and stifling me with kisses.

"Hilda! What are you doing? don't let him push it in! Oh! Oh! Oh!"

Hilda with her sly cunning had trapped me. It was she that opened the lips of my cunt, pushed in the head of his prick and then held it by the roots.

At each thrust he cried: "Sweet Katie—sweet pet—you have it now—in your delicious cunt—fuck—fuck—fuck! Hold my balls Hilda! Slap my arse, slap hard!"

At every smack she gave his bottom I felt his prick rush up with increased vigour into my cunt. I began to wriggle and heave.

"Ah, little one, you like it now—ah—oh, it comes—there —there it is."

He then put himself in order and hurried on deck to take his share of the night duty.

When I stood up I could hardly walk, so Hilda supported me into my cabin and helped me to undress.

When she had settled me in my berth she kissed me and wished me good night.

I stopped her and said: "It was a shame, Hilda, to allow me to be so treated."

"Don't mind, dear," she replied, laughing. "You are nothing the worse. And if I am not much mistaken you will enjoy it better before you leave the ship. Good night."

Though I was tired yet I was too excited to be sleepy.

After a short time I heard someone open the door of Hilda's cabin.

"Oh, Carle, what do you want here at this time of the night?"

"I want you, my pet, I can't live without you."

"Sure you have me all day."

"But I want you all night, too."

"But that you can't have yet, you know."

"Why not, love, don't you trust me?"

"Wait until we are married, Carle. You will have enough of me then. Go away now, there's a dear fellow. There, you've kissed me enough already to serve for a month. Well, I will sit on your knee just for a moment, if you promise to go away at once. Ah, where is your hand stealing?"

"Let me, my pet, I am curious to know if you are as nice here as I expected."

"And if I am not, what then?"

"Well, let me try anyway—there—open."

"Will you swear on your soul that you will marry me at the end of this voyage?"

"I will, indeed, dearest, on my soul. Thanks Hilda. Now I love you more than ever because you have confidence in me. You are very nice indeed, my sweet pet, you have a darling little pussey. Oh, how soft and warm it is. Now put your hand here and you will find something that is just made for it. Move it up and down, my love, it is all your own. Feel how strong and hot it is; it's longing to make acquaintance with its friend here. Won't you let them kiss, just to touch those loving lips?"

"Ah, Carle, it's not kind of you; you know I am so fond of you! You won't hurt me?"

"Open your legs more—there—it's in—in your sweet cunt. Darling Hilda, don't you like to feel my prick there, fucking, fucking?"

"Yes, but push gently, there's a dear."

"My love—oh, my love!—How my prick loves to fuck your sweet cunt."

Then they went on hugging and kissing for ever so long.

After a while I heard her asking questions about his prick and balls. "Now it is beginning to get large again. There, see how it has stiffened up. Would you like me to put it into my mouth and suck it?"

"Yes, my love, that would give me great pleasure. Thanks, darling Hilda, your mouth is almost equal to your cunt. That's delicious."

"But who can tell what queer places this has been in. How many girls have you had, Carle?"

"Ah, Hilda, don't be getting jealous. I have fucked, as you know, a good many girls. And if you are a wise little wife you won't object to my fucking a few more besides yourself, even after we are married. Now, let us make an agreement, love, which I am certain will tend to our mutual happiness. Give me perfect liberty and I will promise never to do anything without your knowledge and consent. I will give you the same liberty to have anyone you please and as often as you please, on the same conditions. I am satisfied we will love each other better and enjoy each other more than ever when we are not tied up exclusively to each other. Do you agree?"

"Well, Carle, I don't desire any liberty myself but if it will make you happier and cause you to love me more, I agree. But, remember, the condition must be carried out."

("Just a moment, Kate! Were they married afterwards, and did they follow that agreement?"

"They were, and the last time I met them, I thought I never saw a happier or more loving couple."

"Another word: what do you think of the arrangement yourself, Kate? I ask you because Mr. T has proposed the same thing to myself, that is, if I marry him."

"Well, dear, it is hard to give an opinion. Most women like to have a man all to themselves and as a rule they are satisfied with one; but in cases where either party has led a free life before marriage, I can quite understand that such an arrangement would be expedient and wise. But you may have an opportunity of judging for yourself as your papa intends inviting them here as soon as Carle returns from his present voyage."

"Oh, that will be delightful. I am longing to see Hilda and we may have Mr. T also, for he says he can't wait any longer for me and he has written to papa. But go on, dear Kate, and tell me what happened next.")

Just this: The following day Carle told the Captain of his engagement with his niece and that he had promised to marry her as soon as they arrived in port.

The Captain replied: "All right, old fellow, I congratulate you. She is a thorough good girl and will make a jolly wife. But you may have her at once so far as I am concerned, if you sign the marriage contract in my presence, which you know has legal force in Danish law."

Carle jumped at the idea. So the contract was drawn up and signed by Hilda and himself, the Captain and I adding our names as witnesses.

"Now," said the Captain, "I pronounce you man and wife together, etc. Have at her as soon as you like, my boy! And as we have witnessed the wedding it would be only fair that we should witness the bedding too."

Carle found her in his arms and placed her on his knee. The Captain caught hold of me and moving his leg under me, said: "Kate, you will have to be my niece now." And in spite of my struggles he forced his hand up between my legs.

Carle was not slow in following his example, and soon amidst many "Ah, Carle," "Stop Charlie" our cunts were taken in full possession of by exploring hands while two standing pricks boldly upreared their rosy tips.

Finding that they were bent on enjoying us openly, we saw no use in further resistance and so let them have their way.

The Captain smiled when he saw how skillfully and lovingly Hilda caressed Carle's noble tool, and under cover of a kiss placed my fingers on his own. "Now, Carle, lay her on the locker and don't spare her maiden-trap. Kate will guide the bird into the nest and I will look on, and see fair play and no favour."

Carle laid her back and tenderly lifting her dress uncovered her belly and thighs. Then raising her legs, he spread her thighs widely apart and paused to admire her cunt, fringed

with golden hair, and cosily placed himself between her luxuriant thighs. He then leaned over her so as to place his prick
upon its opened lips.

"Kate, now pop it in and hold it firm."

I stooped forward and taking hold of Carle's bounding tool
pushed its head into her soft recess. In doing so my bare
bottom became exposed to the Captain's view.

He caught me round the hips and cried: "Oh, lovely arse!"
He kissed it and I felt his warm pliant tongue playing in and
about my cunt and penetrating my bottom-hole itself. Then
quickly rising up he thrust his rampant prick into my cunt
and fucked away all the while leaning over my back, watching
Carle and crying out at every thrust: "That's the way, old
fellow! Send it home—rattle your bullocks against her arse—
fuck—fuck—fuck—ah, oh!" And we all fell together, our
cunts overflowing with the discharge from their excited
pricks.

After lying over her for a few moments Carle began to
heave his bottom again and gave her the benefit of a second
fuck, without taking out his prick.

This pleased the Captain greatly. He stooped over his
niece and kissing her asked how she liked being fucked.

She smiled, and stretching out her hand took hold of his
prick, now soft and hanging down.

Carle laughed to see her frigging her uncle's prick and
went on slowly driving his own in and out of her cunt.

The Captain's prick began to stand; he pushed it towards
her face. She drew it to her lips and calling me, raised my
clothes and placed Carle's hand on my cunt, then looking up
she said: "Now we are quits."

He kissed her and said: "Darling Hilda, you are the best
and sweetest of wives, you will never regret it."

Then bending down he asked me to lean back and open
my thighs. He kissed my cunt and sucked the clitoris all the
while with a slow and measured stroke, fucking Hilda's cunt.

"What are you doing to Kate, Carle?"

"I am sucking her sweet cunt while I am fucking yours.
And what are you doing to the Captain?"

"I am sucking his prick and squeezing yours in my cunt."

The Captain now heaved his great heavy bum and worked
his prick in and out of her mouth, just as Carle with increasing vigour drove his prick in and out of her cunt. She heaved

up and down, and in the height of her excitement, grasped one of the cheeks of my bottom and at every thrust of Carle's prick gave me such a squeeze that I could hardly suppress a shout.

But I felt nearly as excited as herself, for the action of Carle's lips and tongue in my cunt was almost as exciting as that of his prick in hers, while the view of his fine bottom rising and falling between her wide-spread thighs, and the Captain's tool darting in and out of her mouth, caused me fully to share in the general form of excitement.

The Captain feeling the tide of pleasure rising to the flood, cried: "Fuck her, Carle—fuck her cunt."

Carle replied: "Suck him, Hilda—suck his prick."

Whilst I, I pressed my cunt against Carle's mouth and spent on his tongue, called out the names—prick—cunt—arse—frigging—sucking—fucking—oh!

Carle went on deck and the Captain soon after tumbled into his berth. Hilda and I retired to our cabins and were soon fast asleep.

(To be continued.)

THE GOOD NOBLEMAN.

Air—"There was a Little Man."

Respected near and far,
There was a noble
Marquis, and Wallsend was the title that he bore, bore, bore,
Who left his brother-swells
To follow little girls,
And tell 'em not to do it any more, more, more.

Said he: "A man's affair
Isn't meant to go in there!"
And his Lordship put his finger on the spot, spot, spot;
But the wicked girls appalled
The nobleman, and called
On God to paralyse each limb they'd got, got, got.

"Your private parts, or cunny,
         Should not be let for money,
They're only meant to pee with," did he preach, preach,
    preach,
         His ears he almost doubted,
         When the little creatures shouted:
"God blind us into bloody corpses, each, each each!"

         "You always should endeavour
         To stop a young man ever
On any grounds from creeping up behind, hind, hind."
         And this noble thought he dreamed,
         When the little creatures screamed:
"God strike us deaf, lame, dumb and blind, blind, blind!"

         "You dissembling, bleeding, rotten,
         Bloody, cankered, misbegotten
Lump of shit, rubbed over with a little spend, spend, spend!"
         The little children cried,
         For a cockstand they espied
Within the noble breeches of their friend, friend, friend.

         They were tearing down his breeches,
         And his bitter cries and screeches,
And his blushes would have melted hearts of snow, snow,
    snow.
         And the little creatures found,
         When they dragged him to the ground,
That, while lecturing, he'd shot his noble roe, roe, roe.

FLUNKEYANIA; or BELGRAVIAN MORALS.

By Charles.

Chapter II.

It was rather late in the afternoon when we arrived home,
and I was in my apartment making some slight alteration in
my attire before attending my lady at the dinner table, when,

enters Justine! Without tapping or giving any other intimation of her approach.

I remonstrated with her, with mock gravity on her great impudence, representing to her that under the present circumstances my attire was grossly disarranged and that there was a great possibility that she might have found me in a state totally unfit to be seen by any young woman whatever.

To which the saucy girl replied that she did not know what state that was, unless I was sewn up to the neck in a strong sack; and even then, she continued, she thought that a loving woman with a sharp pair of scissors might overcome the difficulty and make me a presentable member of society —fit to be seen by herself anyway.

I think I was going to put this experiment to the practical test, and that without the adjuncts of the sack and the scissors,when Justine stopped me by saying that she had a very particular message for me from Her Ladyship.

This appeared to be that I was not to mention to anyone, least of all to the Earl, the circumstances of the Countess's having taken "Miss Courtney for a drive."

"For a ride," said I, correcting her with all possible gravity.

"Well, then, for a ride, if you like, you saucy boy," replied the sweet girl, giving me a slight box on the ear. "You know a great deal too much, sir; but you will promise not to tell Ernest, darling, won't you?"

Now, I was resolved to tease her a little. So I said that really I considered Miss Courtney a very fine girl. That she had given me a couple of sovereigns when she got out of the carriage. That she was just the sort of a girl that I was sure His Lordship would like: tall and long-legged, in fact exactly like a young fellow in girl's clothes. He's very fond of boys and would be delighted in finding Adam's needle instead of Eve's bit of old hat, when he put his hand up her clothes— and I was chafing away at a great rate when my pretty visitor stamped her foot with vexation, and then began to cry!

Of course upon this there was only one thing to do, and that was to comfort my young lady in every way that I could, and I succeeded so well that from sobbing, pouting, pushing me away and calling me a tantalizing, cross wretch, she began to return my kisses after the most approved fashion. Then she clasped me round the neck, sighing on my shoulder and murmuring incoherently all the loving epithets that suggested themselves on the spur of the moment, yielding herself as she did so to the loving clasp of my arms.

Almost undressed as I was, my natural feeling got the better of my discretion. It was too plain what the Countess's soubrette sighed for at the moment, and could any young fellow refuse such an appeal to his gallantry, especially when that engine of love which knows no conscience was bursting with impatience.

My hands raised her clothes as I threw her back on the edge of my bed and for a few minutes we revelled in the delights of love.

When we were getting more composed and able to converse like reasonable beings, I gave Justine willingly enough the promise her mistress had told her to get from me. While she informed me that the Earl was particular, almost to jealousy, of anyone using his beautiful chestnuts, unless they who used them belonged to the family.

I could not help wondering if he would be equally jealous of anyone "using" his beautiful chestnut-haired wife! And whether I was to be considered "one of the family"?

I could not help hinting something to this effect to Justine, in as discreet a way as the object admitted of. And to my surprise instead of being exposed to a lecture, for my brazen impudence, for daring to entertain such ideas, or a storm of jealous reproaches for my cruelty in so thinking of anybody but herself, after what had just passed between us —and that not for the first time—instead of this I received from the faithful femme de chambre no slight encouragement.

She told me that she was sure the Countess was very fond of me. That she had questioned her (Justine) about my private habits, how I looked when in dishabille.

"You see, Ernest," said the arch girl laughingly, "that she supposes that I know all about it."

Then she told me that the Earl, although not at all an unkind husband, was habitually neglectful, and that, as the girl very shrewdly remarked, ladies considered even worse. That they will bear with a great deal of flirting, infidelity, and other bad conduct on the part of their lovers or husbands, as long as they themselves are not neglected. But that is the one offence not to be forgiven.

I do not mean to say that Justine expressed this sentiment

precisely in these words, but this was the sense of what she said, and very good sense, too.

The upshot of her conversation was that I was to be ready and bold; but not too knowing or forward. To look my best, and to watch for a favourable opportunity which she felt sure my Lady would afford me when she could. Indeed, Justine went on to say that the present occasion would not be at all an unfavourable one, when I could take the opportunity of assuring my mistress of my inviolable secrecy as to the "Miss" Courtney transaction, and my eternal devotion to her service.

"But," said Justine, "I dare say my Lady may feel rather fatigued with the exercises she has taken today—and as for you, sir; it is, or ought to be entirely out of the question!"

I begged to assure Justine that she was never more mistaken in her life, for the taste of love she had just given me only whetted my appetite for a fuller feast, which was perfectly true; for what, with the girl's beauty before me, and the peep which I had had that afternoon into the closed carriage, the warm blood throbbed in my veins so that between reality and imagination I was in a highly efficient state; and all of this I might have given Mademoiselle Justine another and immediate proof of, had not the Countess's bell rung just at this juncture.

Our tête-à-tête was interrupted, Justine exclaiming: "Let me go directly, you dear, naughty fellow—don't you hear my Lady's bell? I promised her to be back in five minutes, and here I've been five and twenty! How you have tumbled my dress, to be sure! Do get along with you! But I must kiss the dear boy first, who has given me such a proof of his vigour!"

Her hand was under my shirt in a moment, and grasping the reanimated object of her desires, she stooped and took it in her mouth for a moment or two, tickling the ruby head with her lascivious tongue as her cherry lips pressed deliciously around it. But just as I felt the crisis coming on, she suddenly rose from her stooping position and, slapping my posteriors with no light hand, exclaimed with a laugh: "Ah, would you, sir? I know what you are going to do!" and bounced out of my room, saying as she closed the door, to be ready for Her Ladyship's commands in half-an-hour.

Reader, what could I do in the excited state in which she left me, but pass my hand two or three times up and down on my bursting affair, till the seed spurted over the floor and satisfied my raging lust for that moment.

(*To be continued.*)

LADY POKINGHAM; OR THEY ALL DO IT:

Giving an Account of her Luxurious Adventures, both before and after her Marriage with Lord Crim-Con.

CHAPTER VI.

After luncheon I ordered Charles to take several shawls and a floor-stool into the summer-house of the garden, as I wished to take a nap, and was sure the open air was more conducive to refreshing sleep than the close atmosphere of a room on a warm sunny day.

Annie and Patty exchanged significant glances as I gave the order, but my uplifted finger stopped any further manifestation of intelligence.

We had a fine large garden at the back of the house, in some parts beautifully shaded by umbrageous elms of a venerable age, especially on the banks of a small circular pond about twenty yards in diameter, where, facing the south, the summer-house stood under the trees by the side of the small lakelet.

I followed Charles as he carried out my orders, and arriving at our destination, ordered him to spread the shawls over a sofa which stood there, for fear the leather might be damp. Then he fetched a pillow, and placed the foot-stool at my feet.

I had nothing on but a loose morning-wrapper, with my chemise and drawers underneath.

"How very oppressive it is," I exclaimed, as I languidly sank back on the couch as soon as he had prepared it, allowing as I did so, a most negligent exposure of my neck and a slight glimpse of the orbs of love beneath.

"Ah! Oh, oh! My goodness; the dreadful cramp!" I almost screamed, as bending down in great apparent pain, I pulled up the robe to rub the calf of my right leg. "Ah, oh! what torture!"

Charles was on his knees at my feet in a moment.

"Oh, my Lady, is it so very bad? Let me bend up your toes!"

"No, no, not there, rub the calf, as hard as you can, Charles, there's a good boy!" I replied, my face wincing under the pain. "Higher, rub along my leg, the foot's no use!"

Somehow the toe of my bad foot touched his trousers just outside the most interesting part of his anatomy; the slipper had fallen off and I could feel his prick quickly harden and throb under my toes, whilst his face flushed all over, and I thought quite a perceptible tremor passed through his frame, as he went on rubbing my leg below the knee, and I need not say how my own lustful temperament was affected by the contact.

My robe had opened down the front so that he had a full view of legs, drawers and bosom, perhaps the wrinkle of love itself.

My blood was in a boil and I could no longer resist the impulse to enjoy such a beautiful Adonis.

"Get up, Charles, it's better now," I said in a low voice, "and pray don't tell what you've seen by accident. That cramp threw me into such an awful agony I did not know how I tossed about!"

"Dear Lady, your secrets are always safe with me," he replied, looking down bashfully as he rose to his feet. "I could kiss the ground under your feet to prove my devotion!"

"No, you are such a kind boy that just for this once, Charles, only this once, mind, I will give you a kiss myself instead. Come closer to me! What a fine boy you are. Now don't be bashful, really I mean to kiss you, if you promise never to tell."

"Ah, Madame, how kind of a great lady to a poor page-boy like me! I shall never forget such a favour and would die for you any time!" he said with bashful excitement.

"Come then," and I took his handsome face between my hands and kissed him repeatedly. "Why don't you kiss me, Charles?"

"Oh, Lady, and may I take that liberty?" he asked, his

warm lips almost sucking the breath from me, so earnest was his kissing.

"Yes, yes," I murmured, "you may kiss me now, dear boy! And would you be faithful, Charles, if I trusted my life, my honour to your keeping?"

"Those kisses have made me your slave forever, dear Lady. Nothing could ever wring a secret of yours from me."

"Then, Charles, I will tell you I'm in love with your figure! I know you must be a perfect Cupid, and should you like to strip quite naked, that I may enjoy the sight of a living statue? Will you do so, no one will ever know?" I asked.

His face was crimson and I could see that he actually trembled under my gaze. "Now Charles, make haste, and if you do that for me I'll give you a sovereign and a new suit of clothes."

Slipping off his jacket I began to unbutton his trousers. Turning them down, my eager hands wandered under his shirt, feeling the firmness of the ivory-like flesh of his deliciously rounded buttocks whilst my eyes did not fail to detect how his linen stood out in front and was saturated with his spendings.

He seemed to understand me now and almost quicker than I can write it, he was naked as Adam in Paradise.

My roving hands took possession of his beautiful little prick, quite six inches long, and ornamented round the tight-looking balls by just a shade of curly brown hair.

"What's this, Charles, are you often wet like this?" as I called his attention to the glistening sperm on my fingers. "What a big fellow this is, quite enough for a man. Did you ever make love with a girl?"

"No, my Lady, but I wanted to try it with Patty, only she never would."

"Then you shall with me, Charles, now. And I'll try to get Patty for you afterwards, I should so like to see you two together," I said, drawing his prick to my lips and sucking it deliciously for a moment or two till I felt he was getting near a second spend.

"Now, sir, kneel down and kiss me," I said, letting him go as I reclined on the sofa and opened my legs whilst his hands opened the slit in my drawers and exposed the lips of my cunt to view. His mouth was glued to it in a moment, and ah! oh! how his lascivious tongue made me spend in a second or two whilst my unslippered foot was rolling his prick on his thigh. But I was afraid of losing the next emission of his love juice, so I gently drew him over my body and directed his dart of love into my cunt.

He was hardly up to his business, but the instinct of nature seemed to prompt him to shove in.

What ecstasy as I felt the slow insertion of his virgin prick! How it seemed to swell inside the luscious sheath which received it lovingly.

At first we lay motionless, billing and cooing with our lips, till I began a slight motion with my buttocks, to which he was not slow to respond.

How I enjoyed that boy! The knowledge that I had a really virgin prick within me added such a piquancy to my enjoyment that I fairly screamed from excess of emotion as I spent and felt his balsam of life shoot into my longing womb.

He had to fuck me three times before I would let him dress and go about his business. He had been with me over two hours, but the time was well spent in making love and worming out of him all about himself and the other page who slept with him, Sam, who although good-looking had so much Indian blood in him that his complexion was almost black.

In answer to my questions Charlie informed me that they often played with each other, and rubbed their cocks together till the thick white stuff squirted out, and he added: "Dear Lady, would you believe it, his affair is two inches longer than mine; besides, it is the blackest part about him!"

"Do you think he would like a game with us?" I asked.

"Oh, certainly. He is just the fellow! It was he who taught me all I know, and I must tell you what he told me, that his last master, Colonel Culo, who had brought him over from Calcutta, had him sleep in his cabin all the way home and seduced him by handling and sucking his prick, which was so nice that at last Sam let the Colonel fuck him in the bottom-hole. The Colonel wasn't very big, you know, and easily got into him by using a little pomade. Then, when Sam left him because the Colonel was afraid he might get about his daughters if he kept him in his service, he was presented with a present of fifty pounds. He often wants me to let him get into my bottom as he said it felt very nice, but I never would go further than playing with cocks."

"Well then, this very night, about an hour after all the rest are in bed, bring him with you to the girls' door. You will find it ajar and mind only to come in your shirts and be sure not to disturb the cook and housekeeper."

With these orders I kissed and let him go, then went in to dress for dinner.

Just before we went to bed I treated Cookie and the housekeeper to a good glass of port in which I put a rather stiff narcotic to make them sleep well so that in case our revels with the two pages should prove noisy they would be too sound asleep to hear anything of it.

Patty and Annie were all nervous excitement and expectation after I told them of my arrangement. We were all naked and they hot as possible, and could not resist pressing their naked bodies against me, while with tears and blushes they expressed their fears of the pain of losing their troublesome virginities.

At last I heard a slight noise in their bedroom which so startled them that they flew to go and hide themselves underneath the bed, whilst I opened the door and entering their room, which was in darkness, found my two young men in the dark hesitating to tap at the door.

"Slip off your shirts and slippers," I whispered in a low voice. "Feel, I am quite naked myself, all is to be free between us now," as my hands groped for their pricks. I found them to be as stiff as possible, and could not resist pressing their naked bodies against my own belly, where the contact of their throbbing pricks had such an effect on me that selecting Sam by the size of his affair, I backed towards the girls' bed and drew him upon me. What a luscious bit it was! So large that my cunt was fairly gorged with the delicious morsel, which spent almost before it was well into me. My arms held him firmly round the waist as my body rested against the edge of the bed so that without withdrawing he had to go on with the delicious fuck, and I begged Charlie to put his prick into Sam's behind, to make him do his work well with me. The latter was nothing loath, and although the want of lubricant was rather an obstacle, Charlie soon succeded in spite of his wincing and flinching a little.

The effect was to give my cavalier quite double energy. My hands passed behind him and played with Charlie's prick and appendages as he fucked Sam's bottom delightedly.

This was another virgin prick I was enjoying. Fancy taking the maidenheads of two handsome youths in one day. It fired me with the most lustful sensations! How my cunt throbbed on his glorious black prick. How we spent in torrents of that elixir of love which makes us die in ecstasy at each fresh emission. What heavenly joys to spend together, as we did, three times without withdrawing. I knew such excesses were only tending to shorten my life, but reason is powerless to resist the attraction of such Cytherian joys.

At last it was finished and we entered my room where the lights of a dozen candles showed everything to the best advantage. The figures of the two youths reflected in the looking-glasses round the room seemed to fill my apartment with lusty young fellows, half dark and half fair, all with limp and glistening pricks, just as they had withdrawn from the combat of love.

"Listen, my dears, cannot you hear the heavy breathing of the two girls under my bed? I'll wager they've been frigging each other whilst we had that glorious fuck in the other room!" I exclaimed. "But let us first refresh our affairs with a cold douche and have a glass of champagne! Then see if we won't drag them out in the light, my boys!"

We laved ourselves, and a couple of glasses apiece immensely revived our flagging energies. I had a nice little dog-whip with a long lash on it. So telling the boys to lift up the curtains of the bed, I slashed under on the surprised and timid beauties so effectually that I had only time to give about a half-dozen cuts before they sprang from their concealment and ran screaming round the room as I followed and plied my whip smartly over their tender bottoms. The sight of the thin weals which every cut drew on their tender skin, the shrieks of pain and the blushing effects on both faces and bums, so excited us that the boys' pricks stood again immediately and I longed to see the two pages ravish them as roughly as possible. Yes, I confess, that at that moment I felt awfully cruel and should have liked to see them suffer the most dreadful agonies under their defloration.

I know that with many men their delight is intensified if they can only inflict pain on the victims they ravish, but for a woman to gloat over such a sight is almost incomprehensible. Yet it is so, I was literally mad with lust of blood and torture!

At last I made them kneel down and kiss the boys' pricks as they begged of them to take their maidenheads.

Charlie had Patty and Sam had Annie. I ordered them to lay the girls on the soft Turkey carpet in the middle of the room with pillows under their buttocks. Then my two young champions, kneeling between their legs, opened the lips of the girls' spending cunts and proceeded to insert the heads of their pegos within the vermilion clefts of the victims.

It was a most delightful sight for me as I witnessed the blushes and enjoyed every painful contortion of their faces as the pricks were ruthlessly shoved into them under the influence of my whip, which I used without pity to push the boys on to victory. At last it was done and I could see that the boys had spent into them and I was sorry it was so soon over.

The tears of the girls were changed to loving smiles as by my directions they all had another wash. Then we sat down to jellies and wine, indulging in all manner of freedoms and jokes, till my young men began to feel their feet again and I could see that both of them were enjoying and eyeing me most amorously.

My blood was up and nothing would do but I must enjoy them both at once with the girls joining in the best way they could.

Sam and Charles sat on either side of me, and I could feel both pricks ready for action. So I made the former sit on the edge of the bed and take me on his lap, and as soon as I felt properly sitted on the fine black prick, I called Charlie to shove his cock into me from behind, along with Sam's. This was not quite so easy to do, as Sam quite filled my sheath. Yet I was determined to have it so, and with the assistance of the girls, Charles succeeded in accomplishing my erotic fancy. Then by my orders, Annie and Patty tickled my clitoris and the lips of my distended cunt, as well as the cocks and balls of my two lovers.

(*To be continued.*)

————————

THE PEARL,

A Journal of Facetiæ and Voluptuous Reading.

No. 15   PUBLISHED MONTHLY.   Sept. 1880

LA ROSE D'AMOUR;

Or the Adventures of a Gentleman in search of Pleasure.
Translated from the French.

CHAPTER VII.
(Continued.)

I felt considerably enervated for a day or two and refrained from again entering the lists of Venus until I had fairly set sail on my projected cruise in search of love and beauty in the Hesperian climes, where I hoped for the most exquisite pleasures in the arms of the ardent ladies of Cuba and Spanish Main.

I coasted round and put into Bordeaux for the purpose of giving the sailors a chance of getting themselves girls.

In two days they were all mated, and we put off for Havana, intending to stop there a short time, as I had heard much of the beauty of the women of the island.

Arriving at Havana, I took some rooms at one of the best hotels, giving orders to the Captain to keep the brig in sailing order so as to be able to sail at a moment's notice.

At the *table d'hôte* I noticed a handsome, vivacious brunette, evidently an inhabitant of the island. Her eyes were fairly hidden under a mass of deep black hair which overshadowed them; but I could perceive whilst at the table, she was continually glancing at me, and the moment my eyes met hers she would suddenly drop her eyes on the plate or look in another direction. From this I augured favourably and deemed success certain, thinking that I had made a conquest.

In the evening I attended the theatre accompanied by the Captain, and both of us well armed. I there saw the lady in a box in company with a couple of elderly gentlemen.

The one whom I took to be her husband was a cross-grained, ugly looking fellow.

I followed her home with the intent to win her.

In the morning I got an introduction to Señor Don Manuel Vasquer, the husband of Donna Isabel, my lovely vis-à-vis at the table.

I told him I was a gentleman of rank and fortune, traveling for the pleasure with a vessel of my own, and invited him down to the harbour to look at the brig.

He accepted the invitation and was very much pleased with the neat cleanliness of everything on deck, and with the luxury displayed in the fittings of the cabin.

I had a lunch set out and plied him well with champagne so that when he left the vessel, he was in very high spirits. On reaching the hotel he invited me up to his apartment and introduced me to his wife and a couple of other ladies we found with her.

I endeavoured as well as my looks could express to let her see that I had taken particular notice of her, and was much smitten by her charms.

After conversing for a short time I retired to my room to dress for dinner and penned a declaration to the Donna Isabel, declaring my passion for her and imploring her to grant me an interview, as I had read in her eyes that I was not disagreeable to her.

After dinner I joined her and her husband and slipped my note into her hand, which she immediately hid in the folds of her dress. I then went to my room to wait for an answer, which I felt sure would soon be sent to me. Nor had I to wait long, for in a couple of hours a negro-wench opened the door, poking her head in to ascertain if I was in the room, threw a note to me, and shutting the door without saying a word, retired.

I hastily picked up the note and opening it found my expectations confirmed!

She granted me an interview. Her note stated that her husband would go out to his plantations the next day and that at three o'clock in the afternoon she would be alone taking her siesta.

The evening, night and morning hung heavily on me, and after dining, I retired to my room, laid my watch on the table and sat gazing at the dial to see the weary hours pass away; but as the minute-hand pointed to three; the same black wench again opened the door, poked her head in, looked round and drew back, leaving the door open.

I jumped up and followed her to the rooms of her mistress.

Here I found Donna Isabel reclining in an elegant dishabille, on a sofa. She held out her hand to me in welcome, which I took and pressed to my lips.

She invited me to be seated and I placed myself on a footstool at her side. Taking her hand between mine, I disclosed my passion for her, imploring her not to refuse my love. At first she pretended to be much surprised that I should make a declaration of my love to her and appeared half angry. But as I proceeded with my tale of love and pressed her for an answer favourable to the passion which was consuming me, she appeared to relent, and rising from her reclining position made room for me to sit beside her on the couch.

As I sat down by her side I dropped an arm round her waist and drawing her to my bosom I implored her to grant me her love—even to leave her husband and fly with me to some remote corner of the earth where we could while away our years in the soft dalliance of love.

I told her that her husband was an old man with whom she could not enjoy life, and from whom a young woman like herself could not receive those tender attentions, and the soft and real pleasure which she could enjoy in the arms of a young and devoted lover.

She sighed and hung her head on her breast, saying she never knew what it was to receive those delicious and tender pleasures from her husband that I had just spoken of. That from the time of her marriage to the present moment, her whole time was taken up with drinking and gambling. That he left her to amuse herself as best she could in the house, for he was so jealous that he would never allow her to go out except in his company. She sighed again and wished that heaven had given her such a man as myself.

I know not how it was, but when she stopped, I found one of my hands had opened the front of her dress and slipped beneath her shift and was moulding one of her large hard breasts, and my lips were pressed on hers.

My leaning against her had insensibly moved her backwards till, without our knowing it, her head was resting on the cushion of the sofa and I was lying on top of her.

Whilst I was assuring her of eternal love and constancy
and begging her to allow me to give her a convincing proof
of my tenderness and affection, and also to let me convince
her that as yet she had had the mere shadow of the ecstatic
pleasure of love, but that if she would allow me I would give
her the real substance and a surfeit of those pleasures of
which I felt convinced she had received but a taste from her
husband, I had been gradually drawing up her clothes, till my
hand rested on a large, firm, fleshy thigh. Isabel had closed
her eyes, her head hanging to one side, her lips slightly apart
and her breast rising and falling rapidly from the quick pulsations of the blood caused by her fierce and amorous desires.

I raised her shift still higher till it disclosed to my sight a
large tuft of long black hair. I then unbuttoned my pantaloons and with a little gentle force parted her legs, and got
between her thighs.

Parting the lips with my fingers, I inserted the head of my
engine of love, and in a few moments we both died away
amidst the most exquisite transports of love.

I lay heaving and panting on her bosom while she lay
motionless under me, till finding that my stiffness had scarcely
diminished and knowing by the short motions and jerks of
the head that he was once more ready for the field and impatient for the word to start again, I commenced moving
in her.

"Beautiful creature," I cried, "what delicious sensations!
What pleasure! My God!" said I, "you are almost virgin.
How lusciously tight your sweet flesh clasps my rod!"

Her arms were clasped around my neck, her thighs around
my back, her moist rosy lips glued to mine. Our tongues met.
With what vivacity, what voluptuousness she moves up to me,
giving me energetic heaves for my thrusts. I felt from the increased motion of her bottom that again she is about to dissolve herself into bliss. I too feel it.

"Ah, my God! Oh! what pleasure! I come; there, there,
dear love, you have it now—joy, love, bliss unbearable!" And
I was swimming in a sea of pleasure, in a perfect agony of
bliss.

When we recovered from our delirium, I arose and drawing her clothes down slowly over her legs, I pressed her to
my side. Planting a soft kiss on her pouting lips I folded her
in my arms and asked her how she liked the reality after be-

ing fed for more than a year on the mere shadow of that delicious substance she had just largely partaken.

The answer was a kiss that sent a thrill of pleasure through every vein.

"Oh, my dear, this is nothing to what you would enjoy were you to link your fortune to mine and fly with me to France. Then we would live a life of love and pleasure such as you have just tasted. Our whole lives would be nothing but love and pleasure, morn, noon and night it would be love, all love. There should be nothing around us but love—nothing but pleasure!"

Isabel rang a small bell and the same piece of ebony who had twice placed her head in and out of my chamber-door entered.

Her mistress told her to bring in some lunch and she soon returned with an elegant cold repast and some delicious wine.

After eating and drinking we again turned our attention to love. Rising from the chair I led her to the sofa, and drawing her on my knees, I stripped her dress and shift from her shoulder and loosening the strings of her petticoats toyed and played with her breasts, which were really beautiful, large and firm, and tipped with two most tempting strawberry nipples.

Nor was my companion idle, for whilst I was thus engaged she had unbuttoned my pantaloons and taken out my genitals, which she admired and toyed with, capping and uncapping its red head till she had brought it to a most beautiful state of erection.

I raised her on her feet and all her clothing slipping on to the floor, she stood in all her naked beauty before me.

What charms, what beauties did my eyes and lips feast on as I turned her round and round. Her soft round belly, her plump bottom and then her dear little cleft, that masterpiece of beauty, how I hugged it to me. What kisses I lavished on it, all of which she repaid with interest.

She sinks down on the floor between my legs. She caresses my pego, she presses it to her lips. They pout and she puts its large red head between them. I push a little forward, it enters her mouth, she sucks it, her soft tongue rolls it over and over. She continues tickling it with her tongue. Feeling that if she continues I must spend, I jerk back and drag it from her mouth. She again wants to keep it. I lay her down on the floor with the cushions under her buttocks. I get on her with my head between her thighs, my prick and stones hanging over her face. Again she takes it in her mouth, while I put my tongue between the lips of her cunt and frig her clitoris with it.

The motion of her rump increases! I find she is about to spend and I suddenly rise up, seat myself on the sofa, and she sprang after me, jumped on the sofa, her cunt touching my face, tightly clasping her arms round my neck.

She slowly let her bottom come down, till it touched the head of my pego. I directed it aright and she impaled herself on it.

A few motions and I most plentifully bedewed her with the nectar as she was paying down her own tribute to the God of Love.

When she rose off me, the sperm dropped from her salacious slit in large gouts upon me, attesting the bountiful measure with which nature had endowed both of us with the elixir of life.

In the evening she sent her black to order her supper to be sent up into her rooms, and after quietly supping we retired to bed and I spent the most agreeable night that I ever passed with any woman.

Her husband returned the next day, but I found an opportunity to meet his wife in the evening and renewed for a short time the transport we had enjoyed the day before.

A few days later, her husband had invited a party of six young ladies and the same number of young men to visit his wife and take dinner with them. I also was invited.

Immediately after receiving the invitation I sent word to the Captain to raise steam and be ready to sail at a moment's warning.

I joined the party at dinner and found three of the invited girls to be very handsome and the other three very good-looking.

After the dinner was over, I invited the party to visit my yacht and take an evening's excursion with me.

The husband of my mistress was very loud in his praises of the beauty of the yacht and of the rich and elegant manner in which she was fitted up and joined his solicitations to mine; the party consenting, we ordered carriages and drove down to where the yacht lay. Getting abroad we sailed up the harbour and ran up the island.

After we were out of sight of the city, I took the Captain aside and told him that towards night I wanted him to run the brig in towards the shore; and that I intended to seize the seven men and land them in a boat and make off with the women. I told him to go and speak to the crew about the matter and have them in readiness to obey my signal.

A little before dusk, we ran close in shore at a place where there was no plantation visible. I had ordered some lumber to be strewn about the greater deck and commanded the Captain to send the sailors to carry it away.

Sixteen stalwart fellows came aft and suddenly seized on the men and bound their arms and legs. I then told them what I intended to do, ordering the men at the same time to take the women below. Their execrations and implorings for the girls who were their relatives, I would not listen to, but I had them put in a boat and sent ashore. They were unbound and let loose. The boat returned to the brig and we set sail for France.

The girls did nothing but sob and weep for a day or two but I soon brought them to their senses. Immediately after setting their companions ashore I went into the cabin, and bringing Ibzaidu and Mary out of their hiding places, I introduced them to the company.

When supper was served they all refused to sit at the table and eat. But I told them if they did not comply with all my wishes that I would hand them over to the sailors to be used by them as they chose. This had its effect on them and they seated themselves at the table.

I rang a bell and two of the handsomest women belonging to the sailors entered stark naked, as I had ordered them to wait on the table.

The Spanish girls were all about to rise up, but putting on a fierce aspect, I threatened them the first who should rise would be passed forward to the men. This had effect on them and they sat still.

Whilst the servant was pouring out the coffee I arose and went to the side-table as if to fetch something, but in reality to pour a few drops of a certain liquid into each cup of coffee.

The quantity put in each cup was enough to set any woman's amorous and licentious desires on fire.

They all drank their coffee and in about half-an-hour the effect was very visible, as all the coyness of modesty had disappeared and they languishingly cast their lascivious glances at me, joking the servant-girls on their nudity, and whenever they came in reach of them, pinching, slapping them, etc., so great was the effect produced by the drug I put in the coffee.

When the supper was over and the tables were cleared, I commenced playing and tussling with them. Rolling them about on the floor and playing them a thousand amorous tricks which they repaid with interest—throwing me on the floor, falling in a heap on top of me while I would catch a kiss from them, squeeze a fine bubby, slide my hand along a thigh, or slip it up under their petticoats and grasp a large calf or a well-turned knee. I ordered in some wine of a very strong quality, well drugged with the love-potion.

I plied them with the wine of which they drank very freely and in a couple of hours all reserve and modesty had left them.

I took the Señora—the wife I had seduced at the hotel and whose husband I had set ashore with the others—on one side and invited her to step into one of the staterooms with me, I then asked her if she could forgive me for robbing her from her old cuckold of a husband. She threw herself into my arms and with a fervent embrace and kiss sealed my pardon with her lips.

(To be continued.)

It has without doubt been Truscott's ambition
To get the new Temple Bar in position.
He thought of it by day, dreamt of it by night,
And one morning woke in a terrible fright.
"I dreamt, my dear love, that this thing came to pass,
That the public had shoved Temple Bar up my arse;
That they greeted me loudly with hisses and calls
And the dragon grew lively and bit off my balls."

AN UNFORTUNATE FAMILY.

Miss Jones, whose father was a wealthy alderman, and thought nobody but a rich city man was good enough for his daughter, took the precaution to allow young Brown to get her in the family way.

When the youngster was about three months on the road she one morning appealed to her papa to sanction their engagement and she asked for a speedy marriage:

"Egad! Do you think I'll ever have that penniless puppy?"

"Oh, oh, Papa! But the puppy's had me and there's a baby coming!" sobbed Miss Jones, covering her crimson face with her hands.

"Well, I'm buggered!" exclaimed the alderman.

"Father! Father! Don't say that; we're such an unfortunate family!"

HOAR FROST.

A Yankee travelling on the London and North Eastern Railway the other day, had for his vis-à-vis a gentleman who had lost his nose. The disfigured countenance so fascinated his gaze that at last his fellow-passenger, getting impatient at what he considered an impertinence, exclaimed in a rage: "Really, sir, you are very rude and insulting to look at me so! Did you ever see a person before who had had the misfortune to have his nose frost-bitten?"

The Yankee apologized for his seeming want of manners, and re-assured the annoyed person by informing him that he was going to alight at the next station. However, after leaving the train he continued to walk up and down the station-platform in seeming thought, till just as the train was on the move, his curiosity again came over him and thrusting his head through the carriage window with a meaning grin on his face, he said: "I guess, stranger, that must have been a darn sharp Hoar Frost!"

Lord E. T——e, when a youth, asked his mother the following question: "Mama dear," said he, "what is the meaning of the word bugger?"

"Bugger, my child? Why do you ask?"

"Because I heard my tutor call the coachman a damned bugger."

"Well, my child," replied the Marchioness, "a bugger is a person who does his fellow an injury behind his back." —Cough.

MY GRANDMOTHER'S TALE; or MAY'S ACCOUNT OF HER INTRODUCTION TO THE ART OF LOVE.

From an Unsophisticated Manuscript Found Amongst the Old Lady's Papers after her Death, Supposed to have been Written about A.D. 1797.

CHAPTER IV.
KATE'S NARRATIVE CONTINUED; THE VOYAGE; CAPTAIN LEMBERG AND HIS NIECE HILDA

I need not tell you that after all reserve was laid aside amongst us we certainly enjoyed ourselves amazingly.

Carle and the Captain seemed to delight in fucking us turn and turn about, but everything was done openly and by general consent.

The books and pictures were freely used and we tried to act the scenes depicted or described.

The Captain would lay Hilda on her back across the table. Then, placing me over her so that her face was between my thighs while my feet rested on the floor, he would produce his prick, and Hilda looking up, would pop it into her cunt and hold it while he fucked.

Carle would be at the other side of the table between Hilda's uplifted thighs, while I, stooping forward, would take his prick and stick it into her open cunt and then handle his bottom and balls. The Captain leaning over my back would watch the operation with great interest, and, waiting until Carle's prick was all absorbed within the hairy lips, would cry:

"Now, old fellow, let us make a fair start! Draw out first, and when I say one, push."

"ONE."—The two bottoms heaved, driving the two pricks deep into the recesses of our cunts.

"TWO."—Another energetic shove, making our breasts and bellies rub together.

"THREE."—A vehement push; the Captain's belly smacked against my bottom, and Carle's balls banged against Hilda's rump.

"FOUR."—The two excited pricks rushed with delicious force into our throbbing cunts, making us bound to meet them.

"FIVE."—We felt the pricks rammed home, they seemed to reach our very hearts.

"SIX."—A flood of boiling seed burst into our cunts and filled our reservoirs so that they overflowed and the hot sperm poured out, saturating pricks, ballocks, and cunts in love's sweet juice.

The next time that Hilda and I were alone she pointed to some whipping scenes among the pictures and suggested that we should make a trial of the boasted efficacy of the birch rod in producing emotion.

"But where shall we get a rod on board ship?" I asked.

She at once replied: "Oh, I know where there is a broom without a handle. I can easily abstract some of the twigs and tie up a rod with enough for our purpose."

So, that evening, when I was in my nightdress, Hilda came into my cabin and showed me a rod which she had prepared and neatly tied with ribbon.

I was a little frightened at the sight of it and said:

"Won't it hurt?"

"Oh, it may a little at first, but when one begins to get the feel, the pain will be turned into pleasure. However, begin with me, I am not afraid."

She then placed herself on the sofa with her naked bottom up, and making me tuck up my shift, she put her arm round my hip and told me to whip away.

I touched up her beautiful white posteriors while she played with my cunt.

"You may hit harder than that, Kate," she said, wriggling her bottom about.

I began to enter into the sport and struck her so smartly

that the cheeks of her bottom assumed a rosy hue like two blooming apples.

"Oh," she cried, as she rolled over, "my cunt is on fire—put your finger into it, Kate. How I would enjoy being fucked now. How I wish Carle was here."

"Well, you have your wish," he said, as he stepped in quite naked and holding in his hand his fine red-headed prick in stiff erection.

He seized her round the waist and making her stoop forward he plunged his prick into her cunt from behind.

"Stay a moment, Carle," she said. "Kate is to get her whipping now, and lest you should cover it with your hands let me tie them here."

And without asking my leave she secured my wrists and tied them firmly to the legs of the sofa, and then to keep my legs apart, she tied my ankles, too. I did not quite like my position but as I was helpless I only said:

"Remember, you must stop when I tell you."

Then she leaned forward and Carle introduced his prick into her cunt from behind.

They both laughed while she played away at my poor innocent bum. At first I tried to bear it as patiently as I could; but Carle became more energetic in his strokes, and she imported more force to her blows. At last I said: "I say—Hilda—stop! Hilda, you wretch, what do you mean? You cruel girl let me up, you are torturing me!"

My whole bottom felt in a flame. I made frantic efforts to release my hands and I began to sob. Just then she fell forward, and Carle pressing against her bottom discharged into her cunt. Then, coming to me, she untied my hands and laying her cheek against mine, said: "Forgive me, dearest Kate, I was so excited. I am just burning!"

"Oh, Hilda, you cruel girl, how could you? Oh, I am so hot; I am just burning!"

"Where are you so hot, darling Kate?"

And I felt a hand slip up between my thighs and press the lips of my cunt. Looking up I saw the Captain's good-humoured cheery face.

"Never mind, Kate, we will punish her for this. Let me give you what relief I can."

Then, gently separating my thighs he pushed in his prick while Hilda kissed away my tears. The soft head of his prick had a most soothing effect on the terribly excited folds of my cunt and as it gradually passed up I forgot the pain of the whipping in the intensely amorous excitement I now experienced. I never felt anything more delicious than the sweet friction of the Captain's cock in my fevered cunt; it made every nerve thrill again with pleasure.

"Does not that repay you?" Hilda whispered.

"Oh, yes," I replied. "Push it in; drive it home, fuck me—fuck me. Oh, fuck—fuck—fuck!"

The Captain now declared that Hilda ought to be well whipped for her cruel treatment of my poor bottom.

"Very well," said Carle, "but as I am the real offender I will bear it in her place."

So putting the rod into my hand he leaned over the berth and stuck out his great fleshy rump, while Hilda sat below him, holding his prick and sucking it in her mouth.

"Now, Kate," said the Captain, "lay it on strongly; don't spare his impudent backside, hit him, hit him hard! Don't mind, he used to be flogged every day at school!"

I whipped away and soon his bottom began to glow, his balls were tightened up and his prick swelled and stiffened. He heaved gently so as to work it in and out of her mouth and then with a tremendous "Oh!" he spurted his seed down her throat.

Now, sweet May, that must do for the present. Good night, my love, good night.

Chapter V.
Kate's Narrative Concluded.

Before I resume Kate's narrative I must tell something that happened to myself the following night.

Kate was later than usual in coming and when she did I was in bed, my lamp out and the room quite dark. When she got into bed she put her hand on my cunt, and asked if I had ever any longing for a prick now. I told her I had but that I was waiting for my lover to come and then I should have plenty of fucking.

"But would not any other prick do you as well as his," she asked, all the while frigging my cunt until she had it in a glow.

"Well, Kate, you have so excited my cunt with your finger that I could enjoy being fucked by most any prick."

"Well dear, your finger has done the same for me. Let us try to relieve each other and as the night is hot let us get outside the clothes. Come, lie over me."

And placing herself on the edge of the bed with her feet on the floor, she put me astride over her, my breast and belly resting on hers, and my bottom turned out. Then she threw her arms around me and thrusting her tongue in my mouth held me firm. I felt something touch my bottom and then a soft round stiff thing poked against my cunt. I spluttered out: "Let me up, Kate, I am sure there is someone behind us."

"Nonsense," said Kate, "it is only your own overheated imaginative mind."

"I tell you it is no imagination. Oh!—it is pushing in—let me up—there is someone fucking me. Oh, Kate, I feel his prick, my cunt is filled with it, do let me up."

But she held me tighter than ever.

"Don't be foolish, keep your bottom quiet. It is only my finger."

"No, it is a prick, I feel its head—in—ever so far. Oh!"

"What is it doing?"

"It is fucking, fucking, fucking, fucking. Oh, there the feeling comes, how delicious!" And I lay motionless on her bosom. Then the prick was suddenly drawn out and must have been thrust into her for I felt a belly with hair on it rubbing against my bottom as the prick was worked in and out.

Then a pair of strong arms clasped us both together and after holding us for a moment, quickly withdrew.

After we had returned to our usual places in the bed I asked: "Who was it, Kate?"

"Oh, never mind, let me go on with my story."

"Both the Captain and the mate had good voices and they sometimes sang for us when taking their grog in the evening.

"Our custom was to sit reclining on the broad stern locker which was well covered with cushions. Carle was generally between Hilda and me, and with a hand on each of our cunts. I would be occupied petting his prick and balls while she would be similarly engaged with the Captain. The latter while sipping his grog would strike up one of his favourite ditties in a bold rollicking tone, and Carle would quickly follow suit. After which there would be a general fuck such as I have already described.

"I only remember two of their songs, which I will repeat for you as specimens if you like."

"Do please, I would like to hear them."

THE CAPTAIN'S SONG.

I care not what squeamish lovers may say,
 The maiden that best suits my mind
Is the sweet girl that will meet me half way;
 And while she is free, be as kind.
With her rich beauties I never am cloyed,
 Fresh pleasures I find at her side;
I don't love her less because she's enjoyed
 By many another beside.

Shall I try to describe all her merit,
 I feel that I'd never have done;
She is brimful of sweetness and spirit,
 And sparkles with freedom and fun.
It is bliss then to hold her and win her,
 She never proves peevish or coy;
But the farther and deeper I'm in her,
 The fuller she fills me with joy.

She opens her thighs without fear or dread,
 She points to her sweet little crack,
Its lips are so red, and all overspread
 With hair of the glossiest black.
Reclined on her breast, and clasped in her arms,
 With her my soft moments I spend;
And revel the more in her melting charms,
 Because they are shared with a friend.

THE MATE'S SONG.

My Jamie is a lover gay,
   He is so very funny.
When last we met to sport and play,
   He took me by the cunny.
Then drawing out his sturdy prick,
   Right in my hand he placed it,
And said 'twould be a jolly trick,
   If in my mouth I'd taste it.

I kissed its bright and rosy head,
   And then began to suck it;
He felt about my cunt, and said,
   He wanted now to fuck it.
Down on the bed he laid me,
With bursting balls, and prick's round head,
   Love's sweetest debt he paid me.

Let maidens of a tim'rous mind
   Refuse what most they're wanting;
Since we for fucking were designed,
   We surely should be granting.
So when your lover feels your cunt,
   Do not be coy, nor grieve him;
But spread your thighs and heave your front,
   For fucking is like heaven.

When Kate had repeated these songs she asked me what
I thought of them.

I told her they were excellent, especially the mate's, and
that I certainly should learn that one and sing it to Mr.
Trevor. Kate then continued her narrative:

I ought to tell you that during our voyage my maid Nina
had not been idle. She attended me every morning to assist
in giving me a sponge-bath and in dressing me. She amused
me by the recital of her adventures with the sailors who
coaxed her to come to them at night in their hammocks. She
said fucking in that position was quite new.

She had an adventure which I must repeat to you. Our
passengers were a sailor, Jim Murphy, sent home on sick-leave,
his wife and her sister Jenny, a buxom damsel about twenty.

Now, Mrs. Murphy kept a sharp look-out on Jenny, with whom the boatswain soon fell in love, and he tried to find opportunities of being alone with her to press his suit, or in plain language, to get a fuck out of her.

Mrs. Murphy had at times to be in her husband's cabin to give him medicine or attend to his wants, so she told Nina in her absence never to leave Jenny alone with the boatswain.

Nina faithfully promised and kept her word in the following manner.

One evening Mrs. Murphy was sent for to attend to her husband and the moment she was out of sight the boatswain came and sat down by the side of Jenny and Nina and asked Jenny to sew a button on his shirt.

"Yes," said Jenny.

"Then come to my cabin and I will give it to you."

Nina said: "Yes, Jenny, we will both go."

So all three went into the boatswain's little cabin and Nina said: "Now if you want to show Jenny your prick Mr. Boatswain, now's your chance, and I will unbutton your breeches for you." And suiting the action to the word she did so, and released his noble pego from prison. His swelling head stood proudly erect, and Nina, taking hold of it, said: "Look, Miss Jenny, here's a noble plaything for you to put in your cunt."

Jenny blushed scarlet all over neck and face, and said: "Oh, for shame, Nina, to talk about such names!"

BOATSWAIN.—"Well said, Nina! You know a thing or two and pretty Jenny here will soon know how pleasant it is to make love. Come sit on my knee, darling, and give me a kiss before your mother comes back. You know, I want to make you my wife if you will marry me as soon as we get ashore. And then I have a nice little house of my own we can live in. Give me a kiss and sit on my knee, there's a darling."

Jenny did both and the boatswain made her grasp his prick with one of her hands while one of his own quickly slipped under her dress and touched her knee. Jenny called out, "Don't, don't," but the hand goes further up until the bower of bliss is reached and one finger gently intrudes and tickles her slit.

"Say yes, darling Jenny, and I swear to marry you and to give you a silk dress and a home of your own. For I am very sure your mother is cross to you."

JENNY.—"Yes, that is true, she is cross, but I'm afraid."

NINA.—"Now Jenny don't be a fool! Do you expect to get a better husband than the boatswain who earns more than a pound a week? You do all he asks and I will be a witness for fair play! You will find it most delicious to have his sugar-stick stirring you up—you will like it so much that you will ask for it afterwards."

"But will you be certain to marry me, Mr. Boatswain?"

"Yes, by the Holy Virgin, I will, as soon as ever we get on shore and can find a priest to marry us."

"I should like a house of my own and to live away from mother, for she is very cross at all times."

"Then that is all settled, darling Jenny! I consider you my wife; and now I will teach you a wife's duty. Lay down on my bed here, dear Jenny, I suppose you know a wife and husband occupy one bed?"

JENNY.—"Yes."

BOATSWAIN.—"Now, Nina, keep watch at the door. There now, my prick is getting into Jenny's cunt. Oh, it's heavenly! Why, Jenny, what is the meaning of this? Where's your maidenhead?"

"Oh, the priest took that when I had my first communion. Mother knows all about that."

"Well, I'm going to have a good fuck now."

And Nina said it was half-an-hour before he left off and she saw Mrs. Murphy coming. I went into the boatswain's cabin and Mrs. Murphy followed me and saw him fucking her daughter.

"Oh, you villain, you dirty blackguard!" she exclaimed: "you have ruined my daughter, my precious Jenny! Stop your fucking this minute," trying to pull him off and turning to me: "As to you, you promised to keep a close watch over Jenny, you wretch!" And she gave Jenny a look and Nina a blow on the shoulder with her fist that stretched her on the floor.

(To be continued.)

FLUNKEYANIA; OR BELGRAVIAN MORALS.

By Charles.

Chapter III.

It may seem an extraordinary circumstance to some of my readers, and did not at first seem natural to me, that a spoony girl, such as Justine, should not only have not felt jealous at the prospect of a liaison between her mistress and myself, but should even do her best to foster and encourage it. But moments of reflection will, I think, serve to dispel partially, if not entirely, the idea of there being anything peculiarly uncommon about the matter.

In the first place, Justine regarded the Countess of Pomeroy as quite a superior being, so far above her as to render anything like rivalry out of the question. Moreover, in a certain way, she perfectly adored her and regarded everything Her Ladyship did as right.

Then again, the shrewd girl had sense enough to know that neither she nor I had any money to speak about, and that if we left the Countess under Her Ladyship's displeasure, we were neither likely to get any other situations. Whereas, if we were serviceable to my Lady, especially in the way of amours or secret fancies, our devotion and faithful attachment would very likely be rewarded in our ultimate marriage and an establishment in the shape of a good shop or perchance a fine boarding-house where we hoped not only to reap substantial profits but get an occasional cut in with our superiors, as we ministered to their lecherous appetites by favouring assignations for amorous dalliance.

These ideas floated through my brain as I dressed myself with more than usual care to attend upon my Lady. Adding, however, to my reflections a pretty strong conjecture that if my dear little soubrette were to catch me visiting anybody else but her Lady with such ideas in my head—say Sophie, the pretty chambermaid for instance, the young woman's cheeks and my hair and even a more sensitive part would most likely come to grief.

These meditations brought me to the door of my Lady's dressing-room where Justine admitted me, and I found my noble mistress lying on her sofa, attired in a most graceful dishabille, dressed in a morning-robe of light blue silk so negligently open at the front that I could see the orbs of love, whilst one beautiful leg, hanging carelessly over the side of the sofa, as she reached sideways, displayed to my gaze a ravishing calf, ankle, and tiny foot encased in pink silk stockings and Turkish slippers, for she did not intend to appear at the dinner-table that day.

She looked rather pale and languid but my entrance caused a slight perceptible flush to pass over her beautiful features and I also perceived an increase of palpitation on the part of those ivory bosoms as she seemed to draw a long breath before addressing me. She began by saying:

"Justine has told me, Ernest, that you have promised to be true and faithful and to keep secret my clandestine interview with Miss Courtney today; I have a particular wish that it should not be known." Here she slightly coloured again. Then she continued:

"May I depend on you faithfully?"

With this she extended her white hand to me which I kissed with as much devotion as if it had been a Queen's, indeed I should say with a great deal more. This did not seem to cause her any displeasure, for she remarked that it seemed on my part an act of homage, devoting my service.

To this I replied that if kissing her feet could better express my devotion I should be happy to do so.

As she smiled at this and did not object, I took silence for consent and proceeded to kiss her lovely foot and ankle and, well—perhaps a little higher. At any rate, my lady readers must form their own opinion from the Countess's saying to me, half laughingly:

"I perceive, Master Ernest, you are one of those greedy people who, when given an inch, must take it all."

"My Lady, I would rather give you all than take an inch," I exclaimed, to which she replied:

"If this kind of thing goes on you must submit to have your eyes bandaged! Justine, bandage his eyes with your handkerchief!"

Now, the truth of the matter is I was grossly infringing on my tacitly permitted privilege of foot-kissing, having slightly raised the blue silk robe, till I found she was minus underskirt or drawers and I almost saw the heaven of love itself while my bursting pego felt the soft slippered foot gently pressing upon it, but as Justine seemed in no hurry to obey the cruel order of her Lady—indeed, I strongly suspect that her binding would not have been effectual—I availed myself of the delay to beseech the Countess in the most devotedly affectionate terms that I could use consistent with respect, not to be so cruel, that as I had already been partially admitted to the gate of paradise, it was very great severity to deprive me of a glimpse of it, with some more extravagant nonsense to the same effect which seemed to amuse Justine amazingly, and actually did not seem to displease Her Ladyship, for she said something, if I recollect rightly (for I was very far from being in a condition to pay correct attention to what was said), about my being a foolish boy, but that as I had vowed myself to secrecy and her interests, and as it would be an insult to offer me money—why, why I must choose my own reward!

At least I know if I have not exactly reported my Lady's words, that was the practical termination of her speech; indeed I fear I took advantage of the kind tendency of her words before she had quite brought them to an end.

My fingers had already got possession of her clitoris and were revelling in the juicy moisture with which the vermilion lips of her aristocratic crack was already bedewed in anticipation of the fresh bit of meat it was her intention to devour. The effect was electrical. Justine had guessed the propitious moment and her busy fingers let loose the engine of love from the restraint of my breeches. With a bound I threw myself on Her Ladyship as I raised or opened the robe which had hitherto presented a slight obstacle to my view. Her legs mechanically opened and I was in paradise, Justine keeping her fingers busy titillating the parts in conjunction, as she knelt by the side of the sofa, and really seemed to enjoy the sight of our transports. And what was my astonishment when, after three emissions I withdrew exhausted for the moment, to see the soubrette bury her face between the thighs of her mistress and greedily suck from the love-spot all that her tongue could lick up of the mingled sperm which oozed from that delicious aperture. It was a scene of voluptuous enjoyment such as my youthful ideas had not previously entertained.

The ice fairly broken, all ceremony (except outward form) was at an end. But these it was of course highly necessary to observe, if possible, with more strictness than before, so that in the course of an hour or so I was sent with an order to the housekeeper to provide something light and delicate for her Lady, who was an invalid and would not dine at the family table. This of course was promptly supplied but I was sorry to observe (for I was retained to wait on Her Ladyship,) that the order had been so literally observed that the Countess, who was really only languid and no invalid at all, actually required nourishment and was likely to come off second best under this sick-room regimen.

I suggested this at once to Justine, who perceived the error made and volunteered to supply the deficiency. She showed herself a capital forager, for she returned speedily, bringing not only several dainties herself, but also accompanied by one of the under-footmen who bore a tray containing a capital supper with a bottle or two of wine.

This, the clever girl asserted, had been ordered by the Countess for her two attendants who were, after their duties were over, to have supper in the anteroom.

By this manœuvre the Countess obtained the supper she absolutely required, but there was also plenty left over for Justine and myself, when (Her Ladyship having concluded her repast) we sat down to enjoy it in the anteroom.

I mention this little circumstance to show how familiarity was cemented and kept up between the Countess and us two, her special servants. Indeed, she expressed herself warmly on the subject to me for suggesting the idea and to Justine for executing it. There was yet another cause for mutual congratulation and it was this.

What our beloved, but supposed to be invalid, Lady would have done on a wing of chicken, some jelly and the ghost of a glass of wine and water, I cannot tell, and shudder to think of, but I think we all three congratulated ourselves upon the effect produced by such condiments as tongue, potted meats, to say nothing of two or three bottles of good wine.

The colour returned to my Lady's pale cheeks, her languor gave way to vivacity and high spirits, and her eyes sparkled with the combined fire of passion and champagne.

Justine exhibited similar symptoms in a modified degree while I, thanks to my youth, strength and strong constitution, felt as if nothing particular had happened.

I had reason to bless my stars that I had partaken of a

good supper, for after a little laughing talk, the Countess dispatched Justine to my room with orders to lock the door and bring her the key, exclaiming: "Now, Ernest, where do you suppose you are to pass the night?"

Under any other circumstances this might have been a puzzling question, but as Her Ladyship asked it, flung herself upon my knee and began kissing and hugging and fondling me in a style more becoming to her passion than her rank as a Countess, her question answered itself or rather her behaviour supplied an answer to it.

Not that I was ungrateful, however, for these proofs of endearment, far from it; on the contrary, I reciprocated them with all my heart and soul and repaid them with interest both physically and mentally. So that when Justine arrived with my bedroom key she was not at all surprised to receive an order to prepare her mistress for bed, to prepare another for herself in the anteroom and to call me at five o'clock in the morning, before any of the household were up. However, as the Earl was absent on a visit to the Duke of Dashwood, and nobody else had claim on my services, there was little fear of my being wanted or of any exposure consequent thereon.

I rather suspect that putting the Countess to bed was a longer business than usual, and I am afraid that Justine found me a nuisance rather than otherwise, for I was so proud of my newly invested privileges and other important offices, which I considered myself entitled to, that I insisted on acting the part of a chambermaid to a somewhat indefensible extent. And the beauty of it (in every sense of the word) was that the Countess rather backed me up in my vagaries than otherwise, until at last Justine lost all patience and vowed that if I did not retire into the anteroom and leave her alone with her mistress for a few minutes, I should go back to my own room as I deserved.

"Now, she's jealous, throw her on the bed, Ernest," ordered the Countess, "and do her over at once. I shall be delighted to see two such handsome persons playing the Adam and Eve game: besides, I've got a little tickler here to increase the fun and add to our enjoyment."

My affair was again in prime condition. So, throwing Justine over the edge of the bed I was into her in a moment. "Ah! ah! oh! Pray don't, my Lady!" I called out almost in a scream, as one, two, three slashing cuts of a heavy birch rod warmed my bottom behind. Justine held me to herself like a vice and I could hear the Countess laugh as she plied the merciless rod, till presently such a beautiful glowing sensation, added to an extraordinary bursting stiffness in my piston-rod, drowned all sense of pain as I shot such a profuse emission into my sweetheart that I almost fainted from excess of emotion.

And here it was my intention to draw the veil, or more correctly speaking, to drop the curtain and to balk the necessity of my friends by giving no further record of the proceedings of that delicious night; but I think in common gratitude to my beautiful Lady Pomeroy I ought to acknowledge that I was in a state of exquisite bliss and I may say without vanity that my lovely companion owned to something very like that enviable state herself.

We were both a little *too* happy, for when Justine came to call me in the morning I was almost exhausted. And the faithful girl could only rouse me by insisting that her mistress was faint, that I must leave the room while she administered restoratives.

(To be continued.)

THE OLD DILDOE.

Tune—"The Mistletoe Bough."

The beds were all made in the bawdy house fine,
And the whores were rejoicing in gin and wine;
And the old bawd herself, dressed out so gay,
Was making them drunk on Xmas day.
And there was "Peg Watkins" the brothel's delight,
Got lewd on a cove, as was there that night.
And said she to herself: "If I don't have a go,
I'll content myself with the old Dildoe."

Chorus—Oh! the old Dildoe, oh, the old whore's Dildoe.

"Oh! I am weary of lashing," Peg now did cry,
Come upstairs with me Joey, and let's have a shie."
But Joey determined to stick to the gin,
And wouldn't leave his liquor to have put in.
And Peg cursed him and told him to go to hell;
But drunk as a fart, from the chair he fell.
So away she ran with her blood in a glow,
Determined to try the old Dildoe.

Chorus: Oh! the old Dildoe, oh! the old whore's Dildoe.

To the old bawd's bedroom at once she went,
To seize upon the implement.
She looked in the cupboard, she looked in the pot,
She searched high and low but found it not.
She rushed to the couch, she searched the bed,
Underneath the pillow she spied its head.
She seized it and cried: "Full well I know,
Far better than Joe's the old Dildoe."

Chorus—Oh! the old Dildoe, oh, the old whore's Dildoe.

She flew with the treasure into her room
(Its size was the handle of a broom).
Oh! what ecstatic moments she passed there,
As she threw up her legs on the back of a chair.
Through each vein in her body the fire lurked,
Surely and quickly the engine worked;
Face her, back her, stop her no! no!
Faster and faster flew the old Dildoe.

Chorus: Oh! the old Dildoe, oh! the old whore's Dildoe.

Minutes soon passed and the hours flew by,
When there suddenly came a fearful cry,
Which was followed at once by a fearful scream,
Which awoke the whores from their drunken dream.
They all jumped up in a hell of a fright,
In an empty gin-bottle they stuck a light;
And the old whore herself away did go
To look after the safety of the old Dildoe.

Chorus: Oh! the old Dildoe, oh! the old whore's Dildoe.

But the old whore very soon did return
With a look of agony and deep concern;
For her heart was filled with dire remorse,
As she told the whores of her fearful loss;
She questioned them all and implored them to tell,
Where the treasure had gone that she loved so well;
When one of them said: "I think I know,
Peg Watkins is using your old Dildoe."

Chorus: Oh! the old Dildoe, oh! the old whore's Dildoe.

Away they all flew to Peggy's room.
But, ho! 'twas filled with smoke and fume,
And a terrible stench came forth from the bed,
Where poor Peggy lay all burnt and dead.
Sad, sad, was her fate, when, instead of a fuck,
With the old Dildoe she had tried her luck;
And when at the short digs she so hard did go,
It caught fire with the friction—the old Dildoe.

Chorus: Oh! the old Dildoe, oh! the old whore's Dildoe.

An old and favoured servant of two maiden ladies had been frequently reprimanded by them for his free behaviour with the female servants. Caught one day in *flagrante delicto*, he was summoned to their presence, and while the girl was sacked, he was told that if he did not do better and turn over a new leaf, much as they valued him—his next escapade would be the last. He promised amendment and matters went on very well for a time. One evening, he was not to be found when wanted, and on a search being made, was discovered in the beer-cellar, buggering the page boy.

"How now," he was asked, "is this your amendment? You promised to turn over a new leaf." "So I have" said he, "only I have begun *at the bottom of the page!*"

History does not give the conclusion of the matter.

LADY POKINGHAM, OR THEY ALL DO IT;

*Giving an Account of her Luxurious Adventures both Before
and After Her Marriage with Lord Crim-Con.*

PART VI.
(Concluded.)

Description fails me in endeavouring to picture the excessive voluptuousness of this conjunction, *trio in uno*. My profuse spendings so lubricated their pricks that they were soon quite comfortably rubbing together up and down, up and down inside my delighted cunt, and then: "Ah! Oh! Oh! I spend! I die in ecstasy! Where am I? Ah! heavens! Oh! God, what bliss!" That is how I screamed out and then almost fainted from excess of emotion, only to awaken directly to find them also in the frenzy of their emission.

The excitement was so great that my champions retained their stiffness and kept their place whilst the girls, not to be outdone, jumped up on the bed, and Patty, turning her bottom to my face, buried Sam's face between her thighs as she pressed her cunt to his mouth for a gamahuche; Annie straddling and lying over her to present her cunt and bottom to my lascivious tongue, which did not fail to seize the opportunity to revel both in her cunt and little wrinkled pink bum-hole.

This went on until sheer exhaustion compelled us to separate, and how I hugged and kissed them all, when at last I let them retire to their respective rooms.

Next day I was very ill and the day after that a medical man had to be called in, Patty going by my express desire to a doctor with very limited practice whom I thought would not be exhausted by his lady patients.

As soon as he arrived my servants all retired and left us alone.

"My dear lady," said Mr. Loveshaft, "what has brought you to this state of unnaturally prostrating excitement? Tell me all. Don't keep anything back if you wish me to do you any good."

"Oh, Doctor," I replied in a whisper, "pray, put out the light, the fire is quite enough to see by, and put out your ears close to my lips. I can only whisper my confession, and don't want you to see my blushes."

This was done and his face was close to mine when I threw my arms nervously round his neck and drew his face to my feverish lips and I kissed him more wantonly, saying:

"I want love; there's no one to love me. Oh! Oh! Fuck me first and physic me afterwards. I know you must be a gallant man, and mine's a real case of nymphomania!"

Whilst one hand still held him in a most amorous embrace, the other wandered to his prick, which my impassioned appeal had brought to a sense of its duty in a moment. What a fine fellow he was too, both long and thick, as opening his trousers without resistance he let me take it.

"Throw off your clothes, there's a love of a man, and let me have this first, and the medicine afterwards," I exclaimed, thrusting my tongue into his mouth.

He was a most amiable doctor and it was nearly an hour before the consultation was over.

I rapidly declined after this and in spite of the doctor's unremitting attentions, both to my health as well as my cunt, I grew worse and worse and had to be sent to Madeira for the winter. So I shall conclude my long tale with my adventure on shipboard on the voyage out.

My housekeeper, whom I shall call Miss Prude, went with me as companion. We had arranged to have a fine large state-cabin in the stern of the steamer, with sleeping beds, or more strictly speaking, berths for four, as I engaged Patty and Annie to accompany us as servants. At any rate, Miss Prude thought so, but I had a deep design to seduce that virtuous young lady in spite of herself. So, by a little bribery, Annie was induced to stay behind and let my dear Charlie take her place in female attire.

As you journey to Southampton at night, we embarked at a very early hour before daylight, my companion being with me in a first-class carriage whilst the servants travelled in another part of the train and looked after the shipment of our luggage. Miss Prude never for a moment suspected the change while she and I retired to our berths as soon as we got on board, leaving everything to the girls.

For the first two days sea-sickness quite prostrated us all, especially my companion, but on the third day she was quite lively and the supposed Annie kept as much as possible out of sight till we all retired to rest. The servants had got into their berths and appeared to be asleep. Miss Prude and myself were both undressed and sitting side by side on the ottoman. I asked her to put out the lamp and as she did so I put my arm around her waist and drew her gently down by my side.

"Isn't it lovely now we've got over the sickness? What a beautiful sensation the motion of the vessel gives. Oh, if you were but a nice young man now, my dear!" I said kissing her most amorously and thrusting my tongue into her mouth whilst one of my hands wandered under her nightdress and invaded all those delicious hairy parts, so sacred to virginity.

"Oh, for shame, my Lady! How can you be so rude?" she exclaimed in a loud whisper.

Still I found she did not repulse me and from the heaving of her bosom she was evidently in considerable confusion.

"What is your Christian name, darling? Miss Prude is so cold," I asked, between my lascivious kisses.

"Selina, but pray, don't, my Lady!" she said almost with a sigh as my fingers found out her little clitoris between the pouting lips which her yielding legs had allowed me to titillate.

"What a love of a name; Selina! and you must call me Beatrice, will you—there's a darling? And we must sleep together in the same berth, there's room for both. I must kiss you all over to prove my love—even there, darling," I said indicating her pussey with my finger, which was on the spot at the time, "and you shall do the same to me. Or, if you don't like, you shall see how Patty loves to kiss my crack. Ah! Ah! you'll soon learn Selina, to know what is nice, even if it seems horribly rude to think of."

"Did you never guess, my dear," I continued, "why some girls are so awfully fond of each other? Well, I will tell you —it is because they are in the habit of procuring from each other all those forbidden joys which married people alone are supposed to enjoy."

She was all atremble. My fingers were fairly buried in her slit, as far as they would go, and making her spend deliciously.

"Oh! Oh! I must suck it, every pearly drop that distills from your virgin recess is worth its weight in diamonds!" I said excitedly, throwing her back at full length on the ottoman, whilst I fell on my knees between her yielding thighs and glued my lips to her cunt. My tongue revelled in that

thick creamy emission which only real virgins give down, for
when their love-juices have not secreted so long, they are
far more creamy than the spending of a woman is after often
being fucked or frigged.

She enjoyed it immensely. How she wriggled and twisted
in the excess of her excitement.

At last I got up and woke Patty. Then returning to my
ladylove, I whispered in her ear: "Selina, darling, I am going
to give you a real taste of what a man is like. Patty is going to
put on my dildoe and fuck you with it, while she tickles my
bottom-hole and you gamahuche my cunt. Won't that be a
delightful conjunction, my love?"

"You frighten me, Beatrice dear. What is a dildoe, will it
hurt?" she whispered in a low tone.

"Exactly like a man's affair, Selina! And although it can
shoot a delicious soothing emission into you at the ecstatic
moment, there is no fear of getting in the family way," I
softly replied. "Now Patty is ready; let me straddle over your
face and present my cunny to your sweet lips for a sucking
kiss. You will like it. It will excite you so, to the unmistak-
able joy the dildoe will give when it once gets in," suiting
the action to the word by placing myself over her.

Her blood was in a boil. She eagerly thrust her tongue into
my longing cunt which almost instantly rewarded it by a
copious spend which Selina seemed to relish as much as any
epicurean gamahucher would have done; her legs lasciviously
wide apart, which Master Charlie was not slow to avail himself of; the position in which I was over her effectually preventing the longing virgin from seeing the impending ruin.

Opening the lips of her spending cunt gently with his
fingers, the fellow cunningly frigged her with the ruby head
of his prick, until poor Selina got so excited that she began to
bite me and wriggle about in such an extraordinary way, as
well as moan and sob out: "Oh! Ah! shove, shove! Do push
it in further, Patty dear! I feel I must have it. Oh! Oh! Ah-h!
It hurts now! Pray, don't!" as he commenced to force the
maidenhead in earnest. I pressed my cunt upon her mouth so
that she could not scream and intensely enjoyed the pain we
put her to; for she was awfully tight and Charlie was not to
be denied. He pushed and rammed at her in lustful fury,
spending, but still going on, till he got the whole of his manhood fairly into her sheath, then he rested for a few mo-

ments, making his prick throb in its tight receptacle till all sense of pain seemed to be lost to our victim; and the natural lubricity of her nature asserted itself once more, and answered with a wanton heave of her bottom to every thrust of her partner. There seemed no satisfying her greedy cunt, now it had once got a taste of the real thing.

At last we got off her, and lighted the lamps once again, let her see the dildoe for herself and guess! How astonished she was to find it was real life, instead of a hateful substitute, but she forgave us for the deception which had afforded her such exquisite pleasure.

After refreshing our parts with cold water, she thoroughly enjoyed the sight of Charlie fucking the amorous Patty, and with her own hands handled his balls and tickled them as well as Patty's cunt during their encounter.

As we could not expect to have more than another two nights on board ship, I determined to make the best of the time, especially as I had a particular fancy for a good-looking youth in preference to men; and there were a couple of young middies on board I had quite fallen in love with as they had shown me many delicate attentions when I was so ill for the first few days.

A fine bright morning saw us on deck directly after breakfast.

"Good morning, my Lady," said young Simpson raising his cap with a knowing, wistful look.

"Come here, you impudent-looking boy," I laughed, and as he approached, said, in a whisper:

"Can you keep a secret?"

"My bosom is as safe as an iron chest, if Your Ladyship has anything to confide," was the reply.

"I am going to leave you soon, you know, and would like to give you and young William a treat in my cabin tonight, if you can manage to come after all are retired and you are off duty then, I think."

"Yes," he replied, "from 10 P.M. to 6 A.M. and you may depend on us being very quiet."

Putting a finger to my lips as a sign of strict secrecy, I glided away from him and sat on the poop for the greater part of the day, looking at the water in a dream anticipation of the fun I hoped for at night.

I had made ample preparation for them and bribed the

stewards not to take any notice if they heard noises in my cabin, as I was going to give a little party to two or three young lady passengers before going ashore at Funchal, the port of Madeira.

After supper, myself and companions lay down to rest in our clothes, leaving the lamps burning and the refreshments all ready to hand. After a while, when all was quiet, our cabin door opened softly and the two handsome boys in their best uniforms quietly saluted us as they entered, both of them kissing me before I could rise from the couch. The door was bolted by Patty, who laughingly told them to mind how they behaved, or they would get served out. In reply to which both of them caught her and kissed her in spite of her pretended resistance.

The middies were hungry and soon did ample justice to a game-pie washed down with several bumpers of champagne as they toasted us, from the servants to myself.

I drank glass for glass with them. My veins were on fire, consumed by my lustful longings to enjoy two such handsome youths, and as soon as they had finished their repast, I begged them to sit by my side on the ottoman. And just as Simpson was in the act of sitting down I drew him upon my lap, saying with a laugh:

"What a nice baby he was to nurse, what a pretty little dear; kiss its dear mama."

My lips met his in a long-drawn osculation which seemed to make him quiver all over with emotion as he lay on my bosom.

"Did you ever have a sweetheart, dear boy?" I asked.

"Yes; such a pretty girl at the Cape. I have rare fun with her when I go ashore."

"What! Are you impudent enough to take liberties with her?"

"Yes, she even let me get into bed with her."

"You impertinent little fellow to mention such a thing to me! Here, Miss Prude, and you girls, tie him up and pull down his breeches! I've got a tickler that will make his bottom smart for this!" I exclaimed, pushing him from me with great apparent disgust.

"What a lark! I should like to see them do it. Here, Peter, old boy, help us or these girls will really master me," and he began to find himself rather overmatched.

A smile and a gesture from me only turned his chum Peter Williams to our side and it was fun to see how foolish he looked when he found himself really tied up to one of the berths and his breeches pulled down in spite of all he could do. How he blushed as they tucked up the tail of his shirt and exposed a very pretty white-skinned bum which was soon rosy enough under the hand-slapping he got from the whole party, thoroughly enjoying the joke.

"Stand aside all of you," I said sternly, "and let me pay him the desserts for his impudence," advancing birch in hand.

He was a plucky little fellow and distained to cry out although I saw two or three big tears roll down his crimson face under my infliction, and I could also see that his cock was as stiff as a poker. He was released, and without even waiting to pull his breeches up, rushed forward to help us as we stretched his friend Peter on the ottoman, and then by my direction he sat on his back, whilst I gleefully let him have a due share of the birch till he begged hard to be let off.

When they thought to adjust their clothes we all began to laugh and joke them about the beautiful red weals we could see, pulling up their shirt-tails and taking such liberties that in a short time they were quite undressed and we had two youths in a state of nature with standing pricks to look at.

"Well, I wouldn't give much for those toys of yours if that is all you have to show the girls!" I said laughingly, as I switched the parts indicated with my rod. "Why Annie here has a better cock than any of you. We'll all strip and you shall see."

This was the expected signal and all further restraint on our impulsive passions was thrown aside in a moment.

I think those two handsome middies had never really had a girl before and that I really took their maidenheads. In fact, I indulged in my letch for having two pricks in my cunt at once, whilst Charlie fucked Miss Prude before our eyes, till she had hysterics from excessive lubricity.

We kept it up till nearly five o'clock, fucking, gamahuching and indulging in every fancy we could think of. I even made Charlie get into my bottom with Simpson in him. Peter Williams also postillioning her companion with his prick in his fundament, whilst Miss Prude and Patty tickled and helped to excite us the very best way they could.

At last they were obliged to leave us and I may say that was the last lustful orgy I was ever able to indulge in, for my constitution broke down rapidly even during my stay at Madeira and I returned to England in the following May, since when, dear Walter, you have been my constant and loving attendant, and seen how rapidly this consumption is carrying me to my grave. Oh! I would that I had strength to do it once more and that you were my manly champion in that combat of bliss which I shall never taste again. Would to Heaven I might die in spending as I felt your very soul shoot into my vitals, but, alas! it cannot be! Still, if there is bliss in the world to be, I feel assured of an everlasting fuck.

Amen! I am unable to hold my pen any longer.

CONCLUSION.

SWEET POLLY.

Oh, do you remember sweet Polly, Ben Bolt,
    Sweet Polly with a cunt soft and brown;
How she'd grin with delight when you gave her a quid,
    And how quickly she'd fetch a prick down?
That girl has now gone to decay, Ben Bolt,
    That soft, luscious quim is now dry;
And that lump of delight is now a bag of dry bones,
    That wouldn't please you, Ben, or I.
Had she stuck to the Navy, I vow, Ben Bolt,
    She'd alive be and kicking today;
But a bloody big soldier got round our poor girl,
    And turned the poor mot into clay.
He gave her no coin, but he gave her the pox,
    He whacked her while we were away;
He fucked her to death, and true to his set,
    He often got in the back way.
Now she's gone dead, and he's off abroad,
    And there the cuss had better stay;
For if he comes near me, my toe in his arse
    Will remind him of his comrade's play.

THE BURIAL OF SIR JOHN THOMAS.

Not a sound was heard, but the ottoman shook,
   And my darling looked awfully worried,
As round her fair form I a firm hold took,
   And John Thomas I silently buried.

We buried him deeply at dead of night,
   The tails of our night-shirts upturning;
With struggling raptures and fits of delight,
   The night-lights dimly burning.

No useless French Letters enclosed his crest,
   For ne'er in such rubbish we bound him;
But he went like a warrior taking his rest,
   With naught but his fur coat around him.

Few and short were the sighs we gave,
   Though we oftentimes groaned as in sorrow,
As at each stroke for the joy we'd rave,
   Ne'er giving a thought for the morrow.

But as yet he had not nearly done,
   And ne'er had a thought of retiring,
When suddenly to groan we again had begun
   Through John Thomas silently firing.

And we thought, as he came from his narrow bed,
   As lifeless and limp as a willow,
How lowly he hung down his diminished head,
   And how gladly he'd rest on his pillow.

THE PEARL,

A Journal of Facetiæ and Voluptuous Reading.

No. 16   PUBLISHED MONTHLY.   Oct. 1880

LA ROSE D'AMOUR,

Or the Adventures of a Gentleman in Search of Pleasure.
Translated from the French.

I then asked her to undress, and told her that in a moment I would return to her. I went out and gave an order to Mary and returned, finding my mistress stripped to her shift.

I undressed, and taking off my shirt, gave her a kiss, and drew her shift over her head and we both stood naked. I opened the room-door and picking her up carried her into the cabin amongst the girls.

Isabel had by this time got drunk as well as the girls who had come on board with her. With what shouts of laughter did they receive us, tickling us, pinching us, slapping us against one another, catching at my genitals and pulling the hair that surmounted the notch of my mistress, patting our bare backsides, throwing us on the floor, putting us on top of each other, etc., whilst I would catch them, pull up their petticoats, pinch their buttocks, flap the head of my enormous machine against the lips of their hairy little slits, force it into their hands and make them play with it.

I caught one and with the help of Ibzaidu and my mistress soon stripped her naked, handing her clothes to Mary, whom I ordered with Ibzaidu to put away her clothes, and who were as naked as I, who locked them up in one of the rooms, and in a few minutes I had stripped the whole of them stark naked.

Oh! then what amorous, wanton tricks we sportively played each other, they tickling my large bags and stones, playing with my penis and rubbing it, I moulding their beautiful titties and with the tip of my finger tickling their cunts.

One little devil who could not have been over fourteen I made spend. What fun this was to the rest, to see her re-

cline her head on my shoulder, spread apart her thighs, and
gasp out her exclamations of delight. Her oh's and ah's and
me's, as she gave down the generous fluid which ran down
my fingers and wet my whole hand.

While I was thus with my finger frigging the dear little
maid, Isabel had squatted herself down between my legs and
had taken my pego in her mouth and was frigging me in that
way. I did not notice it until the delicious creature who was
reclining on my shoulder had done spending. But I felt that
I too was about to spend, and trying to draw my penis from
her mouth, she clasped her hands around my buttocks and
squezed me up close to her mouth, till my stones and bags
tingled against her chin and neck.

I exclaimed: "My God! Let go. I'm going to spend!"

But instead of doing so she hugged me still more and
tickled its head with her tongue more and more.

The crisis seized me, the short convulsive jerks of my backside announce that the fluid is coming.

"I'm spending; here it is. Ah, my God! what pleasure! How
exquisite! What bliss! Oh, God, quicker! Oh, bliss! Heavenly
joy! I'm spending," and I fell to the floor fairly fainting away
through excess of pleasure. My flesh quivered and danced, my
whole body was in motion, as though attacked with St. Vitus'
dance.

Never, no, never in the world was a man so frigged by
woman. Never before did man experience such voluptuous
pleasure. Never was there such bliss so heavenly, so ecstatic,
imparted to man by woman, as I received from my mistress
as I let flow the pearly liquid into her mouth. Never did the
most exquisite sucking and friction of a cunt produce the
same amount of such intense ecstasy as I felt when spending.
As the pearly liquid spurted from me she placed her tongue
on the head, rolling it over and over it, producing in me
feelings of bliss so delicious as to throw me into convulsions
of pleasure.

It was some time ere I recovered myself, and then it was
through the teasings and ticklings of my lovely tormentors. I
had a pallet made on the floor of the cabin from the beds in
the staterooms, and putting the lights out, we lay down. I
was in the arms of Isabel and soon well repaid her for the
pleasure she had given just before.

Thrice did I spend into the most secret recesses of her

notch the warm and generous fluid which acts so powerfully on women, and then composed myself for sleep.

After sleeping for I should judge about two hours, I was awakened by feeling someone rubbing and playing with my member, which was in fine standing order.

I found it was Isabel, who had her rump stuck close to the hollow of my thighs and was rubbing the head of my penis against her culo. She wet it every now and then and the sliding of it between her fat buttocks caused a most agreeable tingling sensation to pervade my whole corporeal system.

Wishing to aid her in her intentions, still pretending to be asleep, I aided her all in my power so far as regarded position, etc.

I clasped my arms around her waist and one thigh, which I lightly raised.

"Oh," she said, "you are awake and want more pleasure!"

I made no answer and guided the head of my prick to her little hole au derrière. I thrust forward but it would not penetrate. With her fingers she moistened its head with spittle and again placed it aright; but as it was an awkward position to lie in I rolled her on to her belly, placing a cushion under her to raise her rump high up. I opened her thighs, got between them and tried the back entrance. I forced it in. She squirmed and wriggled about gasping with pleasure and I could hardly keep in her.

Her wriggling about and the delicious contractions of her culo brought down from me a copious discharge of the electric fluid which I injected into her.

"Oh, God!" she exclaimed, "what pleasure. I feel it rushing into me! How hot it is, my dear love. Again, and quicker. Now I come, too; it is running from me. My God! 'tis heaven! What pleasure. Ah, what lus—lus—luscious pleasure!"

The words died on her lips. As I was fucking her in her slit, and had frigged her clitoris at the same time, thus procuring her the double pleasure.

Here was an entirely new source of pleasure opened to me by the libertinism of my new mistress. Already I had enjoyed her in three different places, and I found that she had penetrated into the inmost recesses of my breast, creating a sensation there which I felt could never be effaced by any other female.

What a luxury it was to see the wild, stupefied astonishment of the charming girls who surrounded me to find themselves lying with me stark naked, and it was somehow increased, I venture to say, by seeing me on top of Isabel, giving her an appetite for her breakfast with the morning draught which she sucked in with great delight.

They all sprang up looking for their clothes or something with which to hide their nakedness, but in vain; no clothes were to be seen, as I had them safe under lock and key.

The ravishing little creature in whose arms I had spent the night nearly laughed herself into fits at witnessing the dumb terror of the girls and commenced railing them, telling them everything that had occurred during the night, recalling to their minds all the follies and extravagances they had been guilty of, and tried to induce them to take their good luck, as she said, with fortitude, describing to them all the pleasure she had received from me during the night and begging them to submit to whatever I would desire with good grace and it was better for them. I then spoke to them, telling them where I was taking them to, and that at the least resistance made by them I would hand them back to the fierce desires of the common sailors; but on the contrary, if they acted as I wished them, everything should be well with them. That they could not form the slightest desire but what would be instantly complied with. The most delicate attentions should be paid them, and I ended by telling them of the life of luxury and blissful love they would lead with me, and on the contrary, of the dreadful life they would spend if by remaining refractory they caused me to give them away to the brutal lusts of the sailors.

This had considerable effect on them as I could see fear and horror plainly depicted on their countenances.

I then rang a bell for a servant and told her to bring me a bottle of wine, telling the girl where to get it.

When she brought it in I filled the glasses and asked the girls, who were huddled together in one corner, to come and take a glass each.

They did not stir, and putting on a frowning aspect, I commanded them to come and drink.

They came forward to the table and drank the wine.

I told them to seat themselves on the sofa while breakfast was being laid. I seated four on one sofa and attempted to lay myself down across their knees, but they all jumped up and ran into a corner. I determined to terrify them at once, so they would be perfectly subservient to my desires. Calling a servant, I sent her to call my mate, one who officiated as my valet.

When he entered the cabin I ordered the girls to resume their places on the sofa, which they tremblingly did.

Then I told the mate to seize on the first one of them who attempted to move, drag her on the deck and give her to the sailors.

I went up to them and sitting on one of them for a moment, lay down with my belly and face towards theirs. The one on whose thighs I rested my feet I bade to part her legs and with my toes I tickled the lips of her bushy notch. The one on whose thighs my cheeks rested I also made to part her legs so that I could drop my right arm between them. I then frigged her clitoris occasionally with my little finger, tickling her just inside the lips; she began to wriggle about on the sofa. The girls on whom rested my buttocks and thighs I made play, one with my stones and the other with my Jacob's staff.

At breakfast I put into the cup of one of the youngest and prettiest girls enough of the tincture of cantharides to make her libidinous desires show themselves pretty strongly.

After we had finished eating I took her to a sofa and drew her on my knees, and as the drug began to take effect on her, I took all the liberties I desired with her, kissing and sucking her pretty lips, the nipples of her breasts, handling her buttocks, frigging her clitoris, drawing my grand machine up between her thighs and rubbing the lips of her pussey, till I felt myself able to succeed in making an entrance into any place no matter how small. She the while hugged me in her arms, giving me kiss for kiss, rubbing and screwing her bottom on my thighs, giving evidence of the raging fever which was consuming that part of her.

Her companions, none of whom had seen me drop the tincture into her coffee, regarded her manœuvres with me in perfect wonder, little thinking that they each would do the same before they were two days older.

I fixed a cushion and pillow on the sofa so as to properly support her head and bottom, and laying the lecherous little devil down I opened wide her legs and laid myself down be-

tween them. She aided me with good will in getting it well
fixed, so as better to operate.

Mary and Ibzaidu came to act as pilots to steer my noble
craft safe into the harbour of Cytheria. The entrance to the
haven was very narrow, making the way rather difficult till
Donna Isabel ran up to me and slapping me hard on the
bare buttocks drove me up to the hilt, causing the delicious
creature whom I was deflowering to scream out with the
pain. The blood flowed from her and the sperm from me,
mingling most delightfully.

Resting for a moment, I recommenced the delightful race
and soon had the joy to know that the dear girl was reaching
the very acme of human enjoyment whilst I at the same time
again drowned my senses in another discharge of that peculiar
fluid the flowing of which drowns one in such ecstacies.

Three others did I serve in the same manner before the
close of the day, ravishing them of their dear little maidenheads, of no manner of use to a woman, and of which I am
particularly fond.

One I forced to give up to me her virginity by the aid of
the tincture without taking way her senses. Oh! they were
bliss, doubly refined, her fierce struggles to free herself from
my lascivious embraces. How sweetly musical to my ears
were her yells of agony and shame. With what transports did
I force her to resign her sweet body to my fierce desires.
How ravishing was the pleasure I felt in ripping and tearing
up the tender outworks, the inner gates, the bulwarks, everything. And at last, despite her continued struggling and
screaming, to drive full tilt into the very temple of Venus,
triumphantly plucking off her virgin rose from its stem, causing the blood to flow in profusion. Oh, how I gloated on the
ruins of all that is held dear and honourable by her sex—her
virtue.

Ye Gods! it was a fuck so altogether exquisitely delicious
that it was a full half-hour before I was sufficiently recovered
to enter again into the little grotto of Venus, the road to
which I had just opened.

Lovely creature! Three times did I experience in your arms
that fierce transporting pleasure which intoxicates the soul
and drowns the mind in those voluptuous ecstacies which can
only be experienced in the close embrace of the two sexes.

Abstaining from cohabiting with any of the girls for a

couple of days, I felt my strength renewed and invigorated, and on the fifth day after carrying them off from the island, I had ravished the whole six of their dear little maidenheads I had cruelly forced them to give up to my lechery. But once having lost them, which they held so guarded, they entered into all my whims and pleasures with the passion and ardor that characterizes the females of the south.

Once the Rubicon was crossed they became the greatest libertines I ever met with. They would hang round me day and night, trying every means in their power to keep my prick in a constant state of erection. They would lay me down on the floor stark naked, like themselves. They would fairly fight for the possession of my genitals. One would gently squeeze my stones, while another would be playing with my penis, which she would by the gentle friction of her soft, delicate hand bring to an erection.

Then would she precipitate herself on me and devour the rich morsel, palating it with those exquisite contractions and inward squeezings which at the time women are about to spend render the act of copulation so exquisitely delicious.

Then, when one was mounted on me, would the dear creatures show forth the full fire of their lechery.

Two of them would seize on my hands, one on each, and, running my fingers into their salacious slits, would thus procure for themselves a semblance of the pleasure their more lucky rival was enjoying and receiving from the friction of the stiffly red-tipped horn which sprang out from the bottom of my belly.

Isabel would rush into the arms of Ibzaidu, to whom she had taken a great liking. Tumbling on the floor in each other's arms they would press each other, squeeze breasts, suck nipples, force their tongues into each other's cunts. Their hands would play and twine in the bushy hair that shaded the mounts above their notches. Their fingers would slide lower down, would enter the sacred grotto, and then running them in as far as they could, they would commence the titillation, and with the finger of the left hand at the same time they would frig the clitoris, which would soon bring them to that delicious state of annihilation which causes the soul to dissolve itself in a sea of bliss.

At other times they would seize on the languishing Fanny, who yet retained her maidenhead but of which she was very anxious to be rid, and throw her on the sofa or floor, and while Ibzaidu would be squeezing or sucking her breasts, pressing her own lovely titties to her mouth, kissing and sucking her rosy lips, and thrusting her tongue into her mouth, Isabel would be between her thighs, frigging her clitoris with her fingers and with her tongue between the lips, so titillate her cunt as to give her the most delicious pleasure. The dear Fanny would spend, pouring down the liquor of which she possessed a superabundance, amidst sighs, long and deep.

Nor would her hands be idle, for those who were procuring her the pleasure did not forget themselves.

They would force her hands into their own glowing furnace and send down such a flow of liquid as would wet the hands of Fanny all over.

Then would these two try their best to procure for Fanny those pleasures which all around her were continually being received from me but of which I had as yet deprived her. But she was not long to be burdened with that which all maids are anxious to get rid of—her virginity.

Giving myself one day's rest, I lay down in the cabin by myself on a mattress. The girls always made their beds on the floor and we lay together. After I had been asleep for sometime, I was awakened by feeling someone playing with my private parts. Isabel and Ibzaidu were lying on either side of me, their heads resting on my thighs. Isabel had taken that piece of flesh of which she was so fond in her mouth and was tickling it with her tongue. The other was feeling and playing with the curious bag which hung low down between her thighs, gently rubbing and squeezing the stones.

My machine was proudly erect as a mast, its red head glowing through the darkness.

"Come," said Isabel, "Ibzaidu has lived for five days on the shadow of the substance which the other girls have been so gorged with, and it is but fair that you should recompence her for starving, while others have been living in plenty. Come you, stand! Your prick is in fine condition. You must spend this night with her and me for I have not partaken of the flesh for some time."

I laid Ibzaidu on her back and getting between her legs I entered my prick into her parts. The moment she felt the head within the further recesses of her cunt she spent most plentifully. I worked away in her for some time, holding back my own liquor as long as possible so as to give her as much pleasure as I could, and she spent three times more. Just as she was dissolving her very vitals into sperm, I met her and injected the seed into her womb.

I got off her, lay between the two. Without giving me any time for recruiting, Isabel commenced playing with my staff, which she hugged, pressing it to her breasts, squeezing it between them, pressing it against her cheeks, gently frigging it with her hand, and taking its uncapped head between her lips, softly biting and tickling it with the end of her tongue.

Then stopping till it sank down again, small and shrivelled up, she would take it and thrust the whole of it into her mouth, and by her exquisite palating and sucking and tickling cause it to start into life, proudly erecting its head till her little lips could hardly clasp it.

I laid her down on her belly, placing a pillow under the lower part of her body, and then entered her au derrière, put my left hand under her thighs and inserted my fingers into her cunt, holding them stiff, whilst I worked in her arse-hole.

The motions of her bottom, caused by the fall of my thighs against her backside, made her frig herself on my fingers. Thus did she enjoy a double pleasure.

Nor was Ibzaidu without share in this beautiful scene. She had lain down with her belly to my breast, her bush and slit rubbing against my side, with her right thigh thrown over my head.

Drawing her closer to me I kissed the lips of her cunt. I tickled her clitoris with my tongue, I put it between my lips and titillated her so deliciously with them that she died away in pleasure, at the same time that Isabel was losing her senses from the convulsive transports into which my double frigging had thrown her.

After this performance was over, we lay completely exhausted in each other's arms for about two hours, at the end of which time I began to feel myself somewhat revived.

While we were lying dormant in each other's embraces, Isabel had been describing to Ibzaidu the intense pleasure she had enjoyed when I enlarged her au derrière, and she prevailed on her to make me frig her in the same manner, making her lay her head between my thighs to play with my little thing and make it start into new life.

The beautiful, delicate and voluptuous Ibzaidu took my

tickler in her mouth and by the tickling of her tongue and the sucking she gave it she soon made it to stand most beautifully erect, upon which she let it go.

I soon placed her in a convenient position for the attack which was to ravish her of her second maidenhead, and she was perfectly willing to surrender at once.

I placed her on her right side, partly lying on her back. I then lay down on her left side and prepared to enter her. Isabel had lain herself down in front of Ibzaidu, her cunt touching her face, and her head between the thighs of her companion.

She took the head of my enormous machine into her mouth which she wetted well with spittle and then guided it to its destination. But the place was so small that I made many attempts before I could penetrate.

At last I felt it enter. I shoved slowly and steadily, and at length felt it impossible to reach any further.

Ibzaidu writhed and twisted about so much after I was in her that I could hardly keep myself upon her. Isabel had put the fingers of her right hand into the cunt of the beautiful creature whom I was stroking behind, and the motions of her back as we worked together made her frig herself with them.

At the same time she put her own arms round the buttocks of Isabel, and drawing her slit up to her mouth, she put her tongue into it and frigged her so well in this way that Isabel spent before either of us, wetting the tongue and lips of the beautiful Circassian with the pearly drops.

The crisis now seized me and at the same moment the frigging of Isabel's fingers caused Ibzaidu to spend at the very moment I was squirting a stream of boiling sperm into her very vitals.

"Ah, dear sir, have mercy on me! I feel it here in me! I too—oh, goodness, I am spending! Oh, heavens, what a pleasure. I die—I spend again—again! I am spending!" She relaxed the convulsive grasp she had of Isabel's bottom. Her flesh quivered and danced and she lay convulsed with pleasure such as gods never dreamt of.

In three weeks we reached the coast and harboured in the little creek. I immediately went ashore, taking the women with me and went to the chateau.

Heavens! What a welcome I received. How the lively, rampant, lecherous girls crowded round, and with what embraces did they receive me. I was fairly devoured by the hungry creatures who crowded to embrace me.

And, *La Rose d'Amour!* Ah, dear Rose, as I pressed you in my arms and received your burning kisses, what a thrill did they not send through my whole body.

And you, beauteous Laura, how your little heart beat as I pressed your bosom to mine; what fire flashed from your languishing black eyes as you put one of my hands on your cunt and your own on my already stiff pego.

Then came Rosalie, the delicate, fair-skinned, blue-eyed Rosalie. With what fierce delight did she spring forward, light as the burning gazelle, and into my arms. What lustful fires sparkled in her half-closed eyes. Her lips meet mine—they are glued together. She forces open her mouth, her tongue meets mine. She rubs the lips of her cunt against my thigh, she clasps her arms tight, her breast rises and falls in quick succession, she wriggles her bottom, her backside convulsively jerks, and she says: "Oh—oh!—God!" and sliding through my arms she sank upon the floor.

There, there at the further end of the room I see Caroline entering. Caroline, that very goddess of voluptuous beauty. She has heard of my arrival. She advances towards me, perfectly naked except for a pink gauze drawn round her waist— I too am naked, for the girls had stripped me on entering the room. My prick is hard and stiff, standing erect against my belly. Caroline sees it, she fixes her eyes on it, and remains perfectly still, fascinated by the charming sight. I fly to her, I take her in my arms, her emotions overpower her, she sinks on the floor on her back, she drags me with her. As she falls, her legs part and I fall between them, and five times did she spend ere she recovered from her fall.

When she rose up what a brilliancy sparkled in her eyes. Her gait was light and elastic as a fawn's.

When I rose up from my fall with the lovely Caroline, I met the gaze of the licentious Nubian, who was advancing to meet me, holding in her hand a glass of wine. She was perfectly naked and twisted and screwed her thighs together. I meet, accept the glass and drain the wine. The moment I drank it I knew that it was mixed with the tincture for exciting and creating amorous propensities.

The lovely creatures I have just been naming gathered

round me, they embraced me in every part; some a leg and a thigh; others hung round my neck; some seized on my hands with which they frigged themselves, one seats herself on the floor between my legs and playfully squeezes my stones and strokes my once more rampant prick. The luscious Celeste has her arms clasped round my neck and I am about to impale her with my prick, but Fanny comes forward and urges her claim in favour of her little maidenhead, which is consuming her with a burning fever.

I clasp her in my arms and lay her down, falling upon her. One of the girls hastens to place a cushion under her bottom and then guides the dart to its sheath. I shove and thrust, and one of the girls, giving me a couple of hard slaps over my backside, drove me in up to the hilt and the sweet girl at once sucked in the delicious poison she had been longing for.

The wine which I had drunk contained so much tincture that my pego continued standing.

The Nubian next came in for a good stroking. Three times while I was in her did she spend. Caroline, Laura and Rosalie came in their turns; each received an exquisite frigging.

I then went to bathe, taking with me only four of the girls: Caroline, Celestine, Laura and Rosalie.

Whilst in the bathroom I twice more frigged Rosalie and Laura, and then dismissed them to their apartments, remaining with the other two.

I had luncheon brought into the bath to me, and determining to sacrifice myself to the libidinous desires of my two lovely mistresses, I drank more of the wine containing the tincture. Sufficient to enable me to give the two who were with me as much cock-broth as they could sip through the night.

After remaining in the bath for a couple of hours, we came out and went to the bedchamber.

I led them into the state bedroom, and letting down the hangings, jumped into bed.

The two girls followed me and I was buried to my utmost length in the fiery furnace of Celestine. Four times did this amiable creature let fly her mettle and in such profusion did it come from her that the sheet under her bottom was all wet with it.

In her turn did Caroline take in and gorge her greedy little cunt with my morsel.

Thus did I spend the night, first frigging one and then

the other, till they were entirely spent and worn out with
the delicious fucking which I had given them.

I now determined to give up searching for any more
maidenheads, and gave myself up to the dear girls I already
possessed, than whom I could find none more beautiful,
more voluptuous or more devoted to my capricious pleasures.

I now live happily surrounded by the sweet creatures, but
I hear someone calling me from my private bed. I am in good
condition, having abstained for three days. I fly to her, I
jump into her arms and drown myself in a sea of bliss, in
the arms of *La Rose d'Amour.*

THE END.

THE BLUE VEIN.

A True Welsh Story.

Ye fun-loving fellows for comical tales,
Match this if you can, truly current in Wales;
The Bible so old, and the Testament new,
Having none more authentic, more faithful or true.
Four frisky maidens, young, handsome and plump,
Who could each crack a flea on their bubbies or rump,
Took it into their heads just to bother the tail
Of Ned Natty, a groom, so they jalap'd his ale.

Now Ned on red herrings that evening did sup,
So he drank every drop of the gripe-giving cup.
Soon his guts 'gan to grumble and shortly Ned found
His bowels give way, and his body unbound;
The buckskin's gay leather, by gallus confin'd,
Could not be cut down 'till indecently lined;
This made Neddy's Pego, accustomed to sprout,
Shrink into his belly, and turn up his snout.

The time this damn'd jalap in Ned's belly lurked,
No post horse like Neddy was ever so worked.
Three nights and three days he lay squirting in bed.

And neither could hold up his tail nor his head.
The storm at length ceasing, purg'd Ned 'gan to think
On some revenge sweet for this damnable stink;
"For I'm damn'd," exclaimed Ned, "if these bitches shan't
    find,
That I'm cabbaged before, tho' I'm loosened behind."

'Twas early one morn, exercising his steed,
Ned saw an old gipsy-hag crossing the mead.
Straight he hailed her and said: "Woman, where do you
    hie?"
She replied: "To tell fortunes of females hard by."
Now these females Ned found were his japlaping friends,
So he thought it the season to make them amends.
Then he brib'd for the cant and the gipsy's old clothes.
Thus equipped, said Ned: "Trick for trick: damn me, here
    goes!"

First Molly, the cook-maid, he took by the hand,
From her greasy palm told her what fortune had plann'd.
She was soon to be married, each year have a brat.
"Indeed," cried the cooky, "how can you tell that?"
"I'll tell you the number," said Ned, "let me see
The blue vein that's low plac'd 'twixt the navel and knee."
When she pulled up her clothes, Ned exclaimed: "I de-
    clare
Your blue vein I can't see, 'tis so cover'd with hair."

Next dairy-maid Dolly, of lechery full,
Swore she was then breeding, for she'd had the bull.
To the gipsy, said Doll: "Can you, old woman, tell,
Whether bull or cow-calf makes my belly so swell?"
When he viewed her blue vein, he said, "Doll by my troth,
You must find out two fathers, for you will have both."
For the squire and the curate, when heated with ale,
Doll Dairy had milk'd in her amorous pail.

Now Kitty the housemaid, so frisky and fair,
Who smelt none the sweeter for carrotty hair,
Presenting her palm to the gipsy so shrewd,
Was candidly told that her nature was lewd.

While feeling the vein near her gold-girded nick,
Kate played the old gipsy a slippery trick,
So that Kate, who had ne'er been consider'd a whore,
Was told she'd miscarried the morning before.

Then came Peggy the prude, who no bawdy could bear,
Yet would tickle the lap-dog while combing his hair.
"Is the butler my sweetheart," said Peggy, "sincere,
And shall we be married, pray, gipsy, this year?"
Quoth the gipsy: "You'll have him for better or worse,
But you'll find that his corkscrew is not worth a curse.
So when you are wed, 'twill be o'er the town talk'd:
There goes Peggy, a bottle, most damnably cork'd."

Now Ned, thus revenged, bid the maidens good-day,
But, curious, they ask'd him a moment to stay.
"For," said Molly the cook-maid, "we all long to see,
If you've a blue vein 'twixt the navel and knee."
Ned pull'd up his clothes, sir, when, to their surprise
They beheld his blue vein of a wonderful size.
The sight, Kate the carrotty, couldn't withstand;
She grasped the blue vein till it burst in her hand.

So alarm'd the prude Peggy fell into strong fits,
Frightened cook and Doll Dairy went out of their wits.
Then carrotty Kitty to gipsy Ned spoke:
"We'll each give a guinea to stifle the joke."
But Ned swore that no money should silence his tongue,
That the tale should be told in a mirth-moving song:
"As a caution," cry'd Ned, "to all Abigails frail
That there's more fun in f——g that jalaping ale."

The story like wildfire o'er Cambria spread,
From the borders of Chester to fam'd Holyhead.
In a vein of good humor, the vein that is blue,
Will long be remembered by me and by you;
Then fill a bright bumper to honour this vein,
A bumper of pleasure to badger all pain;
So hear us, celestials, gay mortals below!
Drink c——t, the blue vein, wherein floods of joy flow.

MY GRANDMOTHER'S TALE; or MAY'S ACCOUNT OF HER INTRODUCTION TO THE ART OF LOVE.

From an Unsophisticated Manuscript, Found Amongst the Old Lady's Papers, After her Death, Supposed to have been written about A.D. 1797.

Nina got up and said: "And so I did keep close to Jenny and I have watched over her, and I it was who saw Mr. Boatswain's prick slip in and out of her cunt, and I have been watching her while he did it! What could be closer watching than that, Mrs. Murphy?"

"But he has promised to marry me," called out Jenny.

"Yes," said the boatswain, "I swear I will, but she must let me have a fuck every day until we are ashore."

Mrs. Murphy was obliged to give her consent as she saw the mischief was done.

All our love-matters went on in much the same manner, until at last our brig reached London docks, when we wished Jenny and the boatswain good-bye, and with Nina and our luggage, Captain Lemberg took us to the hotel, where he usually put up when he returned from his voyages.

Captain Lemberg was very kind and chose a bedroom for myself and Nina next to his own, and both opened into a parlour intended for our mutual use.

Captain Lemberg decided I should remain a week or two at the hotel with him, to rest after the voyage and to see some of the sights of London, before I went to the school. In fact he told me he did not think I need go to school until he was obliged to return to the brig, which would be a couple of months, and I told him I would prefer to obey my father's wishes. So we decided I was to go to school in a week.

My father had given me a letter to hand to Madame Stewart, the school-mistress, who lived at Hampton Court.

Captain Lemberg took us to the theatres, which pleased me extremely, also to the Tower and Monument and British Museum.

The time passed very rapidly away in seeing the wonders of London by day and the theatres in the evening, and then we had nice suppers at our hotel and Nina and I retired to our bed, soon to be followed by Captain Lemberg to continue those loving fucking matches like those on the ship.

At last the week ended and Captain Lemberg took me in a coach to Madame Stewart together with Nina, who was to continue to wait on me as lady's-maid.

We had a little fucking in the coach and at last arrived at the school, which was a large house surrounded by ornamental grounds and gardens, enclosed by high walls. The grounds sloped down to the Thames, on the banks of which, of course, there was no wall.

Madame Stewart received the Captain and myself and Nina in a large drawing-room, and I handed her my father's letter and told her Nina was my servant.

She told Nina to retire for the present to the housekeeper's room.

Madame was a fine-looking woman of about fifty, with dark hair and eyes and a fine bust.

After reading the letter she kissed me and said she was acquainted with my father many years before and would try to make me happy, provided I obeyed the rules of her establishment.

Captain Lemberg then paid her £100 for one year's fees in advance and asked for a receipt.

Madame asked him to step into the next room with her as she kept her writing materials there, and she wished to ask him a few questions in private.

So pouring me out a glass of wine and giving me some cake and a book of pictures, they withdrew into the next room and shut the door.

You may be sure my eye was at the keyhole in a moment and I saw that the Captain had pulled out his prick! And I heard him say:

"Madame, I am entitled to the usual commission for bringing you a new pupil and I will take it in dog-fashion."

"Hush!" said Madame, "or the young lady will hear you."

"Nonsense—now get down on all fours so as not to derange your dress."

Madame did so and the Captain tossing up her clothes exposed her bottom, and standing behind her, leant over her back and fucked her in that position.

When this was over they each took a chair and I overheard the following conversation:

MADAME S.—"Is this young lady a virgin?"

CAPT. L.—"Yes, as much as you are!"

Madame S.—"Shall I read you the letter her father has sent me?"

Capt. L.—"I shall be delighted to hear it read."

Madame then read the letter aloud, and I heard every word that follows:

My Dear Madame Stewart:

These will be handed to you by my daughter Kate, a fine girl just over twelve years of age. Captain Lemberg has kindly undertaken to see her safely to your house, and I have authorized him to pay you for the first year's expense, one hundred guineas.

My daughter's education has been neglected in such matters as penmanship, grammar, drawing, and music. Be pleased to spare no pains in instructing her in these.

In some other things she is in advance of her years. On account of living all her life on a slave plantation she has always seen boys, girls and women in a state of nakedness, so the difference in sex is familiar to her. She has seen men and women in the act of coition.

You will please pay special regard to her religious duties, and also try to inculcate that modest demeanour which is such a characteristic to your own movements that I shall never forget being struck with on occasion of my last visit to your school some fifteen years ago when I had the felicity of watching you slowly strip naked at noon before a large mirror in your dining-room previous to your honouring my pego with a visit to your fine quim.

Alas! Madam, these remembrances quite overpower me and make me regret the distance that separates us!

I have sent a very fair mulatto-girl named Nina, to wait on my daughter.

> From your obedient servant,
> Sebastian de Lorme.

P.S.—Nina is not a virgin although she is very tight in her cunny. She may be useful at your conversations. Neither Kate nor Nina have ever been birched."

Capt. L.—"What a very interesting letter. Do you use the birch still, Madame?"

Madame.—"Certainly, when my young ladies deserve it."

Capt. Lemberg then insisted on having another fuck, for

reading my father's letter of his interview with Madame Stewart had given him a cockstand.

So they had another bout and the Captain said he must leave. So I hastened from the keyhole and was apparently absorbed in my book when Madame and Captain entered the room.

The Captain kissed me as he bade me good-bye and thrust his tongue into my mouth as he did so, bidding me obey Madame in everything and all would be well.

He promised to take me for a day's holiday before the brig sailed if Madame would kindly consent.

I promised to endeavour to please Madame, and with another kiss he departed.

Madame Stewart then had a long talk with me and urged me to be candid and truthful in my answers to her questions. She asked: "Have you ever seen the slave men quite naked?"

"Yes."

"And the slave women?"

"Yes."

"And is it true that neither of them ever have any hair on their private parts?"

"Do you mean their cocks and cunts, Madame?"

"Yes, my dear."

"Then it is not true, because I have seen short curly hair on those places, and in the case of the men, quite as much as was on my dear father's prick."

"Do you mean to say you have seen your father's prick?"

"Yes, Madame, and felt it too!"

So I told her all my history, at which she was delighted and wanted to look at my cunny. I complied and she complimented me on my rich growth of hair.

She told me I must never let a man's prick enter my cunny without her consent being first obtained as she was desirous of shielding me from harm whilst I was under her roof; but she promised I should have all the coition that was good for me at proper times if I was diligent in my lessons.

You may be sure, dearest May, I was pleased with this intelligence and gave the required promise, thinking what a wise and kind schoolmistress she was.

I told her my father had fucked Nina and sent her to be my waiting-maid, and as we were very fond of each other I hoped she would allow us to be together as much as possible.

She agreed to this saying she quite understood from my father's letter that it was his wish Nina should be with me. She made me repeat the tale I had told her about my taking Nina's place in the garden with my father and also the scene with him just before the brig sailed.

Nina was then called into the room and I told her that Madame Stewart was a very kindly lady and was willing we should occupy the same room like we did at home.

Poor Nina was profuse in her thanks and asked permission to kiss Madame's feet as a token of her gratitude.

Madame then told us to follow her upstairs, and she took us down a long passage with bedrooms opening from both sides of it. Here she pointed out a room and told us it was ours, but shared with another girl, the daughter of a wealthy baronet, Sir Thomas Moreton.

The room had three narrow beds in it, as Madame said her rule was for each pupil to have a bed of her own.

Madame then kissed me and told me to read the rules, a copy of which was fastened on the wall. As nearly as I can recollect they ran as follows:

Rule I—Every pupil, before retiring to rest, must strip naked and wash her person in every part.

Rule II—No pupil may examine her secret part before the mirror.

Rule III—No pupil must occupy a bed that is not her own.

N.B.—The penalty for breaking either of these rules is one dozen stripes with the birch.

When Nina heard me read these rules she said: "But how will Madame know if we break them?"

I replied: "Perhaps the other girl will tell tales on us! Or, perhaps she will be a nice girl and we can do as we like."

"Hush!" said Nina.

And Madame entered our room with Miss Moreton, saying, "Let me introduce you young ladies, as you will occupy this room together. Miss Moreton has been in this establishment for two years, so she knows all the girls and all the customs. You will soon get acquainted."

Madame withdrew and Miss Moreton asked my age and who my father was and we were soon chatting away glibly.

She said she was sixteen and should leave the school next

holidays. Her name was Alice. She asked me if I had ever had a lover. I told her yes—Captain Lemberg—and that my father had sent me in his ship from home to England.

"Oh!" said Alice, "then you had a fine time together, I know! Please tell me all about it."

I said I would someday, but now I wanted to know all about the girls at school as I was never at school before.

Alice was surprised at this but I informed her my mother died when I was young and my father would not part with me, but preferred teaching me himself.

Alice told me Madame was very strict with the new girls until she had the chance to whip them a few times, after which she was very indulgent.

She told me that Saturday evening was punishment time and she had found out that gentlemen were admitted to Madame's room to peep at the girls punished. I enquired how she knew that. She said I had no doubt noticed that the grounds reached the water's edge.

Well, said Alice, one Saturday Madame sent me into the garden to get some fruit the gardener had forgotten and I saw two boats stop at the boat-house. I hid behind some bushes and saw four gentlemen, muffled up in cloaks, walk up the path which leads to the side entrance of the house. They were admitted by Mrs. White, the housekeeper. My curiosity was excited, so I quickly brought Madame the fruit and ran into her private room, and crept under the sofa to listen, thinking I would be certain to find out something. Nor was I wrong in my conjecture, for in a few minutes Mrs. White ushers in the four gentlemen and two of them sit down on the very sofa I was under. They talked to each other about the superior manner in which Madame's establishment was conducted. Two of them said they had daughters at present in the school and hoped they would have broken some of the rules that week.

This remark astonished me but my surprise was greater when by the voice of the next speaker I recognized my own father, Sir Thomas Moreton! He had visited me that very morning, gave me a supply of pocket money, wished me good-bye and said he was going back home at once; and here he was in the same house!

The other speaker was the rector of the parish church, the Hon. and Rev. Algernon Stanley. I knew his voice, for in the course of the conversation he was addressed as Stanley by my father.

Evidently the party of four were acquaintances, for they all chatted away on good terms.

In a few moments I heard my father's voice:

"Well, gentlemen, I will bet you five pounds that when you see the punishment this evening you will allow my daughter's bottom to be the plumpest and most exciting of any you shall see tonight!"

RECTOR.—"But suppose your daughter is not birched to-night?"

SIR MORETON.—"Then we will let the bet stand over till some other Saturday when she is flogged and we all are here."

Here, dear Kate, was a revelation to me! My father and three other gentlemen evidently were here for the purpose of witnessing the punishments about to be inflicted on the schoolgirls' bottoms! And my father must have seen my bottom on some previous occasion, or how could he make this bet! I knew I was to be punished that evening for my name was on the blacklist.

How should I escape from under the sofa and reach the schoolroom? For my ambition was fired by my father's words of admiration about my plump bottom and I wanted him to win that bet!

Fortunately for my intentions, Madame came into the room and invited the gentlemen to adjourn upstairs.

Directly they were gone I crept from my hiding place and ran up to the schoolroom by the back staircase and seated myself at the piano and commenced practicing my exercises.

In a short time the German governess, Fraulein Hoffman, came to me and said:

"My dear you must prepare for punishment."

"Yes, Fraulein," I answered.

And, according to the custom, I retired to my bedroom, took off my form, skirts and corset and returned to the schoolroom in chemise, drawers and stockings, which was the regulation dress for punishment.

Three other girls were to be punished; one rebelled from Fraulein's order and had to be dragged to her room and undressed.

At last we heard a bell ring and each of us, the culprits, was escorted by a governess to the room especially used and fitted up for punishment. It was lighted from the roof and had ladders, Berkeley horses and other appliances, such as ropes from the ceiling, rings in the floor and ceiling to which to fasten refractory culprits.

On this occasion we were made to slowly take off our drawers and then kneel on a kind of table with our heads low down and our posteriors sticking well out, with our hands and ankles tied securely.

Next, our offences were read out to us by Madame as follows:

"Margaret Stanley, your offence is as usual peeing in bed. I give you notice that I intend telling the worthy rector, your uncle, of this most disgusting habit of yours.

"Emmeline Chesterfield, your offence is greediness in eating up the cake you brought from home, and not sharing it with your schoolfellows.

"Constance Le Ray, you were discovered viewing your naked person in the glass; such vanity must be checked by the rod."

And then Madame read my name.

"Alice Moreton, your offence is one against decency. It is that of having received a letter from a lover whom you obstinately refuse to name or give any information as to how you have carried on this clandestine correspondence.

"I will read it aloud to you, Miss Alice Moreton, and I hope your cheeks will blush with shame as much as the cheeks of your bottom will blush under the rod, presently. This is the horrid letter:

My Dear Alice:

How I do long for another kiss on the lips of your pussey! The last I had was delicious! I dream of you every night and sometimes fancy I am in one of those high pews at church with your naked bottom sitting in my face, so I can kiss and suck your pussey! At other times in my dreams you catch hold of me by the cock and sing: "I will not let thee go, unless you fuck me!"

You cannot wonder at these dreams, sweetheart, for they are only repetitions of the facts of the day!

Give my love to Madame and asked her to notice the beauty of your cunny!

From your devoted love,
Henry.

Madame having finished the letter told the governesses to commence flogging us, and to strike as she called out, One, Two, Three.

They were stationed close to our heads so they had to strike over our backs to reach our bottoms, which were turned towards the end of the room at which Madame was seated on a dais, raised up six steps above the level of the floor.

I remembered the conversation of the gentlemen and the bet of my dear father, and I had no doubt they were watching us from some secret peep-hole, or were perhaps under the dais. So at every blow of the rod I writhed and twisted my posteriors as much as possible, in order to display all its beauties.

Margaret received fifty stripes, Emmeline sixty, Constance eighty, and I, the greatest offender, received one hundred, which caused me to faint away.

What do you think of that, Kate dear?

I told her I thought it was a great shame and asked if the gentlemen ever came again.

Alice said no doubt they did although she had never had an opportunity of proving it; still, on Saturdays occasionally she had slipped into the garden and found boats moored to the boat-house. "However, my dear Katie, I have told you all I know, perhaps someday we will make more discoveries."

Kate said she warmly thanked Alice for telling her all the circumstances, and they kissed and went to bed.

Chapter IV.
A Letter from Susey.

About this time I received a letter from Susey, who, when the vacation commenced, went to her uncle in Scotland, and I may as well give her adventures in her own words:

My Darling May:

You remember the morning you took leave of me, I had to walk a mile to meet the coach. John Cox, my sister Jane's intended husband, came to start me off, and he carried my box on his shoulder as we walked across the fields and down to the crossroads where the coach takes up passengers.

John told me he and Jane were soon to be married, and he said her belly was so big that it looked beautiful.

I asked him what made it so big and he laughed as he said: "Why, Susey, because I have made a baby inside of it to be sure, you little goose!"

John also said that he was now obliged to fuck Jane behind, because her belly sticking out quite prevented his approaching the front.

He told me that he had a special message from Jane to me which was to be sure to do my pee just before getting on the coach, as I should have to ride for many hours and it was very painful to be obliged to hold your water.

"So," says John, "you had better squat down at once, and I can see your little cunt at the same time."

So I got close to some bushes and had a good pee and John had a good look at my cunny, and afterwards kissed and sucked it. Just then we heard the guard's horn announcing the near approach of the coach. So I had only time to give John's prick a farewell kiss, and then we hurried to the little ale-house at the crossroads.

The coach was full inside so I had to take an outside seat, and as there was no ladder I climbed up as well as I could. But I felt John's hand on my thigh as he stood beneath me.

When the coach started I looked at my fellow passengers and saw there were two gentlemen—one evidently a clergyman and the other, from remarks made, was his son, apparently about my own age. He asked me how far I was going and I replied, to Scotland.

"Have you never been there before?"

"No, sir," I replied.

"They have some very curious customs in Scotland," he said.

"What are they?" was my enquiry.

"The wearing of the kilt, for instance," said he.

"I do not know what a kilt is," was my reply.

"I will show you a picture of a Scotsman dressed in his kilt," said he, taking a book from his coat-pocket, and turning over the leaves, he showed me the picture of a tall man with naked knees and a short petticoat which he explained was the kilt.

I laughed at the odd figure in the picture and asked: "Do

the Scotch girls and women dress like that too? If so, they must be cold."

"I wish they did," said he, "don't you, father?"

"Well, my son, it would have a very delightful effect, no doubt," said the clergyman.

I interposed: "But the poor man must feel very cold here."

"Not at all," said the clergyman. "When I was at college as a young man, I wore that dress once at a fancy ball and found it very comfortable."

"Did you waltz in your kilt?" I asked.

"Yes, certainly, and why not?"

"Because I should think the whirling motion of dancing would cause your kilt to fly up and expose your . . ." and I stopped suddenly—laughing.

"Bottom, you were going to say, my dear! And where would be the harm in that? Ladies like to get a glimpse at a man's bottom sometimes," said he.

"I'm sure they don't," I replied.

"Oh," said the son, "you think the ladies would rather look at him before than behind, eh? Well, what do you say at this picture," and he moved aside the kilt, which was a separate piece of paper, and showed me the Scotsman's prick in full erection.

"That's more in your way, my dear," said he. Then speaking to the clergyman, he said: "Father, this young lady, evidently, from her blushes, thinks a man's prick is more beautiful than his bottom."

"I am very glad to hear it," said he, "for it proves that her education has not been neglected and that she has learnt from her catechism: 'What is the chief end of man?'"

(*To be continued.*)

FLUNKEYANIA; OR BELGRAVIAN MORALS.

BY CHARLES.

CHAPTER IV.

That I have not ere this alluded to the Earl of Pomeroy, by whom I was specially engaged and to whom my services were due as well as to the Countess, must be attributed to the fact that almost immediately on my entering upon my duties, as recorded in this veracious narrative, His Lordship had joined a shooting-party at the Duke of Dashwood's, with whom the Earl was particularly intimate. Indeed, common report went so far as to say that His Lordship was still more intimate with the Duchess and that his Grace seemed to be perfectly indifferent on the subject.

Report as a general rule is a sad liar, but I strongly suspect (indeed, I had reason subsequently to know) that in this instance there was a good deal of truth in the rumour. Be that as it may, their Graces, accompanied by their daughter, the Lady Georgiana, were making a return visit to the Earl and Countess of Pomeroy, both of whom (very sensibly, as they might have need of my services) took care to make me acquainted with certain peculiarities of their noble guests.

As the Countess's remarks and suggestions were by far the more concise, I shall take them first in order.

She commenced by saying that she hated them all three. Father, mother and daughter. His Grace she described as a great heavy man, fond of good eating, hard drinking and riding, and that in matters pertaining to women he was a gross sensualist.

People had even been kind enough to couple her name with his, which she need not say was a base fabrication.

"Of course, my Lady," I ventured to interrupt.

She then went on to say that nothing would induce her to have anything to do with such a brute and that she would leave him to his liaisons with chambermaids and housemaids, whom he had the bad taste to prefer and to whom he conducted himself in such a style as to render him a nuisance in any country-house where he happened to be staying.

"On the last occasion when he was here," my Lady continued, "he had the impudence to make improper advances to my maid Justine, but I very soon put a stop to that. Indeed, I think that Justine herself had too much good taste to permit such a thing."

Here I may notice, en passant, that while I cordially subscribed to Justine's good taste as far as I was personally concerned, yet I had my private doubts about that young lady resisting temptation, especially if a heavy bribe were offered.

But I am interrupting the course of the Lady's remarks.

"If his Grace condescends to make paramours about the girls' bedrooms, generally it's no business of mine, as long as the housekeeper does not call my attention to the degrading circumstances. If the girls get into mischief I am sorry for them and they must leave, that is all."

This was all my Lady had to say about his Grace of Dashwood, and pretty much too, you'll say.

The Duchess came next in consideration. She, it appeared, was very handsome, though dark. This was quite true, her Grace presenting a marked contrast in appearance to my mistress, who, as I think I have before noticed, had bright brown hair. The head and front of her offence was, in Lady Pomeroy's opinion, not only that she, the Duchess, kept up a constant and most undisguised improper intimacy with the Earl, but had the effrontery to presume to be on the most affectionate terms with herself, the Countess.

"Just as if," continued that indignant lady, "she could fancy me so stupidly blind as not to perceive what was going on almost under my very nose. Why, the very fact of not concealing it is an insult in itself!"

And I must say that I quite agreed with her there.

As to the Lady Georgiana, my mistress considered her a handsome aristocratic young lady, who had nothing but the accident of her birth to justify her excessive haughtiness and who affected to consider all other people, and the male sex in particular, as so much dirt under her feet.

"That part of the business," continued my Lady, "I am convinced is all sheer nonsense, and in reality she is as sensually inclined, body and soul, as either her father or mother, and that will be found out someday, I feel perfectly certain."

As the Countess emphasized the last remarks, I could not help fancying that she glanced at me in a peculiar way.

Could it be that she had designed me as the instrument for lowering the pride of the haughty Lady Georgiana?

As to the characters of the gentleman's valet and the lady's femme de chambre, she merely premised that they were a trifle worse than usual among persons in their situations. The rest I might find out for myself.

Then reminding me of my pledge of secrecy and the peculiar bond by which she had secured my fidelity, we forgot for a few minutes our relative positions as Lady and servant.

I had been standing respectfully in front of Her Ladyship, but at the conclusion of her explanatory remarks on the virtues and vices of her guests, she motioned me to draw closer as she wished to ascertain for herself if I had been wasting on others that which I ought to keep so as to be always in readiness to minister to her requirements.

Opening my trousers with her own delicate hands, she pulled out my rapidly rising organ of pleasure, and drawing back the foreskin, exclaimed: "Ah! you have been good! I can easily tell if the prepuce is all red that you have been obliging someone else within five hours. But this jewel is pale and I see no traces of recent excitement."

I fell on my knees and offered the devotions of my tongue at her shrine of love, then followed that up by a most salacious sucking, till she was content and graciously dismissed me, in order that I might be in immediate attendance on the Earl, who summoned me, and as his guests had just arrived, I lost no time in waiting on my master.

As of course the new arrivals were at once shown to the apartments destined for them, it afforded a capital opportunity for my Lord to order me to follow him to his dressing-room. The private instructions and directions I there received were, as the reader will see, slightly different to the suggestions thrown out by Lady Pomeroy.

To begin with, His Lordship expressed his strong opinion that the Lady was guilty of infidelity and that the partner of her misdemeanour was no other than his most intimate friend, the Duke of Dashwood.

Of course, I knew better than this, but as I was supposed to know nothing, I said nothing.

I think His Lordship tried hard to persuade himself that the case was such, in order to try and make some small excuse for his conduct with regard to the Duchess. This, indeed, he hardly tried to conceal.

He was far from entertaining the same opinion of Monsieur Duroque and Mademoiselle Juliette, the valet and femme de chambre of the Duke and Duchess, which was held by the Countess. Indeed he represented that couple as the most valuable and trustworthy of their class, especially recommending Juliette to my notice. She and I would, it appeared, be the means of communication between the Duchess and himself in the way of verbal messages, notes or otherwise,

and therefore it was highly desirable that I should cultivate
the young woman's acquaintance.

"You have my full permission to fuck her, and make yourself as agreeable as possible. Then I can depend upon you
both. There's nothing like that to ensure discretion in love
matters," he added.

This, from the estimate I formed of her character and
judging from her personal appearance, I considered I should
not have much difficulty in doing.

My final instructions were not to fail in my attendance
on my Lady and to report to him anything worthy of notice,
particularly between her and the Duke.

This I faithfully promised to do, feeling pretty confident
that I should notice nothing in that quarter, and mentally re-
solving that any other eccentricities of my Lady as developed
in respect to myself should not be considered worthy of
notice.

So far, so good. And when my services to Her Ladyship
were concluded, little did he guess in what some of those
services consisted, or with what pleasure they were given.

I was to attend His Lordship in his dressing-room as he
would most likely require me.

Upon this I bowed and withdrew, and my Lady having a
good deal of company to entertain at dinner, subsequently
retired rather fatigued about eleven o'clock. I was at liberty
to retire and repaired at once to my Lord's dressing-room.
There I waited until nearly twelve when, making his appearance, he demanded if anyone had called there with a note
for him.

I was in the very act of replying in the negative when a tap
was heard at the door and opening it, entered Juliette.

She hesitated a little on seeing me, but on the holding out
of his hand as if expecting something, she placed in it a small
note. On reading it, he nodded his head and smiled, saying
to the bearer, "Your mistress is retiring, I suppose?"

On receiving an answer in the affirmative he further asked
whether his Grace was in bed or making any preparations for
going to bed?

To this the clever soubrette replied that she had just seen
Duroque, who had informed her that the Duke had taken a
good deal of wine and seemed quite disposed for bed and
would probably sleep soundly.

Upon receiving this information, my Lord dismissed me, as there was little possibility of my services being required that night in the espionage department, and it is to be presumed that he could manage anything else perfectly well without my assistance.

CHAPTER V.

Tired as I was, I was undressing myself very leisurely but had nearly concluded that operation, when, lo! the door of my room quietly opened.

I never locked it for fear of being suddenly and secretly summoned.

Who the opener might be, of course, I could not tell, but I certainly did not expect to see Mademoiselle Juliette.

Putting her finger to her lips as a sign of silence and secrecy, she informed me that the Duke was up and evidently bound on some nocturnal ramble, and that she, being in the Duchess's room, Lord Pomeroy (it is to be presumed that he was there too) had begged her to awake me, and desire me to look after his Grace as there was every reason to fear that his destination was the apartment of the Countess.

"So don't sit there staring like an owl in the sunshine," exclaimed the impudent black-eyed girl. "Get up and put your breeches on and I'll help you."

Now I beg to assure my kind readers that at this moment I was in that particular costume in which Charles Lever describes his hero, Harry Lorrequer, being discovered when the bell rang to draw up the curtain at some private theatricals: to wit, a shirt and silk stockings.

Nothing more, upon my honour!

And I leave it to any to say whether it was a delicate operation for a modest young man to undergo to be assisted in pulling on his breeches by an impudent black-eyed soubrette.

The chastest Joseph that ever lived must have yielded to the temptation, and the stupidest gawky of a piously brought-up lout must guess what followed.

I picked up my trousers from the chair upon which they had been flung as I undressed, and pretending to bungle as I bashfully attempted to hide John Thomas, who at the bare idea of a bit of anything fresh, was in his usual unruly state.

"La!" she exclaimed as her hand touched my projecting shirt, "is it anything that will bite?"

"Yes love, but not anything to hurt a darling like you. Won't you stroke his pretty head? It's a pet with all the ladies," I replied, pulling up my shirt and presenting the Vade mecum of pleasure to her eyes.

Juliette at once flushed crimson as she covered her face at the sight, ejaculating: "How dare you, sir? I'll tell the Countess!"

"Not before you've enjoyed it, however, and then you can give me a reference for gallantry as well, which may do me a great service. You're in for it, now, Miss Juliette," I said, shoving her towards the bed, and in spite of her resistance, I soon had her clothes up and got between as beautiful a pair of thighs as I ever saw (she had no drawers on). It wanted only the electric touch of Mr. Pego to make her surrender all discretion. Ah, what an engagement we had, yard-arm to yard-arm, as Jack Tar would say! In fact I fired into her port-hole till she surrendered and went off into a faint of ecstasy.

I shall never forget it, short as the fuck was, it was one of the most enjoyable I remember. Time was precious and she soon kissed and forgave my boldness, for, of course, it was only what the young lady had hoped and expected, and so I trust she was satisfied. But now I had to attend to business.

Finding that the Duke had indeed left his room, I proceeded in search of his Grace, not in the direction suggested by Juliette, but in quite another direction than towards my Lady Pomeroy's apartments, to where the under-servants slept. Comfortable rooms enough they were, too.

Now I was perfectly aware that Sophy and Lucy, the two housemaids, slept in one room. There I thought would be my mark, and there, sure enough, I found his Grace evidently on the most affectionate terms with the two young women, whose charms, though not of the most aristocratic class, were by no means to be despised; for he was paying them very liberally in advance, and so I had to remain and see whether he fell into the snare which sometimes awaits the bad paymasters who pay in advance, or I should make but a poor report to my employers. But, no, I had the gratification of witnessing through the medium of the keyhole (after rather a tedious observation, however, for were there not two young women?) that "there is honour among housemaids" and that

if his Grace of Dashwood did not get his money's worth it
was not the fault of Sophy and Lucy!

(*To be continued.*)

NURSERY RHYMES.

There was a young bride of Antigua,
Whose husband had said: "Dear me, how big you are!"
    Said the girl: "What damn'd rot,
    Why, you've often felt my twot,
My legs and my arse and my figual"

    There once was a young man of Bulgaria,
    Who once went to piss down an area,
        Said Mary to cook:
        "Oh, do come and look,
    Did you ever see anything hairier?"

A CURIOUS FACT FOR NATURALISTS.

The Editor has received the following from a subscriber:
"One often hears: 'No standing pricks this weather,' or,
'It's a difficult thing to find it, etc., during a severe winter,'
but one intensely cold morning, just as we were getting up,
my wife looking out of the window, drew my attention to a
poor cat which had been out all night, expressing her sympathy for the poor beast. Presently I looked into the back-
yard for myself, when, lo! there were two cats, the feminine
rolling on her back in the most approved fashion of cat-
courtship, when the lady is agreeable to the gentleman's
attentions. The thermometer at twenty-six degrees below
freezing made no difficulty with him. He was on to her and
into her in a moment, the only difference being that he, and
in fact both of them, were more ready than on a warm sum-

mer's night, when we all know to our cost, the long preliminary caterwauling, scratching, etc., necessary to bring Mr.
Tom to the point."

N.B.—I suppose scratching with cats has the same effect as
birching on human beings.

THE LOVER'S KISS.

"Give me, my love, that billing kiss,
    I taught you one delicious night,
When, turning epicures in delight,
    We tried inventions of bliss.

Come gently steal my lips along,
    And let your lips in murmurs move;
Ah, no—again—that kiss was wrong,
    How can you be so dull, my love?"

"Cease, cease," the blushing girl replied,
    And in her milky arms she caught me;
"How can you thus your pupil chide?
    You know 'twas in the dark you taught me!"

AMENITIES OF LEICESTER SQUARE.

Girl to Ponce:—Go along, you bloody Mary Ann, and
tighten your arse-hole with alum.

English Whore to French Woman:—Yah, you foreign
bitches can only get a man by promising them a bottom-fuck!

French Woman:—Yes, I do let the English gentlemen
have my arse-hole but my cunt I do keep for my husband.

TOASTS.

Gent:—The first four letters of the alphabet—A Big Cunt Daily.

Lady:—In with it, and out with it, and God work his will with it.

THE PEARL,

A Journal of Facetiæ and Voluptuous Reading.

No. 17   PUBLISHED MONTHLY.   Nov. 1880

MY GRANDMOTHER'S TALE; or MAY'S ACCOUNT OF HER INTRODUCTION TO THE ART OF LOVE.

From an Unsophisticated Manuscript, Found Amongst the Old Lady's Papers, After Her Death, Supposed to Have Been Written About A.D. 1797

"My dear father," said the young man, "we have the back part of the coach to ourselves and the guard is sitting with the coachman, so we are quite private here. Would it not be a good opportunity for letting this young lady look at your reverend prick?"

"Most certainly, my son," replied the clergyman, unbuttoning his trousers. "I am always ready to please the ladies."

So he pulled out his noble tool, fondly stroking it. "There, Miss, there is something for a man to be proud of, and I am proud to have such a father."

"I hope you may have just such another someday," I said.

"Thank you, my dear," said he, "I will show you what I have at present."

And he exhibited his own prick. I told him it was as big as he had any reason to expect, and he quite agreed with me and then regretted the fact that our being outside the coach would prevent his father and himself from looking at anything I would like to show them. "But," continued he, "the coach will stop to change horses in a few minutes' time, and then the passengers generally get down and go inside the inn for half-an-hour for refreshments. But my father, the rector, is well known to the landlord and we will ask for a private room and take our refreshments there; and then, Miss Susan, you will have the wished-for opportunity."

By the time he had finished speaking we arrived at the Royal George, and the parson and his son helped me down from the coach, and I soon found myself in an upstairs parlour with them. They told me their journey terminated there, as they had to drive in a gig to their home, five miles distant, and they both begged me to lose no time.

I replied: "I am in your hands, gentlemen! Only don't harm me."

They promised they would not, and the father then raised my clothes, called his son's attention to my white thighs and the pouting lips of my cunt.

Both father and son kissed and sucked it for a few minutes and then the father insisted on his son having a fuck before he had one.

By the time each had finished, the horn blew the warning to get ready. So hastily swallowing a glass of wine, I arranged my clothes and bade them good-bye.

They accompanied me to the coach and this time I was able to get inside, there being one place vacant, and the parson kindly paying the difference in fare.

With mutual farewells the coach started again and I looked at my fellow passengers and found one who appeared young, the other two being grey-haired gentlemen.

They all accosted me very politely and hoped we should have a pleasant journey together.

The young man enquired how far I was going and when I replied to Edinburgh, he expressed his pleasure that we should be going to the same city.

"What a fortunate circumstance," said he, "that you were not travelling by this coach last week."

"How so?"

"Because the notorious Dick Turpin and his gang stopped the coach just a little way from here and robbed the passengers, and used the ladies very cruelly."

"Oh! how you frighten me! Do tell me all about it," said I.

The elderly gentleman opposite now spoke and said:

"I can give you the correct account, for I was one of the passengers and one of the victims, I may say."

"Oh, do tell me if there is any danger of Dick Turpin coming again today?" I asked.

"Not the slightest," said the old gentleman, "and that is the reason why I am travelling again so soon. Besides, I am armed with my horse-pistols."

"Oh," said I, "don't show them to me, I am so terribly frightened! But tell me about the villains."

The old gentleman continued: "It was just about three in the afternoon when, as we were bowling along, as we are now, I heard several horsemen ride up on each side of the coach and call to the coachman to stop or he should be shot. And two shots were fired at him, and one wounded him, the other broke the lamp.

"Of course the coach was stopped and the robbers then called: 'Stand out and deliver your money and valuables, or you are all dead men.'

"There must have been ten or twelve men—some on foot, and some on horseback.

"I should mention that the inside of the coach was occupied by some girls going to York to school. There were four besides their mistress and outside there were four more girls—that makes nine ladies, and there were six men passengers besides the coachman and guard.

"I should say that two of the misses were my grandchildren, aged about thirteen and fourteen.

"Well, the villains first looked inside the coach and made the madame give up her gold watch and rings, then they made us men come down and stand in the road while they searched our pockets, one man standing with the muzzle of a pistol pressed close to my forehead while he searched my pockets.

"When this was done, they abused us for giving them so much trouble for so little money and declared they would be revenged on the women for it.

"I begged them to spare my poor grandchildren.

"'Point them out,' said one of the villains.

"I did so, thinking that he was going to listen to my requests, but no; to my surprise he tied their hands behind them and then lifted up their clothes and threw them over their heads, exposing their bodies from the waist downwards!

"I rushed forward to replace their clothing when two of the villains caught hold of me and tied my hands behind my back, and then to my indignation, they actually cut open my breeches in front and pulled out my prick."

"Horrible!" I exclaimed.

"Monstrous," said the young man.

"Yes," continued the old man, "and that is not all. There is something more horrible to tell."

"Oh, do tell," said I.

"Pray," said the young man, "continue."

"Well, the villains made me kneel down and kiss the slits of my two granddaughters and made me suck them and push in my tongue! Then they uncovered the poor girls' faces, and tying their clothes tight under their arms, ordered them to suck my cock! In vain they and I protested. A loaded pistol fired off close to our ears was the warning of what our fate should be if we disobeyed. So first one and then the other dear girl went through the task. And the villains made me say the sucking was pleasant!"

"And what did you say?"

"Of course I told the truth, that the sucking gave me great pleasure."

"And what became of the other men who were passengers?"

"Oh, they were made to suck the slits of the schoolgirls and to submit to have their pricks sucked in turn."

"And how did the school-madame fare?"

"Oh, the villains grossly insulted her by examining her cunt, and telling her she was too old to allow them to give her any pleasure of that kind, so they cut a bunch of twigs from the bushes and forced her on all fours, bared her backside and gave her a good flogging."

"Do you mean to state that all these outrages took place on the high-turnpike road?"

"Well, yes, that is to say, close to it, for there was a piece of turf or grass-land rather wide at the side of the road at this place. In fact, there were a few trees and bushes growing there."

"Did no person pass in travelling along the road, while this took place, for it must have taken some time?"

"Yes, it took an hour or more, but a farmer with his wife riding behind on a pillion, and one wagon loaded with hay accompanied by the wagoner, were all that passed by during the time. Part of the hay was unloaded to serve for beds on which to extend the unfortunate lady-passengers and the farmer was compelled to fuck his wife in public."

"Did Dick Turpin take part in these outrages?"

"No, he told his men to fuck any way they took a fancy to,

but he kept watch most of the time and gave the necessary directions to his men so that several of them kept watch in turn, while the others committed these outrages on their victims."

"Do you mean to say that the ten schoolgirls were all raped and their maidenheads taken?"

"Certainly; if they had any to lose! They were all fucked before my eyes."

"How did it all end?"

"Oh, after a while Captain Dick said: 'That's enough for this time, boys. Mount and away!' And so they rode off leaving all the victims tied and bound until some passer-by should come and relieve them. Of course we called for help directly after our tormentors had left us and in half-an-hour some foot passengers and also the returning mail-coach came by and released our bonds and we all made the best of our ways to our destinations."

The young man now spoke. "It is all quite true, Miss, I assure you; I was one of the passengers by the down-mail on that occasion and I saw the condition of the ten schoolgirls as described by our friend here. They were all tied to trees with their arms behind them, and their clothing raised and tied close to their shoulders so as to expose their bellies and all below.

"I could not help being delighted with the sight, although of course I pitied the poor things, and I delayed helping to release them in order to have a good view of their naked charms. I was much amused at the remarks of a worthy tradesman and his wife who were also looking at those schoolgirls. The wife spoke sharply: 'Well, Mr. Jones, I am ashamed of you to stand staring like a stuck pig at those naked shameless young hussies. Why don't they put their dresses down?'

"'Well, my dear,' said her husband, 'they have their hands tied behind their backs and can't help themselves, and as to my looking at them, my excuse is I never saw such a sight before! Why, there are ten naked bellies for me to look at and four have hardly any hair on their slits and the others all have black hair on them, but one, and she. . .'

"Here his wife angrily interposed: 'You have made good use of your eyes for these few minutes, Mr. Jones; I must say I am astonished at you, a married man and the father of six girls and four boys, so to demean yourself! Why don't you shut your eyes until this disgraceful exhibition is over?'

" 'No, Mrs. Jones, I am not going to close my eyes! I may be called as a witness against the villains if ever they are caught, and if I shut my eyes how am I to describe to the jury the cruel state in which the girls are left?'

" 'Well,' said his wife, 'had you not better try and catch those villains?'

" 'No, my dear, my duty does not lie in that direction.'

" 'Nor your inclination either,' retorted his wife, 'for evidently you prefer the safer course of feasting your eyes on these poor girls' nakedness.'

" 'Well, my dear, you know I am always delighted to look at yours but you so seldom allow me to do so.'

" 'I should think not, indeed,' said Mrs. Jones, 'and that reminds me that last Sunday I saw you take two of our daughters on your knee and I think you had your hands under their clothes!'

" 'Nonsense! Mrs. Jones, only a little play and romping, for my girls are very fond of their old father; besides it is a father's duty to see if his girls' underclothes are clean and in the fashion.'

" 'Now, Mr. Jones, do be quiet. What right has a man to be troubling himself about his girls' clothing?'

" 'Why what I buy and pay for with my own money I have the right to examine, and you know I should never have married you if I had not examined you first!'

" 'For shame, Mr. Jones, to speak about that here in the open air where anyone might overhear you!'

" 'Now Mary Ann, dear, will you untie these poor girls' clothes from their necks and help me undo their hands?'

"So I then offered my assistance to several of the girls and helped to put their clothing down over their bellies, taking care to touch much of their naked bodies in doing so, and getting my hand on each of their bellies in the performance of this duty.

"I ought to mention that the place where these outrages took place was a kind of valley between two hills, and where a house was not in sight for many miles. It was up a lane through this valley that the highway-men came on horseback to do their unlawful work, and when they had completed it they went away down the valley again."

At this moment as the young man finished his account the coach gave a lurch forward, probably from the coachman suddenly whipping up the horses; however, I found myself flung against the elderly man sitting opposite me and he caught me firmly in his arms and kissed me, saying: "God bless me, Miss, don't be frightened, come to my arms, I'll take care of you."

I replied I could not help it and then felt a hand passing up my thighs from behind, and another hand patting my bottom.

I cried out: "Oh, this conduct is most shameful gentlemen, do leave a poor girl alone!"

"Why, what's the matter, my dear?" said the young man.

"Nobody is touching you," growled the old gentleman.

"Well, my dear, I am kissing you," said the one on whom I had been thrown.

"I know that," I replied, "but more than that has been done to me."

"Well," said he, "I am a magistrate and my name is Squire Johnson, and if you will sit by my side and make your complaint you shall have justice done to you."

The other elderly-looking gentleman said: "Well, Squire Johnson you have known me for years as the parson of the parish and my name is the Rev. Mr. Scarlett and I expect you to take my oath against any other person's."

The young gentleman now spoke: "Oh, I am a medical student going home from college. My name is Charley Stuart and I am sure to fall in love with every pretty girl I see, especially such an angel as this!" giving me a most loving look.

"Now, then," said Squire Johnson, "if you, Miss, will give us your name we will proceed."

I replied: "My name is Susan Gardiner and I charge Parson Scarlett and Charley Stuart with touching my naked body."

Squire Johnson wrote this down in his pocket-book and then said: "Miss Susan, you say you charge these gentlemen with an indecent assault! Please state the particulars."

I did so, saying the Parson put his hand on my bottom, "when the coach by that sudden jerk threw me into your arms and you kissed me. The other gentleman, called Charley Stuart, put one of his hands between my thighs, very high up, at the same time."

Squire Johnson.—"Now Parson, what is your reply to those charges?"

Parson.—"Oh, I saw the young lady's petticoats disarranged and I tried to replace them."

Squire J.—"And you, Charley Stuart?"

Charley.—"Oh, I plead guilty and promise not to do it again until the next time."

Squire J.—"Gentlemen, from your replies I am quite satisfied that you are both guilty of the offence charged against you; and my sentence is that you each pay Miss Susan immediately the sum of half-a-crown, that you each beg her pardon and that you each offer to show her your pricks. Come, Parson, you first, out of respect of your cloth, as you are in holy orders."

Parson.—"Never did I hear a more impartial and righteous sentence."

So he paid me the half-crown at once and pulled out his tool; it was short and thick with an enormous red head.

Charley said: "See Miss Susan, I offer you this half-crown for the sweet kisses you gave me. Here, balanced on the head of my prick and it is cheap enough."

And Squire J.—"Now, Miss Susan, I offer you this half-crown, and as it is now four o'clock, before the coach will stop, I propose that you should give us some entertainment —and answer all our questions truthfully."

Parson.—"Also obey us in all our wishes."

Charley.—"And Miss Susan, if you do, you shall be paid a guinea from me."

Squire.—"And another from me."

Parson.—"And I will give another, that will make three golden guineas! Think, what a lot of money!"

Dear May, do not blame me for acceding to their wishes. I knew I was completely in their power, and then the presents of the guineas! It seemed riches indeed to me, who had never possessed more than a few shillings at one time in my life.

So I dried my tears and taking up the three half-crowns, said: "Do not harm me, good gentlemen! I will agree to your proposals and trust to your honour, as I am only a girl entirely at your mercy, but I should vastly like three guineas."

"A very sensible good girl," said the Parson.

"You are an angel," said Charley.

Parson.—"I will ask Miss Susan if she has any hair on her little slit?"

"Yes," I replied.

Squire.—"What colour?"

"Light red"

"Did you ever allow a man to look at your cunt?" said Charley.

"Yes."

Parson.—"And suck it, I'll be bound?"

Charley.—"And kiss it?"

"Yes."

Squire.—"Then Miss Susan shall be laid across the laps of two of us, and the other shall kiss and suck her pretty cunny."

"Agreed!" they all cried.

And this was done in succession, until all three had had their turn. To do this my petticoats and smock were raised so as to expose to view my thighs and belly. Then each gentleman knelt on the floor of the coach and kissed and sucked my cunny.

The Parson asked: "How much time, Squire, do we have before the coach stops?"

"Three hours."

The Parson then said: "That will be ample time for Miss Susan to strip herself naked, and to let us enjoy looking at her charms in the nude state."

"Yes," said the Squire, "plenty of time."

I replied that I should take cold.

"No, I'll take care of that," said Charley. "I will keep you warm. I will give you brandy from this bottle."

"But I shall be seen by passers-by," again I objected.

But the Parson and Squire agreed to keep the curtain of the coach-windows drawn down, sufficient to prevent all chance of anyone seeing me.

"Now," said Charley, "I will be your lady's-maid and disrobe you."

He then took off my bonnet and shawl, then my frock stays and petticoats. I begged hard to be allowed to retain my smock, but all in vain as the Parson said it would interfere with the full view of my naked body; besides, he said: "Eve was naked in the Garden of Eden, so there's Scripture for you, Miss Susan."

I was praised for the whiteness and firmness of my skin, and my shape was much admired.

Two of them sat on one seat of the coach and one on the other, with their knees as close to one another as possible, and on this broad lap I was laid and rolled over and over, their hands roving over my back, shoulders and bosom, belly and bottom, in succession, one pointing out to the other some attraction that he specially admired.

My mouth and both hands were next occupied with three pricks at once, and I was obliged to change from one to the other, until each had his prick sucked.

Next I was seated between two of them on the edge of the seat. Then they raised my legs higher than my head, and told me to jut my belly well forward. This had the effect of exposing my bottom-hole as well as my cunny. Then one gentleman would fuck me in this position and then the others would change places, until all three had fucked me. But I will say, they all withdrew their pricks before spending and spouted their sperm over my belly, as it was solemnly promised by them all that there should be no risk of getting me with a child.

By the time they managed to get a couple of fucks each, the time came for me to resume my clothing, which I was thankful to do. And I was only decently dressed when the guard's horn warned us the coach was about to stop.

I was glad to learn we had to stop one hour for dinner, but was amused at Charley telling the chambermaid I was his wife, and so accompanying me up to the bedroom where he actually produced the pot from under the bed and made me sit down and do my pee, while he, lying at full length on the floor with his head close to my belly, watched the waterfall, as he called it.

Then he went down the stairs with me to the dinner-table, where we all did justice to the repast and had some good wine.

My companions were all very attentive to my wants and paid my score between them.

We then resumed our places in the coach as before, the coachman telling us we should have another four hours without stopping at all.

I noticed the Parson and Squire soon felt the efforts of their wine and good feeding, for they were soon sound asleep and snoring.

Charley said he was glad of that as now he could have me all to himself. So we first had a mutual prick-and-cunt-sucking match, each trying to hold back the juice of love as long as possible.

Next, sitting in Charley's lap with his tool ensconced in my cunny, I gently rode up and down, till he was compelled to withdraw and spend all over my belly.

We tired ourselves out with our varied loving encounters and at last we both fell asleep and were only aroused by the guard's horn announcing our arrival at our destination in Edinburgh.

My uncle was waiting for me at the inn and after thanking my travelling companions for their polite attentions, I took my uncle's arm and walked with him to his home.

My uncle kept talking all the way and enquired the name of my late companions.

I answered truthfully and he was pleased to think I had been in such good respectable society: "For," said he, "now-a-days there are so many villains about that a young girl might be ruined before she knew her danger."

I mentally resolved to act the part of an innocent girl in dear uncle's presence and also I determined to put in practice the instructions of Charley Stuart, who, being a medical student, told me many things about a woman's private parts that I did not know before. One thing he told me was to get a lump of alum and push it up in my cunny and keep it there all night. It would act as an astringent and make it as tight as a virgin's cunny. And he also advised me to use a solution of alum in water with a female syringe as often during the day as was convenient.

Dear May, I advise you to do the same. When you send a messenger to buy the alum you can say it is for a sore throat or to use in dyeing—as it is used for both those purposes. Only, dear May, let me give you a caution—don't let the piece of alum be very large, for I will tell you what a fright I had.

One night I put a lump as large as a hen's egg up my cunny and in the morning I could not get it out! It had caused such a contraction of the inside folds of my cunny that I could barely insert the tip of my finger so you may imagine my dilemma. At last I thought: "Why of course, hot water will dissolve it." So I sat over the bidet for nearly an hour and bathed my poor cunny with warm water and it gradually dissolved some of the alum, and I was none the worse for my fright.

Well, to resume, Uncle and I came at last to his house which was a bookseller's shop with rooms for residence over the shop and a milliner's shop on one side, and a dressmaker's shop on the other, while opposite was an inn called "The Royal Standard," and next door to that was a board-school for young ladies.

I mention these details because Uncle called my attention to them, saying they were all his best customers.

On arriving at Uncle's house he took me upstairs and introduced me to the housekeeper, who was going to leave to get married the following week, and I was to take her place in Uncle's household.

She took me to a comfortable bedroom, and kissing me, praised my good looks and enquired if I would like a bath after my long journey.

I replied it was the one thing I was longing for. So she opened a door leading from my bedroom and showed me the bath, saying she would be back in half-an-hour to help me dress and get ready for dinner.

Oh, May, how I enjoyed that cold bath! I splashed and dashed the water all over my naked body and took the opportunity of removing the alum Charley had considerately slipped into my cunny in the coach, for, said he, who knows how soon you may have to pass for a virgin?

I had just finished my washing and stepped out of the bath and was seated on a stool drying myself when the door opened and in came the housekeeper, Jemima, and rushing up to me, exclaimed: "Oh, Miss Susan, please stand before this pier-glass for a moment!"

I did so and found it was as tall as myself and reflected my figure as large as life.

Jemima now began to rub me with a towel, all the time praising my skin, my back, my belly, and my thighs, in such a loud voice that I began to fancy she intended someone in the next room to hear. However, I kept my thoughts to myself and only said: "Make haste, Jemima, and help me dress for I want my supper so badly."

At last she was obliged to leave off her rubbings and she brought me a clean smock and petticoat which she helped to put on. Then I sat on a low stool and drew on clean white stockings; but Jemima would help put on a new pair of garters, which fastened with a silver clasp. I was so pleased with them that I jumped up and stood before the mirror to admire my garters, and of course had to raise my smock rather high to do so.

"Those garters are a present from your uncle," said Jemima, "you will not forget to thank him presently."

"Of course I shall thank him," I said.

Jemima now put on me a very low-necked blue frock.

"And this also is your uncle's present," said she.

"Oh, what a dear, kind uncle he is! How much I love him already," I replied.

"Well," said Jemima, "now go down to supper and tell him so."

On entering the room downstairs I found supper on the table and Uncle in his dressing-gown and slippers sitting by a bright fire.

(*To be continued.*)

DRAWING-ROOM PASSE TEMPS.

Gent—Have you tried the new medicated paper for the water-closet?

Lady—It is so dreadfully expensive.

Gent—No, really I know a place where you can buy six packets for ten-and-sixpence.

Lady—It is so deliciously soft, I cannot think how I could have put up with old newspapers.

Gent—May I send you half a dozen?

Lady—Thanks very much.

Gent—What a very disagreeable smell, I think our vis-à-vis must have farted.

Lady—No, it's that conceited thing on your left. I saw her cough behind her hand and pull her dress out.

Gent—You must forgive me but, do you know, I thought at first it was you.

Lady—Oh, you naughty satirical man.

Gent—What a troublesome complaint is piles!

Lady—Yes, poor mama and my sisters have them shock-ingly.

Gent—And you, come now, confess.

Lady—No, indeed, and indeed . . .

Gent—Not a little bit?

Lady—No, not a bit.

Gent—Do you find that your bowels act with regularity?

Lady—Quite so, thank you for your kind enquiries, I go punctually every ten days or so.

Gent—Now that is very naughty of you, you ought to go every morning.

Lady—But the seat is so dreadfully cold to sit down on in this nasty weather.

Gent—Might I warm it for you?

Lady—What would mama say?

(*Here you see, the conversation is gliding into a flirtation and should be diverted unless you have honourable intentions. If you have, it may continue as follows:*)

Gent—Your mama would say we were two cozy dicky birds to bolt ourselves into the water-closet.

Lady—But you would go away after you had warmed the seat, would you not, because I might make a little noise?

Gent—If it played a pretty tune I would love it.

Lady—And would you rumple the paper for me?

Gent—All day long.

Lady—For little me only and for no one else?

Gent—For no one but you would I rumple a particle of paper. Is it not extraordinary that there are no public urinals for ladies?

Lady—You men would be always standing about the doors.

Gent—But you ought to have them built like ours, you know, with the trough projecting a little further.

Lady—Butter-boat fashion, how very nice.

THE BANKRUPT BAWD.

Tune—"Vicar of Bray."

Near Jermyn Street a bawd did trade
　　In credit, style and splendour,
Well known to every high-bred blade,
　　And those of doubtful gender.
How nature once, in marring mood,
　　Her body formed, I'll tell ye,
Upon her back a swelling stood,
　　To mock her barren belly.

CHORUS:

For some succeed and others fail
　　That into commerce enter.
So few are chaste and many frail
　　In this great trading center.

In coney skins her commerce lay,
　　A charming stock she'd laid in;
She ne'er to smugglers fell a prey,
　　Her practice was fair trading.
These skins when dressed were red and white,
　　The fur of each fair creature,
Of different hues, as day and night,
　　Kept warm man's naked nature.

Chorus:　For some succeed, etc.

The trading stock of this old bawd
　　A vital stab sustain'd, sir,
The news like wild-fire flew abroad,
　　Each customer complain'd, sir.
Some coney skins lay with a lot
　　By caution uninspected;
So quarantine, alas, forgot,
　　Foul plague the whole infected.

Chorus:　For some succeed, etc.

Now old and young her shop forsook,
  Insolvent was her plight, sir,
When Habeas Corpus catch-pole took
  Her body off by night, sir,
From Banco regis civil law,
  To liquidate her debt, sir,
Between the sheets this old bawd saw
  Of London's fam'd Gazette, sir.

Chorus: For some succeed, etc.

To give each creditor his due,
  Three men, the Lord's anointed,
Jack Wilkes, Lord Sandwich and Old Q
  Were assignees appointed;
But luckless bawd! the after day
  Her stock on fire they found, sir;
So 'twas agreed she could not pay
  A condom in the pound, sir.

Chorus: For some succeed, etc.

The skin (her own) this bawd had left,
  Each assignee did handle;
'Twas found of all its fur bereft,
  By singeing flame of candle;
Same butter'd buns concealed within,
  Old Q's keen eye beset, sir;
So Wilkes defin'd this coney skin
  A fund for floating debt, sir.

Chorus: For some succeed, etc.

By headlong lust her claimants led,
  They seized her mortal treasure;
The furious coney skin was spread,
  A dividend past measure.
Now all came in, not one stood out;
  The bawd was set at large, sir;
Her coney skin (of worth, no doubt),
  Did every man discharge, sir.

Chorus: For some succeed, etc.

FACETIAE.

Cease, foolish painters, Hercules to draw
With wooden club, inspiring man with awe;
A different club that here should adorn,
This god's most powerful weapon is the horn;
No mightier spear than that the champion hurls,
With which one night he fucked three score of girls!
A crowd of grave enquirers made resort,
To where the learned doctors held their court;
And asked them who had been that serpent brute,
Which tempted mother Eve to eat the fruit?
"Ye silly men," the sages did reply,
"Why do you waste your time and ours, oh, why?
Eve's tempting snake was but a long and thick,
Great, knotty, ruddy, massy, mighty prick!"

Always, except on Sabbath days,
Nell with her busy needle plays;
    But not the milliner's needle, Miss!
No, 'tis the sailor's needle, dear!
That shows the mariner how to steer
    Right through the ocean of her piss.

The Editor of the *Standard* is a good-natured fellow, ever ready to attend the wants of his customers, more especially when they happen to be good-looking members of the fair sex.

The following conversation which recently took place in the office of the *Standard*, fully carries out our assertion:

ENTERS LADY:

Lady—Is the Editor in?

Editor—Yes, Madame, what can I do for you?

Lady—I desire an article inserted and should like you to put it in for me.

Editor—Certainly, with pleasure, if you will first show it to me, so that I may see what it is like.

Lady—I wish a situation as a wet nurse and should like to get a good healthy boy.

> (*Editor prepares this advertisement and shows it
> to the Lady, who likes the look of it and wishes it
> to be put in at once, and asks the price.*)

Editor—How often shall you want it put in?

Lady—Well, I cannot tell! That will depend whether it is taken or not; but what will you charge for inserting it three times?

Editor—One dollar for putting it in three times.

Lady—Oh, how dear! You might do it for me for less!

Editor—No, Madame, we have so many ladies to oblige, that is our lowest price for inserting three times such an article as you ask for.

Lady—Well, suppose you do not get me a baby in three times, how much will you charge me for three times more?

Editor—Why Madame, if you can manage to keep the affair standing after that, for one dollar more I will put it in as often as you like, till I get you a child; that is, of course, provided the ink continues to flow.

FLUNKEYANIA; OR BELGRAVIAN MORALS.
By Charles.

Chapter VI.

Honour amongst maid-servants, you would have thought so, had you but seen how Sophy and Lucy, after receiving the Duke's retaining fee, worked for his pleasure in hopes of getting a refresher when he retired.

Nor were their labours in vain. Yet, I verily believe he had stimulated himself by a dose of tincture of cantharides, phosphodyne, or something of that sort, for he was a perfect goat.

Lucy in her nightdress was sitting on the edge of the bed with a finger between her thighs, evidently trying to impress upon his Grace the necessity of another bit of flimsy for her bedfellow; and from what I could only partially hear, he made that depend on how they pleased him first.

Although I could not hear all that was said, what I saw will enable me to supply the dialogue.

Lucy now proceeded to business by suddenly throwing the bedclothes off Sophy, whose chemise she turned up, and began to smack her lily-white bum before she could very well help herself.

I could see the red marks flush on her tender skin at every slap. This seemed greatly to please the Duke, who did his best to prevent the helpless girl from getting up.

Sophy struggled desperately, looking both flushed and cross but afraid to call out for fear of making too much noise.

His Grace had gone on his expedition in slippers and dressing-gown. So when this slapping was over; he slipped off his only coverings, and dropping the slippers, had nothing but his stockings on as he jumped on the bed between the two girls, his great affair as stiff and ready as possible.

Sophy was the first to take possession of that red-headed prize. She was evidently excited by the rough usage of her posteriors and begged to be comforted at once.

"So you shall, my dear," said the Duke, "and let your bedfellow straddle over my face, that I can tickle her up with my tongue whilst you ride my cock."

This was a luscious sight and raised all my own lustful feelings quite to burst point, till, as they all seemed to come together, I actually emitted in my breeches.

After this, each of them sucked his prick and balls by turn, till he mounted Lucy and fucked her like a satyr; Sophy all the while kissing and fondling his testicles and working one finger in his arse-hole to excite him to the utmost.

Even this did not exhaust him, for he gamahuched them by turns, and even did the "La Rose" trick of the French women, by frigging their bottoms with his long tongue, which seemed to drive them almost mad. They got his prick in a glorious state again, and at his request, both knelt down on hands and knees, presenting their bottoms to him. What a surprise I had, for he buried that great bursting prick of his in each arse-hole in turn, and then for a change, in their cunts. He made it last awfully long and I could see plainly by their wriggles of delight and the subdued ejaculations of pleasure which I heard, such as: "How nice—lovely—delicious. How you do make me come. Oh, do spend into me," etc., as each girl was also busy frigging herself as well.

At last it was over. I saw him taking the second fiver out of his dressing-gown. So, turning from the keyhole, I retraced my steps. Everyone to his taste, I reflected, as I quickly and cautiously descended the stairs on my homeward journey. And yet again, I thought, a man might do worse; and if I had not been so exceptionally fortunate, as I am, I might be very glad of two such buxom lasses as Sophy and Lucy.

These reflections brought me to the door of the Duchess of Dashwood (quite in another part of the house from that of the Duke), and here I essayed to make my knocking with my knuckles.

But whether Juliette was in the arms of Morpheus or of one of our young footmen, or of M. Duroque, or of all three, I cannot tell; but at any rate, I could not obtain admittance, until I heard the bolt withdrawn and the voice of the Earl, my master, telling me to come in.

I entered accordingly and made a full report of what I had seen, much to the pretended surprise of His Lordship, but not at all to the surprise of the Duchess, who declared with considerable emphasis, "It was just like him!"

She, then totally oblivious of my presence, as it seemed and of her own dishabille, which might be charming but was somewhat remarkable for her own peculiar situation, that is to say, a married woman comfortably in bed with another woman's husband—totally forgetful of all these trifles as it seemed—she began to expatiate upon the enormities perpetrated by his Grace of Dashwood.

Of the valuable impulse he had given to the population in his neighbourhood through the medium of the farmers' daughters and pretty cottage-girls; that she never could keep a decent-looking chamber-maid or housemaid in the castle—that in London he was worse, if possible—that she suspected him of improper conduct with Mademoiselle Juliette, the best soubrette she ever had, and was getting on at a great rate, when the Earl politely reminded her that my presence in the room was no longer required and suggested that I should be allowed to retire, which her Grace cordially agreed to, commenting at the same time upon my manners and general appearance in a style which I may be forgiven for not repeating, but which suggested my having found favour in her eyes.

As the reader may believe, I took particularly good care to report to my Lady on the following morning all that I had seen regarding the Duke and Duchess.

As concerned the proceeding of the former there was no embellishment required; a plain unvarnished statement of facts was all that I dared venture on and it was enough in all conscience.

But where her Grace and my Lady's husbands were concerned, I must plead guilty, I fear, to having thrown in a little colouring, suggested a few natural touches in fact, that brought out (so to speak) the prominent features of the picture into high relief.

The trifling episode about Juliette coming by herself into my room and assisting at my toilet, I thought it judicious to say nothing about whatever.

My report produced, as might be expected, a variety of conflicting emotions in the mind of Lady Pomeroy.

But while she was reflecting, I suppose as to what opinion to express, Justine, like a favoured girl, took the liberty to open the ball with: "Pray, Master Ernest, when you were bound on such an errand why did you not call at my room and take me with you? Two witnesses would have been better than one, you know."

I replied with as much gravity as I could, though I could hardly suppress a laugh, that I could not think of introducing such youthful purity to such a scene of licentious sensuality.

At this remark, notwithstanding her vexation, my Lady Pomeroy fairly smiled, and I think that Justine would have boxed my ears if she had dared.

Then she continued her examination by asking if: "That wretch, Juliette, was in the room when I made my report to the Duchess?"

"No, she was not," I briefly answered.

"And where the dev—(it was nearly out)—was she then?"

"How should I know?" was my reply. "Rocking somebody to sleep, I presume; Lady Georgiana, or M. Duroque, or somebody else."

"Hush, Justine," said the Countess now laughing, "you are too forward, and as for your report, Ernest, it is all very disgusting of course, but it is very painstaking and faithful on your part, and it is a comfort to know that I shall not be bothered with the attentions of that brute of a Duke, while he is here; and I'll take care that Justine is not annoyed. As for those two fools of housemaids, I shan't take any notice of their conduct; it would only create a general scandal. Of course I knew that my Lord misbehaved himself grossly with the Duchess but did not know that she abandoned herself so completely when there was a third party, and a handsome young man, in the room. What is your opinion on the subject?"

To this I replied with all becoming indifference that it was a subject on which I hardly felt competent to express an opinion, when in the presence of such a good judge as Her Ladyship, but as far as my own personal feelings were concerned, that her Grace's self-abandonment and forgetfulness of the barriers which modesty might have interposed in the presence of a third party, produced no effect whatever. And that I had lately been taking lessons in an academy of such a very superior grade to that in which it appeared her Grace had taken her degrees, that I consider myself too proficient to require instruction from her in any branch of learning whatever.

Of course this speech was understood precisely as I intended it to be.

Justine laughed and my lovely mistress smiled and coloured and said that I was "a silly, flattering boy," but seemed very much gratified nevertheless.

I was then dismissed for the present, under directions to attend her Grace when she took Lady Georgiana out for a drive in the afternoon.

I could not help laughing in my sleeve, as I wondered whether they would drive in the direction of her Lady's nurse, who lived in a certain obscure street, or if Miss Courtney would be picked up anywhere and make a third inside passenger.

According to the old adage a third makes bad company, but under these circumstances I do not think that either of the ladies would have objected to the addition.

However, I may as well say at once that nothing of any consequence occurred during the drive. That is, nothing at all ostensible to speak about.

If any conversation took place between the ladies that produced some effect on them shortly afterwards, I cannot tell for a certainty, as of course I could hear nothing of it. But, judging from the hints thrown out by my Lady Pomeroy to Lady Georgiana and her longing to see her haughtiness and scorn of men brought down to a proper level, and connecting these suggestions with a mysterious adventure which befell me the day after the ladies drove out together, I cannot but think that Her Ladyship had some hand herself in bringing about the fulfillment of her own predictions.

On that day as it happened, or most probably it was selected on purpose, the Duke and Duchess and the Earl had gone to the theatre; the Countess desiring to remain at home and lady Georgiana stayed to keep her company.

It become quite late in the evening and as my services were not required, I was sitting by myself, when Juliette came in without knocking, silently and mysteriously, as once before, but not with the same results. She merely came, as she said, to tell me that my presence was required.

"Where?"

Never mind, I was required that was enough, and very flattering to me!

Moreover it was absolutely requisite that my eyes should be bandaged.

Now, I was no fool and I was pretty certain that no harm could come to me in the Earl's mansion at any rate. Moreover, if my eyes were bandaged, my hands were free; besides, I may as well confess to my readers that my last association with my eyes bandaged, or more nearly proposed to be bandaged, was an extremely agreeable one; so after a faint show of objection I submitted, having a pretty strong notion of the object of the grand adventure.

I was then led by my conductress up one passage and down another, evidently for the purpose of puzzling me, and this was successful, for on being ushered into a room, I certainly could not make out where I was. That the room was comfortable and with some luxurious articles of furniture in it, there was no doubt. Also that there were two or three females in it, I was persuaded, for I heard low whisperings, some of an argumentative character. Some as if fun, and some seemed made in allusion to me in connection with some sport or other.

But I was not such a fool as not to make a shrewd guess as to what sort of sport was likely to take place, when a few merry young women have got a handsome young man in a room among them, with his eyes bandaged, and awaited my fate with becoming fortitude.

I had not long to wait.

I heard someone give a whispered persuasion, some more giggling and then violent hands were laid upon me. I don't mean to say that I was hurt or that the hands laid upon me were particularly rough, but at any other time I would have protested against indignities offered to me; under the circumstances I considered it wiser and pleasanter to hold my tongue and submit to my fate.

So I did. So would my reader if he had such a chance. Fancy yourself blindfolded as I was, and fancy several pairs of delicate soft hands pulling off your clothes, till there was no rag on your body except your stockings and the handkerchief over your eyes. How would you like to hear a soft, gentle voice as pleasant as a rippling brook, say: "Look at that beauty, won't you kiss its ruby head?" Then a soft hand takes John Thomas, gently draws back the foreskin and you first feel the warm breath, then the touch of the velvety tongue of some beauty who, you instinctively know, feels her blood at that moment in a boil of voluptuously longing excitement.

You are drawn softly to a couch, laid gently on your back, and some delightful creature splits herself upon your rod, rides it with spirit, till just the ecstatic moment; her lips are glued to yours in long lusciously amorous kisses, as the soul-dissolving emission mixes the male and female semen in one life-giving stream of pleasure.

She rolls aside and another fair creature takes her place before you have time to lose your stiffness. (Fresh cunt, fresh courage.) On you go for a steeple-chase of love again, again you come together! Each time I tasted the heavenly bliss of coition, if possible, in a more delightful degree, for I had four of them, one after another, before they allowed me to get up.

Then the darlings dressed me, but made such a pretended muddle of getting on my trousers, as they laughingly tried to put my limp prick away comfortably in its place, it got so handled and squeezed that I had the horn as ever. So, seizing the first one I could hold, I bore her to the floor, up with her dress and into her reeking cunny in less time than it takes to write it.

This was a delicious bout, for the others laughed and slapped our bottoms all the while as we wriggled on the carpet. I was so delighted I am sure I made my partner spend three times before I was subdued, and she lay listlessly beneath me in the after lethargy of satisfied desire.

Whilst feeling her beautiful legs my hands came upon a small loose strap which I slyly slipped into my trousers as I put away the limp engine of love, thinking perhaps to make out my antagonist when I examined the colours I had captured on the sly.

I was kissed and sent away in charge of Juliette and soon found myself in my own room again.

It was a most mysterious story, but I had obtained a slight clue, a very slight one certainly, when my conductress advised me to put myself in order as I should probably be required to wait upon my mistress and Lady Georgiana at the supper-table.

But no sooner was her back turned than I inspected the little waif or stray I had secured in my pocket and found, as I expected, that it was neither more nor less than a lady's garter, and one of a colour and make that I had never seen before.

Anyhow, the next morning Mlle. Juliette was making anxious enquiries about one of her Lady's elastics which I at once offered to restore on condition of being allowed to replace it. And if anyone considers this affords a clue to my mysterious adventure they are welcome to it. I have no opinion to offer except that it is time to wind up my story.

The Earl of Pomeroy and the Duchess of Dashwood never visited the theatre on the eventful evening I have just described; the Duke, who could not obtain a divorce, filled his house with such bad company that his daughter, the Lady Georgiana, has obtained permission to live under the protection of her particular friend, the Countess of Pomeroy.

Justine and I, being so comfortably fixed and quite young as yet, think it would be folly to marry at present and so we retain our confidential stations.

THE END.

MEMORANDA FROM MR. P——.

Mr. Reddie used to call me Petro, as a short familiar name; but whilst he lodged with me at my house, Brecknock Crescent, Camden Town (N.B.—This is where I first was introduced to Mr. Reddie), I was continually afraid he would bring himself or both of us into serious trouble.

Once, I remember, we went to Margate for a few weeks at the seaside, and the landlady of the house where we stopped had a very good-looking son, a youth not over fifteen, if quite so old. Mr. Reddie was in love at once, but how to win the boy over was the difficulty.

"Petro," he would say, "I must fuck that boy or go out of my mind from frigging myself as I lie in bed and think of him. How can we manage it, old boy?"

I recommended patience, and an opportunity would be sure to turn up.

"Treat him well, and let's take him out for a bathe or a walk with us whenever he will go," I said.

My advice was taken. Young Frank was soon quite at home in our rooms and evidently pleased at being made such a favourite by the lodgers, who were always treating him to cakes, wine or fruit.

We took several promenades with him as companion, and in a few days he also regularly accompanied us and shared the same machine with us when we bathed.

How we joked him about his little doodle, asked him if it would stand stiff and about boys playing with each other's cocks at school. This was of course done very carefully and gradually, and we began to think him discreet enough as he had often assured us that he told no tales out of school, when we gave him shillings or half-crowns.

His mother was a buxom woman of about eight and thirty, who had been left a widow for some years, her husband having been in the Civil Service, but died after they had been married about ten years.

Now Mrs. Glover was decidedly more to my taste than the boy. So I made assiduous courtship of her on my own account, for Mr. Reddie couldn't even bear for a woman to touch him.

Her bedroom was next to mine, and I had a peephole so that I could watch all her movements as she dressed or undressed, and had often noticed how she sometimes looked at her cunt in the glass and seemed to sigh as if thinking of past joys. One night in particular, before sitting on the chamber-pot as usual before getting into bed, she seated herself on the bedside drawing up her night-chemise to her navel, whilst she at first gently frigged her clitoris with a couple of fingers. I could see the little piece of flesh stand out quite excitedly. Her fingers worked nervously for a moment or two, as her face began to flush, and her bosom to heave with emotion, when all of a sudden, she fell backwards on the bed in the act of spending, her legs wide open, allowing me to see clearly a few pearly drops glistening on her busy fingers.

Now was my chance. I had observed she never locked her door. My prick was rampant for such a glorious fuck, as I believed she would be, and having only my shirt and stockings on, I noiselessly opened my door as well as her own so quietly as to be quite unperceived by my luscious victim, as she lay gasping on the bed, from the effects of her copious emission. I had previously well oiled the locks of both doors on the sly.

Stooping down, so that she would not see my approach and having neither boots nor slippers on my feet, I soon was kneeling between her open legs and gazing my fill at the delicious throbbing cunt of my landlady. She still lay with two fingers right in, but not frigging. The mark was fair and open, so, slowly rising, I brought the nose of my impatient prick within an inch of the spot. It was then very gently touched. There was a kind of spasmodic twitch of sympathy, but she did not otherwise seem to notice it, and I could see her eyes were closed.

Mr. Peaslin went on gently to insinuate himself and fortunately for my game-cock, the spending had oiled her so that I gained an inch or two, and then with a sudden plunge as I clasped her round the hips, I was three-quarters entered in a moment.

What a start she gave, but seemed to have the presence of mind not to scream.

"Oh, heavens, sir, what are you about? I'm ruined! Leave me, you wicked man, this instant!" she exclaimed, as I could see the tears start to her eyes, and the deep blush of shame overspread her face.

"Not yet, my darling Mrs. Glover! I had a peephole and

the sight of you fingering yourself drove me quite mad with desire. Now, won't you forgive me? I couldn't help myself," I replied, as I seized the opportunity to push on to victory, and felt myself buried to the hilt in her throbbing sheath.

I lay on her kissing and imploring for forgiveness, making my prick throb inside of her as I did so, and at last she faintly smiled my pardon. I need not tell you more, how we used to sleep together every night, and that our liaison quite blinded her to our intentions regarding Master Frank.

We soon proceeded to all sorts of indecencies with the youth. Mr. Reddie and myself would compare the immense difference in the size of our pricks before him in the bathing-machine (Reddie's was a very small one, not five inches). We asked him to feel and judge for himself. The very touch of his delicate soft youthful hand made the seed shoot from me, which you may be sure immensely surprise the lad, and made him blush scarlet, so that we were afraid of having gone too far.

Another morning Mr. Reddie gamahuched him till he spent in his mouth and seemed to enjoy the sucking, after which we handled each other's pricks and he amused himself with them, until we emitted our juice, mine spurting all over his belly as he stood in front of me. Then we went into the sea to refresh ourselves and afterwards made him a present of half a sovereign, which his innocent mother, I believe, thought was only a delicate way of pleasing herself.

A day or two after this, Mr. Reddie pretended to be obliged to return to town for two or three days and we easily per-suaded Mrs. Glover to allow Frank to go with us, and I prom-ised to show him all the sights, while Mr. Reddie was attend-ing to his business; this she also took as another kindness to herself and we started on our journey.

We took apartments in town at the house of a Mrs. Ander-son (an old friend of Mr. Reddie's where he was always safe to do as he pleased). They consisted of a sitting-room and bedroom adjoining, the latter with two beds in it so that Frank had to sleep with either one of us.

Then we showed him a fine collection of coloured plates of boys and girls, boys with boys or men, etc., some of the latter plainly showing they had got their cocks in their part-ners' bottoms.

"You'll let him do it to you, Petro, won't you?" appealed Mr. Reddie as he whispered in ecstasy: "I shall soon be landed now!"

There was no object on my part; his little cock couldn't hurt me. Besides, I had a great fancy for it at the moment, and told him he must put his arms around my waist and handle my cock and make it come.

Frank was quite pleased to try. His youthful affair was quite stiff and hard at the idea of having a man.

We threw off everything and I knelt down on all fours on the hearth-rug. Then, Mr. Reddie guided Frank's prick to my arse-hole and he soon wriggled it in whilst his hand clasped and frigged my big cock in front. It was so extraordinarily exciting to my ideas that I spent at once, and clasped one of my hands round each of his wrists to make him frig quicker; also to secure him in case he flinched from Reddie's assault.

My friend had already got a finger well greased with cold cream up Frank's fundament which the boy seemed to enjoy rather than not, as I might judge by the increasing activity of his little prick in my arse.

"Now, Frank," said Mr. Reddie, "you will let me try to have you, won't you, you dear boy? It won't hurt."

I had previously taken a looking-glass from the dressing-table and placed it on the floor, so I could see every motion of both of my companions. With one hand Reddie was caressing the cock and balls of the boy, as he fucked my bottom, whilst his right hand presents his prick to the tight little pink arse-hole which kept bobbling towards him.

Frank winced a little at the attack; but Reddie being small, as I have said, had no difficulty in effectually getting into him. How his face flushed and his eyes sparkled with delight as he almost screamed out: "I'm in, oh, delicious! I'm landed at last, Petro, my dear fellow! I'm coming—I can't stop!"

This made me come again and I also felt Frank spend at the same moment. We kept our places and had another splendid bottom-fuck before separating.

My prick was too big to get into either of my companions; but I loved to have the boy fuck me, and frig me whilst Reddie had him.

The very thought of that adventure makes my old pego stand at any moment.

The Rev. Kettle of Battersea met on the Rhine-boat a lady who had not seen him for years. "How do you do, Mr. Kettle, I heard you were married. Any family?"

"Yes, Madame, six."

"Six, dear me! how many are boys and how many girls?"

"The number is divided, Madame, there are six little Kettles, three with spouts, three without."

THINGS I DON'T LIKE TO SEE.

I'm a modest young man, I'd have you all know,
And I can't bear to hear or to see anything low;
From a child all my friends could not fail to detect,
That my notions were moral and strictly correct.

Now some of you, doubtless, may think me an ass,
And declare my confession is naught for a farce;
Still, to what I have said I'll religiously stick,
And, to use a low phrase, stand my ground like a brick.

Stop, a few minutes you are able to spare,
A bit of my mind I intend to lay bare;
Tho' with my way of thinking you'll p'raps not agree,
I'll tell you a few things I don't like to see.

I don't like to see vulgar girls in the town
Pull their clothes up, and stand to be goosed for a crown;
Nor a man with light trousers, of decency shorn,
Stop and talk to young ladies while having the horn.

I don't like to see women wear dirty smocks,
Nor a boy of fifteen laid up with the pox;
And I don't like to see, it's a fact by my life—
A married man grinding another man's wife.

Nor I don't like to see—you'll not doubt it, I beg,
A large linseed poultice slip down a man's leg;

Nor a gray-headed sinner that's fond of a find,
When a girl under twelve he is able to grind.

In church, too, believe me, I don't like to see
A chap grope a girl while she sits on his knee;
Nor a lady whose visage is all over scabs,
Nor a young married lady troubled with crabs.

Nor I don't like to see, through it's really a lark,
A clergyman poking a girl in the park;
Nor a young lady, wishing to be thought discreet,
Looking in print-shops in Holywell Street,

I don't like to see, coming out of Cremorne,
A girl with her muslin much crumpled and torn;
Arm in arm with a fellow who's had the mishap,
To forget, when he shagged her, to button his flap.

Nor I don't like to see, though some think it a treat,
A young woman scratching her thing in the street;
And a boarding-school miss, with no sense in her pate,
Sit and chalk a man's tool on the back of her slate.

I don't like to see, in the bright face of the day,
A man stand and piss in the public highway;
Nor a Newfoundland dog, without any disguise,
Tied fast to a bitch not a quarter his size.

Nor I don't like to see, little sisters and brothers
Get playing at what they call fathers and mothers;
And I don't like to see, though at me you might scoff,
An old woman trying to toss herself off.

I don't like to see—it's a fact that I utter—
That nasty word ——— written up on a shutter:
And I don't like to see a man, drunk as an Earl,
Getting into a lamp-post thinking it's a girl.

I don't like to see, 'cause my feelings it shocks,
Two girls busy playing with each other's c———;
Nor I don't like to see, though it may be a whim,
A hole like a pit-mouth in place of a q———.

But I fear I'm encroaching too much on your time,
So I'll put an end to my quizzical rhyme;
Though with my way of taste you'll perhaps not agree,
I've told you the things I don't like to see.

A' THAT AND A' THAT.

Put butter in my Donald's brose,
    For weel does Donald fa that;
I love my Donald's tartan hose,
    His naked prick, and a' that.

    For a' that and a' that,
    And twice as mickle as a' that:
    The lassie get a skelpit gnat,
    But wan the day for a' that.

For Donald swore a solemn oath,
    By his first hairy gravat,
That he would fight the battle there,
    And fuck the lass and a' that.

    Chorus: For a' that and a' that, etc.

His hairy cock, both side and wide,
    Hung like a beggar's wallet;
His prick stood like a rolling-pin,
    She nicker'd when she saw that.

    Chorus: For a' that and a' that, etc.

And then she turned up her cunt,
    And she bade Donald claw that;
The devil's dizzen Donald drew,
    And Donald gave her a' that.

    Chorus: For a' that and a' that, etc.

FACETIAE.

Boss returning from the wars,
Wearied out with wounds and jars,
Tells the tale of blood and strife,
Woe and suffering to his wife;
"Never mind, dear Boss," she said,
"Your tool is safe—let's go to bed."

Through my brain strange musings ran,
Deeply pondering: "What is man?"
Still the question I resolve,
Philosophic doubts to solve:
"What is man? I'll tell you true,
He's but a pizzle's dirty spew!"

LINES FOR VALENTINES.

What a fate this poor girl in her lovers befalls,
A prickless old man, and a youth without balls.

Boast not that you have won a rich wife,
Length of tool, not of purse, makes the comfort of life.

Your prick is so useless for love's pleasant game,
   Your nose long and hooky and fuck of such muck,
Go, stick then your nose in the cunt of your dame,
   And you'll have at one go both a blow and a fuck.

To his bed he went sleepy and drunk, oh, very!
   He wanted to piss, felt about for the jerry,
Took up by mischance a big mousetrap instead,
   Which snapped off, alas! his old gentleman's head!

ADVERTISEMENTS.

To Be Sold—A Bargain
A MAIDENHEAD
(Slightly Soiled)

The owner being about to get married is willing to sell the above by auction. Further particulars will be announced in the next number of THE PEARL.

TO THE LOVERS OF GOOD THINGS.

Messrs. Rogers, Rosencrantz and Co., Importers of Foreign Females, and other Curiosities, beg to announce the arrival of a cargo per steamship *Orient*, direct from Zululand, of young girls of all ages from 8 to 16 years of age, all genuine virgins which will be offered for selection any time next week. Terms—C.O.D.

N.B.—As this class of goods is extremely perishable buyers must remove their purchases at their own risk.

Orders from the country per post carefully attended to; and the girls sent sealed with our trade-mark over their cunnies, without which we do not guarantee them.

RELIGIOUS.

Rev. Newman Hall will lecture on "The Conduct of Lot and His Daughters," December 20. Illustrated with Dissolving views of the Paternal Pego entering the Daughters' Cunts.

Also January 7: "Solomon in All His Glory," with 700 wives and 300 concubines; being an attempt to elucidate the mystery of how he gave satisfaction to them all.

Rev. J. Spurgeon will Address the Young Women's Christian Association on the subject of:

CIRCUMCISION.

With practical examples of the advantage of removing the hood or foreskin from the penis.

Admission to women only. No collection.

THE PEARL,

A Journal of Facetiæ and Voluptuous Reading.

| No. 18 | PUBLISHED MONTHLY. | Dec. 1880 |

MY GRANDMOTHER'S TALE; or MAY'S ACCOUNT OF HER INTRODUCTION TO THE ART OF LOVE.

From an Unsophisticated Manuscript, Found Amongst the Old Lady's Papers After Her Death, Supposed To Have Been Written About A.D. 1797.

SUSEY'S LETTER CONCLUDED.

Uncle got up and came to meet me, saying: "Welcome, Susey, I am glad you have come! How blooming you look! You must want your supper after such a long ride."

I threw my arms around his neck and kissing him, said: "Thank you, dear Uncle, for all your great kindness and especially for this lovely silk dress and the pretty garters you gave me."

"Does the dress fit you, my dear?" he asked, placing his hands on my bosom and squeezing it gently.

"Yes, Uncle dear," I said.

We then had supper, and Uncle insisted on my drinking four glasses of the champagne, which I found warmed up my blood as doubtless Uncle intended it should do.

After supper he said: "Susey, if you love me, show me your garters."

"Oh, Uncle!" I replied blushingly, "would that be decent and proper?"

"You are an ungrateful girl to refuse the first trifling request I make," he said.

"Not ungrateful, Uncle," I replied; "see here, please examine my pretty garters," and I stretched out both my legs as I continued sitting in my chair.

Uncle was on his knees between my legs in a moment, and put his hands first on one garter and then on the other, unclasping them and kissing my thighs just above the stockings.

Then he said: "Dear Susey, do you know that your mother was my favourite sister? And that as children we used to sleep together, and were fond of taking off each other's nightdress and of examining the difference in our naked bodies, and making water in the same pot. And now, dear Susey, I want to tell you that your dear mother on her death-bed confided you to my care, and I have paid for your education and maintenance all your life; and now I hope you will love me and be a comfort to me in my declining years."

"Yes, dear Uncle," I said, "you may depend on my doing everything in my power to give you pleasure."

"That's a good girl," said Uncle. "But now you can do something this minute to please me, and that is to show me your cunny!"

I told him he could look at it if he wished. So as I was seated in an easy-chair he lifted one of my legs over an arm of the chair and telling me to hold my clothing and chemise out of the way, he exposed my cunny and bottom-hole to his delighted view, and covered both with kisses, sucking and putting his tongue as far as possible into both places. The end of this, of course, was that I gave down my liquor of love over his tongue and he greedily sucked up every drop, declaring it was most delicious.

After this he pulled out his prick and pretended to me that he had fucked my mother, therefore he had a right to do the same to me!

I laughed at this reasoning and feigning ignorance of his meaning asked him to explain everything.

He then laid me on the sofa before the fire and undressed me and also himself, all the time praising the whiteness of my skin, and then, dearest May, he fucked me, and fancied he was the first that had penetrated my virgin slit, as he fondly called it.

Now I must close this letter, hoping you have had as much pleasure as I have in the way of fucking.

By the way, dear May, why don't you get your father to fuck you? Uncle says you would find it delicious, for he knows your father well and says he remembers that his cock is both long and very thick!

I remain, darling May, your loving friend,

SUSEY.

P.S.—Be sure and keep this letter a secret and don't let your father see it for the world! Write soon and tell me everything.

I put this precious letter in my pocket and then remembered that Kate had never told me how she first became acquainted with my father. So I went into the dining-room in search of her and found her and papa sitting on the sofa, with their private parts exposed and each was fondling and touching the other's genitals.

Papa caught sight of me and called out: "Come in May, I want you most particularly."

I went up to him.

He continued: "I want to see if the hair on your cunny is as fine and silky as this on Kate's cunt. Now be a good obedient girl and I will give you a silk dress and you shall choose the colour yourself."

How this promise dazzled me! I had had only one silk dress many years before and now the promise of choosing one myself conjured up visions of beauty to my mind's eye.

I replied quickly: "Yes, dear papa, I will do all you require," and I raised up my clothing as I stood in front of him.

"That is not convenient," he said. "You had better slip off your clothes except the chemise. Kate will help you."

So in a few moments my dress and petticoats were on the ground and I was en chemise as I did not wear drawers in those days. In taking my dress over my head my pocket was emptied on the carpet and the letter caught my father's eye.

"Oh, a love letter," he cried, "fine goings on, Miss May! I must read this letter from your favoured lover!" and he picked it up and commenced to read it.

"It is not a love letter," I said, "but one from my schoolfriend Susey who is in Scotland with her uncle."

"All the same I shall read it aloud," said my father.

And he did so. And Kate whispered to me: "Don't be afraid of anything, May dearest, I will take your part."

My father was delighted with Susey's letter and as his breeches were unbuttoned as he sat on the sofa I could see his pego rise to a fine erection as he came to some of her descriptive passages.

At last he came to the end where she advised me to get my

father to fuck me, and then he cried out: "Sensible girl this Susey! I wish she were here now. I must invite her and her uncle, my old friend, on a visit this summer, and we will have glorious times! But at present I am concerned to examine closely my daughter's cunny! And if she consents, willingly will I fuck her for I cannot use force to my own daughter, I love her too well for that! Only if she cheerfully consents to let me have my will, she shall have five guineas in addition to the silk dress and I will take her to the theatre one night each week!"

I exclaimed: "You dear kind papa! How much I love you! Yes, do whatever you like with me and teach me how to give you pleasure. I hope, dear Kate will not be jealous of poor little me?"

"No, no, dearest May," said Kate. "I shall never be jealous of you or any other girl your papa wished to fuck; in fact I should like to see him fuck all the girls in the parish, if he wanted to!"

Papa said: "Generous-hearted Kate, you shall never have cause to regret such unselfish conduct. It was the perfect nobleness and disinterestedness of your character which attracted me to you, and the more I see of your mental superiority the more I bless the hour we first became acquainted with each other! Now May, I am ready to fuck you!"

"And I, dear papa, am ready to be fucked," I replied smiling.

Kate insisted on papa stripping himself perfectly naked and also on removing my smock. She then told papa to lie flat on his back with his prick standing erect; she then made me lie on top of him and she slapped my bottom in time to papa's heaves and thrusts until the crisis came and my womb was deluged with paternal sperm.

I was swimming in delight and could not help calling out: "Thank you a thousand times, dear papa, for this delicious treat!"

"And thank you, my darling child, for giving me such exquisite pleasure," replied papa.

In the next bout our positions were altered and Kate took part in the pastime, placing herself in such a position that papa could see her cunny while he fucked mine.

We changed positions many times until papa said he must rest from his labours of love, and after partaking of refreshments we all three went to papa's bedroom and fell asleep on his bed, one on each side of him.

In the morning I asked papa to tell me how he became acquainted with Kate, and he replied as follows:

"Last Christmas I went up to London for a holiday and at my club I met with several old friends, who had daughters at school with Madame Stewart at Hampton Court. Sir Thomas Moreton, my neighbour, was one of the party, and while drinking our wine, we talked about our experiences in fucking, and afterwards the conversation turned to the subject of schoolmistresses whipping their scholars' bottoms. I argued that it was not done nowadays but might have been done years ago.

"Sir Thomas laid me a £50 bet that I was wrong and offered to take me to Mme. Stewart's to prove it.

"I accepted his wager and on the following Saturday evening accompanied him to Mme. Stewart's to put his wager to the test.

"We were conducted to a room fitted up with all kinds of punishment apparatus and at one end was a raised dais or platform, under which we seated ourselves, and the door being closed we found the front of the platform was pierced with peepholes in all directions so we had a perfect view of the room, which was brilliantly lighted up with wax candles whilst our recess was dark.

"Presently six girls were brought in by the governess and Madame Stewart ascended the dais over our heads and gave orders for the number of stripes and read the list of offences.

"The fair culprits were placed with their bottoms towards the dais so we had a full view of their struggles and wrigglings as the rod fell on their thighs and bottoms and we had many a peep at the tender cunny which peeped from between their legs.

"My Kate was one that was punished on that occasion and I was especially attracted by the quivering of the lips of her cunny as the rod fell on her lovely bottom. At last I was sure I could see the dear girl give down the pearly drops in pleasurable emission. Such sensitiveness charmed me, and when the punishment was over I made an offer to Madame Stewart to take Kate home with me as a fucking-piece, offering her a bribe.

"Madame demurred at first then said the matter should be left to Kate's decision.

"She was called into the room and I told her how I was smitten with the sight of her naked charms and wanted her to come and live with me a few months every year.

"She first looked at my standing prick and then enquired if it would be any advantage to Madame Stewart and that if it would, she would come with me.

"I told her I offered Madame £50.

"'Then,' said Kate, 'I will go with you and trust in your honour as to your treatment of me.'

"Such disinterested conduct is most uncommon in this money-loving age and I love and honour Kate for it."

I told my father I was sure he would be generous to both Kate and myself.

He told me he was anxious I should be married to a gentleman of his acquaintance, an elderly rich widower.

I enquired how he knew anything about me and what was his name? To which my father replied his name was Mr. Sinclair and it was his cock I had become acquainted with, that he was over eighty years old, so I should be a rich widow probably in a few years. That the old gent was able to do a fair amount of fucking, but if I wanted more I could easily get a young man for a pound a week to do it for me.

I consented to my father's propositions and we invited Mr. T (the resident tutor at the school mentioned at the beginning of my tale), to come to the wedding. We also invited Susey and her uncle.

They all came and I was marired one fine May morning out of compliment to my name. After the ceremony the clergyman asked permission to have the first kiss on my cunny, which I granted him in the vestry.

We went for our wedding tour to the Isle of Wight for a month during which time my husband was satisfied he had got me with a child. He then gave me permission to have as much outside fucking as I wanted.

I told him I should wait until we got home as I was longing for a taste of Mr. T's noble tool and also for my dear father's prick.

My husband was pleased with my determination and engaged Mr. T as librarian, and in that capacity he remained until the lamented decease of Mr. Sinclair at the age of ninety, who left me with one daughter nine years old, and all his money.

As soon after his death as was decent I married Mr. S—— whom I found to be one of the best husbands.

Susey often pays us a visit and brings young girls with her to please Mr. T who has a penchant for the unfledged cunny, and often has a game of blindman's buff with the naked children, and a romp with my little Agnes when she is naked. The little darling is now twelve years old and very proud of being able to make "her new papa's cocky get big," as she says, by rubbing her little cunny against its head.

Mr. T anticipates the pleasure of taking her maidenhead when she is fourteen. I tell him that it is too early and that he ought to wait until she is fifteen, but he is so impatient that I fear he will have his own way.

So good reader, both lady and gentleman, farewell!

> And may you never want a fuck,
> Nor yet a prick or cunt to suck.

FINIS.

ACROSTIC—MADRIGAL.

C ome love and dwell with me
U nder the greenwood tree,
N o one can happy be,
T han I shall be if bless'd with thee!

P laced near your mossy grot,
R ises a rustic cot.
I would bear thee to that spot,
C ool when the sun is hot;
K ind fair one, linger not!

F lowers bloom their brightest there!
U nknown fragrance fills the air!
C ome, sweet Chloe, grant the prayer,
K neeling I make to thee!

ACROSTIC—THE MARTYR.

F irm as a rock the noble martyr stood,
U nbending as a rod of tempered steel;
C almly he sees the touch ignite the wood,
K nowing the agony he soon must feel.

M ighty the influence which makes the body
Y ield prompt obedience to the power of will!

C onscious of being right, this is the motto,
U pon his banner writ in words of light.
N o other motive can supply the power,
T o cheer the martyr in his dying hour!

D ying because he would maintain the right,
E ver should rule in place of boastful might!
A nd so the martyr's name shall never die,
R ound the whole world the stirring tale shall fly.

P eoples unborn his noble name shall learn,
A nd his example make their bosoms burn;
P atriots shall hail him as a brother true,
A nd write his history for all to view!

THE DISAGREEABLE PASSENGER.

A Yorkshire excursion train the other day contained a rather morose-looking individual, who being offered the newspaper, grumpily replied: "I don't read!"

"Will you take a cigar then?" asked another passenger.

"I don't smoke!"

Presently a third offered him his flask.

"I don't drink!

This happened in a carriage with open compartments, so a clergyman who had overheard it all and thinking that perhaps a little intellectual conversation would be more to his taste, leaned over the back of the seat and said: "Would you like to step over here with us, there is only myself, wife and daughter?"

"I don't fuck!" was all he got for his kind intention. And we need not say that he was both disgusted and chagrined as the laughter of the others pealed through the carriage.

A QUESTION OF LUNACY.

A lady the other day, wishing to get an imbecile son into an asylum, consulted a doctor about a certificate and he naturally enquired as to the actions of the alleged lunatic.

Lady—I must tell you that lately at Christmas he would get up at night and eat all the mince-pie in the pantry.

Doctor—That is only gluttony.

Lady—There's something awfully shocking to tell: The other day he threw the servant down the stairs and fucked her!

Doctor—Mere depravity, that's all. Now allow me to explain the difference to you, Madame! If you had told me that your son had eaten the servant and fucked the mince-pies there could have been no doubt about the necessity of confining him in an asylum.

THE SULTAN'S REVERIE.

An Extract from the Pleasures of Cruelty.

This brings to my mind, says Lucidora, a tale I have heard of the late Sultan, who, being middle aged and worn out with the amorous exertions in the well-filled seraglio, determines to seek some fresh excitement; everything seems so insipid and blasé to him.

At first he is at a loss how to amuse himself, but one day, discussing with his chief eunuch the arrangements and routine of the harem, a circumstance which never gave him a thought before suddenly gives him an idea that he may get both satisfaction and excitement from cunt, viz., that when he came to the throne (he was a nephew of the previous Commander of the Faithful), he left the Sultana Valide unmolested, who in the lifetime of his predecessor had intrigued in every possible manner to set aside his succession in favour of her own son contrary to the usual Osmanif custom. Since which time the baffled Sultana, a beautiful lady of about thirty, had peevishly shown her hatred of him by keeping the strictest seclusion, only walking by herself quite unattended in the most secluded part of the extensive gardens of the seraglio,

The Sultan had heard of the once famous beauty of this proud lady and was assured by the Chief of Eunuchs that she was still surpassingly lovely and was suspected of indulging in every variety of voluptuousness with the ladies of her suite in private.

SULTAN.—"At what hour does she generally take her walk in the garden?"

CHIEF OF EUNUCHS.—"About seven in the morning, your Majesty; she is an early riser and first goes to the Mosque then walks in the garden for an hour or more or sits under the trees reading some exciting French work, but retires as soon as the eunuch gardeners disturb her."

SULTAN.—"Well, good; keep the gardeners from that part of the garden tomorrow. I will have a private interview with her Majesty."

CHIEF OF EUNUCHS.—"Her Majesty would feel insulted to be addressed in the garden even by the Sultan. Consider, Sire, her late position, and what deference would she expect even from your Majesty yourself."

SULTAN.—"By the beard of the prophet! I'll bring her to her senses without even telling her who I am. She has never seen me. It will afford infinite satisfaction to witness her haughty, proud indignation, at a stranger's intrusion on her privacy. But leave me to consider her dignity, all I want is that you keep out all intruders, and be sure to awaken me early enough in the morning."

Next day, at an early hour, the Sultan is ready for his anticipated excitement. It is a lovely morning in early spring;

and he thoroughly enjoys the invigorating, soft sea-breeze which rustles the leaves of the trees over his head.

Seating himself on the grass behind an Oleander thicket, close to a pretty little lake, so as to command a long vista of one of the principal walks, he gives himself up to a reverie of his chibouque. "Ah, to think I never thought of her before, the beautiful haughty. Oh, Allah, what a fine revenge for all she did against me. What a delicious time of day. How curious that although I can scarcely get my poor cock to rise at the prettiest of my odalisques, one always awakes in the morning with a standing pego. What is the cause of it? Perhaps it indicates the proper time of day for voluptuous indulgence. Ah, yes! That must be so for I always notice how I am, especially if I have indulged in too much Frankish brandy overnight. That's our only stimulant. Ah, Allah! why did the prophet forbid us the glorious wine? Spirits were not known then or he would have put a veto on that also. Women, women, nothing but women for good believers! What a man that prophet must have been and after all nothing else for us in heaven! Shall we not be exhausted or cloyed with pleasure there? Ha! Ha! Ha! Of course I'm a true Musselman, but it takes a big faith to believe all that, or about Isa either. Religion is a manufactured article in all countries, a monopoly not to be interfered with lightly; but no one will know the mystery until after death. How true the saying of Solomon: 'That the only real good is to enjoy your life and thank God for it.' There is but one God, whoever is his prophet; we were never intended to make ourselves miserable.

"Ah! Xerxes must have been like myself when he offered such rewards for a new pleasure. He had found himself all used up. 'Vanity of Vanities' said the preacher who had three hundred princesses for wives and seven hundred concubines.

"It was Xerxes who married Esther. Queen Vashti reminds me of the Sultana Valide; how I will humble her and enjoy her humiliated rage as she finds herself helpless in my power.

"Esther, they say, won the king's heart through the voluptuous instruction imparted to her by Mordecai. All the other virgins only just submitted themselves to the Royal Ravisher; but Esther not only did that but when he was spent with his first efforts played with him and sucked his affair, and after all presented her beautiful bottom to his aroused priapus,

which so excited him he was obliged to ravish that also, and
finally put the crown on her head, not as one of the most
beautiful of all virgins but simply to reward the erotic excitement she had raised by her dalliance. Oh, that I had such
a nice girl in my harem; they are all duffers. Ha, there she
comes up the walk," catching a glimpse of the beautiful Sultana coming towards him unveiled and book in hand evidently
intent on seating herself under a tree close at hand. Watching
all her actions, the Sultan continued to enjoy his smoking
and after a little while the lady seated herself on a little
mound of grass under a shady tree, proceeding to peruse her
book, soon being so absorbed in its contents that she did
not perceive his stealthy approach from behind, so that he
actually stood at her back looking over her shoulder and reading the same page as she was feasting on. The title of the
work was Le Diable au Corps, a most erotic and sensual book,
which seemed so to excite her that she sighed and swayed
herself about whilst one hand was quite lost under her clothes,
and seemed to the Sultan to be very curiously engaged somewhere. She reads and she sighs, and he sighs, but unnoticed
by the beautiful student.

What charms he can see all down her neck and voluptuously rounded bosom, having just under his eyes the dazzling
white skin, and blue-black hair streaming down in three long
plaits along her back, the lovely delicate hands, and plump
rounded arms.

How curious it is that anything improper or forbidden has
such an exciting effect on all mankind. Here the Sultan, who
could feast unmoved by the delicious charms of hundreds of
lovely girls in his harem, is strongly excited by the charms
of one so unwittingly exposed to view.

His manly weapon rises in all its forgotten vigour. The
Sultana has thrown back the light shawl which covered her
shoulders, so as to leave her neck quite exposed. He frigs
himself over his unsuspecting victim when she suddenly drops
backwards at full length, her eyes closed, her sensuous smile
of enjoyment on the lips, rather apart, with one knee bent
upwards and the hitherto unseen hand evidently working
something under her clothes. As she sighs and almost sobs
with pleasure, her beautiful legs are quite exposed with nothing on them, but delicate slippers on the feet. Drawers are
quite wanting in the royal apparel.

Sultans are mortal, and however he might have wished to prolong and enjoy the sight, it was impossible for him to restrain his own emotions. The ecstatic moment had arrived, he directs his swollen excited member downwards and showers a good stream of sperm all over her face, neck, and bosom, laughing: "Ha! Ha! Ha! by the prophet you are a wanton woman. What the devil have you got under your clothes?"

Thunderstruck, crimsoning with shame, the Sultana's eyes start open. Then she hides her face in her shawl, shrieking: "Ah! Ah! Help! A man! A man!"

The Sultan gave her a vigorous kick: "You may scream but who's to help you? Do you want to expose your own shame, or do you really want a man?"

She springs to her feet and attempts to fly but he dexterously catches the tail of her dress and in the endeavours to effect her escape pulls her clothes over her head so that she is quite uncovered, her arms helpless, whilst every part of her beautiful body from the waist downwards is fully exposed.

What a sight meets his gaze! A splendid swelling mount all covered with long, black, curly hair, extending far over her beautiful belly, and some inches down on the inside of her thighs, most extraordinary large rounded buttocks, quite out of proportion to her size, but so exciting to behold and replete with voluptuous pleasure.

SULTANA, shrieking.—"Ah! Ah! How shameful! Oh! Oh! Let me go, or your life will pay the forfeit!"

SULTAN.—"Ha, ha! Will you, indeed, spare my life, lady?" whilst still keeping her head and hands in a helpless condition. He inflicts a furious kick on her bottom, which he repeats again and again, as she begs and cries for mercy, promising everything she can think of to be released; her bottom bruised all over and slightly bleeding in places.

SULTANA.—"Oh! Oh! Allah! Have mercy. Deliver me from this demon!"

SULTAN.—"Ha, ha! Cry away to Allah. You ought to be one of the Peris in the Prophet's Paradise. A wanton woman like you would be properly employed there. What's that instrument I see lying in the grass dropped from you just now? Tell me this instant what it is or I will murder you."

SULTANA.—"Oh, oh, mercy! It's only a French godemiche!"

SULTAN.—"A godemiche? What's that for? Speak up" (giving another furious kick).

SULTANA.—"Oh! Oh! We ladies use it to excite ourselves.
Oh, if you only knew who I am!"

SULTAN.—"Indeed Madame. Tell me, pray, perhaps I may
show you some respect."

SULTANA, hopefully.—"You little think, for I'm the Sultana
Valide, it will be fearful for you if anyone should come and
catch you."

SULTAN.—"Ha! Ha! You wish me to believe that, you
wanton! Now tell me true, are you not one of the lower
women of the palace?" (Kicking again, this time her belly,
almost making her faint with the shock.)

SULTANA, shrieking.—"Oh! Oh! Mercy! I am indeed the
Sultana. Oh! Mercy! Oh!" (as kicks follow in quick succession).

SULTAN.—"So you are really the Sultana and you wish me
to believe that, do you?" (Taking advantage of her ceasing
to struggle to tie her to a tree with her clothes still over her
head, helpless as before.) "Now, you lying woman, I'll teach
you to pass yourself off as the Sultana. Here" (placing the
godemiche in her cunny) "I'll give you pleasure; tell me how
you feel, if I do it nicely or not, or I'll murder you on the
spot. Wait a little. I've got a better idea; you must do it
yourself; feel my knife," said he again, pricking her bottom
and making the blood to run freely. "Resist and I'll kill you;
turn around!"

So he alters the fastening till she is extended full length
on her back, still secured to the little tree. Then with his
knife he cuts a hole through her clothes. She can just put in
one hand and use the godemiche.

"That will do; work away at once! I'm going to make a
nice little switch from this prickly shrub to keep you up to
your work."

The poor Sultana, nearly dead with fright, does her best to
obey. His rod of prickly shrubs cuts and scratches her hips
and thighs, and sometimes the mount, drawing drops of blood
at every stroke. She frantically works her instrument, presenting to his view, as he kneels close in front of her, a most
luscious and voluptuous sight, for she is one of those rare
women who are splendidly furnished with an enlarged clitoris
and prominent pouting lips to her cunny, which are now
plainly seen as they draw out and recede, clinging lasciviously
to the working godemiche. Dropping the switch he amuses

himself by pinching and nipping her clitoris and all around the gaping luscious mouth of her vermilion gap.

His touch seems to electrify her. She screams with delight: "Oh, oh, oh! You make me come! How hot I am! Good heavens! Allah! Allah!" and she spends with such profusion that it shoots all over his fingers as the godemiche is still worked by her nervous hands.

SULTAN.—"Now, withdraw that nasty thing and let me inspect your wanton crack; you're never a modest woman to have behaved as you have. Give me that godemiche, I'll put it in my pocket."

SULTANA.—"Oh, pity me! Let me go now. Do have mercy!"

SULTAN.—"You bitch of a dog, who are you? Now confess or you shall be more and more punished."

SULTANA.—"Oh! Oh! Mercy! I am indeed the Valide! If this was found out nothing would save me, for the Sultan is my enemy!"

SULTAN, laughing ironically.—"Ha! Ha! Ha! You think he would have you thrown into the Bosphorus in a sack, do you not? How many poor girls have you served so in your times?"

SULTANA.—"Oh, none! I was never cruel or jealous like some of the favourites."

SULTAN.—"Such lies convince me you are not what you pretend to be; now speak the truth will you? I might as well tell you I am the Padishah himself! Did he never have you? They say he's been a regular goat in the harem."

SULTANA.—"You won't believe me; oh, mercy! mercy! I've been a chaste woman all my life."

SULTAN, beginning to flog her again with the prickly twigs. —"Chaste, chaste, chaste—I should think so after what I have seen—" (giving scratching switches at every word).

The poor woman kicks about and writhes in agony. Her flesh is soon covered with blood which only seems to excite his fury the more. She screams wildly for mercy, sobbing for mercy: "Oh! Ah! Allah! Allah! Mercy, holy prophet! I shall die! Oh, finish me!"

His excitement is now at its highest. He throws himself upon her, exclaiming: "Holy Prophet, holy Prophet, that puts me in mind of your bottom-hole!" Throwing her legs over his shoulders, he first plunges his bursting instrument into her cunny, well to lubricate it, then presents the head to her dark brown fundus; he thrusts furiously and soon gains a partial insertion. "Oh! Oh! You'll split me!" she screams; "not there, not there, I never would allow the Sultan to do that. Oh, oh! Never. What shame! What filthiness!" she sighs as he pushes on and on, to complete possession, and he rests a little after his exertions, but the nervous nippings and contractions of the fundamental canal are too exciting. He spends a stream of his essence into her bowels which she involuntary meets with a slight heave of her bottom. Both of them exhausted, they remain quite still for some few minutes, affording him infinite pleasure, as he causes his dilated instrument to respond to the contracting pulsations of her anus.

SULTAN.—"Are you finished now, you wanton?" withdrawing from her body with a noise something like the drawing of a cork so tightly is the muscle of her bottom contracted around his still inflamed affair. "Ah, ha! how tightly you hold! Haven't you had enough? Ha! Ha! I'll take a love token from you, just to remember your pussey when I look at it." So saying, he cut off a good lock of the fine, long, black curly hair of her cunny. "I must have enough to make a bracelet for my wife, she will little think where it came from," he said, hacking away again and again, causing excruciating pain.

"Oh! Ah! Ah! help! Oh, do have mercy! My God!" she sobs. "I shall never be able to take a bath; my assistants will see, it's all gone! Oh, oh, pity me!" she screams, but he cuts on, enjoying her screams and sobbings till the mouth of her crack looks like a chin unshaved for a fortnight.

"You lying woman, I've made a nice Sultana of your pussey for you, and now I'll really finish you off and let you go."

"Holy Prophet! be merciful! Oh, what more misery can you inflict?" sobbing and screaming.

SULTAN, stuffing a tuft of grass up her fundus.—"That will keep out the cold! Be a pity for a Sultana to catch cold!"

Her legs are wide open showing the red lips and clitoris of her pussey all smeared as they are with blood and sperm; then gathering several tufts of grass with the earth clinging to the roots he proceeds to pelt her cunny with them until one fairly sticks in the entrance. The poor woman is almost unconscious, moaning and sighing, incapable of any efforts to save herself.

With a brutal laugh he shoves his toe into her crack, saying: "Now the cold will keep out of there, too!" Then unloosening her clothes and allowing her to uncover her face he enjoys the spectacle of her tearful, pitiable looks as she sobs and moans in her exhausted state. "Ha, ha! a little water will revive you, you wanton Sultana. You'd better pick yourself up and go back to your apartment," said he, making water all over her and even into her gaping mouth.

She chokes, gasps and falls back in a lifeless swoon. This last indignity had finished her.

So leaving her to recover as best she could he retires from the scene.

A few days afterwards the Sultan requests an audience of the Sultana Valide, as he hears she has been indisposed, and when ushered into her apartment she receives him unveiled in consequence of his exalted rank as her sovereign.

THE SULTAN, refusing to be seated.—"Madame, hearing you were ill I have brought you a present which I hope may restore your animation a little; especially if you use it vigorously as I have seen you do." And he places in her hands a casket of Morocco leather, ornamented with gold, which contains her godemiche. "If your Imperial Highness will look, you will see how I have improved it." (He had put a quantity of her own hair on the india-rubber to make the instrument look more natural.) "I have still enough left to make myself a keepsake," said he, inclining his head as he withdrew from her apartment. "Au revoir, I have repaid you for all your former kindnesses to me."

You may imagine the angry, furious looks of indignant hate which she cast at him as he looked steadily at her, enjoying her shame and confusion whilst giving his present.

HOW HE LOST HIS WHISKERS.

An Episode in the Life of Steve Broad.

You didn't know Steve Broad? More's the pity! A jollier, better-heard and manlier fellow never pissed against a wall.

He was my constant chum from the time we occupied some diggings in Camden Town. Till he went to Australia we were together.

The Siamese Twins, Castor and Pollux, were not more inseparable.

Old Jack Falstaff and Prince Henry and Poins loved each other because "their legs were both of a bigness."

Shall I whisper the secret or one of the secrets of our attachment? Our pricks were both of a length and our arse-holes the same gauge. Don't infer too much from that admission. It was not often that we fucked. There, I will tell you a story that will show you the sort of fellow he was.

Steve had a pal, Alf Nugent, and he and Alf had lived together as chums. Alf occasionally receiving a visit in his lodging from a pretty sister, Lettice, as they called her from Letty Nugent, a charming little blonde with oh! such shoulders; a mouth humid and peachlike and a pair of eyes that would entice the bark off a tree.

It was not long before Steve and Letty struck up an acquaintance. Steve could make love like a Romeo.

Letty was "willing" as Barkis, and the brother Alf was not one to spoil sport, so the three got on charmingly together. Alf often gave a pleasant little party. I was invited. Steve had made my acquaintance in the city, and took me there. I introduced a young girl Kitty Marshall, and Alf brought his inamorata, Nellie Grover. So that the six of us formed a pleasant little gathering and rare fun we had.

Let me sketch for you one of our social meetings after a recherche supper, prepared by the nimble hands of Letty Nugent, who turned out every article as palatable as Ruth Pinch's Steakpie.

The table was cleared of all but wines and fruits, the couches were drawn up to the fire and the six of us would go in for a little fun.

Steve would warble in his rich manly voice a polly song, such as:

> There's a thing that bears a well-known name,
>   Though it is but a little spot;
> Its smell sets my heart and my brain in a flame,
>   And its touch makes my prick grow hot.
> 'Tis the sweetest thing this world can show,
>   To praise it can't be wrong;
> 'Twill set your blood in a fervid glow,
>   Make your prick grow stiff and long.

'Tis a woman's cunt. Her glorious fan,
Oh, a cunt is the pride of an Englishman.

That cunt will not be treated with shame,
    But calls for proper respect;
And though mostly fit for a fucking game,
    Yet it sometimes in mourning is decked.
Then beware how you go with the darling then,
    Or perhaps sorely punished you'll be;
For cunt won't be the sport of men,
    When it wants its privacy.
For caprice is part of cunt's own plan
To enhance its joys to an Englishman.

But when cunt is ready, I give you the tip,
    No half-hearted play can it stand;
It likes to be fondled with tongue and with lip,
    And shuns not the touch of your hand.
But the glorious Prick sets Miss Cunt in a thrill,
    She loves a prick, long, thick, and firm.
And she'll wriggle and pant till you madly fill
    Her bang full of glowing sperm.
You may frig and gamahuche and try every plan,
But fair fucking's the pride of an Englishman.

Of course a song like this was well received and quickly
followed by a practical illustration.

My little lady, Kitty Marshall, warmly defended gamahuching and so did I; for laying Kitty down on the couch and
parting her beautiful legs I displayed to the others a cleft
that an angel would think it a new joy to suck. Soon the
whole six of us were engaged in an amorous orgy, and Steve,
who certainly could boast the most magnificent priapus that
ever adorned a man, took pretty little Letty in his arms and
gave her what you may call an "Exhibition Fuck." His balls
knocked against the entrance of her lovely quim and at last
when she wriggled and panted and hugged him into a spend
he poured such a libation into her that we could see it overflow and they mutually lay entranced until we revived them
with some glorious wine.

Then we would go in for a game of blindman's buff, all
being stripped naked and armed with birch; we would scamper

about the room, cutting right and left, and endeavouring to land some smart blows on each other's glowing posteriors, until thoroughly exhausted; we would sit down on our smarting arses for a good story or song.

Apropos of our game of blindman's buff, Alf told us a good story.

A respectable-looking old buck was brought before Mr. Norton, the magistrate, charged with dog stealing or rather enticing ladies' dogs to follow him with the intention of stealing them.

"Well, sir," said Mr. Norton, "what have you to say to this charge?"

"If your honour will allow me to explain it in my own way and give you a little bit of my history I think I can prove it is all a mistake."

"Well," said the magistrate, "go on."

"Well, your honour, a year or two ago I had a little money and wishing to see life I took a walk late at night in the neighbourhood of Haymarket, and got into the company of one of those girls."

"One of what girls?" said Norton.

"A whore."

"Well, sir, your expression is far from elegant, but I understand you."

"Well, your honour, this girl enticed me home and there I found a lot of her companions and a nice little spree we had. At last we proposed a game of blindman's buff, and as I was the only male present it was proposed that we should all strip and then the ladies should be blindfolded and a prize given to the lady that caught me. Oh, it was jolly fun to see the girls running about naked and catching hold of each other and their slipping their hands down to the proper place to feel if it was the man they held; but they kept giving me such jolly slaps on my bottom that I tried to run out of the door when one of the girls picked up my umbrella which stood in the corner and made a lunge at me (the devil must have looked). Oh, the tip of the umbrella entered my fundament as it was turned to her and as she withdrew it the ferule was left behind, and there it is now, and every time I sigh—"

"Every time you what?" asked Mr. Norton.

"Well, every time I fart, if you like, the ferule whistles and the dogs follow me and I can't help it."

Mr. Norton laughed heartily at this explanation, told him not to diet windily, and let him go.

But, however, to return to Steve. He soon got to be really in love with Letty, proposed marriage to her and had the full consent of her brother Alf, and the promised consent of her father; and it was arranged that on the return of Alf and his sister to their country home, Steve should come on a visit and get the old boy's consent.

The old gentleman invited him to get a look at him.

The time came. Alf and Letty went home and Steve was soon to follow.

At last the day arrived and he went.

After picking up his traps, bidding his landlady good-bye, and giving the slavey a farewell grind on the kitchen-dresser, he took himself down to the station, booked for Fairbanks, and was soon seated alone in a first-class carriage.

Alone! Yes, all but a delightful companion—the last number of *The Pearl* with which and his favourite meerschaum Steve whiled away the time as the stations flew past.

It was a beautiful day but he heeded not the aspect of the country, so thoroughly was he absorbed in the doings of Lady Pokingham and Miss Coote, etc.

All this excited his imagination until he got in a most furious state, not knowing how to ease his torment, and only wishing that he had a companion on the journey, whether male or female, he would have heeded not. He was in such a pitch of excitement that he would have got into a kangaroo, when—

The train stopped at Bellevue, and—

A young lady got on board carrying a rather large bundle which she placed under the seat and then sat down.

Steve's heart bounded as he noticed her light flowing hair, her airy step, and her little figure. But she was closely veiled and as yet he could not see her face, but the lovely swell of her bosom, the creamy whiteness of the little bit of her throat that was visible convinced him that she was young and lovely.

The train sped on. Modestly the young lady kept her veil down and Steve thrust *The Pearl* in his pocket and was soon deep in the *Times*.

Oh, how that veiled face piqued him! Again, again and again he cast his eyes to it over the *Times* but the veil was still down.

"Does the draught annoy you?" said Steve, pointing to the partly opened window.

"Not at all, thank you," replied a sweet voice behind the veil.

Something in the voice thrilled Steve through. He had heard it before he felt sure, and he was more anxious than ever to see the face it belonged to.

At last as they passed a certain station with a sigh of relief she threw up her veil and turned her face to her hero.

"Good heavens, Kate, is it you?"

"Why, Mr. Broad, who would have thought of seeing you. Oh, I am so glad. You know that odious old lawyer, that wanted to marry me? Well I am positively flying from him and until I passed this station I felt they would pursue me. That is why I kept myself veiled but now I am quite out of my trouble, I think; for I have got a disguise which I shall put on. I tried all I could to get into an empty carriage but the guard assured me there was not one, but now you can help and not hinder me."

Let me tell you now, that Steve and the lady were old friends. They had met the first time at some private theatricals. Steve made love to her in the character of a French Count on the stage, and in his character of an English lover off the stage, he managed to make a first appearance in Kate's delicious cunny. In fact he took her maidenhead and many a delightful love-fuck they had, until Kate went abroad. And now they had met again under such strange circumstances.

"Let me tell you quickly," said Kate, "I am engaged to Paul Jellocombe, you remember him. Well, love, you won't be jealous when I tell you we are going to be married as soon as ever I am of age. I have escaped from home and mean to stay with Paul's folks until a few weeks elapse when I shall be my own mistress. And now for my plan: I have eluded them so far, but for fear they should dispatch a message to the telegraph station and stop me I have brought a disguise, and now, help me on with it, quick. You shall be my lady's-maid."

Before Steve had time to get his breath the charming, volatile girl took off bonnet and cloak, undid her dress, whipped it off around her feet, exposing a lovely pair of white shoulders and two glowing breasts, small for her size, but round, polished as marble.

If Steve's priapus had before been excited it was now delirious.

Jumping from his seat he helped her take off her petticoats, etc., until she came to her drawers.

"Stop sir, that will do," said Kate, "I don't want any further undressing. No! No! Don't be foolish. I can allow no liberties. Quick, I know this line well, you have only just time to turn me into a middy before we get to the next station.

Stooping as she spoke she undid the bundle at her feet and quick as her nimble fingers could move and with Steve's assistance, she was soon dressed as a middy. Her light hair was tucked cleverly up, a short crisp wig assumed. Her cap stuck jauntily on her head. She looked as smart and trim a middy as ever saluted the quarter-deck.

The transformation was no sooner completed than the train stopped at a station, and they both jumped out for refreshments.

The rollicking girl, her walk, her gait, showed her well fitted to play her part. She was indeed no mean actress.

As soon as they were back in the carriage, which Steve adroitly secured for themselves by puffing a tremendous cloud of smoke in the eyes of an old lady who would have entered, Steve took the middy on his knee.

"Well, Kate, love, this is quite an adventure and I tell you, it is a long way to the next station, and as it has been one of the great ambitions of my life to fuck a midshipman this is too good an opportunity to let it pass."

Kate offered no resistance. Thrusting his hand into the bosom of her jacket he first felt her round and polished breasts, pinched her nipples and fired her with his wanton touches and the hot burning kisses he printed on her lips. Then unbuttoning his trousers he allowed his splendid staff d'amour to display itself before her.

"Oh, Steve, how it has grown since I saw it last," said Kate mischievously as she took it in her hand.

"Yes," said Steve, who could not resist a pun, "I have heard him groan for a taste of your darling cunny. Come, let me feel how it is getting on?"

As he spoke he slid his hand into her trousers and felt her cunt, moist and mossy, tickled her clitoris, and roused all her warming passions.

As the train sped on they abandoned themselves to all that their impassioned natures could suggest.

Steve knelt down on the floor of the carriage and opening wide Kate's legs he pressed his hot lips to her creamy cunt, and gamahuched her, until she spent in delirious pleasure.

And then when all his feelings were working up to such a pitch of excitement that he could no longer contain himself, he laid her supple form over the seat and getting into her from behind he thrust his prick to the very hilt in her reeking cunt. One, two, three thrusts and as he clasped her to him with a convulsive thrill he poured out his manly balm in an ecstasy of enjoyment.

"Hi, hi! Stop that you infernal scoundrels! Oh, you dirty rascals!"

In a sudden bewildered start of alarm they looked round to see a red, round, indignant face, ornamented with a bristly white moustache and surmounted by a tuft of white hair that made the upper part of the head look like an infuriated cockatoo.

His face was peeping on them through a window in their compartment, which being concealed by a curtain the same colour as the carriage they had not noticed.

The passenger in the next compartment, reaching something from the back over his head, was prompted to draw the curtain and his restless, listless curiosity was rewarded by seeing Steve ram his hungry prick into Kate's writhing cunt, but as the old boy thought, into the arse.

In a minute Steve and Kate arranged their costume, and were sitting down whilst the passenger continued to glare at them muttering subdued imprecations and swearing he would charge them at the next station.

Without turning his head Steve whispered to Kate to get out at the next station, to bolt through for the highroad and leave him to detain the old boy until he could join her.

Quick as thought, as they neared the station, Steve bolted out, using a railway key he always carried. He locked the compartment in which the old man was alone and he and Kate dashed through the station before the fat old duffer could cause them to be stopped.

Quickly as they could they made for the country and had a parting rural fuck which they thoroughly enjoyed.

There is really something delightful in rural out of doors, al fresco fuck, the music of the birds, the babbling of the nearby stream, the fresh air fanning your face, and invigorating your frame, seem to me to always give great zest and vigour to the performance. I know for myself the thrusts I give are more vigorous, the sperm I spend is more copious and the thrill always more delightful when I have a glorious country-fuck in the open air.

"Good-bye, I am sure it will not be long before I see you again," said Kate. "And married or not, remember, there is always a loving, dear, affectionate little cunny to welcome you whenever you see me."

"Farewell," said Steve, "and be sure my prick will always stand your true friend."

So they parted.

A hearty welcome awaited Steve at the hands of Alf Nugent and his charming sister Letty.

They were alone in the house, their father being expected shortly, so they made him quite free.

After a jolly meal for which his long walk had given him an appetite, Alf said: "Now let me show you our private boudoir."

Following him, Steve soon found himself in a most tastefully furnished little room. A pianoforte stood in one corner, other musical instruments were about the room, splendid pictures of voluptuous scenes adorned the walls and a glorious couch that seemed fit for a seraph to recline on stood the chief object of attention.

"And now," said Alf, "before my father comes home, and he will not be long, he has only some slight business in the town, let us see if you are in good form. Letty is dying for a fuck and I shall have great pleasure in seeing you operate."

Steve was quite reinvigorated. It took but a little time for them to undress the lovely girl and lay her at full length on the soft spring-couch.

In a few moments Steve was on her, and his prick buried to the hilt in her luscious cunt.

"Go to it, Steve," said Alf. "Give it to her. The young hussey has some good stuff to spend, I know, for she sucked my prick three times yesterday. There now, you are getting slow but I'll warm you up, I warrant," and suiting the action to the word, Alf seized a birch from a corner and laid it smartly across Steve's arse.

This quickened his strokes and soon a shiver shook their bodies and Letty and he melted in a glorious spend.

"Oh, poor Alf, look at his prick," said Letty.

And turning around as he slid off her, Steve certainly noticed the stiffness of Alf's prick and it was in a most painful state of excitement.

Whilst Steve readjusted his clothes, Letty dropped quietly to her knees, and taking Alf's prick between her ruby lips, soon sucked it into a state of quiesence whilst Steve looked on highly amused at the look of gratified pleasure which soon spread over Alf's countenance.

"Hark!" said Alf, "what is that! A carriage, as sure as I live, it must be father. Look, Steve, from the window, who is it?"

Steve looked out.

"It is an old gentleman coming up the garden walk, Alf. Is that your father?"

Alf peered out.

"Yes."

"Then for heaven's sake don't let him see me, I must disguise myself. I cannot stop now to tell you how, but something must be done to destroy my identity or I am done for. Quick, Letty, you go down and meet your father; Alf and I will join you presently!"

Letty soon disappeared, though burning with curiosity. She was docile and did as she was bidden.

"Now, Alf," said Steve, "you're guv'nor saw me in the railway carriage fucking a lovely girl, but as I was having her backwards and she was disguised as a sailor—a tale hangs to it but I can't tell you now—I expect he thought I was doing a bit of backdoor work and as he may be a particular old boy he must not know me again."

Steve was a young man of decision. Although it cost him a sigh, his beautiful whiskers were soon sacrificed. His tact and skill soon changed his whole appearance and when he descended to join Letty and Mr. Nugent, but for a sign from Alf, Letty would not have known him. Much less did Mr. Nugent recognize the bold fucker of the railway.

That's how Steve lost his whiskers.

A curious sequel hangs to the story.

After dinner, when the gentlemen were alone, the old gentleman began:

"A very curious circumstance happened to me this morning when in a railway-train. I happened accidentally to look through the window of the compartment and saw a young man actually in the act of indecency with a midshipman; the rascals escaped by locking me in the carriage. However, in the carriage he had left, the young villain dropped a book. I took charge of it; as I had no spectacles I did not look close at it but as it doubtless contains some clue to the rascal, look at it for me."

Steve saw in a moment it was *The Pearl*; but knowing no clue to his identity was in it, he just glanced at it, handed it back, advising old Nugent to look at it more closely in the privacy of his chamber.

The old chap retired presently for his afternoon nap, taking the book with him, and soon after they heard peals of laughter from his room. Then he was heard walking up and down and soon his voice was heard calling Patty, his favourite servant.

Alf and Steve peeped through the keyhole after she had entered the room and saw him reading passages from the book. Then taking her in his arms he laid her on the bed, and raising his shirt-tail, he displayed his prick, stalwart and strong. In a few moments it was lodged in her creamy cunt. And both Steve and Alf were convinced that the old boy knew the way there.

In the evening old Nugent called Letty and Steve, joined their hands and said: "Bless you my children! A delightful little work I have been reading today has put fucking in such a beautiful light that I at once give you my consent to commence it as soon as possible. I have quite altered my opinion about that young fellow I saw and am convinced that to give his prick a treat is the first duty of every man at all times. I propose now that your nuptials shall be celebrated by a glorious fucking tournament."

This was done. Happiness was the lot of them all that evening.

Old Nugent never found out Steve's escapade. He died soon after and left them a heap of money, and so amorous was the old boy to the last that they had to send for the servant to toss him off, before they could get the lid on the coffin.

Kate married and is quite happy and I long to see Steve and have another laugh with him over: "How he lost his whiskers."

The ladies in America have taken to dabbling on the Stock Exchange.

The following telegrams passed between two lady friends and rather puzzled the telegraph officials.

"Dear Louise, a bull here has a large concern for which he is anxious to find an opening. Can you accommodate him?"

The reply was:

"I cannot at present as my monthly settlements are on, but if the bull can keep it standing for a week, I have no doubt I can find a vacancy for it."

Q.—When is a newly married lady like the Victory at Trafalgar?

A.—When her cock-pit is full of bloody semen.

THE NOVICE.

A pretty little novice in her convent woke at dawn,
And looking from her lattice she spied upon the lawn,
    A handsome shepherd quite intent
On playing with his instrument, his instrument so long!

She raised the window softly and watched him for a while,
Delighted with his movements, then asked him with a smile:
    "Oh shepherd, pray, my wish consent,
And say what is that instrument, that instrument so long?

You play with it so nicely, it gives me joy to see,
So dear, I implore you, to teach the same to me;
    Oh, kind young shepherd, pray consent,
I'll finger well your instrument, your instrument so long!"

He looked up to her lattice with pleasure in his eye,
And cried: "Come down, fair maiden, for there you are too
high,
      Far, far too high for the extent,
That I can stretch my instrument, my instrument so long."

She tarried not a moment, but swiftly rushed below,
And with the handsome shepherd she learned her lesson so
      That soon she played most excellent
Fantasies on his instrument, his instrument so long!

The first sweet lesson over for her too fast, she then
In winning tones addressed him: "I'd like to play again."
      Once more her fingers to work went,
Which made him use his instrument, his instrument so long!

But strangers seemed approaching, the fair girl bid him fly,
And cried: "Oh, don't forget me, whene'er you travel by,
      Oft, oft, come back, and we'll invent
Fresh tunes for that dear instrument, that instrument so
long!"

A GENTLEMAN'S WIG.

Tune—"Derry-Down."

I sing not of despots, or slaves who submit,
Not of farmer George, Jenky, Dundas, Fox or Pitt!
My ballad's the bantling of laughter and gig,
'Tis of an old cock in a c—— tified wig.

'Gainst the poll tax of Pitt this old codger did rave,
Like a felon transported, it forc'd him to shave.
"Tho' tried for my life," said th' old buck, "I'll rob
The tail of some Dolly to build a brown bob."

Near Somerset House he fell in with a tit,
And he thought for his purpose the c——tling was fit;

But when he examin'd her parts; d'ye see,
All the hair of her c——t wouldn't make a toupee.

The same night he picked up a merry-ars'd wench,
The hair-quantum stuff of the wise-wig'd bench;
Whilst on her back, sleeping as fast as a top,
He with keen cutting scissors her c——t made a crop.

Away went the thief, and the barber received,
The booty, for which a final caul he had weav'd;
But strange! whilst old razor the wig had in hand,
The pole in his breeches did constantly stand.

Well pleas'd with his plight, Razor laid by his work,
And lather'd the beard of his wife like a Turk.
"Keep the wig," said she, "love, don't expose it for sale.
'Tis bob for your head and a bob for my tail."

The wig frizz'd and curl'd, closely shav'd Codger's nob;
Away went the barber to try on the bob;
But the box waxing warm, Codger's passions did rise,
Which brought tears in his breeches instead of his eyes.

In rampant condition he flew to a fair,
And perchance met the Dolly he'd robb'd of her hair;
She whipp'd off the wig, cloth'd his parts with the caul,
So in went his dry bob, and wet bob, and all.

Now we know to be true what anatomists state,
That the fountain of love is supplied from the pate;
'Twas the jasey provoking, sirs, mark what I say,
Made his fountain of love's bason to play.

Then take my advice, ye old cocks of the game,
Whenever you find your wild passions grown tame,
Get a wig made of hair from the spot ye all prize,
And in spite of your prudence your pego will rise.

————————

ACROSTIC.

Come father dear! now lay your body down
Upon your daughter's naked belly white,
Now raptures soon shall our embraces crown;
This is the only road to true delight!
I know the lessons I have learnt from you,
Sweet lessons in the flowery paths of love!
Sure I'll remember all I ought to do,
When I am under and you are above!
Enter at once, dear father, to my bower,
Each movement of your prick will give me bliss!
'Tis joy to me to know I have the power,
With you to share sweet rapture such as this!
How often you have praised my cunt's tight grip!
Each time you fuck 'tis better than the last!
Now from my cunt your prick will never slip!
Your legs and mine entwined shall keep it fast!
Only a father's love such joy can give,
United thus, forever I could live!
Nor envy those who boast a husband's love.
Give me always this prick, I ne'er will rove,
And never wish for any other man.
No prick with this, I'm certain, can compare!
Does it not take both of my hands to span?
Then what a wealth he has of curly hair!
Each morn upon my cunt his burning kisses fall,
Night after night his tongue enters my quim so small.
Do it again, papa, I can't forbear to call,
Even my mother laughs and says: "My husband dear,
Ram in your prick at once, and end this wild career."

THE WEDDING NIGHT.

When John and Sue had tied the nupital bands,
Like ardent lovers, join'd their hearts and hands,
Hymen prepared his torch to bless the two
And in them centered his peculiar care.

The blissful hour arriv'd, Sue to his bed
By buxom damsels joyfully was led;
One with officious hands her stays unlac'd,
While standers-by extoll'd her lessening waist;
Her garters some with eagerness untied,
And all by turns were variously employ'd.
Susan, with bashful modesty array'd,
Like to a prudent and virtuous maid,
Now plac'd in bed, these dubious thoughts arose:
"I fear this night I'll have no repose;
To bed with man; methinks is vastly odd,
Tho' matrimony was ordain'd by God.
Oh, how my virgin frame will shake with fear,
When am'rous John in glowing hopes draws near;
If my fair front to his I shall incline,
And all my blooming charms at once resign,
He'll say I'm bold and turn his head aside,
And think he's purchas'd a lascivious bride.
To him, my parts posterior if I turn,
He'll charge me with indecency and scorn—
But here he comes:—Oh, how shall I behave,
To show myself his true and faithful slave?
A medium I'll observe, fall which way it will;
Of his fair Susan John won't take it ill,
And that I no apology may lack.
I'm e'en resolved to lie upon my back."

GOD SAVE QUEEN CUNT.

God save our great Cunt! our Queen!
For ever may she reign,
    Supreme o'er all!

Her praises we will sound,
True bliss in her is found,
She long ago was crowned,
    Queen of the world!

Adam in Eden's bowers,
With choicest fruits and flowers,
    Felt all alone!

Only his prick to frig,
When it was hard and big,
Till he felt with fatigue
    Weary and worn!

Our Queen saw his distress,
And swift to his redress
    From heaven she came.

Told him her name was Eve,
And asked him to believe
That she would relieve
    Prick's burning flame!

Adam at once replied:
"For something I have sighed,
    I knew not what!

This cunt you show to me,
New strength puts into me,
And yet it seems to me,
    My prick's more hot!"

Great Cunt, our Queen, then said:
"On this bank in the shade
    I will lay down.

Put your prick in the slit,
Never fear the tight fit,
Push, and it will admit,
    Your cock so brown!

Up and down move your bum,
In which I'll put my thumb,
    To keep good time!

Shove your cock in and out,
Until from his blunt snout

The sperm shall madly spout,
    'Tis bliss divine!"

Can I describe our Queen?
Her beauties must be seen
    To be well known.

Lips that are lecherous,
Perfect and amorous,
And odoriferous!
    This is her crown!

You will find her great chink,
Lined with skin quite pink,
    God bless Queen Cunt!

Never in man or beast,
Will you find such a feast,
If with your tongue you taste
    Her juicy cunt!

Emp'rors and kings bow down
To her power and renown,
    Queen Cunt they love!

Their pricks with joy they push
Into her hairy bush,
And with a furious rush
    With joy they shove!

The Pope of Rome, I know,
Cunt's claims cannot forgo,
    But owns her sway!

Cardinal, monk and priest,
From greatest to the least,
All love her luscious feast,
    Both night and day!

Mankind of every race,
Where'er their dwelling place,
    Get the stiff prick.

Chinese or Negromen,
Zulus or Englishmen,
Irish or American,
  Love Cunt's sweet nick!

Ever since Adam's day
Cunt has maintained her sway
  Over the world!

Never by piety,
Or any dignity,
From her authority
  Has she been hurled!

Cunt's greatest foe has been,
One that is quite obscene:
  A tight arse-hole!

Conquered now is this foe,
Perfect his overthrow!
In sight he dares not show,
  To save his soul!

God save great Cunt, our Queen,
Let her throne be between
  Sweet woman's thighs!

And may the curling hair,
Gracefully clustering there,
Man's pego still ensnare,
  Until he dies!